*Unity and Diversity in
Development Ideas*

United Nations Intellectual History Project

Ahead of the Curve? UN Ideas and Global Challenges
  Louis Emmerij, Richard Jolly, and Thomas G. Weiss

Quantifying the World: UN Ideas and Statistics
  Michael Ward

UN Contributions to Development Thinking and Practice
  Richard Jolly, Louis Emmerij, Dharam Ghai, and Frédéric Lapeyre

Political Economy for a Divided World: Trade, Finance, and Development
  John Toye and Richard Toye

Unity and Diversity in Development Ideas

Perspectives from the UN Regional Commissions

Edited by Yves Berthelot

Indiana University Press

Bloomington and Indianapolis

This book is a publication of

Indiana University Press
601 North Morton Street
Bloomington, Indiana 47404-3797 USA

http://iupress.indiana.edu

Telephone orders   800-842-6796
Fax orders   812-855-7931
Orders by e-mail   iuporder@indiana.edu

The paper used in this publication meets the minimum requirements
of American National Standard for Information Sciences—Permanence
of Paper for Printed Library Materials, ANSI Z39.48-1984.

Manufactured in the United States of America

Library of Congress Cataloging-in-Publication Data

    Unity and diversity in development ideas : perspectives from the UN regional
commissions / edited by Yves Berthelot.
      p.   cm. — (United Nations intellectual history project ; 2)
    Includes bibliographical references and index.
    ISBN 0-253-34335-6 (cloth : alk. paper) — ISBN 0-253-21638-9 (pbk. : alk. paper)
     1. Economic development projects—Case studies. 2. Economic development—
Cross-cultural studies. 3. Developing countries—Economic conditions. 4. United
Nations—Economic assistance. 5. United Nations—Technical assistance. I. Berthelot,
Yves. II. Series.
    HD82.U57 2004
    341.7'59—dc21   2003009550

1 2 3 4 5 09 08 07 06 05 04

Contents

Boxes and Tables

Boxes

Tables

Foreword

It may come as a surprise to many that no comprehensive history exists of the United Nations family of organizations, neither institutional nor intellectual. True, a few of the funds or specialized agencies have written, or are in the process of writing, their institutional histories. This is, indeed, what all UN organizations should do, along with enhanced efforts to organize their archives so that independent researchers can also document and analyze dispassionately the problems and contributions of multilateral institutions in the last half-century.

Faced with this major omission, which has substantial implications for academic and policy literature, we decided to undertake the task of beginning to write an *intellectual* history—that is, a history of the ideas launched or nurtured by the United Nations. Observers should not be put off by what may strike them as a puffed-up billing. Our working assumption behind this effort is straightforward: Ideas and concepts are a main driving force in human progress, and they arguably have been one of the most important contributions of the world organization.

The United Nations Intellectual History Project (UNIHP) was launched in 1999 as an independent research effort based in the Ralph Bunche Institute for International Studies at The Graduate Center of The City University of New York. The project also maintains a liaison office in Geneva. We are grateful for the enthusiastic backing from the Secretary-General and other staff and governments within the UN system. Generous financial support from five foundations and eight governments ensures total intellectual and financial independence. Details of this and other aspects of the project can be found at our website: www.unhistory.org.

The work of the United Nations can be divided into two broad categories: economic and social development, on the one hand, and peace and security, on the other. The UNIHP has committed to produce fourteen volumes in the first arena and a further three volumes if sufficient resources are mobilized to include the latter. These volumes will be published in a series by Indiana

University Press. In addition, the project also has completed an oral history collection of some seventy-five lengthy interviews of persons who have played major roles in launching and nurturing UN ideas—and sometimes in hindering them! Extracts from these interviews will be published in 2004 in *UN Ideas: Voices from the Trenches and Turrets*. Authors of the project's various volumes, including this one, have drawn on these interviews to highlight substantive points made in their texts. Full transcripts of the oral histories will be disseminated in electronic form at the end of the project to facilitate work by other researchers and interested persons worldwide.

There is no single way to organize research, and certainly not for such an ambitious project as this one. The way we have structured this history is by selecting topics—ranging from trade and finance to human rights, from transnational corporations to development assistance, from gender to sustainability—and to tease out the history of ideas under each of these topical headings. We have selected world-class experts for each topic and given them freedom and responsibility to organize their own research, analysis, and presentation of material. Guidance from us as the project's directors, as well as from peer review groups, is provided to ensure accuracy and fairness in depicting the original ideas, what happened to them within the UN system, and what happened afterward.

As lifelong participants in and observers of multilateral development work and diplomacy, we are convinced that the UN story deserves to be better documented if it is to be better understood and appreciated. The Bretton Woods institutions, in this respect, are far ahead. The World Bank published two massive histories—one on the occasion of its twenty-fifth anniversary and the other (two volumes and more than 2000 pages) on its fiftieth. The International Monetary Fund (IMF) has an in-house historian who captures its place in history with regular publications.

We are pleased to be part of what we hope will be a long and varied journey for the world organization. As Secretary-General Kofi A. Annan kindly wrote in the Foreword to *Ahead of the Curve? UN Ideas and Global Challenges*: "With the publication of this first volume in the United Nations Intellectual History Project, a significant lacuna in twentieth-century scholarship and international relations begins to be filled."

Unity and Diversity in Development Ideas: Perspectives from the UN Regional Commissions is another step in this intellectual odyssey. We are extremely lucky to have persuaded our friend and colleague Yves Berthelot to not only write the chapter about the Economic Commission for Europe, which he directed from 1993 to 2000, but also to act as the editor for this crucial vol-

ume. He heads up our project's office in Geneva and has been intimately associated with the UN as a senior staff member for many years. His task, to
orchestrate chapters from authors around the world, must be seen as a significant contribution to this intellectual history. Moreover, his introductory chapter goes beyond a mere synthesis of material to provide a passionate
and lucid portrait of past contributions and a plea for what they could be in
the future.

This is the only edited volume in the series. When the topic of assessing
regional contributions to UN development ideas was suggested by the project's
International Advisory Council, we were unable to imagine how any single
author or small group of authors could write knowledgeably about all the
regions in the world. Hence, we decided to call upon experts to bring to bear
their knowledge about how development discourse and policy were shaped
by the UN presence in important geographical regions of the world. After
considerable debate, the most sensible way to organize this discussion was
through the lenses of regional commissions that were on the front lines in
debates within each region. While we have been careful throughout the project
to avoid "institutional" histories, in this case it was the most logical way to
proceed.

Yves Berthelot's team consisted of two other leading development practi-
tioners who also served as executive heads of UN regional commissions, for
Africa and for Latin America and the Caribbean, respectively. We could not
have found more insightful contributors than Adebayo Adedeji and Gert
Rosenthal; they are among those rare analysts whose views are informed by
both solid scholarly training and hands-on experience. They were joined by
Blandine Destremau and Leelananda de Silva, whose own research and practical experience is considerable in Western Asia and in Asia and the Pacific.
The analyses and conclusions of authors about each region are a personal
interpretation of a very diverse region and experience. Other authors would
certainly have a different take on these issues, but we are extremely pleased to
be in a position to place in the public domain the first comprehensive overview of development ideas as they emerged from important regions over the
last half-century.

We hope that readers will enjoy this journey through time. As they proceed, they should keep in mind a challenging observation from Midge Decter:

> Ideas are powerful things, requiring not a studied contemplation but an action,
> even if it is only an inner action. Their acquisition obligates a man in some way
> to change his life, even if it is only his inner life. They demand to be stood for.
> They dictate where a man must concentrate his vision. They determine his

moral and intellectual priorities. They provide him with allies and make him enemies. In short, ideas impose an interest in their ultimate fate which goes far beyond the realm of the merely reasonable.[1]

Louis Emmerij
Richard Jolly
Thomas G. Weiss
New York, December 2002

Acknowledgments

This volume would have not existed without the wisdom of the UNIHP International Advisory Council, which suggested assessing the UN regional contributions to development ideas, and the decision of the co-directors to go ahead despite the institutional perspective that views from the regional commissions would introduce in a history of ideas.

My thanks therefore go to the members of the Advisory Council—Galal Amin, Margaret Joan Anstee, Lourdes Arizpe, Eveline Herfkens, Enrique Iglesias, Andras Inotai, Thandike Mkandawire, Gert Rosenthal, John Ruggie, Makoto Taniguchi, and Ramesh Takur—for their vision and for the important suggestions they made to improve the first draft at a review meeting hosted by the Dag Hammarskjöld Foundation.

I am greatly indebted to the co-directors, Louis Emmerij, Richard Jolly, and Tom Weiss, for their decision and for their continuous support and advice. I was honored to have been asked to serve as editor and pleased that they selected such talented, competent, and patient authors for each chapter. It was stimulating to work with Adebayo Adedeji, Blandine Destremeau, Paul Rayment, Gert Rosenthal, and Leelananda de Silva.

I thank the governments of Canada, the Netherlands, Norway, Sweden, and the United Kingdom as well as the Carnegie Corporation of New York, the Ford Foundation, and the Rockefeller Foundation for their generous contributions to the project. I address special thanks to the government of Switzerland and to the République et Canton de Genève for their interest in this volume and their important contribution to the project, which permitted the project to open an office in Geneva and to benefit from the presence in this city of many present and former actors in UN intellectual life.

The hospitality offered by the director general of the UN office in Geneva, Mr. Sergei Ordzhonikidze, and by the director of the library, Pierre Pelou, gave the project access to the richness of the wonderful Library of the Palais des Nations and to its archives. I am extremely grateful to both and to their very helpful staff.

I am grateful to the executive secretaries of the five regional commissions, K. Y. Amoako, Kim Hak-Su, Jose-Antonio O'Campo, Brigitta Schmögnerova, and Mervat Tallawy for facilitating access to staff and documents and for commenting on the first draft of the chapters covering their respective commissions. They made key suggestions and, at the same time, fully respected the independence of the project and the judgment of the authors.

Special thanks go to Paul Rayment, who not only wrote the ECE chapter with me and made substantive suggestions for, and contributed part of, the introductory chapter but also carefully read the whole volume and helped in its editing. Carla Bellota did a wonderful job in revising and completing the endnotes and in harmonizing the presentation of the six chapters and Effie MacLachlan provided extremely valuable assistance in getting the book into its final publishable form.

During the two years through which this volume took shape, I benefited from constant encouragement and stimulating questions from Dosithée Berthelot-Yeatman, my wife; Susan Bartolo, my special assistant when I was in the ECE; Tatiana Carayannis from UNIHP; and Sophie Theven de Gueleran and Frédéric Lapeyre, both attached to the UNIHP Geneva office. They helped me find information, facilitated contacts, and relieved me of other tasks. Without them the completion of this volume would have been much delayed.

Yves Berthelot

Abbreviations

AAF-SAP	African Alternative Framework to Structural Adjustment Programmes
ACDA	Asian Centre for Development Administration
ACDESS	African Center for Development and Strategic Studies
ACPR	Advisory Committee of Permanent Representatives
ACU	Asian Clearing Union
ACW	African Centre for Women
ADB	African Development Bank
ADB	Asian Development Bank
ADF	African Development Forum
AGF	Africa Governance Forum
AGR	Accord européen sur les grandes routes de trafic international [European Agreement on Main International Traffic Arteries]
AIDMO	Arab Industrial Development and Mining Organization
AIEDP	Asian Institute for Economic Development and Planning
ALALC	Asociación Latinoamericana de Libre Comercio [Latin America Free Trade Association]
ALECSO	Arab League Educational, Cultural and Scientific Organization
ALTID	Asian Land Transport Infrastructure Development
AOAS	Arab Organization of Administrative Sciences
APDC	Asian-Pacific Development Centre
APEC	Asia-Pacific Economic Cooperation

APPER	African Priority Program for Economic Recovery
ASEAN	Association of Southeast Asian Nations
ASI	Asian Statistical Institute
ASMO	Arab Standards and Metrology Organization
ATRCW	African Training and Research Centre for Women
AU	African Union
CAEC	Central American Economic Community
CAEU	Council for Arab Economic Unity
CCEET	Centre for Co-operation with European Economies in Transition
CEC	Central-American Economic Council
CEET	Centre for East European Economies in Transition
CEFAS	Le Centre Français d'Archéologie et de Sciences Sociales [French Centre for Archaeology and Social Sciences]
CENDE	Centro de Estudios del Desarrollo [Center for Development Studies]
CEPAL	Comisión Económica para América Latina y el Caribe [Economic Commission for Latin America and the Caribbean]
CEPU	Central European Payment Union
CERMOC	Centre d'Etudes et de Recherches sur le Moyen-Orient Contemporain [Centre for Study and Research on the Contemporary Middle East]
CGPRT	Centre for Grains, Pulses, Roots and Tubers
CIB	Centre Internationale du Batiment [International Committee for Building Research]
CIS	Commonwealth of Independent States
CMEA	Council for Mutual Economic Assistance
CNRS	Centre National de la Recherche Scientifique [International Center for Scientific Research]
COCOM	Coordinating Committee for Multilateral Export Controls
CPC	Committee for Programme and Coordination

CPSU	Communist Party of the Soviet Union
CSCE	Conference for Security and Cooperation in Europe
CSIS	Canadian Security Intelligence Service
DESA	Department for Economic and Social Affairs
ECA	Economic Commission for Africa
ECAFE	Economic Commission for Asia and the Far East
ECCAS	Economic Community of Central African States
ECE	Economic Commission for Europe
EC-ESA	Executive Committee on Economic and Social Affairs
ECITO	European Central Inland Transport Organization
ECLA	Economic Commission for Latin America
ECLAC	Economic Commission for Latin America and the Caribbean
ECO	European Coal Organization
ECOSOC	Economic and Social Council
ECOWAS	Economic Community of West African States
ECWA	Economic Commission for Western Asia
EEC	European Economic Community
EECE	Emergency Economic Committee for Europe
EFTA	European Free Trade Association
EMU	European Monetary Union
EPTA	Expanded Program of Technical Assistance
EPU	European Payments Union
ESCAP	Economic and Social Commission for Asia and the Pacific
ESCOR	Economic and Social Council Official Records
ESCWA	Economic and Social Commission for Western Asia
EU	European Union
EURATOM	European Atlantic Energy Community
FAL	The Final Act of Lagos
FAO	Food and Agriculture Organization
FDI	foreign direct investment

FLNA	Frente Nacional de Libertação de Angola [National Front for the Liberation of Angola]
FOB	free on board
FRG	Federal Republic of Germany
G7	The Group of 7 (Canada, France, Germany, Italy, Japan, United Kingdom, and the United States)
G77	The Group of 77 developing countries
G8	The Group of 7, plus the Russian Federation
GA	General Assembly
GAOR	General Assembly Official Records
GATT	General Agreements on Tariffs and Trade
GCC	Gulf Cooperation Council
GDI	gender-related development index
GDP	gross domestic product
GDR	German Democratic Republic
GEM	gender empowerment measure
GNP	gross national product
HDI	human development index
HIPC	heavily indebted poor country
IBRD	International Bank for Reconstruction and Development
ICTs	information and telecommunications technologies
IDA	International Development Association
IDB	Inter-American Development Bank
IDEP	Institut pour le Dévelopment Economique et la Planification [Institute for Economic Development and Planning]
IDS	International Development Strategies
IEP	Institut d'Etudes Politiques
ILO	International Labor Organization
ILPES	Instituto Latinamericano y del Caribe de Planificación Económica y Social [Latin American Institute for Economic and Social Planning]

IMF	International Monetary Fund
ISO	International Standardization Organization
ISPs	Internet service providers
ITC	International Trade Center
ITO	International Trade Organization
ITU	International Telecommunication Unit
JIU	Joint Inspection Unit
LAFTA	Latin American Free Trade Area
LPA	The Lagos Plan of Action for the Economic Development of Africa 1980–2000
LRTAP	Long-range Transboundary Air Pollution
LTPS	*Sub-Saharan Africa—From Crisis to Sustainable Growth: A Long Term Perspective Study*
MAP	Millennium Partnership for the African Recovery Programme
MIT	Massachusetts Institute of Technology, Cambridge
MULPOCs	Multinational Programming and Operational Centers
NATO	North Atlantic Treaty Organization
NEPAD	New Partnership for African Development
NGOs	non-governmental organizations
NIEO	new international economic order
NNP	net national produce
NOx	nitrogen oxides
OAPEC	Organization of Arab Petroleum Exporting Countries
OAS	Organization of American States
OAU	Organization of African Unity
ODA	official development assistance
OECD	Organisation for Economic Co-operation and Development
OEEC	Organization for European Economic Cooperation
OEP	overall economic perspective

OIOS	Office of Internal Oversight Services
OPEC	Organization of Petroleum Exporting Countries
OSCAL	Office of the Special Coordinator for Africa and the Least Developed Countries
OSCE	Organization for Security and Cooperation in Europe
PANAFTEL	Pan-African Telecommunication Network Plan
PLO	Palestine Liberation Organization
PTA	Preferential Trade Area for Eastern and Southern African States
R and D	research and development
RCM	Regional Coordination Meeting
RICAP	Regional Interagency Committee for Asia and the Pacific
SAARC	South Asian Association for Regional Cooperation
SADC	Southern African Development Community
SALT	Strategic Arms Limitation Talks
SAPs	structural adjustment programs
SECI	Southeast Europe Cooperative Initiative
SIAP	Statistical Institute for Asia and the Pacific
SIPRI	Stockholm International Peace Research Institute
SITC	Standard International Trade Classification
SMEs	small and medium-sized enterprises
SSA	Sub-Saharan Africa
SSR	Soviet Socialist Republic
TAB	Technical Assistance Board
TAI	technology achievement index
TIR	Transport International Routier [International Road Transport]
TQM	Total Quality Management
U.S.	United States of America
UDEAC	Union Douanière et Economique d'Afrique Centrale [Customs and Economic Union of Central Africa]

UN	United Nations
UNAIDS	Joint UN Program on HIV/AIDS
UNCTAD	United Nations Conference on Trade and Development
UNDAF	United Nations Development Assistance Framework
UNDP	United Nations Development Programme
UNEP	United Nations Environment Programme
UNESCO	United Nations Educational, Scientific and Cultural Organization
UNESOB	United Nations Economic and Social Office in Beirut
UNFPA	United Nations Fund for Population (originally the United Nations Fund for Population Activities)
UNHCHR	United Nations High Commissioner for Human Rights
UNICEF	United Nations Children's Fund
UNIDO	United Nations Industrial Development Organization
UNIFEM	United Nations Development Fund for Women
UNIHP	United Nations Intellectual History Project
UNIN	United Nations Institute for Namibia
UNITA	Uniao Nacional para a Independencia Total de Angola [National Union for the Total Independence of Angola]
UN-NADAF	United Nations New Agenda for the Development of Africa
UN-PAERD	United Nations Program of Action for Economic Recovery and Development
UNRRA	United Nations Relief and Rehabilitation Administration
UNSIA	United Nations System-wide Special Initiative on Africa
UNTACDA	United Nations Transport and Communications Decade for Africa
URBAMA	Centre d'Etudes et de Recherches sur l'Urbanisation du Monde Arabe [Center for Study and Research on the Urbanization of the Arab World]
US$	U.S. dollar

WHO	World Health Organization
WMO	World Meteorological Organization
WTO	World Trade Organization
WWI	World War I
WWII	World War II

Unity and Diversity in Development Ideas

1

Unity and Diversity of Development: The Regional Commissions' Experience

Yves Berthelot

- **The Major Contribution of the Regional Commissions: A Regional Culture**
- **Five Battles for a Single Mandate**
- **Responding to Regional Needs: Cohesion, Development, and Integration**
- **The Regional Commissions as the UN's Regional Arm**
- **Looking toward the Future: Are the Regional Commissions Still Needed?**

The Major Contribution of the Regional Commissions: A Regional Culture

In the constellation of the United Nations (UN), the regional commissions are very special stars. Multisectoral, they illustrate the sectoral richness and complexity of the development process; regional in scope, they stress by their very existence the importance in development of initial conditions, institutions, and the societal dimension; and by the regional representation of their governing bodies, they bring to the UN an authentic regional voice. They recall the necessity of understanding the historical context of the socioeconomic problems for which they are searching for effective policies and strategies. Automatically, they go against the neoclassical approach that, in its tendency to prescribe "one-size-fits-all" policies, plays down the role of cumulative socioeconomic processes as a constraint on policymakers' freedom of action. By the same token, they go against a tendency of some entities in the UN system to jump to global conclusions without first assessing whether the regional building blocks really add up to a coherent global approach.

For these reasons, the regional commissions are similar and different. This chapter highlights both their differences and their similarities by examining in turn a regional culture; battles for mandates; cohesion, development, and integration; actions as the UN's regional arm; and visions of the future. It draws on the five following chapters while not pretending to offer a systematic summing up of their content. In fact, each regional chapter should be considered as self-contained and this introductory chapter as a reflection of the views of the author, enriched and amended by those expressed in the regional chapters. The aim of this volume being to assess the regional commissions' contribution to the intellectual history of the UN, it is appropriate to make some general points about the approach followed. This will clarify the multiple links between an institution and the ideas it produces.

Regional Commissions: The Intertwined Histories
of Ideas and Institutions

Writing an intellectual history of an institution is an extraordinarily difficult task. As with an individual, such a history cannot be restricted to asking whether or not important new ideas were produced in the course of its work. Significant contributions are in any case difficult to identify: Their recognition is subject to variable time lags, their relative importance is frequently revised (especially in the social sciences), and disputes over parentage are not uncommon. Most innovators stand on the shoulders of their (often forgotten) predecessors, and diligent scholars usually have little difficulty in finding historical precedents for even the most radical of "new" ideas. Any claims to originality must therefore be tentative and made with considerable care and modesty. But it must also be questioned whether the production of new ideas and original contributions is actually the most appropriate criterion for assessing the intellectual contribution and influence of an international economic institution. Influence may derive not from specific, seminal ideas but from a particular mindset or general approach to analyzing problems and making policy recommendations. Such a mindset would comprise not only a conceptual apparatus but also assumptions about how economies actually work and value judgments, explicit or implicit, about such matters as income distribution, the acceptability of specific tradeoffs (inflation versus unemployment), and general questions concerning the social outcomes of economic activity. Such a perspective on the economic and social world may be very influential, and when it is accepted by large numbers of those subject to its influence, and especially when it reflects the views of the most powerful members of the economic system, it begins to approach a type of Gramscian cultural hegemony. Thus, there is hardly anything that can be regarded as original among the individual components of the neoliberal or Washington Consensus as formulated after the debt crisis of the 1980s, but, whether or not one agrees with it, it would be difficult to deny that the synthesis has had a major influence on economic policies in much of the world in the last two decades. But even here there are still questions: Does the particular mindset arise from work done in the institution itself or is the institution a conduit for diffusing ideas from its member governments or from the academic world? And can we trace a relationship between the economic analysis and policy proposals made in international bodies and the economic policies actually pursued in individual countries? International officials often like to claim (or seek) a direct influence on national policymakers, but they should heed Professor Winch's warning that this involves "both an over-optimistic conception of the technocratic status of economics, and a naïve view of the processes of political decision making."[1]

Much of the economic analysis carried out in the regional commissions, and in most other international organizations for that matter, is unlikely to turn up in the usual citation indexes of academic work that tend to reflect specific contributions to relatively narrow fields of specialization.[2] In contrast, one of the main tasks of such organizations is to assess what is currently happening in the regional or global economies, to judge how matters may develop in the next eighteen months or so, to review the appropriateness of current policies, and to warn of possible dangers. Such regular conjunctural analysis, if given a sense of direction by a coherent mindset, can help to develop a general framework of ideas, which may have a significant influence on national and international policymakers. The propagation of neoliberal ideas in the 1980s and 1990s was greatly assisted by the regular biannual assessments of the current economic outlook published by the IMF (International Monetary Fund) and the OECD (Organisation for Economic Co-operation and Development). At the same time, the regular analyses of departments within the UN, such as the regional commissions and the United Nations Conference on Trade and Development (UNCTAD), although they appear to be much less influential, have helped to maintain a degree of skepticism toward much of the Washington Consensus and thus to preserve a measure of healthy debate over economic policies. Whether the latter bodies will gain in influence will depend to a large extent on economic developments and whether the ruling consensus is seen to remain relevant to the problems that require solution. From this point of view, it is important that coherent alternatives or amendments to the current consensus are readily available when the need for change is recognized.

Thus, it is important that at least some institutions recognize what Seamus Heaney has called "the necessity to confront the ruling intellectual pressures with a counter reality,"[3] even at the risk of being unfashionable or, at least in the short run, without apparent influence. This is an apposite injunction for the secretariat of the UN, the charter of which opens with "we the peoples of the United Nations," not "we the governments." This implies, to twist an observation of Montaigne, that we must pay attention to those who are subject to policy and not just to the governments that make it. Bulent Ecevit once remarked that progress is only possible with "constructive skepticism," which is only possible with "free thinking that allows one to perceive the changes taking place in the world more quickly than someone who inclines to be committed to certain fixed explanations and stands."[4] This is a disciplined, not a destructive, skepticism which is given a sense of direction by a clear understanding of the ultimate purposes of the economic system and of the value premises which underpin them. Of all the outstanding people who led the UN secretariat in the early postwar years, the one who articulated this point of view most clearly was Gunnar Myrdal, the first executive secretary of the Economic Commission for Europe (ECE). And in assessing the intellectual contributions of the various departments of the UN to international policy discussion, at least one of the attributes we should be looking for is a capacity for "constructive skepticism."

Institutions, as von Hayek and von Mises insisted, evolve, and in general they evolve gradually. Their history and the initial conditions in which they were created are therefore important. Both their agendas and policy orientations show strong continuities over time. There would appear to be good reasons for this. First, many of the fundamental problems are never "finally" solved—instead they constantly resurface in one form or another. How should change be managed and the costs of adjustment be distributed? How can productivity be improved? Can government intervention improve economic outcomes? How far should domestic economies adjust to the dictates of the international economy? How should the international monetary system be managed? Second, secretariats acquire comparative advantages in certain areas, and these specializations are reinforced over time. And third, institutional memory involves, among other things, the transmission from one generation to the next of certain intellectual attitudes and approaches, often implicitly. In the case of the regional commissions, initial conditions and their first years of activity have had a considerable and long-lasting influence on their activity, and for this reason it was not always possible to clearly separate the history of ideas from the history of the institution itself.

Five Regional Cultures

In subsequent chapters, the reader will discover that each of the regional commissions has developed its own culture that has guided its actions, analyses, and policy recommendations.

- Under Gunnar Myrdal's leadership, the Economic Commission for Europe (ECE) from its earliest days sought a middle way between the neoclassical approach and the Marxist alternative, which continental Western Europe translated into the so-called social market economy of the 1950s–1960s. The secretariat believed in indicative planning and state intervention to correct market failure and guide economic development. For more than fifty years, it sustained the idea of an undivided Europe by constructing and maintaining a bridge between its western and eastern halves, even when no other institution was able or willing to do so and when the prospect of achieving it was far more remote than it appeared at the end of the 1980s.
- Under P. S. Lokanathan's leadership, the Economic Commission for Asia and the Far East (ECAFE), despite the immensity of its territory, the lengthy decolonization process, the divisions of the Cold War, and the outbreak of actual wars, had a profound sense of the necessary unity of the region and held firmly that decisions concerning it should only be made by countries in the region. The ECAFE secretariat was convinced that member countries were responsible for their own development and, therefore, had to design their strategies and mobilize their own resources, public and private, through planning. Regional integration was seen as an indispensable complement to this process. In becoming the Economic and Social Commission for Asia and the Pacific (ESCAP) and focusing more on technical assistance, the commission lost its institutional and intellectual leadership. But, borrowing the title of a pamphlet that Lokanathan published in 1954, it continued to be "The Economic Parliament of Asia."[5]
- Under Raúl Prebisch, the Economic Commission for Latin America (ECLA), sought to modify the region's integration into the world economy by overcoming the asymmetry of trade benefits in favor of the developed countries through industrialization and regional cooperation. Benefiting from its relative homogeneity, ECLA developed, and maintained when it became ECLAC, the Economic Commission for Latin America and the Caribbean, an exceptional level of

policy debates within the secretariat and between the secretariat and member states. It is the quality of these debates that permitted the commission to adapt its model to new circumstances and to reject a narrow technical view of economics in favor of an interdisciplinary approach integrating economics, sociology, and politics.

• Created in 1958 after protracted debates, the Economic Commission for Africa (ECA), was effectively deprived from 1960 to 1963 of the leadership of its first two executive secretaries, successively Mekki Abbas and Robert Gardiner, who were sent to Congo as the special representatives of the UN Secretary-General. Nevertheless, in its resolute fight for decolonization, it forged the conviction that Africa alone should decide the future of the continent. Marked by the political decision to respect the boundaries inherited from the colonial era and conscious of the narrow economic base of so many small countries and the cultural diversity in the continent, the ECA was equally convinced of the necessity for regional and subregional cooperation. It never abandoned these convictions and created a large number of integrating entities. But, faced with the multiple needs of its members and the multiple pressures exerted on African governments by donor countries and the international financial institutions, the commission failed to establish clear priorities, confused resolutions with action, and waited too long before forging a coherent African strategy of self-reliance. Although adopted, the strategy was not implemented, in particular because, contrary to the World Bank, the commission lacked the financial resources to back it. In the 1990s, the commission turned to more concrete priorities such as strengthening the managerial and negotiating capacities of its members and increasing their awareness of the strategic choices to be made in particular domains.

• Despite the small size of its region and the common cultural and religious heritage of its members, the Economic Commission for Western Asia (ECWA), was conscious of the tensions within the region that frequently resulted in wars and civil strife. Its first executive secretary, Mohammed Said Al-Attar, and his successors were therefore convinced that the main role of the commission was to promote regional cooperation, a conviction reinforced by the fact that many natural obstacles to development could be effectively addressed only in a regional context. Divergences among member countries were such that reference to UN global decisions was the only way to reach agreement on certain issues. This, combined with the fact that the secretariat was not inclined to develop specific development paradigms for the region, encouraged ECWA and then ESCWA, the Economic and Social Commission for Western Asia, to seek a role in the dissemination and adaptation of UN economic and social principles, values, and policies to the region.

This brief introduction to the contributions of each commission brings out both similarities and differences. The culture of each commission—consisting of ideas, value judgments, and institutional mechanisms—was shaped by the circumstances of the region, the leadership of their executive secretaries, and by the dominant ideas of the time. The culture specific to each commission may be the most distinctive contribution that they have made to the intellectual history of the UN. Each culture has nurtured ideas that highlighted the double dimension of each commission's contribution. First, they developed responses to the specific needs of their region, which sometimes proved to be globally applicable; second, they adapted to the conditions of the region ideas developed by the UN at the global level.

Depending on the circumstances of the region or of the problem being addressed, the ideas could be more or less original, more or less sophisticated. For example, in analyzing the external trade of Latin American countries with their developed partners, ECLA noted asymmetrical benefits and developed the center-periphery thesis on which it based a development strategy, including industrialization by import substitution, which later inspired several countries of Asia, the Middle East, and Africa. The ECE, confronted with the division of Europe between two antagonistic blocs that were opposed by their ideologies and their views on how to organize the economy, took a functionalist and pragmatic approach to developing East-West cooperation on well-defined technical matters of common interest. Several of the norms and conventions which resulted from this approach became global or were extended to neighboring countries of the ECE region.

The ECA, reflecting both on the increasing marginalization of the continent in the world economy and its excessive dependence on foreign capital, foreign skill, and foreign technology, forged an alternative strategy of collective self-reliance in order to increase the participation of the mass of the people in the production. Later, its criticism of structural adjustment programs obliged the Bretton Woods institutions to review their rhetoric, if not their practice. ESCWA, concerned by the inequalities between its member countries and the impossibility of addressing particular problems such as water management in a purely national context, sought regional solutions. Some of its achievements in water management and the fight against desertification could prove useful in other regions affected by similar problems. ECAFE, noting that its member countries lacked the sense of belonging to the same region, created a set of institutions to establish links between these countries while addressing specific problems. Subsequently, the ECA adopted a similar strategy.

These are just a few examples of the hundreds of ideas produced over several decades by the regional commissions in responding to the needs of their regions in their sectors of competence. It would obviously be impossible to describe them all. The authors of this volume have emphasized policies developed in response to the most pressing political, economic, or social problems that each commission had to address. Indeed, the first task of the commissions was to try to assess what was happening, what might happen, and, in light of that knowledge, which was admittedly imperfect and often provisional, to review existing policies and make suggestions for improvement. The emphasis on the comparative approach encouraged national policymakers and analysts to see their own country in an international setting and perspective. This habit of comparing achievements and assessing the effects of interdependency has been consolidated over five decades, so it is perhaps taken for granted; but it is one of the important foundations for effective cooperation in general. The ECE initiated it and was emulated by the other commissions.

As a result, the authors have not highlighted the many specific solutions developed in response to the many technical problems arising between countries of the same region. Readers are thus spared the tedious enumeration of practical details. At the same time, they may miss the fact that by promoting such ideas, the commissions facilitated economic relations within their regions and prevented hundreds of misunderstandings that, in times of political tension, could have degenerated into more damaging conflicts. For example, who owns the electricity produced by a hydropower station built on a river that separates two countries, and how should downstream countries be compensated for possible disturbance to the flow of water?

Cooperation on technical issues, however narrow in scope and however obvious and modest the underlying ideas may sometimes appear, not only provided practical benefits but also cumulatively strengthened the habits of cooperation. This contributed to the creation of a common mindset, which, for an institution, is probably one of the most important factors in achieving the objectives for which it was created in the first place.

Although for some problems there were solutions benefiting all parties with visible results, in many cases it is difficult to assess the impact of an idea and to allocate responsibility for ambiguous results to its inadequacy, its partial implementation, or unforeseen events. Among the difficulties are the lags between the formulation of an idea and its acceptance—that is, an idea received at first with skepticism may later enjoy general acceptance, and vice versa. Such an assessment is perhaps more easily made at the regional level, and the authors have exercised their own judgments on the impact of the ideas and actions of each commission. While no further consideration is made in this chapter on the impact of ideas, interested readers are referred to the general considerations developed in the first volume of the United Nations Intellectual History Project (UNIHP) series.[6]

When it comes to disseminating more general or "global" ideas in the regions, the contribution of the commissions has been equally important. While ideas do not have to be conceived anew, their adaptation to a particular region requires a deep understanding of what is essential in the ideas and how they could be perceived, received, and applied. Despite the fact that they may have been negotiated and adopted by all or at least a majority of the members of the UN, a number of these "global" ideas originated in the Western developed countries and inevitably reflected their vision of the world and their political interests. Civil and political rights, gender equality, and the environment, for instance, now part of the development agenda, were marked by their origins. Therefore, their adaptation and implementation in each region required, and still requires, particular sensitivity to the culture and history of the region concerned. ESCAP, ECLAC, the ECA, and mainly ESCWA have devoted some attention to this issue. In contrast, the ECE did not devote energy to ideas dear to the South—such as economic, social, and cultural rights; the new international economic order (NIEO); the stabilization of commodity prices; or human-centered development—that were internationally agreed upon but often resisted in the North.

Within the UN system, developing an idea to meet some regional need or adapting a global idea to the specificity of a region is not a priori the exclusive prerogative of the regional commissions. In fact, most UN specialized agencies, funds, and programs have also established regional offices or bureaus. The crucial difference, however, is that, contrary to the regional commissions, they do not respond to regional intergovernmental machinery. This important point explains why this volume does not describe the intellectual contribution of the UN as a whole to the needs of the regions but focuses on the contribution of the five entities that are the regional commissions. Compared with the other volumes of the United Nations Intellectual History Project, this one introduces a strong institutional dimension, although it does not pretend to be an institutional history of the commissions but rather an illustration of their intellectual contributions. But this institutional dimension is important. The framework of ideas and values particular to the secretariat of each commission and the general mindset developed between governmental

representatives and the staff of the commissions through a multitude of negotiations are two sides of the same fact. For an institution to be creative and
effective, it needs to develop a sufficiently broad basis of shared ideas and
practices which enable its staff and its "customers" to interact constructively.

"Shared ideas" does not imply *la pensée unique*. An international secretariat has a responsibility to present to its member countries the range of
approaches to a particular problem, to insist that there are always alternatives
(albeit involving different costs), and to allow member countries to decide
what is best for themselves. At the same time, if the secretariats have a clear
analytical standpoint, they also provide a benchmark for comparing the alternatives. Secretariats should maintain a "constructive skepticism" to all policy
ideas, including their own and those of global entities.

The debates that surrounded the creation of each regional commission
provide a first example of how institutional and intellectual histories are intertwined. These influenced their subsequent responses to three issues each
of them had to address—the cohesion of the regions, development strategies,
and the dual trend toward globalization and subregional cooperation—and
which illustrate their diversity while pointing to their main contributions.
Similarly, diversity emerges from their role in preparing and implementing
global initiatives. Finally, the institutional dimension reemerges from an account of their relations with UN headquarters in New York.

Five Battles for a Single Mandate

The founders of the UN had not envisaged the establishment of regional
entities when they created the organization and its specialized agencies. Even
after the creation of the ECE and ECAFE in 1947, it took twenty-six years to
establish the five regional commissions (ECLA, 1948; ECA, 1958; and ECWA,
1973) and forty-four years to include each country that wished to become a
member of a commission—Israel, which was excluded from ECWA, had to
wait until the end of the Cold War before being accepted as a member of the
ECE in 1991.

What Is a Region?

In the debates concerning the creation of the regional commissions, the
issue of what is a region was never raised despite the impact it could have had
on their role and membership. The definition of "region" may have been
obvious to the negotiators, but the dictionary shows how malleable this concept is. "Region: a relatively large territory, possessing physical and human

characteristics that make it a unity distinct from neighboring regions or within a whole that includes it."[7] Indeed, the definition fits with the practice of using "region" to refer to a part of a country as well as a group of countries, small or large, depending on the unifying characteristics retained. The members of each of the five regional commissions share sufficient common geographical, historical, or cultural characteristics to separate them into five more or less distinct units. Because the purpose of the commissions is to facilitate concerted action for development, each country within a region should be a member, and the only choice of membership should have been for countries at a regional boundary to decide to which region they wanted to belong. There may be, of course, some degree of political opportunism in joining two commissions or more. For example, the presence of former colonial powers in the membership of ECAFE, ECLA, and the ECA was initially justified by their remaining responsibilities over territories in the region. Later, the five newly independent states of Central Asia were automatically attached to ESCAP when the Soviet Union was dismantled, but within three years all had also joined the ECE. Similarly, the three countries of the Caucasus attached to the ECE have since decided to also join ESCAP.

The table in the appendix gives, year by year, the membership of each commission. It shows how each commission grew over time with decolonization and the dismantling of nations, large and small, including people who decided to divorce despite their economic and historical links. It shows also how long it took for the membership of each commission to fully cover its territory and how many countries chose to belong to more than one commission.

The Rationale for Regional Commissions

Economic, institutional, or practical considerations could justify the existence of regional commissions, but none of these was thoroughly addressed in the debates that preceded their creation.

The economic rationale lies in the conviction that cooperation between countries of a region is beneficial to all and could help to prevent a repetition of "beggar thy neighbor" and other non-cooperative policies of the 1930s. It was decisive in the creation of the ECE and ECAFE. Latin American countries used the same argument and the precedent of the ECE and ECAFE when they sought the creation of ECLA. Subsequently, and in order to establish the ECA and ECWA, the independent countries of Africa and the Middle East used the same argument again.

The argument that wherever international cooperation and policy coordination are required policies should be formulated at a level that internalizes

the externalities or spillover effects of particular problems provides an institutional rationale. The optimal level of cooperation will not necessarily coincide with existing institutions or structures, but regional approaches are more
likely in practice to be closer to the optimum than are top-down global initiatives or simultaneous multiple bilateral negotiations. Nonetheless, the resistance of most institutions to delegating responsibilities upward or downward
is fairly universal. The European Union (EU) refers frequently to the principle of subsidiarity but has tended to resist it throughout its history. This is
illustrated today in the discussions about the distribution of functions between member governments and the commission and in its preference for
bilateral dialogue with non-EU members in Europe rather than in the context of pan-European institutions such as the ECE, the Organization for Security and Cooperation in Europe (OSCE), or the Council of Europe.

Finally, from a practical point of view, the benefits from cooperation with
close neighbors are usually more immediately obvious than those from global agreements. Many, if not most, of the urgent issues demanding effective
international cooperation are those affecting neighbors. Regional institutions
usually are well placed not only to bring about solutions to specific issues but
also to develop strong habits of consultation and cooperation. As discussed
above, member governments resort to them automatically whenever problems arise.

These rationales were neither seriously addressed nor challenged when the
first commissions were established. Some countries did not consider it necessary to create the ECE and ECAFE for the sole purpose of taking over the
tasks of the United Nations Relief and Rehabilitation Administration
(UNRRA) that was due to be dismantled in early 1949. The Ukraine SSR, for
instance, thought that existing UN institutions could assume UNRRA's responsibilities and that, for the reconstruction of war-torn areas, free relief
and soft loans were what mattered. Canada, Australia, and New Zealand wondered if it was appropriate to create geographical divisions when trying to
build a unified world. They also feared that divergences could occur between
policies advocated in a region by the commission on one side and by the
specialized agencies on the other. This risk never seriously materialized, but,
depending on the personalities involved, constructive cooperation or acrimonious territorial disputes marked the relations between regional commissions and specialized agencies. In fact, both have their role, which makes an
either-or choice inappropriate here as in many other organizational matters.
For example: Should ministries of foreign affairs be organized by subject or
region? Should multinational corporations be structured by product lines or
regional markets?

Political Resistance

In every case, there was resistance and delay in the creation of the regional commissions. The reasons were largely political, although there was some reluctance to assume the cost of new institutions. Political reasons often hide behind apparently reasonable considerations. One of them, often used in the world of international institutions, is the risk of duplication. The United States initially opposed the creation of ECLA on the grounds that it could duplicate the existing Pan-American Union's Inter-American Economic and Social Council. The United States, however, could better control a pan-American organization than a Latin American one. Conversely, Western countries did not worry about duplication when they set up a Centre for East European Economies in Transition (CEET) at the OECD in the wake of the collapse of communism in Eastern Europe in 1989, even though the ECE had detailed knowledge and experience of both market and planned systems and already had an institutional structure in place for policy advice and practical cooperation.

In the 1940s and 1950s, there was no question of duplication in the case of Europe, Asia, or Africa, because none of these continents were covered by pan-regional organizations: The Conference on Security and Cooperation in Europe (CSCE) was created only in 1977 and the Organization of African Unity (OAU) in 1963; there is still no pan-Asian political structure. Western Asian countries, in contrast, felt that cooperation between ECWA and the many existing Arab organizations would be mutually beneficial. This shows the limit of the duplication argument. The view that the UN regional commissions were losing their raison d'être with the emergence of non-UN regional or subregional institutions reemerged in the 1990s.

Political considerations delayed the creation of ECA and ECWA for one and two decades, respectively. The principle of universality argued for opposition to the Arab states that wanted a commission that would exclude Israel. In response, they argued that their region should not be discriminated against, and they finally obtained the creation of ECWA. There was no principle to be opposed in the creation of the ECA, simply the desire of the colonial powers to avoid any interference in the management of their colonies. Participation by former colonial powers and their colonies did not raise particular problems in ECLA. The former were full members of the commission and the latter could become associate members on presentation of their request by the member responsible for its international relations. Similar solutions were adopted for ECAFE soon after its creation and, later, for the ECA. But in these two regions, there were fewer than ten independent countries when they were

established, and the participation of the colonial powers soon led to controversies. In ECAFE, they were reluctant to propose their territories as associate
members and had to be invited in 1951 not to oppose economic proposals
supported by the majority of the countries in the region. In 1961, the ECA
considered a more radical proposal that the colonial powers cease to be members of the commission and participate only in a consultative capacity. This
was rejected by the UN's Economic and Social Council (ECOSOC). But in
1963 these powers had to accept the status of associate members together with
the territories that were still under their control. The ECA and ECWA are
today the only commissions in which France, the United Kingdom, and the
United States are not full members. Adebayo Adedeji, in chapter 5, suggests
that, in the present circumstances, it would be in the interests of the ECA for
the major powers to be granted full membership. Interestingly, at the end of
the 1980s, the Cuban delegation, always irritated by the presence of the United
States, raised the matter of why a Commission for Latin America was not
limited to Latin American membership. The secretariat and many member
states felt that ejecting the developed countries from ECLAC would seriously
weaken the commission; they argued that it was a positive thing to have an
intergovernmental forum where the region could meet and discuss development issues with its main partners from the unique vantage point of Latin
America. Using this logic, Japan, Germany, and Italy were invited to join the
developed countries who were already members of ECLAC. Only Italy accepted and joined in 1990.

In the context of the Cold War, the participation of the independent non-
member states of the UN and of the territories under the control of the Allies
were a source of considerable controversy between East and West. The Soviet
Union wanted the independent non-member states of the UN to be admitted
in a consultative capacity for the consideration of matters affecting them. This
suggestion was rejected in a vote, but several countries became members of a
regional commission prior to joining the UN. The case of countries occupied
by the Allied countries after World War II was even more controversial. The
Soviet Union wanted a solution whereby the Allied Control Authority would
represent the occupied country. This was accepted. But the Western part of
Germany, with the authorization of the Western Allies, was systematically associated with the work of the ECE. When the Federal Republic of Germany
(FRG) was created, ECOSOC accepted it as a full member of the commission
in 1956. The Soviet Union continued to represent Eastern Germany, and when
the German Democratic Republic (GDR) was created, Western countries opposed its participation in the ECE until its admission to the UN in 1973. Like
the Federal Republic of Germany, Japan joined ECAFE as a full member in

1954 prior to joining the UN in 1956. In all these cases, the united West won the argument against the East in ECOSOC, while the colonial powers alone had to defer to the will of African states.

The Mandate

If political and institutional debates delayed, sometimes for years, the creation of one or another of the regional commissions, they were all given the same core mandate. It derived directly from the UN Charter, Articles 1.3 and 1.4. and, as such, the commissions were instrumental in pursuing its basic purposes. From the outset, they were the regional arms of the UN. With some variation in the wording to take account of the time elapsed since the end of WWII, the commissions were asked to:

- Initiate and participate in measures for facilitating concerted action for the economic reconstruction (and development) of [the region], for raising the level of economic activity, and for maintaining and strengthening the economic relations of the countries [of the region] both among themselves and with other countries of the world;
- Make and sponsor . . . investigations and studies of economic and techno-logical problems and development [within the region]. . . .
- Undertake or sponsor the collection, evaluation and dissemination of such economic, technological and statistical information as the Commission deems appropriate.[8]

On two points—the social dimension and technical assistance—different mandates marked the evolution of thinking about development. As underlined in the forthcoming UNIHP volume on development theory and practice,[9] social development was not the priority in the aftermath of WWII. This explains why only the latecomers, the ECA and ECWA, were asked "to deal as appropriate with the social aspects of economic development and the interrelationship of economic and social factors." Later, ECWA became ESCWA and ECAFE became ESCAP, the "S" in their titles underlining the social dimension of development. In contrast, ECLA and the ECA stayed with a lonely "E," but they managed to add the quoted sentence to their mandate. Only in the ECE did governments continue to resist the idea that social and economic matters were intimately linked. Before 1989, social issues would have been so divisive for the ECE—composed of two blocs with different economic and social systems, with both committed to overcoming the other—that it could have undermined cooperation on other matters. Social investigations would have shown weaknesses that the East wanted to hide. After 1989, there were some, but not the ECE secretariat, who thought that too much attention to

social considerations could have delayed reforms and legitimate state intervention. Instead of the ECE, the United Nations Children's Fund (UNICEF)
forged ahead with excellent work on the social dimension of transition, frequently producing East-West comparative studies. This said, the most elaborate analysis by a regional commission of the interaction between the social
and the economic were produced by ECLAC in the last decade.

Initially, it was not envisaged that the regional commissions would act as a
channel for assistance to their region. The first meeting of the ECE took place
in May 1947, the month before General Marshall's famous address at Harvard
University. For a few weeks, the ECE was considered as the possible secretariat for managing what became the Marshall Plan, but this plan did not
materialize. Only years later, in the mandates of the ECA and ECWA, was a
modest role given to the provision of technical assistance to their member
countries. They were invited "to perform such advisory services . . . as the
countries of the region may desire" with the ritual reminder that such services should be provided "within available resources" and avoid "overlap with
those rendered by the Specialised Agencies." In other words, they were invited
to find a niche for their technical advisory services that would not infringe on
the turf of other agencies rather than take a lead in the assistance to their
regions.

In the 1970s, the discussion and the adoption in UN resolutions of the
NIEO prompted debates on the capacity of the UN system to put into place
such a new order. Decentralization became fashionable, but vested interests
remained strong. Finally, in January 1979, the General Assembly decided in
Resolution 33/202 that "the Regional Commissions shall have the status of
executing agencies, in their own right"[10] for intersectoral, subregional, regional,
and interregional projects. It foresaw their participation in coordinating
mechanisms and confirmed, as already expressed in General Assembly Resolution 32/197, that "they should exercise team leadership and responsibility
for co-ordination and co-operation at the regional level."[11] However, nothing
significantly changed. Later, in the 1990s, encouraged by the two Secretaries-
General, Boutros Boutros-Ghali and Kofi A. Annan, the executive secretaries
convened coordinating meetings where the situation of their regions was discussed in order to harmonize the views of the agencies and the interagency
technical assistance programs. But the commissions never imposed themselves
as "team leaders"; at best they were recognized as facilitators for regional cooperation.

More important was the impact of technical assistance activities on the intellectual contribution of the regional commissions. In theory, serious action-
oriented research can be rooted in technical assistance, which gives the staff

practical experience with specific development issues. And, indeed, it happens. But, Leelananda de Silva, in chapter 3, also sees in Resolution 32/197 (quoted above) the source of the intellectual decline of ESCAP. Technical assistance can be perverse as it gives more immediate satisfaction to all the actors concerned than does the conduct of rigorous analysis or participation in lengthy negotiations. It gives autonomy and means to professional staff who have the impression of doing something concrete. Ambassadors or delegates offer more thanks for bringing experts and resources than for transmitting a study or a resolution. When technical assistance becomes the priority, the need for resources to assist countries to implement the policies and conventions developed by the commission gives way to the demand for resources for technical assistance. Donors are put in the driver's seat and can impose policies and projects. There is little incentive for the secretariat to develop genuine new ideas; instead, it is encouraged simply to conceive of projects that please a solicited donor, and, as such, are often subject to fashion.[12]

It is not easy to hold the line that technical assistance by the commissions should focus on helping countries implement policies adopted and agreements reached collectively or on providing information for action-oriented research. The regional commissions, as do other entities or agencies of the UN, have not always resisted the temptation to go beyond this limited but important role.[13] Regrettably, the United Nations Development Programme (UNDP) failed to stick to its initial role of providing resources to agencies. Instead, it began to develop assistance programs of its own that were often disconnected from the policies and conventions adopted through international negotiation and tended to hire external experts who ignored the accumulated experience in the UN system.

Responding to Regional Needs: Cohesion, Development, and Integration

The five regional commissions share quasi-identical mandates. In each of them, governments decide on the program of work, and their secretariats enjoy a broad autonomy vis-à-vis UN headquarters. This autonomy was exercised in different historical contexts and in different economic, social, and political circumstances. While addressing broadly similar issues, the regional commissions followed different paths and made very uneven contributions to the intellectual history of the UN.

The ways in which the regional commissions addressed three problems highlight their differences and similarities. First, if concerted action among countries was to facilitate reconstruction and development, how could the interwar tradition of making decisions at the national level without consulting neighboring countries be changed? How could ideological differences be overcome, and how could regions prevent political tensions from degenerating into war? In other words, how could regions create a sense of belonging to the same family and maintain cohesion? Second, which development strategies and economic management models needed to be conceived or adopted to best fit the specific circumstances of each region? Third, as the trends toward globalization and subregional integration intensify, what issues are usefully addressed at the regional level?

Securing the Cohesion of the Regions

The five secretariats shared the conviction that in order to accomplish their missions they had to secure the full participation of all countries in the region and create and maintain the unity of their region. If all the interests involved were represented and cooperative activities multiplied, unity would be reinforced. Each region had colonies or occupied territories, or even independent countries that were not members of the UN, but each commission found ways to associate them with its work before they became members of the world organization. As an extreme example, Switzerland joined ECE in 1972 but waited until 2002 to join the UN. Since 1989, the newly independent countries have joined the regional commission of their choice as quickly as possible, which reflects some recognition of the useful role performed by the commissions.

History, geography, culture, politics, and economic interests influenced the countries' sense of belonging to the same entity. ECWA was created after several Arabic organizations had been established. The ECA was born when the pan-African movement, initiated by the African diaspora in 1900 with George Padmore and William E. B. Du Bois, took roots in Africa with Dr. Nkrumah and the independence of Ghana. In the meantime, it had become a political force for the emancipation of the African people. The geographical and cultural unity of Latin America inspired the creation of many regional groupings after countries had become independent from Spain or Portugal. This was a deeply rooted ideal which had been pursued, but without sustained success, since the independence of the Latin American countries. Despite its record of wars and conflicts, Europe had a strong historical sense of unity as expressed by Michelet in the sentences quoted at the beginning of the chapter on the ECE. The size and history of ECAFE, however, were such that its secretariat felt it necessary to give priority to building regional unity.

It could be said that the comments above do not take into account the U.S. participation as a founding member of the ECE and ECLA, a fact that formally breaks the geographical and historical unity of these regions. But the words "Europe" and "Latin America" in the very name of the commissions weaken this remark. The United States played a key role in establishing the ECE in 1947 at a time when the economic recovery of Western Europe was essential to its medium- and long-term interests. But in general, the United States has not played a leading role in promoting the interests of these regions. It has acted rather as a controller, making sure that the commissions' activities do not harm its own interests. The same could be said of its participation in ECAFE.

In response to their mandates, the regional commissions developed intergovernmental machinery from which emerged networks of officials and experts. These constituted the topsoil in which ideas related to the problems of the regions grew and matured. This intergovernmental framework became an instrument of unity.

In parallel, ECAFE, and subsequently, ECLA and the ECA, created an infrastructure of regional institutions. This was not necessary in the case of ECWA, where such institutions existed before its creation; nevertheless, the commission was instrumental in encouraging the creation of a few new institutions. The ECE did not create any such institutions, although from a legal point of view, the conventions it developed were independent institutions which relied on the ECE secretariat to service them. The institutions created by the other regional commissions had two different fates. The more famous and successful, such as the regional development banks or some research centers, loosened their links with their sponsoring commissions and became financially autonomous and intellectually independent. The least successful became a burden on commissions that did not have the means to support and revitalize them, for reasons spelled out particularly in chapters 4 and 5. But, despite unavoidable failures, the institutional infrastructure promoted by the commissions as well as by the intergovernmental machinery that they developed were powerful instruments of unity. They raised the consciousness of belonging to a common space where cooperation could be mutually beneficial.

Maintaining regional unity, or creating it in the case of ECAFE, was not an easy task. None of the regions were immune from interstate conflicts or tensions or from civil strife or wars. Hundreds of conflicts since WWII have affected each of the five regions: in Europe, the East-West divide and later the Balkans conflict; in Asia, the Korean and Indochina Wars and the recurrent Indo-Pakistani conflicts; in Latin America, several brutal dictatorships, the

Falklands War, and many border disputes; in Africa, the struggle against apartheid, the wars or civil wars that affected and still affect nearly half of the continent; and in Western Asia, the Iran-Iraq War, the civil war in Lebanon, the
invasion of Kuwait, and, above all, the permanent tension created in the region by the occupation of Palestine by Israel. These violent confrontations as
well as conflicts of interests, trade disputes, and innumerable irritating differences over fishing rights, international waters, transboundary pollution, and
the like appealed to nationalistic instincts and made regional cohesion more
difficult. But the most pervasive and divisive influence was the Cold War, with
its ideological opposition between two different political, social, and economic
systems. Particularly acute in the ECE region, it permeated all the other regions as the antagonistic Western and Eastern blocs actively sought clients in
order to strengthen their own standing vis-à-vis the other camp.

To maintain the cohesion of Europe despite the Cold War, Gunnar Myrdal
pioneered the idea that confidence-building must start with small steps, especially with those seen by the population of the region as bringing practical
benefits. The supply of coal and wheat were among the first concrete cases of
practical East-West cooperation in the immediate aftermath of WWII when
ECE took over from UNRRA in Europe.[14] Soon after, the ECE initiated negotiations on norms, standards, and conventions to facilitate border-crossing,
to simplify trade procedures, to design a network of roads and railroads linking the north and south of the region and the west to the east, to harmonize
road signals and improve road safety, to reduce the risks of motorcar accidents and limit their damage, to speed up relief in case of accidents in the
transport of dangerous goods, to reduce air and water pollution, to minimize
the impact of transboundary industrial accidents, to improve the quality of
perishable goods on the market, to manage gas storage, and so on and so forth.

The achievements were considerable: More than two hundred conventions
and protocols were successfully negotiated despite the Cold War. Each country
was free to participate and could join the negotiations or adopt the results whenever it wanted. This was not always harmonious, and for several years the Eastern bloc shunned the negotiations. However, the process was transparent and
the success of the negotiations, the access to technical information which they
made possible, the networks they created, and the usefulness of the results
convinced the East European countries to participate. The norms, protocols,
and conventions became links that kept the region together. The functional,
gradualist approach initiated by the ECE was subsequently adopted and extended by the West European countries. This led them from the European
Coal and Steel Community in 1951 to the European Union. Most of the ECE's
conventions and norms became elements of the *acquis communautaire* and

are therefore rigorously applied by all the countries wishing to join the European Union, which sometimes did not apply them as rigorously before 1990.

A major source of tension has disappeared with the end of the Cold War, but other dividing lines have emerged or deepened between the well-off countries and the relatively poorer ones. Similar cleavages separate regions, but there are vast disparities within regions as well. Tables 1.1 and 1.2 summarize this reality. The evolution of GDP per head for each region from 1958 to 1999 confirms the widening gap between regions (table 1.1). The percentage of the population living below $1 a day ranges from close to zero in the ECE region to over 46 percent in sub-Saharan Africa (table 1.2). But these averages hide large intercountry differences: in the ECE, the proportions range from zero in Western Europe to more than 11 percent in Moldova; in ECLAC, the range is from less than 2 percent in Chile and Uruguay to more than 24 percent in Honduras; and in ECA, the range is from 3 percent or less in several countries of North Africa to more than 70 percent in Mali.[15] These differences are echoed in trade structures. The ECE region accounted for 55 percent of world exports in 2000 and more than two-thirds of Western Europe's trade was with other West European countries. At the other extreme, Africa's share of world exports is less than 2.5 percent, and more than two-thirds of its trade is with Western Europe and North America. In the other regions, intraregional trade ranges from 49 percent of the total in Asia to 17 percent in Latin America and 7 percent in the Middle East, as indicated in table 1.3.[16]

Economic differences, of course, are not the only ones. The number of member countries in each commission in 2000 was, with the exception of ESCWA (13), fairly similar: 41 in ECLAC, and 52, 53, and 55 respectively in ESCAP, the ECA, and the ECE. But their populations vary considerably, from 3.5 billion in ESCAP to 158 million in ESCWA.[17] Political systems, which can have a major influence on economic performance, also vary considerably. Measuring such differences is a controversial matter, but the widely cited "state of freedom and democracy" by Freedom House focuses on the rights and freedoms enjoyed by individuals, and these are regarded as important factors promoting enterprise and economic performance in general. On the Freedom House indicator, two-thirds or more of all the countries in the Americas and Europe are rated as free, while for the Middle East and Africa the proportions are 7 and 17 percent, respectively.[18]

Education and research and development are indicators not only of current levels of development but also of the base for future development. There has been considerable progress in raising enrollment rates at all levels of education over the past thirty years, but although the gap between Europe and some of the other regions (Asia and Latin America) has been closed in primary

Table 1.1. Income: Per-Capita Gross Domestic Product, by Regions (in current dollars)

Per-capita gross domestic product, by regions (in current dollars)

Year	World	ECE			ESCAP			ECLAC	ECA	ESCWA
		Europe	Northern America	ECE Total	Asia	Oceania	ESCAP Total	Latin America[a]	Africa[b]	Western Asia
GDP per capita										
1958	480	780[c]	2,320	1,348	104[d]	1,270[e]	133	330	110	230
1975	1,570	3,567	7,080	4,394	616	5,171	691	1,097	430	1,228
1999	5,157	13,156[f]	32,276	18,823	2,240	15,218	2,350	4,102	729	2,303
Highest GDP per capita 1999										
	41,188	41,188	33,666	41,188	34,742	20,834	34,742	14,999	7,116	29,159
	Luxembourg	Luxembourg	United States	Luxembourg	Japan	Australia	Japan	Bahamas	Seychelles	Qatar
Lowest GDP per capita 1999										
	107	249	19,835	249	182	732	182	466	107	387
	Burundi/Ethiopia	Republic of Moldova	Canada	Republic of Moldova	Tajikistan	Kiribati	Tajikistan	Nicaragua	Burundi/Ethiopia	Yemen

Source: UNCTAD, *Handbook of International Trade and Development Statistics* (New York and Geneva: United Nations, various years). From 2000 onward: UNCTAD, *UNCTAD Handbook of Statistics* (New York and Geneva: United Nations, various years).

Notes: In the absence of official values, UNCTAD's secretariat has proposed estimates for some regions and applied them, whenever possible, in order to ensure comparability at the total group levels. Highest and lowest per-capita GDP for each region consider only the countries for which official estimates exist.

[a]Includes the Caribbean. 1975 and 1999 totals also include Bahamas, Barbados, Belize, Guyana, Leeward Islands, Trinidad and Tobago, Windward Islands, Bermuda, Falkland Islands, French Guyana, Greenland, Guadeloupe, Jamaica, Martinique, Netherlands Antilles, Surinam, U.S. Virgin Islands.

[b]Includes South Africa (South African per-capita GDP representing US$401 [1958], US$1,384 [1975], and US$3,286 [1999]).

[c]Western Europe only. Excluding Albania, Bulgaria, Czechoslovakia, Eastern Germany, Hungary, Poland, Romania, the Soviet Union, and Yugoslavia.

[d]The total for Asia (East and Southeast) excludes China (Mainland), Mongolia, North Korea, and North Vietnam.

[e]Australia and New Zealand.

[f]Does not include the five republics of Central Asia that are in ESCAP.

Table 1.2. Poverty: Population Living below $1 per Day[a] in 1998, by Regions

	Western Europe	Central Asia	East Asia	South Asia	Latin America	Middle East and North Africa	Sub-Saharan Africa	Total
			Population Living below $1 per Day in Each Region in 1998 (%)					
Poverty Rate (%)	< 1.00	5.14	15.32	39.99	15.57	7.32	46.30	24.27

Source: Information is available at the World Bank's website at www.worldbank.org.

Notes: The World Bank considers only the developing countries and gives no information about Western Europe and Northern America. The regional grouping given by the World Bank has been kept. The international poverty lines are based on nationally representative primary-household surveys conducted by national statistics offices or by private agencies under the supervision of government or international agencies and obtained from government statistical offices and World Bank country departments.

[a] Population below $1 a day corresponds to the percentage of the population living on less than $1.08 a day at 1993 international prices (equivalent to $1 in 1985 prices, adjusted for purchasing power parity).

Table 1.3. External Trade: Share of Intraregional and Interregional Trade Flows in Each Region's Total Merchandise Exports, 2000 (by Percent)

Region	ECE			Asia	Latin America	Africa	Middle East	World
	North America	Western Europe	Central and Eastern Europe, Baltic States, and the CIS					
ECE								
North America	**39.8**	18.5	0.6	21.6	16.5	1.1	1.9	100.0
Western Europe	10.8	**67.8**	5.3	8.2	2.3	2.4	2.5	100.0[a]
Central and Eastern Europe, Baltic States, and the CIS	4.4	54.2	**26.6**	7.4	2.2	1.1	2.6	100.0[b]
Asia	25.7	16.9	0.9	**48.9**	2.5	1.3	2.5	100.0[c]
Latin America	61.3	12.5	0.8	5.8	**17.3**	0.8	0.8	100.0[d]
Africa	17.9	49.7	0.7	17.2	2.8	**7.6**	1.4	100.0[e]
Middle East	15.6	18.3	0.8	47.9	1.1	3.8	**6.5**	100.0[f]
World	22.7	39.4	3.7	23.1	5.6	1.9	2.4	100.0[g]

Source: World Trade Organization, *International Trade Statistics 2001* (Geneva: WTO, 2001), 40, Chapter III, Trade by Region, Table III.3; also available at http://www.wto.org

Notes: North America, Western, Central, Eastern Europe, Baltic States, and the CIS are presented in separated groups in WTO, *International Trade Statistics.* But here it has been grouped in the second column. Unfortunately, the others regions cannot be detailed.

[a]Errors and omissions equal 0.7.
[b]Errors and omissions equal 1.5.
[c]Errors and omissions equal 1.3.
[d]Errors and omissions equal 0.7.
[e]Errors and omissions equal 2.7.
[f]Errors and omissions equal 6.0.
[g]Errors and omissions equal 1.2.

schooling it still remains considerable for secondary and tertiary education. Tertiary enrollment has increased sharply in Europe over the last thirty years, and although it has also risen in the other regions, the gap between them and Europe has increased considerably: Against 43 percent in Europe, the ratio was 19 percent in Latin America and just under 4 percent in Africa. Not surprisingly, the latter difference is reflected in the shares of GDP allocated to research and development. In Europe, this reached as high as 3.8 percent in the 1990s (Sweden) and just over 3 percent in Japan, but the largest shares in the ECE (South Africa) and ESCWA (Kuwait) were under 1 percent.[19] The three indicators in table 1.4—GDP per capita, human development index, and share of arms expenditure in GDP—confirm the disparity between and within regions and also that the classification of a country within a region varies depending on the indicator used.

Differences between regions are not more important than disparities within each region. The magnitude of such differences is highlighted in table 1.2. Differences between countries of the same region are not in themselves a source of tension or a threat to the unity of the region. But they could become so if they widen, if no prospect for improvement exists, or if some countries feel that, in addition to being among the least favored, they are treated inequitably and are marginalized in the institutions of the region. The low participation of the poorer countries in the sectoral meetings of their commission, because of a lack of resources but also of interest, is worrisome. It is vital for the unity of the regions, and therefore for their security and stability, that the weakest countries be able and willing to voice their concerns and that they are listened to in the regional forums. This view is shared by the secretariats of the commissions. But they encounter increasing difficulty in translating it into practice in a world in which the dominant common wisdom suggests that countries have to bear the full responsibility for their success or failure and in which two superpowers are no longer competing to attract clients and allies.

A comment is in order about the sources of the data cited in this section. Later in this chapter, the remarkable statistical work accomplished by the regional commissions is praised. The reader might wonder why the data cited here emanate from so many other sources. The regional commissions, however, have not always produced the same statistical series and when they did, the data were not always comparable. Moreover, part of the statistical work is unpublished and is used only for internal purposes. This is regrettable and reflects a more general weakness of the UN; namely, that it does too little to publish and promote its analysis and statistics, often leaving the Bretton Woods institutions as the dominant source of information on development.[20]

Table 1.4. Gross Domestic Product per Capita, Human Development Index, and Military Expenditure: The Three Highest and Lowest Countries in Each Region

Region	Gross Domestic Product per Capita (in 1999 dollars)		Human Development Index (1999)		Military Expenditure, as % of GDP (1998)	
ECE						
3 highest	Luxembourg	41,188	Norway	0.939	Israel	8.7
	Switzerland	35,443	Canada	0.936	Croatia	6.2
	United States	33,666	Sweden	0.936	Greece	4.8
3 lowest	Bosnia and Herzegovina	703	Turkey	0.735	Malta	0.8
	Ukraine	625	Albania	0.725	Latvia	0.7
	Republic of Moldova	249	Moldova	0.699	Republic of Moldova	0.6
ESCAP						
3 highest	Japan	34,742	Australia	0.936	Brunei	7.6
	Singapore	24,116	Japan	0.928	Singapore[a]	5.1
	Australia	20,834	New Zealand	0.913	Pakistan	4.2
3 lowest	Bhutan	213	Bhutan	0.477	Japan	1.0
	Nepal	210	Laos	0.476	Papua New Guinea	1.0
	Tajikistan	182	Bangladesh	0.470	Nepal	0.9
ECLAC						
3 highest	Bahamas	14,999	Barbados	0.864	Colombia	2.6
	Barbados	9,789	Argentina	0.842	Chili	1.9
	Antigua y Barbuda	9,432	Uruguay	0.828	Bolivia	1.8
3 lowest	Guyana	758	Honduras	0.634	Guatemala[a]	0.7
	Haiti	485	Guatemala	0.626	Costa Rica[b]	0.6
	Nicaragua	466	Haiti	0.467	Mexico	0.6
ECA						
3 highest	Seychelles	7,116	Mauritius	0.765	Mozambique[a]	40.2
	Libyan Arab Jamahiriya	5,131	Tunisia	0.714	Angola	14.9
	Mauritius	3,682	Cape Verde	0.708	Eritrea[c]	13.5

3 lowest	Democratic Republic of Congo	115	Burundi	0.309	Nigeria	0.7
	Ethiopia	107	Niger	0.274	Gabon	0.3
	Burundi	107	Sierra Leone	0.258	Mauritius[c]	0.2

ESCWA

3 highest	Qatar	29,159	Bahrain	0.824	Saudi Arabia[d]	12.8
	United Arab Emirates	18,874	Kuwait	0.818	Oman[a]	11.6
	Kuwait	15,590	United Arab Emirates	0.809	Jordan	9.6
3 lowest	Iran	1,501	Jordan	0.714	United Arab Emirates	3.3
	Jordan	1,175	Syria	0.700	Lebanon[d]	3.2
	Yemen	387	Yemen	0.468	Egypt	2.9

Source and Notes:

For Gross Domestic Product per capita: United Nations Conference on Trade and Development, *UNCTAD Handbook of Statistics 2001* (New York and Geneva: United Nations, 2001), 286–291. In the absence of official estimates, UNCTAD's secretariat has proposed estimates for some regions and applied them, whenever possible, in order to ensure comparability at the total group levels. Highest and lowest per-capita GDP for each region consider only the countries for which official estimates exist, and which are members of the corresponding regional commission.

For Human Development Index: United Nations Development Programme, *Human Development Report 2001* (New York and Oxford: Oxford University Press, 2001), 141–144. The Human Development Index (HDI) calculated by UNDP is a composite index based on three indicators: longevity, as measured by life expectancy at birth; educational attainment, as measured by a combination of adult literacy (two-thirds weight) and the combined gross primary, secondary, and tertiary enrollment ratio (one-third weight); and standard of living, as measured by GDP per capita (purchasing-power parity in US$). The HDI has been calculated for UN member countries with reliable data in each of its components, which means that some countries could not be considered for this table.

For Military Expenditure: United Nations Development Programme, *Human Development Report 2000* (New York and Oxford: Oxford University Press, 2000), 214–217. For military expenditure, UNDP used data published by the Stockholm International Peace Research Institute (SIPRI) in its *SIPRI Yearbook 2000—Armaments, Disarmament and International Security* (Oxford: Oxford University Press, 2000). For SIPRI, "military expenditures" includes all expenditures of the Ministry of Defence and other ministries on recruiting and training military personnel as well as on construction and purchase of military supplies and equipment. Military assistance is included in the expenditures of the donor country.

[a]Data refer to estimates deemed uncertain by SIPRI 2000.

[b]Data refer to estimates by SIPRI 2000. Data refer to expenditure on border guards and air and maritime surveillance. Data refers to 1997.

[c]Data refer to 1997.

[d]Data refer to SIPRI 2000 estimates.

Building a Regional View of Development

Both Gunnar Myrdal and P. S. Lokanathan shared the view that cohesion and concerted actions among member countries were mutually reinforcing and would facilitate reconstruction and development. A few months after the creation of the ECE and ECAFE, both had the idea that their member states needed to be fully informed about their common problems and about the negative impact that purely national approaches would have on their growth and welfare. This was in line with the ideas that had presided over the creation of the UN and the Bretton Woods institutions. With this in mind, they both decided to produce a survey of current economic conditions in their respective regions.[21] Gunnar Myrdal stressed that the analysis should emphasize "those problems that are common to the nations of Europe rather than those which are peculiar to individual countries."[22] Similarly, the first *Economic Survey of Asia and the Far East* feared that in a disjointed Asia "the Survey, instead of being an analysis of common problems, [might] become in large part an examination of the situation in respect of each country."[23] ECLA, the ECA, and ECWA followed suit. And over the years, the various executive secretaries have maintained the emphasis on common problems and comparative analyses of country situations. Only the ECA, in its first survey, covering the period 1950–1963, chose to conduct its analysis of Africa's problems in a subregional context. But this choice was made because it was judged more realistic than a pan-African approach "in order to aid thinking and planning on the line of multinational co-operation."[24]

Written by secretariat teams and published under the sole responsibility of the respective executive secretaries, the surveys have constituted a unique vehicle by means of which their ideas could be identified and promoted. It is striking to see how in the first two or three surveys of each commission, the obstacles to development in each region and the strategies to overcome them were clearly spelled out. It is even more fascinating to discover the conviction of the secretariats that there were always solutions to apparently intractable situations. There was no question of according priority to the restoration of macroeconomic equilibrium at the expense of growth and the improvement of welfare. On the contrary, the task was to encourage growth and restructuring in such a way that equilibrium could be restored in the long term.

STATISTICS

Before elaborating a strategy, it was necessary to have a reliable analysis of the region's economic situation. The first invaluable achievement of the five secretariats was to collect statistical data. In the first surveys, and often highlighted in the forewords signed by the executive secretaries, were remarks about the poor quality of the available data and the efforts needed to harmonize statistics in order to make comparative analyses possible. Gunnar Myrdal devoted the entire preface of the first ECE survey to this issue. He reverted to it in the third survey noting that because of the reduction in the number of series published, it had been necessary to reconstruct part of the data related to Eastern Europe from "speeches and reports of a summary character where it [was] not always possible to determine clearly the definition . . . or the relationship to previously published series."[25] Similar difficulties occurred in other regions. Even today the collection and organization of reliable data for the surveys continues to be a demanding task but one which, when rigorously done, provides researchers with a unique and recognized source of information. Honestly prepared, even if fallible, the supply of internationally comparable statistics have made a crucial contribution to the professional reputation and integrity of the secretariats. It is regrettable that the limited distribution of the surveys has deprived policymakers and researchers of valuable material for the decision-making process.

Among the statistical series collected toward the end of the 1940s, two deserve particular mention because they drew the executive secretaries of ECAFE and ECLA, and thereafter the secretariats and the commissions, into uncharted waters and had an important influence on policies in these two regions. Analyzing the data related to population, employment, and agricultural production, the authors of the 1947 *Economic Survey of Asia and the Far East* noted that all the efforts toward industrialization had not resulted in any appreciable reduction in the dependence of the population upon agriculture. There were not enough resources within each country to transfer part of the population from high-density toward low-density areas and there were limited possibilities of migration within the region because the newly independent countries had the "understandable desire to restrict the number of . . . immigrants." Therefore, this "outlet for surplus population being closed, one way by which the pressure of population may be reduced would be a reduction in the rate of the natural increase of population, but here the position [was] discouraging." At that time it was not possible to answer the question of "whether or not birth-rates would decline in the countries concerned even during the first stage of their economic development."[26] ECAFE's work helped governments to consider introducing population policies, which they finally did under the pressure of necessity and with the help of some bilateral aid agencies.

More famous are three tables in the 1949 *Economic Survey of Latin America*; namely, "Latin America: Population, Exports and Capacity to Import (1925–

1949)"; "Terms of Trade and Total Import Coefficient of the United States (1900–1949)"; and "Terms of Trade and Total Import Coefficient of the United Kingdom (1870–1949)." These tables were the basis of the major conclusion that Latin America's capacity to import, and therefore its capacity to invest and develop, was constrained by the downward trend in its terms of trade. In addition, the volume of Latin American exports was influenced by real income in the major industrialized countries—and the import restrictions that the latter imposed to address national problems. This conclusion, drawn from observation of the long-term statistical series and linked to further statistical observations on productivity and the structure of employment, led Raúl Prebisch to elaborate a development strategy that would have a great influence in Latin America and in most parts of the developing world.[27]

THE FIRST DEVELOPMENT STRATEGIES

The development policies or strategies recommended by the other regional commissions may not have been so famous as that conceived by Prebisch, but they had in common a preoccupation with detailed statistical and comparative analysis. Because of the continuous observation of economic developments in the regions, these strategies were adapted over the years in response to new realities. This is a valuable and distinctive feature of the contribution of the regional commission to the intellectual legacy of the UN.

The common aspiration after WWII or after independence was to improve standards of living. Europeans referred to the pre-war period and the United States; the underdeveloped countries, as they were called at the time, looked to the standards prevailing in the United States and Europe. In a desire to emulate the industrialized countries, whose standards of living were associated with the diversification of production and industrial development, the key words were growth, diversification, industrialization, and productivity. Diversification was also necessary to absorb the increase in the labor force resulting from population growth and productivity gains in agriculture, despite the pessimistic view of ECAFE about the capacity of industry to offer enough jobs. On this point, the view of ECLA was that migration was not a realistic alternative, which gave it the opportunity to challenge the existing division of labor and the established order with some humor: "The logical consequences of the premises of mobility of productive factors, which is the postulate on which the theoretical concept of the international division of labor is built up, are very far-reaching and must be borne in mind in any attempt to interpret the significance of this reality by theory."[28]

Integrating these different components in a coherent vision, ECLA developed the most articulate and comprehensive development strategy of all the regional commissions. This strategy was presented in the first part of the 1949 *Economic Survey of Latin America*. The style of this survey is unusual. It appears as the presentation of the results of economic research, an economic treatise for the use of governments, and a plan for the development of Latin American countries. The strategy proposed became generally known as the "import-substitution strategy." It is well described in chapter 4 of this volume and, for the purpose of this introduction, only a brief mention is made of the main elements. Drawing on the statistical observations mentioned above and aware of the unrealistic assumptions of the theory of the international division of labor, ECLA saw in the development of industrial production not only an engine for growth and a source of employment for the workers released by the increase of productivity in agriculture but also a way to reduce, in the medium term, the need for imports that were restricted by the deterioration in the terms of trade. It noted that "measures . . . of a protective nature . . . have always been adopted by countries in the process of development" and cautiously admitted that "since there [was] no other way . . . activities which [could] be developed by protective tariffs [did], within certain limits, give rise to an increase in real income."[29] Only later would ECLA recommend and actively promote regional or subregional arrangements that would strengthen industries by allowing them to reap economies of scale.

The import-substitution strategy was reproduced in most countries of all the regions, but perhaps most successfully in those that would become the "Asian tigers." Korea and Taiwan offer the best examples. Agriculture was modernized in order to increase food security and the income level of the peasants. Industry was then developed under tariff protection to absorb the increase in labor supply due to demographic growth and the labor power released by the modernization of the agriculture. The difference with the policies followed in Latin America, where industries were aimed at the national or regional markets, was that industrial products were designed not only to respond to domestic needs but also to meet the quality standards required to be competitive on the world markets. This was not so much in contradiction with the ECLA recommendations as with the rather narrow interpretation by some governments of import substitution. Import-substitution strategies have been heavily frowned upon during the past twenty years, but they were followed by all present developed economies, and often for a long time. For instance, the U.S. average tariff rate was 40 to 50 percent in 1875 and 48 percent in 1931.[30]

As indicated earlier, ECAFE was more pessimistic than ECLA about the capacity of industry to absorb an increasing and active population. It concluded that development would be helped if the natural population increase were reduced. This conclusion, brave for the time, had an impact not only in Asia but also on the decision of the UN to create the UN Fund for Population (UNFPA).

In the meantime, for ECAFE at the end of the 1940s, the restoration of agricultural production to pre-war per-capita levels was the most pressing problem. Such an objective would respond to the primary demand of the people and loosen the balance-of-payments constraint. ECAFE reminded governments of the importance of agricultural development, which was of great importance for the success of industrialization, since the growing income of peasants provided a domestic market for industrial production.

To increase productivity and diversify output required imports of technology such as equipment, inputs, and, as income increased, consumption goods to meet the needs of populations. In the initial phase of development, domestic savings were insufficient to finance investment and imports naturally grew faster than exports, so that most countries faced severe balance-of-payment problems and difficult choices in the allocation of resources between consumption and investment and in investment among sectors. To meet the first challenge, financial resources from abroad were necessary, and to meet the second, planning appeared to be the most effective solution. All regional commissions concurred in this broad judgment.

ECAFE calculated the region's financial needs and estimated the gap between investment needs and domestic savings. A better fiscal policy could only marginally reduce the gap, and to wait for voluntary savings would aggravate the difficulties confronting the economy. Faced with this situation and the dollar shortage, in ECAFE's 1949 *Economic Survey of Asia and the Far East,* Lokanathan wrote that strengthening the region's economic and financial relations with Europe, particularly the former colonial powers, could offer a partial solution.

This echoed the view expressed, for similar reasons, by Myrdal that "Europe could participate to its own advantage in the economic development of overseas countries, not only through its exports of capital equipment but also through the provision of financing."[31] Not surprisingly, this proposal left those concerned by the immediate overseas balance-of-payments problem of Europe rather skeptical. But Myrdal insisted on this point because he anticipated the reduction and eventual disappearance of Marshall aid. He feared that this would leave Europe with a deficit in dollars that it would not be able to finance if the United States maintained high tariffs on Europe's industrial exports.

Myrdal's vision materialized in a way through the grants and loans that Europe, the United States, and then Japan provided to developing countries. But those were guided by political considerations rather than by a clear understanding of the economic interdependence of the North and the South. That interdependence, which Myrdal recognized, would later be named and promoted by UNCTAD, a story told in detail in another UNIHP volume.[32]

Managing the technicalities of financial issues, important as this was, was not the strong point of the regional commissions. They considered financial issues in relation to growth and development. In a balanced way, they encouraged countries to improve the rate of domestic savings but without entering into recommendations about fiscal policy itself, and they recognized the necessity of foreign aid and investment. Here they contributed to the debate on the advantages and disadvantages of foreign direct investment (FDI). They highlighted the conditions under which foreign investment would contribute to the transfer of technology and the increase of net exports. Case studies helped governments to have more realistic expectations and eventually to design more efficient policies. The commissions never took radical positions on these issues. Instead they followed the evolution of the general mood from the reticence toward foreign investments in the 1950s and 1960s to the attitude of the 1990s that "the only thing worse than foreign investments is not getting any." Even the *dependentista* theory at the end of the 1950s, and later the collective self-reliance advocated by the ECA in the Monrovia Strategy, did not diminish the role that foreign finance could play (see chapters 4 and 5). The ECE entered the debate in the 1990s over the role of FDI in the economies in transition. Contrary to much official opinion in the early 1990s, the ECE *Economic Survey of Europe* argued that FDI was unlikely to make a significant contribution to Eastern development until the processes of reform and transformation were well advanced. The commission saw the insistence of Western governments on largely business-type financial relations with the transition economies as mistaken since private investors did not regard themselves as prime movers in the transition process. The ECE argued that official assistance, financial and technical, was key in the early stages in order to create the institutional frameworks of the market economy that were a precondition for attracting FDI. Moreover, were the rush to attract FDI to be successful in a few cases, the result could be counterproductive in the presence of missing or ineffectual institutions: "As long as they have security of title to their assets and guarantees of profit repatriation, foreign enterprises, like sportsmen, will be happy to play according to whatever rules are in place. If markets are not competitive, there can be no presumption that the activities of foreign companies will automatically contribute to a more efficient allocation of resources."[33]

The Rise and Decline of Planning

None of the regional commissions felt that the allocation of resources between sectors and states, consumers, and investors could be left entirely to market forces. Each was convinced that government was the key actor in building up an economy that could meet the needs of people and establish balanced relations with the rest of the world. The instrument for guiding the action of the government was planning. Until the middle of the 1970s, this belief was not controversial. In the Europe of the late 1940s, countries were encouraged to present their requests for Marshall Plan aid in the context of a medium-term plan, and the World Bank cooperated with the regional commissions in advising countries on planning. The regional commissions never advocated the sort of planning that characterized the centrally planned economies of the Soviet bloc. Rather, they viewed plans as an instrument to clarify and prioritize goals, to link them to the resources, and to identify the relations between the different sectors of activity. Coherence between objectives and policy instruments, institutional change, and proper sequencing characterized the messages about planning from the commissions. The implicit model was certainly more the French than the Soviet Plan.

In the 1960s, one of the first moves of the ECA was to organize the training of African civil servants who would serve in their national planning systems. It created IDEP, the Institute for Economic Development and Planning, in Dakar. Samir Amin recalled that when he became the director of the institute, his main priority was not so much to teach the techniques of planning as to encourage the students to answer the questions "What are the goals? What are the obstacles? How to overcome them?"[34] These were essentially the same questions asked of the Europeans in 1948 by the Marshall planners. The ministers of planning also met yearly under the auspices of the ECA. Initially the debates, exchanges of experience, and technical assistance focused on the development of more realistic plans and on their implementation. But it soon became evident that more was needed. Stimulated by the challenges of the NIEO and convinced that the development policies inspired by the experience of other continents were inadequate for Africa, the ECA decided to formulate development strategies that better fitted African realities. This generated strong support from African ministers of planning. From 1976 to 1989, the ECA drew up several major strategic documents that Adedeji considers to be the main intellectual contribution of the ECA. The economic debates with the champions of liberalization and adjustment, from the adoption of the Monrovia Strategy to the Lagos Plan of Action, are described with some passion in chapter 5.

For its part, ECWA, created at the time of the first oil shock in the early 1970s, insisted on realism and implementation. It encouraged planning as a way to prepare for the post-oil era. This proved to be wise, since even if oil remained the main resource of the region, its price had fluctuated so much that it was worth planning for diversification.

ECAFE, having insisted that priority should be given to agricultural development and food production, praised the increasing role accorded to this sector in the plans elaborated at the end of the 1940s. But, keen to avoid controversies between socialist and market-oriented countries, it was mainly content to compare the different national plans. Nevertheless, important and pioneering recommendations were made, including the "need for proper proportion between projects which yield immediate visible results and those whose results take longer to appear but provide essential preliminary development." Indeed, long before Walt Rostow analyzed the necessary conditions for an economy to "take off," ECAFE had already written that "once the process of development gets under way, its effect becomes cumulative." It showed how development in agriculture, transport, and power would facilitate industrialization. Equally important, ECAFE noted that there was no single pattern of industrialization: It would "vary from country to country depending primarily on the availability of resources and the institutional set-up."[35]

The ECE and ECLA focused more on methodology. ECLA created the Latin American Institute for Economic and Social Planning (ILPES) in 1962, which made a particular contribution to the planning of public expenditures. In 1961, the ECE set up the Senior Economic Advisers to the governments of the ECE. The group, which originally included eminent economists such as Jan Tinbergen, discussed the methods used in long-term social planning, the elaboration of projections, and the use of econometric models.

By the mid-1970s, the vogue of planning was in decline. In Western Europe, "indicative planning," as opposed to planning as conceived in centrally planned economies, appeared unable to "reduce uncertainties" in countries overwhelmed by the problems of adjustment that followed three decades of sustained growth and the first oil shock. In Eastern Europe, countries had failed to reform their planning methods and their economic difficulties became better known abroad, raising serious doubts throughout the world about planning as an effective instrument. The work of the ECE's senior economic advisers was redirected toward long-term forecasts and the identification of crucial issues likely to arise in the future. At the end of the 1990s, the group was dismantled. In Africa and Latin America, the reduction of state intervention demanded by the new economic orthodoxy, or Washington Consensus, in the framework of structural adjustment programs led to the disappearance of

ministries of planning or to their marginalization. In ECAFE, planning followed the fate of planning in India, and its success in the "Asian tigers" was
not acknowledged. Irma Adelman once remarked that "there would not have
been an East Asian miracle" had the Washington Consensus been imposed on
the countries of East Asia while they were building up their economies.[36]

By the end of the 1980s and the fall of the Berlin Wall, the Washington
Consensus was established as the new common wisdom. But if the brand
name was new, the content was essentially the policy outcrop of the neoclassical school. Liberalization and privatization would secure correct relative
prices. Non-intervention by the state in the allocation of resources would reduce uncertainties, and the free decisions of the enterprises and consumers
would secure an optimal allocation of resources. Time-consuming institutional development could be postponed to a later stage and would then be
facilitated by the demand for rules emanating from the enterprise sector. The
hypotheses behind this scheme diverged from those underlying the strategies
that the regional commissions had recommended since their establishment.
Basically, the latter were skeptical about the spontaneity of the response to
the right prices and thought that institutional and coordination failures would
block or weaken the mechanism of reallocation of resources, let alone the
broader development process. They had consistently seen a major role for
government in building the institutional framework for a market economy
and in getting the development process under way.[37]

CRITICIZING THE WASHINGTON CONSENSUS

Did the commissions change their line in the 1990s? For the ECE and
ECLAC, the answer is "yes" and "no." Certainly they integrated the changes in
the world economy and both became more explicitly market-friendly, although
the underlying philosophy in the ECE remained firmly in the Myrdal-Kaldor
tradition. At the same time, they challenged the simplistic assumptions of the
Washington Consensus that, as William Lazonik put it in the 2001 ECE Spring
Seminar, "failed to understand modern capitalism."[38] Both challenged the idea
that stability is the central piece of the development process. The neoliberals
believed stability to be a necessary and sufficient condition for economic
growth and generally harmonious development. Both commissions believed
that it was necessary to a degree—certainly not hyperinflation, but the pursuit of inflation rates of 2 percent was dogma. They believed that efficient
product and factor markets would be the outcome of successful development
rather than a precondition for it. As early as 1990, the ECE underlined the
risks of shock therapy and consistently throughout the decade stressed that

market-economy institutions were necessary if liberalization and privatization were to yield the expected results. Similarly, ECLAC was favorable to a gradual dismantling of trade barriers and an orderly process of privatization. Both were favorable to the inflow of long-term capital but had serious reservations about the liberalization of short-term capital movements. They considered that the latter were often destabilizing and obliged governments to pay excessive attention to macroeconomic equilibrium at the expense of growth. After the Asian crisis, ESCAP joined them in articulating this line. All the commissions warned about the social costs of reforms and crises and the need for sharing the costs of adjustment equitably in order to reduce the risk of political crises. But again, ECLAC went farther in offering a holistic framework articulating growth and equity, private and public responsibilities, and micro- and macroeconomic dimensions for the short and long term. Gert Rosenthal, who led ECLAC in the 1990s, describes this approach in the last section of chapter 4.

Guided by statistical evidence and by close relations with member states, the commissions adapted their vision of development to changes in their regions and in the world. Theoretical debates and the dominant streams of thinking naturally influenced them. But throughout the years, they adhered to the idea that growth facilitated change rather than the reverse and always tried to place short-term problems and responses in a longer-term perspective. They believed that the state had to remain a central actor, not only to put in place institutions and guarantee their good functioning but also as a catalyst and a direct participant in the building of economic and productive infrastructures. Essentially they did not believe that one solution could be applied in all cases. Intellectually, the more creative were ECLA, the ECE, and the ECA; the two other commissions were more influenced by the dominant conventional wisdom emanating from Washington and Brussels. ECLA had the greatest impact because of its strong intellectual leadership and the interaction between the secretariat, the academic community, and the region's political elites. Some governmental decisions were clearly influenced by its recommendations. The ECE was respected in academic circles for its work on the factors of growth and its analysis of the centrally planned and, later, transition economies. The economic advisers of governments and the economists of the EEC (European Economic Community), CMEA (Council for Mutual Economic Assistance), and OECD secretariats read its surveys with attention. They were a source of information for all those who had access to them in Eastern Europe. On development strategies, the ECA engaged in dialogue with ministers of planning who had little impact on actual decisions and actions. ESCWA elaborated agreements on elements of development strategy that were rarely put into practice. De Silva (in this volume) attributes the absence of a visible impact of ECAFE/ESCAP to certain discretion among intellectual leaders and their deferential attitude toward governmental development decisions. But this commission and the four others did have an important impact if only because they contributed essential public goods, such as information, analysis, debates, and long-term forecasts. In doing so they reduced uncertainty to some extent and provided governments with elements for designing development policies that would meet the needs of their countries.

Between Subregional and Global Integration

Initially the regional commissions had three reasons to promote regionalism. First, as part of their mandate, they were invited to facilitate concerted action between their member states. Even if the formulation was weak, it gave direction, or at least a dimension, to the efforts toward reconstruction and development. Second, industrialization, so important for catching up with the developed countries, called for regional and subregional arrangements. Third, the dependence of the South on decisions taken in the North and the apparent impossibility of changing the existing economic order as long as so many countries were still under colonial rule led to the idea that regional or subregional integration would reduce this dependence. In sum, as a first step, regional integration was seen as a priority to facilitate and rationalize the development of the participating states.

REGIONAL OR SUBREGIONAL INTEGRATION

The secretariats of the five commissions were convinced that regional cooperation was necessary not only for the maintenance of regional cohesion but also as a condition for development. Depending on the different circumstances of each region and the relative weight given to regional unity and economic development, this cooperation took different forms. ECWA's secretariat, because of the small size of the region, the obvious complementarities between oil-producing and non–oil-producing countries in terms of human capacity and financial resources, and the fear of a split between them, advocated regional cooperation, while member states were more keen to establish bilateral links with Western countries. The ECE, even though one of its studies was a formative influence in the creation of the Coal and Steel Community and thus on the European Union (see chapter 2), favored the unity of the continent and, therefore, the negotiation of regional sectoral norms and standards. ECAFE, equally concerned with the unity of the Asian region, did not become involved in the creation of subregional arrangements before the 1980s. In the 1940s and 1950s, it recommended that industrial planning be organized among neighboring countries but did not actively pursue the proposal.

ECLA and, later, the ECA were strong advocates of subregional cooperation and agreements. The preference for such arrangements was purely practical. In Latin America, the differences between subregions would have made it difficult to set up an overall regional scheme. In the ECA, the disparities within the region were even greater, and subregional arrangements were seen as steps toward stronger regional cooperation. The economic rationale for the creation of subregional arrangements was twofold. First, national markets were often too small for certain industrial activities to be economically viable. Subregional arrangements were expected to enlarge such markets while permitting the protection of infant industries. Second, the fear that ruinous competition between new enterprises would lead to a waste of already scarce resources for investment argued in favor of subregional cooperation.

The ECA's commitment to subregional cooperation never wavered, but the institutions that it created proved difficult to manage because of the lack of competent staff, including in the ECA secretariat itself and its member governments. Nevertheless, "the very fact that [ECA] did advocate, and lay the groundwork for regional arrangements had important consequences . . . for the future of regional capacities in Africa."[39] It created a climate favorable for the creation of several subregional arrangements such as the Economic Community of West African States (ECOWAS) and the Southern African Development Conference (SADC). ECLA not only elaborated the intellectual arguments for subregional arrangements but was also the only regional commission to be actively involved in the creation of such arrangements, in particular the Latin American Free Trade Association (LAFTA), the Central American Common Market, and the Andean Pact.

The actual impact of the subregional groupings on development was disappointing for several years. One reason for this was excessive ambition: From the outset, the aim was to achieve a level of integration that the European Economic Community or European Free Trade Association (EFTA) had reached only after a succession of modest steps interrupted by setbacks. More often than not, the terms of the agreements were not respected. For instance, tariff reductions decided at the ministerial level were ignored by customs officers. The fear that one group of countries might benefit more than others from an agreement also created acrimonious and unproductive tensions. In addition, when it came to the location of enterprises, the idea of having a fair distribution of investments among countries conflicted with the preference of investors for concentrating industrial activities and services in the same

place. As Robert W. Gregg noted in 1966, "If recent experiences with integration yield any lesson, it is that urban-industrial societies with a relatively high
level of economic diversification are better candidates for more rapid progress
toward union than are underdeveloped, mono-cultural societies. Ironically,
the integration movements in Europe . . . are probably an important factor in
spurring experimentation with economic unions in areas which otherwise
fail to meet some of the criteria for integration."[40]

This judgment may be understood to mean that regional integration is
facilitated by development rather than the reverse. Yet it was not the intention
of the author to discourage attempts at sectoral or subregional integration.
Rather, he wanted to caution against excessive enthusiasm and to convey the
message that integration was more likely to yield results if it focused on specific sectoral activities (such as basin-river management or international highways) and if it limited itself to a small number of countries.

Regionalism: The Political Argument

The successful negotiation of the NIEO and its subsequent failure provided an additional political rationale for regionalism. The NIEO attempted
to open the way to fundamental changes in the international economic system, which Prebisch and the ECLA secretariat and, after them, UNCTAD and
many theoreticians considered a prerequisite for development. Many of the
issues raised in the 1949 *Economic Survey of Latin America* were addressed in
a worldwide context: the terms of trade and access to technologies, markets,
and financial resources. Although temporary success had been obtained with
the adoption of the Common Fund for Commodities, it was not possible to
carry it forward. No individual commodity agreement was accepted linking
its fate with others under the umbrella of the Common Fund. Both developing and industrialized countries are to be blamed for this failure. However,
the failure of the Common Fund illustrates a general strategy of the industrialized countries to stop the NIEO from producing concrete changes. Conscious that the unity of the developing countries and the links that they were
able to establish between different sectoral issues had obliged richer countries
to give in to their "general demand that they work toward an NIEO, the industrialized countries have sought to disaggregate demands." The developed
world dealt with countries on a case-by-case basis and resisted addressing
interrelated issues in a single negotiation. Other examples of this tactic can be
found in the treatment of the debt problem and the refusal to draw the consequences of the link between rural poverty and the international trade of sub-
sidized food products.[41]

Despite its failure, the NIEO raised awareness of their collective strength among developing countries, which in turn gave a new dimension to regionalism. Countries in a given region saw more clearly that they had common interests or concerns that could be better defended in international forums if they were united. The regional commissions were the obvious place to articulate and develop common positions and programs. In the preparation for and the follow-up to the global conferences of the 1990s, their contributions helped to better distinguish between what was universally applicable and what had to be left to the regions. They also became the forums where the policies pursued by the Bretton Woods institutions could be discussed or challenged. In most cases it was also the occasion of a constructive exchange of ideas with UNCTAD.

ECLAC and the ECA were the two most active commissions in uniting their member countries to bargain for concessions on the international scene. The Asian countries, which used the financial resources available in the 1970s to finance investment rather than consumption, were able to manage their debt in the 1980s. But Latin American and African countries suffered from the surge of interest rates in the 1980s and the painful conditions imposed for rescheduling debt. ECLAC challenged the adjustment that it judged recessionary and viewed the debt-alleviation schemes as offering too little too late. The ECA went a step farther. It reacted vigorously against structural adjustment policies. Taking up where the dependentist theoreticians of the 1960s at ECLA left off, the ECA thus proposed a strategy of collective self-reliance but did not exclude external financing and FDI. The commission prepared special programs for Africa and succeeded in having them discussed and adopted by the General Assembly. The UN Program of Action for Economic Recovery and Development (UN-PAERD, 1986–1990), followed by the UN New Agenda for the Development of Africa (UN-NADAF, 1991–2002), were the results of two programs discussed and approved by ministers of planning in the framework of the ECA. UN-PAERD was the first program adopted by the General Assembly on a geographical basis; previously, special programs had aimed to address the problems of a category of countries, such as the least developed.

From the end of the 1940s, regionalism had been seen primarily as a way to overcome the limits imposed by a purely nationalist approach to development. In the 1970s, it emerged also as a means for countries to have their views considered and taken into account in global debates, and this dimension remains valid. It is unclear whether the first dimension of regionalism will continue to be relevant in the new century with the globalization of the world economy. The five regional commissions had the opportunity to address this question in the documents that each prepared for UNCTAD X (2000) and that served as a reference in the public debate their executive secretaries had with the secretary-general of UNCTAD on this occasion.[42]

Toward Regionalization or Globalization

The least expected conclusion of the UNCTAD debate mentioned above, given the relentless publicity given to the "global village" and global markets, was that the evolution of external trade of the ECE, ECLAC, and ESCAP regions was toward a much closer integration of the countries within each region rather than toward a more global engagement. In the case of the ECE, the regional concentration of trade was repeated, if a little less sharply, in the pattern of foreign investment. Regional concentration of trade has been a long-standing phenomenon in Western Europe, but it increased especially during the years that immediately followed the first oil shock. It developed in the two other regions with the diversification of their economies. Certainly technical progress has lowered the material content of GDP, and the consequent falling share of primary commodities in external trade, compounded by the deterioration in the commodity terms of trade, has increased the share of industrial products in the external trade of the ECE, ECLAC, and ESCAP. For the ECA and ESCWA, the very low level of regional integration reflected the continuing dependence of the countries of these regions on a few commodities. These observations confirm Gregg's opinion that regionalism is reinforced by development, but at the same time this raises the question as to why this should be so.

Trying to explain the fact that international trade in manufactures was increasingly "intra-industry" as opposed to "inter-industry," the ECE also looked at why regional trade developed faster than global trade:

> Economies of scale and of co-ordination allow the intermediate parts and processes required in the production of manufactured goods to be separated and entrusted to specialist producers. This dynamic division of labor could in principle be extended on a global basis . . . but in practice it is likely to proceed more rapidly among countries with similar levels of income per head and hence similar industrial structures.[43]

In answer to the question of whether the multiplication of subregional arrangements introduced a bias in international trade, the regional commissions admitted that it might have diverted exporters from searching for openings on the world market. But they were unanimous in thinking that these arrangements did not undermine the multilateral trading system and would rather reinforce it. ECLAC had forged the expression of "open regionalism" (see chapter 4), and the other commissions endorsed it. ECE argued that the tendency toward a greater regional concentration of trade was less the effect of regional agreements (although these may have some diversionary impact) than of more fundamental forces related to the economies of conglomeration. The view that increased regionalization was somehow a deviation from a more optimal allocation of global resources was a reflection of basic flaws in the traditional theory of international trade, which continues to underlie general thinking about globalization but which excludes scale economies and any gains from concentrating economic activities in a particular location or region. In the heated controversy about whether the welfare gains from subregional arrangements were smaller or greater than those resulting from liberalization on a multilateral basis, the secretariats were clearly on the latter side.

Not only was open regionalism not undermining the multilateral trading system but, in the view of the secretariats of the commissions, it was reinforcing it. Each regional or subregional arrangement establishes rules and practices that introduce a minimum of fairness and equity in their relations. On the contrary, the commissions thought that the multilateral trading system was undermining itself because of its failure to bring fairness to international trade and financial relations. This has been one of their constant concerns. After the early denunciation by ECLA of the asymmetry in trade relations, each commission analyzed the consequences of the deterioration of the terms of trade for commodity exporters for the economies of their region. Later they denounced the asymmetry between those developing countries that, deliberately or under pressure, liberalized imports and the obstacles that their exports of more competitive products continued to face in the markets of major industrialized countries. The ECE also contributed to these denunciations about trade with the United States in the early 1950s and the decline of commodity prices and inflation. After the 1990s, the ECE criticized the obstacles to Eastern European exports of textiles, steel, aluminum, and equipment. The commissions were convinced that a more equitable trading system required both a strong World Trade Organization (WTO) and appropriate rules. Hence, developing countries would have to "formulat[e] their own proposals and counterproposals in their favour aimed at correcting existing imbalances and asymmetries."[44]

Before and after the financial crises of the 1980s and the 1990s, the regional commissions cautioned against the free movement of short-term capital. They argued that the constraints that it would impose on macroeconomic policies would undermine growth without securing the necessary national financial resources. Indeed, the evidence suggests that the presumed benefits of free capital movements have fallen rather short of expectations. The ECE noted that, contrary to theory and expectations, "domestic investment and domestic savings rates tend to be closely correlated across countries: different rates of return on capital persist and are not equalized by foreign capital flows."[45] After the crises in Asia, Russia, and Latin America, the respective commission secretariats analyzed their causes and impacts, and they also challenged the way they were handled by the existing international mechanisms, particularly by the IMF. They adhered to the view that, in the future, adequate provision of liquidity would be crucial in preempting crises, minimizing contagion, and mitigating adverse impacts. They considered that in Asia and Latin America, the IMF provided liquidity assistance only after the countries had been hit by the crisis, and were subject to the fulfillment of conditions that delayed its actual provision when it was urgently needed.

ECLAC and ESCAP proposed or supported the creation of regional funds designed to disburse funds rapidly and focus on immediate stabilization measures. Their existence, together with the additional liquidity made available, could in itself reduce the probability and intensity of future financial crises. Closer to the countries than the IMF, they would be better placed for prevention. Both commissions also think that the regional level is more appropriate for setting prudential norms and sharing information. In other words, ECLAC and ESCAP, with the assent of the other regional commissions, believe that the international financial system should be rebuilt and that regional institutions and mechanisms should be among the essential building blocks to reduce the risks of new crises and avoid having the poor bear an excessive share of the costs of adjustment.

Globalization is currently both an alleged description of economic reality and a set of normative goals. As a description of reality, it is exaggerated, since trade and financial flows tend to be more regional than global. In its normative aspect, "the globalization agenda turns out to be the traditional neo-classical, neo-liberal agenda up-dated for a world where geographic distance is alleged to have little significance for business activity."[46] Finally, it was Henry Kissinger who highlighted the political dimension of the debate over globalization versus regionalism when he stated that "what is called globalization is really another name for the dominant role of the United States."[47] This suggests, perhaps, another countervailing force behind the growth of regionalism.

The Regional Commissions as the UN's Regional Arm

The interaction between globalization and regionalism in the economic sphere has an institutional echo within the UN system. The relationship be-

tween global and regional entities that was evoked in the debates surrounding the creation of the commissions has continued to preoccupy delegations
and secretariats without, however, leading to an effective division of labor. As
theory was called on to support economic interests, organizational principles
were invoked in aid of institutional interests. Viewed positively, this could be
said to reflect the dedication of the staff to the institutions they serve and the
attachment of countries to the institutions from which they benefit. Viewed
negatively, this can be seen as diverting attention from substantive issues in
which real political and economic interests are at stake. In any case, what is
certain is that a more explicit commitment on the part of the management of
all the organizations involved is as important as more resolute decentralization and better coordination if the flow of ideas and cooperation within the
UN system is to be strengthened.

Ideas do circulate between the regional commissions and global entities.
Prebisch's analysis of the deterioration of the terms of trade may have benefited from Hans Singer's work on the issue, but it was he and ECLA who
transformed the ideas into a development strategy that inspired the other
regional commissions, the economic department in New York, and, later,
UNCTAD.[48] ECAFE pioneered work on population and prompted the UN
entities and specialized agencies to integrate the population dimension into
their activities. When the UNFPA was created, it took over responsibility for
population policy and actions in the UN, and ESCAP cooperated closely with
the new body. Several of the conventions and norms or standards adopted in
the ECE became global, such as the Convention on the Transport of Dangerous Goods, or were adopted by neighboring countries, such as the Convention on International Road Transport (known from its French acronym as
the TIR convention). The protocol on the emission of heavy metals served as
a reference in the preparation of a global effort to reduce this form of pollution. The Aarhus Convention, called "Access to Information, Participation in
Decisions and Access to Justice in Matters Related to Environment," has retained the attention of both the United Nations Environment Programme
(UNEP) and the Office of the High Commissioner for Human Rights
(UNHCHR). The work of the ECA inspired UN-PAERD and UN-NADAF
and contributed to the UN's views on structural adjustment.

Conversely, global initiatives such as the Development Decades or global
ad hoc conferences invited contributions from the regional commissions and
drew them into areas that they had not previously explored or that would
have been difficult to tackle without the authority of UN resolutions and global events. Contributions to the development decades initially mobilized the
secretariats of commissions to convey visions about development that had

matured in the regions to the rest of the world. But it soon appeared that in designing the development decades, a sort of multilateral diplomacy was winning over economics and leading to long catalogues of measures, the merit of which was that they were acceptable to the West, the East, and the South, but which no one was really committed to implementing. Participation by the commissions thus turned into a series of routine exercises.[49]

More important were the impulses provided by the global thematic conferences. The successive conferences on population or human settlement drew on the work already done by the commissions and gave new direction and impulse to their work in these domains. Work on the environment started in 1950 in the ECE, which had even scheduled a pan-European conference before the 1972 Stockholm meeting was decided. But in the other commissions, environmental activities started only after Stockholm and grew in importance with the increased sensitivity of member countries to their impact on and relationship to development.

If the ECE had an impact beyond its region on some technical international agreements related to the environment, the ECA's pioneering work on women influenced the actual conception of the UN system. As pointed out by Margaret Snyder, in the early and mid-1960s, the ECA had organized meetings on the Role of Women in Community Development, the Role of Women in Urban Development, and Participation of Women in National Social and Economic Development, long "before anybody was talking about women in development"[50] and "long before Americans had any such concepts."[51] The women-and-development approach brought in by the ECA complemented the gender-equality approach championed by the North American feminist movements and the legal approach of the Commission on the Status of Women. The ECA's work contributed directly to the first Women's Conference in Mexico and led to the creation of the United Nations Development Fund for Women (UNIFEM). Subsequently, the commissions progressively raised awareness of the problems facing women in their regions and contributed through their statistical and conceptual work to changes in the status of women.[52]

Blandine Destremau in chapter 6 gives a fascinating description of how the ESCWA secretariat was able to address the very sensitive issues of women, population, conditions of labor, and migration because these themes had been addressed at the global level. Of course, it adapted global analyses and recommendations to the specificity of the region, but ESCWA, deliberately and more than any other commission, played the role of a regional arm of the UN.

Thus, ideas moved back and forth between global entities and regional commissions, the former stimulating or helping the latter, and vice versa. But it was not always the case. Development decades were a missed opportunity and, more generally, it is regrettable that in an organization with such limited resources, the scattered teams of economists have rarely, if ever, joined forces in a common undertaking. If it had taken advantage of the country experiences, the statistical evidence it collected, and the theoretical analyses it developed, the UN could have built a development paradigm to compete with that promoted by the Bretton Woods institutions. The UN often criticized the approach of the World Bank and the International Monetary Fund, but it failed to present a convincing and comprehensive alternative to the Washington Consensus. An initiative taken in the Executive Committee on Economic and Social Affairs (EC-ESA) to put together the building blocks of a constructive dialogue with the World Bank after the crises of the late 1990s failed for lack of leadership and the will to succeed. Excellent pieces of work, such as *Recasting the International Financial Agenda,* by José Antonio Ocampo, ECLAC's executive secretary, were never published under the UN secretariat's authority.

Rather than mobilizing talents to elaborate a UN vision of development, there were a number of calls for centralized coordination of the regional economic surveys for the sake of consistency in statistics and forecasts. Fortunately in this case, this did not succeed either. There should never be a monopoly of the analysis of current developments and policies, not even in an organization as large as the UN. Maintaining several independent centers of excellence and analysis is essential in areas where there is inevitable uncertainty and where value premises, usually hidden, heavily influence conclusions and recommendations. It is not irrelevant to note that in the major industrialized countries several independent research institutes, often with very different perspectives, are maintained, most with government support. A diversity of independent sources of analysis is also important to maintain the "constructive skepticism" that should be applied to all received analysis and recommendations, especially as these are inevitably influenced by the interests of the powerful and, not least, by fashion. The regional commissions' economic surveys, UNCTAD's *Trade and Development Report,* and the Development of Economic and Social Affairs' (DESA) *World Economic Survey* secure the necessary diversity. There should be no pressure for harmonization, only for high quality.

Relations between the regional commissions and headquarters, for the most part, have been mutually beneficial. Some regional ideas or achievements became global, and some global visions were adapted to regional circumstances. But more attention to ideas and less attention to bureaucratic considerations could have contributed better to the intellectual recognition of the UN on development issues. Better use could be made of the inputs from the regional commissions, and the diversity that they represent should be better integrated into global thinking.

Looking toward the Future: Are the Regional Commissions Still Needed?

The ECE, ECAFE, and ECLA were reconfirmed in their mandates in 1951, their usefulness never being seriously questioned by their member states. Objections and support were often purely political. They were given responsibility for granting voting rights to member countries who were not members of the UN, a politically important decision. In 1972, the *Regional Co-operation Study on Regional Structures* by the UN secretariat, based on a questionnaire addressed to all the member states, again confirmed its support for the commissions. The study proposed that the commissions be given some coordinating responsibilities over UN agencies at the regional level and "executing agency functions for subregional and regional projects."[53] But the mobilization of the formidable but dispersed intellectual potential of the UN on development was not addressed. After the fall of the Berlin Wall, at the initiative of Willy Brandt, a Commission on Global Governance was convened whose report, *Our Global Neighborhood,* analyzed the situation created by the end of the Cold War and globalization. The report proposed a thorough reform of the UN to adapt to the changes that had occurred since its creation fifty years earlier. The report, which praised the contributions of the regional commissions, "notably ECE and ECLAC," recommended that "the continuing utility of the Commissions now needs to be closely examined and their future determined in consultation with governments in their region."[54]

The main argument of *Our Global Neighborhood* regarding the very existence of the regional commissions started with the observation of the dynamism of regionalism and the spread of open regional groupings. The report went on to say that the UN should prepare itself for the time "when regionalism becomes ascendant world-wide, and even help the process along." It concluded that this "objective could be helped if resources now spent on the Regional Commissions were diverted to the support of these [regional and subregional] organizations and their activities."[55] One response to this could have been that the regional commissions were already cooperating with, or had themselves created, these independent subregional or regional organizations and that it would be simpler and more efficient for UN headquarters to deal with this blossoming nebula of organizations through the commissions rather than directly with them.

In practice, at the initiative of each executive secretary, governments were consulted. As a result, governments confirmed their strong support for the continuation of the commissions and discussed reforms with the secretariats. From an institutional point of view, the initiative of the executive secretaries and the reforms that followed were timely and may have changed the fate of the commissions. Indeed, in the mid-1990s, some UN senior officials and governments that were looking for savings took up the argument of the report of the Commission on Global Governance and considered the possibility of abolishing the regional commissions.

But beyond bureaucratic considerations, the institutional raisons d'être of the commissions are more fundamental. The commissions are an instrument for the unity of the regions and as such have the added advantage, more than any other regional grouping, of being part of the UN and benefiting from its moral authority. Their neutrality on divisive issues reassures the weakest countries, which are able to voice their concerns and receive attention. Therefore, the regional commissions need the UN. Conversely, the world organization needs the commissions to be able to integrate the diversity of the economic and social world and to distinguish between what is universally applicable and what should remain regional or local. In this respect, the issues are no different from those facing, for example, the members of the European Union in their relations to the European Commission in Brussels or within individual countries concerning the distribution of power and responsibility between the capital and the regions. The common thread is the discovery, or rediscovery, of the limits of centralization in an increasingly complex world.

As suggested above and demonstrated in the following chapters, the regional commissions have played an important and useful role in the realm of ideas. Creative, they developed ideas that responded to the needs of their members and, sometimes, to those of the larger global community. Receptive, they have adopted global views or principles and advocated them in their region. Examples have been given above, and many others are found in the following chapters. It is unfortunate that the opportunity was missed to build on the wealth of the diverse experience in the commissions' secretariats and forge alternative approaches to development that would challenge the ruling paradigm. The need remains and the potential exists. The regional commissions, their member states, and their secretariats together have developed cultures and mindsets and accumulated experience which provide the building blocks for a bottom-up process to improve development thinking. The pieces need to be brought together, but who will have the talent, the modesty, the courage, and the leadership skills to do that? A Myrdal or a Prebisch could have done it, but even they would have a much more difficult task today in overcoming the institutional complexity and bureaucratic obstacles that constitute a major constraint on substantive work in the present UN. The question remains open but it will need to be answered if the UN is to recover an influential and constructive role in economic policy in the future.

2

The ECE: A Bridge between East and West

Yves Berthelot and Paul Rayment

- **Contrasting Lessons from Two Postwar Periods**
- **A Structure of Cooperation for a Divided Europe**
- **The Achievements of the Early Cold War Period, 1947–1953**
- **The Search for Sustained Growth, 1953–1989**
- **The Transition Era: Entering Uncharted Territory**
- **Conclusions**

> *L'Europe n'est pas un assemblage fortuit, une simple juxtaposition de peuples, c'est un grand instrument harmonique dont chaque nationalité est une corde et représente un ton. Chacune est nécessaire en elle-même, nécessaire par rapport aux autres. En ôter une seule, c'est altérer tout l'ensemble, le rendre impossible, dissonant. . . .*[*]
>
> —Jules Michelet (1798–1874)

Contrasting Lessons from Two Postwar Periods

When the **Second World War** (WWII) ended in Europe on May 8, 1945, the continent was in a devastated state. More than 50 million people had died, five times more than in the First World War (WWI).[1] In addition, there were more than 11 million displaced persons—10 times more than after WWI— needing food, shelter, and medical attention.[2] The material destruction was far greater and more extensive than at the end of WWI: Villages and cities throughout the continent were in ruins; road, rail, and other physical infrastructures had suffered large-scale destruction and disruption; much of the merchant shipping fleet had been lost; and there were serious shortages of

---

[*]"Europe is not a haphazard collection, a simple juxtaposition of peoples, it is a vast harmonic instrument in which each nationality is a chord with its own tone. Every one is necessary in itself and in relation to the others. Take one away and you alter the whole, rendering it unviable, discordant. . . ."

food and raw materials. Networks of international trade had been broken or disrupted, and virtually everywhere trade and capital movements were subject to direct government controls.

An unprecedented aspect of WWII was the extent to which the civilian population was directly affected, accounting for perhaps half of all casualties—far higher than in any previous conflict. "Policies on genocide were but the most extreme forms of a war which targeted civilians and the very structure of pre-war society. Reconstruction after 1945 was, therefore, a very different enterprise from that of the 1920s: this time there could be no thought of going back."[3] But what was the way forward? Stalin presciently declared, "This war is not as in the past. Whoever occupies a territory also imposes on it his own social system. Everyone imposes his own system as far as his army can reach. It cannot be otherwise."[4] As a result, Europe—and consequently the membership of the United Nations Economic Commission for Europe (ECE)—divided into two blocs, on the one hand liberal democracies with market-based economies and on the other communist people's democracies with centrally planned economies—a division that was to prevail for more than forty years.

In 1945, Western Europe was a collection of highly regulated economies, mainly but not entirely the result of wartime planning, so policymakers were faced not only with the tasks of reconstruction but also of reconversion to market-based economies that would avoid the failures of interwar capitalism. There were fears that the postwar expectations of the population would be higher than the capacity of the system to satisfy them, thereby increasing the risks of social unrest and political instability. All this was set against the background of increasing East-West tensions. The tasks and prospects of reconstruction after WWII looked far worse than those prevailing after WWI, and yet not only was the recovery much faster than most people expected but it led to the golden age of the 1950s and 1960s, whereas the period after 1918 ended in the depression of the 1930s. The post-WWII recovery and transformation of the West European economies also stand in contrast to the experience of the former centrally planned economies of Eastern Europe and the former Soviet Union after 1989: After a decade of transition, and allowing for the statistical problems in making such comparisons, many of them had not regained the levels of output prevailing before the "shock of transition" and only a few had found their way to sustained rates of output growth.[5]

What was different about 1945 in contrast to 1918? In the first place, it should be noted that the damage to productive capacity from bombing was less than expected: In fact, capacity at the end of the war was greater than at the start, and, despite the tremendous loss of life, the West European labor force was as large as it was before the war.[6] But the potential for recovery is one thing; its realization is another. In 1918, Europe's leaders were mostly anxious to reestablish the world that existed before 1914; they looked back to a golden age—and to the gold standard. In general, policies were focused almost entirely on financial stability, and this priority implied restrictive fiscal and monetary policies, balanced budgets, and constraints on government spending. Wartime controls were rapidly abandoned, leading to sharp increases in prices; an early example of what, in the 1990s, would be called "shock therapy." As suggested above, no one in 1945 wanted to return to the prewar situation; in fact, avoiding the failures of interwar capitalism was seen as crucial for restoring and maintaining liberal democracy and the market-economy system. Most policymakers in Western Europe in 1945 probably followed Keynes in believing that while the decentralized market economy provided the best foundation for democratic and dynamic societies, government action to reduce poverty and unemployment was necessary to maintain support for such a system. Consequently, macroeconomic policy now gave priority to economic growth and the reduction of unemployment. Investment was encouraged by tax and other incentives, and the commitment to full employment encouraged the corporate sector to look beyond the short-run fluctuations in the business cycle. In moving from wartime controls to a peacetime market economy, West European governments were much more gradualist than their predecessors in 1918 (and the advisers to East European governments in the early 1990s). This helped to avoid the inflationary spiral that occurred after WWI, but it was also an implicit recognition of the need to avoid severe shocks to the population and to build a consensus for the new postwar economic and political system.[7] Indeed, the search for a more consensual basis for economic policymaking is one of the key differences between the two postwar periods: In contrast to the 1920s, the aftermath of WWII saw considerable efforts throughout Western Europe to introduce institutions and practices that would encourage wage moderation and preserve the social peace (the welfare state itself, co-determination, indicative planning, etc.). Although it is difficult to quantify the impact of such measures, many judge them to have made a key contribution to the economic performance of the 1950s and 1960s.[8]

There were also major differences in approach to the international economy in the two postwar periods. As was the case with domestic policies, attitudes in 1945 were shaped by the perception that the economic failures of the interwar years had been a major factor behind the slide into the disaster of WWII. "The 1944 Bretton Woods conference and the institutions it spawned represented an effort by the allied governments to create post-war structures that would help to prevent a repetition of the global economic catastrophe and the 'beggar-thy-neighbor' policies of the 1930s."[9] The revolutionary idea, embodied in the Articles of Agreement of the International Monetary Fund (IMF), was that "because exchange rates were matters of international interest, they should be subject to international scrutiny and normally to international agreement."[10] Although the Havana Conference, held between November 21, 1947 and March 24, 1948, failed to establish the International Trade Organization (ITO), it formulated the General Agreements on Tariffs and Trade (GATT) that guided international trade relations for more than forty years and provided a framework of rules for the conduct of trade and for negotiating further trade liberalization.

This boost to international institutions and international cooperation in both economic and political affairs owed a great deal to the United States, which played—and sustained—a very active role both in building the overall postwar international institutional framework and in supporting the recovery of Western Europe. Follies, such as the Morgenthau plan for the "pastoralization" of Germany, had been abandoned by the end of the war and been overtaken by a conviction that European economic recovery was essential to the long-term interests of the United States, as Keynes had argued in 1919.[11] That recovery would not be possible if German industry were suppressed. This argument was greatly reinforced by the perception in Western Europe and the United States that the major threat to security lay in the growing tensions between the Soviet Union and the Western allies, not from Germany. Instead of trying to punish a vanquished state with demands for heavy reparations, a policy that had failed in the 1920s, the objectives of peace and prosperity in Western Europe were to be pursued by creating a "united states" of Europe which would reconcile German recovery with the security needs of other West European countries. Originally it was hoped that a return to free trade and multilateral settlement within the framework of the new Bretton Woods institutions would suffice to get a sustained European recovery under way, and the rapid recovery of industrial output in 1946 supported such hopes. But a series of European dollar crises, the premature enforcement of sterling convertibility in 1947, and fears in the winter of 1946–1947 that the immediate postwar increase in activity might be running out of steam led to the introduction of the Marshall Plan.

There has been much questioning of how far the Marshall Plan was responsible for the postwar recovery. It was in fact already clear to Nicholas Kaldor (see box 2.1) and his research team in the ECE that when Marshall aid arrived, a strong European recovery was already under way as a result of domestic efforts,[12] but the assistance probably helped to ensure that it could

continue without being prematurely checked by balance-of-payments constraints and other bottlenecks. The strong U.S. commitment to European recovery also helped to boost business confidence and expectations, not least in
Germany, and thus to encourage the growth of fixed investment (which was
much stronger than in the aftermath of WWI). The Marshall Plan was also
important in insisting on cooperation among the European recipients of
Marshall aid in its distribution, in developing regional projects, and, through
the European Payments Union (EPU), in liberalizing their trade and payments in a gradual but purposeful manner. In contrast to the lack of cooperation among the European states in the 1920s, the Marshall Plan played an
important role in promoting the process of close interaction and cooperation
which has characterized the European region ever since and to which the ECE
has made a significant contribution. Just over fifty years later, the ECE secretariat would return to the Marshall Plan and draw some salutary lessons for
helping the countries of Eastern Europe in their transition from centrally
planned to market economies. (This will be discussed later in this chapter.)

These, then, are some of the salient features of the world in which the ECE
was created in 1947 and some of the broad lines of thinking about economic
policy that were shared by the economists who joined the new institution.
Despite the considerable changes that have occurred in the region, many of
the fundamental issues and concerns have remained or resurfaced, not least
with the collapse of central planning and the transition to market economies
in Eastern Europe and with the challenges and tensions created by globalization. How should change be managed and the costs of adjustment be distributed? How far should domestic economies adjust to the dictates of the
international economy? Can government intervention improve the prospects
for growth and employment or should it be kept to a minimum? How should
the international monetary system be managed? The answers given to these
and other questions of economic management in the postwar period of reconstruction and in the 1950s and 1960s no longer seemed adequate to
policymakers in the three decades or so after 1973. But there are now increasing doubts as to whether the neoliberalism of the 1980s and 1990s has all the
answers to the development problems of developing and transition economies or can respond effectually to problems such as environmental degradation or chronic economic inequality.

A Structure of Cooperation for a Divided Europe

Against this general background of new ideas and policy approaches, the
immediate problems in Europe in 1945 were practical and the priorities clear:

to provide food, clothing, shelter, and medical care to large numbers of suffering people; to rebuild houses and infrastructure, especially transport; and to remove the obstacles to a recovery of production and international trade. The United Nations Relief and Rehabilitation Administration (UNRRA) provided humanitarian relief without discrimination, an effort described by one historian as "the biggest piece of first aid in history."[13] To confront the immediate problems of economic dislocation (and, by extension, the risks of social unrest), three intergovernmental bodies were set up, outside the framework of the United Nations (UN), on the initiative of the United States and Britain. These were the Emergency Economic Committee for Europe (EECE), the European Coal Organization (ECO), and the European Central Inland Transport Organization (ECITO).[14] Known as the "E-organizations," their main tasks were to organize the supply and equitable distribution of basic materials, especially coal, and remove bottlenecks in the transport system. Membership in the three organizations was open to all European countries except the defeated powers and Spain, but the Soviet Union only participated to a limited extent in ECITO. Poland and Czechoslovakia, however, were active participants in the ECO and ECITO. ECITO had a broader mandate than the other two: It was to address production and distribution problems in a wide range of activities, including agriculture, timber, and machinery, and to discuss and make recommendations concerning reconstruction policy and longer-run development.

Creating the Economic Commission for Europe

The "E-organizations" did useful work that contributed toward the "surprisingly rapid recovery of industrial production in the eighteen months following the cessation of hostilities,"[15] but they had little time to grapple with the larger economic policy questions facing the region. By the end of 1945, it was clear that a different organizational structure was needed to address the longer-run problems of reconstruction and economic development in Europe. No doubt there were many who recalled that the various institutions for economic cooperation established after WWI had failed to tackle the major problems of reconstruction, which had serious consequences for the economic development of the region as a whole. Such concerns led the Polish minister of labor and social welfare, Jan Stanczyk, to submit a resolution to the First Session of the General Assembly in February 1946 concerning the "Reconstruction of Countries Members of the United Nations Devastated by War." Stanczyk stressed that reconstruction had to be addressed as a special problem in its own right—it could not be handled through the humanitarian program of UNRRA nor would it be brought about simply through the restoration of international trade and financial networks, as proposed by the Bretton Woods institutions. He also argued that the reconstruction of the ruined countries was beyond the resources of most of them and was not simply a matter for them alone but "a problem of [the] world economy."[16] A new approach was therefore needed to better organize and accelerate the process. The Polish resolution was adopted unanimously by the General Assembly, and this proved to be the first step toward the founding of the ECE just over a year later, in March 1947.

In the long series of debates and negotiations which took place in the Economic and Social Council of the UN (ECOSOC) and various working groups and subcommittees,[17] a number of themes and arguments were raised that would reappear time and time again in the following decades. Not every member of ECOSOC was in favor of creating regional entities within the UN. The Ukrainian SSR thought priority should be given to assistance and credits on favorable terms to the war-devastated countries through UNRRA and the International Bank for Reconstruction and Development (IBRD), and its delegates probably shared the initial fears of the Soviet Union that such a regional body would seek to interfere in the internal affairs of its members. It wondered how, in a Europe where two economic systems coexisted, an organization could make meaningful recommendations while respecting the sovereignty of governments. But the Soviet Union eventually supported the creation of an ECE and in fact proposed a number of amendments to the terms of reference which would have increased the autonomy of ECE vis-à-vis ECOSOC and other UN organizations. It may have been that once the Soviet Union saw that the creation of the ECE was unavoidable, its interests lay in having as great an influence as possible in the commission. A different line of opposition came from some countries such as Canada that argued that "the San Francisco Conference had expressed itself—wisely and after ripe reflection—in favor of functional rather than regional organizations."[18] The debate on the respective virtues of regional versus global approaches thus first arose in the postwar context and has continued to the present.

In supporting the original Polish proposal, the representative of the United States made remarks about foreign aid that would constantly reemerge in all discussions on aid policy: "Aid across national boundaries depends upon domestic policy and its ingredients of enlightened self-interest and the natural instincts of friendliness, generosity and humanity,"[19] but "it is manifestly impossible for any country to pledge itself in advance, no matter how indirectly, to a programme or policy which would ultimately demand a contribution of its national resources, without examining in each particular instance for what uses and for what purposes such contributions were being asked."[20] The representative of the United Kingdom agreed in emphasizing that "countries cannot live for ever, or even for long, on charity, however generous. They must be helped to help themselves."[21] These arguments would be heard again not only a year later in the context of the Marshall Plan but also over fifty years later in the discussions about assisting the transition economies of Eastern Europe.

In one of the earliest reports to ECOSOC making proposals for reconstruction, the Nuclear Economic and Employment Commission stressed the complexity of the task insofar as the "basic task of reconstruction is combined in most countries with programmes designed to modernize the structure of industry and to modify the character of the economic system. . . . The short-run process of primary reconstruction is thus overlaid by a process of secondary reconstruction which has long-range aims. . . . Reconstruction, both in the narrower and wider sense of the term, merges into the general problem of the economic basis on which a new and lasting peace may be built."[22] This is remarkably close in concepts and tone to the analysis of the ECE secretariat in response to the collapse of communism in Eastern Europe in 1989 and in discussing the prospects for economic revival in the Balkans after the Kosovo conflict of 1998.[23]

Another important and contentious issue in the negotiations concerned the treatment of European countries that were not members of the UN. Above all, the argument was over Germany. The Soviet Union's delegate asserted that "the occupation authorities alone were responsible for economic development in the area concerned and he opposed any mention of the German economy in the terms of reference of the Economic Commission for Europe."[24] Moreover, he "did not want to see the competence of ECE extended either to the whole of Europe on the one hand, or to non-member States of the United Nations on the other." But Germany was crucial for the European economy, and the Soviet proposal[25] to limit the domain of the commission was outvoted. Paragraph 10 of the terms of reference thus remained unchanged: It stipulated that "the Commission may consult with the representatives of the respective Allied Control Authorities, . . . be consulted by them . . . and advise them."[26] The practice that developed in this regard was for experts from Germany to take part, initially with the authorization of the then occupation authorities, in the full range of the activities of ECE subsidiary bodies, though not in the public sessions of the commission itself. In fact, the authorities and the experts of the western zones of Germany participated in the work of the commission roughly from the beginning of its practical work, while those of the eastern zone did so, after Stalin's death, from the spring of 1953. After the establishment of the Federal Republic of Germany (FRG) in May 1949 and of the German Democratic Republic (GDR) in October 1949, the question of their participation in the sessions of the commission was raised in 1954 and 1955, but a majority in favor of this was lacking. Finally, on February 21, 1956, the FRG became a member, but it was only in 1973 that the GDR joined the UN and then the ECE. Despite the political difficulties created by such a situation, the secretariat managed to fully involve experts from the GDR in its technical meetings and to include the GDR economy in its statistics and comparative economic analysis of the countries of Europe.

As for the European nations that were not members of the UN,[27] Article 8 of the ECE's mandate stipulated that the commission could admit them in a consultative capacity, without limitation, to "the consideration of matters specially affecting them," as suggested by the Soviet Union. In fact, Gunnar Myrdal, the first executive secretary, decided to invite all of them, except Spain, to participate in all meetings of the commission, its committees, and their subsidiary bodies. The pan-European character of the ECE was reinforced when, in 1951, at the initiative of the commission, ECOSOC amended Article 8 in such a way as to authorize the ECE to decide whether to grant voting rights to European countries that were not members of the UN. This was done[28] three years before all these countries became members of the UN.[29] These arrangements and practices concerning Germany and other non-members of the UN "made ECE an all-European organization right from the start, at a time when the question of admission to membership of the United Nations of a number of countries was unresolved."[30] This enabled the ECE to address the issues of reconstruction and the development of Europe in a comprehensive and meaningful manner and to develop a framework of practical cooperation that spanned the entire region.

The ECE and the Marshall Plan: A Path Not Taken

Thus, after just over a year of arduous negotiation, the ECE came officially into being on March 28, 1947, and a week later, on April 4, Gunnar Myrdal, then minister of trade of Sweden, accepted the Secretary-General's invitation to become the first executive secretary. The achievement was a remarkable one: The case for a regional commission within the UN system had been argued and won and the ECE had been set up with a broad mandate, considerable room for initiative, and the possibility of involving all the countries of Europe if it so wished. Moreover, the new commission had the strong support of the Western powers and especially of the United States, which had taken "the initiative and exercised strong leadership" in the entire process of setting up the ECE.[31] However, East-West relations had been deteriorating steadily and the differences were widening rapidly over Germany. In retrospect, Myrdal judged that, given the intensification of the Cold War, the ECE had only just made it: Had the decision to create it not been reached by March 1947, it is likely that it would never have been reached at all.[32]

At the beginning of 1947, neither the United States nor Britain had yet assumed that the breach with the Soviet Union was final, but internal and external factors were pushing them toward state-building in the "Bi-zone" (i.e., the American and British occupation zones of Germany which had been combined the previous December).[33] Internally, many Germans were starving after the 1946–1947 winter and, externally, the attempts to maintain quadripartite policymaking were collapsing. On March 12, President Truman set out the Truman Doctrine, which described the world in sharp bipolar terms and promised to resist any threat from communism anywhere. Soon after, in April, the foreign ministers' conference in Moscow failed to reach any agreement over Germany: U.S. Secretary of State George Marshall concluded "that Stalin, looking over Europe, saw the best way to advance Soviet interests was to let matters drift."[34] The report of the U.S. delegate to the First Session of the ECE in May described "the calamitous condition of Europe"[35] which both reinforced fears that the Soviet Union might expand its empire in Europe and increased the incentive for the Western allies to strengthen the institutions of the "Bi-zone." On June 5, Marshall delivered his historic speech at Harvard, which led to the Marshall Plan. In their contribution to Marshall's speech, the economic staff of the State Department suggested "a co-ordinated European recovery program assisted and primed by the United States. . . . The initial approach should be Europe-wide in order to avoid undesirable psychological repercussions in Western Europe and to attract, if possible, the Soviet Union and the satellites. The Economic Commission for Europe was suggested as the most appropriate agency for handling such a program."[36] But in his speech, Marshall did not mention the ECE: He simply invited the Europeans to work out a plan and present it to the United States. During the weeks that followed, discussions continued in the State Department as to whether or not the ECE would be asked to design and implement such a plan, but it was left to the Europeans to decide whether or not to involve the ECE. The debate moved to Europe, particularly to the United Kingdom, where partisans and opponents of the ECE were being given responsibility for the plan. In the end, the British Foreign Office and the Board of Trade concluded that there was a danger

> that action will be obstructed and perverted by Russia and her satellites. . . . It ought not to be too difficult to keep the matter outside the purview of the

ECE. . . . The simplest course, if it can be managed politically, would seem to be for us and France to issue an invitation to a conference on the basis of a . . . draft plan which we might square informally in advance with like minded countries. . . . This does not, of course, exclude keeping the ECE in touch with developments, nor bringing them in more positively at later stages.[37]

On June 27, the foreign ministers of France, the United Kingdom, and the Soviet Union met in Paris to discuss a common response to the American initiative. This proved impossible: Molotov left Paris, and the British and French governments decided to press ahead with organizing a reply to Marshall's proposal, whether or not the Soviet Union was prepared to join them. On July 4, the two governments invited twenty-two European countries to a conference whose principal task would be to prepare a response to Marshall by setting out the needs of Europe and a plan for economic cooperation. A letter to the Soviet authorities expressed the hope that their refusal to participate in the organization would not be final. Albania, Bulgaria, Finland, Hungary, Poland, and Romania refused the invitation. Czechoslovakia at first accepted and the following day refused. In mid-July, the Conference for European Economic Co-operation began in Paris and adopted its report in September and transmitted it to Washington. The final outcome was the creation, in April 1948, of the Organization for European Economic Cooperation (OEEC) to organize the European Recovery Program. At the Second Session of the ECE in July 1947, the delegates of France and the United Kingdom made it clear that "their Governments did not propose that the Commission should at the present time take any specific action with regard to this matter; the organization to be set up would, however, maintain contact with the Commission."[38]

The reasons behind the decision to organize the European Recovery Program outside the ECE—and the UN—have been surrounded by much the same controversies as those surrounding the Marshall Plan itself. The French and British foreign ministers have been accused of deliberately engineering the Soviet walkout from the Paris Tripartite Conference of June 1947 in order to exclude the Soviet Union from the Marshall Plan. However, Paul Porter has pointed out that it was the French foreign minister, M. Bidault, who proposed giving the ECE the responsibility for the European response to Marshall, but Molotov rebuffed him. Porter argues that given the high standing of the UN in public opinion in 1947, it would have been impossible for the British, French, and U.S. governments to reject a Soviet proposal to use the ECE.[39] But the Soviet Union did not make such a proposal, perhaps because it had different objectives and perhaps from a reluctance to enhance the status of an organization where it would always command fewer votes than the Western allies.

But whatever the reasons for this outcome, the effects on the ECE and the UN as a whole were significant. The responsibility for the financial and macroeconomic aspects of the recovery program were given to the OEEC and the Bretton Woods institutions, while the ECE was asked to focus on technical aspects, especially those inherited from the three "E-organizations." The latter were—and are—important, but this institutional division of functions meant that the ECE never became a forum where ministers of finance and economy from the whole of Europe would meet regularly to address the broader economic problems facing the region. Such a forum still does not exist, although a strong case can be made for one given the growing income gaps among the various countries of the region—Western versus Central Europe and the latter versus the Balkans and the CIS (Commonwealth of Independent States)—which risk becoming a serious source of tension. The UN as a whole was also weakened insofar as the senior ministers of the G7 countries dealing with economic affairs largely withdrew from the UN to discuss major issues among themselves or with similar developed countries in the Organisation for Economic Co-operation and Development (OECD). Had the subsequent work of the OECD been developed within the UN, not only the ECE but also ECOSOC would have been greatly strengthened.

A similar development to the Marshall Plan outcome was to be repeated in 1989 when the ECE was largely ignored as an institution that could play a significant role in helping the countries of Eastern Europe in their transition to market economies. Among those who thought that the ECE should play a larger role in the post-1989 transformation of Europe were Willy Brandt,[40] the former West German chancellor, and Walt W. Rostow. Rostow wrote that the "ECE was also a distinguished center for research on Europe's post-war problems and possibilities. . . . The Research Division of the ECE should become a center for the analysis of [the transition] process and the relinkage of East and West."[41] But, distrustful of the UN in general, the leading industrial countries created a new Centre for Co-operation with European Economies in Transition (CCEET) within the OECD in March 1990. Ten years later, the center was closed down and some of its activities maintained in the OECD Centre for Co-operation with Non-Members.

The Decisive First Years: Setting Principles and Methods

Having lost responsibility for the Marshall Plan, which would have given it much greater power and political visibility, the ECE had to find a way to carry out the tasks it had been given and respond to the needs of a region divided by the Cold War and composed of two fundamentally opposed economic and political systems. Myrdal and his team successfully met this challenge. In a divided Europe, they established a dialogue based on serious economic and technical analysis. Confronted by two different economic and social systems, they developed a common understanding of the need for international norms and standards. Without financial resources to distribute, they built upon the common interests of member countries, leading them to concrete cooperation. Taking to heart the UN Charter, which stipulates that the paramount consideration in the employment of staff is the necessity of recruiting only those people who meet the highest standards of efficiency, competence, and integrity (Article 101.3), Myrdal was able to attract an outstanding group of talented and dedicated economists. Unlike his successors, he was in full control of all appointments and did not have to face an obstructive set of rules and bureaucratic behavior.

At its first session, there was already one indication that the commission might succeed in fostering an East-West dialogue. Following a plea from the Soviet Union delegate, who noted that there were 250 million Russian-speaking people in Europe, Russian was adopted as a working language of the ECE together with English and French. This helped Russian-speaking delegates feel at home in the ECE and facilitated exchanges in the technical committees, where delegates from the East rarely spoke any other working language.

But a key factor was that the new executive secretary deplored the Cold War and the lack of East-West cooperation. He was strongly opposed to economic nationalism and disliked the term "Western Europe" insofar as it was used to imply that East and West did not share a common European heritage. Myrdal was firmly committed to developing cooperation on a pan-regional scale, and he immediately set about trying to improve East-West relations in the belief that increased trade would improve the prospects for peace. One of Myrdal's first acts was to appoint a Russian as his deputy, not, as was rumored at the time, as a result of Soviet pressure but because he wanted to gain the confidence and support of the Soviet Union in his efforts for regional cooperation. Myrdal was disappointed that the Marshall Plan was not given to the ECE to administer because he feared that a separate institution focused on the West would increase East-West tensions and undermine his efforts to build cooperation across the divide. It was *not* the disappointment of a frustrated bureaucratic empire-builder.

Perhaps the major achievement of the ECE in the forty or so years from 1947 was to keep alive the idea of a larger and older Europe that transcended the boundaries of what was to become the Common Market and the European

Community. It did so by building and preserving a bridge between its western and eastern halves when no one else was willing or able to do so and when the prospect of reuniting them was so distant as to appear quixotic. Much of the credit for this must be given to Myrdal's leadership in the early and politically difficult years of the new commission. It is against the background of this "big idea," the pursuit of European economic integration across the divide of the Cold War, that the ECE conducted much of its economic analysis, made policy recommendations, and developed intergovernmental cooperation over a wide range of technical issues. The latter were often narrowly defined and individually might appear relatively modest, but their practical benefits were significant and, equally important, they strengthened the habits of cooperation among countries with very different social systems and outlooks and made an important contribution to the economic integration of the region.

In Myrdal's approach to building the ECE we can identify three major pillars. Perhaps the most important idea that he brought with him to his function was that

> a research group, and consequently also the secretariat of the ECE insofar as its research work is concerned, should be a free and independent scientific agent, which approaches the problems and reaches and states its findings guided only by the inherited and established standards of the profession, without sideward glances at what would be politically opportune. . . . In scientific inquiry governments cannot be granted any monopoly of truth. This implies among other things that official statistics and assertions by governments about facts and causal relations cannot be accepted at their face value, but have to be scrutinized in a scholarly manner.[42]

The secretariat was governed by this idea in making investigations and studies of economic and technological problems and in collecting and evaluating economic and statistical information, two tasks assigned to the commission in its terms of reference.

The main outlet for the economic analysis of the secretariat since 1948 has been the annual *Economic Survey for Europe*.[43] The governments never formally asked for a survey; this was an initiative of Myrdal, who thought that governments needed such a publication, not least because no one else at the time was providing a comprehensive overview of what was happening to the European economies. At the end of the second session of the commission in July 1947, he said that the *Survey* "[would] not aim at reproducing in voluminous form the rather hackneyed material which [was] available in so many places. It [would] much rather attempt to produce a selective survey of European problems, acting as an alarm clock to draw the Commission's attention to impending troubles and complications."[44] The *Surveys* have always been produced under the sole responsibility of the executive secretary, who never submits them to governments prior to publication. Successive executive secretaries have preserved the independence of the secretariat in this regard and, consistently over the years, have refused to alter them when governments, as they have on many occasions, challenged the analysis on political grounds. Before 1989 such demands for correction came primarily from the East, but since then they have come either from North America or, more frequently, from Brussels. Nevertheless, it is fair to say that Myrdal's claim in 1956 that "the independent status of the ECE secretariat, so far as its research work is concerned, has, rather astonishingly, come to be accepted in the Commission, and has become an institutional tradition"[45] remains valid. Addressing the Forty-first Session of the commission in 1986, following pressure by the GDR on the secretariat to delete its analysis of declining productivity trends in Eastern Europe and the Soviet Union from the 1986 *Survey,* the ambassador of the United Kingdom said:

> We cannot agree with every aspect of the secretariat's analysis. That, however, is not the point. . . . In the light of the differences between our economic systems it is important that the *Survey* continues to be a product of independent, objective research, against which we can all measure our own policies. This work is an asset to member countries whatever their economic persuasion and its independence should be carefully preserved.[46]

Myrdal would have been pleased with that, not least with the willingness to tolerate honest disagreement, and he could legitimately say: "There are few things in my life I feel so proud of as having had a role in building up and defending this tradition of independent truth-seeking in an international secretariat."[47] The ECE and the UN secretariat in general enjoy here a privilege that not all secretariats of international organizations can claim; while many of them may have larger and stronger research teams, their publications are subject to prior scrutiny and amendment by governments.

It is perhaps worth taking this point farther. One factor that helped Myrdal create an independent analytical capacity in the secretariat was that if the Western countries wanted an independent assessment of developments in the centrally planned economies, they could hardly object to the same approach being applied to their own. That balance of interest was upset by the collapse of communist regimes in 1989; since then, most of the effort to censor the secretariat's economic analysis has come from the West. Thus, Canada tried to suppress a study of the free trade agreement between Canada and the

United States (which suggested there might be some flaws in the arrangement as well as benefits)[48] and the European Commission has repeatedly objected to the secretariat's discussing enlargement of the European Union (EU),[49] raising questions about the employment effects of the Maastricht Treaty or the timing of the start of the European Monetary Union (EMU). These attempts failed. More recently, the EU commission has opposed suggestions that the ECE secretariat take up the question of the effects of EU enlargement on the transition economies that will remain outside. In all of these cases, the main objections seem to be either that negative aspects of official policies should never be raised or that they are none of the ECE's business despite their obvious concern to the ECE's non-EU members.

Myrdal's case for secretariat independence in research is effectively, and above all, an argument for openness and transparency as key ingredients of the policymaking process in democratic societies. But there are also practical issues involved, insofar as forcing consensus in economic policy analysis may not only be very difficult to achieve but may also be counterproductive. The secretary-general of the OECD has conceded that the "OECD tradition of publishing reports only when the content is approved by all member countries . . . has sometimes fostered diluted compromise positions or, in some cases, prevented rich and much-debated analysis from ever becoming public when any country had objections."[50] This is particularly important in the area of economic and social policy, where there is no scientific consensus on many issues and where to pretend otherwise is to foster delusions or to provide a cover for special interests or for hidden value preferences. Nor, on many issues in a democratic society, is there a unique compromise to be discovered between the various competing interest groups or between the ideal and what is practicably attainable. Again, to pretend otherwise is to risk reducing complex issues to binary choices, either "for" or "against"—the fallacy of the excluded middle.[51] The practical application of Myrdal's approach is to focus on actual important policy problems, to assess the pros and cons of different solutions and compromises, and, while being open about the analysts' own preferences and values, to leave it to individual countries to decide what is most appropriate for them in light of their particular circumstances. International institutions lose credibility and the confidence of the outside world when they give way to backstairs pressure from individual governments (or business corporations) to ignore "awkward" facts or to tilt their conclusions in one direction or another. And they also become less useful to the community at large if they succumb to such pressure. Comparing an early ECE *Survey* with a similar report from the OEEC, an American economist disagreed with many of the conclusions of the ECE study but nevertheless found it more interesting because of its penetrating analysis, its wider range of vision, and its more provocative conclusions.

> In considerable part, no doubt, these differences reflect the fact that, whereas the ECE report is mainly the independent expression of the views of [its] research staff . . . the OEEC report required the full agreement of the representatives of the various participating governments. This helps to explain the cautious wording of the latter study, its tendency to indulge at times in platitudes and generalities, and its obvious effort to avoid offending national sensibilities.[52]

In the contemporary world, where strong pressures to conform to a particular vision of economic and social arrangements have been accompanied by increasing disillusionment with established institutions, there is perhaps a salutary lesson here for the UN as a whole, especially as it still appears to command more trust than other international institutions on macroeconomic matters.[53]

The academic community has been regularly asked to assess the quality of the *Survey*, and it has consistently rated it as the most reliable source of information on Eastern Europe, even after 1990, when many other organizations started publishing analysis of the economies in transition. The reputation of the *Survey* for serious and balanced research had a considerable impact on academics as well as on government advisers in Eastern Europe in the years before 1989.[54] Stanislaw Raczkowski, vice chairman of the Committee on Economics at the Polish Academy of Sciences, has written that "during the dark days of the 'Cold War' this was the only place in the world where the countries of the two confronting political camps cooperated peacefully, solving many economic problems. The quarterly Bulletins of this Commission were always carefully studied in Poland by both the government and the academic community."[55] In the same vein, responding to a question about the impact of the *Survey*, a minister from a country of Central Europe noted that during the communist era the *Survey* represented a second opinion for officials and academics, although in public they had to say what Moscow wanted. He added with some humor that today nothing had changed except that "what has to be said in public is what Brussels wants." These anecdotes reveal that the work of the ECE was perceived as honest and independent and not as propaganda material in the service of the East, the West, or a particular ideology. The post-1989 readership surveys indicate this is still the case. It may also be one reason why, in the mid-1990s, when Western governments were looking for savings in the ECE budget and arguing that there was plenty of information published on OECD countries and that the *Survey* be limited to the countries of Eastern Europe, the latter insisted that the ECE was a pan-European body and that they looked to the *Survey* for analysis of both the Western and Eastern economies and pan-European economic problems.

The second pillar of Myrdal's approach to developing the ECE's activities was a set of principles for practical cooperation among the member governments. The phase of postwar rebuilding was hampered by acute transport difficulties and by the scarcity of the most basic materials, including coal, steel, and timber, and of certain critical industrial products such as silicate bricks, ceramic insulators, and ball bearings. Eliminating these bottlenecks required international cooperation. This was an obvious task for the commission in line with its general mandate. Paragraph three of its terms of reference stated:

> Immediately upon its establishment, the Commission should consult with the member governments of the Emergency Economic Committee for Europe, the European Coal Organization and the European Central Inland Transport Organization with a view to the prompt termination of the first, and the absorption or termination of the activities of the second and third, while ensuring that the essential work performed by each of the three was fully maintained.[56]

Such a clear mandate was most useful because it helped to overcome the reticence of both Western and Eastern countries. The former, because of the Soviet attitude, feared that the efficiency of the last two "E-organizations," if transferred to the ECE, would be jeopardized, and the latter feared that some of these activities would be dominated by Western interests. At its second session, the commission "decided which of the essential functions now being performed by European emergency organizations should be maintained and what machinery it would establish for that purpose."[57]

The transfer of the activities of the "E-organizations" was a success, but it had to be consolidated by concrete results. Very rapidly, the principles were established that would make the work of the subsidiary organs of the commission practical and acceptable to all parties. First, "big and general problems, which are set forth in their terms of reference, are tackled in their technical aspects, by dividing these wider problems into their composite parts, so clearly stated and defined that government experts can usefully and effectively discuss them between themselves and seek agreement on practical solutions."[58] Second, "no meeting is better than a bad one."[59] Third, "Issues are as a rule not brought to a vote in the working organs of the commission. This practice is founded upon a common recognition of the fact that no economic problem and, indeed, no important problem whatsoever concerning sovereign governments can be solved by a majority decision in an inter-governmental organization, but only by agreements between as many governments as are willing to consent."[60] These three principles are still applied today. The first ensures that endless discussions of general considerations are avoided; the second may not have been applied often enough but, generally speaking, it avoids the frustration of delegates wondering why they have come to Geneva; and the third allows interested governments to go ahead and develop international instruments that others can eventually adopt. Although widely accepted today, these principles, when first articulated and applied at the end of the 1940s, broke new ground in facilitating cooperation in a deeply divided Europe and when the tensions of the Cold War were at their peak.

The third pillar of Myrdal's legacy was his vision of the relative roles of governments and the secretariat in an intergovernmental organization. He imposed it upon his arrival but developed it at some length in his introductory statement to the eleventh session of the commission, on April 5, 1956:

> First, I have always believed in the administrative principle of having a hard-working staff with a minimum of unused resources. . . . The pressure of work is a useful discipline, keeping a Secretariat above the demoralization of futility and frustration and leaving it little time for petty intrigues. . . . Second, I feel, as a citizen of our troubled world not less than as a United Nations official, that if there are any additional budgetary resources to spare for work in the economic field, they should be devoted rather to building up the personnel of the other two regional commissions. . . . My third and most important reason for self-restraint in this staffing question stems, however, from my basic conception [that] ultimately the work which needs to be done, is *work by the Governments themselves.* . . . It is a sign of a weak and inefficient international organization when too much of its activity becomes work of the Secretariat.[61]

This vision materialized. First, Myrdal attracted an outstanding group of economists (with "due regard to geographical balance") and a secretariat composed of high-quality staff. If Robert Marjolin did not accept the responsibility of the research division, Nicholas Kaldor did, and Hal B. Lary became his deputy and eventually his successor.[62] Robert Mossé, Wladeck Malinowski, Albert Kervyn de Lettenhove, Walt W. Rostow, and Evgenyi Chossudovsky were among the first to join the secretariat.[63] Second, the number of substantive staff of the ECE remained smaller than that of the other regional commissions except ESCWA. Third, and more important, governments responded as Myrdal wanted, and the accumulated wealth of ECE conventions and norms is the result of the work of national experts sent by their governments, facilitated by the staff of the secretariat.

In following the line so described, the ECE successfully carried out a range of useful tasks that helped Europe in all the stages of its postwar history, but much of the work was technical and was hidden from the general public, which benefited considerably (but obscurely) from it, and was increasingly ignored by the senior politicians in the member countries.

The Achievements of the Early Cold War Period, 1947–1953

As suggested in chapter 1, the intellectual history of an organization is as much, if not more, about the general outlook and values of those employed in the institution, and how they contribute to the analysis of problems and proposals for action, than about specific major contributions to economic thinking. Both Myrdal and Kaldor were major theorists (see box 2.1), but both were probably more interested in policy issues and applied problems. They shared an almost classical belief in economics as a moral discipline, and both believed that intelligence and rational analysis could improve economic outcomes and diminish the prevalence of "stupidities" such as unemployment and poverty. Their approach to the market economy was essentially pragmatic and non-dogmatic. Their focus was on practical policy problems—how to move an economy from A to B—and they were well aware that there were no quick market solutions to economies wracked by severe structural problems and institutional deficiencies.

Myrdal basically saw the ECE as a two-track organization with research and policy analysis constituting one major area of activity and technical or operational functions the other. The two tracks were in part distinguished by their operational modalities: In the former, the secretariat pursued its activity under the sole responsibility of the executive secretary and without prior approval by governments before publishing the results; in the latter, the search for consensus among governments was de rigueur, however slow and painstaking it might be, and there was no question of countries being forced to adopt norms or standards as a result of majority votes.

Economic Analysis: Labor Shortage, Inflation, and External Deficit

One of the principal tasks of the ECE's *Economic Survey* was to provide a regular assessment of the current situation and outlook in the region, and as Myrdal put it, to maintain "a vigilant watch on economic trends in Europe."[64] This was a difficult task in the 1950s, when statistics, especially quarterly data, were less abundant and took longer to appear than now. Nevertheless, it is clear, both from their reception at the time and the references to the early *Surveys* in the economic histories of the period, which are now appearing, that this work was brilliantly successful. There is no space

Box 2.1. Gunnar Myrdal and Nicholas Kaldor

In Gunnar Myrdal, the first executive secretary, and Nicholas Kaldor, the first director of economic research (or, as it was known then, the Research and Planning Division), the nascent ECE had two of the outstanding economists of the twentieth century. Both men had not only powerful intellects but also strong personalities and gifts for leadership. The team they put together in the first three years of the ECE's existence was exceptional: six of them (Gunnar Myrdal, Nicholas Kaldor, W. W. Rostow, Hans Staehle, Ingvar Svennilson, and Pieter Verdoorn) rate entries in the latest edition of the *Palgrave Dictionary of Economics and Law,* and well over half of the original group went on to professorships or to produce important books and papers.[65] Myrdal would receive the Nobel prize for economics in 1973, and many in the economics profession think that Kaldor should have been given one as well.

There is insufficient space here to give any more than a brief overview of the ideas that these two leading figures brought to their work in the ECE. Both men had established reputations before joining the ECE, both had made significant contributions to pure theory, and both were highly critical of the neoclassical general-equilibrium school. Moreover, both had expressed fears for the postwar period and were not overconfident that recession and unemployment would be avoided.[66] By the time Myrdal took over the ECE, he was known as an institutional economist and in a major work, *An American Dilemma,*[67] which appeared in 1944, had demonstrated his strong attachment to interdisciplinary research and his belief that it was illegitimate to isolate economic variables from their political and social setting. Among his original contributions to theory were the concepts of *ex ante* and *ex post,* which emphasized the role of expectations and uncertainty in the economy, and the role of cumulative and circular causation.[68] Both ideas broke away from the traditional static framework of economic theory, and both are important when considering the process of adjustment and structural change and the relative roles of the market and the state. A key element in his approach to research was his view that no research is ever free of political and moral preferences and that therefore value premises should be stated explicitly.

Kaldor had made major contributions to Keynesian theory before joining the ECE and in 1939 had made a seminal contribution to welfare theory in proposing the compensation principle; namely, that if those who gain from an economic or policy change could potentially compensate the losers and still be better off, then the change must be for the better (since productivity must have risen). His work had also focused on imperfect competition, economies of scale, the functional distribution of income, growth, and technical progress. Like Myrdal, Kaldor rejected the neoclassical assumptions as a useful description of the real world in which economic policy had to be formulated, and he was also to develop the principal of cumulative causation in his later work on economic growth and productivity. (It is significant, given the later development of the Kaldor-Verdoorn law, that Verdoorn was a member of Kaldor's team that produced the *Survey* of 1948.)

here to assess the record in any detail, but one example of the "vigilant watch" is how quickly the *Survey* picked up the fact that the setbacks to output in early 1947 were temporary and that by the time Marshall was making his speech at Harvard, the recovery resumed at the same momentum as before. Thus, part of the recent revisionist assessments of the Marshall Plan—that it assisted a growing economy rather than lifted it from the morass of stagnation described by Marshall—was already clear at the time to Kaldor and his team.

The focus on short-run issues was inevitable and proper, since if the short-run problems were not overcome there would not be much of a long run to enjoy (this was the serious moral point behind Keynes's quip that "in the long run we are all dead"). But the short-term analysis was not merely descriptive. Most reviewers recognized that the approach to the analysis was held together by a coherent set of ideas and, also crucially, that it identified the big problems and improved the general understanding of them. And one of the key merits of this analysis was to encourage the readers, especially the official ones, to view their economic problems and policies in a European rather than a purely national perspective. Of the many reactions to the early *Surveys,* three will be sufficient to give the general tone. In the United States, one reviewer wrote that "for the last three years, the annual publication of the *Survey* has been the most important event in the field of regional economics. . . . Its combination of abundant factual and statistical material with theoretical analysis of the highest order has set a standard never before reached by similar works."[69] Two years later, a senior British economist and government adviser judged that the *Survey* "remains the best guide through the tangle that makes up one year of modern history. By getting the tangle sorted out earlier in the year, the *Survey* makes it correspondingly easier for the intelligent but breathless European to keep pace with events and even catch a glimpse of where they are taking him."[70] One of the many virtues of the *Surveys* was that reviewers were able to praise the assessment and analysis of developments while disagreeing with the policy recommendations. This was particularly the case (although not exclusively) with U.S. readers who felt that the *Survey's* skeptical attitude toward trade liberalization and other matters betrayed a lack of faith in the working of a free market economy.[71]

Whether these *Surveys* had a direct influence on policy in the region is a question too complex to attempt to answer here. But it is clear that the *Survey* had a wide and enthusiastic (but critical) audience in the 1950s when in fact it had hardly any competition. This would change in the early 1960s, when the OECD started its *Economic Outlook* and short-term forecasting in the national research institutes of Western Europe expanded rapidly.

In the eighteen months following the cessation of hostilities, industrial production had recovered quickly and had exceeded its prewar level by the last quarter of 1947. The major macroeconomic problems, however, were inflation, low productivity, and disequilibria in the balance of payments.

A major constraint on increases in production, to which the *Survey* had already drawn attention in early 1948, was the exhaustion of labor reserves. Greater efforts therefore had to be made to increase productivity. Despite increases in 1946 and 1947, it was still below prewar levels and far below those in the United States. This dimension was well understood by the countries of Western Europe that, in the framework of the Marshall Plan, sent "productivity missions" to the United States to learn from the achievements of U.S. enterprises. The problem of labor shortages also became clear to Eastern European planners at the end of the 1960s, and this stimulated reform efforts that are addressed later in this chapter.

The rate of inflation differed widely from one country to another, but it was possible to distinguish two groups of countries. In the first, inflation was suppressed by direct controls on prices, consumer rationing, government controls on the allocation of scarce materials, and, in some cases, restrictions on the free movement of labor. In the second, inflation was open, the rise in prices absorbing a surplus of cash holdings. In the first group were most of the Western European countries; in the second were a few Western countries, including France, and the countries of Central Europe. In the second group, the competition between wages and profits through strikes and price increases led to a worse income distribution than before the war, while in the first, distribution of income was more egalitarian. There was no complacency about inflation in the *Survey*: "Both open and suppressed inflation damaged productive efficiency"; suppressed inflation reduced the attractiveness of earning money and blunted the incentives for productive effort, which in turn could "become a serious factor, hampering the recovery of output"; open inflation "sharpened the incentives to productive effort, but, together with a more unequal income distribution, lowered the general efficiency of industry by making rational cost calculations extremely difficult and by diverting resources to unproductive uses." The *Survey* recommended a mix of budgetary, monetary, and income policies "to bring the real value of cash holding to a more normal level."[72]

Throughout the late 1940s and 1950s, a recurrent problem for Western Europe was its balance-of-payments deficit vis-à-vis the dollar zone. Despite fluctuations due to the Korean war, the deficit was essentially structural and needed to be tackled urgently because Marshall aid was due to be reduced and phased out. The analysis and suggestions made in the 1953 *Survey* in this context are of particular interest because they raised a number of issues of international development and proposed policies that later would be at the heart of the North-South debate. It was generally agreed, at the time, that the solutions to Western Europe's external economic problems were to be found in Europe itself, in keeping inflation under control and in demonstrating greater flexibility and adaptability in the use of resources. In the same spirit, the *Survey* felt that "quantitative controls over trade and payments [did] exert perverse effects on the allocation of resources, on incentives in production and trade, and on business profits and ethics,"[73] familiar language today. A footnote to this text is worth quoting as it refers to an issue that today has gained considerable international attention: "The special advantages thereby conferred on those favored with import licenses provide an inducement for corruption. Similar problems arise in other ways under exchange controls."[74] But to this classical view of the causes of and remedies for balance-of-payments problems, the *Survey* added the idea that a solution for Europe alone was inadequate; a worldwide approach was needed. The problem was "to lay the foundation for a new equilibrium in international trade and payments and to make the fundamental changes necessary for a more regular and normal functioning of the world market."[75] In what appears to be a criticism of the work of the Conference for European Economic Co-operation, the 1953 *Survey* noted that those who developed the European Recovery Program in 1947 in response to the invitation contained in Marshall's speech had "failed . . . to recognize how deeply rooted was the distortion in the whole pattern of world production and trade."[76] And because of this, it could be said that Marshall aid had contributed to the stalemate of the early 1950s "by making less apparent and less pressing the need to pursue alternative policies aimed at decreasing European dependence on imports from the dollar area."[77]

The authors of the *Survey* were conscious of the fact that before any policy line could be adopted to address this problem, it was crucially important that the politicians and responsible senior officials reach a common understanding of the fundamental nature of the imbalances and the magnitude of the adjustment to be sought. With that aim, the *Survey* provided background analysis and suggestions as to what could be the main elements in a coherent program. The first possibility, "an increase in western Europe's dollar earnings from sales of goods and services to the United States and other dollar countries,"[78] would have implied not only some adjustment of the European economies but, mainly, a change in U.S. commercial policy. In order to strengthen their competitiveness, the Europeans were pressed either to reduce their internal costs or to further depreciate their currencies. But, as noted in the *Survey,* "even with the modifications brought by the Reciprocal Trade Agreements programme, United States commercial policy [was] still explicitly designed to limit narrowly the scope within which competition [could] produce its effects and to prevent serious disturbance to any existing American production."[79] Here again, from the point of view of development thinking, is a footnote that contains elements of the future theory of "unequal exchange": "A general reduction of the internal price level or in the foreign-exchange values of the currencies of European countries affect not merely their exports to the United States, but also their exports, six times as great, to other countries as well, even where their prices are now fully competitive, and thus means a significant further deterioration of their terms of trade."

The second possibility, "an increase in production of food and raw materials both in western Europe and in other non-dollar areas with the double aim of meeting the needs of expanding population and industry in the world generally and of reducing the present one-sided dependence on dollar sources of supply,"[80] was favored by the authors of the *Survey.* In commenting on what the conditions would be for success along this line, the authors made suggestions that anticipated the vision of what could have been a North-South partnership. Europeans, preferably with the Americans, should enter into "purchase contracts" with their partners in the rest of the world and "supply part of the investment funds required" to increase the production of food and raw materials. It was recommended that "foreign investment should be justified primarily by the needs and potentialities for economic development of the capital-receiving countries"[81] and by the requirements of investing countries for the exports supplied in return. Prophetically, the limitations of foreign direct investments, concentrated on a limited number of countries, sensitive to political hazards, and linked to the exports of capital goods from the investing country, were stressed. And, while advocating the financing of investment abroad from public funds, a macroeconomic point was made that seems to have anticipated current discussion on the financing of development: Public finance "makes no greater real demands on the national economy than an equivalent amount of private investment would impose," but, of course, it "is inevitably vulnerable to the pressure to reduce public spending."[82]

The shortage of basic raw materials also continued to threaten rising production, thus prompting the ECE secretariat to prepare a series of medium-term forecasts of supply and demand (as well as actions described below) in order to facilitate intra-European exchanges. But, more generally, the revival of intra-European trade was seriously hampered by a lack of the means to finance continued trade deficits. European countries were thus moving toward a strict bilateral balancing of their accounts with one another with all its obvious inconveniences. It was frequently argued, at the time, that the solution would lie in arrangements permitting freer convertibility of European currencies. The *Survey* argued that this "would not alter the fundamental causes of balance-of-payments disequilibrium" and "on the contrary, . . . might well itself constitute a further restricting and distorting influence."[83] Fearing that each country would try to reduce its imports and increase its exports in order to obtain dollars to settle trade deficits with their neighbors, and recognizing that the dollar would continue to be the currency most sought after, it suggested that safeguards be erected to prevent a ruinous competition for dollars. It would then be possible to develop "a structure of trade under which each country may have both import surpluses and export surpluses in its trade with other European countries, the one being offset against the other, and, secondly, by making it possible for countries whose positions require it to have import surpluses in the immediate present, offset by export surpluses in [the future]."[84] This analysis anticipated the European Payments Union, which operated from 1950 to 1958 (with the support of Marshall aid) and allowed a gradual and orderly liberalization of trade among the Western European countries and the multilateralization of payments. It also led to further debates in the ECE's Committee for the Development of Trade when it finally started meeting in 1954 and to the establishment in 1957 of a voluntary multilateral compensation system for East-West trade "whereby governments [might] use the ECE secretariat as agent in order to reach quarterly agreements on the transfer of bilateral balances among national banks."[85] In the twelve years during which this compensation system was in operation, it helped governments to arrange transfers to a value of about $136 million. It was terminated in 1969 when the extension of automatic transferability removed the need for such a facility.

The Development of Practical Cooperation

As indicated above, sustaining the postwar recovery required a solution to Europe's severe balance-of-payments problems. The authors of the first *Surveys* quickly identified this as the crucial issue facing European policymakers, but they also argued that the problem was essentially structural and could not be solved by quickly moving to convertibility and letting the exchange rate bring about the correction. Borrowing was judged unlikely to be possible on a sufficient scale. The next alternative would be to reduce the rate of growth and thus reduce the demand for imports, but this would have led to increased unemployment, which, in the immediate postwar years, would have carried considerable risks for political stability and the recovery of democratic institutions. The authors of the *Survey* were well aware of such risks, which is why they settled on the remaining option of seeking a large increase in exports. But adjustment would take time and, together with the preceding considerations, this explains why the *Survey*'s approach was gradualist and emphasized direct action and government intervention to tackle bottlenecks and other constraints on increasing export capacities and competitiveness. Not everyone agreed with this diagnosis, and in the United States there were many who thought market forces should have been given greater freedom more rapidly, but the *Survey*'s analysis was coherent and realistic—and it provided the intellectual underpinning for both direct action to deal with the bottlenecks and shortages that were to occupy the ECE's technical bodies in their early years and for the subsequent development of intergovernmental cooperation.

The few examples given below illustrate how the secretariat and governments interact in addressing technical problems and may come up with practical ideas that change attitudes and permit durable cooperation.

ORGANIZING TRADE AGREEMENTS

Even without a multilateral compensation mechanism in place, East-West trade should in principle have developed strongly. Poland and the Soviet Union had coal, and the agricultural potential of the Eastern European countries was large. But in fact, the volume of East-West European trade declined sharply each year from 1946 to the summer of 1953. The ECE established a Committee for the Development of Trade in May 1949, but less than a month later it was in deadlock. "The western countries considered that the first task of the Committee should be to form a clear conception of the goods available and required for trade, while the Eastern European countries stressed the futility of any effort to exchange information as long as discriminatory export licensing policies were practised against them."[86] Confronted with this situation, Myrdal decided not to convene the committee until a basis for agreement had been reached. The committee did not meet again until October 1954. In the meantime, he consulted member governments and made several proposals. In November 1949, he outlined a multilateral trade framework in which "subsequent bilateral negotiations could more effectively take place."[87] Under such an agreement, Western countries would buy, over several years, cereals and possibly other goods at prices fluctuating between agreed-upon lower and upper limits. The export revenues could then be used for the purchase of goods from lists to be agreed upon. On this basis, in November 1950, an ad hoc meeting on grains permitted the exchange of information on availability and requirements but failed to examine the question of counterpart deliveries. In August 1951, there was a similar meeting on grain and timber at which concrete trading proposals were considered. A Consultation of Trade Experts took place in 1952,[88] but practical measures and procedures to expand trade did not materialize until April 1953, when "for the first time in post-war history, a practical multilateral discussion of east-west trade problems took place without political recriminations."[89] In the summer of that year, East-West trade increased rapidly, reversing the downward trend that had existed since the war. Although it is not possible to ascribe this result directly to the consultation organized by the ECE, a number of experts who attended it reported subsequently to the executive secretary that in their judgment the substantial increases in the areas of trade for which they were responsible "were traceable to the contacts made at the 1953 Consultation."[90] The consultations became part of the regular meeting of the trade committee until it was felt that East-West trade mechanisms were sufficiently well established. The consultations took place under the chairmanship of the executive secretary, who decided on the agenda and made and delivered the report to governments under his own responsibility.

Meeting Energy Needs

In intra-European trade, there was one product, coal, for which the exchanges between the two parts of Europe were conducted very smoothly, and it may be that this example inspired Myrdal when he outlined the agreement for grains. The Coal Committee, established in July 1947, took over from the European Coal Organization (ECO) in April 1948 and inherited the "invaluable sense of co-operative effort"[91] that had developed in the ECO at a moment when a "liberated Europe was threatened by coal shortage." Between April 1948 and September 1950, the Coal Committee, in which two major eastern producers, the Soviet Union and Poland, participated, allocated to countries in need 60 million tons of solid fuel from European sources. In doing so, and in order to ensure that no country suffered a dramatic coal shortage, the committee took into account the equivalent quantities sold through bilateral agreements. After 1950, however, there was a swing from acute shortage to temporary periods of glut, putting in question the committee's long-term efforts to increase output.

The ECE Coal Committee did not attempt to develop such an ambitious degree of intervention as had been proposed by the Economic Committee of

the League of Nations in 1927 and 1929.[92] But it did work out a production
and consumption policy of which the essential elements were to increase pro
duction potential, to develop instruments for adapting production to the requirements of the European economies, and to adapt consumption to available
supplies through a more rational use of solid fuels. To implement this policy,
the statistics on supply and demand, developed initially by the secretariat for
allocating scare resources, were an essential instrument of stabilization of the
coal market. Also, the technical meetings of the ECE helped to exchange information and to issue recommendations on ways to better use the different
varieties of coal, to promote the wider use of control instruments, and to
improve the yield of heating and power equipment. But the most innovative
achievement of the committee may have been to prepare and adopt an international classification of coal[93] in order to facilitate a better flow of information among all the operators in the coal industry. This was not an easy task,
and many attempts to evolve a workable classification system had failed before the war. It required patient efforts and a strong spirit of cooperation so
that "the many thousands of different types of European coals [could] be
described in a common language."[94]

While technical and limited in scope, the Coal Committee's policy was not
only an important contribution to the better functioning of the coal industry
in Europe but also a contribution to one of the basic aims of the UN: to develop a common language as the first step toward mutual understanding and
joint undertakings. The system has been regularly revised and in 1997 was
recognized by the UN's Economic and Social Council. It is today available in
seven languages, the translation having been financed by a number of interested developing countries. Thus, certain activities which originated in a highly
interventionist environment have retained their importance in a more market-oriented economy, a point which underlines the fact that some of the
institutional foundations of both systems are not dissimilar.

The consumption of electricity had been growing rapidly between the
two wars, and in the early postwar period there were serious shortages of
generating-plant and interconnection facilities. The ECE Committee on
Electric Power was established in July 1947 to deal with the shortages and
bottlenecks. Looking for ways to reduce the costs of equipment, it recommended specifications for turbo-alternators that were submitted to the International Standardization Organization (ISO). To increase supply, it
considered a number of development possibilities which offered prospects
for international cooperation. Some countries thought that a supergrid system would provide the most economic solution to the supply problem: a
rational idea, but almost impossible to realize in the political context of the

time. The gradual extension of cross-border links was shown to be the more practical and useful approach. The construction of hydroelectric power stations on rivers bordering two states as well as the exchange of electricity between countries raised considerable administrative difficulties that the committee tried to overcome with practical recommendations to governments. One result of these was an agreement in 1954 between Yugoslavia and Austria to control the waters of the Drava River, which permitted further hydroelectric development. Subsequently, on the basis of the committee's recommendations, other agreements led to the formation of joint companies or undertakings by two or more interested countries. For example, the Yougelexport program involved Austria, the FRG, Italy, and Yugoslavia. Thus already in the early 1950s, the ECE was promoting subregional/cross-border cooperation that in recent years has been extensively developed by local authorities thanks to increased decentralization.

FACILITATING TRANSPORT IN A FRAGMENTED EUROPE

Just as essential as the availability of energy is the efficiency of the transport network. ECITO had already addressed many of the bottlenecks in the flow of national and international traffic by the time the Inland Transport Committee of the ECE was set up in July 1947. It took over the residual activities of ECITO but also addressed longer-term problems arising from the rapid growth of road transport in Western Europe, technological change in all modes of transport, and the intensification of international trade in a Europe where borders are numerous and intricate. The exchange of experience, as in other sectors, was certainly useful in improving national transport systems and in disseminating more efficient technologies. But the key contribution of the Inland Transport Committee from its inception was to address systematically all the elements that contribute to the facilitation of the international transport of goods and people: tracks, security, customs operations, and transit.

Today the numerous agreements and practices developed by the Transport Committee seem obviously sensible, but after a decade of growing protectionism in the 1930s and a devastating war followed by the division of Europe, this was not so clear at the end of the 1940s and during the early 1950s. In 1957, Paul Levert, then director of the ECE Transport Division, concluded his assessment of what the ECE had achieved in his sector:

> In the technical field, there is now a widespread conviction that routine procedures are out of date, that the comparison of ideas and exchange of experience

are indispensable, and that a country is not necessarily lowering itself by adopting international standards. In the economic field, the same feeling is gaining ground and countries are beginning to understand that it is not always in their interests to cling to established practices, and that in complying with the recommendations of an international forum they add to their own authority that of the organization making the recommendation. One of the advantages of the meetings of the Inland Transport Committee and of its subsidiary bodies lies in the development of this spirit of co-operation.[95]

Discussion about the economics of transport, however, proved to be more difficult and less conclusive than those on technical or administrative matters. The committee established model accounting methods for calculating the economic costs of the different transport modes, but there was little agreement on how to proceed, and the strikes of road carriers and the ongoing discussions about the privatization of railways at the start of the twenty-first century continue to echo the debates of the early 1950s.

INSPIRING THE MONNET-SCHUMAN PLAN[96]

With reconstruction, the demand for steel was growing rapidly, but production was hampered by shortages of raw materials, such as metallurgical coke, scrap, manganese ore, and nickel. This was the first problem addressed by the ECE Steel Committee between the fall of 1947 and early 1949. Because of the considerable investments required to create new production capacity, the secretariat undertook a study of long-term demand in a worldwide perspective. The results were published in 1949 in *European Steel Trends in the Setting of the World Market*. The study concluded by stressing the risks of overcapacity. Not surprisingly, some governments, fearing that it could weaken their arguments for financing new steel plants under the Marshall Plan, tried to stop its publication. But the study was to have a major impact on the future of Europe, as described by Myrdal:

> When it was in a draft form, it was already one of the main inspirations for the launching of the Schuman Plan. M. Jean Monnet, when sometime later he set out to draft a practical plan for cooperation in the coal and steel field, needed independent expert advice and, at the request of the French Government, the Director of the ECE Steel Division and his assistants were instructed to give whatever help they could.... The first draft of possible technical clauses for the creation of a European Coal and Steel Community was worked out in ECE by the then Director of the Steel Division, though naturally without our taking sides on the political issues involved.[97]

After a period of spectacular growth, the coal and steel industries, as a result of changes in demand, overinvestment, technological innovations, competition from developing countries, and growing concerns for the environment, were forced to restructure, to develop more sophisticated products, and to use cleaner technologies. The ECE provided a forum where specialists met to discuss these problems, and this continued even when the OECD opened its committees on steel and chemicals to non-OECD members.

CREATING THE EUROPEAN TIMBER CLUB

As in the case of steel, wood products (sawn timber, pit props, plywood, pulpwood, and firewood) were in great demand at the end of the war, and the priorities were to reequip forest industries and raise production, to halt overcutting, and to ensure that the products reached the areas where they were needed. Some of these problems had been addressed by the EECE, one of the three "E-organizations," but in April 1947, the UN's Food and Agriculture Organization (FAO) convened a European Timber Conference that recommended that the ECE tackle the problems of the European timber shortage while the FAO concern itself with the long-term development of the European forest. This gave rise to a particularly successful cooperation between the two institutions that continues today, with FAO and ECE staff jointly servicing the Timber Committee. It was at the time of a slight recession in the industry in 1949 that the ECE secretariat produced the first of a series of studies of long-term trends in European timber production and consumption. The most recent of these, which have always provoked intense debate, was completed in 2000. As with the steel study, the first timber study (written by Walt W. Rostow and Alfred Maizels) had an important practical impact. It indicated that sawn-wood needs would rise, but at a lower rate than industrial production, while the consumption of pulpwood would grow faster. Even with vigorous output growth in Europe, supplementary supplies of timber from North America and the Soviet Union would be necessary. However, at that time, the Soviet Union was facing serious reconstruction problems and was no longer able to export to Western Europe. Opposed to importing from other regions, while at the same time conscious that too-high prices would encourage the further use of substitute materials, the European producers decided to raise supply without increasing prices. As a result of this study and the debates it stimulated, the Timber Committee became "The European Timber Club," where Swedish and Finnish shippers, together with British importers, set the tone. "At no time did any delegate feel that the interlocutors he would have chosen were absent"[98] from the committee meetings.

Promoting the Industrialization of House-Building

At the end of the war, the stock of housing was far from sufficient to meet the needs created by internal migration and the growth of population. The first task of the ECE Housing Committee, which took its responsibilities from the EECE in 1947, was to draw the attention of governments and the public to the seriousness of the problem at a time of competing claims for investment resources. The committee's inquiries showed that even if the prewar rates of construction were doubled, it would still take on average twenty years to meet current housing needs.[99] The committee therefore recommended the industrialization of house-building and the establishment of national organizations for building research that subsequently had a considerable practical effect. Later on, in 1953, to provide an effective link between the national organizations and to facilitate the exchange of experience, the committee helped to create an International Council for Research and Innovation in Building and Construction (CIB). More controversial was the question of housing finance and the related problem of rent controls. A secretariat report, *European Rent Policies,*[100] analyzing the actual situation in most ECE countries, concluded that any form of rent control should be abolished, a view that should at least qualify the perception in some quarters that the secretariat was unduly hostile to the free play of market forces. This somewhat extreme view, however, helped the committee to conclude that, so long as there was a general shortage of houses, rent control should *not* be abolished, nor, for that matter, should subsidies on housing. But it recognized that rents in a number of countries had been frozen for too long at too low a level. Finally, as suggested in the secretariat's report, it was recognized that rent policy was an integral part of housing policies and was closely related to the matter of housing subsidies.

Pioneering Steps in Statistics Coordination

Almost as important as the restoration of international trade, the availability of raw materials, and the removal of key bottlenecks, reliable statistics were essential if governments were to effectively discharge their economic responsibilities. In Eastern Europe, the adoption of central planning required the collection of huge amounts of data. In Western Europe, data were necessary not only because governments had assumed responsibilities for reconstruction but also because they were now expected to run the economy in such a way as to avoid unemployment and the mistakes of the 1930s. This required a close monitoring of developments. In addition, they had to prepare the plans required in order to obtain Marshall aid. More generally, statistics were now seen more clearly as a public good to be used by enterprises, unions, and the media. ECOSOC arranged that, under the responsibility of the UN Statistical Commission, the statisticians of each region would meet among themselves in order to discuss their specific needs and resources. The European statisticians met in 1949, 1951, and 1953. At the end of the last meeting, the participants felt the need for closer and more systematic exchanges among themselves and for better coordination between the international agencies active in the field of European statistics. They therefore created a permanent body, the Conference of European Statisticians, whose members are the directors of the central statistical offices of the countries of the region, with a full-time secretariat provided by the ECE. The bureau of the conference included the director of the UN Statistical Division as an ex officio member. Thanks to the conference, the statistics produced became richer, more reliable, and more precise, even if, according to Barrie Davis, the first head of the Statistical Section of the Research and Planning Division, it was easier to reach agreement on the statistics to be collected and the definitions and classifications to be used than on the methods of collecting them. He thought that "much of the value of the work [of the conference came] not so much from precise recommendations that statistical offices are expected to put into immediate effect as from the general stimulation derived by exchanging experiences and views on common problems at meetings"[101]—another example of how the ECE both generates and disseminates ideas.

The origin of the conference led to it becoming a model of cooperation between regional and global entities, with the conference both adapting the standards developed in New York to European needs and elaborating new and sophisticated standards that were then taken up by New York. For example, the ECE contributed concepts for the global revision of the national accounts system in the 1960s. Its original mandate and the active participation of the directors of national statistical offices made the conference a powerful instrument of coordination of statistical activities in Europe. This role of coordination culminated in 1992 with an agreement that the statistical activities in the ECE region of the ECE itself, the EU, the OECD, the IMF, the World Bank, the FAO, and the International Labor Organization (ILO) would be presented in parallel in a single document. For each activity described, the long-term objectives, the expected outputs, the list of meetings, and the data to be collected are indicated. This permits the parties to the agreement to organize joint meetings and to avoid duplication in data-gathering by adopting joint questionnaires. More important, it provides a clear picture of current statistical work and thus a basis for identifying gaps and making the necessary adjustment to meet the needs of European society.

The ECE on Track

On March 15, 1953, a few days after Stalin's death, Malenkov set forth the doctrine of peaceful coexistence, arguing that in the nuclear era, the competition of ideas should be substituted for the force of arms. The climate was ripe for more substantial economic cooperation between the two parts of Europe: The period of reconstruction was over and Europe was ready for years of sustained economic growth. Despite the division of Europe, all countries shared a conviction that their development depended upon the development of their partners and the dynamism of international trade. This perception was also favorable to cooperation. The ECE was firmly established as the unique pan-European forum for economic cooperation. It could claim concrete achievements in allocating scarce resources and in establishing conventions, norms, and standards that would facilitate economic relations between its member countries. In promoting exchanges of experience regarding domestic policy and technical problems, it helped to diffuse the knowledge, and often the use, of more advanced techniques and to harmonize practices; more important, it helped to create extensive networks among specialists and decision-makers in their areas of activity. In the ECE, more than in any other part of the UN, the governments decided, and still decide, on the details of their program of work and contribute effectively to its implementation. But

> the practice of requesting the Secretariat to produce particular studies does not, *per se*, infringe upon the freedom of the Secretariat in research, as long as it is recognized that the Secretariat also has the right independently to decide, on its own initiative, to undertake studies, and that a Committee cannot forbid the Secretariat to study a particular problem. In ECE this is, and has always been, the constitutional situation. Its formal basis is simply a paragraph in the ECE's rules of procedure that "the Executive Secretary can, at any time, make an oral or written statement."[102]

For more than fifty years, the secretariat has exercised this right with the support of member governments and their economic advisers in both national administrations and the universities.

Thanks to Myrdal, the basic principles and approaches that would characterize and guide the work of the commission, its subsidiary bodies, and the secretariat were well in place by the end of the ECE's first two years of activity. He and his colleagues are to be praised for this, as well as for having maintained them with such a determination that, by the time of his departure in 1957, they had become so embodied in the institution that it would have been difficult to overturn them without destroying it.

From the end of the Cold War until today, the ECE has continued to produce surveys, bulletins, and special studies and to develop conventions, norms,
and standards in response to the needs of the region as perceived by its member governments or the secretariat. Their simple enumeration would exceed
the number of pages remaining for this chapter. Selection is therefore necessary, and the studies referred to in the second part of the chapter are limited
to those that developed ideas that contributed to development thinking; similarly, the conventions mentioned are those that had, or could have, a worldwide impact in view of the problems they address.

The Search for Sustained Growth, 1953–1989

Between 1953 and 1989 there were dramatic economic and political changes
in the ECE region. East-West relations, at the heart of the commission's work,
moved from the Cold War to the signing of an agreement on economic cooperation between the Soviet Union and the European Economic Commission
on November 27, 1989, less than three weeks after the fall of the Berlin Wall.
But this development was not straightforward and it was often marked by
setbacks.

The Context

The period was dominated, on the one side, by the necessity for the communist regimes to gain access to goods and technologies produced or developed in the West to limit the increasing costs of armaments and to maintain
power over their peoples. An evolution dominated, on the other side, at least
initially, by fears of the attractiveness of communism to various sections of
the population as an alternative to capitalism, by concern that incidents could
degenerate into open conflict in Europe, and, later, by the need to diversify
sources of energy. On both sides, the whole period was marked by mounting
regionalization and globalization.

KEY POLITICAL ELEMENTS

On the political side, the first step forward was, as already mentioned, the
doctrine of peaceful coexistence (1953), followed, during Khrushchev's official visit to Belgrade, by the recognition of the plurality of roads to socialism
(1956). Then, on the other side, the Eisenhower Doctrine offered economic
aid and military assistance against any threat of communist aggression to the

countries of the Middle East (1957). At the 21st Party Congress, Khrushchev boasted that the Soviet Union would catch up with and surpass the United States, but a few months later he warned the Chinese of the danger of testing the strength of the U.S. capitalist system that he did not regard as a "paper tiger." The Brezhnev Doctrine on the limited sovereignty of the countries of the Warsaw Pact (1968) was used to justify Soviet intervention in Czechoslovakia in 1968. In the meantime, in the 1960s, Willy Brandt had inaugurated the "Ostpolitik" as part of the process of normalizing relations with the East. By 1973, the year Solzhenitsyn published *The Gulag Archipelago*, the majority of people in Western Europe, according to public opinion polls, had ceased to consider the balance of Soviet achievements as positive. But a year later at the Fourth Summit of the Non-Aligned Movement, in Algiers, President Boumédienne declared the Soviet Union the natural ally of the movement, a title it lost when it invaded Afghanistan in December 1979. In 1975, the Helsinki Declaration concluded the first Conference on Security and Cooperation in Europe, at which the signatory states expressed the will "to broaden, deepen and make continuing and lasting the process of détente."[103] Yet two years later, in London, Helmut Schmidt expressed his fear that the security of Western Europe might be decoupled from that of the United States because of the deployment of the SS-20 missile and the implications of the SALT II (Strategic Arms Limitations Talks) negotiations then underway (1977). Subsequently, Henry Kissinger stated in Brussels that the SALT II agreement (1979) signed by President Carter opened a window of vulnerability of the United States to a Soviet first strike. Trust was still lacking when Ronald Reagan qualified the Soviet Union as an "evil empire"[104] ready "to commit any crime, to lie, to cheat"[105] in order to reach its goals. Relations definitely changed for the better with the arrival of Mikhail Gorbachev as general secretary of the CPSU in 1985 and head of state in 1988. After the Geneva Summit with Ronald Reagan, Gorbachev declared at the Supreme Soviet that "the European house is a common house where geography and history have intimately linked together tens of States and peoples" (1985).[106] Thereafter he introduced, on Soviet television on January 15, 1986, the concept of *perestroika*, a radical program of reform and restructuring of the Soviet economic and political system that, within a few years, would lead to the breakup of the Communist system and of the Soviet Union itself.

On the economic side, key developments include the trends toward regionalism and globalization, the shift in priorities in the West from growth and social welfare to the fight against inflation and a freer reign for private enterprise, and the successive failures of reforms in the Eastern economies.

MOUNTING REGIONALIZATION AND GLOBALIZATION

The Marshall Plan initiated economic cooperation among the West European countries while the Council for Mutual Economic Assistance (CMEA), created in January 1949, was intended to integrate the centrally planned economies. The first step in the construction of what is today the EU was taken in April 1951 with the signing of the treaty establishing the European Coal and Steel Community. The rejection by the French Parliament in 1954 of the European Defense Community slowed down the process of political integration, but the construction of the European Community continued as initiated by Jean Monnet, sector by sector.[107]

The European Monetary Agreement was signed in 1955 and on March 25, 1957, the treaties establishing the European Economic Community (EEC) and EURATOM (European Atomic Energy Community) were signed in Rome. Thus began a long and complicated process that would lead to the introduction of the Economic and Monetary Unions and, at the beginning of 2001, a single currency. By contrast to the functionalist approach in the West, the CMEA attempted to organize the "socialist division of labor" in an authoritarian way. The initial idea was to assign each country a production sector for which it was best endowed with natural or human resources. But this plan failed because of the desire on the part of the member countries to equip themselves with their own heavy and metallurgical industries. National interests, as perceived by each country, eventually won over the ambition of socialist integration. The CMEA received its charter only in 1959 and had no permanent institutions before 1962. While integration was progressing in Western Europe, Eastern Europe was approving programs (1970), plans (1975), or long-term objectives (1979) for integration. The results were modest, and the international trade that a rational division of labor might have generated was constrained by the rigidity of the payments mechanism and national priorities.

Three years after the signing of the Treaty of Rome, and one year after the CMEA had its charter, a number of other regional groupings were created throughout the world that were inspired by similar reasons: the European Free Trade Association (EFTA), the Latin American Free Trade Association, and the Organization of Petroleum Exporting Countries (OPEC). Other groupings followed, including the Association of South East Asian Nations (ASEAN, 1967). Hopes for economic success or political considerations stimulated adhesions to the EEC and the CMEA. Mongolia, Cuba, and Vietnam joined the latter respectively in 1962, 1972, and 1978. The EEC benefited from successive waves of enlargement: Great Britain, Ireland, and Denmark in 1973;

Greece in 1981; Spain and Portugal in 1985; Austria, Finland, and Sweden in 1995 after it had become the EU. During the last decade of the twentieth century, all the countries of Central Europe, the Baltic States, Ukraine, and Moldova had applied to, or had expressed a wish to join the EU.

The trend toward globalization was also dynamic and sustained. A succession of trade rounds marked the first steps. The Dillon Round of negotiations ended, in 1962, with an average lowering of customs tariffs of 7 percent; the Kennedy Round (1964–1967) achieved a reduction of 40 percent; and the Tokyo Round (1973–1979) a reduction of 30 percent. The Uruguay Round (1986–1994) enlarged the scope of international trade rules. Not only did it cover new ground such as services, intellectual property rights, and investment matters related to trade but, more important, it introduced rules related to national policies affecting international competition. It is regrettable that these developments, which facilitated globalization and established certain ground rules, were made without China and most of the countries of Eastern Europe that were not members of the GATT. East-West trade, until 1990 and even after, remained restrained by systemic and administrative obstacles that the ECE tried to reduce. In the monetary domain, the major event was the declaration by President Nixon, on August 15, 1971, that the United States would suspend all sales and purchases of gold, thus ending the link of the dollar to gold. Attempts were made to maintain a system of foreign-exchange rates, but by March 1973 these had all failed and the Bretton Woods system was ended. This effectively meant the privatization of exchange-rate risk, and for the financial markets to be able to handle that, they required large-scale deregulation. The United States abandoned all controls on international capital flows on January 1, 1974, and was followed by most of the other Western market economies over the next decade. Deregulation thus opened the way to the globalization of capital markets.

Key Studies

With the most pressing problems of the recovery period solved by the early 1950s, the interest of governments shifted to long-term economic growth, intra-European trade and integration, the development of the less industrialized countries of Southern Europe and, later on, of the Third World countries. The ECE secretariat pioneered research on many of these issues which was published either in the *Surveys* and *Bulletins* or as independent studies and discussed at the annual sessions of the commission or by the Senior Economic Advisers.[108]

THE FACTORS OF GROWTH

Growth and Stagnation in the European Economy was published in November 1954. Prepared by Professor Ingvar Svennilson of the University of Stockholm in cooperation with the ECE secretariat and financed by the Rockefeller Foundation, this study has become a classic. It starts with a beautiful remark on the necessary consistency between long- and short-term changes, "since the longer period is composed of a number of shorter periods. . . . The difference between a study of long-term changes and one of short-term variations can therefore only be one of emphasis. In the analysis of long-term changes, certain factors and causal relations are brought into sharp relief, while others are dimmed or left in the background."[109] The study first set out a theory of long-term growth. It criticized the works of Cassel and Marshall, the first for not introducing technological change and the second for his overoptimism about technological progress and the assumption of a high rate of saving in a society with uneven income distribution. This led to the conclusion that "output, labor and capital equipment [could] not be treated as homogeneous totals once we introduce technological change as an important factor in economic development."[110] Svennilson proposed the following explanation of long-term economic growth:

> • National economic growth is dependent on the transformation of the national economy;
> • This transformation is partly induced by national economic growth;
> • Investment is an important aspect of the transformation process.
> The aggregate level of investment forms one of the main determinants of the level of employment, which again affects the level of output.[111]

This approach differed from the Schumpeterian business-cycle theory by its emphasis on long-term growth itself in promoting investment and transformation rather than on exogenous innovation. As such, it was clearly related to the concepts of the Kaldor-Verdoorn law and cumulative causation.

The data on which the study was based covered the whole of Europe and the period 1913–1938 with some consideration given to data as early as 1880 and as recent as 1950. One of the key findings reinforced the view that trade restrictions were responsible for the stagnation of the interwar period and provided an additional argument for the development of intra-European trade:

> The arbitrary combinations of resources within smaller or larger national areas had a decisive influence on long-term growth of Europe as a whole. It is likely that the existence of this national structure slowed down, not only the

growth of the less favoured countries, but also the general development of Europe's joint resources. This effect was reinforced by the inter-relations of trade and payments of various countries.[112]

A subsequent ECE study, *Some Factors in Economic Growth in Europe during the 1950s,* was published in 1964, a few months after the publication of Denison's pioneering study, *The Sources of Economic Growth in the United States.*[113] Both attempted to shed light on the factors behind the growth of production other than capital and employment. The ECE study (to which another well-known development economist, Heinz Arndt, who was in the secretariat in 1960–1961 and was one of the first to tackle the question of "Why do growth rates differ?" contributed) significantly added to the knowledge base on the subject. Comparing the growth performance of European countries, it identified among the "residual" factors the pressure of demand and the supply of academically trained engineers as significant factors. It was not possible to find links between the rate of growth of output and either the level of total research outlays or the proportion of national resources devoted to education as explanations of differences in growth rates. The supply of engineers, however, was a significant variable in both the centrally planned and the market economies. The demand factor in the former economies was mainly a decision of the planning authorities; therefore, "the more efficiently the future pattern of 'demand' on resources could be planned or foreseen, the more effectively supplies of materials, productive capacity and labor could be planned to meet the demand."[114] In the market economies, the most important factor was "the influence of government policies in creating a general 'climate' favorable or unfavorable to a strong investment demand—depending upon the degree of success achieved in maintaining a steady overall demand expansion and in ensuring that any checks to expansion which might be necessary (to protect the balance of payments or for other reasons) had the minimum discouraging effect on investment."[115] In the absence of abundant and easily accessible international credit, and taking into account the agreement among the West European countries not to resort to competitive devaluation, the burden of adjustment fell on domestic policies designed to restrain costs. "Thus the problem of 'incomes policy' [came] to be seen as one of the main keys to a solution of the general problem of maintaining economic growth in most of the industrialized countries."[116]

From these two major studies on long-term growth emerged a strong conclusion which has remained deeply rooted in the thinking of the secretariat; namely, that growth, or rather the expectation of growth, is a key factor of long-term growth. This apparent tautology stresses that it is growth expectations that induce the necessary investment required to adopt new technologies and adapt to new demands and changes in the international environment. Growth and structural change are thus intimately related in a process of cumulative causation. These ideas reappear in a 1977 study of structural change in European industry,[117] and more recently the secretariat criticized the cautiousness of monetary policy in the Euro zone for failing "to recognize the dynamic interactions between growth expectations, fixed investment, rising productivity and employment—and mild or falling inflation rates."[118]

GROWTH AND INCOME DISTRIBUTION

Income policies as a condition for maintaining long-term growth could, in line with the analysis referred to above, be understood as a search for an optimum distribution of income in order to secure enough saving for the financing of investments and a sufficiently sustained demand to stimulate production. At the same time, income policies could be used to limit the recourse to restrictive policies, which are damaging to employment and growth, in dealing with inflation or balance of payment deficits. It was this latter objective that was given priority in the immediate postwar period, although "such policies, as so far conceived, have not proved strikingly effective instruments of economic management."[119]

The ECE secretariat reviewed these policies in great detail in a major study, *Incomes in Postwar Europe: A Study of Policies, Growth and Distribution,* published in 1967, in which Eastern and Western Europe were necessarily treated separately. In the centrally planned economies, the major task of incomes policy was "to lay down the rules which would result in promoting the desired allocation of resources," while in market economies the problem was how to "[persuade] enterprises and trade unions to observe and enforce certain standards in determining pay and prices."[120]

Starting with Western Europe and taking incomes policy in its broadest sense, the first issue was to determine the expected change in the general level of prices. It had been "common to base the norms on the assumption of no general price increase at all."[121] This was obviously unrealistic. But the study went farther in suggesting that zero price increases might be undesirable as well, because some increase helped to alleviate the debt burden and the risk of investment and because structural changes affected the weight of the different components of the price index. High rates of inflation, on the other hand, created injustice that governments had to correct. What was finally "more important, from the point of view of growth and welfare, [was] that the general price tendency should [have been] more or less predictable and under con-trol."[122] The difficulty was that if the government announced a reasonable and tenable increase in the price level, the behavior of enterprises, unions, and workers would automatically result in a larger increase in prices and wages than what was expected.

The second question concerned the distribution of incomes between la-bor and profits and the related problem of the allocation of resources be-tween private consumption, public expenditure, and private investment. The objective of keeping the shares of labor and capital unchanged—in other words, that pay per capita in real terms increased in line with productiv-ity—would "be valid for the longer term only if there [was] reason to be-lieve that the existing distribution [represented] a satisfactory, and lasting, equilibrium and [was] consistent with economic and social progress."[123] The most common perception was that any shift in favor of labor would reduce savings, since the marginal savings ratio of households was lower than that of enterprises and, as a consequence, would weaken investment and growth. This implicitly assumed that the self-financing of enterprises was more conducive to economic efficiency and underestimated the potential role of financial institutions. In fact, to reach a desired private investment ratio and a given growth rate, an essential step would be to adapt the institutions of the capital market to provide adequate incentives to raise household savings and channel them toward the financing of enterprise investment. A shift of income between labor and capital would therefore not be an obstacle to long-term growth, and policy could aim at changing management percep-tions of what the normal rate of return on capital should be. Having reviewed the various instruments, from persuasion to the taxation of profits or direct controls, the study concluded: "In practice, price regulation has been the only instrument extensively used (apart from rent controls) to influence incomes other than pay."[124]

The third question was the distribution of pay between industries, degrees of skill or training, and occupations. The experience was that, whatever the incomes policy and despite economic and social change, pay structures tended to maintain a remarkable stability. In this matter, incomes policy might be guided by two conflicting principles: equity, which unions translated into equal pay for equal work; and efficiency, which linked productivity and pay. The study recommended that representative organizations of management and workers be encouraged to reach a consensus on explicit and coherent poli-cies. A possible approach would be to agree on the use of standard methods of job valuation, but these implied that agreement could be reached on the inevitably subjective weights to be attached to the particular characteristics of each job and that it would be acceptable to depart from the existing pay structure. Despite these difficulties, the study concluded that this approach could introduce more uniformity and rationality into pay structures and limit the excessive reliance on age-old tradition and practices.

In Western Europe, an incomes policy, in the broad sense defined in the study, would obviously be technically and politically difficult to implement. The ECE secretariat thought that nevertheless this should be attempted, both for its economic advantages:

> What an incomes policy offers is the possibility of two gains: a way of balancing total incomes with resources, which avoids the waste, the disturbances and the loss of potential growth in living standards associated with alternative ways of restraining money demand in conditions of full employment; and, in the longer term, the opportunity for introducing more order, stability and rationality into income distribution, and of applying socially acceptable standards to it.[125]

and for political considerations:

> It may be held that the important question is not how much effective freedom of action would be sacrificed, but whether the criteria of income distribution determined by social decision would be preferable to the mixture of market forces, custom and group pressures by which income distribution is now governed.[126]

The description of the difficulties encountered in Eastern Europe is more of historical interest than of use for development policies today, but the reflections on Western Europe are of renewed interest when the income distribution is worsening in many countries and when, in some, there has been hardly any improvement in the mechanism for setting incomes. It can be argued that one of the reasons for the instability and high inflation rates of the 1970s was that the oil shocks triggered a bitter struggle over income shares and that it took another decade for a socially acceptable distribution to re-emerge. Whether the significant increases in income inequality in the 1990s will lead to a similar struggle over relative incomes remains to be seen, but it is unlikely that capitalism has escaped from the basic tensions described in the study. In any event, it remains the most comprehensive review of income policies ever made and may well be worth revisiting in the coming years.

SOUTHERN EUROPE: PIONEERING IDEAS ON DEVELOPMENT

In the ECE, interest in the development of less-developed countries was initially linked to the search for solutions to the dollar shortage in Western

Europe. Countries not belonging to the dollar zone were seen as partners able to supply needed food products and commodities and provide markets for European manufactured goods and equipment. But ideas on development policies were developed at the end of the war for the countries of Southern Europe. The analysis of past experience, current weakness, and the potential of Portugal, Spain, southern Italy, Greece, Turkey, and Yugoslavia led to a set of considerations aimed at helping these countries to formulate development strategies adapted to their specific conditions. They were published in the 1953 *Survey*. If these considerations do not constitute a comprehensive development theory, they have qualities that are often missing in such theories: They are realistic, they are practical, they indicate the pros and cons of different solutions, and they correctly leave the policy decision to the national politician. After fifty years of development failures and successes throughout the world, the 1953 *Survey* still offers sensible proposals for those countries, and they are many, which do not yet have a diversified industrial sector.

On the basis of detailed analysis of each country, the secretariat refused to consider southern Europe as overpopulated but argued instead that poor social organization was responsible for the underutilization of labor. They did not therefore advocate emigration that would have deprived these countries of young people at an age when they became productive, and, indeed, once the development of Southern Europe got under way, emigration diminished drastically.

In countries where half of the labor force was in agriculture, agricultural and industrial development were intimately linked, a fact too often neglected in the 1960s and 1970s. "Just as a policy of industrialization is in danger of being frustrated at some point, unless supported by a growing market provided by higher real income in agriculture, so agricultural progress is impossible unless . . . the peasant is given the incentive of a growing demand for his products. Agriculture and industry can either progress or stagnate together."[127]

Development policies must therefore address obstacles to progress in both agriculture and industry. In the former, three interrelated factors explain why its potential was not exploited: the social structure, the poverty of farmers, and the "technical inertia of a largely illiterate farm population."[128] Agrarian reforms to break up the *latifundia* were one way to increase production by giving each peasant the minimum amount of land required to support a family. But the ECE drew the attention of politicians to the possible conflict between this goal and the necessity to avoid compromising long-term productivity gains. To permit poor and illiterate farmers to acquire new techniques of production, a program including services to teach modern methods and the provision of financial subsidies for fertilizers, seeds, and the building of silage tanks was recommended. The research needed for developing agricultural techniques, seeds, and efficient fertilizers called for cooperation among Mediterranean countries enjoying similar climate and soils.

Inadequate home markets, deficient social services and public utilities, the shortage of skilled labor, and the lack of capacity to mobilize the little savings that were available for industry were among the common features that impeded industrial development. Whereas home markets would improve with increases in peasants' income, a better-educated labor force and the improvement of public utilities should be the responsibility of the state. Specific industrial policies touched upon issues such as protection and the criteria for allocating investment funds. On protection, the ECE was unambiguous. "At exchange rates which secure over-all equilibrium . . . [there] is little scope for industrialization in these economically retarded countries, unless a fairly high protection against foreign competition is given."[129] The issue was therefore to choose between protection in selected sectors and non-discriminatory protection. National producers obviously thought that their own sectors should be protected, but for the sake of long-term development, the ECE advocated a uniform ad valorem duty.

The *Survey*'s argument that "the maximizing of private profit provided poor guidance for investment" is another sign of that lack of complete confidence in market forces that worried many of the publication's readers in the United States. It recommended that projects should be preferred which promised, over their whole life, either "to give maximum net social returns per unit of capital invested" in order to reduce underemployment or "to exert the most favorable effect on the balance of payments" in order to alleviate balance-of-payments constraints.[130] As a consequence of the first objective, labor-intensive rather than capital-intensive techniques should be preferred, while the second would lead to import substitution since the Southern European countries were not competitive in foreign markets for industrial goods. But such objectives should not be pursued in a rigid way because "it should be remembered that economic development must, in the longer run, be an all-round process in which all broad branches of activity are represented so that they provide external economies for one another." Similarly, if carried beyond a certain point, the rejection of the most modern techniques "may become a hindrance to the diffusion of the standards of efficiency and of technical knowledge which is necessary for industrial growth."[131] So as early as 1953, the ECE secretariat had anticipated the limits of import-substitution strategies and the debate on appropriate technologies. Nineteen years later, when the countries of Southern Europe had diversified their industry and entered into intrabranch exchanges with the rest of Europe, the secretariat did not think it possible to draw clear-cut lessons from their experiences about the most efficient way to acquire modern technologies. Direct foreign investments and the purchase of patents and licenses both had advantages and disadvantages. National or subregional research should be encouraged, but such research raised the issue about which sector the state should allocate public money to. Although it was recognized that it would be "impossible from theoretical and analytical considerations alone to determine in detail in what products or branches the 'comparative advantages' of a given economy were most likely to lie in the future," the secretariat judged that "the hazards of selecting the 'wrong' lines for specialized development may well be less than the risks of an undifferentiated and over-extended approach to industrialization."[132]

On international trade, the secretariat made a specific contribution that would eventually become famous with the UNCTAD General System of Preferences. The idea of asymmetrical obligations in favor of developing countries was present in the following statement:

> There is no inconsistency in advocating protection as regards the imports of less-developed countries and free trade as regards their exports. If contradiction there is, it is only a manifestation of the more fundamental contradiction that highly developed and less developed countries exist side by side and have to trade with one another, reaping benefits from the international division of labor but without compromising the basic aims of their economic policies.[133]

Import protection combined with an outward export orientation was to be an important feature of Korea's successful and rapid development some years later. The role of the state was not seen as an ideological issue. State intervention was presented as a necessity due to the circumstances of these countries. Economics was not regarded as a science that was universally applicable but a mix of universal rules and changing behavior according to circumstances. For instance, since it appeared that "the improvements in agricultural methods were unlikely to come about solely by market forces, as an effect of growing demand from the towns"[134] the ECE recommended that public programs focus on ways to increase productivity. Similarly, attempts to reduce disparities between regions "have failed to produce any marked effect, at least when they were not accompanied by more direct intervention to create public utilities and social capital." For the industrial sector, public lending and shareholding and mixed forms of ownership were not a priori ruled out, but the commission cautiously noted that "whilst the development of mining production in the last three decades suggested that public enterprise or public sponsorship in some form was an essential prerequisite for rapid progress, such a generalization would not hold for manufacturing."[135]

For the state to play its role, it needed resources that should come first from a reduction of the considerable amount devoted to military expenditures, up to 20 percent of GDP in Yugoslavia, but also from higher rates of taxation: "Higher rates of taxation are all the more necessary as economic development is bound to require as well an increase in the rate of current civilian government expenditure, to provide not merely a larger and more efficient civil service, but also for an expansion of education and health services, which are at least as important for future productivity as investments in physical assets."[136] That being said, governments should resist the temptation "to enforce collective saving at a rate which leaves individuals with too little incentive to greater effort."[137] Here again, the ECE secretariat held very pragmatic views based on observations of diverse experience of issues that would later become subject to ideological debates based on overly simple theoretical considerations.

It is interesting to note that out of the thirty-nine pages devoted to the development of the less developed countries of southern Europe in the 1953 *Survey*, only six were focused on external capital assistance and access to European markets. This emphasized the message, often stressed by Myrdal, that development is first of all a domestic affair. Forty-seven years later, the *Survey* of 2000, considering the factors of long-term growth and the issue of catching up, again insisted on the importance of domestic factors and therefore on the need for a specific policy mix in each country.

Addressing Potential Obstacles to Growth

The other dimension of ECE activity, intergovernmental cooperation on technical matters, developed throughout this period. Whether or not it was inspired by the analyses of the *Surveys,* it aimed at alleviating bottlenecks that could affect growth.

Improving Planning Methods

Before the war and immediately after it, planning in the East had some successes in priority sectors but at huge human and material costs. By the end of the 1950s, growth was slowing down, and at the same time, it was becoming very difficult to plan economies once the stage of extensive growth had ended. The failures were attributed to excessive centralization, and reform of the planning system was put on the agenda. A fundamental problem, however, was that reforms required decentralization of decision-making, but this implied a shift in power from the center to the periphery. As soon as local power increased to the point where the dominance of the Communist Party could be challenged, the reforms were checked. The large enterprises, nevertheless, became powerful enough to negotiate their targets with the planning authorities after the mid-1970s, but their aim was not to increase market shares, efficiency, or profits. Indeed, like the Party, "they wanted to preserve power positions, which were measured in terms of control on resources: how to get higher allocation of investment goods, how to be permitted to hire more workers so as to supply a greater volume of output."[138] This is why the revolutions of 1989 had to be political and not just economic.

But one regrettable consequence was the rejection of any suggestion of the need for planning. "The plan was linked with the party to such an extent that the transition governments rejected any concept of a plan, even indicative, even strategic, even drafted and implemented within decentralized and really autonomous enterprises. 'Plan' will be a dirty word for a long time."[139]

The blame for the failure of reform attempts in the planned economies has to be put on the Party rather than the planners, who were constantly improving their methods. The meetings of the senior economic advisers to ECE governments became the occasion for them to meet their colleagues from the West. From 1967 to 1977, they discussed the difficulties encountered in long-term and multilevel planning and in handling technical progress, social and distributional aspects, environmental consequences, and so on. In 1973, they began to develop an overall economic perspective (OEP) for the ECE region: That for 1990 was issued in 1977 and for 2000 in 1988. In the early 1970s, the original intention was to produce forecasts. Later, with the uncertainties created by the oil-price shocks and, more important, by the rapid development of technical change, their ambitions became more modest. "The OEP [was] thus meant to be neither a forecast nor a plan but an aid to decision-making, helping policy-makers and planners in the region to focus attention on crucial issues likely to arise before the end of the century, and on their policy implications."[140] Many governments from East and West had agreed with the analysis of the factors of economic growth referred to above, and, thus, one of Europe's leading experts in technology and technical change observed that it was "not altogether surprising that uncanny similarities had been noted on science and technical progress made respectively by the Communist Party of the Soviet Union and the Republican Party of the United States."[141]

Eastern Governments were compelled to try to improve productivity in the face of diminishing labor-power reserves and West European governments were compelled by the fact that the levels of productivity in their countries were lagging behind those in the United States. A priori, the policy problems were different in centralized and decentralized economies, but Eastern specialists were conscious that technological development in production needed such a tremendous amount of specialized information and knowledge that no central organ was able to master it, a point that had been made by the Austrian school of economists in the 1920s. Similarly, in the market economies, governments felt that the lack of coordination between ministries and agencies was costly and was not giving research and development (R and D) the priority it deserved. The general goal was clear. But "neither in the centrally planned economies nor in the market economies was there anything approaching an adequate theoretical framework to guide decisions makers in the execution of their responsibilities."[142] Little progress had been made in practice since 1825, when Emperor Franz Joseph wrote a note to Metternich in which he proposed removing the Rothschilds from the list of court bankers because of their support for a railway project north of Vienna, the Emperor judging it unreasonable because few people used the stagecoach on the route. A wise decision would have required economic and technological forecasting as well as normative value judgments. In 1967, the senior economic advisers raised many questions but provided no definite answers. What was the appropriate level of aggregate expenditure on R and D and scientific activities to accelerate technical progress? What criteria should be used to determine an optimum combination of autonomous research, imported technology, and participation in international projects? How to arbitrate between multiple policy goals? In both East and West, decisions, in practice, were the result of political compromises and "it might be doubted whether the information available to decision makers on social opportunity costs and potential benefits of major decisions had been in any way adequate."[143] The senior economic advisers recommended the use of cost-benefit analysis and checklists of questions to guide choices and to develop internationally comparable statistics—relatively weak conclusions that reflected the general lack of knowledge of what went on inside the "black box" of technological progress.

The difficulties of forecasting or anticipating longer-run developments led to talk of multidisciplinary approaches: "The assumptions underlying formalized growth models of working hours, innovations, productivity or consumption cannot be validly established without psycho-sociological analysis of behavior patterns."[144] But Jacques Baudot, the author of this quotation, instead of making the traditional routine endorsement of the multidisciplinary approach, raised a pertinent question: "How can long-term thinking have recourse to psychology and sociology, which are sciences of immediate observation, without implicitly assuming a permanence of behavior patterns, attitudes and social structures over a period of time? On that assumption, is not long-term thinking likely to be a factor making for conservatism?"[145]

It is interesting to note that by the late 1990s, similar criticism was being made in the corporate sector of "strategic planning," which was seen as reducing the flexibility of corporate response to unexpected and unforeseeable events. The debate on methods thus joined the debate on ideas. As early as in 1966, the Senior Economic Advisers had discussed optimization models and the impossibility of specifying social aspirations in a numerical "objective function." They noted "as Arrow has argued, there might exist no preference ordering that balances the conflicting aims of different parts of the community in a satisfactory (consistent, non-dictatorial) way."[146] The relatively simple and clear objective of maximizing GDP helped to sideline these conceptual and political difficulties and was more easily accommodated both by the planners and the politicians. The events in Paris of May 1968 were an early reminder that societies might need rather more, and subsequent environmental concerns were another reminder, but boosting GDP with few constraints has still not been ousted in practice as the easiest objective.

The issue of long-term growth was taken up in a quite different perspective by E. Lundberg, L. P. Blanc, B. Horvat, E. Mason, J. Pajetska, C. T. Saunders (former director of the ECE's Economic Analysis Division), J. R. N. Stone (Nobel Laureate), and J. Tinbergen (Nobel Laureate) at a seminar organized in December 1973 by the Senior Economic Advisers at the initiative of Jacques Royer, then director of the Projection and Programming Division of the ECE. The report of the Club of Rome had just been published, the first oil shock had just taken place, and the gap between poor and rich was again in the headlines. Jan Tinbergen was the only member of the panel who felt that "the development of the rich countries should be slowed down gradually" and that there was "some sort of natural limit to what we as human beings should want and ask for." For Saunders, the desire for growth and material progress was "pretty deep in human nature and likely to continue to be so." But growth had social and environmental costs. The social costs were still neglected by economists who did not appreciate the stress created by the structural changes that growth implied (Blanc) and by the separation of personal relations in work and the artificial life in big cities (Stone). For all the participants, nevertheless, growth increased the scope for social and economic choices and, in particular, facilitated income-distribution policies at least within a country if not necessarily between countries (Pajetska).[147] This view was strongly repeated in 1977 when unemployment and poverty were again becoming serious problems in Western Europe: "The reduction of unemployment through coordinated expansionary policies in these countries is a prerequisite for further development and resolution of many distributional problems in the region."[148]

As for poverty, the views that were expressed in 1972, when the Senior Economic Advisers debated distribution policies in the context of long-term development planning,[149] were further developed. Existing policies aiming at increasing the welfare of the poor were qualified as humanitarian and were opposed to egalitarian policies designed to achieve equality in the distribution of personal resources or equality of access to social resources: "Poverty is often defined and measured too narrowly, as reflected in the level of income of an individual, a household or a family. . . . Instead, the measurement of poverty ought to encompass a wider range of welfare constraining factors such as economic and cultural inherited capital, environmental conditions, working opportunities and social relations."[150] Thus, some of the concepts and policies that would nourish the preparation of the Copenhagen Conference in 1995 had already surfaced in the 1970s in the debates of the regional economic advisers.

The costs of pollution could no longer be ignored, and Stone suggested that clean air and water should be considered as final rather than intermediate goods. Two years later, in 1975, the Senior Economic Advisers and senior advisers to ECE governments on environmental problems joined forces to discuss the ecological aspects of economic development planning, a few months after the Cocoyoc Declaration had been adopted under the auspices of the United Nations Environment Programme (UNEP) and the United Nations Conference on Trade and Development (UNCTAD). The discussion focused on how to make growth more sustainable, although that now-fashionable word was not used. If growth had negative as well as positive impacts on the environment, then the questions of tolerable impacts and of development policies and planning were important. On the former issue, there was no agreement between those who advocated the standstill principle, which implied the maintenance of the present ecological diversity, and those who favored the concept of staggered development. On the second, there was more agreement that an environmental impact statement as part of the preparation and selection of projects was a valuable instrument. Better information and a better understanding of the interaction between human activities and the environment were needed, but so were strong regulations and institutions. Tinbergen and several participants were "ahead of the curve" in raising sensitive issues such as the need for changes in lifestyles and the relationship between world demographic trends and the capacity of the biosphere to bear the level of agricultural activity required.

In the debates over methods and, later, in discussing long-term forecasts, the Senior Economic Advisers contributed to the clarification of ideas about medium-term development issues for the region, and this work was disseminated in governmental circles as they were themselves high-level officials or influential advisers in their countries. Their meetings ceased in 1997, when budgetary constraints forced reduced resources to be concentrated on the secretariat's economic analysis and the *Surveys:* The Senior Economic Advisers had anyway by then lost much of their influence and the *Surveys* were reaching a broader audience. But the value of bringing senior government advisers to Geneva to discuss economic issues in a more academic than official environment had been recognized. In April 1988, the secretariat introduced the first "Spring Seminar," which brought together government economists and other officials with academics and independent researchers. This stimulus to a free and open discussion of important policy issues (conducted without country nameplates in front of officials) has proved popular with both officials and academics and is an effective way to extend and raise the level of communication between these two groups, both of which have important degrees of influence on the policymaking process.

PRACTICAL APPROACHES TO STIMULATING LAGGING EAST-WEST TRADE

The ECE felt that expanding East-West trade was one important way to narrow the division of the continent, and an early initiative, already mentioned, was the secretariat's operation of a voluntary multilateral compensation system between 1957 and 1969. A second contribution toward facilitating trade procedures was to develop standard contracts and general sales conditions for a number of products and services. This work began in 1949 for the export and import of engineering equipment and since then has been applied to a wide range of activities. These sales conditions, standard contracts, and guides are now widely used in international business. Their practical value is that they simplify the conclusion of contracts, prevent conflicts of laws between different national systems, reduce misunderstandings and litigation, and help to balance the interests of buyers and sellers—all of which help to lower transaction costs. To handle disputes, the ECE prepared a Convention on International Commercial Arbitration. Today the executive secretary of the ECE is still invited to designate arbitrators two or three times a year.

Nevertheless, in 1969, East-West trade still represented no more than 6 percent of total intra-European trade, far below its potential. Governments asked the executive secretary to prepare "an analytical report on the state of intra-European trade which would enable mutually acceptable recommendations on the removal of economic, administrative and trade-policy obstacles" to be made.[151] The report, prepared by the Economic Analysis Division and issued in 1970,[152] developed some concrete proposals that were implemented. One suggestion was to harmonize norms and standards "so as to assure equal access on import markets to all suppliers of the same products and spare parts."[153] A second suggestion concerned administrative practices. These were, to say the least, "inconsistent with the interest attached to east-west trade by Governments and economic organizations."[154] On the Western side, slow delivery of licenses or import permits; delays in customs clearance; non-recognition of certification provided by Eastern laboratories; arbitrary subdivisions of quotas by periods, countries, and importing firms; and difficulties in obtaining visas for engineers and businessmen were among the devices used to limit imports which were judged "unfair" because their prices did not supposedly reflect their costs of production. On the Eastern side, obscure and arbitrary decision-making demonstrated that long-term economic interests, and declarations of intent meant little in the face of political distrust and administrative inertia. These issues have been debated in the Committee on the Development of Trade for many years. But little progress has been made, and many of the obstacles mentioned above were still being quoted in the early 1990s as hampering the growth of exports from the East to the West.

More promising has been the development since the mid-1960s of "industrial co-operation," taken to mean agreements between enterprises which go beyond the straightforward sale or purchase of goods and services to include a whole range of operations (development and transfer of technology, marketing, etc.) extending over a number of years. Entrepreneurs obviously have more incentive to remove, on a case-by-case basis, administrative obstacles than bureaucrats have to change their habits for the sake of what to them may be an abstract improvement in the economy.

The analysis in the *Survey,* however, has not always been successful in stimulating the technical work of the commission. The 1956 *Survey* contained a broad review of European transport problems, including a detailed analysis of the relative cost structures of road and rail transport and "the extremely irrational distribution of traffic" between the two.[155] Regrettably, the *Survey*'s analysis failed to promote a debate among the transport specialists on the broader issues of European transport policies. They preferred to develop their cooperation on precise questions within their technical expertise and, above all, were not disposed to debate about the respective merits of each mode of transport. Conscious that they were not likely to comply with the provisions of the Rio Conference's Agenda 21, the ECE member countries finally decided in 1997 to hold a Conference on Transport and Environment in Vienna where this issue was discussed.

Pre– and Post–Oil Shock Attempts at International Energy Cooperation

In the second half of the 1950s and in the 1960s, the abundance of energy at low prices distracted governments from paying attention to the global demand for energy or to the constraints that insufficient energy supply or higher costs might impose on the growth of production.

The secretariat had taken the initiative of preparing a study in the mid-1950s on the price of oil in Western Europe because of concerns expressed in the Committee on Coal about the competition over oil products, but this immediately touched the sensitivity of the oil companies.

> In this instance representatives of oil interests prior to publication expressed their concern over the analysis they feared would make a problem full of delicacy for them. When the study was published and turned out to be a sober presentation of important facts, hardly in dispute but hitherto difficult to document, the excitement abated and the way was open for a more dispassionate consideration of the problem.[156]

Indeed, this study raised interesting issues. It described how the FOB (free on board) price of oil from the Middle East was aligned with the FOB price of Texas Gulf and concluded: "The wide divorce which persists between prices and production costs in the Middle East suggests that, if this link were severed, the price charged on sales to European countries by the Middle East could be significantly lowered without adverse effects on the further development of its crude oil production."[157] But it went on to say that "the present division of margin of price over cost between royalties and profits is both arbitrary and likely to change."[158] The study regretted the lack of attention given to the problems this situation created and suggested an approach that would "explicitly recognize the interests of all Governments, consuming as well as producing."[159] The Coal Committee invited the secretariat to promptly publish the study "in Geneva and New York . . . on its own responsibility."[160] This was done. But when delegates more politicized than the experts attending the Coal Committee saw the study, they insisted upon its withdrawal. The story, as reported by two different witnesses, was that the United States, the United Kingdom, and the Netherlands made strong representations to Dag Hammarskjöld, who intimated to Gunnar Myrdal that the study should be withdrawn. The study was not distributed, and the already-printed copies disappeared within a few days from the public places where they were left.

By the end of the 1960s, it was evident that energy problems needed to be addressed in an integrated manner, so the secretariat submitted to the commission in April 1970 a proposal "to deal with the energy situation as a whole

on the basis of an econometric model for the European energy economy" and
"to define this model after those existing in ECE countries have been suitably
compared."[161] Such a European model was never built. But the comparison of
national models was made, and it concluded with a prescient remark in early
1972: "The supply of oil and its price is generally considered as an exogenous
variable which will not be influenced by the demand originating in a particular national economy. . . . This assumption may be true for many individual
countries, but it may not be true for entire economic regions, as combined
demand for such regions can greatly influence quantities and prices on the
supply side."[162] This prompted the executive secretary, Janez Stanovnik, to
indicate that in his view the energy problem had become an issue of major
urgency requiring special efforts of regionwide cooperation[163] and to prepare
a report in which the links between energy and growth were analyzed. This
was done, and the secretariat concluded, in early 1973, that, considering that
the ECE region was the major consumer of energy and, with the exception of
the Soviet Union and to some extent the United States, had to rely on imports, and given that supply was not a constraint on demand: "It would seem
that limitations on availabilities of energy over the next decades are not geological in nature, but economic, technical or political. In addition, limitations
may be imposed in the long-term by the need to preserve man's biosphere."[164]
This was another prescient conclusion.

   Beyond its contribution to the debates on energy and growth that took
place between 1971 and 1976, the secretariat had sketched an ambitious program to address energy issues after the first oil shock.[165] Such a program would
have encompassed long-term agreements on energy supply, East-West exchanges, the development of gas and oil pipelines, the organization of research on energy saving and energy efficiency, and assistance to oil-importing
developing countries. But this attempt to give the ECE a central role in energy
policy failed because of the opposition of ECE governments and the New
York secretariat. Some ECE governments were favorable to the creation of a
committee for the general problems of energy, but others "felt that the time
was not ripe to take this type of decision."[166] Jacques Royer, who participated
in the team that produced the report and the proposals, recalled in a conversation with one of the authors the intervention of Under-Secretary-General
for Economic Affairs Philippe de Seynes, who felt that global energy problems were not a responsibility for the regional commissions but for the secretariat in New York.[167] But this also failed to materialize as the major oil
companies and, in consequence, their governments would never accept that
oil be addressed in the UN. Western governments instead created the International Energy Agency within the OECD in November 1974, and the ECE

continued to address technical issues with particular emphasis on energy efficiency and saving.

ENVIRONMENT: FROM A BURDEN TO A GOAL

The attention given to the environment in the region came first from the heavily polluting sectors, energy and transport, as they were concerned that the damage generated by their activities could limit their own expansion. But curiously, it was at a meeting of experts on inland waterway problems in 1955 that the issue of pollution was raised for the first time in the ECE. Inland water vessels played a minor part in the pollution of European rivers, which was mainly caused by enormous quantities of urban and industrial waste. It was therefore decided to place the issue before the commission, and as a result a conference on water pollution in Europe was held in 1961 that highlighted the urgent problems and called for rules for the control of pollution on international watercourses. By the end of the 1950s, the coal industry had also become aware that the environmental problems it created risked reinforcing the attractiveness of oil, which was already less expensive and less polluting. The Coal Committee therefore initiated work in the 1960s in a number of areas to reduce pollution. By the end of the 1960s, other ECE subsidiary bodies had included projects relating to environmental problems in their programs of work, and the ECE had become a forum for studies, exchange of information, and the development of recommendations on a diverse range of issues related to the environment.

In spring 1967, the Czechoslovak government suggested the convening of an ECE meeting of governmental experts to examine the escalating environmental problems in a comprehensive and long-term perspective. This initiative was the precursor to a similar proposal by the Swedish government to the General Assembly, which led to the United Nations Conference on the Human Environment in Stockholm in 1972.[168] The ECE Symposium on Problems Relating to Environment took place in Prague in May 1971 and served as a preparatory meeting for the Stockholm Conference. The most important conclusion in its report was the recognition of the "potential conflicts between the maximum increase of material production on the one hand and general welfare, including a satisfactory quality of the environment, on the other."[169] Such environmental disruption had tended to be downplayed in the context of a rather narrow concept of the standard of living and welfare, but now it appeared that "a reallocation of resources in favor of the quality of the environment might therefore significantly raise the standard of living."[170] In the subsequent debates that took place in the ECE during the 1970s, the range of issues was extended, not least to the admission that environmental degradation was caused not only by production but also by consumption, for example by the use of motor cars, and therefore the improvement of the environment would require changes in the lifestyles and hence the support of the whole population. Thus, by early 1971, the ECE had done pioneering work across several sectors in bringing to the fore substantive concepts that would nourish subsequent international debates on the environment.

Two issues that would become important in later UN debates emerged in the Prague symposium: the international dimension of the environment and responsibility toward future generations. On the latter, "a new moral approach was needed, in which mankind would be seen as the custodian of resources, for its current use and that of future generations."[171] On the former, the fact that "problems in one country could easily affect other countries"[172] should have led to a strong commitment for international cooperation. Instead, the symposium report was very cautious because "national and international questions should be distinguished, the major responsibility for action resting on national Governments, while international co-operation should facilitate and enrich national measures."[173] This attitude was not due to the traditional reticence of Eastern Europe vis-à-vis any intrusion in their national affairs; it was an attitude shared by all the member countries that, as in the case of oil, were not ready for imposed decisions on what they considered to be strategic economic issues.

Air is as vital as water. But waters go downstream while air goes in all directions, depending on the wind. This may be why countries that were not ready to subscribe to obligations on water management felt they had a more common interest in reducing air pollution. The history of the Convention on Long-Range Transboundary Air Pollution (LRTAP) and its protocols illustrates the complex interrelationships of general politics, country leadership, and scientific concerns. Air pollution had been discussed in the ECE since the beginning of the 1960s and a conference devoted to it was held in Strasbourg in 1964 that led to technical work on measurement, methods of investigation of damage, standardization of maximum permissible emissions, and cooperation with the World Health Organization (WHO) and the World Meteorological Organization (WMO).

The political impulse toward an international convention was given by the Final Act of the Helsinki Conference on Security and Cooperation in Europe and the proposal by Leonid Brezhnev to hold a series of all-European congresses on the question of cooperation in the fields of protection of the environment, development of transport, and energy. The consultations conducted by the ECE secretariat on the Soviet proposal led to a High-Level Meeting on the Protection of the Environment, where the Convention on Long-Range Transboundary Air Pollution and a Declaration on Low and Non Waste Technologies were adopted. "The creation of the convention was largely a product of the atmosphere of *détente*," and, indeed, the convention "was weak on substantial commitments" but "proved to be more important in its institutional role and its function as an impetus to the negotiation of future regulatory protocols."[174]

Until 1982, the Nordic countries had taken the lead on air pollution because of the acidification of their lakes that caused the reduction of fish stocks. Other countries, less affected by this phenomenon, were opposed to any international control of air pollution. The United Kingdom even argued that the hypothesis of transboundary pollution was fraught with scientific uncertainties, a familiar argument today of opponents of measures to deal with global warming. When German scientists produced evidence that acidification was responsible for the damage to the Central European forests, Germany became a strong advocate of international commitments to the reduction of sulfur emissions. "The vivid and scary image of the *Waldsterben*, especially concentrated to the Black Forest," induced "a policy shift . . . of the same magnitude as the reports on the ozone hole over the Antarctica."[175] In 1983, the opposition of France, the United Kingdom, the United States, and the Eastern bloc prevented an agreement on a protocol to the LRTAP convention that would have mandated a reduction of 30 percent in sulfur emissions. But the "30 Percent Club" recruited new members in 1984, and the protocol was signed in 1985 by twenty-one countries. It opened the way to the adoption in 1988 of a new protocol to freeze NOx emissions at their 1987 (or earlier) levels by 1994. Here again economic interests were at stake. Germany supported it because its motor-car manufacturers were already obliged to install catalytic converters; France, Italy, and the United Kingdom argued for lean-burn engines which were better adapted for smaller cars. The importance of these protocols lay in the acceptance of international commitments and controls. But they did not stipulate emission reductions that would have been larger than those achieved by national legislation and changes in the structure of production.

By the end of the 1980s and early 1990s, significant progress had been made in the ECE in securing agreements among governments to deal with transboundary air pollution and, more slowly, transboundary water pollution. Reaching such agreements often involves long and complex negotiations requiring a determined and sustained commitment by member governments. The ECE's work on air pollution began in 1964, but it took eleven years to agree on a methodology for measuring it and another two to settle monitoring and evaluation procedures. In analyzing current problems and coming up with new ideas to solve them, an international secretariat needs to be well ahead of the curve if only because intergovernmental agreement on what to do lags so far behind.

A Time of Modest Contributions to Ideas

Neither the secretariat of the ECE in its *Surveys* and other publications nor the Senior Economic Advisers created an overarching development model for the countries of the ECE region. They did not aim to do so, and in any case it would have been impossible in an ideologically divided Europe. They contributed to the intellectual debate in a more modest but perhaps more useful and scientific way than by proposing ready-made models. In comparing national policies, methods, and outcomes, they added to knowledge and understanding of many aspects of development. The exchange of ideas and experience in debates and publications and the gathering and assessment of a range of expert views are the proper methods of scientific progress. In an uncertain science such as economics, the question marks are as useful as the conclusions, particularly for decision-makers. That did not prevent the ECE secretariat from holding strong views about growth, how to overcome the resistance to change, and how to meet the needs of the less-favored sections of the population. At the same time, it reconciled its advocacy of growth with a pioneering concern for the environment through a conviction that technological progress, combined with international rules and conventions, could lead the way to sustainable development.

While contributing to the intellectual and policy debate on development, the ECE tried to address some of the needs of the region by following Myrdal's recommendation to take up, among a large number of complex and political issues, those problems for which solutions appeared feasible within a reasonable time span. Most of the ECE's committees were able to agree on a large number of recommendations to guide domestic policies. Many produced internationally agreed-upon standards or norms. Some negotiated soft international laws and, sometimes, legally binding agreements. By the end of the 1980s, a major problem was that these instruments were unequally applied. Well respected in Western Europe, where the European Community had transformed them into *directives communautaires,* they were, in general, poorly put into practice in Eastern Europe. After 1990, the situation changed in those countries that wanted to join the EU, as these instruments represent in some sectors more than a quarter of the *acquis communautaire.*

The Transition Era: Entering Uncharted Territory

"The extraordinary—and it must be added, totally unexpected—developments in Eastern Europe and the Soviet Union in 1989 constitute a major turning point in Europe's post-war history."[176] Symbol of the division of Europe, the Berlin Wall fell on November 9, 1989. This had been preceded by the opening of the boundary between Hungary and Austria, permitting thousands of people to leave the GDR through Hungary. In one way or another, the people of Eastern Europe had made it clear that they wanted a decisive change in the way their political and economic affairs were conducted. On July 1, 1990, Chancellor Kohl declared the economic and currency union of Germany, and political union was decreed on October 3, 1990. The other Western European countries accepted this once the Bundesrat recognized the Oder-Neiss boundary with Poland. The Warsaw Pact was formally dismantled in 1991, although it had effectively ceased to function in late 1989. The Soviet Union was crumbling through 1991 and finally ceased to exist officially when the CIS was founded on December 21, 1991.

From Plan to Market: A Case for a New Marshall Plan

The factors behind the collapse of the communist regimes in Eastern Europe and the Soviet Union, and why they collapsed when they did, are matters of considerable controversy that will keep scholars busy for many years to come. But from the economic point of view, the ECE secretariat had been recording a steady weakening of economic performance over a very long period. After rapid rates of growth in the 1950s and 1960s had led to the full utilization of the existing reserves of labor, the official strategy was supposed to bring about a shift from *extensive* growth (i.e., based on a simultaneous expansion of labor and capital) to *intensive* growth (i.e., based on a more efficient use of resources and a more intensive use of capital). Fixed-capital formation did increase quite rapidly from the mid-1960s and 1970s, although it slowed down sharply from 1979 as a result of the second oil-price shock and the subsequent debt crisis. However, despite the considerable increase of investment in the 1970s, the earlier slowdown in rates of output growth continued, as did the growth in labor productivity. In 1986, the ECE secretariat calculated that capital productivity had been falling in most of Eastern Europe since 1971, and the contribution of changes in total factor productivity to the growth in total output (NNP) in the first half of the 1980s was smaller than in the early 1970s.[177] (This was the study the GDR tried to suppress.) The

consequences of this chronic deterioration in productive efficiency were manifold, but above all it reflected a failure of the planning system to react effectively to economic changes, whether they were internal (exhaustion of labor
reserves, CMEA integration) or external (oil-price shocks, competition in
export markets, coping with the debt problem). Thus, observing the situation
in April 1990, the ECE secretariat warned "the present situation in eastern
Europe and the Soviet Union is not so much a cyclical or short-term phenomenon as the most recent stage in a general deterioration in performance
which stretches back over two decades or more."[178] By the time of the collapse
of the Berlin Wall in the autumn of 1989, it was apparent that the Eastern
economies were facing not only severe stabilization problems but chronic
structural disequilibria as well.

The ECE insisted, from the beginning of the transition, that stabilization
and structural and institutional reform could not be isolated from one another. Macroeconomic instability will undermine investment and micro-
reforms, while obdurate supply-side problems and weak or missing institutions
will make macroeconomic policy ineffectual. Consequently, a strategy for the
transition process had to be pursued on a wide front and institutional reform
could not be postponed to some later date. Of course, not all the institutions
to be found in a market economy could be tackled at once, and all institutional reform takes time, but key deficiencies needed to be attacked very early,
especially those affecting the efficiency of monetary and fiscal policy and the
incentives to private investment. In contrast, the orthodox approach in 1990
(and the "shock therapists") upheld the perennial optimism of the neoclassical school that institutional problems would not be a significant deterrent to
investment and structural change as long as markets were freed and relative
prices were "correct." The ECE's more pessimistic view of the likelihood of
such spontaneous adjustment, however, implied a major role for government
in building the institutional framework for a market economy—as has been
the case historically in all the present developed market economies—and in
getting the development process under way. But the problem here was that
the public administration itself was in urgent need of reform in all the transition economies, and the public mood in the immediate aftermath of the 1989
revolutions was not very supportive of measures to boost the effectiveness of
government. It was for these reasons—the scale of the structural problems in
the transition economies and their limited resources to handle them—that the
ECE was the first to suggest that what was needed was another Marshall Plan.

The problem of moving from a system of central planning to a market
economy was largely without precedent. Nevertheless, there was some relevant experience in the reconversion of war economies to normal peacetime

functioning in the second half of the 1940s. Indeed, in the immediate after-math of WWII, the economies of Western Europe were highly regulated and were faced with considerable problems of reconstruction and restructuring, the solution of which was hampered by large deficits in current accounts, overvalued currencies, open inflation, and high levels of foreign debt. A net-work of bilateral trade relations restricted intra-European trade and special-ization. This resembled in many respects the situation in Eastern Europe at the end of the 1980s and even more so after the dismantling of the Soviet Union two years later. But "a crucial and fundamental difference between the transformation problems facing west European countries in 1945 and those facing the eastern countries . . . was that the former did not have to recon-struct market economies from first principles."[179] This led the ECE to analyze what makes a market economy work and how support from the West should be designed to help bring it into existence in the East:

> It is often overlooked, even by many economic agents in the market econo-mies, that the actual functioning of markets and market economies depends on a detailed infrastructure of property rights, corporate and non-corporate law, an extensive array of specialized financial institutions, regulations and regu-latory bodies, labor law and procedures for settling disputes, and so on. Much of this infrastructure is embodied in institutions, but important elements are embedded in cultural and social traditions and in the conventions of business practice. Although all the leading market economies today share a number of basic characteristics . . . there is no single, homogenous model of a market economy.[180]

In these few lines lay all the differences between the views of the ECE sec-retariat on the transformation of the centrally planned economies and the common wisdom of 1989. The fact that there was no unique model of an efficient market economy and that policies should be adapted to the specific-ity of countries was, and is still too often, forgotten in practice. But in 1989, a notable difference concerned the assumed time path of reforms. Because changes in institutions, economic infrastructure, and behavior take time, the ECE proposed a more evolutionary approach than the rapid "shock therapy" widely advocated, especially by those who feared that the recent political changes could be reversed. For the latter, rapid reforms, including liberaliza-tion and privatization, would create an irreversible situation. (It is still a puzzle as to why such fears were so prevalent so early when the regimes that had been overthrown had failed on virtually every criterion of success—political, economic, and social—and were generally seen to have lacked popular legiti-macy. Perhaps the Cold War Manichean view of communism in the West also

needed time before it could be shaken off.) The ECE, for its part, feared that
the excessive optimism of those who believed that reforms could be achieved
rapidly would raise unrealistic expectations and that this could create an explosive social situation when reforms would prove to be painful and results
would take time to materialize: "The argument that the legal and financial
infrastructures of the market economy must be put in place *before* markets
can perform as expected suggests that the *order* in which reforms are introduced may be more important than the pace of reforms."[181]

Admittedly, many policy measures were urgent, not least to avoid accelerating inflation and balance-of-payments problems. This is where foreign assistance can be especially helpful—by easing current-account constraints,
financing part of government budget deficits, and reducing the high levels of
inherited foreign debt, it can allow countries to focus on the more time-consuming structural problems. Financial help is essentially about buying time
for hard-pressed governments—and that is what the Marshall Plan did for
Western Europe in the 1940s. Marshall aid for Western Europe consisted largely
of financial assistance (largely grants) with a relatively small proportion of
technical assistance. But given the scale of structural and institutional problems in the transition economies, the ECE suggested "that these proportions
need to be reviewed in any assistance program for the East. In other words,
the Marshall Plan should be turned on its head."[182] This was obviously a point
about the structure of such assistance; it certainly did not imply, as some commentators reported, that financial help was not important!

A program of Western support along the lines of a new Marshall Plan was
important for the ECE's argument for the need for gradualism in most areas
of reform. The ECE naturally shared the consensus with respect to the need
for price liberalization, but it recalled that after WWII, West European prices
had been liberalized progressively as uncertainties over supply responses were
reduced. The process was not fully completed before 1957. This line was generally followed by the transition economies. Similarly, on trade liberalization,
the ECE secretariat also advocated progressiveness: Transparent tariffs and
quotas should, as a priority, replace the direct controls in place under central
planning, and then a program should be drawn up for their reduction and
eventual elimination. In favor of gradualism, the authors of the *Survey* quoted
the precedent of the EPU, the series of trade negotiations under GATT, and,
not least, the authority of Adam Smith. "Humanity may in this case [if labor
mobility is low] require that the freedom of trade should be restored only by
slow gradations, and with a good deal of reserve and circumspection."[183] Unfortunately, trade liberalization that was too rapid, associated with overvalued
currencies and the invasion of Western products, impoverished the peasants

and, by giving little time for adjustment, made large fragments of the industrial sector obsolete overnight. In the second half of the 1990s, when currencies had stabilized at more reasonable levels, many national enterprises demonstrated that they were able to adjust to changing demand.

The ECE also noted that the success of privatization in the West had been linked to the degree of competition prevailing in the relevant sectors. It warned that in Eastern Europe, without reasonably accurate estimates of the net worth of the enterprises to be privatized, there was a considerable risk—a risk which later materialized too often, particularly in Russia—"that social assets would be sold off at prices which would imply large transfers of wealth either to the old managers and to former members of the *nomenklatura* or to newcomers from the west."[184] Therefore, if the creation of new private enterprises was to be encouraged, the privatization of large public enterprises was not the immediate priority. In the following years, the *Surveys* contributed to the debates on privatization. They expressed views on the aims and modalities of privatization as well as on the need to restructure enterprises prior to or immediately after their privatization. When, to justify the priority given to privatization, the argument was developed that privatization created a constituency for market institutions and laws, the ECE agreed that, to be effective, institutions had to have a constituency. But it pointed out that private enterprise could adjust to almost any legal environment provided it was stable and that it was the responsibility of the state to formulate the necessary rules of the game that would ensure respect for the common interest and, indeed, maintain popular support for the market system as a whole. At a time when slogans against the "bloated" state were flourishing, especially in the West, the ECE constantly reminded its readers of the need for a strong and reformed state to build institutions, conduct reforms, and uphold the rule of law. By the mid-1990s, the anti-state anthem began to soften, as too many states had proved unable to enforce their own laws. However, it was only after the disastrous financial crisis of August 1998 in Russia that the importance of institutions began to move to the top of the agenda.

In the minds of the decision-makers of the West and the East, the Marshall Plan was associated with massive transfers of financial resources. Contrary to what is still believed, an equivalent effort in the early 1990s would have not been out of reach. Assuming that the same amount per capita would be provided to the six East European countries and the Soviet Union as during the four years of the Marshall Plan, the ECE secretariat estimated the cost at $16.7 billion a year at 1989 prices. At the same time, Jacques Delors, president of the Commission of the European Community, indicated that if the six East European countries alone were given the same support as the EC provided to its own depressed regions, it would amount to $14 billion a year.[185] However, the question was not so much "What amount?" but "For what purpose?" As mentioned above, the ECE secretariat advocated that a new Marshall Plan should have a major component of technical assistance. But financial transfers would also be necessary, and a number of urgent objectives were suggested: improving the transport and communication infrastructures, which would increase the attractiveness of the transition economies for foreign capital; and improving the disastrous state of the environment. Another suggestion was to finance a temporary Central European Payment Union (CEPU), modeled on the EPU of the 1950s, in order to avoid a precipitate collapse in trade among the former members of the CMEA. This suggestion was dismissed by a number of politicians in the East as an attempt to keep them locked into the CMEA structure—which of course it was not. Instead, intra–East European trade collapsed rapidly and exacerbated the transition recession.

Another key but often-forgotten feature of the Marshall Plan, which the ECE emphasized, was that it invited each recipient country to draw up a four-year outline plan for recovery. The plans were coordinated in the OEEC. This framework reflected Marshall's insistence that the European countries themselves should assess their requirements for aid and that there should be a minimum of cooperation among them. Similarly, the ECE recommended that Eastern countries should be invited to do the same.

The main substantive recommendations were made already in April 1990 and are summarized in box 2.2. They were repeated and developed in subsequent *Surveys* in the 1990s. Time has demonstrated that the ECE was largely correct in its analysis, as it proved impossible to undertake all the reforms at the same time and, even when laws and regulations were adopted and decided on rapidly, it took time for them to be effectively applied. However, the ECE may have overestimated the risk of destabilizing social tension, just as others overestimated the danger of a return to communism. In Central Europe and the Baltic States, democracy has proved to be resilient: Successive elections brought new majorities as a result of popular dissatisfaction, but reforms continued to be pursued and there was continuity in macroeconomic policy. However, social tensions do not always appear as a "big bang": Sometimes they may simmer at a level that inhibits governments from implementing painful but necessary policy measures, and sometimes they may be reflected in large numbers emigrating or seeking asylum abroad, a preference for "exit" rather than "voice." Both manifestations are currently present among the transition economies, especially those in Southeast Europe and in parts of the CIS. Had ECE recommendations been applied with a greater sense of urgency and with more rapid and generous support from the West, they might have

Box 2.2. Economic Reform in the East: A Framework for Western Support*

1. The recipient countries should identify themselves their needs for assistance. They should produce coherent programmes showing how they intend to reach their structural adjustment objectives.

   The constituents of any technical assistance programme will depend on the particular circumstances of each recipient country, but it is suggested that a number of elements be given priority since they will play an important role in creating the credibility of the reform programmes and calibrating the expectations of economic agents with a realistic pace of structural reform. The suggested priorities for technical assistance are:
   - The creation of the legal, financial and institutional framework essential for the operation of a competitive market system;
   - The provision of comprehensive and reliable statistical and economic information services for both government and enterprises;
   - The development of the various marketing skills required for boosting exports.

2. For improving the competitiveness of East European countries, Western countries might usefully:
   - Eliminate all quotas and other quantitative restrictions on imports from reforming Eastern countries according to a precise timetable;
   - Monitor the effects of western COCOM (Coordinating Committee for Multilateral Export Controls);

   And the Eastern countries should:
   - Convert the present administrative controls on eastern imports into the most transparent devices of tariffs and quotas and draw up a timetable for their gradual elimination.

3. Effective technical assistance will increase the eastern capacity to absorb new capital funds and technology. Nevertheless, there is still a need for financial assistance in the immediate future, and especially for grant aid that would avoid any addition to existing debt levels. The priority objectives for such financial aid should be:
   - Radical improvement of transport and telecommunications systems;
   - The rapid reduction of environmental pollution;
   - The creation of a Central European Payments Union to facilitate Eastern countries transition to a system of free trade and multilateral settlements.

*This box contains only quotations from ECE, *Economic Survey for Europe 1989–1990* (New York and Geneva: United Nations, April 1990).

avoided mistakes and reduced the welfare costs of adjustment. In assessing the results of policy, the criterion cannot simply be whether it succeeded but whether it succeeded at least cost to those who had to bear the pain of adjustment. So the question raised in the first publication of the United Nations Intellectual History Project, which begs a response, is why the ECE's views had little impact.[186]

Obviously, it is too early to pretend to have a definitive answer when the records of the principal actors are still closed, but a number of elements appear to be important. First was the fact that the *Survey* was going against the stream of economic-policy thinking in the leading market economies.[187] In 1989–1990, neoliberalism was triumphant and there was a widespread conviction that the policies of liberalization, deregulation, and privatization pursued in the "Anglo-Saxon" countries provided an appropriate model for transition economies. Associated with this approach was a belief that government should interfere as little as possible in the workings of the economy. "Get the government out of the economy" was the simple message from the West. Rapid price and trade liberalization, together with speedy privatization, would unleash domestic entrepreneurial energy and attract foreign investors eager to get in on the forthcoming boom. Implicit in this approach was that the market economy was somehow immanent even in Soviet-type economies and would become apparent once all the shackles on private initiative were removed.[188] It was also attractive to Western governments because it implied that the basic tasks of restructuring would be undertaken by foreign direct investment and, therefore, there would be no need for large-scale official assistance along the lines of a Marshall Plan. Professor Rudiger Dornbusch of MIT is among those who now see this rejection of a Marshall Plan approach as a major strategic error.[189]

Second, the majority of Western finance ministers simply did not want to hear of suggestions for a Marshall Plan for Eastern Europe, although a number of other senior politicians thought it was desirable.[190] Fiscal consolidation, in part a legacy of the 1980s and the fight against inflation, was high on the agenda and would be reinforced in the EU by the Maastricht Treaty of December 1991 (which was already foreshadowed by the abolition of remaining capital controls in the EU in July 1990). Essentially, Western Europe was largely preoccupied with its own concerns, and the message of the Washington Consensus, that the transition to a market economy was largely a matter of liberalization and foreign capital, was a welcome relief. Third, the neoliberal policy stance was widely attractive in the transition economies. Although there were many economists and officials who sympathized with the ECE view, most of them were not in the first post-1989 governments. It must be admitted that "getting the State out of the economy" was an attractive message for those in the East who identified the state with repression and economic failure. Arguing for reform of the state to undertake different but necessary tasks in a market economy was more difficult and less welcome. Rapid liberalization and privatization was also attractive to the members of the *nomenklatura:* Far from wanting to turn the clock back, they were happy to get a head start in grabbing state assets at fire-sale prices—and when things went wrong, early liberalization of the capital account enabled them to move their newly acquired capital to safety abroad.

A fourth reason for the ECE's lack of influence reflects both the marginalization of the UN itself in international economic policy debates as well as attitudes toward Eastern Europe within the UN. The G7 had made it clear that the Bretton Woods institutions would be largely responsible for the response to the transition, and these institutions were determined not to yield their role to another "Marshall Plan," as they had been forced to do in 1947. Also, many East European governments were now more interested in joining NATO and "Western" organizations such as the OECD than in seeking more influence for the UN. Within the UN itself, there were a number of reasons why no coherent contribution was made at the highest level to the policy debates on transition. The only senior official in New York who expressed agreement with what the ECE was saying was Göran Ohlin, who saw transition issues as an opportunity for the UN to regain a more authoritative voice in international policy discussion. Against this were several forces. The developing countries were fearful that the transition economies would divert assistance, private investment, and general attention away from themselves and were therefore suspicious of any move that might suggest that the UN was itself diverting resources to the East. Transition was a problem for the rich men's club. These views were shared by the Secretary-General at the time, who appears to have taken little interest in what was happening in Eastern Europe and the former Soviet Union.[191] Second, the various UN agencies and departments were engaged in a traditional bureaucratic struggle for parts of the new piece of turf that had appeared with the collapse of communism. The ECE is a very small department within the UN and with no coherent approach coming from UN headquarters on Eastern Europe and the former Soviet Union, there was little chance that the ECE's analysis would be amplified by becoming the voice of the Secretary-General.[192]

Nevertheless, it cannot be concluded that the ECE should have saved its breath or that in order to be more influential it should have confined its analysis to the politically possible. When everyone does that they usually end by saying the same thing, which is not very helpful to those responsible for policy and who need to consider all the options. It would also have been a rejection

of the principles laid down by Myrdal and the tradition of "constructive skepticism" maintained over the years in the ECE.[193] Moreover, one of the objectives of thinking ahead of the curve must surely be to transform the politically
impossible into the politically feasible.

Enlarging the European Union

Access to the EU was seen by most of the countries of Eastern Europe as
essential, not only for providing the foundations for sustainable long-term
growth but even more for underpinning their new democratic institutions
and increasing the general security of the region. Psychologically, they saw
membership in the EU as providing confirmation of their "return to Europe"
and putting an end to the period when they were subject to a foreign hegemony. Thus, soon after the fall of the Berlin Wall, the countries of Central
Europe expressed their wish to establish close links with the EU. In 1990–1991
most of them signed Association Agreements with the union and, when Brussels had clarified the procedure, all of them formally applied for membership.
Later, in 1998, two countries of the CIS, Ukraine and Moldavia, as well as
those emerging from the breakup of the former Yugoslavia and Albania also
indicated their wish to join.

Box 2.3. Steps to Enlargement

The Association Agreements

The Association Agreements form nowadays the legal framework for association
between the applicant countries and the EU and cover political and economic relations. Between 1991 and 1996, such agreements were signed by Poland and Bulgaria
(December 1991); Romania (February 1993); Bulgaria (March 1993); the Czech Republic and Slovakia (October 1993); Estonia, Latvia, and Lithuania (June 1995); and
Slovenia (June 1996). Even before 1990, Turkey, Malta, and Cyprus, respectively in
1963, 1970, and 1972, had signed association agreements, the aim of which was the
establishment of a customs union.

1993: The Membership Criteria

The Copenhagen European Council approved the principle of the EU enlargement
and adopted three sets of criteria:

• Political criteria: democracy, the rule of law, human rights, and respect for and protection of the minorities

• Economic criteria: a functioning market economy and the capacity to cope with competitive pressure
• Adoption of the *acquis communautaire*

In December 1994, the Essen European Council set a pre-accession strategy, which was reinforced in 1999 at the Berlin European Council with the creation of two pre-accession instruments—a structural instrument and an agricultural one, a financial framework for these instruments, and the doubling of pre-accession aid.

Between 1994 and 1996, ten countries with economies in transition submitted their application for membership in the EU: Hungary and Poland (1994); Bulgaria, Estonia, Latvia, Lithuania, Romania, and Slovakia (1995); and the Czech Republic and Slovenia (1996). Turkey (1987) and Cyprus and Malta (1990) had already submitted their applications.

The Accession Negotiations

On 16 July 1997, the European Commission published the *Agenda 2000,* which addressed in particular the issue of enlargement and to which are attached the commission's opinions on the situation of applicant countries with regard to the accession criteria. In December 1997, the Luxembourg European Council approved the report and decided that the accession negotiations should be launched with the Czech Republic, Estonia, Hungary, Poland, and Slovenia. It also established a financial framework for supporting the pre-accession process. On 30 March 1998, the accession process started for six countries—the Luxembourg group, composed of the five countries mentioned above and Cyprus.

In December 1999, the Helsinki European Council noted that certain candidates would not be able to meet the Copenhagen criteria in the medium term but nevertheless decided to convene bilateral intergovernmental conferences in 2000 with a view to opening negotiations with Bulgaria, Cyprus, Latvia, Lithuania, Malta, Romania, and Slovakia.

Negotiations started in 2000 with ten transition countries (plus Cyprus and Malta). At Laeken in December 2001, the European Council judged that many of them would likely be able to complete negotiations by the end of 2002 and become full members of the EU by 2004. The start of negotiations and the requirements of the accession agenda gave a strong boost to the reform process in these countries.

In December 2002, at the European Council meeting in Copenhagen, the negotiations were completed with ten countries: the Czech Republic, Estonia, Hungary, Latvia, Lithuania, Poland, Slovakia, Slovenia, Cyprus, and Malta. All ten are expected to become full members of the EU by May 2004. In addition, the Copenhagen summit endorsed the goal of Bulgaria and Romania to become full members in 2007.

The ECE is not involved directly in the enlargement process, although all the conventions and norms developed in the ECE are part of the *acquis communautaire*. In the 1990s, the secretariat developed some "operational" activities, mainly to assist transition economies in adopting and implementing these conventions and norms, but these were not focused only on candidate countries. The ECE, however, has at various times reviewed aspects of enlargement in the *Survey,* although its views were not always well received in Brussels. First, the ECE argued early on that the EU should have a comprehensive and transparent pre-accession strategy, which would require more than simply informing the candidate members about the complexities of the *acquis* and the sequence in which the various rules and regulations might be introduced. Such a strategy should make it "possible to reduce or attenuate some of the costs of adjustments and anticipate many of the benefits of membership by strengthening both policy credibility and the expectations of economic agents, especially investors and entrepreneurs, in both transition economies and Western Europe."[194] At the same time, the ECE advocated that the EU should facilitate market access for exports, including sensitive products, from Eastern Europe. It also argued that financial transfers be better targeted to avoid the buildup of external debt, help build market institutions, and promote trade among the transition economies. These proposals did not please Western countries, but it is interesting to note (see box 2.3) that these recommendations, made in 1996, were echoed in the decisions made in 1997, although it is not claimed that the ECE had a direct influence on this development. By contrast, the candidate countries did not like the view of the secretariat that it was not in their interest to accede too soon to the union:

> A rushed and premature entry of the transition economies into the EU is unlikely to be in their longer-run economic interests if they are unable to face full-fledged competition in the single market. In such a case, they would risk being confined to low value added activities, subject to increasing competition from transition economies farther east and from the developing countries.[195]

This view was expressed in 1996 when Western politicians, seeking popularity in the East, were forecasting the first admissions for 2000. At that time, the ECE considered that further enlargement was unlikely to occur before 2005—which looks as if it will prove to be the most accurate of all the forecasts being made at that time.

At a time when the EU was still hesitant about the potential extent of enlargement, various diplomats suggested that the ECE might be a "waiting room" for the second wave of candidates for membership. This was thought to be a useful idea since a significant part of the *acquis communautaire* originated in ECE norms and conventions and many of these countries were not yet respecting them fully. This would have required some resources to be channeled through the ECE for technical assistance. But, more important, it would have implied that the EU and the concerned countries would agree to discuss a number of trade, financial, and general issues of common interest within the ECE framework. The EU was not willing to do this and was not prepared to go beyond technical and environmental negotiations in the ECE. This restrictive attitude has not changed. At the end of 2001, Russia suggested that the secretariat organize a seminar to explore the consequences of enlargement for the rest of Europe, but the EU refused to support the proposal.

Marginalization and Reconstruction in Southeast Europe

While countries in the "first wave" of candidates for membership of the EU had more or less regained by 1998 the levels of production of 1989, the countries of Southeast Europe (other than Slovenia) had still not yet recovered from the sharp fall in their GDP between 1989 and 1993. On the eve of the Kosovo crisis, the GDP of Yugoslavia was at 50 percent of its level in 1989 and in the other Balkan countries it was around 70 percent and clearly not on a rising trend. The breakup of the former Socialist Federal Republic of Yugoslavia and the ensuing conflicts disrupted trade, devastated some economies, and left the region mired in uncertainty. In the newly independent states as well as in the other countries of the Balkans, fluctuating policies and a lack of continuity in the reform process have discouraged investment, and they have tended to fall farther behind the rest of Europe.

The idea that countries or groups with opposite or competing interests nevertheless share common problems that they can better solve by cooperation has continued to inspire the efforts of the ECE in the region. The first attempt to facilitate dialogue among the countries of ex-Yugoslavia was stillborn because they vehemently rejected the slightest suggestion that they might have anything in common for the future. Janèz Stanovnick, former executive secretary of the ECE, who was president of Slovenia at the time of the breakup of Yugoslavia, warned the then executive secretary of the ECE that any initiative to bring together the former components of Yugoslavia, even to discuss technical matters of common interest, such as circulation on the Danube, would only unite them against the commission.

The second attempt, however, was made in the context of an informal seminar in the ECE in 1999 that brought together experts on and in the region and without the participation of member states. Among the experts were several opposed to President Milosevic, who would later occupy important positions in Yugoslavia. Mladjan Dinkič, who later became governor of the Central Bank, participated in this seminar.

For the third attempt, the ECE drew on the lessons from the first attempt and tried to involve all the countries of Southeast Europe, those from ex-Yugoslavia, and also Hungary, Bulgaria, Turkey, and Greece. But because of its exclusion from UN debates, the Federal Republic of Yugoslavia (Serbia and Montenegro) did not participate. In the aftermath of the Kosovo War, the U.S. administration wanted to convince Congress that it had not only an immediate objective of maintaining peace in the area but also a long-term development perspective for the region. The idea was that all the countries of the Balkans, whether or not they were affected directly by the Kosovo War, have small economies of limited interest for outside investors and that their future would be more promising if they were more closely integrated with one another. The ECE, because of its expertise in intergovernmental issues of trade, transport energy, and the environment and its networks in the region was identified by the United States and the countries of Southeast Europe as the best organization to support this policy. The Southeast Europe Cooperative Initiative (SECI) was established in 1997 and managed to speed up the removal of obstacles to border-crossing and the harmonization of transport regulations and, more important, to initiate and develop a dialogue among the countries of the area over a broad range of technical and political issues.

SECI was the result of an interesting combination of U.S. pressure on the governments of the region orchestrated by Ambassador Richard Schifter; the dynamism of Dr. Ehrard Busek, former vice-chancellor of Austria, who chaired hundreds of meetings; and the capacity of the ECE to develop and formulate projects and policies and to gather around the same table experts from countries with accumulated grievances. As it was perceived as a U.S. initiative, some EU members were reluctant to cooperate and questioned the ECE's involvement. The EU subsequently launched the Stability Pact, which raised great expectations because it was taken as a signal that the EU was concerned about the marginalization of the region and that financial resources would be forthcoming. At the end of 2001, Dr. Busek was appointed co-coordinator of the Stability Pact while retaining his role as co-coordinator of SECI, thus uniting the two approaches.

SECI provided the ECE with the possibility that its ideas on the development of the region would be discussed by all the interested parties. The ECE was concerned that emergency relief and reconstruction would distract attention from addressing the chronic and deep-seated structural problems of the region; namely, a large share of the capital stock that was economically non-viable, a poor physical infrastructure, and an incomplete structure of market-economy institutions. It therefore proposed a long-term strategy whose components would include a realistic time frame; national programs of re-construction and institutional reforms formulated by the governments to take into account specific sensitivities and avoid the standard international ap-proach of "one policy fits all"; coordination of national actions and interna-tional assistance in areas where there are public goods, externalities, and economies of scale; and rapid delivery of public assistance with *ex post* con-trol that intermediate targets have been met. Some features of the Stability Pact are consistent with this approach, but it still falls short of the broader framework for national and regional development proposed by the ECE, which again drew on the methods of the Marshall Plan for inspiration.[196]

Convergence in Europe

The issue of convergence has gained renewed interest in Europe in relation to the transition process and the enlargement of the EU. But the findings of ECE research on convergence between and within the United States, Western Europe, and Eastern Europe are of more general interest.[197] Spontaneous move-ment toward convergence would indicate that market forces might eventually lead to similar living standards across countries; persistently large or widen-ing gaps between rich and poor countries would support the need for na-tional and international policy measures to stimulate a catch-up process.

According to ECE calculations, the real-income gap between Western Eu-rope and the United States was reduced significantly in the 1950s and the 1960s as productivity grew more rapidly in Europe. There was little further progress after 1973, and the gap widened slightly in the 1990s. In 1998, the real per-capita GDP of the EU was 33 percent below that of the United States. The fact that the productivity gap is smaller than the GDP gap "points to the role that physical and human capital accumulations have played in maintaining the United States' lead in per capita GDP."[198] In Western Europe, there was a strong convergence in real GDP per capita in the 1950–1973 period, but during the subsequent long period of stagnation or weak growth performance became more unequal, even among EU member countries, as a result of the specific interactions between domestic and international factors on the growth of in-dividual countries.

Similarly, in Eastern Europe and the Soviet Union, there was convergence of per-capita incomes only in the 1950s and 1960s. It stopped during the 1970s and was followed by a rapid divergence during the 1980s. Since 1989, the di-verging trends have become even more pronounced. With the exception of a few countries in Central Europe, which from the mid-1990s began to catch up with West European levels of GDP per head, most of the transition economies have continued to diverge from one another and to fall farther behind the income levels of Western Europe. A number of studies have estimated the time required for these economies to catch up with Western Europe, and despite differences in their methodological approach, the general conclusion is that it will take decades, even for the most advanced of them. Moreover, the experience of the fifteen members of the EU during the 1990s suggests that EU membership by itself will not be sufficient for a more rapid rate of catch-up.

The conclusion drawn in the *Survey 2000* on the issue of catch-up can serve as a general conclusion on the difficulties, conflicts, and hopes of the transition era:

> . . . regrettably, neither economic theory nor policy practices have discovered "easy fixes" and practical recipes for success in accelerating the process of catching up. Past experience has shown that previous "growth miracles" have always combined country-specific factor endowments, prudent and forward-looking public policies, specific geographic location and, often, a lucky coincidence of circumstances, all of which have always been placed in a specific historic context. *Ex-post,* growth miracles can be explained but it is next to impossible to reproduce them; new success stories may draw from the lessons of past ones, but they will always contain unique and innovative elements. What is clear, however, is that the potential for catching up and economic convergence in Europe exists, and it is up to imaginative political leaders and creative policy makers in the transition economies to find the keys to success.[199]

Conclusions

The ECE was created by the General Assembly, and its budget is regularly adopted as part of the UN budget. But its work and its contributions to ideas and development have been guided, almost exclusively, by the decisions of its member states in Geneva and the initiatives taken by the executive secretaries and the secretariat. Principles and directives emanating from New York have had little impact on the substance of its work, at least for much of its history.

There is some arrogance attached to this assertion. The arrogance comes from the fact that ECE members consider themselves to be the initiators of most of the values, policies, and principles adopted by the UN and that therefore there is little point for the ECE to act as the "regional arm" of the organization in promoting them in the region. When the UN gave prominence to development, ECE member countries considered themselves to be already developed and, at least until the end of the 1980s, not directly concerned by the development debate. They never considered, for instance, that it would be worth discussing in the ECE the potential costs and advantages for the region of the development of the Third World countries, the opening of their markets to the exports of the South, or the stabilization of commodity prices. The secretariat occasionally discussed some of these questions in the *Survey* and made some contributions and recommendations as described above, but member states were first of all concerned with their own problems, which in a way is the raison d'être of the regional commissions.

This arrogance does not imply, however, that the ECE did not recognize the importance of being part of the UN system. On the contrary, in the mid-1990s, when some delegates were considering dismantling the ECE and transferring its most valuable activities to the Organization for Security and Cooperation in Europe (OSCE) or other institutions, two arguments put an end to the suggestion. The first was that because the ECE was part of the UN, ECE members were guaranteed that each of them would be treated on an equal footing and could make its views known. This is unique and key for the full participation of the weaker countries. The second is that the instruments developed by the ECE—its conventions, norms, standards, and technical concepts—could be adopted or adapted by non-ECE members far more easily than if the ECE were not a UN organization. A few examples have been given in this chapter. Sometimes, but not often, ECOSOC has recommended to the rest of the world that an ECE instrument be adopted (as in the case of the transport of dangerous goods) or a global entity has taken up an ECE convention as a reference for a worldwide negotiation (as did UNEP with the protocol on heavy metals to the LRTAP Convention). More often, in practice, a country interested in a particular instrument has taken advantage of its automatic status of observer in any UN body to attend relevant ECE meetings in order to inform itself, follow the negotiations, and, eventually, if it so wishes, adhere to the convention or norm. Thus, the fact that the ECE belongs to the UN adds to the influence of the region when neighboring countries and others in the rest of the world decide to adopt some of its instruments. And this happens in the best possible manner: Because the ECE has neither means of coercion to apply nor incentives to offer, in contrast to what happens in other institutions or in bilateral negotiations, countries adopt ECE instruments freely simply because they judge them to be in their interest.

Myrdal's original conception of the ECE as a two-track organization proved to be very robust for more than five decades. On the one hand, it has a research or "think tank" function carried out under the sole responsibility of the executive secretary, who exercises an independent judgment of what needs to be analyzed in the interests of the region, and on the other it is a set of operational functions driven by the practical interests of member govern- ments and based on a search for consensus. In the first decade or so of the ECE's existence, the relationship between the two tracks was quite close with analytical studies highlighting issues in the fields of agriculture, timber, en- ergy, steel, engineering, transport, and housing. Studies in all these areas ap- peared in the *Survey,* the *Economic Bulletin,* or as special monographs. The ideas and proposals discussed were not always taken up, or indeed welcomed, by the intergovernmental bodies, but they helped to provide a broader per- spective for each of the specialized areas of work—just as the *Surveys* aimed to provide a broader international perspective for national economic policy- makers. Some of these special studies (on steel and oil, for example) had an influence and resonance that reached far beyond the technical bodies in Geneva. The interaction between the two tracks, however, has tended to weaken over the years, partly because of large cuts in the absolute resources allocated to economic analysis—cuts which coincided with the expansion of the ECE's East European membership from eight to twenty-seven countries—and partly because the principal subsidiary bodies tend to be dominated by technicians engaged in long-term processes of negotiation over norms, standards, and so forth. As shown earlier, these can take years to reach a conclusion, and once the process has been started resources are preempted and there is little scope for changing direction or taking new studies on board. There are also very few working economists now in the operational divisions of the ECE, and that weakens interaction with the Economic Analysis Division. This is per- haps part of the life cycle of any institution, but although understandable given the nature of technical cooperation, it can weaken the overall response of the organization to new developments in the region. Thus in 1990, when a new Marshall Plan for Eastern Europe was proposed, and in 1999 when a strat- egy was outlined for postwar reconstruction in Southeast Europe, it was not possible to back them up with sectoral studies in transport, energy, and the environment, key problem areas for the countries concerned and areas of spe- cial expertise in the ECE. Had this been done, the overall impact of the ECE's analysis might have been much greater.

A detailed assessment of the economic analysis track over fifty years was impossible in a single chapter, and only selected issues have been highlighted here. But it should be understood that one of the principal functions of eco- nomic analysis has been, in Myrdal's words, to keep "a vigilant watch on eco- nomic trends in Europe." Until the 1960s, the ECE had little competition in this area, and its assessments of both Western and Eastern Europe were at a very high level of competence and were probably influential throughout the

region. In the late 1960s and 1970s, a certain routine began to affect the current analysis, although that of Eastern Europe and the Soviet Union retained
its virtual monopoly position and remained the key source for both academics and officials, not least in the East, in following developments in those countries. This falling off in the current analysis was partly due to the diversion of
resources to large special studies, but this was reversed in the 1980s and 1990s,
leading to a much sharper and livelier assessment in the *Survey* of developments in the region. Myrdal's instinct here seems to have been sound: It is
through the careful analysis of current developments that the well-trained
independent economist can hope to spot changes in the underlying developments, highlight the risks, and make recommendations for changes in policy.
The *Survey* team has never had the resources to build its own short-term forecasting model, but this has proved to be an advantage since it leads to a more
critical assessment of the "consensus" forecasts based on knowledge of the
assumptions in the standard models and of the relatively important judg-
mental inputs which go into most forecasts. The ECE's record in assessing the
conjunctural outlook over the past decade or so in both Western Europe and
in the transition economies has been very respectable.[200]

The purpose here has not been to sift through the ECE's very large analytical output to find what have been its original contributions to economic thinking, although roughly at the ends of the time span considered here, we may
mention the origin of the Kaldor-Verdoorn law in the first *Survey*[201] and, forty
years later, probably the first suggestion that intra-industry trade was being
driven by the fragmentation of production systems, an idea that was taken up
in the academic literature in the second half of the 1990s.[202] Sometimes the
contributions have been technical but essential for a better understanding of
developments,[203] but more generally the *Survey* has continued to be marked
by a "constructive skepticism" which insists on looking more closely and
critically at the conventional wisdom, whether it concerns allegations about
the greater rigidity of wages in Western Europe compared with North
America[204] or, as described in chapter 1, exaggerated claims about the extent
of globalization.[205]

In its economic analysis, the ECE has never been attracted by overarching
economic models, not least because it has usually been aware that the economy
is an integral part of a more complex political and social reality. The preference of ECE economists for market economies and democratic systems has
always been clear, but there has never been an unquestioning belief in the
overpowering wisdom of the market or of member governments. Moreover,
the ECE has more recently insisted that there is no single model of a market
economy and that transition and developing countries should be encouraged

to develop arrangements for the conduct of their economic and social affairs that are best suited to their histories and their present conditions. One policy or model for all is ultimately a recipe for disappointment and conflict.

The ECE's second track, consisting of close intergovernmental coopera-tion on a wide range of practical and technical issues, gives the lie to the old saying that the UN is "just a talking shop." The key areas were mentioned earlier and there is no need to summarize them here. But it should be empha-sized that these activities, which are frequently very obscure for the outsider, yield considerable economic benefits. Thus, the work devoted to facilitating the electronic exchange of international trade documentation has led to sig-nificant reductions in the transaction costs of international trade, which seem to be not only larger than the estimated benefits of the Uruguay Round but have been achieved without the diplomatic drama surrounding that and simi-lar higher-profile events.[206] Large gains, but unfortunately not estimated by the secretariat, will also have been made by the various conventions to facili-tate the transport of goods across the various frontiers of Europe. More gen-erally, in setting norms and standards, the ECE has helped to ensure that international economic relations in the region are non-discriminatory and market-extending rather than distorted by national protectionist forces, as was the case in the 1920s and 1930s.

Most of the ECE's operational work in its principal subsidiary bodies con-sists of what has sometimes been described as "necessary multilateralism" or, less grandly, "nuts and bolts cooperation," that is to say, cooperation on issues where all parties can envisage practical solutions to international problems and where the evident possibility of benefit to all encourages the parties to work together. But the larger significance of the ECE's experience is that this "necessary cooperation" developed among countries that were bitterly divided over broader political, economic, and social values. It is often thought that the way to peaceful coexistence and cooperation is to seek to reconcile or eliminate the differences between countries and peoples. But this may some-times be mistaken. The ECE's experience shows that cooperation can move ahead by *accepting* certain differences in preferences and values. This does not imply accepting murderous behavior and violations of human rights, but it does imply recognition that there are differences and preferences that may not be reconcilable and should therefore be accepted and respected by others.

Although the Europe of today is no longer divided by antagonistic ideolo-gies, it remains marked by the heritage of history, by different religious affili-ations, by different preferences, and by differences in the conduct of social and political affairs. There are also potential sources of tension, not least in the growing economic disparities between countries. At the same time all member countries of the commission, with the exception of the United States, the Russian Federation, and the countries of Central Asia, are either members of the EU or have membership as a central policy objective. Some have already entered into accession negotiations, while for others the prospect of integration may be too far off to be an effective stimulus for change. Increasing disparities and, for some countries, uncertainty about joining the union may create frustration and bitterness, and efforts will be needed to ensure that these do not lead to a new division of Europe. Among the potentially positive factors, the energy resources of Russia and Central Asia could be both a factor of development for these countries and of increased security of supply for the European importing countries.[207] In such a context, there is a need for a vision of Europe in which national preferences and values do not disappear into an amorphous larger entity, but one in which each country retains a significant role and a future. Such a vision has to be developed in independent forums where each country and the representatives of civil society can voice their views. Three pan-European forums, the ECE, the OSCE, and the Council of Europe, have the neutrality, the competence, and the experience to facilitate such an undertaking. The ECE experience, founded on Myrdal's basic approach, shows that the acceptance of a diversity of values and preferences is compatible with economic cooperation and progress. That, perhaps, is an encouraging lesson for other parts of the world.

3

From ECAFE to ESCAP: Pioneering a Regional Perspective

Leelananda de Silva

- **The Changing Context**
- **The Early Days: Creation and Consolidation**
- **A Culture of Regionalism**
- **Regional Action at the Sectoral Level**
- **Summing Up: Rise and Decline**

The Economic Commission for Asia and the Far East (ECAFE) was born to another world. In 1947, there was hardly an Asian region of independent sovereign nations. Countries in Asia looked more toward the West than the East. The United Nations system was in its infancy. There was no experience of multilateralism in the region. Regional and subregional institutions did not exist. It was a struggle to establish ECAFE, and it was even more daunting to consolidate it. The first ten years of its life were taken up in building its own systems and procedures. However, much was done in these early years.

This was the period in which ECAFE was an important factor in the region's international relations. ECAFE provided the forum for regional member countries to cut their teeth in a new world of multilateral action. Until its name change in 1974, ECAFE continued to be creative and versatile and provided leadership to a region struggling to be born. Its first twenty-five years was its golden age. Since then, the role of the Economic Commission for Asia and the Pacific (ESCAP) has diminished for diverse reasons—the emergence of a more complex multilateral and UN structure; the proliferation of regional and subregional institutions; the impact of globalization and the growing irrelevance of a region as large as ESCAP; the increasing role of ESCAP as a branch of the UN bureaucracy instead of being a more indigenously rooted regional body;

and the diminishing quality of ESCAP's leadership in recent years. Overall, during its 50-year history, the commission has been a pragmatic and practical institution.[1] Economic theorizing was not its forte. The economic and social theories and ideas which it adopted and absorbed in its analysis and prescriptions were derived from other, mainly UN, sources. It was behind the curve, rather than ahead of it.

There have been several histories of ESCAP. David Wightman wrote an extensive and impressive history of its first fifteen years.[2] The first three executive secretaries were anxious to put the record straight and Wightman was commissioned for the task. As an outsider from Harvard, he had the independence and objectivity to analyze and discuss issues more critically than could have been done by an insider. Five years later, there was an official history which provides an exciting, factual, and partly analytical report of these formative years in ECAFE's history.[3] On the occasion of its twenty-fifth anniversary another history was written; coming soon after the earlier one, it focused primarily on the regional institutional infrastructure that the commission was creating at the time.[4] In 1987, forty years after ECAFE's birth, another record of its achievements—part history, part snapshot was published, which provides many insights into how ESCAP made a sharp change of direction in the mid-1970s, becoming more an operational technical assistance agency and the regional development center of the UN instead of the indigenous regional organization that it once was.[5] The decline of ECAFE is most evident in the document published on its fiftieth anniversary, which is largely a pictorial wall chart which doesn't provide any sense of its history.[6]

The paper that follows is not a history along chronological lines, although the sequence of sections is chronologically linked. The first section provides a brief history of the changing context in which the regional commission has functioned for over fifty years. The second section focuses on the first fifteen years, when ECAFE was a key factor in Asian relations. There was a strong political dimension to its activities during that period. If it can be so described, this was the period when ECAFE was engaged in the higher realms of international diplomacy. The third section addresses issues primarily, but not exclusively, pertinent to issues that emerged during the first twenty-five years of the commission's existence which led to the unfolding of a culture of regionalism. The fourth section, on sectoral issues, encompasses the commission's work in sectoral tasks and technical assistance over the 50-year period. This section is largely a collection of microhistories of key sectors. A concluding section briefly examines the rise and decline of a regional commission.

The Changing Context

The commission, more than any other UN institution, has been the creature of its context. It is not an institution that has appreciably changed the regional climate; instead, it has been dominated by the climate of the region. Probably the one occasion it changed the regional climate and context was when it was instrumental in creating the Asian Development Bank (ADB).

At least four historical aspects of contextual change must be considered as having influenced its path and direction. The politics of the region and global politics both had a major influence on ECAFE until the mid-1970s, after which the political context diminished in importance. Probably that coincided with the diminishing role of ESCAP itself. The global and regional economic context has had a major influence all through its 50-year history. The commission has largely reacted to economic developments within and outside the region. ESCAP is part of the UN system, and changes in the UN system and associated multilateral regimes have had a major impact on the commission; ESCAP's programs of work are shaped by developments within the UN system. Since the early 1970s, ESCAP could not avoid taking note of the emergence of subregionalism. The expansion of its membership beyond what was regarded as the traditional Asia of the 1940s has also shaped its activities. ESCAP now represents 60 percent of the world's population. Is it still a region? Or is it half the world? The rationale for such a regional commission is now in question.

Political Context

Asia was largely a war-torn region in the mid-1940s. China and Southeast Asia were in the throes of political instability and civil war. Japan was an occupied state. The relatively stable part of the region was the Indian subcontinent, although it was marred by major civil disturbances. In 1945, there were only six sovereign states in Asia—Afghanistan, China, Iran, Japan, Nepal, and Thailand. Between 1945 and 1960, most Asian states achieved their independence. Also during this period, China ceased to be actively engaged in the UN system; controversy surrounded China's seat in the United Nations. The Korean War had also increased tensions considerably in Northeast Asia. During the period up to about 1960, colonialism and the influence of the former colonial powers were felt strongly within ECAFE, while Japan's role was highly restricted.

From about the mid-1960s to the mid-1970s, the Cold War had a significant impact on the politics of the region. In the 1960s and into the 1970s, the

Cold War was experienced in the most acute form in the Indochina region, the Vietnam War dominating international politics. The Cold War created significant tensions among the region's member countries, thereby retarding efforts at regional cooperation.

From the mid-1970s, although the Cold War was still an important influence, countries in the region began to assert themselves on regional issues. Three great regional powers—China, India, and Japan—were emerging, and by the 1990s they had even become global powers. The role of Japan within regional institutions, including ESCAP, was increasing. During this period, the climate for regional cooperation was far better than in the 1960s. When the Cold War ended in 1989, ESCAP took the opportunity to enlarge its membership into Central Asia.[7] Although it had been unstable in the 1940s, most of the region in the 1990s could claim a degree of political stability unique in its history.

Economic Context

Complementing its political instability in the 1940s was the stark poverty which could be observed throughout the region. Japan had a per-capita income of only about US$100 in the late 1940s. Other countries were even poorer. Agriculture was the major occupation of the vast majority of people, and food security was the primary concern of most governments in the region. Agricultural development was therefore their major task. There was little manufacturing, and only Japan could be considered an industrial country. China and India could claim only modest levels of industrial activity. There was little intraregional trade at the time, and trading patterns were skewed in favor of the West. In these early years, most Asian economies were similar and not complementary. Economic diversification lay in the future. From the 1940s to the 1960s, a major concern of ECAFE was to stimulate "induced complementarities."

In the 1950s and 1960s and even well into the 1970s, most countries of the region were aiming to develop their economies largely on the basis of dirigiste models of development. The state was considered to be the central actor. The prescriptions for economic development were either based on the Russian experience, suitably modified, or on the Indian model, which, although it was predicated on central planning, allowed the private sector an important role. Planning was the fashion in this period: ECAFE itself believed in it and, through its publications, promoted policies largely based on the Indian model of planning. ECAFE promoted regional integration and regional cooperation as an important adjunct to these national planning models.[8]

A major economic transformation in the region can be observed from about the 1970s. By that time, countries in the region were more comfortable with each other and the opportunities for enhanced intraregional economic transactions were clearly evident. Japan was emerging as a global economic power and an economic powerhouse of the region. China and India had achieved high levels of industrialization. The Korean peninsula was also becoming highly industrialized. Many Southeast Asian countries pursued their own policies for economic development and sought to move away from state-focused planning models toward market-oriented approaches and greater global integration. There was an enriching diversity of economic experience within the region. By the 1990s, with the end of the Cold War, Asia's role in global politics and in the global economy was rapidly changing. There were now at least three regional powers—China, India, and Japan—with a strong global outreach that were on the verge of emerging in the front rank of global political and economic power.[9] These dramatic changes of the last two decades also influenced ESCAP's activities. In its economic prescriptions, it moved away from economic planning and toward a more open regionalism, taking account of the rapidly advancing phenomenon of globalization. ESCAP today is situated in a world totally different from the one in which it was conceived.

The UN System

The UN system has changed considerably over the last fifty years, and this has been a major factor in bringing about change in the commission. There was no systemic provision within the UN system for regional commissions covering the entire world. Instead, they emerged one after the other, and now it is the norm that every part of the world be covered by a regional commission.

At the time of ECAFE's birth, the UN system was a relatively lean organization. The specialized agencies were all there, except for the United Nations Industrial Development Organization (UNIDO). Apart from the United Nations Children's Fund (UNICEF), other funds and programs had not yet been established. The United Nations Development Programme (UNDP) was established in the early 1960s, although its predecessors include the Expanded Program of Technical Assistance (EPTA) and the Technical Assistance Board (TAB). The United Nations Conference on Trade and Development (UNCTAD) was established only in the mid-1960s and the United Nations Fund for Population Activities (UNFPA) in the 1970s. These are major partners of ESCAP now, but they did not exist in the 1950s.

The commission is a generalist organization, addressing a range of tasks over a wide range of development activities. The relationship with specialized agencies is therefore a vital factor in its effective operation. There is some rivalry and some overlap between the commission and the specialized agencies. One of its first concerns in the early 1950s was with agriculture and food security, an area of major concern to its member countries, but also one to which ESCAP has probably made the least contribution. This is largely due to conflicts of interest between the Food and Agriculture Organization (FAO) and the commission. The FAO was unwilling to work alongside ECAFE in the field of agriculture: It established its own regional office in Bangkok and barely cooperated with ECAFE. The outcome has been that the commission has virtually phased itself out of agriculture and food security issues. The experience with the FAO is exceptional, however.[10] The commission has had closer working relationships with the United Nations Educational, Scientific, and Cultural Organization (UNESCO) and the International Labor Organization (ILO), especially in the late 1980s, when it became active in the field of human resources development.

A major influence on the commission has been UNCTAD. It has worked closely with UNCTAD on international trade issues and there is a fairly clear division of labor between the two organizations. UNCTAD focuses on global issues and works with ESCAP to develop a regional dimension and regional perspectives on international trade. Both organizations appear to view themselves as complementary bodies.[11] ESCAP has also developed a sound working relationship with UNIDO. Trade and industry were two areas in which ESCAP was actively engaged prior to the establishment of UNCTAD and UNIDO. It had built up its own track record within its committee structure on trade and industry. However, UNCTAD's agendas and perspectives have heavily influenced the commission's analysis and prescriptions from the late 1960s. Similarly, population was an important area of activity of the commission prior to the founding of the UNFPA. As will be seen later, the commission was in the forefront of population issues at a time when they were not considered appropriate for international action. With the establishment of the UNFPA, appropriate working relationships have developed between the two bodies. Regrettably, with UNFPA's establishment, ESCAP lost its autonomous and initiatory role in population issues.

For most of its existence, the regional commission and the UNDP, and its predecessors (the EPTA and TAB), have worked together closely, primarily in implementing intercountry activities. The UNDP supported most of ECAFE's initiatives in the 1960s and 1970s to create an infrastructure of regional institutions. ESCAP and other regional commissions were empowered by General Assembly Resolution 32/197 of 1977[12] to begin executing agency functions for regional projects for the UNDP and the UNFPA. This was a turning point in

ESCAP's history. It became largely an operational agency undertaking technical assistance, primarily on behalf of the UNDP, although this was to change
later. In the 1990s, with changing orientations in the UNDP, its collaboration
with ESCAP almost ceased at the operational level.[13]

UN General Assembly Resolution 32/197

UN General Assembly Resolution 32/197 of 1977 had a dramatic impact on
ESCAP. It designated ESCAP and other regional commissions as the main
regional economic and social development centers within the UN system for
their respective regions. It also provided the authority for regional commissions to function as executing agencies for programs and projects funded by
UN agencies and bilateral donors. Member countries did not express any reservations about the possible implications of this resolution on the autonomy
and indigenous nature of ESCAP.

At the time, they probably did not visualize its far-reaching implications.
Since then, ESCAP has been particularly concerned with the mobilization
of extrabudgetary resources. It is now largely a technical assistance agency.
It is also more integrated with the UN system, implementing many activities
which either precede or follow UN global decision-making processes. The
room for ESCAP to maneuver and make its own decisions and programs of
work has been significantly diminished. ESCAP's 40-year history, published
in 1987, had this to say of ESCAP's function: "ESCAP's most important roles
are as a provider of technical assistance, an intergovernmental forum, a leading research facility and a development information source."[14] It also speaks
of ESCAP acting as the regional counterpart of global programs under the
responsibility of central UN agencies and organizations. In other words, it
is the regional department of the UN, taking its directions from the global
system.

Regional and Subregional Bodies

In 1947, ECAFE was the only organization for the region. There was the
prospect that if it were not for ECAFE, the governments of the region might
have established their own regional organization outside the UN system, as
was the case in Latin America and Africa. The Asian Relations Conference of
1947 considered such an organization but it is probable that ECAFE preempted
its emergence. Since that time, many other regional and subregional bodies
have been established, and they have clearly influenced the activities and the
role of ECAFE.

The ADB was established by ECAFE in the 1960s. At first it was under ECAFE's shadow but it now overshadows ESCAP and is a more influential organization in the region. The ADB has developed into a major multilateral financial institution. Governments of the region attach significant importance to it because it is a critical source of financing, and they are more engaged with ADB than with ESCAP at higher and more substantive levels. Its influence on economic policymaking in the region is clearly evident, and Japan, the major economic player in the region, attaches great importance to the ADB. The ADB has strong research and analytical capacities,[15] produces high-quality publications, and is now a serious rival and competitor of ESCAP.

The growth of subregional organizations has also had an important impact on ESCAP. The Association of Southeast Asian Nations (ASEAN) is the most important of these subregional organizations. In the early days of ASEAN and well into the 1980s, ESCAP had little contact with ASEAN. This was largely due to ESCAP's philosophy at the time—that it should focus on regional instead of subregional issues.[16] In a way, ESCAP largely neglected these subregional organizations. Since then the policy has changed and there is greater interaction with them. ESCAP now feels it has a role in stimulating inter-subregional cooperation by bringing together the various subregional bodies in the region.

ESCAP is also more inclined to adopt subregional approaches in its activities,[17] as regionwide approaches with such a large membership are probably untenable, especially in operational activities. However, ESCAP has missed many opportunities by not being involved with non-UN subregional organizations at their birth.

An Evolving Membership

In 1947, ECAFE could hardly be described as a regional organization: It had nine member countries, of which only three were from the region. There was considerable acrimony in those early days about the membership of the organization.[18] It was only in 1960 that ECAFE became a truly regional organization that expressed the wishes of regional member countries. In 1960, in the Lahore Declaration, member countries agreed that only countries in the region should decide on substantive issues and that non-regional members, while they could express their views and opinions, would refrain from exercising their vote.[19] Late in the 1960s, it was also decided that Australia and New Zealand would be considered regional members, thereby adding to the developed-country dimension of the organization, hitherto represented only by Japan. ECAFE's membership evolved from nine member countries in 1947 to twenty-nine by 1973 (when ECAFE changed its name). By 2000, ESCAP's membership had grown to more than fifty countries.

These changes in membership have had a considerable effect on ESCAP's policies and activities. In the first two decades of ECAFE, the South Asia region was the dominant influence. ECAFE's first three executive secretaries—and they were the only executive secretaries of ECAFE—were all from the Indian subcontinent. Since then, the focus has changed. There is a greater involvement with Northeast and Southeast Asia and with the Pacific. A Pacific regional center has been established.

In the 1990s, with the addition of member countries from Central Asia, there is another new geographical dimension. The Central Asian countries have economies in transition from centrally planned to market-oriented economies and ESCAP is therefore required to address these transitional issues. Whether ESCAP as a body is now too large and unwieldy is an issue worth consideration. With a membership which includes half the world's population, it is certainly in another league from the other regional commissions, at least in terms of population.

The Early Days: Creation and Consolidation

Although today regional commissions appear to be natural and integral components of the UN system, there was nothing inevitable about their establishment in the mid-1940s. Regional commissions that covered the entire globe were not viewed as a necessary part of the UN vision. Once the Economic Commission for Europe (ECE) was established, it gradually became inevitable that other regions might also require a similar mechanism. Even then, there was no clear concept of what a regional commission might do apart from addressing the short-term needs of reconstruction and rehabilitation in the aftermath of war.

In these early days, the regional commissions were not necessarily considered permanent organs within the UN system. In the immediate aftermath of the establishment of ECAFE, there were considerable disputes over various aspects of its organization and function, its mandates, its membership, its structure, and even its location. The arguments at the time also reflected the divisions within the world and within the region, especially those resulting from the emerging Cold War and the tensions emanating from a resurgent Asia, where there were various conflicts between colonial powers and emerging nations and among the emerging nations themselves. The experience of ECAFE in this early decade is particularly enlightening; it was probably the only period of its history when the issues surrounding it achieved importance in mainstream international relations.

The debates surrounding ECAFE at its foundation also need to be placed in the context of the ferment of ideas that was clearly evident, both at the global and the regional level.[20] Both developed and developing countries (although these terms were not yet in vogue) were groping for ideas and mechanisms for the establishment of a new world order. The UN had been created and there were several specialized agencies. The Bretton Woods institutions were established. It was also perceived that mechanisms would need to be created to channel assistance to poorer and war-torn countries. The Marshall Plan had generated tremendous excitement, and other regions felt that such mechanisms as the Organization for European Economic Cooperation (OEEC) should not be confined to Europe. For the Asian region itself, although a little later, there was the Colombo Plan, which was adopted in 1951 by seven independent Asian countries in the Commonwealth and later extended to other former British colonies in Asia and the Pacific. Although it was not the Marshall Plan, it pointed in the same direction. Estimates were made of the capital and technical assistance needs of the Asian region. At the time of the birth of ECAFE, there was a distinct hope that ECAFE might play a key role in channeling assistance from developed countries to the Asian region. It was clearly seen as having a development-assistance dimension, at least in the minds of the top officials of ECAFE and in most developing-country governments in the region. Apart from these global and North-South considerations, within Asia itself there was a growing demand for better understanding and cooperation among the countries of the region. The Asian Relations Conference (New Delhi, March 1947) was probably the first time that the Asian nations had met. It was a major and even a dramatic event at a time when international conferences were rare events. If it were not for ECAFE, it is entirely feasible that the Asian Relations Conference would have led to the creation of an intergovernmental organization outside the UN system.[21]

The origins of ECAFE are to be found in the concerns expressed within the UN in New York about the urgent need for economic reconstruction in war-devastated countries. Europe received priority in this regard, partly due to the fact that European countries were more articulate and they represented themselves, while in Asia there were only three countries (China, India, Philippines) that were sovereign states and members of the UN and had the capacity to express the demands of the region. The Temporary Sub-Commission on the Economic Reconstruction of Devastated Areas, established by the UN's Economic and Social Council (ECOSOC) in 1946, consisted of twenty members, of which twelve were from Europe, two were from North America, two were from the Far East (Australia and New Zealand), three were from Asia (China, India, and the Philippines), and one was from Africa (Ethiopia). No wonder, then, that Europe's concerns were uppermost and Asian concerns were relegated to the background.[22]

This, however, was only part of the explanation. The working group established for Asia and the Far East, which had only a few Asian member countries, was extremely slow in presenting its reports. In its report to the subcommission, the working group for Europe proposed the creation of an Economic Commission for Europe, among other recommendations.[23] This is probably the genesis of all regional commissions. When the Second Committee of the UN (on which there was a majority of developing countries) discussed the Temporary Sub-Commission's reports, these developing countries argued strongly for regional commissions for other regions. China was particularly active in this regard. An important argument for the establishment of a regional commission for Asia was that the United Nations Relief and Rehabilitation Administration (UNRRA), which was responsible for relief work in Asia, was about to be disbanded and a substitute institution was required to continue its tasks. China had been one of the major recipients of UNRRA assistance, and its needs were continuing and widespread. While the European members were not inclined to favor a regional commission for Asia, Latin America offered strong support. The General Assembly Resolution 46/1 of December 1946 approved the establishment of ECAFE.[24]

There was another aspect to ECAFE's establishment. Although the General Assembly approved it in principle, it was ECOSOC that established ECAFE in March 1947.[25] While the General Assembly's decision was guided largely by the relief, rehabilitation, and reconstruction needs of the region, ECOSOC's decision, based on the report of the working group for Asia and the Far East, had an extra dimension. The working group felt that mechanisms were required to promote and coordinate reconstruction in the broadest sense and that therefore it was necessary to bring international aid activities into the region within a common framework. ECAFE could be the mechanism for this. In these early days, there is thus the clear impression that ECAFE was seen as a coordinating body for development assistance in the region.

The Politics of Membership

At the First Session of ECAFE, held in Shanghai in June 1947, there were only ten member countries—four Asian (China, India, Philippines, and Thailand) and six non-Asian countries (Australia, France, the Netherlands, the

Soviet Union, the United Kingdom, and the United States). It was therefore obvious that ECAFE was an organization for the region but not of the region. It took a few more years for it to emerge as a truly representative regional body. In these early days, when most countries were still not self-governing or even members of the UN, other ways had to be found to include more regional members, and there was considerable debate for about three to four years over these membership issues.[26]

Broadly, there were two views regarding membership. The United Kingdom suggested that non-self-governing countries could become associate members without voting rights. Countries such as India wanted the countries of the ECAFE region to be represented in ECAFE as full members that were nominated by their own national governments. The Soviet Union proposed that countries which were not members of the UN could be associated with ECAFE in a consultative capacity, a position not dissimilar to the one they took at the time concerning the relations of a divided Germany to the ECE. The UN Legal Department more or less agreed with the United Kingdom's view that full membership could not be accorded to non-self-governing countries, as full membership could be granted only when the obligations of UN membership were also accepted. ECAFE therefore adopted the associate member approach. There then followed the other issue of how to nominate the representatives of non-self-governing territories. The Indian position was that the nomination must be made by the territory itself. The United Kingdom's position was that the power responsible for international relations (in other words, the colonial power) should make the nomination. The problem was overcome when France, the Netherlands, and the United Kingdom immediately nominated most of their colonies for associate membership (North Borneo, Brunei and Sarawak, Burma, Ceylon, the Indochinese Federation, Hong Kong, the Malayan Union and Singapore, and the Netherlands Indies). This list of territories is a virtual roll call that is now a part of Asia's history. It should be noted that Japan was not yet a member of ECAFE, as it continued to be an occupied power until 1950.

There were also disputes regarding associate membership. France proposed Cambodia and Laos for associate membership, but the Soviet Union questioned the representative character of their governments. The admission of Burma, Ceylon, Hong Kong, Malaya, and British Borneo was also opposed by the Soviet Union on the grounds that these non-self-governing territories should make their own applications for membership rather than being proposed by a colonial power and moreover that they should only be admitted in a consultative capacity. The most vexing membership problem arose with regard to the Republic of Indonesia, which the colonial power (the Netherlands) did not recognize. While countries such as India, Pakistan, the Philippines, and the Soviet Union supported its inclusion, China abstained, mainly because of the harsh treatment of the Chinese in Indonesia. After further acrimony, the Republic of Indonesia was admitted to associate membership in December 1948 along with an entity defined as "the rest of Indonesia."

The Netherlands opposed this action vehemently and withdrew from the commission's sessions that year.[27] The admission of the Republic of Indonesia to ECAFE was an important victory for the Indonesian nationalist cause. However, by May 1950 Indonesia became independent, was admitted to the UN, and became a full member of ECAFE. The admission of Vietnam also created significant tensions, which were more ideological in nature; even Asian nations were opposed to its admission. There was also the problem of China; the Chinese People's Republic had been firmly established in October 1949. Every commission session up to 1957 saw formal motions from the Soviet Union to include the People's Republic of China, but they were not successful. Japan entered ECAFE after the signing of the Treaty of Peace in San Francisco in 1951. The membership of ECAFE was expanding, and by the late 1950s it was a truly regional organization. Countries which had joined as associate members were now full members. In 1958, Iran applied to join ECAFE, in the absence of a commission for West Asia. Many regional countries were unhappy with Iran's application, and although it was accepted, ECAFE was alerted to the danger of any further extension of its geographical scope. This is intriguing in the light of the admission of Central Asia in the 1990s. In the late 1950s, it was recognized that ECAFE should not overextend itself, but that is exactly what it did.

For ECAFE to be a genuinely regional body, its regional members should be the determining influence in its decision-making processes. In view of the membership pattern in its early days, ECAFE was far from being a truly regional organization:

> The dominating role of the Western powers might have been more tolerable to Asian delegates if it had been more constructive. In fact, it was essentially negative. They consistently opposed proposals for extending ECAFE's functions beyond those of collecting information and publishing studies. Only very reluctantly did they capitulate to the Asian demand for a committee on industry and trade. They poured cold water on all ideas for facilitating an expansion of intra-regional trade. They opposed the development of heavy industry in Asia, on the grounds that iron and steel supplies were becoming more plentiful and cheaper in Europe and the United States. Indeed, so equivocal did their approach to Asian industrialization seem, that the Philippines urged the Commission in

1950 to put itself on record as clearly favoring the region's industrial development. In Asian eyes, their outlook mocked the purpose of ECAFE as an instrument of Asian aspirations.[28]

This was the type of situation that demanded a vigorous response from
Asian countries if ECAFE was to be representative of their interests. The executive secretary submitted a memorandum to the 1951 ECAFE session in
Lahore proposing that non-regional members should exercise restraint in
voting on matters predominantly concerning the region and not directly involving member countries outside the region. This led ultimately to the Lahore
Agreement, whereby it was agreed that non-regional members would refrain
from voting on proposals indigenous to the region. As noted in the ECAFE
report to ECOSOC:

> Member governments feel that the time has come when clearer recognition
> should be given to the principle that member countries belonging to the re-
> gion should take their own decisions in the Commission on their own eco-
> nomic problems; and that in doing so, they should take full account of the
> views of the associate members in the region, to be ascertained when not known
> by referring any specific resolution to a committee. In pursuance of this prin-
> ciple, the member countries of the Commission not in the region would be
> willing as a general rule to refrain from using their votes in opposition to eco-
> nomic proposals predominantly concerning the region, which have the sup-
> port of a majority of the countries of the region.[29]

This decision finally established ECAFE as a genuinely regional organization,
representing the interests of its regional member countries.

Expanding Mandates and Tasks

As noted earlier, when ECAFE was established there was no reason to believe that it would be a permanent instrument of the UN system. Therefore,
the immediate focus was on urgent issues confronting the region, especially
reconstruction.[30] From the start, however, the region's member and associate
member countries had a larger view of ECAFE as a permanent regional organization, concerned not only with short-term issues but also with long-term
and structural aspects of economic organization in the region. The executive
secretary, P. S. Lokanathan, certainly hoped to increase the involvement of
ECAFE in the critical development issues of the region.

In 1947, at the Second Session of ECAFE held in Baguio (Philippines), he
proposed that the commission examine a range of issues relating to food and

agriculture, industry, energy, transport, and monetary issues. In particular, he suggested a joint ECAFE/FAO committee on food and agricultural production.[31] The Western countries were not inclined to support the expansion of ECAFE's mandate in these directions. They warned that ECAFE should not usurp the functions of other UN bodies. This has been a recurrent theme in the relations between generalist bodies (such as ECAFE) and specialized agencies. However, at the 1948 session, ECAFE was entrusted with the tasks of reporting on industrial development and transport plans in the region and taking joint action with other agencies in fields such as agriculture and technical training.[32] It was also given authority to establish a Trade Promotion Section within the secretariat and to address statistical issues in the region. The publication of an annual economic survey of Asia and the Far East was also approved.[33]

At this time, there was also an effort by the regional member countries to involve ECAFE in their pursuit of external development assistance. The report of the Working Party on Industrial Development had estimated that national economic development programs in the region would require around US$14 billion over a five-year period, of which about half was in foreign exchange. Many countries saw this estimate as the basis for a kind of Marshall Plan for the region. The Western powers did not view these proposals with favor.

There were other occasions on which regional member countries preferred ECAFE to play a role in external development assistance. They believed that ECAFE could help governments prepare proposals for financing by the World Bank. Western countries were opposed to this suggestion. With the establishment of the United Nations Expanded Programme for Technical Assistance (EPTA, predecessor of the UNDP), there was also a prospect for ECAFE to channel requests for technical assistance to member countries. This proposal of the executive secretary was discouraged by UN headquarters and even the commission itself was not supportive. However, the commission and UN headquarters both saw a role for ECAFE in EPTA activities; it could help governments formulate proposals for technical assistance.

Ultimately, none of these proposals were implemented, and ECAFE, like other regional commissions, was barely engaged in any intermediary role in UN technical assistance.[34] There is some evidence that the countries in the region itself were not favorably inclined toward making ECAFE a technical assistance intermediary. This is an illustration of governments taking up contrary positions on the same issue in different forums, partly due to conflicts of interest among government departments.

At the same time, Western countries were averse to establishing permanent subsidiary bodies of ECAFE and instead relied on working groups and working parties. The executive secretary's proposal to set up a committee on industry was not accepted. What is more intriguing was the fate of the proposal for a committee on technical training. This was not approved, largely because of the intervention of the ILO, which informed ECAFE that it planned to establish a tripartite labor-power committee for Asia and to open an Asian field office. This is an early example of a constant and continuing irritant to ECAFE, namely, the specialized agencies establishing their own regional presence. The first permanent subsidiary body to be set up within ECAFE was the Committee on Industry and Trade.[35] The committee reflected the fact that ECAFE was no longer concerned with reconstruction and that its focus was shifting to economic development. Along with the establishment of this committee, other committees and subcommittees were progressively established— on transport, on energy, on iron and steel. A Bureau of Flood Control was also established.[36]

The late 1940s and early 1950s was also the time when ECAFE was searching for a home of its own. Initially, ECOSOC declared Shanghai to be the temporary home for ECAFE. At the Second Session of ECAFE in 1947 in the Philippines, the host country proposed that Baguio should be the headquarters, but China insisted that it should remain in Shanghai. In 1948, Malaya (supported by the United Kingdom) proposed Singapore as the venue,[37] Pakistan suggested Karachi, and there were other offers from Burma, Ceylon, India, and Thailand. Because of civil unrest in China, ECAFE had to move from Shanghai and settled in Bangkok, once again as a "temporary" arrangement. In 1951, when ECOSOC established ECAFE as a permanent body, it also decided that it should be located in Bangkok "until such time as the site of the office of the United Nations in Asia and the Far East shall be determined."[38] Since then, it has remained in Bangkok, which is now its permanent home.[39]

A Culture of Regionalism

The commission's primary contribution has been to develop a culture of regionalism in the Asia-Pacific region. Although it is less emphasized these days, the theme of regional cooperation dominated the first twenty-five years of ECAFE. Since then, that focus has been somewhat diluted by the emphasis on technical assistance, although it remains one of the two pillars of ESCAP activity. Most technical cooperation involves some elements of regional cooperation, and the analytical work undertaken also offers regional perspectives which should lead to improved policymaking for regional cooperation.

However, it is the work of the first twenty-five years in creating that culture of regional cooperation that has been most valuable. In the 1940s, there was hardly any experience of such cooperation, and ECAFE was therefore the path-finder in promoting it. The contribution of the commission over its fifty-year history might best be explored under three themes—prescribing policy and developing common positions for the region, building an autonomous infra-structure of regional institutions, and creating its own institutional machin-ery for regional dialogue.

Regional Policy Development

When the countries of the region emerged as nation-states, freed from their colonial constraints, their primary aim was to develop policies for their na-tional development. Their external economic policies were largely focused upon trade and aid, and addressing these issues primarily meant developing working relationships with their main trade and aid partners, which were almost exclusively the developed countries. In the 1940s and 1950s, there were no distinctive regional policies for these new nation-states. The important role ECAFE played therefore needs to be seen in this context. Until about the late 1960s, only ECAFE had a strong commitment to developing regional poli-cies and stimulating its member states to consider and develop their own re-gional approaches to economic development.

The development of regional policies has been a continuing task of ESCAP, which it has undertaken in several ways.[40] First, its annual survey has addressed the question of feasible forms of regional economic cooperation. Second, it has done considerable analytical work on aspects of regional cooperation, both broadly on the economic front and at the sectoral level.[41] Third, the com-mission has been the mechanism to transmit and translate globally agreed-upon agendas and perspectives, generated largely within the UN framework, so that they are further developed in a regional context. Fourth, the commis-sion has helped member countries develop common positions in relation to global issues.

The 50-year period can be divided into roughly four phases of policy de-velopment. The early days of ECAFE, until about the late 1960s, were domi-nated by planning based on the Indian and Russian models and were also probably influenced by the types of socialist planning undertaken in the West.[42] This was also a period when ECAFE's policy analysis was starting to be placed in the context of the international development strategies of the UN, a trend which continued well into later years.

The second period, starting from about the early 1970s, was largely influ-enced by the issues and the thinking of UNCTAD, which was at the forefront of the North-South debate of the time. From about the early 1980s, a third phase can be identified when ESCAP was influenced by UN policy orientations on social and environmental issues. Starting in about the mid-1970s, ECAFE's strong focus on economics was diluted by these new agendas. Since the early 1990s, ESCAP's economic thinking has moved in a more market-oriented direction and toward a more open regionalism. It has become highly sensitive to World Trade Organization (WTO) issues; now, instead of UNCTAD, the predominant influence appears to be the WTO.

In ECAFE literature from the 1940s to the 1960s, especially the annual *Economic Survey of Asia and the Far East* and other associated publications, it is clear that ECAFE's regional policy prescriptions centered upon the state playing the lead role in economic development. A major concern was savings and foreign exchange and, on the basis of the two-gap model,[43] ECAFE continually estimated the shortages for the region. It emphasized public investment and saw industrialization as the appropriate strategy for creating employment.

ECAFE was partial to heavy industry. It advocated protectionist policies for industry, and public enterprises received priority in its policy- and capacity-building efforts. The developed countries made continuing demands for tariff preferences. Regional planning was needed to harmonize industrial policies and thereby stimulate intraregional trade in manufactured goods. One of the aspects ECAFE focused on was the potential for trade between Japan (which was emerging as an industrial power) and the rest of Asia. During this period, although social investments (education and health) were considered to be useful, they were justified largely by their contribution to economic growth. ECAFE was continually preoccupied with foreign-aid issues and argued for improvements in quantity and quality; it was also seeking a role for itself as a channel for some types of external assistance or, at least, involvement in various aspects of project implementation.

Within the UN system, the dominant concern in the 1970s was with issues relating to the new international economic order (NIEO). There were also major global conferences on food and agrarian reform and a strong emphasis on employment, such as in the World Employment Programme of the ILO. The influence of these concerns and activities was widely felt in ECAFE/ESCAP and in the discussions of the commission and its subsidiary bodies. Especially when addressing NIEO issues—and particularly with regard to primary commodities—UNCTAD was the dominant influence. The commission aligned itself largely with UNCTAD perspectives on North-South issues and there was a detectable bias against the prescriptions of the World Bank and the International Monetary Fund (IMF). ECAFE/ESCAP ideas during this period were largely derived from other parts of the UN system, particularly from

UNCTAD. In the area of primary commodities, one of its main concerns was to translate UNCTAD recommendations for producer cooperation into practical forms of regional cooperation. During this period ESCAP intensified its efforts to stimulate cooperative arrangements among regional producers of products such as natural rubber, rice, and timber. ESCAP's view appears to have been that regional cooperative arrangements among primary producers would contribute to the strengthening of producer cooperation at a more global level, although this assumption has not generally been borne out by experience. ESCAP's annual survey for 1976, for example, focused on regional cooperation and emphasized collective action at the regional level within a framework of collective self-reliance. The 1970s also witnessed ESCAP's continued engagement with food and rural development issues, which were again a reflection of the work of global conferences at the time.

Since about the early 1980s, ESCAP's policy engagement has broadened to include social and environmental issues.[44] ESCAP has facilitated the development of regional positions at various global summits and in UN discussions on human development, the environment, population, social issues, gender, habitat, children, and so on.

A new dimension to regional cooperation emerged as a result of these activities. For example, ESCAP initiated the publication of a report on the state of the environment in the Asia-Pacific region, which has appeared at regular intervals and has been useful in enhancing environmental awareness in the region. Similarly, ESCAP's policy analysis of women and of gender issues in the region was stimulated by the increasing emphasis the UN system placed on these issues. Most of the policy analysis was undertaken at the national level.

However, unlike regional economic cooperation, there was no significant basis for practical cooperation among countries at the regional level. Since 1957, ESCAP has included a special theme in the second part of its annual survey. Of the forty-four surveys published between 1957 and 2000, there are only three in which topics other than economic issues have been addressed. ESCAP's key role continues to be in the field of economic development.

In the 1990s, there was a major change in ESCAP's policy prescription and policy analysis. With much of the rest of the world, it has moved toward a more market-oriented approach to economic development. More emphasis is now placed on the role of the private sector, foreign investment, and the liberalization of trade. ESCAP was actively engaged in helping member governments prepare for the Uruguay Round of Multilateral Trade Negotiations. Since the establishment of the WTO, a major concern of ESCAP has been to assist member governments in exploiting the opportunities it presents and enabling them to conform with its provisions.

ESCAP has also focused on financial issues in recent years, but its thinking on a new international financial architecture largely reflects the views of the UN system elsewhere. The experience of the East Asian model, both before and after the financial crisis of 1997, has had an important influence on ESCAP thinking in recent years.

It is important to emphasize that ECAFE, and more particularly ESCAP, has avoided issues that would create political differences among its members in its policy recommendations. It represents a heterogeneous region and has focused largely on providing analysis of and information about regional economic trends, whether it be in trade, investment, technology, the environment, gender, or other issues, rather than prescriptions of its own. It has largely confined its recommendations about economic ideas and policies to translating into regional terms the global policies advocated elsewhere in the UN system, whether it be the UN General Assembly or organizations such as UNCTAD. It has also avoided any conflict with the ADB on policy issues. Regional economic cooperation has been ECAFE/ESCAP's primary focus; its analysis and proposals tend to look upon what is positive in such forms of cooperation without necessarily examining in depth why countries in the region are not actually collaborating more closely with each other.

Creating Autonomous Regional Institutions

The first fifteen years of ECAFE was largely a period of consolidation. Beginning in the early 1960s and continuing for a period of about ten years, there was a period of intense creative activity during which the commission pioneered the establishment of a wide range of institutions for the Asian region. It was thus creating a regional Asian institutional infrastructure. This intense spell of activity was driven by its executive secretary at the time, U Nyun of Burma (1957–1973). The first ministerial conference on regional economic cooperation held in Manila in 1963 adopted what is known as the Manila Resolution, which authorized ECAFE to explore a broad range of institutional arrangements to stimulate regional cooperation. It called for institutional arrangements for trade liberalization, export promotion, primary-commodity price stabilization, and the establishment of an Asian Development Bank (ADB), among others.[45]

The most outstanding achievement of ECAFE was the establishment of the ADB.[46] It is now a major multilateral financing institution and has very little contact with ESCAP. In the 1960s it was different, though; it was ECAFE that proposed the establishment of the ADB in the early years of that decade. For a brief period the proposal was frowned upon by some of the Western

powers and was only discreetly mooted by the executive secretary, who kept it
in the forefront of his quiet diplomacy. In 1965, at ECAFE's twenty-first session in Wellington, New Zealand, a resolution was adopted on the ADB. The
Secretary-General of the UN at the time, U Thant, was also Burmese and a
friend of U Nyun. Their common Asian and country background led them to
view the ADB as a potentially important institution which they should do
everything to support. U Thant sought the assistance of President Lyndon
Johnson. Eugene Black, the president of the World Bank, also extended his support, and Under-Secretary-General for Economic and Social Affairs, Philippe
de Seynes, at the UN also gave strong support and used his good offices to
convince European countries. Japan was then emerging as an important Asian
regional power, and its support for a regional bank was decisive. The ADB
was finally established in 1965. Until the early 1970s, the ADB reported to the
annual sessions of ECAFE. It is clear from the resolutions adopted by ECAFE
that at that time a close working relationship was envisaged between the two
institutions and that the ADB would be inclined to seek ECAFE's assistance
in developing proposals for financing.

An important initiative of ECAFE was the establishment of the Asian Institute for Economic Development and Planning (AIEDP) in 1964. The objective of this institute was to create a strong cadre of high-quality economic
planning professionals and to undertake research and provide advisory services. It was described as a "regional staff college for senior officials, who help
to formulate and administer policies, programmes and projects of economic
and social development in their countries."[47] Over a period of about ten years,
the AIEDP proceeded to develop courses and to provide a wide range of training in the region, and by the end of 1973 it anticipated moving from its temporary headquarters in Bangkok to a new campus in Singapore. The prospects
for the AIEDP looked promising in the early 1970s, but by the end of the
decade its time was running out. In 1970, another institution was established,
the Asian Centre for Development Administration (ACDA),[48] the proposals
for which were drawn up by a UNDP/UN/ECAFE mission. The objective of
this center was to train development managers. By the early 1980s, the AIEDP
and the ACDA had merged to create the Asian-Pacific Development Centre
(APDC), located in Kuala Lumpur.

In the early days of the AIEDP, ECAFE saw it as the training arm of the
ADB. There was a significant complementarity which could have been exploited. But as the paths of the ADB and ECAFE diverged, any such linkage
became impractical. It is intriguing to note that nearly twenty-five years later,
the ADB established its own Asian Development Institute in Tokyo. The merged
APDC has continued to survive on a small budget; it lacks the resources to

undertake any coherent set of activities. Economic development issues have been largely relegated to the background[49] and the region's training needs are met by others, particularly through arrangements with bilateral donors.

In 1970, as a result of ECAFE's efforts, the Asian Statistical Institute (ASI)[50] was born and located in Tokyo. The Asian region needed trained statisticians, and the institute was one of the mechanisms for mounting a major training effort. The institute was strongly supported by the UNDP. Above all, it has had the continued support and blessing of the government of Japan. For over thirty years, it has helped governments in the region build their statistical capacities. At each annual session of ESCAP, it has reported on its work programs and the proceedings of both the annual sessions and the Committee on Statistics demonstrate that the institute is considered an important entity in regional cooperation. After nearly twenty-five years, UNDP support has almost ceased, and the institute has mobilized a modest amount of resources from its member countries. The support of the government of Japan, however, has been the key to its survival as an effective institution.[51]

Two other significant innovations of the early 1970s were the Asian Clearing Union (ACU) in 1973 and the Bangkok Agreement on Trade in 1976. The ACU is a mechanism for monetary cooperation and has a membership of ten countries in the region. It provides for the multilateral settlement of payments, and currency transactions cleared through it have increased to about US$1 billion, thus reducing to some degree the pressure on the foreign-exchange reserves of its member countries. What the ACU also illustrates is that it is extremely difficult to expand the membership of this type of organization to a larger number of countries in the region. The Bangkok Agreement started with seven member countries and provides tariff preferences on selected products for its membership. It is only a modest effort in regional cooperation, although it holds prospects for further expansion.[52]

Several other initiatives of the commission in the field of trade and finance deserve notice. A noteworthy proposal, which never materialized in spite of early enthusiasm, was for the establishment of an Asian reserve bank (1972). The proposals were drafted by Robert Triffin, the architect of the European Payments Union. In the late 1990s, there were proposals from outside ESCAP for the creation of an Asian monetary fund and for various other exchange facilities among central banks. The stillborn proposal for an Asian reserve bank, however, was a lost opportunity for the region, and ESCAP is no longer in the picture in developing regional financial and monetary initiatives. The Asian Re-Insurance Corporation was established in 1979 to reduce the foreign-exchange outflows of member countries for the payment of insurance premiums, an objective which has been relatively successful.[53]

ECAFE also encouraged, and was active in establishing, several regional commodity bodies: the Asian Coconut Community (1969),[54] the Association of Natural Rubber Producing Countries (1970), and the Pepper Community (1972), which later became the International Pepper Community. Another institution, the Asian Rice Trade Fund,[55] was set up in 1973 but failed to mobilize adequate support for its continued functioning. ESCAP also established the Centre for Grains, Pulses, Roots and Tubers (CGPRT)[56] in Indonesia in the late 1970s, which has continued to function despite continuing financial constraints.

There were other regional initiatives from the commission. One of the most imaginative was the establishment of the Mekong Committee,[57] consisting of four riparian countries (Khmer Republic, Laos, Thailand, and Vietnam), to manage the resources of the Mekong Basin. This was probably one of the first international arrangements for the management of water resources. The Mekong Committee has now been transformed into the Mekong River Commission, although it is set up outside of ESCAP. There was also the Asian Highway as well as the Trans-Asian Railway and the Asian Telecommunications Network. In the late 1970s, the Asian-Pacific Centre for the Transfer of Technology was established in India.[58]

This phase of creating a regional institutional infrastructure, which characterized the 1960s and 1970s (it virtually ceased after 1973), was unique in the annals of the commission. The initiatives for it were due to the active leadership of the then executive secretary. The establishment and operation of these institutions was also partly due to the financial support provided by the UNDP, which was then actively engaged with ECAFE in searching for promising regional projects and programs. This was a situation that did not last beyond the 1980s. Could ESCAP have maintained such an active leadership role? Another history of ESCAP reckons not:

> Thus, within a short period of 10 years ESCAP, acting on the impulse of a wide range of global and regional initiatives, transformed itself into a multi-faceted organization that could support cooperative institutions over the entire spectrum of socio-economic development. This was not, however, a sustainable period, for at some point the centrifugal force of so many independent activities could have fragmented the organisation and undermined its basic role as a focal point for development in the region. It became apparent, therefore, that a re-assessment of the approach, with its emphasis on institution building, would be necessary.[59]

This is not a conclusion with which one has to agree. More regional institutions need not have fragmented ESCAP. And even if new institutions were not being created, there was still ample scope for other types of initiatives for regional cooperation. What is disturbing is that after the mid-1970s, ESCAP ceased to be a regional fount of ideas for institutional innovation. Was this due to a lack of leadership or to circumstance and changing times or a combination of the two?

Regional Cooperation Machinery within the Commission

ECAFE used to be referred to as the "Parliament of Asia," a favorite phrase of Executive Secretary U Nyun.[60] Lately, ESCAP has also stressed its role as a regional development forum. The commission's extensive machinery—the annual sessions, the meetings of its subsidiary bodies (sectoral and, now, thematic committees), other associated intergovernmental forums, the Regional Coordination Meeting (RCM), and the Advisory Committee of Permanent Representatives (ACPR)—contains numerous meeting places of various kinds for policymakers and senior officials from the region. These bodies, in their discussions and in their recommendations and decisions, have been an important and integral part in the process of generating a culture of regionalism. Here, we examine briefly how these institutions have emerged over time.

The annual session is the highest policymaking organ of the commission, and from its inception it has attracted high-level policymakers. Because it is a generalist body, the agendas of the annual sessions have been broad and diffuse and there is no way for a government to be represented there by a range of experts that can adequately cover all the issues. The annual reports of the annual session indicate that the discussions are of a very general nature. In fact, there is little debate on the issues, and governments tend to make statements that simply reflect their own positions.

Observers see these annual sessions as probably more important as a place for policymakers to get to know each other and less as a forum for the exchange of substantive ideas on regional issues. The annual sessions in most alternate years are held outside Bangkok and, as a result, the commission has been hosted by many countries in the region. That has been a stimulating experience, both for the organization and for the host countries and has probably led to the closer involvement of ESCAP with these countries. Host countries have also used the opportunity to develop their own views on regional policies. An illustration of this is provided by the ECAFE forum in Sri Lanka in 1974, when, at the opening of its thirtieth annual session, the prime minister of Sri Lanka mooted the idea of a world fertilizer fund, which was then taken up at the World Food Conference the same year in Rome and led to a

UN General Assembly Resolution (jointly sponsored by New Zealand and Sri Lanka) establishing the International Fertilizer Supply Fund, which is managed by the FAO.[61]

When ECAFE was established in 1947, there were no subsidiary bodies, and it took a great struggle to establish the first one. Developed countries in ECAFE were opposed to the idea of permanent subsidiary bodies and preferred to function through working groups and expert committees, thus reducing the role of government in the technical work involved. It was only after considerable pressure that the first committees, on industry and on trade, were established. By the 1960s, there was a panoply of subsidiary bodies, and by the end of the 1970s, there were at least nine committees—Agricultural Development; Development Planning; Industry, Technology, Human Settlements and the Environment; Natural Resources; Population; Shipping and Transport and Communications; Social Development; Statistics; and Trade. This structure of subsidiary organs, each of which focuses on a sector, was attractive to governments whose own machinery was organized on sectoral lines. Specialists from the relevant national agencies could be represented on these subsidiary bodies.[62]

In 1992, there was a major change in the overall structure of these subsidiary organs.[63] In place of sectoral committees, five thematic committees were instituted—Regional Economic Cooperation; Socioeconomic Measures to Alleviate Poverty in Rural and Urban Areas; Environment and Natural Resources Development; Transport, Communications, Tourism and Infrastructure Development; and Statistics. This thematic approach, which was the fashion in the 1990s, particularly within the UN system, made it extremely difficult for the relevant government organizations to be represented appropriately. Organizing the structure of subsidiary organs along these lines led to a degree of confusion in ESCAP, which so far has not been overcome. The "Report of the Task Force on ESCAP Reform" (1997)[64] was highly critical of this structure. It noted that the broad agendas of these committees had led to superficiality of discussion and inappropriate participation by governments and had failed to enliven the deliberations of the commission. Nevertheless, these committees continue to function.

The ACPR, established in 1974, was an important mechanism "to maintain close co-operation and consultation between the members and the secretariat of the Commission; to review the draft calendar of meetings; to exchange views with the Executive Secretary on the provisional agenda for the Commission session."[65] It was expected to be an advisory body to the executive secretary, but recently its role has been changed such that it now advises the commission. The records of the meetings of the ACPR clearly indicate that it is primarily concerned with procedural rather than substantive issues. It has become increasingly active, and its meetings have increased from about six each year in the 1980s to about thirteen each year in 2002. Observers have queried whether the ACPR is of any value to ESCAP and question whether it has tended to interfere too much, to the detriment of a more autonomous role by the secretariat. Moreover, the ACPR is dominated by the countries that are represented in Bangkok and by the smaller number of missions which have the capacity to engage actively in such issues. Because it is represented by foreign-ministry personnel from member countries, the ACPR also has a tendency to be more influenced by foreign-policy perspectives than by the substantive aspects of regional cooperation.[66]

Almost from its beginning, the commission has aimed to be the coordinating agency of the UN system at the regional level, but this has not been accomplished; most UN agencies did not like the idea of being coordinated. UN agencies, funds, and programs wish to be represented at the annual sessions and in the appropriate subsidiary bodies, but this is the limit of the extent to which they are prepared to coordinate their affairs with the commission. In the early 1990s, a body known as the Regional Interagency Committee for Asia and the Pacific (RICAP) was established to bring together UN agencies at the regional level under the leadership of ESCAP. It was not a success, and it has been discontinued. Instead, a Regional Interagency Coordination Meeting (RCM) has been established recently, meeting annually under the aegis of ESCAP but chaired by the Deputy-Secretary-General of the UN in New York. This probably takes it out of the ESCAP mandate, as the RCM is virtually an instrument of the Office of the Deputy-Secretary-General.

Since the late 1980s, ESCAP's history has largely been one of reforming its own institutions. There has been considerable tampering with its internal structures. Instead of sectors, there are themes. Many task forces and working groups have been established. The change in internal structures has also been driven by similar developments elsewhere in the UN system. The ACPR is indeed active, as this is the kind of work which greatly interests its members. But whether all these changes are productive or of any importance to the governments which ESCAP serves has not been adequately assessed. Nor has there been any in-depth consideration of whether there are other institutional arrangements that might be more appropriate to the Asia-Pacific situation.

Regional Action at the Sectoral Level

Since 1947, the commission has implemented a wide range of tasks at the sectoral level.[67] In the ECAFE phase, sectoral activities had a strong dimension of regional cooperation. Most of its work was undertaken through its subsidiary organs, which focused on specific sectors. The work of these bodies led to further activities such as regional conferences (of planners, statisticians, industry officials), working groups, and expert bodies. There was also a fair amount of technical assistance, especially in the form of advisory services. During this phase, the technical assistance of ECAFE was largely integrated with and projected the decisions and work plans of these subsidiary bodies in the region.

Technical assistance was largely funded from the regular budget and took only a small share of total ECAFE expenditure. After 1977, when ESCAP placed itself as an operational agency, technical assistance emerged as the most important sectoral activity; the subsidiary organs of ESCAP also became more concerned with programs and projects that focused on technical assistance.

Subsequent to UN General Assembly Resolution 32/1974, ESCAP undertook a large program of technical assistance, initially funded primarily from UN sources but subsequently funded, for almost the same amount, by bilateral donors. The greater dependence on extrabudgetary resources had an obvious impact on ESCAP's activities and relationships. Increasingly, its agendas had to conform with the priorities of the funding agencies. The increasing role of technical assistance also led to a greater focus on activities at the level of individual countries where the regional dimension was not particularly significant. Also, technical assistance was increasingly directed toward social and environmental sectors, which do not lend themselves to active forms of regional cooperation.

An important characteristic of deliberations in the commission and its subsidiary bodies is that the challenges and the constraints confronting member countries—whether they be in economic and social development, trade, industry, statistics, population growth, transport, the environment, or natural resources—are largely approached through the opportunities they offer for technical assistance.

ECAFE/ESCAP has focused on the provision of technical assistance to meet the challenges facing member countries. There is little, if any, extensive analysis of the comparative experience of countries, especially in relation to the numerous economic models in the region and their relative successes and failures. For example, no analytical work appears to have been done on the Japanese experience.[68] The value of ESCAP's technical assistance might have been significantly increased if there had been more comparative and critical analysis of the experience across countries and of the various policy prescriptions in order to determine what has been relatively successful.

Statistics

ECAFE has been engaged in statistical development from its earliest days and has made an enormous contribution to the evolution of statistics in the region. Part of its work has been undertaken in close collaboration with the United Nations Statistical Office, although most of its work has been for the region, guided by regional statistical bodies such as the Asian Statistical Conference. Since 1970, it has also worked closely with the ASI,[69] which itself was a creation of ECAFE.

The Statistics Section was formed in 1949 with two objectives in view—the improvement of national statistics and the compilation of regional statistics, primarily for use in the regional analytical work of ECAFE. There was both a national and a regional dimension in ECAFE's approach to statistical development. A large amount of practical work was undertaken in these early days, especially in building up files of basic statistical series on production, trade, finance, prices, transport, and so on. Regular statistical series started to be published in the quarterly *Economic Bulletin for Asia and the Far East.*

There was close interaction with national statistical agencies, and the flow of advice and information helped to improve the quality and timeliness of statistics. One of the earliest regional workshops, held in 1950 in cooperation with the UN Statistical Office and the IMF, addressed issues in trade and balance-of-payment statistics. This workshop also led to a working party to discuss the adaptation of the Standard International Trade Classification (SITC).

ECAFE also convened the Regional Conference of Statisticians, renamed the Conference of Asian Statisticians in 1957. This became a permanent body, so its work programs were established on a regular basis. The conference also acted as the forum to discuss issues pertaining to the FAO's 1960 World Census of Agriculture and the 1960 World Census of Population. A range of other tasks were undertaken in which expert groups examined special issues such as sampling (1959), capital formation (1959), training (1960), and national accounts (1965 and 1966). There has also been a range of seminars in areas such as industrial statistics, statistics for economic and social development, national accounts, trade, population, and housing, among others. Manuals have been prepared for training purposes. All these activities were accompanied by the provision of advisory services to individual countries. The ESCAP Committee on Statistics (formerly the Conference of Asian Statisticians) has made an important contribution to the statistical development of the region. This has largely taken the form of institution- and capacity-building in member countries and enabling the reconciliation of statistical methodologies and statistical outputs from diverse sources.

Economic Planning

Economic planning was the accepted norm in the region in the late 1940s. Many governments had their five- and six-year plans, and economic development was generally considered to be achievable through government direction and the public allocation of resources. ECAFE was greatly influenced by the development thinking of the time, and its first two executive secretaries (who were from India) were probably influenced greatly by Indian planning methodologies. ESCAP undertook research into issues of economic development and planning, publishing its analysis in its annual *Economic Survey* and publications such as the quarterly *Economic Bulletin for Asia and the Far East*. A Working Party on Economic Development and Planning met annually between 1955 and 1960 and examined different sectors. In 1961, the first session of the Conference of Asian Economic Planners recommended the establishment of the Asian Institute for Economic Development and Planning. Various other aspects of planning, for example programming and projection techniques, were pursued through expert groups, the first of which was chaired by Nobel Laureate Jan Tinbergen (1959).

An important aspect of ECAFE's work in planning was the regional harmonization of production patterns within countries. It was believed at the time that "the guiding principle should be intra-regional and international specialization in production, on the basis of mutual agreement, of a kind that would assure mutual benefits and equity to all participating countries."[70] This led the commission to convene the First Working Group of Planning Experts on Regional Plan Harmonization (1966). During the first twenty-five years of ECAFE, a major training effort was made to strengthen planning capacities at the national level through various seminars and workshops. These activities of ECAFE did not, however, result in any tangible division of labor in the output of the region.

International Trade

The sectoral activities with the highest profile are those undertaken in the sector of international trade, which is where the primary thrust of the commission's work on regional economic cooperation was made. There was a great deal of activity in promoting trade and improving trade information in the 1960s. The first-ever Asia-Pacific International Trade Fair was organized by ECAFE and the government of Thailand in Bangkok in 1966. Immediately afterward, the Trade Promotion Centre was set up within ECAFE. In the Tokyo Declaration of 1967, it was proposed that the Council of Ministers for Asian Economic Co-operation should be revived, on the premise that it would focus on international trade issues. In 1970, at a meeting of the council in Kabul, a proposal was made to launch a major trade development program for intraregional trade and to establish institutions such as the Asian Clearing Union (founded in 1974) and the Asian Reserve Bank (still under consideration). All through this period and right up to the present day, the Council of Ministers' major tasks have been the regular analysis of trade patterns within the region and the generation of more subsector and product-specific trade information (as is done, for example, by the Trade and Investment Information Service Network, TISNET). The commission, however, remains the primary source of information on intraregional trade. Also in the 1970s, the Bangkok Agreement, which is still a major institution for regional economic cooperation, was negotiated.[71] In the 1970s, partly reflecting the emerging global concerns expressed by UNCTAD and its Integrated Programme on Commodities, ECAFE developed an intense interest in commodities, which led to the establishment of several regional commodity bodies.

The last two decades have featured intense technical assistance in various activities related to international trade. ESCAP actively assisted member countries of the region in the Uruguay Round negotiations. Since the establishment of the WTO in 1995, a major shift in ESCAP's work programs is evident; WTO agreements constitute the framework for its Trade Policy Work Programme. Most developing countries in the region are confronted with complex issues in negotiations and in adjusting their national trade policies to conform with WTO provisions. ESCAP has collaborated closely with UNCTAD and the International Trade Center (ITC) in analytical work on these issues and in assisting member governments. ESCAP's work program during the last decade reflects the decline of UNCTAD as a negotiating forum and the primacy of the WTO in trade negotiations and in the shaping of national and regional trade policy. ESCAP has not done any extensive analysis of the trade barriers within the region, which are an obstacle to a more dynamic pattern of intraregional trade.

Industry

In the 1950s, ECAFE expressed strong support for the development of heavy industry in the region. This was an important aspect of its overall approach to national planning. In emphasizing heavy industry, ECAFE and its member countries (and the Soviet Union) found themselves opposed by the Western powers, who were not convinced of the rationale for the expansion of iron and steel production, as supply was improving rapidly in Europe and the

United States. The ECE was also concerned about overcapacity. The conflict on this issue was also a reflection of the broader differences of approach to national planning between West and East.

At this time, another major concern of ECAFE was the harmonization of production in key sectors among countries in the region. Iron and steel was a key sector, and India was particularly concerned with this issue. ECAFE undertook exploratory activities in this field in the 1950s—it sponsored study tours to Japan and Western Europe, it published its findings on best practices for production harmonization, and it facilitated the exchange of technical experience.

Other noteworthy aspects of the commission's activities in industry include its work on the organization of state enterprises and the development of human resources. It also paid attention to the development of the chemicals and petrochemicals industries, including the fertilizer industry, the pulp and paper industries, the manmade fibers industry, and small-scale industry and handicrafts. In 1965, the first Conference on Asian Industrialization was held in Manila, which led to the establishment of the Asian Industrial Development Council. ESCAP has continued to work in these areas, focusing on feasible aspects of regional cooperation.

Natural Resources

The commission has pursued a wide range of activities in the areas of water, minerals, and energy. Primarily, the work has involved information generation, analysis, publications, the exchange of information and experience, training, and advisory services. These are areas in which, in its early years, it had few rivals in the rest of the UN system. In the 1950s and 1960s, when water and international riparian concerns were not rated as high-profile issues, ECAFE was intensely involved with them and can be credited with considerable foresight in addressing issues such as the flooding of the Mekong River Delta. Flood control was an important concern at the time, and ECAFE established its Bureau of Flood Control in 1949. It was also very involved in assisting in the development of hydrological data, water legislation, and methodologies for unified development of river basins. These are activities which were of immediate interest to many countries which were planning major schemes for irrigation and agricultural development.

By 1950, ECAFE had also developed a geological map of the region, and it undertook a comprehensive review of coal and iron resources in the region in 1950. The first Regional Conference on Mineral Resources Development was held in Tokyo (1953); this was the first time that geologists from the Asian region were brought together. In 1958, ECAFE organized a Symposium on Development of Petroleum Resources, held in New Delhi.

ECAFE also did considerable work in electricity and power generation. In all these areas, it provided assistance to countries to help them build up their own technical capacities and their own national institutions. The study tour of Europe (including the Soviet Union) is illustrative of the type of assistance for institution-building. The United States arranged for Asian electrical engineers to study the latest technical advances in the design and operation of power plants. An important outcome was the recognition that the region must standardize its equipment and practices in the electric power sector.

Transport and Communications

From its early days, ECAFE was concerned with developing the transport infrastructure of the region, which was pivotal for improving regional economic cooperation. The commission has undertaken two broad types of activity in this field. First is a set of high-profile projects—the Asian Highway and the Asian Railway Network—which aim to link countries within the region and facilitate such linkages through standardizing and filling current gaps in the road and rail networks. Since the 1970s, the commission has undertaken an enormous amount of technical work. Second is the technical assistance supplied to member countries to upgrade their road and rail systems, ports, and shipping. No other UN organization is dedicated to addressing these issues (with the exception of UNCTAD's work in transport) and, consequently, member governments have relied on ESCAP as a source of technical advice and information. In 1992, ESCAP endorsed a "new vision" to develop an Asia-Europe transport system. At the same time, it also endorsed an integrated approach to Asian Land Transport Infrastructure Development (ALTID), which brought together the Asian Highway and the Trans-Asian Railway projects. By adopting this approach, ESCAP shifted its focus to facilitating the transport of goods instead of concentrating on modes of transport (marine, rail, or road).

Population

ECAFE has addressed population issues since the early 1950s, long before the establishment of the UNFPA. It organized seminars on population issues in Bandung, Indonesia, in 1955 and Bombay, India, in 1960. One of its key achievements was putting together the Asian Population Conference in New Delhi (1963), one of the first occasions when population was discussed at an intercountry level. The recommendations of this conference led to the adoption of ECAFE Resolution 54 (XX) in March 1964, which asked "the United Nations and the specialized agencies to expand the scope of the technical assistance they are prepared to give, upon request of governments, in the development of statistics, research, experimentation and action programmes related to population."[72] This resolution marked a notable initiative by ECAFE to lead the UN on population issues. In 1966, an expert working group examined the feasibility of establishing a regional population center. Once the UN General Assembly had adopted Resolution 22/11 (XXI) on population and economic development, ECAFE followed with its own Resolution 74 (XXIII)[73] and obtained a mandate to expand its activities in the field of population, especially to undertake an expanded program of research, training, information, and advisory services. By the end of the 1960s, ECAFE had established a sizeable Population Section within the Social Development Division. This section also functioned as a regional clearinghouse for population information.

Since the establishment of the UNFPA in the early 1970s, there have been many changes in the role of ESCAP in this field. These include a close working relationship with the UNFPA, on which it is now largely dependent for funds. Previously, ESCAP had obtained funds from other UN and bilateral sources. ESCAP projects and activities reflect the UNFPA's priorities for the region. A noteworthy contribution of ESCAP since 1979 has been the organization and distribution of population information through the Asia-Pacific Population Information Network. ESCAP has also continued to organize the decennial Asian and Pacific Population Conferences. Overall, the commission has made a distinctive contribution to the adoption of effective national and regional policies in the field of population.

A Miscellany of Tasks

The sections above have described briefly the key areas in which the commission has been engaged, but there are many other issues that ESCAP has addressed. In recent years, one of its important concerns has been with gender issues, its main task being to generate information and analysis on the situation of women. It has also undertaken work in relation to the measurement and evaluation of the paid and unpaid work of women. ESCAP's contribution has primarily been to upgrade national capacities to address these issues. Similarly, it has been engaged in many aspects of the environmental agenda, particularly in following up global agreements. There have also been many activities in the broad field of social development; it has given particular attention to disability issues. ESCAP's work in all these areas is primarily linked to either facilitating preparatory work for global conferences or to following up their decisions and recommendations.

What is also interesting is what ESCAP is not engaged in, especially in the context of new approaches to development. It has barely been involved in matters such as governance and human rights, although they have become major items on UN agendas in recent years. There is also a clear lack of attention given to agriculture and food security issues, a reflection of earlier disputes over turf with the FAO.

Summing Up: Rise and Decline

There are clearly two phases in the commission's history. The first virtually ends with the demise of ECAFE in 1974; the second covers the period of ESCAP. More than just the name changed in 1974. Many other aspects of the organization changed as well. The first phase of ECAFE can be further divided into two parts. Until about 1960, ECAFE was consolidating and expanding its membership to the core group of Asian countries. It was then an organization providing research and analytical advisory services to individual countries while it was taking initial steps to create a culture of regional cooperation. The period from the early 1960s to 1974 was a period of active engagement in creating a regional institutional infrastructure. Many ideas were generated at the time for practical forms of regional cooperation. Since the mid-1970s there has been a relatively sharp change of direction, which has led to a broader concern with issues beyond the field of economics and a strong focus on technical assistance. The commission became more of a branch of the UN system in New York and lost much of its regional character with the expansion of its membership to more than fifty countries that cover a vast geographical expanse.

Up to the mid-1970s, ECAFE was the major regional organization and was the only place where a broad range of economic issues could be discussed. Governments in the region then attached more importance to it as a key regional organization than they do now. Gradually since the mid-1970s, ESCAP's role has diminished. The ADB emerged as a rival that addressed issues of regional economic cooperation and development and had strong analytical capacities and the resources to back its prescriptions. It also attracted the key constituency of senior financial officials of member countries. While ESCAP's annual sessions became more ceremonial and a forum for general discussion, ADB sessions were more purposive. Regional member countries also shifted their attention to their own subregional organizations. ASEAN emerged as a strong force and in the 1980s and the 1990s became the catalyst for expanding various forms of regional cooperation. It quickly expanded its membership to ten countries, bringing in the Indochina-Mekong region, and in the 1990s it initiated the ASEAN + 3 Forum (bringing in China, Japan, and the Republic of Korea). The South Asian Association for Regional Cooperation (SAARC), although not an effective body, has also emerged as a focus of interest for member countries. In the 1990s, the Asia-Pacific Economic Cooperation (APEC) added a new dimension of open regionalism. Member countries of these bodies attach major importance to these new institutions, and consequently they have obtained a significantly higher profile than the routine deliberations of ESCAP. ECAFE largely concentrated on economic issues and on regional economic cooperation at a time when economic growth was the central issue in the development process. By the mid-1970s, development was being placed in a wider context of economic, social, and environmental concerns. The UN was at the center of this development. Apart from changing its name to include "social," ESCAP became increasingly concerned with non-economic issues, primarily in the context of a series of global meetings and summits on social and environmental issues. ESCAP became a forum for developing common regional positions on these matters. Unlike economic issues, social and environmental aspects of development did not lend themselves to active forms of regional cooperation. A regional meeting was not the same as regional cooperation. ESCAP therefore became more of an intergovernmental agency that addressed issues of common interest rather than a regional forum for cooperation. It is intriguing, as noted before, that even with the shift in emphasis to social issues, the commission itself, at least at its annual sessions, continued to focus clearly on economic issues. Social and environmental issues were dealt with either in subsidiary organs or in special regional conferences. The annual survey largely addressed economic issues. ESCAP had a two-tier approach that addressed economic issues, on the one hand, and social and environmental issues, on the other.

Since the UN General Assembly Resolution in 1977, ESCAP has become primarily a technical assistance agency, and most of its projects and programs are funded by extrabudgetary resources. Subsidiary organs of ESCAP have devoted considerable time and attention to these activities. There is only a small element of regional cooperation in this technical assistance, which is intended to build national capacities. Initially, most of the funds for technical assistance came from the UNDP, but in the 1990s the UNDP's engagement virtually ceased, and currently the UNFPA is the larger source of funds. The influence of bilateral donors has also increased, and they now account for most of the financial support for technical assistance. With the increased importance attached to technical assistance, ESCAP's role as the initiator of concrete ideas for regional cooperation has diminished.

Arguably, ESCAP is more of a branch of the UN in New York than ECAFE ever was. In the days of ECAFE, up to the mid-1970s, UN decisions on issues such as the International Development Strategy were followed up by ECAFE, as attested by the numerous annual surveys and the discussions at the annual sessions of the commission, but there were then only a few UN General Assembly and ECOSOC decisions to be implemented. As the UN became more inclusive, taking up a wider range of social and environmental issues, and with the proliferation of global summits, ESCAP became more the creature of UN processes of global decision-making. ESCAP virtually abandoned its 1960s and 1970s role of being a catalyst for institutional forms of regional cooperation. New ideas for such institutions—for example, the Asian Monetary Fund, or the ASEAN Swap arrangements of 1977—emerged from outside ESCAP, unlike the proposal for the Asian Reserve Bank in the early 1970s. The "UN-ization" of ESCAP, instead of making it a more autonomous, indigenous regional institution, has diminished its role. The ESCAP secretariat has virtually given up its autonomous role of generating new ideas, and recent executive secretaries have been followers, rather than leaders, in the pursuit of new forms of regional cooperation. Since the early 1980s, the Advisory Committee of Permanent Representatives has increased its monitoring and surveillance of the secretariat, and this has directly led to a downgrading of ESCAP.

4

ECLAC: A Commitment to a Latin American Way toward Development

Gert Rosenthal

- • **The History of ECLA and Its Intellectual Contribution**
- • **The Prebisch Era (1949–1963): The Seminal Years**
- • **The Immediate Post-Prebisch Years (1963–1972): Variants on (and Some Deviations from) the Same Themes**
- • **The Early Iglesias Years: The Search for Identity in the 1970s**
- • **The Late Iglesias and the Post-Iglesias Years: Short-Term Policies to Deal with the Crisis of the 1980s**
- • **The 1990s and Beyond: The Return to a Holistic Framework**
- • **The Lasting Legacy of ECLA's Intellectual Contribution and Its Impact on the United Nations**

The History of ECLA and Its Intellectual Contribution

While the United Nations Intellectual History Project deals with ideas, this volume adopts an institutional perspective; it delves into the contribution of the regional commissions to the UN's intellectual legacy. Those contributions have had a global impact and, much more so, an impact within the respective regions of each of the economic commissions.

Probably the single most eloquent example can be found in the Economic Commission for Latin America (ECLA).[1] Under the inspired leadership of Raúl Prebisch, this regional commission had a great impact on development thinking in its pioneering years. In this respect, a biography of Prebisch (or "Don Raúl" to his disciples), a history of ECLA, and a history of economic thinking in Latin America converge repeatedly.

Indeed, an extensive literature approaches all three subjects; the common thread is ECLA's exceptional influence on development economics during the

1950s and early 1960s.[2] Clearly, a history of ideas spawned by the UN would be grossly incomplete without exploring ECLA's contribution.

That contribution burst onto the Latin America scene in a spectacular manner. The core of Prebisch/ECLA's original analysis and proposals for the region are condensed in two landmark documents: Prebisch's *The Economic Development of Latin America and Its Principal Problems* (1949)[3] and the commission's *Economic Survey of 1949*,[4] which was prepared under Prebisch's guidance and strongly reflects the ideas contained in his own contribution. These include the secular deterioration in the terms of trade of Latin American economies; the asymmetrical relations between the developed countries of the center and the developing countries of the periphery and the perverse structural effects that such asymmetrical relations have on domestic production, consumption, and savings patterns; and economic and social organization. The documents stress the need to industrialize (even if some limited and temporary protection against imports of manufactured goods is necessary), the critical importance of technological progress, and the active role of the state in development. Much of the work in subsequent years built on this cluster of seminal ideas, including the need to broaden markets through regional economic integration, the desirability of designing development "blueprints" through economic planning, the need to reverse the perverse distributive effects of economic growth, and the understanding of the nature of inflation. The common threads that bound these ideas together were: a) the way Latin American countries related to the world economy; and b) the structural impediments to development (ECLA was largely responsible for spawning the structuralist school of development economics).

It is true that many of these ideas have been questioned over the years, and some have even fallen into disrepute, but that, in itself, does not necessarily minimize their importance and usefulness. For the ultimate criterion of the UN's intellectual legacy in the economic sphere should not necessarily be whether ECLA's ideas proved to be "right" or "wrong." It is equally important to examine how those ideas impacted the ongoing and permanent debate regarding development issues. In other words, it would perhaps be unfair to demand from the UN that it lead the way. A more modest demand would be for it to nurture the debate, clarify the issues, facilitate the decision-making process, and contribute to public awareness on the scope and content of alternative policy prescriptions. These functions all fall within the UN's analytical and normative activities and contribute to the intellectual legacy that is the subject of the United Nations Intellectual History Project. Of course member states have a right to expect the UN's policy advice to be sound, but even here, whether such advice proves to be sound or misleading, it has to be analyzed in the context of the analysis available at the time and not with the wisdom of hindsight.

ECLA was extremely innovative and influential not only in development thinking but also in the way its secretariat interacted with its member governments. Prebisch has been variously described as a thinker, a man of action, and an institution builder.[5] He was also a master disseminator of ideas. He built ECLA as a halfway house between academia and public policy, a place where "thinkers" and "doers" could meet. The in-depth work carried out in countries gave the institution an important presence in the field, and its empirical observations nurtured its ideas about development. Those ideas, in turn, offered a conceptual framework for further action. It would be difficult to find another administrative unit in the UN that had such a decisive impact on so many member countries; many have characterized the body of ECLA's ideas as something akin to a development paradigm.

However, not all of ECLA's proposals were grand overarching strategies. Many consisted of more limited proposals—sometimes a single simple idea—which nevertheless must be credited to the UN's intellectual heritage. One example can be found in ECLA's initial success in furthering the cause of economic integration in Central America in the early 1950s, which it followed up with a proposal for economic integration of all of Latin America at the end of the decade.[6]

Some of ECLA's ideas resulted from in-house brainstorming; others reflected adaptations to the Latin American environment of ideas that originated in other quarters, especially from academics of the developed countries. Some ideas reflected a rationalization of policies that were already being applied in the region; others gave rise to policies. It is difficult to identify clear cause-and-effect relationships between ECLA's ideas and their application in the field, since much of the work was inductive in nature, given the halfway-house qualities mentioned above.

One could argue that ECLA's success as a think tank in its initial years was also the seed of its subsequent relative decline, since some of Prebisch's followers gave credence to the notion that they had developed a theory for economic development. As the region underwent profound changes in the 1960s and 1970s, and as some inherent weaknesses in ECLA's policy prescriptions began to appear, the ECLA secretariat appeared averse, or unable, to sufficiently alter its own development thinking to fit evolving circumstances. Instead, while adapting at least partially to changing realities, it preferred to build those adaptations onto its proposals of the 1950s, showing a reluctance to break with its past, and it made great efforts to defend the validity of the seminal ideas.[7] Thus, by the second half of the 1960s and especially by the 1970s, the institution had lost some of its luster. Perhaps it is no accident that the golden years of ECLA as a center of economic analysis and audacious thinking coincided with Prebisch's tenure (1950–1963) and that arguably its waning influence began even before his departure.

However, the extent of the decline of ECLA in the post-Prebisch era is sometimes exaggerated. Although the quality and relevance of the secretariat's work varied over the years, and circumstances within the UN, Latin America, and the world at large changed dramatically, there were constants during all of ECLA's institutional life that revealed a certain vitality. Thus, even in periods when its influence had clearly diminished, ECLA consistently spawned numerous and creative ideas. It was also able, for better or for worse (depending on the vantage point of individual analysts) to influence policymakers. At the same time, it managed to build a niche in the UN's structure that legitimized policy-oriented analytical activities as fundamentally useful to member governments. It was able to draw on these historic achievements to the extent that there was a moderate recovery of its intellectual role from the early 1980s. In short, the institution clearly deserves a prominent place in the intellectual history of the UN.

Although there were numerous methodological ways to approach the subject, I have chosen to tell the story sequentially; that is, as a function of the succeeding tenures of executive secretaries, which roughly coincide with succeeding decades.[8] Ideas that had both a global and a regional impact are examined. No conscious effort is made to determine whether it was the ideas emanating from ECLA that influenced events in Latin America or whether it was the events in the region that nurtured the conceptual and analytical work of ECLA, since surely both processes were going on simultaneously.

It is implicit when describing ECLA that the main subject of the analysis is the secretariat, although the intergovernmental machinery played an equally important role in shaping and disseminating ideas. This is due to the secretariat's strong propensity to involve leading personalities in working groups, which facilitated the exchange and dissemination of ideas and ended up giving the interested personalities, who were usually linked to their respective governments, a sense of ownership.

It should be stressed that the story being told is about the intellectual heritage of the UN. For purposes of this particular chapter, it is *not* an attempt to write a history of ECLA; it is simply an attempt to link its system of governance to its role in the production and dissemination of ideas. Another point to be emphasized is that the chapter does not attempt to describe in detail all of the proposals formulated by the organization. Rather, a more modest effort is made to selectively explore the considerable contribution that ECLA has made to the intellectual history of the UN through a brief account of its core theses. It should also be added that due to space limitations, no attempt was made to develop each idea in depth, although bibliographical references are offered to those who wish to probe more deeply into the subjects discussed.[9]

The Origins of ECLA and Its System of Governance

Part of ECLA's success as a generator of ideas within the UN can be traced to the nature of its origins and its system of governance, and it is for that reason that this brief review is offered.[10]

Both the Economic Commission for Europe (ECE) and the Economic Commission for Asia and the Far East (later ESCAP) were created to assist in the postwar effort of reconstruction and development in war-torn areas. The creation of a regional commission for the sole purpose of promoting development in the Latin American region was the brainchild of Hernán Santa Cruz, permanent representative of Chile to the UN. He proposed his initiative at the Fifth Session of the Economic and Social Council (ECOSOC) of the UN in July 1947. Santa Cruz believed that this was the least that the UN could do for a region that had been instrumental in its own creation.[11] However, the initiative ran into resistance from various delegations. Among the eighteen members of the council, eight, including the main actors of the Economic and Social Council, were opposed to the initiative. These included the United States, which believed that ECLA would duplicate the Pan-American Union's Inter-American Economic and Social Council. The Soviet Union, the United Kingdom, and France felt that the creation of a new regional commission was not a priority. Canada and New Zealand had gone on record against the regional approach in the world body, while Byelorussia and Czechoslovakia followed the lead of the Soviet Union.[12] However, the delegate of France, Pierre Mendès-France, told delegates privately that France might be willing to support the initiative if European countries were to be involved in the groundwork to create such a commission and, presumably, in the commission itself, were it to be created. As a result of the debate, two decisions ensued. First, the United States said that the matter should be put to the Inter-American Economic and Social Council at its next meeting, to be held in January 1948, in order to ascertain if all countries of Latin America were in agreement with Chile's initiative. Second, given the diversity of opinions in this first round of consultations, an ad hoc working group was created with the mandate to prepare a report to further consider the proposal. The General Assembly also debated the matter and endorsed the creation of the ad hoc working group.[13]

At the same time, the U.S. suggestion was acted upon, and the Inter-American Economic and Social Council included the matter in the agenda of its meeting planned for January but actually held in May 1948.[14] Even before the Inter-American forum met, the Sixth Session of ECOSOC was held (January 1948) to consider, inter alia, the report and recommendations of the ad hoc working group.

Toward the end of the session, on February 25, the council approved Resolution 106 (VI), which created the commission by 13 votes in favor, 0 against, and 4 abstentions (the United States, Canada, Byelorussia, and the Soviet Union). The commission received broad terms of reference, which facilitated its future role in analytical activities. Its mandate included the following responsibilities:

- To initiate and participate in measures for facilitating concerted action for dealing with urgent economic problems arising out of the war and for raising the level of economic activity in Latin America. . . .
- To make or sponsor such investigations and studies of economic and technological problems and developments within territories of Latin America. . . .
- To undertake or sponsor the collection, evaluation and dissemination of such economic, technological and statistical information as the Commission deems appropriate.[15]

Membership of the Commission was open to "Members of the United Nations in North, Central and South America, and in the Caribbean area, and to France, the Netherlands and the United Kingdom."[16]

There is a coda to the story. According to paragraph 16 of Resolution 106 (VI), "not later than 1951 the Council shall make a special review of the work of the Commission with a view to determining whether the Commission should be terminated or continue, and if continued, what modification, if any, should be made in its terms of reference." Thus, by the time ECLA held its third session in Mexico City in 1951, the U.S. government had launched a serious offensive to have ECLA absorbed by the Pan-American Union—which by then had been renamed the Organization of American States (OAS). This offensive was defeated, but barely, thanks to the resistance of many (but not all) Latin American delegations, the quiet resistance of some European delegations (which, under the U.S. initiative, would have lost their right to vote), and a last-minute personal appeal to all delegations by President Getulio Vargas of Brazil.[17] Thus, in a sense, ECLA was created twice; the second time with a more permanent status.[18]

The rather convoluted process of ECLA's creation left as a legacy some important elements that shaped its system of governance and influenced its capacity to generate ideas.

First, the mere fact of belonging to the UN gave ECLA a greater degree of independence than any other regional organization. In addition to the perceived impartiality and moral authority of the UN, it is no small matter to be able to maintain a regional think tank financed by that organization's regular budget rather than by direct government contributions. Independence is enhanced by the fact that the executive secretary is named by the Secretary-General of the UN rather than elected by the governments.

Having said that, there are, of course, limits to the freedom of the secretariat to set its own agenda and express its views. But from personal interviews with the former executive secretaries of ECLA, it appears that those limits tended to be self-imposed, in recognition of the fact that the secretariat was at the service of its member governments. Prebisch always insisted that the institution owed its raison d'être to its member states, and this legacy became part of the secretariat's ethic. The main point is that the absence of a permanent intergovernmental body appears to have contributed to greater independence (or, at least, to less temptation on the part of governments to micromanage the institution), but at the same time the prospect of periodic meetings instilled a sense of accountability in the secretariat's officials.

Another aspect, although unintended, that probably worked in the secretariat's favor was the presence of extraregional member states (originally the United States, France, the United Kingdom, Canada, and the Netherlands; all countries in the Western hemisphere or present in the Western hemisphere through colonies or territories). This forced ECLA to clearly distinguish between the secretariat's core constituency—the developing countries in the region (i.e., the Latin American and, later, the Caribbean states)—and its total membership, which included developed countries. The secretariat, which appears to have developed good antennae regarding the varying demands and limits put on the work program by all member states, managed to navigate reasonably well around the turbulent waters of the North-South confrontations of the 1970s and 1980s. Because they were part of the commission, even the most skeptical governments (usually the United States: first in the pioneering years and again during the Reagan era) could usually be persuaded that the institution played a useful role.

Finally, the relative independence of the secretariat was buoyed by two other facts. First, the periodicity of the commission's meetings—annually until 1951, biennially thereafter—appears to have been a sound decision. The biennial rhythm allows the secretariat considerable leeway to perform its analytical work without formal and frequent reviews with its governments, but they are often enough to subject its work to the scrutiny of governments. In the second place, the physical distance between Santiago and New York, especially during the founding period when electronic communications and jet planes were still undreamed of, meant, in practice, that there was relatively little substantive oversight of the ECLA secretariat.

For all of the above reasons, then, the purely organizational aspects of ECLA—its bureaucratic culture, its institutional identity, and its system of governance—appears to have facilitated the generation and dissemination of ideas.

Common Threads through Fifty-three Years of Intellectual Contribution

Almost everyone would agree that the most exciting and far-reaching contributions of the commission and those that had the greatest international resonance came from its pioneering years. In fact, much of the work of succeeding decades built on the seminal ideas of 1949–1955. These tried to develop a holistic and integrated approach toward the economic and social development of the Latin American countries, based on an exploration of the complex relations between the latter countries (part of the developing "periphery") and developed countries (the "center"). The institution's concern with the asymmetrical nature of that relationship, and with how that relationship helped to shape the structures of Latin American economies and societies, were to become constants (although, of course, with different manifestations) in the secretariat's analysis and proposals throughout its lifetime and up to the present. Among the constants in the commission's concerns are the following:

- How Latin American countries interact with the world economy;
- How to apply technical progress to the productive process in order to achieve sustained growth;
- How to distribute the benefits of growth more equitably;
- How to combine the roles of the market and the state;
- How to overcome structural and institutional impediments to equitable growth with financial stability.

Many observers point out that the commission entered a period of progressive decline from the late 1960s through the 1980s, during which its influence and intellectual output dwindled.[19] However, it is also generally recognized that, while the contribution of the commission over its lifetime has been uneven, it has, by and large, shown a persistent intellectual vitality and élan, even in the worst of times. Ricardo Bielschowsky takes this position and has prepared a matrix of the commission's main intellectual contributions and policy prescriptions for each decade from the 1950s through the 1990s.[20]

A few salient characteristics of each of the periods in which the story is categorized would be in order. The first category covers the tenure of Raúl Prebisch (1950–1963). One can say that he clearly had certain advantages over his successors without in any way diminishing his main asset; namely, his undeniable strengths as a visionary (some would say a prophet) and as an innovative thinker.[21] The period was marked by the mystique surrounding a new and exciting secretariat which was to be built from scratch as part of a broader ideal embodied in the UN Charter. Prebisch was able to attract a small cadre of outstanding personalities to work with him.[22] In the 1950s, ECLA was a rather unique organization; virtually no other regional institution fulfilled its role.[23]

Another important characteristic of the times was the relative weakness of the profession of economics at the national level, especially in the smaller countries. This cast ECLA as somewhat of an intellectual giant, at least in relative terms. Indeed, when Prebisch spoke, especially in the smaller countries, he proclaimed from the mountaintop!

Finally, it was an era of economic growth and of intellectual effervescence at the international level, coming on the heels of the Great Depression of the 1930s, the victory over fascism, and the tremendous impact Lord Maynard Keynes had had on economic thinking.

For all of these reasons, ECLA's initial period is often referred to as its golden years, measured in terms of innovative thinking in the realm of development economics and the influence of that thinking in member countries and the community at large. This is not to say that the institution did not have its detractors. The United States was persistently suspicious and at times hostile to ECLA and its secretariat.[24] And academics questioned the institution's premises early on.[25]

In general, while the industrial sector applauded the ECLA paradigm, more traditional business elites were seriously disturbed by the institution's interventionist stance. Still, in the early 1960s, recognition appeared from unexpected quarters as the Kennedy administration launched its Alliance for Progress. The persistent hostility toward ECLA of previous administrations was abruptly changed, and the alliance, in fact, was at least partially inspired by the conceptual framework prepared by ECLA in the 1950s.[26] It should be noted, however, that the alliance emphasized domestic constraints to development, while ECLA tended to highlight international constraints (and how these impacted on domestic constraints), which the alliance downplayed and proposed to resolve through external financial assistance.

The immediately subsequent period, 1963–1972, on the other hand, was marked by relatively weaker leadership (first that of José Antonio Mayobre of

Venezuela and then of Carlos Quintana of Mexico). During this time, the mystique of ECLA gradually eroded.

New and sophisticated interlocutors began to appear, both at the national level and at the regional and global levels; the growing influence on development thinking of the World Bank in the 1960s and beyond was especially important. ECLA was also being attacked from both extremes of the ideological spectrum: For some, the institution was too interventionist, for others, it was not interventionist enough. Many countries of the region were encountering serious obstacles to economic growth by the end of the 1950s, and the ECLA paradigm was being increasingly questioned. Military regimes were taking over in numerous countries, and most of them were openly hostile to ECLA. At the same time, the Cuban revolution became a source of inspiration for the more progressive forces in Latin America.

Even during this period the institution and its staff spawned ingenious ideas; examples can be found in the institution's conceptualization and advocacy of economic programming or planning, its probing into the structural heterogeneity of Latin American economies and societies, and its greater emphasis on the social dimensions of development. Perhaps the most innovative output of all was a criticism of the seminal ideas of the 1950s, as enunciated in the writings of Fernando Henrique Cardoso and Enzo Faletto on dependency.[27]

The 1970s, which coincided with the ascent of Enrique Iglesias to the post of executive secretary in 1972, were even more troubled. ECLA's original conceptual framework was increasingly being discredited, especially regarding the sustainability of industrialization based on import substitution. The international economy was marked by instability. The ECLA secretariat, always closely influenced by affairs in its host country, was adversely affected by the overthrow of Salvador Allende (whose economic team included prominent ex-ECLA staff) and the emergence of an oppressive military regime hostile to ECLA headed by Augusto Pinochet. It was a period of retrenchment, of a somewhat defensive posture and relative quiescence in the realm of new ideas.[28]

The early years of Iglesias were dedicated to preserving the integrity of the secretariat and even to avoiding its expulsion from Chile.[29] His later years were dedicated to orchestrating a delicate balancing act between the guardians of ECLA's original ideas and the modernizers, who brought a more up-to-date vision of economic policymaking with them and who ultimately prevailed.[30] Thus, the heated debate going on at the time in Latin America—and especially in Chile—between the structuralist approach and the monetarist (some would say neoliberal) approach was reproduced, with nuances, within the secretariat.

But even during these difficult times, the institution continued to produce innovative work that built on its previous reflections. The contributions of Anibal Pinto and José Medina Echavarría on styles of development and the social dimension of development highlighted the inequitable and exclusionary nature of growth patterns in the region as well as the political economy of development. Serious work on the incidence of poverty—absolute and relative—was undertaken, as were the initial activities on emerging issues, such as the links between the environment and development and the status of women. The secretariat was able to document the perverse effects on the economies of the region of the international oil shocks of 1973–1974 and 1979, especially regarding the gradual buildup of debt, a buildup that would come back to haunt the region in the 1980s.

The internal debate within the secretariat persisted, unresolved, through the 1970s and was then overtaken by the severe economic depression of the 1980s; the so-called lost decade for development. The secretariat abandoned temporarily its proclivity to develop holistic frameworks and turned its attention to the crisis and the short term. Drawing on its legacy of professionalism and competence, ECLA produced important contributions on economic policymaking for the emergency, especially in the areas of expansive (or at least non-recessionary) adjustment policies, addressing the debt overhang and hyperinflation. Paradoxically, then, the economic recession had a salutatory effect on ECLA (by then, ECLAC) by temporarily suppressing the internal and debilitating discussion on development paradigms and forcing the institution to address relevant and timely policy questions.

Here again, the institution had an impact in the world of ideas: not holistic overarching ideas on how to approach development, but specific ideas on how to approach distinct development issues. Throughout this period, the institution was still ideologically identified with its past, resolutely avoiding the embrace of the new orthodoxy espoused in the economic realm by Milton Friedman and in the political domain by Ronald Reagan and Margaret Thatcher. However, it could not come up with an alternative to the new orthodoxy, so it found refuge in addressing specific policy questions rather than trying to tackle the big picture. Thus, the ECLAC secretariat was espousing debt alleviation three or four years before U.S. Secretary of the Treasury William Brady announced his debt-reduction initiatives in March of 1989.[31]

Although Iglesias initiated attempts to update the ECLAC message, it was left to his successors to address this latter challenge in a systematic way.[32] They were assisted in this endeavor by three external trends. First, the rather doctrinaire environment of the previous decade was giving way to more pragmatic approaches at the international level.[33] Conservative governments were being replaced by more moderate governments in several countries in Europe and in the United States. In addition, there was increasing recognition that while the market was by far the best mechanism to allocate resources, the right prices were not enough to achieve the conventional objectives of economic policy-making. Second, the demise of socialist realism and the Cold War had a profound impact worldwide. One of its many manifestations was a dramatic transition from authoritarian military regimes to democratically elected civilian regimes all over Latin America; another was the demise of the utopian vision that, for better or worse, had guided the strategies and actions of the Latin American left. And third, the profound economic depression of Latin America was beginning to give way to incipient recovery, assisted by the strong growth of world trade and a fairly successful strategy to deal with the debt overhang.

Thus, by the early 1990s, most Latin American economies had achieved moderate growth in a context of growing financial stability. The ECLAC secretariat was successful in tapping into these trends and combining its specific policy prescriptions on debt and adjustment with a holistic proposal. This proposal combined new policies (trade liberalization, sound macroeconomic management, deregulation, and privatization) with traditional ECLAC concerns (improving the participation of countries in world trade, broadening the application of technology to the productive process, modernizing the role of the state, addressing inequitable growth patterns, and promoting regional cooperation and economic integration). Perhaps the single most important characteristic that distinguished ECLAC from the prevalent orthodoxy was that while it recognized the importance of the market, it held that the market was not enough, by itself, to achieve development. Public policy and sound institutions and organizations were equally important in the quest to achieve growth with equity.

The series of publications under the banner of *Transformación productiva con equidad* (*Changing Production Patterns with Social Equity*) contributed to the debate on how to approach policymaking in the region. Among ECLAC's multiple concerns with sustained and sustainable growth, improving equity, and maintaining financial stability, it emphasized growth.

The present leadership of ECLAC (José Antonio Ocampo) continues to develop and expand on the approach of the 1990s and on the learning process of assessing the economic reforms implemented in the 1980s and 1990s. Ample evidence of innovative work can be found in recent publications and statements of the executive secretary.[34] Contemporary concerns include the need to combine macroeconomic stability with sustainable growth, the need for a strategy for structural change, and an enhanced emphasis on social cohesion and citizenship.

Finally, some common threads run through the institution's intellectual contributions during its 53-year history:

- ECLAC has prided itself on emphasizing the analytical components of its work program. In other words, it likes to think of itself as a think tank, albeit not for the intrinsic value of its research but for its usefulness to policymakers.
- ECLAC has favored a holistic, integrated, and multidisciplinary approach to development.
- ECLAC has tended to explore development issues as seen from the Latin American vantage point; that is, it has shown a commitment to a Latin American path toward development.
- Throughout its lifetime, ECLAC has shown a preference in its analytical work for taking a medium- and long-term view of development policies and strategies, although since the 1980s it has also addressed short-term policy issues.
- ECLAC has consistently stuck to its roots of structuralism, not only in terms of considering the international context as an important factor in defining domestic structures, as well as in determining national policies and strategies, but also in terms of attributing importance to structural and institutional impediments to development.[35]
- ECLAC has looked at development issues from the peculiar vantage point of its main constituency: the developing countries of Latin America and the Caribbean.
- This last aspect has also introduced a bias in ECLAC's work program in favor of those topics that would be relevant to the rather heterogeneous membership, among which the link to the international economy has consistently played a decisive role.
- While ECLAC considers itself technical, its ideas have revealed a conviction of the possibilities of social engineering, and they have also been characterized by an ideological slant toward reformist and forward-looking causes.
- In that context, ECLAC has persistently shown a concern for social justice; its work program, since the 1960s, has been heavy with topics related to income distribution, poverty, social indicators, and equity considerations.

In addition, during its lifetime, the institution has resolved some interesting institutional dilemmas. For example, it considers itself a Latin American and Caribbean organization, but at the same time is part of the UN. As part of the latter, it interacts with foreign ministries; as part of the former, it does so with ministries of trade or finance, central banks, and other economic actors. ECLAC is basically an intergovernmental organization, but it also interacts—albeit insufficiently—with the academic community, and, as stated earlier, it occupies a space between thinkers and doers. In summary, the Economic Commission for Latin America and the Caribbean makes a fascinating case study for the intellectual history of the UN.[36]

The Prebisch Era (1949–1963): The Seminal Years

As stated earlier, it is difficult to divorce ECLA's pioneering contribution from the personality of Raúl Prebisch. For it was Prebisch who single-handedly defined the content and the style of the organization's message and its institutional identity. It is no exaggeration to state that the original proposal formulated by Prebisch in 1949[37] had an enduring impact not only on ECLA's intellectual legacy but on that of the whole UN. The message was further developed in subsequent years,[38] and ECLAC is still capitalizing on that legacy to this day.

ECLA came on the scene during an exciting period of post–World War II reconstruction. It was an era of economic growth and of intellectual effervescence at the international level, coming on the heels of the Great Depression of the 1930s, the victory over fascism, and the tremendous impact Lord Maynard Keynes had had on economic thinking. It was an era of relative optimism that any challenge—including development—could be met if only governments and civil societies put their minds to it. And it was a period in which developing countries were becoming aware of the potential for closing the large gap that separated them from the more developed countries in the Northern Hemisphere.

The ECLA Paradigm

The general thrust of Prebisch's pioneering work is well known. It was born from his empirical observations of how the Great Depression of the 1930s impacted on his own and other Latin American countries. His work was also influenced by European economists, notably John Maynard Keynes.[39] According to Prebisch, countries depending on the export of basic commodities faced inelastic demand with respect to both price and income as well as a systematic bias toward unemployment. Industrialized countries faced the opposite situation: elastic demand that was enhanced by the fact that labor unions were able to participate in part of the gains of increased productivity due to their organized bargaining power. Hans Singer reached similar conclusions in his independent research, especially regarding the elasticities of demand.[40]

Three important conclusions were derived from these observations. First, there was a secular and, in the absence of policy interventions, even inexorable deterioration in the terms of trade for developing countries.[41] Second, the foreign-exchange constraint was an equally or possibly even more important impediment to growth than the domestic-savings constraint, although it was recognized that capital accumulation was an essential element for growth. And, third, there was an asymmetrical relationship between developed and developing countries (dubbed the "center" and the "periphery"), in that gains from international trade accrued more to the benefit of developed than to developing countries.

The latter was due to two complementary but different ideas. The first referred to the effects of the low income elasticity of demand for raw materials on the terms of trade of developing countries. The second was associated with asymmetries in the functioning of labor markets at the Center and the Periphery. Although, in Prebisch's view, these asymmetries were related to the forms of specialization of the various regions, they also played a distinctive role in determining international prices.[42]

The policy prescription derived from these three observations was quite straightforward: Developing countries should industrialize in order to internalize the productivity gains of advanced technology (the phrase Prebisch used is "the application of technical progress to the productive process").[43] This would lead to greater capital accumulation financed through increased savings of the upper- and middle-income groups without placing undue constraints upon the consumption patterns of the poorer segments of society. It would also help to reverse the deterioration in the terms of trade. To Prebisch's credit, he did not prescribe industrialization at any cost,[44] but he did favor barriers to competing imports for long enough to permanently alter domestic relative prices in favor of the industrial sector.

A second set of observations was related to the discontinuities and imperfections in domestic markets and how labor and capital were combined differentially in developed and developing countries. The agricultural sector was deemed to be unresponsive to market signals, given the concentration of land ownership and the abundance of cheap labor; the same could be said for the then-existing industrial sector, which was protected by special privileges and a lack of competition. In general, the private sector did not seem to be responsive to incentives either to invest or to save. These discontinuities and imperfections, which would be further developed in subsequent studies of the commission, were largely the domestic reflection of countries' interaction with the international economy and constituted the structural impediments to development.

The macro and microeconomic conditions sketched above led to a third set of observations: the need for a strong state presence rather than the passive role advocated by Adam Smith and the need to approach development as a long-term proposition. Prebisch emphasized the leading role of the state, although he also recognized the importance of the private sector. But he said remarkably little about short-term policymaking in the traditional realms of fiscal, monetary, and exchange-rate policies, although he briefly touched on the phenomenon of inflation in the 1949–1950 documents in the context of foreign-exchange and savings constraints.

It is difficult to underestimate the impact that these seminal contributions had in the region and beyond. Some observers[45] have pointed out that the scholarship of the commission was deficient[46] and that the commission did not interact enough with the academic community,[47] while others have burnished the original proposals by giving them an ex post facto academic rationale that achieves an intellectual elegance which probably even Prebisch would not have recognized.[48] But both extremes miss the main point: Prebisch was not vying for academic recognition; he was trying to influence policymakers. He presented his case clearly and eloquently in a language and mindset attuned to the level of the technocrats that were beginning to attend UN gatherings at the time. He simplified (some would even say trivialized) complicated notions and made them understandable to public policymakers. In fact, he did it well enough for some of his notions to spill over into respected realms of academia. Certainly the thesis of the declining terms of trade and the tenets of structuralism were treated seriously in prestigious centers of higher learning in Latin America and in industrialized countries. Much of the commission's pioneering work was highly regarded in the emerging discipline offered in schools of economics called development economics.

Some Lines of Inquiry Derived from the ECLA Paradigm

It was not only the paradigmatic quality of ECLA's initial message that should be recorded as part of the UN's intellectual heritage. That holistic framework gave rise to many interrelated ideas that were spawned in the early years of the 1950s and were built upon during the 1960s and beyond:

- The doctrine of industrialization spread rapidly. Industrialization could turn into a strategy for sustained economic development thanks to the technical features of industry: economies of scale, externalities (which included physical infrastructure), transport and

communications facilities, training for the labor force, and the development of new institutions and entrepreneurial classes.[49]
- As a means of contributing to industrialization, and perhaps inspired by the incipient European experience, ECLA promoted the idea of economic integration in Latin America. Its initial efforts took place in Central America.
- The concern about the structural impediments to development (among others, land tenure, weak institutions, segmented labor and capital markets) gave rise to two interrelated activities. The first consisted in the practice, initiated by Prebisch, of undertaking in-depth analysis at the country level; the second espoused economic planning as one of the expressions of a broader, more activist, role of the state.
- The commission undertook significant work in the late 1950s on the structural roots of inflation.
- The commission was one of the first to express concerns that growth would not necessarily lead to improved income distribution or improved social indicators, although the social dimension did not fully come into its own until the 1960s and beyond.
- The commission also addressed the need to mobilize external savings in support of the region's development (a concrete example is ECLA's role in the eventual creation of the Inter-American Development Bank [IDB]).

ECONOMIC INTEGRATION: THE CENTRAL AMERICAN INITIATIVE

One of ECLA's major contributions to the world of ideas, which had tangible results in the case of the five small Central American countries, was to assist them in fostering economic integration. Here, as in numerous other instances, it is hard to discern whether it was ECLA or the Central American governments that took the initiative. According to Victor Urquidi, who from 1952 to 1958 was head of the Mexico City office of ECLA and was directly responsible for economic integration in Central America, it was the governments that took the initiative.[50] According to others, the idea that the small economies of Central America should join their markets to facilitate industrialization originated in the secretariat.[51] In fact, it matters little whether ECLA conceived an idea or whether it took it from elsewhere and then shaped it, gave it coherence, and applied it in the specific context of its member countries.

In the case of Central America, there is no question that ECLA played a major role in fostering economic integration. The fact that it was done by interacting so closely with the governments only made ECLA's role that much more meaningful. Indeed, the pioneering work of ECLA in Central America in the 1950s and beyond reveals a creativity and professionalism that was not confined to the world of ideas. It is also a model of constructive interaction between a part of the UN secretariat and its intergovernmental machinery, what the UN calls "operational activities."

Many facets of this concrete experience are worthy of mention.[52] The first is that neither the national actors[53] nor the ECLA secretariat had a clear vision or blueprint for economic integration. But both recognized that domestic markets were too limited to support industrialization of any significance, at least not beyond the production of the most traditional commodities, such as cement, footwear, and beer. The Central Americans turned to the ECLA secretariat for guidance and technical support, and the secretariat turned to the Central Americans to filter the secretariat's proposals and adopt politically viable policy decisions.

What they came up with in the initial phases was not acceptable to orthodox economists—and was very much opposed by the United States at the time—because it was quite different from generalized trade-liberalization arrangements. Rather, it concentrated on partial and selective arrangements which could be construed as trade-diverting rather than trade-creating, although the ultimate goal appears to have been the creation of an efficient common market.[54]

The initial years of Central American regional economic integration were characterized by a host of bilateral trade agreements between pairs of countries which offered trade preferences or even free trade for a limited number of goods. The rationale behind this scheme was to promote industrialization, which in those times was practically a proxy for promoting development. The most formal and advanced expression of this approach was in the Central American Regime of Integration Industries, which set out to create what, in effect, would be legal but regulated monopolies that were more or less equitably assigned among the five countries. The main incentive for these industries was that they would enjoy free trade within the region and tax incentives and tariff protection during a predetermined period. In order to assure a captive market, these incentives were to be withheld from any competitor for a given number of years (usually ten). But safeguards were also introduced which would allow external competition if the protected industry abused its monopoly position. Two plants were actually set up under this regime (a tire plant in Guatemala and a caustic soda and insecticide plant in Nicaragua), and an additional two plants were designated but never implemented (these would have manufactured pulp and paper and glass containers) before the scheme floundered under the weight of opposition from the public sector to so much intervention (including the firm opposition of the U.S. government). Still, the experience of jointly addressing industrialization on the part of the five governments, with active private-sector participation (the emerging industrial entrepreneurs) and the support of the UN secretariat, left an important mark.

Many other activities were taking place that fostered integration. Institutional machinery was created by the governments to deal with the process, by creating a forum of ministers of economy (the Committee of Economic Cooperation of the Central American Isthmus), for which the ECLA Mexico City office fulfilled the role of secretariat. The committee set up numerous subcommittees which explored cooperative arrangements in many areas, including trade, agriculture, industry, ports, highways, electrification, aerial navigation, and telecommunications. The first regional institutions were created (one to foster industrial technology, the other to train civil servants). And the bilateral arrangements gradually melded into a multilateral trade agreement, which was signed in 1958.[55]

All this led to a strong culture favorable to economic integration, and the ECLA secretariat played a key role in fostering that culture. Perhaps the culmination of ECLA's participation came in 1960 when the five countries signed the General Treaty, which not only consolidated a single multilateral agreement but also aimed at generalized trade liberalization within Central America and the eventual creation of a customs union. In other words, all goods originating in the region, with only a small list of exceptions, would be traded freely within a preset time frame. This instrument was compliant with Article XXIV of the General Agreement on Tariffs and Trade (1947), and, in general, was more market friendly than ECLA's original proposals. However, the secretariat deferred to the governments' more pragmatic response to the pressures exerted by the United States and the more orthodox domestic groups of the private sector.

Finally, and as an indirect measure of how successful ECLA had been in its efforts, the countries created their own secretariat, based in Guatemala City, and relegated ECLA to an advisory role.[56] In fact, the commission continued to exert considerable influence in Central America during the succeeding decades as a backup to the region's own institutions. The Central American experience no doubt influenced the ECLA secretariat in promoting integration at the regional level, as reflected in its landmark document of 1959.[57] The latter not only legitimized the idea of regionwide economic integration but also at least partially legitimized the gradualist and selective approach to the creation of a common market. And as in Central America, governments were closely involved in the 1959 proposal, which took its cue from a "working group on the Latin American Regional Market."

STRUCTURAL IMPEDIMENTS TO DEVELOPMENT

By the middle of the 1950s, and even more so in later years, Latin American technocrats earnestly proclaimed that "profound structural changes" were needed if the countries of the region were to overcome the considerable impediments to development. This conviction, which was gradually assimilated into the collective conscience of all those associated with reformist causes, was at least partially attributable to ECLA's considerable influence. Awareness of the need for institutional and structural change and the need to overcome discontinuities and imperfections in domestic markets appeared in numerous sectoral studies, especially in the areas of industry, mining, and agriculture.[58] In addition, country studies and the biennial flagship documents prepared for the ECLA sessions systematically made the same point.

The growing conviction about the need for structural reforms arose from a series of studies which contributed, in a cumulative fashion, to the conviction that land reform, fiscal reform, and reform of the state were necessary adjuncts to any development policy. While these were perhaps not original ECLA notions, the institution certainly contributed to legitimizing them. The call for structural reforms thus deserves a place in any inventory of important ideas spawned in ECLA. In fact, those ideas had consequences, given the numerous countries that embarked, for example, on programs of land reform (with decidedly mixed results).[59] These initial approaches to the structural impediments to development led to the studies in the 1960s on structural heterogeneity and in the 1970s to styles of development.

THE COUNTRY STUDIES

The original ECLA *manifiesto*[60] of 1949 contains, in addition to the conceptual framework, four economic surveys: on Argentina, Brazil, Chile, and Mexico.[61] An entire section is dedicated to "recent changes in the economic condition of Latin America." But these surveys were only harbingers of things to come. During the 1950s and early 1960s, the institution undertook in-depth studies in numerous countries. These studies, undertaken in the broader context of the secretariat's need to promote economic planning, definitely qualify as part—and an important part—of the UN's intellectual heritage. This was so not only because of the considerable new knowledge that these studies offered to academics, public officials, and the community at large but also because of the discipline they introduced into the production, collection, interpretation, and dissemination of statistical data and indicators.

The country studies were at the same time essential inputs for the secretariat's own understanding of development issues in the region and a vehicle for propagating the ECLA message. They created important partnerships with domestic actors—some of the studies were undertaken jointly by ECLA and a national institution—and permitted the secretariat to identify technicians that were subsequently invited to participate in ECLA's ever-expanding training activities.[62] An additional offshoot of this pioneering work was the basis laid for introducing an internationally comparable system of national accounts. In fact, the first national accounting studies and many statistical offices were set up in numerous countries as a direct result of this pioneering work.

Among the notable country studies that illustrate this type of work under the general title of *Analyses and Projections of Economic Development,* mention should be made of the following: the 1955 study on Brazil, prepared jointly with the Banco Nacional do Desenvolvimento Economico do Brasil;[63] the five-volume study on Argentina;[64] the study on Bolivia;[65] the three-volume study on Colombia;[66] the study on Peru;[67] the study on Panama;[68] and the study on post-revolutionary Cuba.[69] An in-depth study on Mexico was also completed in 1957 but was never published because the Mexican authorities took issue with the findings.[70]

As a result of these and many more national surveys,[71] policymakers came to better understand the functioning of their own economies and the main obstacles to their development. Prebisch often alluded to the national studies to make his theoretical points.[72] The studies explored development issues and alternative policy responses. Sometimes they identified priorities for public and private investments. In short, they had an enormous impact at the time, and they still make for interesting reading today.

THE INITIAL CONCEPT OF ECONOMIC PLANNING

The ECLA secretariat espoused some degree of economic planning very early on in its institutional lifetime. As early as 1952 and 1953, the elements of an "economic development program" were being discussed.[73] This was entirely compatible with the secretariat's views about the active role of the state and its penchant for social engineering. Since this stance took shape at a time when "economic planning" tended to be linked to centrally planned economies, the secretariat took care to clarify that it did not propose a rigorous regimentation of the economy on the part of the state but rather a judicious programming of the public sector's capital outlays in order to complement private investment and contribute to sustainable and dynamic growth.[74] Still, its stance aroused considerable resistance in both academic and business circles.

ECLA promoted its vision of economic planning through seminars and training activities, and by the mid-1950s many governments in the region had established national planning offices (or, in some cases, ministries). It is hard to ascertain a direct cause-and-effect relationship between ECLA's advocacy role and the actions adopted at the national level in numerous countries, especially since the International Bank for Reconstruction and Development (IBRD) and its Economic Development Institute were espousing the same cause, albeit with an even more limited scope.[75] But there is little doubt that the institution had a very strong influence both on the creation of specialized institutions on planning (or "programming") and on the way they carried out their activities. Indeed, the idea of planning for accelerated development took on a life of its own with the explicit endorsement it received from the Kennedy administration under the Alliance for Progress and the Punta del Este Conference of 1961[76] and the creation of the Latin American Institute for Economic and Social Planning (ILPES) in 1962. Thus, the main evolution of ECLA ideas in the areas of planning and their application in the countries of the region occurred in the 1960s.

The Structural Roots of Inflation

The phenomenon of inflation is briefly touched upon in the 1949–1950 landmark documents in the context of foreign-exchange and savings constraints. But inflation was a permanent feature of economic life in the 1950s (and beyond), at least in most of the Southern Cone countries, and at first it did not arouse much interest on the part of the ECLA secretariat. It was only in the mid-1950s that the topic received increasing attention in the yearly economic surveys, all within the context of the perceived separate but interdependent internal and external "gaps" linked to the savings deficit and the external deficit. Inspired by these observations, some of the secretariat staff published, under their own name rather than the institution's, papers which tried to explain the structural origins of inflation, especially based on observations in Mexico and Chile. These studies had great resonance, and at the least had the virtue of putting inflation on the agenda as an important development issue. The first contribution was by Juan Noyola,[77] the second by Osvaldo Sunkel.[78]

There is a legitimate question as to whether these studies can be attributed to the intellectual heritage of ECLAC rather than to the individuals that produced them. At first they did not receive official endorsement. In fact, Prebisch himself issued a report which seemed to be partially at odds with Noyola and Sunkel's premises by calling the confrontation between monetarists and structuralists a "false dilemma."[79] In addition, further work undertaken in the secretariat by Dudley Seers was published only in mimeographed form. However, the authors were, after all, staff members of the institution, and their ideas were at least partially reflected in the secretariat's *Economic Survey* of 1959. Prebisch himself endorsed the key concept that "it would be an error to consider inflation as a purely monetary phenomenon" and to ignore its structural roots.[80] By the early 1960s, the general thrust of Noyola and Sunkel's findings had been inexorably linked with the structuralist school. It therefore does seem legitimate to include the structural roots of inflation in a catalog of the ideas spawned in or by ECLA in the early 1960s.

The main gist of the argument consists of the denial, on the part of structuralism, that orthodox monetary, fiscal, and exchange-rate policies effectively combat inflation. Noyola and Sunkel argued that a reduction in nominal demand would lead primarily to reductions in output, not prices. Tighter credit and higher interest rates would be passed along by firms only through prices, even when a shortage of working capital was forcing them to restrict output. Reduced government expenditures would lead to a contraction of complementary investment and thus of aggregate production. Devaluation would not correct a balance-of-payments disequilibrium by encouraging more exports and fewer imports but would merely succeed in fueling domestic inflation. On the other hand, supply bottlenecks, especially in the agricultural sector, as well as structural rigidities and inflexibilities were equally or more important in explaining sporadic price increases. A careful reading of the documents written at the time suggests a greater tolerance for inflation in Latin America than in other regions on the basis of the tenets of structuralism as well as the long nineteenth-century experience with non-convertible exchange rates.[81] The structural school put greater reliance on price controls and other practices to repress inflation when it threatened the objective of growth.

The main contribution of this novel interpretation of the origins of inflation and the manner in which price increases were propagated was to draw attention to the phenomenon per se and to foster a debate on how to cope with it. It emphasized what perhaps could best be described as the political economy of inflation; that is, the consequences of the struggle between different actors in the distribution of the costs of inflation.[82] This argument had great appeal in the region and provoked a heated debate between structuralists and monetarists; that is, those who base their explanations on the structural and monetary theories of the relationship between inflation and growth. That debate was to persist, with nuances, for several decades and often put ECLA at odds with the IMF in their respective policy prescriptions.

An eloquent expression of the content and scope of the debate was made at the Conference on Inflation and Economic Growth held in Rio de Janeiro on January 3–11, 1963.[83] This debate turned out to be a harbinger of the concerns that would grow in intensity in the 1970s and especially in the 1980s.[84]

THE SOCIAL DIMENSION OF DEVELOPMENT

Two important characteristics of ECLA's initial work which had repercussions in the world of ideas can be classified under the general heading of "social aspects." The first set of ideas appears implicitly in the very first documents, but they are spelled out explicitly in a 1955 paper[85] that argued that development is far too important to be addressed by economists alone. The secretariat suggested that many of the central motivations associated with the development effort "lie outside the usual sphere and working ideas of the economist."[86]

The secretariat appealed to its member governments to launch a multidisciplinary effort involving economists, sociologists, anthropologists, psychologists, and other social scientists. This prescription was followed within the secretariat by bringing sociologists into the staff. The foremost exponent in the secretariat of these matters, José Medina Echavarría, joined the staff in 1952.[87]

The second dimension was the persistent concern of the secretariat—sometimes implicit, at other times explicit—that the fruits of development should benefit everyone and not only a privileged minority. However, the concern for equity came fully into its own only in the 1960s and after. This is suggested by Prebisch himself. In a retrospective publication in the 1980s, he stated:

> Up to this stage (1960), I had not paid sufficient attention to the problem of income disparities, except in the case of the outdated land tenure system. Nor had I paid enough attention in the early CEPAL [ECLA] years to the fact that growth had not benefited large masses of the low-income population, while at the other extreme of the social structure high incomes flourished. Perhaps this attitude of mine was a remnant of my former neo-classicism, which assumed that growth in itself would eventually correct great income disparities.[88]

Cardoso went even farther when he said: "CEPAL trod carefully, up to the end of the 1950s, in proposing socially and politically thorny measures, such as land reform and social equalization policies."[89]

Still, enough was produced under both of these approaches to the social dimensions of development in the pioneering years to lay the groundwork on which subsequent activities would be developed, which were an important wellspring of ideas.

External Financial Assistance and the Creation of the Inter-American Development Bank

Perhaps because ECLA formed part of the UN, whose role includes promoting international cooperation, the commission had always advocated the need for external financial assistance aimed at facilitating development in Latin America. In the 1950s, the institution was favorably disposed toward foreign direct investment (a disposition that became more qualified in the 1960s),[90] but it also consistently sought larger amounts of official finance. This helped legitimize the role of external finance and found concrete expression in two specific instances: the Fourth Extraordinary Meeting of the Inter-American Economic and Social Council, held in Rio de Janeiro, Brazil, in November 1954 and the events leading up to the Punta del Este Conference in 1961, which established the Alliance for Progress.

In the aftermath of the tensions caused within the Inter-American System by the overthrow of the government of Jacobo Arbenz Guzmán in Guatemala, the United States agreed to the convening of a meeting of ministers of finance or economy of the member countries of the OAS. The purpose of the meeting was to address development issues and the need to strengthen development assistance. A measure of the influence that the ECLA secretariat had acquired by that time can be found in the decision, promoted by the Latin American governments, to request the collaboration of ECLA in the preparation and holding of the meeting.[91]

The ECLA secretariat was asked to prepare a report "on practical measures for economic development, the financing of development and problems of international trade in relation to the economic development of Latin America."[92] It was furthermore agreed that the ECLA secretariat would designate a small number of distinguished Latin Americans to constitute a Preparatory Group to formulate recommendations on the basis of the secretariat's document. The group was comprised of Eduardo Frei Montalva as chair, Carlos Lleras Restrepo as rapporteur, and four other distinguished Latin Americans.[93]

This arrangement obviously gave Prebisch and the ECLA secretariat the opportunity to mobilize highly respected Latin Americans to articulate a Latin American perspective vis-à-vis the United States. A perusal of both the pre-

liminary report of the secretariat and the explanatory statement and recommendations of the Preparatory Group attest to just how influential the role of
ECLA was.[94] While the emphasis is on international cooperation, many of the
secretariat's familiar interpretations of the structural impediments to development are present in the reports. Themes that were revisited include the
need for a productivity policy, the essential principles governing trade policy,
and structural obstacles to development. But perhaps the most far-reaching
proposal, at least as it appears in hindsight, was that of creating a special fund
within the Inter-American System in recognition of the fact that direct private investment alone would not meet the region's external financial requirements. The proposal of the secretariat, which was endorsed by the Preparatory
Group, was "to draw up a joint agreement for the creation of an Inter-American Fund for Industrial, Agricultural and Mining Development."[95] The United
States did not support this recommendation during the Meeting of Ministers
of Finance and Economy which was finally held in November 1954.[96] The objection seemed to be, among other things, that the fund would duplicate the
International Bank for Reconstruction and Development.[97] However, although
this was not the first time the idea of a regional financial institution had been
broached, the proposal received additional impetus and momentum from
the ECLA report, an impetus which would culminate, five years later, in the
creation of the IDB.

An Overall Assessment

By the time the organization had reached its fifth year of activity, it had
received ample recognition and had left an important mark among Latin
American policymakers. Extensive proof for this claim can be found in the
proceedings of the commission's yearly meetings, especially in the statements
of the Latin American delegates and heads of state during the opening and
closing sessions.[98] For this reason, the person who perhaps knew more than
anyone else about the UN's work in the economic arena, Sidney Dell, remarked
on "the immense influence that was exerted, both inside and outside the United
Nations, by the group of economists serving ECLA during the early post-war
years."[99] Albert Fischlow put it another way:

> By the end of the decade the Commission's policy emphasis on domestic in-
> dustrialization had found favor in most Latin American countries. An un-
> usual consensus on both the method of analysis and the development strategy
> it implied pervaded the region. Orthodoxy maintained its hold on only a
> small, older generation of economists trained in the European tradition. Al-
> though international agencies defended the tenets of a universal economics

during the 1950s, the heretical structuralists held sway and even gained adherents among sympathetic foreign academics.[100]

In addition to the influence that ECLA had acquired outside Latin America during the 1950s, the central conceptual underpinnings of the original ECLA *manifiesto* were given a global dimension when Raúl Prebisch launched the UN Conference on Trade and Development (UNCTAD). Indeed, Prebisch's main report to the conference, which was held in 1964, starts out with familiar arguments about the declining terms of trade, the differential ways in which technical progress is assimilated in industrialized and developing countries, and the differences between developed and developing countries in the use of labor. It emphasizes the asymmetrical relationship between the "center" and the "periphery."[101] The style of the report and the phrases used are totally reminiscent of ECLA documents. As for the policy prescriptions, these, too, are vintage ECLA. They include, in the first place, the need for developing countries to industrialize, although the reiterated necessity for import substitution was complemented with "the need to export manufactured goods."[102] In short, the ideas promoted by UNCTAD in the 1960s are clearly an outgrowth and an extension of ECLA's seminal ideas of the 1950s.[103]

The Immediate Post-Prebisch Years (1963–1972): Variants on (and Some Deviations from) the Same Themes

By the end of the 1950s, some Latin American economies were showing signs of stress under the weight of a slowdown in world trade and some of the inherent weaknesses of the strategy being followed.[104] Indeed, the policies associated with industrialization based on import substitution provoked distortions in order to induce desired responses, but they did not adequately allow for the indirect, and undesired, consequences of the intervention. The external vulnerability of the economies, instead of decreasing, tended to increase under the weight of overvalued exchange rates, reliance on imported capital goods and intermediate goods, and an implicit bias against export and agriculture. The expectation of higher-paying jobs in industry and the attractions of the cities led to massive rural-urban migrations, but the more capital-intensive industries did not absorb all this labor. Thus, modernization came to be linked to greater inequality and urban squalor. Another imbalance appeared on the fiscal side, as generous tax incentives to industrialization and a shift in the structure of imports toward goods that paid little or no import duties depressed fiscal receipts while ever-greater demands were put on expenditures. The monetization of the deficit contributed to excess demand inflation.[105]

Within the ECLA secretariat, as within Latin America, there were a number of reactions to the changing circumstances at the national, regional, and global levels. One response can be described as business as usual, or more of the same, which is reflected in numerous secretariat documents that appear to assign an unqualified validity to the seminal propositions. A second response was to build on the conceptual framework of the 1950s in such a way as to reflect recognition of those changing circumstances but without a clear change of course. Examples can be found in the secretariat's work on further industrialization, deepening economic integration, economic programming or planning, the social dimension of development, and structural heterogeneity. And a third response was to revisit the ECLA doctrine with a critical look, as reflected in the dependency perspective. More significant, outside the secretariat, but not within it, public policymakers and academics were flirting with a return to orthodoxy (more reliance on the market, less state intervention), which would lead to the monetarist approach of the 1970s.

Some New Departures

Perhaps fittingly, the dividing line between the 1950s and the 1960s can be found in an ECLAC document which was Raúl Prebisch's swan song: the main document presented to the last session of the commission he was to attend as executive secretary (Mar del Plata, Argentina, May 1963).[106] On the one hand, the document contains a reiteration of the seminal ideas of the 1950s, a grand summary of the considerable output of the secretariat during his tenure. On the other hand, it announces, or at least hints at, new departures: the need for greater efficiency in manufacturing, the need for trade preferences, the need for deepening economic integration, a greater concern for the social aspects of development, and newfound doubts about the benefits of foreign direct investment.[107] There is another, more subtle, departure: The tone and mood of the secretariat's documents had changed. In the 1950s, these tended to be optimistic, conveying a message that development was feasible (presumably if only ECLA's prescriptions were followed). In the 1960s, they turned decidedly pessimistic, conveying the message that the obstacles to development were indeed daunting. For example, in the introduction to the 1959 report on the common market, the secretariat notes: "The illusion that might have been cherished in the decade immediately following the Second World War, to the effect that the development of Latin American economy was gaining great momentum, has been completely dispelled."[108] This note of caution and discouragement appears in most of ECLA's documents throughout the 1970s and 1980s, and only in the 1990s does a more positive tone reappear. In the same vein, the documents became more critical of the prevailing strategies and policies being adopted in the region.

INDUSTRIALIZATION REVISITED

Industrialization continued to be a leitmotif during the 1960s and beyond. However, the secretariat recognized the limits of import substitution and the strain that industrialization was placing on the balance of payments. Its assessment of affairs can be gauged from a rather lengthy quotation of a document published in 1961:

> The process of industrialization suffers from three main flaws which have weakened its contribution to improving the standard of living. These are: a) all industrialization activity is directed towards the domestic market; b) the choice of industries to be established has been based more on circumstantial reasons than on considerations of economic yield; and, c) industrialization has failed to overcome the external vulnerability of the Latin American countries. The excessive channeling of industry towards the domestic market is a result of the development policy pursued in the Latin American countries and of the lack of international incentives to exports of industrial goods from the region. Development policies have been discriminatory as regards exports. Assistance has been given—through tariffs or other restrictions—to industrial production for internal consumption but not to industrial production for export. The production of many industrial goods has thus been developed at a cost far above the international level, when they could have been obtained with a much smaller cost differential in exchange for exports of other industrial products which might have been produced more profitably. The same could be said of new lines of primary commodities for export and even of traditional export commodities within certain relatively narrow limits. It would not, therefore, have been enough to place production for export on an equal footing with production for the domestic market. In the large centers, measures would have had to be adopted to facilitate imports of certain industrial goods from the developing countries, thereby giving these countries a greater capacity to import precisely those goods for which there is a greater difference in cost. In this way, a very useful division of labor would have developed in the industrial field, very different from the traditional pattern of trading primary commodities for industrial goods. Until recently, no serious effort had been made to establish such a division of industrial activities among the countries of Latin America.[109]

The secretariat's response, which had an impact on policymakers in Latin America during the 1960s, was threefold. For the larger countries, it advocated backward linkages,[110] thus promoting the manufacture of intermediate and capital goods.[111] Second, a fairly intense effort was undertaken to persuade member governments of the need for greater efficiency and the need to promote the export of manufactures.[112] Finally, an expansion of domestic demand was sought by promoting import substitution on a regional level through economic integration.

The secretariat prepared in-depth sectoral studies, reminiscent of the country surveys, about the possibilities offered by backward linkages and greater efficiency. These studies covered not only capital goods but also some core activities in the region's industrialization: the production of pulp and paper, steel, chemicals, fertilizers, and textiles and the processing of food, for example.[113] The studies were complemented by seminars and symposiums. The foremost example was the Latin American Symposium on Industrialization, held in Santiago from March 14 to 25 of 1966, under the joint aegis of ECLA and the United Nations Industrial Development Organization (UNIDO), as a preparatory activity to a global symposium to be held the following year in Vienna. The extensive documentation prepared for this event by the secretariat and participating governments reveals an almost uniform concern for greater efficiency, promotion of backward linkages, specialization within the regional market to take advantage of economies of scale, and promotion of exports.[114]

The secretariat also worked at the subregional and national levels, for example, in Central America, in the Andean region, and more specific studies in the large countries (Argentina, Brazil, and Mexico). In sum, the secretariat's intellectual commitment to industrialization as a key to development continued in the 1960s. The fact that member states were warned by the early 1960s about the dangers of overprotection deserves recognition. Although this message appears to have had some impact, judging, for example, from the proceedings of the above-mentioned symposium, it also appears that it was insufficient to weaken the influence of the constituency in favor of maintaining protection at the national level.[115] Indeed, chambers of industry tended to prevail upon governments to protect nascent industries to a greater degree and for longer periods than was perhaps warranted. Today, with the benefit of hindsight, it could be argued that the secretariat did not take a firm enough position on the need for the region's industrialization to change course. However, it did, in fact, articulate new messages that pointed in the right direction, a matter that must be included in the intellectual legacy of the times.

ECONOMIC INTEGRATION: THE LATIN AMERICAN COMMON MARKET

ECLAC advocated economic integration as a way to achieve a more efficient industrialization, basically to continue import substitution but at the regional and subregional levels. Inspired by economic integration in Europe and by the Central American experience, the ECLAC secretariat organized, as was its custom, a Working Group on the Latin American Regional Market to undertake the preparatory work for the formulation of a Latin American common market. The combined work of the secretariat and of the working group gave rise to the 1959 landmark document[116] which legitimized the idea of regional economic integration and the gradualist and selective approach to the creation of a common market.[117]

This document and the report of the working group led to the signing, on February 18, 1960, of the Montevideo Treaty, which created the Asociación Latinoamericana de Libre Comercio (ALALC), composed of eleven countries (Mexico and all South American countries). The Montevideo Treaty was open for signature by membership for other Latin American countries, although in subsequent years it became fashionable to talk of "convergence" between ALALC and the Central American Common Market. ECLA was very influential not only in the creation of the ALALC but also in supporting the secretariat created to implement the provisions contained in the Montevideo Treaty. These included the commitment to create a free trade area within twelve years of the treaty's coming into effect. However, initial steps to liberalize trade were partial and progressive, based on positive lists of goods that were to receive preferential treatment between different countries. While this is not the place to assess the outcome of the ALALC's experiences,[118] the main point to be made is the instrumental role of ECLA in its creation and early development. Once more, ideas sown in ECLA would bear fruit—albeit with unintended consequences—in the region.

The topic of economic integration was a priority on ECLA's agenda throughout the 1960s. During this period, the secretariat slowly realized that there were flaws in its conceptual framework, which held that free trade between Latin American countries could promote trade diversion for competitive imports and increase the foreign exchange available for complementary imports from the industrial countries. Trade growth was turning out not to be reciprocal; rather, the large countries could sell manufactures to the smaller countries, but the latter largely exported primary products. Thus, small countries felt that they had simply altered the source of their export earnings rather than their amount. The large countries did not welcome competition from one another.[119]

The secretariat tried to respond to these circumstances within the Latin American Free Trade Area (LAFTA). Simultaneously, a group of governments in the Andean region reacted more decidedly: Dissatisfied with the pace at which ALALC was evolving, they decided to accelerate their own subregional process. Although reluctant at first to sponsor divisions within LAFTA, the ECLA secretariat finally came around and had a second chance to promote its ideas in the design of the conceptual framework which led to the signing of the Cartagena Agreement in May 1969. Again, the institution was committed to working closely with the intergovernmental and common machinery created by the agreement. The Cartagena Agreement sought deeper commitments to integration and a more active involvement of governments to assure that the benefits of integration would be distributed in an equitable manner. The agreement contemplated the joint programming of public investments, some regulation of private investment, and the coordination of national economic policies.[120] A separate decision (Decision 24) tried to regulate foreign direct investment in order to make it more responsive to the joint priorities of the region. In other words, some of ECLA's central ideas—industrialization, planning, achieving policy objectives through an active state—seemed to be embodied in the Cartagena Agreement. While things did not work out as intended, once more ECLA had played a pivotal role in defining and promoting economic integration, this time in the Andean region. And once more, it did so in such close association with the member governments that it is difficult to ascertain where the initiatives originated.

STRUCTURAL HETEROGENEITY

Implicit in ECLA's seminal proposal was the view that Latin America was characterized by dual economies: a modern, export-oriented sector which incorporated modern technology and a subsistence economy which continued with primitive forms of production. In other words, the traditional export sector became an island of development, but the rest of the economy made little progress. The link between the two was cheap seasonal labor. Other social scientists at the time had made the same observations, notably Arthur W. Lewis in the economic sphere and J. H. Boeke in the social area.[121] In succeeding years, and as industrialization progressed, it became necessary to refine this analysis and to explore the heterogeneous characteristics not only of the productive sectors but also of societies and even political interaction.

ECLA made important contributions in this regard, mainly through the work of Aníbal Pinto.[122] It had become clear that most Latin American economies, even the more backward ones, did not respond to the classical link between modern export-oriented enclaves and subsistence activities. Rather, seen from the angle of production, there were numerous intermediate situations, which included modern industrial activities and various intermediate industrial and tertiary activities. Even some agricultural activities were being developed with higher levels of technology. Thus, average productivity showed dramatic deviations from one subsector to the other. In addition, the commission pointed out that modes of interaction between relatively more modern and relatively less modern sectors varied from one situation to another. All this translated into important differences in the capacity of distinct activities to generate employment and accounted for considerable disparities in the wages paid in different activities.

These reflections had a profound effect in Latin America. The expression "structural heterogeneity" crept into the lexicon of technicians and academics. And the concept spilled over into other areas of inquiry of ECLA, such as its work on the segmentation of labor markets and the asymmetrical relationships between urban and rural areas.[123] The concept of structural heterogeneity made it easier to bring together the economists and sociologists in the secretariat. It also became the basis for the work on styles of development undertaken in the 1970s.

Economic Planning Revisited

ECLA had espoused planning since its creation as a mechanism to introduce coherence in public policies and prioritize public expenditure. The institution insisted on its message during the 1950s. Prebisch himself often alluded to the need for planning, which he described as "a conscious and deliberate effort to influence economic and social trends in order to pursue clear goals."[124] He furthermore argued that ECLA-style planning was compatible with a vibrant private sector and with political democracy.[125]

But what gave planning a new boost in the 1960s was the legitimization it was given by the Alliance for Progress. In fact, a fairly complicated machinery was set up, through the establishment of a panel of nine experts to be named by the Inter-American Economic and Social Council, whose role would be to evaluate national development plans. These plans were also supposed to be prepared with the technical support of joint missions, made up of staff from the OAS, ECLA, and the IDB.

One of the institutional expressions of these developments was the creation, in 1962, of the Latin American Institute for Economic and Social Planning (ILPES, in its Spanish acronym). ILPES was created as a subsidiary body of ECLA and was funded entirely by donations (extrabudgetary financing, in UN parlance).[126] Prebisch simultaneously led ILPES and ECLA for a brief period, and he continued to lead ILPES even after he left ECLA.[127]

Both ECLA and ILPES were active in training, providing technical assistance, and undertaking research on diverse subjects related to planning or programming.[128] They also managed to refine their message on the role of planning in the Latin American context and developed what they considered to be relatively sophisticated techniques, especially in the areas of project preparation,[129] budgeting,[130] priority-setting for public expenditures, and goal-setting for macroeconomic indicators.[131] At the same time, national institutions dedicated to planning were either created or strengthened during most of the 1960s.

Clearly, the ideas generated by ECLA/ILPES during this period had great resonance in the region, especially in the initial years.[132] A renewed effort was made in the area of training, which permitted the secretariat to develop its own textbooks[133] and to interact with large contingents of students from all countries of the region. This proved to be an excellent tool for disseminating the ECLA message and for receiving inputs from the field.

THE SOCIAL DIMENSION OF DEVELOPMENT REINFORCED

There are numerous examples during the 1950s of the secretariat's concern regarding the inequitable pattern of growth in Latin America. The yearly economic surveys as well as the in-depth country studies show initial attempts to measure income distribution, and many of the issues raised by the structuralist school revolve around extreme inequalities within the economies and societies. Still, the social dimension of development did not really come into its own until the early 1960s. By then, according to Cardoso, "social aspects were for the first time explicitly discussed and introduced into the explanatory model."[134]

The pioneering work on this subject was done by José Medina Echavarría.[135] This work is unusual not only because of its innovative content, which addresses the sociological and political dimensions of development, but also because it is one of the very few ECLA documents of the time to be published under the responsibility of an individual author.[136] Clearly, the reflections contained in the document—some of which were politically sensitive at the time—could not receive the full official sanction of Prebisch. Still, by allowing the document to circulate at all, Prebisch made a concession to the esteem that Medina Echavarría commanded and at the same time made an important move in the direction of a more integrated approach to development on the secretariat's part.[137]

A more conventional output of the secretariat came out concurrently with Medina Echavarría's pioneering document in the form of *Social Trends and Programmes in Latin America*.[138] This covered population trends, the changing social structure and social integration, the urban-rural relationship, and how to further integrate economic and social development. Rather than a single innovative idea in the area of social development, ECLA's contribution was to bring the social dimension more centrally into development thinking in Latin America. It did so, for example, by trying to establish the distinctive economic behavioral patterns of different social groups, clarifying the special character-istics of marginality, and highlighting the social position of indigenous popu-lations, all seen from the Latin American perspective. "In short, sociology shared the orientation characteristic of ECLA's economic thinking, namely avoidance of the mechanical transposition of existing theories."[139] ECLA also helped to disseminate the notion that socioeconomic conflict was an almost inevitable part of the process of economic development and therefore had to be dealt with.[140]

A Note of Dissent: The Dependency Perspective

The dependency movement represents the revisionist approach to ECLA's seminal ideas. ECLA cannot claim paternity for the movement,[141] which, al-though it was based on an historical-structural method, is much more a con-tribution to sociopolitical analysis than an economic model. But important contributions came out of the ECLA secretariat during the 1960s, particularly through the reflections and writings of Fernando Henrique Cardoso and Enzo Faletto.[142] Indeed, ECLA—or at least Cardoso, who was working at ILPES at the time—can probably lay claim to having spawned dependency studies re-garding development.[143] ECLA's seminal ideas of the 1950s informed Cardoso's work, especially as a point of reference.[144] On the one hand, he endorsed the central tenets of those ideas, but on the other he criticized them severely, ba-sically for not going farther and deeper. For this reason, of all the ideas pro-duced in the institution in the 1960s, dependency in relation to development, although it was linked to the past, also marks the strongest departure into new conceptual territory. Cardoso wanted to refocus the entire debate about Latin America's development, both to add a sociological perspective and to distance it from rigid Marxist and nationalist interpretations. "He wanted to show that there were more possibilities for Latin American development than socialism or underdevelopment with authoritarianism."[145]

The originality of the *dependentistas* derives from using the position of a country within the international system as a determinant of class behavior. It gained ground in the 1960s in response to the deficiencies of modernization theory as well as to the observed limitations of industrialization via import substitution. Dependency theory stood in contrast to the resurgence of or-thodoxy and its external orientation.

In the economic realm, three propositions are central to the dependency perspective. One is the principle of unequal exchange. The second refers to the adverse consequences of private foreign investment. And the third deals with the disarticulation of the peripheral capitalist economy due to its skewed consumption pattern, which is copied from that of the advanced industrial countries.[146]

According to Marxist theory, unequal exchange follows directly from the large wage disparities between developed and developing economies. Low wages artificially reduce the prices of exports produced in the developing countries to the benefit of buyers rather than sellers. According to the *dependentistas,* staying in the international economy is a mistake under such conditions, since trade impoverishes the developing countries as a whole and benefits only elite groups. However, the presence of elite groups explains the strong persistence of these disadvantageous trading relationships.

According to this analysis, open capital markets only accentuate the perverse effects of the free movement of goods. Here the *dependentistas* take issue with the ECLA secretariat's espousal of external financial assistance, especially foreign direct investment. As they see it, foreign direct investment simply provides an opportunity for international firms to pursue their global strategy at the expense of national concerns, usually in alliance with domestic elites. Dependency analysis saw the fatal flaw of the import substitution policy, although it is cloaked in nationalist garb, as the concession of favorable treatment to foreign firms.[147] More than static profits were involved: *Dependentistas* argued that there can be no autonomous development so long as technology is externally supplied rather than indigenously created.

The third characteristic of the dependency perspective is the adverse impact of industrialization on income distribution. Industrial production based on domestic markets is based on income concentration, since it is the middle- and upper-income groups that imitate the consumption patterns of more developed countries, and it is these groups that make up the domestic market for manufactured goods. *Dependentistas* observed that aggregate growth may be sustained, but only at the expense of an unequal, and possibly increasingly unequal, distribution of income. Under this scenario, external bottlenecks are primarily the consequence of the high-import content of such distorted consumption and production structures rather than of insufficient exports.

There is thus a special place within the dependency perspective of the link between income distribution, consumption, and production. While that link is an implicit part of structuralist doctrine, dependency analysts developed it more fully. The relationship ultimately turns on the quantitative sensitivity of the consumption structure to income distribution, the consequent impact on foreign trade, and the productivity growth associated with the resulting production pattern.[148]

Finally, dependency was characterized as much by divergence as by convergence. The rather pessimistic and "no-way-out" implications contained in André Gunder Frank's "development-of-underdevelopment" thesis is not characteristic of Cardoso and Faletto's approach. On the contrary, the latter emphasized the possibility of locally generated change—and not just self-perpetuation—to achieve dynamic development.

An Overall Assessment

The 1960s were by no means as creative as the previous decade. But ECLA continued to develop some of its seminal ideas and made an effort, perhaps belatedly, to adapt them to changing circumstances. And at least one totally new and creative line of thinking developed around the dependency perspective which can be viewed as a serious critique of the seminal ideas; that is, a dissenting voice within the secretariat.

The Early Iglesias Years: The Search for Identity in the 1970s

The 1970s were a particularly turbulent time for ECLA, as indeed was the case for the global economy and, by extension, for the Latin American economies. The UN was entering a period of North-South confrontation, illustrated by the negotiations undertaken around the resolutions espousing the international development decades and the special session of the General Assembly on a new international economic order.[149] The industrialized countries broke with the established global monetary order of the postwar era when the United States ended the convertibility of dollars into gold. The abrupt rise in oil prices had far-reaching consequences and marked a stark differentiation between net oil importers and net oil exporters among developing countries. A related phenomenon was the mobilization by transnational banks of the surplus generated by the oil exporters and the channeling of these funds through direct loans to the governments of the oil importers, thus planting the seed of the debt overhang that would reach crisis proportions in the early 1980s.

In the world of ideas, international monetarism gained sway at the expense of traditional orthodoxy. Not only was money important, but domestic credit management became the central instrument for treating external imbalances, an approach endorsed by the stabilization programs of the IMF. The general thrust of ECLA's central tenets was increasingly cast as a complete inversion of the dominant prescription of prudent credit management, a reliance on the market and the private sector, and export orientation.[150]

Now, with the benefit of hindsight, it appears that the ECLA secretariat was slow to react to these dramatic changes. Rather, for a time the secretariat adopted a rather defensive posture regarding the validity of its seminal ideas, thereby contributing to the debate, but with perhaps less creativity and freshness than had been apparent in the pioneering years. The decade probably marks the low point in the institution's creativity or capacity to generate ideas. Andrés Bianchi diplomatically pointed out that "the first half of the 1970s was not, for sure, ECLA's best moment."[151] And as astute an observer as Fernando Henrique Cardoso remarked: "CEPAL thinking at that time entered upon a phase of relative decline. The consistency and straightforwardness of its prime was succeeded by a period of increasing prolixity and theoretical vagueness in the CEPAL documents."[152]

In contrast, competing think tanks, in the form of new academic centers of excellence, were springing up in some of the larger Latin American countries. Some of them were no doubt influenced by ECLA's earlier years, but they tended to be more rigorous and up to date in terms of the economics being taught in developed countries. Edmar Bacha offers an interesting insight when he describes some of the founders of these centers as *paracepalinos* (crypto-ECLACarians).[153] In fact, by the mid-1970s, some *paracepalinos* were beginning to appear among ECLA's own staff, as a result of a gradual change of generations. This intensified the internal debate slowly taking shape over the following years regarding the future directions of the institution.[154]

Building on the Existing Heritage and Some New Departures

Even in the worst of times the institution showed some vitality in generating ideas. The main areas of intellectual creativity that can be identified in this period are the continuing work on structuralism, this time in the guise of "styles of development"; further clarification of the scope, content, and characteristics of absolute and relative poverty; the initial consideration of some emerging issues, including the environment, development, and the status of women in the countries of the region; and the commission's contribution to the global discussion on development strategies.[155]

STYLES OF DEVELOPMENT

The work produced in the 1970s on styles of development built on previous work in the 1960s and other activities undertaken outside of ECLA.[156]

The main proponent among the economists was Aníbal Pinto, building on his earlier "structural heterogeneity" thesis. The contributions of sociologists Marshal Wolfe and Jorge Graciarena are also noteworthy.[157] This further development of the scope, depth, and characteristics of structuralism was innovative and influential. It also facilitated an integrated approach by the economists and the sociologists of the secretariat.

All of the authors had as a point of departure a deep sense of dissatisfaction with the course of development in the region. They defined the concept of styles of development as "the way in which human and material resources are organized and assigned within a particular system with the object of solving such questions as what goods and services to produce, how, and for whom."[158] Attention was centered on two sets of features. First, those which make up the structural basis of the productive capacity, especially the structure of production and employment between and within sectors, the differentiation between various technological strata, and the way production is linked to domestic and external demand. Second, the more dynamic elements of the system, which are revealed by analyzing the level and composition of demand and its underlying basic factors, such as the level and distribution of income.

In attempting to characterize patterns of production, employment, savings, investment, land tenure, and a host of other attributes of the different Latin American economies, Pinto and his colleagues were revisiting familiar themes of the *estructuralista* school of development in a new and perhaps more coherent manner. For example, in exploring consumption patterns in the region, the authors denounced the conspicuous consumption of upper-income groups as inimical to savings and culturally alienating, since the aim of aspiring lower- and middle-income groups was to imitate the consumption patterns of more advanced societies. These ideas, which also reflect the influence of the dependency perspective, had some impact in the region, and just as the phrase "structural heterogeneity" had crept into the lexicon of academics and even the media in the previous decade, the new term of "styles of development," in a somewhat pejorative sense, was popularized in the 1970s.

ABSOLUTE AND RELATIVE POVERTY

Probably the most lasting contributions of ECLA to the world of ideas during the 1970s can be found in the considerable progress achieved in clarifying, probably for the first time, the extent, characteristics, and scope of relative and absolute poverty in Latin America. While the institution had been dealing with estimates of income distribution since its early years,[159] serious work

at the country level to measure and analyze income distribution, and especially its evolution, had never been undertaken.

Work was begun in 1971, with a joint project conducted by ECLA and the
Development Research Center of the World Bank. Seminars were organized
in Santiago, and work began in twelve countries.[160] The main outputs were
the systematic preparation and publication of statistics on income distribution, the application of a methodology to adapt those statistics to the system
of national accounts, and the provision of a basis of comparison of income
distribution between countries and within countries over time. The household surveys undertaken to support this work were also the basis for ECLA's
initial studies on the incidence of absolute poverty in the region. This work
was pursued jointly with the United Nations Development Programme and
gave rise to several groundbreaking publications.[161]

By the end of the 1980s, policymakers in the region were much better informed about the incidence, characteristics, and implications of poverty in
their respective countries. This was the first stage in targeting public expenditures and, in general, contributing to public awareness regarding the extent of
poverty in the region. The more or less self-contained nature of this work (it
did not need a holistic framework to be useful) was also a harbinger of the
work to be undertaken in the 1980s on short-term policymaking.

EMERGING ISSUES

In 1972, the UN Conference on the Human Environment was held in
Stockholm, which suggested that humanity has the capacity to transform its
surroundings in such a way as to either enhance its well-being and quality of
life or to wreak incalculable harm. Enrique Iglesias, who had been involved in
the preparation of the conference, was inspired to follow up the commitments
adopted by giving them a Latin American and Caribbean dimension. Thus, in
the mid-1970s, ECLAC for the first time seriously introduced the environmental dimension to its activities. Most of the work undertaken during that
period, in terms of research and seminars, is reflected in a publication of the
end of the decade.[162]

Rather than dwell on the multiple ideas that were generated by this work,
what really deserves recognition is the contribution of ECLA to increasing
awareness of environmental issues on the part of policymakers and civil society. This awareness was of course enhanced by the Brundtland Commission's
historic report[163] and especially by the additional momentum provided by the
Conference on Environment and Development held in Rio de Janeiro in 1992.
But after the 1970s, institutions to deal with the issue were created, usually

headed by ministers with cabinet rank. A rapid growth of non-governmental organizations dealing with the environment took place, and moderate progress was achieved in gaining recognition that environmental protection and development were not necessarily at odds with each other. It was increasingly understood that degradation of natural resources and contamination of the habitat could seriously compromise the development effort. To the extent that attitudes have changed, ECLA cannot claim credit for the change, but it certainly made a contribution.[164]

Another emerging issue that the secretariat addressed in this period dealt with women in development as seen from the regional perspective. The topic deserves at least a brief mention because of ECLA's contribution to public awareness in Latin America and the Caribbean on the condition of women and its proposals to further their participation in development. Perhaps inspired by the fact that the first world conference which gave rise to the UN's Decade for Women was held in the region—in Mexico City—ECLA assembled a team of social scientists to explore the status of women in the region. They met first in Santiago and published the results of their deliberations.[165] In the ensuing years, the institution has organized five regional conferences and developed an ample bibliography which aims fundamentally to end discrimination against women and ensure their equal participation in society.[166] It is difficult to measure the impact of this work—part of it is conceptual, part of it more in the vein of advocacy—but it no doubt contributed to bringing about a change in the status of women in Latin American and Caribbean societies. For example, it would today be "politically incorrect" for a government cabinet in any country to exclude women from its ranks, in stark contrast to the situation in 1975. And on other indicators—the proportion of women in higher education, the proportion of women in the work force, the proportion of women in leadership positions—the change, although insufficient, has been quite remarkable. In this, the UN, and ECLA, made a contribution.

THE INTERNATIONAL DEVELOPMENT STRATEGY

Since this chapter covers the ideas generated by ECLA, it would be remiss not to mention, albeit briefly, the work undertaken in the 1970s (and beyond) to assess compliance with General Assembly resolutions regarding international development strategy. More than spawning original ideas regarding development, this endeavor contributed to a work ethic, at the regional level, to participate in a global dialogue (some would say a confrontation) regarding the future course of development. It had a common root with the work going on in the secretariat on styles of development; it also stemmed from a profound dissatisfaction with the course of international cooperation for development.

In general, developed countries tended to approach the dialogue by emphasizing the responsibilities of developing countries and the quality of domestic policymaking. Developing countries, for their part, emphasized the international environment and the asymmetrical relations between North and South (a familiar proposition at ECLA). Resolutions tended to be long, rhetorical, and accusatory.[167] This whole process of multilateral diplomacy in the economic and social spheres is described elsewhere in the Intellectual History Project. The point to be made here is that ECLA, for better or for worse, contributed to legitimizing this approach in its Latin American and Caribbean constituency.

What can be said in the secretariat's defense is that the documents behind the biennial exercise of assessing the results of the International Development Strategies (IDS), especially in their second decade (the 1970s), were prepared with the usual professionalism found in the yearly economic surveys.[168] In fact, the assessments gave the secretariat the opportunity to reiterate its historical interpretation of Latin American development.[169] It also provided an opportunity to interact with its Latin American and Caribbean constituency, but at the same time, it exacerbated the North-South cleavage among its membership along the fault lines of the new international economic order. A case in point is in the Quito Evaluation, in which ECLA assessed the results of the IDS for the first decade (the 1960s) in Latin America and the Caribbean. The U.S. delegation felt compelled to express reservations or at least make comments on thirty-eight of the ninety-one points contained in the document.[170]

At any rate, in the 1970s, the ECLA secretariat continued to play a role in disseminating global issues in its region and in transmitting regional issues to the global intergovernmental bodies. The IDS exercises were one of the vehicles for such a two-way exchange of views.

An Overall Assessment

The 1970s, then, was a period of transition. Some of the activities represent an extension of work carried out in previous decades, while others, by bringing in relatively new topics of the UN, represent the starting point for activities that would be developed in subsequent decades. In spite of the fact that this was a relatively fallow period for the secretariat in terms of its intellectual output, it nevertheless continued to show signs of vitality and creativity.

The Late Iglesias and the Post-Iglesias Years: Short-Term Policies to Deal with the Crisis of the 1980s

The turbulence of the 1970s extended into the 1980s with a vengeance. Important changes were going on in the world economy that would later be characterized as the process of globalization. They were reflected in fundamental transformations in the way the production and distribution of goods occurred in the global economy and in the increasing transnationalization of services. Modes of transport were changing rapidly, and international flows of private capital were growing exponentially. An increasing proportion of trade was controlled by transnational firms, and intrafirm trade was increasing rapidly. Multilateral institutions created to deal with the international economy were slow to adapt, and the major players created their own mechanisms of dialogue and coordination.

The new international economic order was not precisely what the framers of GA Resolution 3201 (S-VI) had in mind; rather, it greatly limited the latitude of sovereign states to design and apply national economic policies and tended to accentuate the divide between North and South. The international marketplace was becoming increasingly competitive and placing ever-greater demands on those that wished to participate. The ideology behind international monetarism was complemented by the imperative of succumbing to the realities of the international economy, which increasingly meant playing by the implicit rules globalization imposed on developing economies.

Clearly, the Latin American and Caribbean countries were not adequately prepared to meet the challenge, although several of them, especially in the Southern Cone, were experimenting with trade and financial liberalization.[171] The term used to describe this process was *apertura,* or opening up the economy.

Most countries had been struggling since the mid-1970s to maintain economic growth in spite of a deteriorating international situation. The terms of trade had turned against them, particularly the net petroleum importers; international rates of inflation were rising, with a multiplier effect in the region; and demand for the region's basic commodities was weakening. During the 1970s, most countries coped with their deteriorating balance-of-payments situation by external borrowing, mostly from private commercial banks; the yearly net inflow rose from less than US$5 billion in 1970 to almost US$27 billion in 1979.[172] Thus, liabilities in foreign currencies, both public and private, grew very rapidly.

These adverse trends all came to a head in the early 1980s as growth slowed down in the industrialized countries and the international economy went into recession with high rates of inflation. Demand for and the prices of

Latin America's commodities were down, and the burden of debt servicing was growing exponentially.[173] The rapid rise of international interest rates aggravated the situation in 1981 and led to the Mexican default of mid-1982. This, in turn, put an abrupt end to the access of Latin American countries to the private international capital markets and ushered in a protracted period—1982 to 1990—during which the region became a net exporter of financial resources. All of these factors were at the root of the profound and prolonged depression of the 1980s, which were known as the lost decade to development.

At first, the region's adjustment and stabilization were approached in a disorderly manner and at an extremely high social cost. A curious mixture of controls and liberalization, of heterodox and orthodox approaches, can be found in the first half of the 1980s. Much was made of the "heterodox" adjustment programs of Argentina, Brazil, and Peru, which sought to control inflation without falling into recession by guiding expectations through price and income controls in the short run and liberalizing markets in the medium term. While they ultimately failed, they offered a laboratory of experiences which ECLAC[174] was privileged to study.[175] Within the secretariat, differing views about how to address the future were still not resolved. Rather, Iglesias was still presiding over a divided house, with one group adopting a defensive position regarding the institution's historical proposals and another advocating a more pragmatic approach.[176] Evolving circumstances in the region seem to have favored the latter view.

The Secretariat Turns to Short-Term Policy Prescriptions

Paradoxically, the disastrous situation for the region's economies had a salutatory effect on ECLA; it forced the secretariat to turn its attention to the dominant preoccupations of the moment rather than attempt to design holistic proposals to address development. While the commission did not totally abandon the quest for an updated paradigm or at least a framework, the emphasis, especially during the first half of the decade, was on dealing with *apertura* and the interrelated management of adjustment, stabilization, and the debt overhang.

APERTURA: THE GRADUALIST APPROACH

The secretariat was critical of the radical liberalization programs that had been promoted in the Southern Cone since the mid- and late 1970s. That was natural enough. In spite of the institution's warnings against excessive

protection of industry, there was strong resistance to the unregulated dismantling of trade barriers and to the untrammeled opening of capital accounts. This conviction was heightened by the barely concealed disdain of
most of the professional staff for the policies—political and economic—
adopted by the Pinochet government in ECLAC's host country. Thus, by 1978,
the secretariat was warning its member governments that "an unfettered opening up of the economy runs the risk of re-establishing, creating or deepening
economic and social features which have long been criticized in Latin
America."[177] The secretariat's gradualist and even cautious approach was at
odds with the shock treatment being prescribed by more orthodox economists, who warned, among other things, that gradualism would give the opponents of *apertura* time to organize political resistance to liberalization
measures, thus compromising their viability.[178]

The secretariat felt at least partially vindicated, having expressed its appre-
hensions and warnings, by the serious financial crisis in its host country between 1981 and 1983, which led the Chilean authorities to revise their economic
strategy. The trade and tariff reforms and the opening up of the capital account of the balance of payments, combined with a progressive currency appreciation associated with a fixed exchange rate and domestic interest rates
that were much higher than international rates all led to a massive inflow of
funds from international capital markets. With the downturn of the economy
in 1981, a major banking crisis erupted, and the government felt compelled to
intervene to help most of the banks.[179] The main point to be made is that the
secretariat persistently questioned the prevailing paradigm—which was generally supported by the International Monetary Fund—on short-term economic policy prescriptions. While the secretariat's views also gradually changed
in response to evolving circumstances, it showed a greater skepticism toward
a rapid shift from relatively closed economies to openness and argued that
protection should be dismantled gradually and that trade liberalization should
precede financial liberalization. It also continued to rely more heavily on public-sector interventions than did the prevailing paradigm. Yet by the second
half of the 1980s, the secretariat did not dispute the need for greater openness
and greater reliance on market signals; the debate revolved around the pace,
the intensity, and the sequencing of the *apertura* process. In this, ECLAC played
a useful role in nurturing the policy debate.

That policy debate was played out through three key and interrelated areas
of policymaking: first, how to bring about an "efficient" or non-recessionary
adjustment of the balance of payments; second, how to control inflation, especially runaway or hyperinflation; and, third, how to deal with the burden of
external debt. The secretariat made important intellectual contributions to

all three areas. A meaningful contribution of ECLAC to the debate was to treat adjustment policies and stabilization policies separately instead of together, as was the preferred approach of the neoliberals.

ADJUSTMENT

The secretariat's critical stance regarding extreme liberalization was connected with a major incursion into a topic which had not been its forte in previous decades: short-term policymaking. A review of the yearly economic surveys, the flagship documents prepared for the biennial meetings of the commission during the 1980s, and specific studies reveals an increasingly sophisticated approach to dealing with the need for adjustment and stabilization.

ECLAC pointed out essential differences between stabilization policies and adjustment policies and recommended dealing with both separately, although in a coherent fashion. Among the differences was the fact that stabilization did not necessarily require a contraction in demand, while adjustment did. Also, it argued that some policies, such as reducing expenditures, could lower inflation and the balance-of-payments deficit simultaneously, while others, such as a monetary devaluation, entailed tradeoffs. The commission questioned the prevailing premise that macroeconomic disequilibrium and price distortions were exclusively the result of excess demand, which many felt was the main factor behind current-account deficits, accelerated inflation, and the distortion in relative prices between tradable and non-tradable goods. Drawing on the spirit of the secretariat's thinking in the 1960s about the structural roots of inflation, and acknowledging the importance of excess demand, it also looked at other reasons for disequilibria. Perhaps the secretariat's main contribution to the policy debate was its criticism of the prevailing ideology for relying too heavily on restrictive monetary policies to dampen demand, reduce fiscal deficits, and control salaries. This led to what the secretariat called "inefficient" or "recessive" adjustments, which entailed unnecessarily high social costs.

The secretariat argued that through a judicious combination of selective policies designed to dampen demand and stimulate supply, "efficient" or non-recessionary adjustments could be attained. It thereby rejected the "one size fits all" approach of dealing with adjustment, arguing that each country merited a "tailor-made" program in response to its specific circumstances.[180] It recommended more emphasis on utilizing installed capacity to increase supply, especially of exportable goods. It also recommended a selective cutback on expenditures to mitigate the impact of adjustment on the poorer strata of society.[181] Most of these proposals became, in time, the norms for policymaking in the region.

STABILIZATION

The secretariat also took exception to the conventional wisdom about how to combat inflation and, indeed, contributed greatly to the understanding of the origin of different types of inflation that formed part of the macroeconomic disequilibria and price distortions of the 1980s. In the first place, ECLAC held that bringing down inflation rates was not necessarily incompatible with economic growth. In fact, it pointed to successful stabilization programs (Uruguay in the late 1960s and Bolivia in the mid-1970s) by which stabilization had been successfully achieved without provoking a recession. The commission offered guidelines on how this was accomplished.

In the second place, a distinction was made between the original sources of inflation—be they excess demand, driven by costs, or of a structural nature—and the way subsequent price increases were propagated through inflationary expectations, especially through institutional arrangements such as indexed contracts (wages, rents, etc.). ECLAC recommended that differential policies be used to deal with both components of inflation.

Third, three types of situation were identified: the so-called occasional inflation, usually brought about by an event, such as a devaluation; high and persistent inflationary processes, fueled by an "inflationary inertia" with fairly predictable rates; and hyperinflation. The secretariat argued that different policy mixes were required to deal with each of these situations. It recommended dealing rapidly with the first type of situation to prevent inertial forces from taking hold; it also found the second type of situation more tolerable and recommended moving gradually to lower inflation rates in order to avoid an unnecessary recession. And it condoned shock treatment to address hyperinflation. As the 1980s evolved and more and more lessons were learned about what worked and what did not, the studies of the secretariat showed an increasing depth and insight regarding the origins of inflation, its varying characteristics, and alternative policy prescriptions to deal with it.[182]

THE DEBT OVERHANG

The third topic on which the secretariat generated important ideas was foreign debt. The phenomenon of overindebtedness and the need for some type of debt relief was recognized early on.[183] The matter received increasing attention in the annual economic surveys and, beginning in the early 1980s, in numerous specific studies. The scope of those studies was intensified with the events of the early 1980s, which led to the Mexican default and the protracted period during which Latin America became a net exporter of financial resources. The work quantified the magnitude of the problem, analyzed its consequences and impact, and increasingly advocated debt relief.[184] It also proposed different modalities that debt relief could take, including debt reduction, the reduction of interest rates, rescheduling of official debt, and dealing with the debt problem on a systemic basis.[185] The secretariat did not propose debt forgiveness, except in one or two cases (Nicaragua and Haiti), anticipating that countries would have to return to private international capital markets in the future. Even after the international community had accepted many of the proposals that ECLAC had been espousing,[186] the secretariat continued to develop ideas on the matter. Perhaps its most complete analysis and proposal was published at the end of the decade.[187]

The Initial Quest for a New Framework

The secretariat was always careful to formulate its policy prescriptions in the broader context of resuming economic growth and redressing the extremely regressive effects of the crisis, which had worsened an already appalling situation in terms of income distribution. Furthermore, there was tension within the secretariat generated by a debate among the staff. One group held that ECLAC was abandoning its traditional and institutional identity by giving insufficient attention to long-term development strategies. The other held that the institution should work with governments in overcoming the emergency before addressing longer-term issues.[188] A by-product of the debate was that it stimulated creativity and had two outcomes worth mentioning in the context of the institution's intellectual heritage.

The first was the result of a question many Latin American social scientists had been asking themselves: Why had some of the East Asian economies performed so much better than their own economies over the last thirty years, particularly in the 1980s? It is to ECLAC's credit that it began research to compare the two experiences over the whole decade.[189] But the secretariat can be criticized for not doing enough in the area of comparative studies and perhaps not seizing the opportunity to do some joint work with its sister institution, ESCAP.[190]

The second outcome was more far-reaching: It evolved from a major seminar, held in Santiago in 1985, which, in addition to being Enrique Iglesias's final event as executive secretary,[191] offered an opportunity to combine short-term policy concerns with longer-term development objectives.[192] The secretariat subsequently built on this initial effort to combine short-term policy concerns with a search for a new development framework. A new opportunity was offered at an extraordinary conference of the commission held at the invitation of the Mexican government in Mexico City in 1987. The document that was produced for the occasion contained proposals in both areas.[193] It took a clear position in favor of opening the economies of the region and eliminating any bias against exporting goods that was left in policymaking. But it also invoked a more activist role for the state than did the prevailing paradigm. These ideas were further developed in the next ordinary session of the commission, held in Rio de Janeiro in 1988.[194] Thus, there was a gradual shift during the 1980s in the secretariat's analytical work; in the first half of the decade the commission emphasized short-term policymaking, while there was a better mix of concerns in the second half of the decade.

An Overall Assessment

There was much trial and error in short-term policymaking in Latin America and the Caribbean during the 1980s and frequent consultations between the "technopols" in charge of those policies. It is difficult to assess to what extent the ECLAC secretariat influenced the course of events, but clearly the institution was present in the policy debate and arguably played a leading role in helping to shape policies in the interrelated areas of adjustment, stabilization, and debt relief. There is little doubt that the most important contributions of the secretariat during this decade were, in fact, in the realm of short-term policymaking, which seems entirely appropriate, given the considerable anguish caused during the protracted period of stagnation, financial instability, and mounting incidence of poverty. But initial steps were also taken to update the institution's overall vision on development, thus preparing the stage for the 1990s.

The 1990s and Beyond: The Return to a Holistic Framework

By the late 1980s, there were clear signs of recovery in Latin America and the Caribbean. The debt-reduction scheme was in place, international inflation—and interest rates—had fallen significantly, and exports were growing as a result of domestic policies and a rapid expansion in international trade. Latin American inflation was decreasing and moderate rates of growth were being registered.

After the doctrinaire approach to extreme liberalization led to disaster, a more pragmatic style of policymaking was adopted in the Southern Cone countries. In fact, a new convergence of views appeared to be emerging in Latin America regarding policymaking. Most countries were moving in the direction of trade liberalization, fiscal discipline, tax reform, monetary disci-

pline, financial liberalization, privatization of most state enterprises, and deregulation to eliminate rules restricting competition, although important differences persisted between countries on the content, scope, and the pace of
application and sequencing of specific policies. Other characteristics of the
emerging model included the deregulation of financial and labor markets,
the elimination of barriers to the entry of foreign direct investment, and the
creation of a legal and institutional framework that strengthened property
rights.[195] Dubbed "the Washington consensus" by John Williamson,[196] this set
of policies and guidelines, which were to be adapted to each specific situation,
became the point of reference for policymakers. A major challenge for the
ECLAC secretariat was how to respond to this framework, which, of course,
involved either embracing it or, more likely, offering an alternative.

Two other aspects of the context should be noted. First, by 1990, the transition from authoritarian military regimes to democratically elected civilian
regimes had been virtually completed in the region, and the process toward
ending civil strife in Central America had begun. The emergence of more
democratic, pluralist, and participatory political systems had important implications for the decision-making process on the part of policymakers, if for
no other reason than that consultations and, sometimes, parliamentary approval tend to be slow and time-consuming. Second, in the second half of the
1980s some governments embarked on new subregional integration commitments, most notably in the Southern Cone.[197] These were spurred on by greater
affinity among democratically elected governments, greater convergence in
policymaking, and the delay in the completion of the Uruguay Round negotiations (the Final Act embodying the results of the Uruguay Round of Multilateral Trade Negotiations was signed in 1993).

The Return to an Updated Framework

This was the background against which the secretariat faced the future. At
least three sets of general initiatives are worth mentioning as part of the
institution's intellectual legacy: the formulation of an updated framework for
development, an updated proposal for economic integration, and an updated
proposal for financing development. These, in turn, gave rise to numerous
specific proposals.

CHANGING PRODUCTION PATTERNS WITH SOCIAL EQUITY

The secretariat was struggling at the end of the 1980s to come up with a
new holistic framework. One publication during this time period that deserves

special mention is Fernando Fajnzylber's pioneering work on the shortcomings of Latin American industrialization, especially when contrasted with industrialization in East Asia. Based on his earlier study, which he prepared while living in Mexico,[198] he finished his work on "Industrialization in Latin America: From the 'Black Box' to the 'Empty Box'" in 1988 after joining ECLAC.[199] The main point Fajnzylber made, which was subsequently embraced by the secretariat, was that the only way to recapture dynamic growth with improved income distribution was by deliberately promoting an internationally competitive productive structure. This was to be achieved by a systemic approach which called for efficiency not only at the level of the microeconomic unit but also at the level of the whole economy. In other words, attention had to be paid simultaneously to all those elements which determined whether a country could compete in world markets, including the quality of human resources, the institutional and legal structure, the capacity for R and D, the depth of capital markets, and so forth.

This approach, which the secretariat incorporated in its landmark document of 1990 titled *Changing Production Patterns and Social Equity*,[200] was a far cry from import-substitution industrialization. It emphasized international competitiveness and had at least some elements in common with the export bias being espoused by other multilateral organizations, especially the World Bank. Where the approach departed from the paradigm in vogue was in its espousal of a more active state presence, albeit a market-friendly state, since, it was argued, international competitiveness would not come about spontaneously but rather required a concerted effort on the part of the public and private sectors. In other words, the right prices were terribly important, but they were not enough to achieve development objectives. While the secretariat was committed to financial stability, it moved away from placing financial stability at the center of policymaking. Rather, it emphasized how sustainable growth that was compatible with financial stability and greater equity could be achieved.

Thus, there were common threads in the secretariat's proposal and the so-called Washington Consensus. It had become clear by 1990 that the international environment precluded a return to industrialization based on import substitution or the persistence of macroeconomic disequilibria. However, there were also important differences. In the debate about what the appropriate mix of state and market should be, ECLAC distanced itself from the so-called consensus in its nuanced preference for the state, while the consensus showed a nuanced preference for the market.

Other differentiating characteristics were to be found in the details, especially regarding the practical application of the different elements of content, pace, scope, and sequence, as well as the overall mix (the "menu") of policies.

The secretariat also proved sensitive to the unique circumstances of each country, rejecting again the "one size fits all" approach to policymaking.

While it was clearly favorable to trade liberalization, ECLAC tended to support the gradual unilateral dismantling of trade barriers, in contrast to those who advocated abrupt reductions. It also favored maintaining differential levels of protection (dispersion) in contrast to the preference shown by some multilateral agencies for a uniform and low tariff on all goods (as applied in Chile). On exchange-rate policies, the secretariat showed a predilection for flexible and administered exchange rates, although it endorsed Argentina's adoption of a fixed exchange rate as a practical way to combat hyperinflation. It was in this area that the institution illustrated most forcibly the fallacy of trying to apply the same policies to each and every country; not even the Washington Consensus contemplated a uniform exchange regime for all countries.

Within this general framework, ECLAC developed an institutional opinion on numerous other development issues and policies, which it gradually worked into the framework. Perhaps most important, the short-term policy prescriptions were placed in the broader context of a longer-term development strategy.

There were four central underlying notions to ECLAC's updated framework. The first was that increasing levels of productivity would have to be the basis of sustained growth. Although this message had a familiar ring to it, since the seminal proposal of 1949 also stressed the application of technology to the productive process, the institution now underlined international competitiveness as an imperative of development, and indeed of survival, in a globalized economy. The emphasis was less on industrialization than on the entire productive system, since it had by now become clear that high productivity could also be attained in primary and tertiary activities. In other words, whether the countries liked it or not, heightened efficiency was something to be taken most seriously for any nation that intended to play by the rules of globalization.

The second notion was that increased productivity would require concerted and simultaneous efforts on many fronts, at both the micro and macroeconomic levels.[201] ECLAC used the metaphor of the chain, whose strength is only equal to that of the weakest link. In other words, in an argument reminiscent of the debate of the 1950s between balanced growth and the "big push,"[202] ECLAC argued that in order to be internationally competitive, it was not enough for a specific enterprise to be efficient. Rather, the whole structure in which that particular plant is inserted needs to function properly: systems of finance, transport, communications, power, labor standards, management, administration of justice, and a host of other variables. This systemic approach needed a sound institutional basis, which then led ECLAC into the whole area of governance for development and democratic governance.[203] The systemic approach also greatly expanded the thematic agenda of the secretariat.

The third notion was also a familiar one: ECLAC argued that growth was a necessary but not sufficient condition for reducing poverty and income inequality and that reducing poverty and income inequality was a necessary but not sufficient condition for achieving growth. Together with the emphasis on higher levels of productivity, the framework underlined the imperative of achieving greater equity and pointed to the East Asian experience as proof that it could be done. This point was stressed in a subsequent document entitled *Social Equity and Changing Production Patterns: An Integrated Approach*.[204] In this document, the secretariat argued that while there were some tradeoffs between policies to achieve growth and those intended to achieve equity, in many cases the opposite was true—that is, that policies could choose to pursue growth and equity simultaneously and that they could even mutually reinforce each other. Investment in human capital in general and education in particular were offered as a case in point, since they supported both growth and a better distribution of income.

The secretariat's commitment to bringing equity into policymaking appeared in all of its documents, from the annual surveys to its in-depth studies that tracked income distribution, poverty, and other social indicators.[205] In 1992, the role of education and knowledge as indispensable tools for both growth and equity was developed in a detailed proposal aimed at policymakers in ministries of education and finance.[206] This document, prepared jointly with UNESCO, had an important impact in the region.[207] It indicated that a complete secondary education is required in most Latin American countries to create a high probability that an individual will escape poverty. It emphasized the content and quality of education. The essential objective of education, the document said, in addition to teaching the traditional academic content, is to develop skills for "learning to learn." It also stressed the need to teach people to handle the new tools offered by information technologies and the need to promote democratic values, tolerance, and the need for a harmonious coexistence of different groups within society.

The fourth notion was also a familiar one: ECLAC continued to favor an active state presence in the development effort, albeit a more market-friendly presence than it had espoused in the 1950s. It argued that growth and the optimal allocation of resources requires more than free prices, for the market needs the support of an active state. ECLAC argued that the role of the state was not only to fulfill its classical functions (supplying social services, maintaining financial stability, providing for the most vulnerable groups, ensuring public security) but also, within the limits of its administrative capacity, to develop market-based institutions (long-term capital and futures markets in foreign exchange), to strengthen incomplete markets (for example, the market for technology), and to eliminate or correct structural distortions (the heterogeneity of the structure of production, the concentration of property, the segmentation of the markets for capital and labor). It further argued that the state had to eradicate or compensate for the most significant market imperfections arising from economies of scale and externalities.[208]

In 1997, the issue of growth with equity was revisited in the context of regional compliance with the Plan of Action adopted at the 1995 World Summit for Social Development. Not only was an analysis presented by the ECLAC secretariat on progress attained and obstacles encountered in the region, but fairly detailed proposals were offered on how to move forward.[209]

Finally, the 1990 document was perceived as a framework to be built on. Thus, in succeeding years, the secretariat developed coherent proposals on a host of issues, including the environment and development[210] and population and development,[211] as seen from the regional perspective.

OPEN REGIONALISM

One of the many spinoffs from the framework of 1990 dealt with economic integration, but integration attuned to the circumstances of the 1990s. During the second half of the 1980s, governments started experimenting with the idea of using economic integration as a springboard for integrating into the global economy. This was the philosophy, for example, behind the Southern Cone Common Market. Simultaneously, as part of its regular work program, the ECLAC secretariat was revising its own thinking regarding economic integration.[212]

As had happened so often before in the history of the organization, it is not clear whether the secretariat was inspired by actions undertaken by its member governments or whether the member governments were inspired by the technical guidance of its secretariat; probably a bit of both was going on simultaneously. The fact of the matter is that the secretariat was able to produce another landmark document in 1994, called *Open Regionalism in Latin America and the Caribbean*,[213] which tried to reconcile unilateral trade liberalization with preferential trade arrangements. The document discusses how to convert subregional or regional trade agreements into "building blocks" instead of "stumbling blocks" to a more open and transparent international trading system. The introduction to the document states that the argument departs from "the core premise that recent integration efforts have generally involved an interaction between two types of phenomena."

> First, the trade liberalization and deregulation policies introduced at the national level by virtually all countries . . . have helped to build up reciprocal trade and investment within Latin America itself, taking advantage of geographical proximity. Second, this "natural," non-discriminatory attitude towards other countries has been complemented by integration based on explicit agreements or policies, which do entail certain preferences with respect to the treatment accorded to other nations. The way in which these phenomena interact is of decisive importance. Depending on their content and scope, formal agreements can prove to be either contrary or complementary to the shift towards a growing interdependence guided by market forces and aimed at better integration with the international economy. The aim, therefore, should be to strengthen the reciprocal links between the two elements in the context of what is termed "open regionalism," i.e., a process of growing economic interdependence at the regional level, promoted both by preferential integration agreements and by other policies in a context of liberalization and deregulation, geared towards enhancing the competitiveness of the countries of the region and, insofar as [is] possible, constituting the building blocks for a more open and transparent international economy.[214]

There is little doubt that the document had a significant impact in the region. For example, in the Fourth Iberoamerican Summit, which brought together twenty-seven heads of state and government of Latin America, Spain, and Portugal, the final declaration committed those leaders to "continuing the international strategy of our countries, aimed at strengthening our integration, in a context of open regionalism as defined by the XXV Session of ECLAC."[215]

Based on the conceptual framework contained in its proposal of open regionalism, the secretariat espoused deeper commitments to interregional economic integration within the formal subregional groups—such as the Southern Cone Common Market (Mercosur) formed between Argentina, Brazil, Uruguay, and Paraguay—as well as wider commitments between groups or individual countries. These new commitments could proceed simultaneously, ECLAC argued. Based on this reasoning, the secretariat supported a simultaneous deepening of commitments to economic integration among the Mercosur countries and some widening commitments among non-member countries (Bolivia and Chile). In the same spirit, the secretariat argued that Latin American and Caribbean integration and hemispheric integration were not necessarily incompatible and supported the creation of a Free Trade Area of the Americas.

In fact, and again based on its conceptual framework, the ECLAC secretariat joined the IDB and the OAS in providing technical support to the governments in carrying out this endeavor.[216]

FINANCING FOR DEVELOPMENT

One of the many consequences of the severe and prolonged economic crisis of the 1980s was an abrupt decline in ratios of domestic savings to GDP from their historical average of around 24 percent to less than 12 percent. Even with the moderate recovery of the early 1990s, the domestic-savings ratio remained depressed. The secretariat pointed out in numerous documents that if the countries of the region were to achieve dynamic growth rates around 6 percent per annum (the minimum required to absorb the new entrants into the labor market), the domestic-savings ratio would have to be on the order of 28 percent.[217] This led to a concerted effort on the part of the secretariat in different areas related to the financing of development, which continues to the present day. ECLAC's work to formulate policy that would facilitate the alleviation of the debt burden has already been discussed. But in addition to its pioneering work on this subject during the 1980s, the secretariat progressively delved into five other interrelated areas which gave rise to numerous ideas and proposals. The first concerns external capital flows and, in general, the liberalization of the capital account of the balance of payments. The second is broader and explores the options available to increase domestic savings and how to channel those savings into productive investment. The third selects a specific area of inquiry, the capitalization of pension funds and health care systems. The fourth concerns public finance. Finally, and only at the end of the decade, the secretariat became involved in studies of international financial reform. All of these activities appear to have had a significant impact in the region.

The secretariat monitored the surprisingly swift turnaround of international capital flows that occurred in 1990, when Latin America passed from being a net exporter of financial resources to the rest of the world to once again being a net receiver of foreign capital. Most countries, particularly the large ones, regained access to the private international capital markets. There were also large inflows of foreign direct investment, some of which were associated with the privatization of public enterprises. Governments were once again able to offer public securities at favorable rates. Although in general, the secretariat recognized the positive role that both private and public capital inflows could play in the development process, it turned its attention away from decrying the negative impact of net capital outflows toward expressing concern about some of the potentially perverse consequences of the large inflows. The commission observed that capital inflows were not making a significant enough contribution to raising the ratios of investment to gross domestic product (GDP).

Rather, it appeared that a large proportion of external finance was fueling the import of consumer and intermediate goods.[218] The secretariat also worried that large capital inflows in some countries were contributing to an overvaluation of the exchange rates, which had a potentially negative effect on the trade account. And perhaps the most important concern of all revolved around the issue of premature liberalization of the capital account and the extreme vulnerability to which countries were exposed by large inflows of speculative or short-term capital.[219] ECLAC was strongly in favor of a gradual dismantling of trade liberalization prior to financial liberalization, especially when a combination of adverse factors was brewing. These usually included an overvalued exchange rate, high domestic interest rates in relation to those prevailing in international markets, and a large stock of short-term obligations. Six months before the Mexican financial crisis erupted in December 1994,[220] the secretariat prophetically warned:

> It should be recalled that Latin American history has been marked by periods of large-scale capital inflows, followed on a number of occasions by periods of debt crisis. This has sparked a wide-ranging debate on the dynamics of the process of opening up the capital account. Today, it is generally agreed that this process should be implemented sequentially, and that it should occur after other liberalization processes, particularly those affecting trade and the domestic financial market, have been consolidated.[221]

To deal with this risk and at the same time benefit from the positive effects of financial inflows, the secretariat recommended tailoring capital-account liberalization to the economy's capacity to absorb and efficiently allocate external resources. In this respect, it recommended facilitating the entry of long-term capital first and discouraging transactions involving short-term financial capital with market-based policies. These were somewhat heretical proposals at the time, but they quickly became the norm after the Mexican financial crisis, and even more so after the Asian financial crisis of 1997.

ECLAC's work on ways to increase domestic savings and channel them into productive investment spanned more than a decade and gave rise to some significant conclusions.[222] First, the level of national savings improves in a favorable macroeconomic and institutional context. Consistent macroeconomic policies contribute to the increase of non-inflationary domestic financing and enable foreign-exchange, money, and goods markets to send stable signals, leading, over time, to a rational allocation of resources. The secretariat argued that progress in institutional development can strengthen the efficiency of financial systems in attracting, coordinating, and allocating resources while ensuring that they are supervised and regulated in accordance with the highest standards. In addition, ECLAC stated that while interest rates do not have a decisive influence on the volume of savings, they contribute to a more efficient use of available resources and to the control of capital movements.

The secretariat also conducted studies regarding the tradeoff between public and private savings, arguing that there is a need for greater complementarity between the two. It also stressed that efforts to promote savings may be fruitless if external conditions place major constraints on growth, citing as an example the transfers of resources abroad generated by external debt. The latter consumed a high proportion of the income which would otherwise have been available as savings, thus reducing the level of investment necessary to ensure sustainable economic growth.[223]

Among the more valuable contributions of the secretariat in this line of work was its insistence on the need to strengthen the institutions that regulated and supervised the financial sector.[224] Again, this was prescient, since various countries of the region experienced serious systemic failures of their national banking systems in subsequent years. The most complete study in terms of proposals was prepared in 1996.[225]

Among the in-depth studies that followed, the most important were in the area of analyzing the impact of the change taking place in some countries—notably in Chile—from existing pay-as-you-go public pension plans to privately administered, individually funded pension systems. While recognizing that, on balance, the capitalization of pension funds had played a positive role in Chile, the secretariat's analysis was more critical than those of the multilateral financial agencies, especially regarding the possibility of transferring the Chilean experience to other countries of the region.[226] ECLAC found four sets of difficulties. The first was the fiscal impact of having the central government absorb the liabilities of the old pay-as-you-go system while the private pension funds received the capitalization. In the case of Chile, this cost was 4 percent of GDP, putting a strain on the public sector's finances. The second was the exclusionary aspect of the new scheme, which left many potential contributors with no pension program at all. The third was the obvious vulnerability of placing a large proportion of savings in pension programs in the hands of a limited number of large private institutions with, at least initially, a weak supervisory and regulatory structure. And the last set of difficulties was the doubt about whether increased financial savings in individual accounts would be translated into higher aggregate savings.

In addition, the secretariat harbored doubts about whether the financial markets were up to the task of channeling the considerable mass of resources mobilized by the private pension funds toward productive investment. On this last point, it appears that Chile was able to meet this challenge, but the peculiar Chilean experience was not readily transmissible to countries with less-developed capital markets. Thus, the secretariat raised the specter of private pension funds mobilizing considerable resources which would then have to be invested abroad, given the lack of adequate low-risk investment opportunities in the local financial markets. The general thrust of the commission's analysis was not to discourage the capitalization of pension funds but rather to alert governments to the risks of blindly imitating the Chilean experience in other countries. It also proposed numerous alternatives, including the possibility of a two-tier system with both pay-as-you-go and capitalization elements.[227]

The fourth area that the secretariat addressed in a systematic manner was that of public finance. A special publication appeared in ECLAC's *Serie Política Fiscal* which covered many aspects of public finance,[228] and a yearly seminar was started which brought together senior officials of the ministries of finance of the region.[229] Through its work, the secretariat exerted considerable influence in bringing about a major shift in the structures of taxation and in the management of expenditures in the region. The culmination of this work appeared in a 1998 publication entitled *The Fiscal Covenant*.[230] By "fiscal covenant" the secretariat meant the basic sociopolitical agreement that legitimizes the role of the state and establishes the areas and scope of government responsibility in the economic and social spheres. It covered consolidating the ongoing fiscal adjustment process, raising the productivity of public expenditures, contributing to greater transparency and participation in fiscal policy, promoting social equity, and encouraging the development of democratic institutions.[231] The work was influential in the region. For example, it was the basis of an important proposal formulated by a blue-ribbon commission (the Preparatory Commission of the Fiscal Pact) in Guatemala in 2000.[232]

Finally, the secretariat got involved with a broader effort begun in the UN in 1998 and which culminated in the Global Conference on Financing for Development in March 2002 in Monterrey, Mexico. In addition to reflecting on the need to increase national savings rates and transfer those savings to productive investments, the work concentrated on the need to strengthen the international financial system in order to prevent crises and manage them better when they do occur. The work also includes an analysis of the advisability of a stronger preventive orientation in the formulation and application of macroeconomic policies at the national level in ECLAC's region as well as proposals of a more systemic nature. The work undertaken has already had repercussions in Latin America and the Caribbean as well as in the preparatory process for the global conference.[233]

MICROLEVEL AND MACROLEVEL ECONOMIC PERFORMANCE

Since its inception, one of ECLA's hallmarks has been its yearly economic survey, which combines an interpretation of the information gathered in each country with an overall assessment of the scope and impact of economic strategies and policies and an analysis of the performance of the corresponding economy. This type of recurrent exercise was deemed of interest to the organization's constituencies and was also a useful instrument in forcing staff members to keep up to date. Although the surveys have not been of uniform quality, the scope and timeliness of these yearly reports has improved over time, and in the mid-1970s a year-end survey was added to the periodic output. This survey has become the most widely read and quoted publication of all the secretariat's outputs.[234]

As an offshoot of this recurrent work, the secretariat became deeply involved in the analysis of economic policies, especially in tracing the effectiveness of the economic reforms initiated from the 1980s onward. This included their effects on economic growth, employment, and income distribution. One of the more compelling arguments the commission developed in the 1990s was that the changes in economic policy have not boosted performance in the way that their proponents had predicted. While most countries had been successful in lowering inflation rates, growth has been moderate and the employment picture has worsened. In the same vein, the incidence of absolute poverty has declined moderately but income distribution has worsened in all but a handful of countries.[235] The work was not confined to the aggregate or country level but also included sectoral and microeconomic analysis. In the latter, the impact of the reforms has been more pronounced, leading to greater differentiation of situations at the level of firms and between different regions. The studies show, for example, that some firms have proven highly successful in becoming internationally competitive, while many have failed or fallen by the wayside. The analysis of the linkages between microlevel and macrolevel economic performance proved to be among the more innovative work of the secretariat in the second half of the 1990s.[236] Probably the most complete presentation of the work in this area appears in the study of Stallings and Peres, which presents the results of a three-year investigation by the secretariat and offers a conceptual framework for analyzing the effects of the reforms in nine countries.[237]

DEMOCRACY, HUMAN RIGHTS, AND INTEGRAL DEVELOPMENT

As the 1990s came to a close and the new century dawned, ECLAC continued to build on its previous analysis, especially its long-held conviction that
development is a holistic process. In that context, it brought into its holistic
framework the concept of citizenship, not only as a right in and of itself but as
an effective means of ensuring that the social objectives of development will
be taken into due account in public decision-making.[238] It also built on its
findings regarding the effects of economic reforms and pointed out that the
continuing difficulties the countries of the region faced were, in fact, a result
of the reforms. In that respect, the secretariat indicated that "it may be necessary to 'reform the reforms.'"[239]

One of the points ECLAC is making at present is the need to look beyond
the narrow definition of macroeconomic stability and to put long-term growth
at the center of macroeconomic management. The secretariat is calling for a
broadening of macroeconomic management to encompass the entire economic
cycle and so permit assertive countercyclical policies. It is also calling for new
institutions and policy instruments to improve the quality of macroeconomic
management. A second line of inquiry develops the need for more assertive
productive development strategies and policies. "An economy's growth performance is closely linked both to macroeconomic factors and to the development of production structures and the institutions that serve as their
framework."[240] And the secretariat has now added the concept of citizenship
and society to its secular concern for greater equity:

> Viewed from an integral perspective, citizenship implies a reciprocal commit-
> ment on the part of public authorities and individuals. The former must re-
> spect the individual's autonomy, accept and promote citizen participation in
> politics and, to the extent that the existing level of development permits it,
> provide opportunities for social well-being and productive opportunities. The
> latter must contribute by participating in public affairs and thereby enriching
> them. This entails a broadening of the public arena.[241]

An Overall Assessment

In the 1990s, ECLAC showed some of the vitality of its earlier years, goaded
on by the sheer weight of the challenges it faced. Its mix of orthodox and
heterodox prescriptions and its discreet (and sometimes not-so-discreet) skepticism regarding the prevailing paradigm contributed to the lively debate in
the region about how to adapt to the exigencies of globalization and how to
recapture the capacity for sustained growth with financial stability with due

regard for greater equity and the consolidation of democratic institutions. During this period, the institution in a way has returned to its roots in proposing an updated holistic framework for development, to be adapted to the particular circumstances of each country of the region, and in concentrating its in-depth research on the relevant development issues of the day. It did so without abandoning the approach of the 1980s of bringing short-term policy-making into its agenda. The secretariat showed a greater capacity to include emerging issues in its work program than it had in the past.

This combination of a long-term outlook and attention to relevant short-term development issues, together with its timely monitoring of economic performance in the region, gave the institution a higher profile in the 1990s than it had in the previous two decades. The presence of the secretariat in the main intellectual seminars dealing with Latin American and Caribbean development and in intergovernmental meetings at the most senior levels and its regular appearance in the region's media attest to its continuing high standing.

The Lasting Legacy of ECLA's Intellectual Contribution and Its Impact on the United Nations

While it has not always been constant in freshness and creativity, ECLAC has nevertheless managed to retain its intellectual vitality for well over fifty years. The high and low periods in the secretariat's creativity are partly a function of the varying quality of the leadership and the staff, but also, more fundamentally, they are a function of its capacity to adapt to changing circumstances within and outside the region, changes which have helped to shape the institution's work program and its relevance. ECLAC's yearly economic surveys have recorded the evolving economic and social situations both within and outside the region. However, the secretariat appeared less adept at adjusting its own work program and proposals, not to mention its conceptual framework, to those evolving circumstances. Thus, during the period analyzed, important lags appear at times—notably in the late 1960s and 1970s—between the major development issues posed by events in the real world and the message being disseminated by the institution.

The secretariat ultimately and invariably did react. Its assessments of traditional concerns were updated from time to time to reflect the changing context, and new topics, such as environmental concerns, were brought into the institution's mainstream. Thus, although the integration of Latin American and Caribbean economies into the global economy has been one of the constants over fifty years or so, the secretariat began with support for industrialization based on import substitution and ended with appeals for international

competitiveness. A commitment to regional economic integration was another constant, but it began with a selective broadening of markets to facilitate the replacement of goods originating in third countries and ended with
an appeal for using WTO-compliant open regionalism as a springboard for
deeper interaction with the global economy. The structural impediments to
development are yet another constant, but the manner in which ECLAC approached them also changed over the period. The same can be said for the
secretariat's constant predilection for an active state, but it has made changes in
how that presence is characterized: from replacing the private sector in some
areas to complementing it; from intervention to facilitation. And of course, the
preoccupation with the distributive impact of development policies is another
constant, but the mix of policy recommendations has changed over time. Finally, during most of its lifetime, the institution has managed to combine a
holistic framework with institutional opinions on specific development issues.

Beyond the substantive ideas contained in the ECLA *manifiesto,* six central
notions appeared in the early ECLA formulations that were to shape the UN's
work ethic and procedures for years to come and were to become profoundly
etched in its ethos. These were the following:

- First, the tactic of using the interaction between Latin American economies
  with the world economy singled out the one common subject that each of
  the countries of the region could easily identify with. The relation
  between the "center" and the "periphery" was as relevant to small as it was
  to large countries. To be sure, the way each country interacted with the
  world economy differed significantly, and the trends in the international
  economy had a varied impact on each country. But the underlying
  philosophy behind the theory of "center" and "periphery" was something
  all countries could relate to. Thus, although "Latin America" then, as now,
  was a rather abstract notion, the commission got away with making rather
  sweeping generalizations about the region as if a single geographical
  entity was under discussion. In later years, ECLAC invariably recited the
  caveat that the region was made up of many different situations and
  circumstances but then proceeded anyway to discuss "Latin America and
  the Caribbean" in the abstract. So, beyond its analytical merits, the center-
  periphery thesis had two important by-products. First, it was a unifying
  theme within Latin America and the Caribbean (and later between
  developing countries). Second, it became the topic par excellence for UN
  analysis, since it made sense for a global institution to address the impact
  of global economic trends on each of its member states, be they developed
  or developing.
- Second, by dividing the world between the "center" and the "periphery,"
  Prebisch and ECLAC hit upon one of the dominant cleavages that has

marked the history of the UN over the years: developing and developed
countries, North and South, rich and poor. The asymmetrical nature of
the relations he described between the two sets of countries implied an
unfair and potentially confrontational relationship. While ostensibly at
the service of all member states, the secretariat nevertheless tended to
present itself as a champion of the South and helped to shape the North–
South dialogue or negotiations in such a manner as to mitigate the
asymmetries. This, in turn, elicited the suspicion of the countries of the
North. Thus, ECLAC turned neoclassical economics on its head. For
neoclassical economists held that it was the small and the poor countries
that would derive the largest relative benefits from international trade and
that world trade would gradually lead to a leveling of incomes between
countries. ECLAC, on the other hand, convinced many generations of
experts and officials that the asymmetrical relations between exporters of
basic commodities and exporters of manufactured goods led to
polarization. In other words, in the absence of policies to mitigate or
reverse this tendency, there was something intrinsically unfair in the
relationship between the North and the South. By the early 1970s, this
notion led to calls for a new international economic order.

• Third, while neoclassical economists did not make any particular
distinctions between developed and developing countries, ECLAC left no
doubt that developing countries were different. Explanations of the
functioning of a highly developed economy were not relevant to
explanations of how a backward economy functioned, and the policy
prescriptions for one and the other differed in very fundamental ways. At
least until the 1980s, when a lively debate arose between
"monoeconomics" and development economics,[242] the idea of the
singularity of developing economies became another fundamental tenet
within the UN.

• Fourth, by looking at development problems through the Latin American
perspective, ECLAC instilled a strong sense of ownership among the
region's governments and academic communities. Up to that time,
economic analysis and policy prescriptions, insofar as they existed at all,
were the product of ideas that were spawned in the highly developed
countries: Europe, and especially England, before World War II and the
United States during and immediately after the conflict. The fact that an
original conceptualization could be constructed from a Latin American
vantage point was a novelty and a source of pride. Indeed, even the Latin
American critics of ECLAC will recognize that the body of work produced
by the commission during its lifetime, especially in its golden years, is part
of Latin America's intellectual heritage. In consequence, when most Latin
American universities started offering degrees in economics, these were
very much inspired by the growing body of ECLAC publications. The fact

that the region's policymakers could identify so strongly with ECLAC's message became a very important asset for the commission and subsequently for the UN as a whole. Indeed, this ownership effect was somehow transmitted to the global bodies: Developing countries appear to feel more comfortable, even today, with the UN's approach to development than with that of any other multilateral organization.

- Fifth, ECLAC's message suggested, implicitly and explicitly, that development did not just occur spontaneously but was the result of a predetermined and well-reasoned strategy. The idea of an active state to move things along and to overcome structural impediments to growth became deeply embedded in the commission's culture, especially in the earlier years. This characteristic earned ECLAC its label as dirigiste early on and subjected the commission to the secular polemic between liberals and conservatives, or between interventionists and the champions of laissez-faire. But the label stuck and was applied equally, with some nuances, to the rest of the UN.

- Finally, ECLAC's insistence on the holistic, integral, and multidisciplinary nature of development was, by and large, adopted by the UN as a whole. Indeed, in the last decade or so, much has been made of the link between the UN's peacekeeping efforts and development: that is, without peace there cannot be development, and without development there can be no peace.[243]

No study of the intellectual legacy of the UN is complete without acknowledging the remarkable contribution of the Economic Commission for Latin America and the Caribbean. To be sure, the most spectacular ideas were generated in the institution's pioneering years, but it has consistently shown vitality and creativity during its lifetime and continues to do so. That is a rather enviable record in the context of the UN as a whole.

5

The ECA: Forging a Future for Africa

Adebayo Adedeji

- **Genesis and First Priorities**
- **From Imported Models to an African Development Strategy**
- **Battles for the African Mind**
- **The Last Decade of the Twentieth Century and the Beginning of the New Millennium**
- **Global Dreams and Regional Visions: The Interactive Impact of UN Global Conferences**
- **African Leaders Take Up the Gauntlet Again**

Genesis and First Priorities

Many problems delayed the establishment of the Economic Commission for Africa (ECA). With the benefit of hindsight, this is symptomatic of the continent's plight during the past century in its multifarious efforts to move forward politically and economically. First, unlike the other three regional commissions—the ECE, ECLA, and ECAFE—whose establishment preceded the ECA, it was a struggle to convince the majority of member states of the UN (United Nations) that Africa deserved its own regional economic commission. This was no doubt partly due to the fact that at the founding of the UN in 1945 there were only four independent African states—the Arab Republic of Egypt, Ethiopia, Liberia, and South Africa. The colonial powers ruled over the rest of Africa. But then, Asia had only three independent states in the region when ECAFE was established, although it was generally known that the independence of India, Pakistan, Ceylon (Sri Lanka), and the Philippines was imminent. The main hindrance was that France, Great Britain, Portugal, Belgium, and Spain were all strongly opposed to the idea as they did not foresee any rapid rise in the number of independent African states.

These colonial powers were among the founding members of the UN; two of them, France and Great Britain, were permanent members of the Security Council. It is therefore not surprising that they succeeded in delaying the establishment of the ECA for thirteen years. Even the compromise proposal of India at the fourth session of the Economic and Social Council (ECOSOC) in 1947 calling for the establishment of an economic commission for North Africa and Ethiopia did not succeed, mainly because doubt was expressed as to whether North Africa and Ethiopia could be regarded as a region even though they had been placed ad interim under the Economic Commission for Europe. The matter of an ECA was brought up repeatedly in 1950, 1951, and 1956 to no avail.

The opponents of a commission for Africa argued that since Africa was not a homogenous continent, such an organization might not be able to cope with the complexities of the region. It is significant that twenty-five years after its establishment, His Majesty King Hassan II of the Kingdom of Morocco, in his message to the commission during the celebration of its silver jubilee anniversary in 1983, went out of his way to contest this argument by reasserting the common history and destiny of the continent in spite of its diversity.[1]

In the commission's very first program of work for the biennium 1960–1961, the secretariat was required to give priority to:

- Problems of the traditional backward sectors of African economies (agriculture and handicrafts) and their integration with the modern sectors;
- Problems of industrialization and transportation in Africa in both national and regional contexts;
- Problems of stabilization of commodity prices, studies of the measures which might be adopted at the national or regional level to reduce fluctuations in world prices, and reports on international action in the field, including an analysis of the effects of such action on African producers;
- Problems of rapid training of professional staff at all levels of development policymaking and planning in member states;
- Problems connected with the social aspects of economic development;
- Problems of financing economic development;
- Problems arising from the lack of adequate statistical data and research.[2]

Also included in the commission's first work program was the convening in 1961 of a regional conference of African businessmen and women to consider a) intra-African capital investment; b) the expansion of trade and markets among African countries; and c) cooperation through joint ventures in the development of natural resources by private enterprise. Thus, right from its creation, the commission left no doubt about its determination to reestablish and strengthen its regional structure and cohesion and to foster and evolve common policy frameworks for commodity stabilization, capacity-building, and holistic human-centered development. It also commenced in earnest to establish its own regional multilateral financing institution, the African Development Bank (ADB).

The second difficulty encountered in establishing the commission was that even after the General Assembly, at its twelfth session in 1957, had recommended its creation[3] and had requested ECOSOC to define its terms of reference, the political battle continued. The difficulties were legal, political, and substantive.

Legally, the colonial powers wanted to ensure that the ECA would not intervene in any of their territories except at their own request; hence their insistence on the inclusion of the clause that the agreement of the "government concerned" must be obtained before the ECA could intervene in a country. Politically, there was a difficult discussion about the membership and the associate membership of the commission. The formula around which a consensus was built was to agree on a list of all the states that could become members. This list included all the state members of the UN which were geographically in Africa (Belgium, France, Italy, Portugal, Spain, and the United Kingdom). Unlike the other regional commissions, on this commission, the United States and the Soviet Union were not eligible for membership.

The admission of non-independent African countries as associate members was subject to the condition that their candidature be proposed by the state responsible for their international relations; that is, the colonial powers. At the request of the United Kingdom and Italy, the list of associate members was comprised of Nigeria, Gambia, Kenya, Zanzibar, Uganda, the Protectorate of Somalia, Sierra Leone, Tanganyika,[4] and the trust territory of Somalia under Italian administration. However, France did not propose any of its territories for associate membership because it was then trying to establish a French Community embracing all of its colonies and metropolitan France. Neither Portugal nor Spain bothered to submit the names of their territories for associate membership.

The major substantive debate concerned the role of the commission with respect to the social aspects of development. It took long and extensive negotiations within and outside the chambers of ECOSOC to incorporate "the social aspects of economic development and the interdependence of economic and social factors" in the terms of reference of the commission. In view of this resistance, the African representatives, led by Mahdi Elmandjra (Morocco), Mekki Abbas (Sudan), Fredrick Akhurst (Ghana), Mengesha Kifle (Ethiopia), and Omar Loutfi (United Arab Republic of Egypt), who negotiated the terms of reference of the commission, felt obliged to universalize the concept of the interdependence between economic and social development and the imperative of articulating social policies by submitting, through the Third Committee of the General Assembly, a draft resolution on "Social Policies and the Interdependence between Economic and Social Development" to the thirteenth session in the fall of 1958.[5] The countries of these five African negotiators on ECA's terms of reference were joined by Liberia and Tunisia and three non-African delegations in sponsoring the resolution which, despite strong opposition, was adopted. The African delegations were so eager for the establishment of the ECA that they committed the Secretary-General to speedy action by including in the new commission's terms of reference the stipulation that its inaugural session be held before the end of 1958.

The third feature of Africa's new commission was that when ECOSOC adopted its Resolution 671A (XXV) on April 29, 1958, which established the commission and decided on the location of its headquarters at Addis Ababa, there were only ten independent African countries: the four African founding member states of the UN—the United Arab Republic of Egypt, Ethiopia, Liberia, and the Republic of South Africa—and six newly independent countries—Libya, Morocco, Tunisia, the Sudan, Ghana, and Guinea. In other words, after thirteen years of struggle, only five countries had been able to achieve political independence. Thus, the ECA, at its birth, had only 19 percent of its current membership of fifty-three states.

Finally, when the General Assembly examined the report of ECOSOC concerning the creation of the ECA, four events occurred during that session which gave the debate on the ECA a special tone and significance. Reference has already been made to the African-sponsored resolution concerning a holistic human-centered conceptualization of development. In addition, Guinea was admitted as the tenth African member state of the UN. Guinea was the only country in the French empire that had dared to defy General Charles de Gaulle by voting for independence rather than becoming a member of the proposed French Community. Third, there was a heated discussion of the Algerian question, as the Algerians were engaged in a large-scale anticolonial war. Finally, 1958 was also the year when the creation of the Special Fund was definitively approved. The idea of a capital fund for development, which had been recommended by the 1948 Havana Conference on trade, was set aside. (This idea reappeared in 1980 in the Brandt Commission report.)[6]

The mandate of UNECA was further strengthened by UN General Assembly Resolution 32/197 of December 20, 1977, which designated the regional commissions as the "main centers of general economic and social development for their respective regions" and required them to "exercise team leadership and responsibility for co-ordination and cooperation at the regional level, taking into account the special needs of their respective regions," as well as by Resolution 33/202 of January 29, 1979, which accorded executing agency status to the regional commissions.

The inaugural session of the ECA, from December 29, 1958, to January 6, 1959, was the first major gathering of Africans, under the auspices of the UN, to discuss African problems on African soil. In addition to the ten African member states of the UN, eight associate members were present, as were observers from seventeen non-African member states of the UN, including the United States and the Soviet Union.

The list of participants at this first session of the ECA is quite interesting. Mekki Abbas, one of those who had been active in the struggle for its establishment and in the negotiation of ECOSOC Resolution 671A (XXV) of April 29, 1958, became its first executive secretary. R. K. A. Gardiner, who became the deputy executive secretary and its second executive secretary, represented Ghana. Other participants included Ismail Toure (later foreign minister of Guinea) and Lansana Beavagui (later prime minister of Guinea); Ms. Angela Brooks of Liberia, who was later elected president of the UN General Assembly; and Taib Slim of Tunisia. The United Kingdom was represented by a minister, J. D. Profumo, while France was represented by G. Georges-Picot, its ambassador to the UN.

Secretary-General Dag Hammarskjöld made a courageous speech in which he insisted on the irreversible trend of decolonization and remarked that the historical process was producing new states whose geographical boundaries were unlikely to be optimal for their economic growth. Accordingly, he pleaded that economic integration should be one of the major objectives of the commission.

The keen desire of the African members to use the commission as the platform for pan-African economic and social transformation was evident. Full and complete political liberation was regarded as a precondition for achieving this. *Concerted action* was the leitmotif throughout the whole session. This concept has acquired other names today—collective self-reliance, endogenous development, regional economic integration, and South-South cooperation. In its formative years, the warning of the Secretary-General that the commission "if it is to be successful, could not disregard the fact that the very elements of the political and constitutional changes which are rapidly taking place in Africa have a direct bearing on the problems of economic development"[7] kept resurfacing.

Indeed, it was not until 1991, when South Africa was weaned of its legally sanctioned apartheid and racism and consequently resumed its seat in the ECA, that all fifty-three African member states of the UN were also members of the ECA. It was at this juncture that the fundamental precondition for true and realistic concerted action could be deemed to have been satisfied. Thus, it took some thirty-three years to achieve the overarching objective of Africa being completely free—free from Cairo to Cape Town and from Lagos to Tenanarive. It was, indeed, "a long walk to freedom."[8]

Political Decolonization in Africa

With only 19 percent of its potential membership able to take their seats as full members, the commission immediately became embattled in the struggle for political decolonization. The member states were in no doubt that the battle against colonialism, racism, and apartheid should be at the top of its agenda, particularly as it was the first-ever pan-African institution and would remain so until 1963, when the Organization of African Unity (OAU) was founded. Born at this historic juncture in the struggle to implement the Human Rights Charter, the commission had no alternative but to pursue its mission of decolonization, without which it would be impossible to bring about the political, economic, and social transformation of the entire region.

Africa's long history of slavery, dispossession, partition, fragmentation, dependence, and marginalization has led to a disjuncture between the Africa that had been dispossessed for more than five hundred years and its precolonial past. It was no surprise that the concerns of the commission at its very first session were decolonization, collective self-reliance, endogenous development, and regional economic integration. Throughout the debates, only non-Africans talked about economic growth.

It was clear to the Africans that what was required was political, economic, and social transformation, without which economic growth would be neither sustainable nor substantial. The African spokesmen were not like the professional diplomats and technocrats who would dominate the next generation. They did not possess the theoretical skills or sophistication or even the self-confidence to put together the development paradigm they thought Africa needed in the language and sophistication of modern-day economists and social scientists. However, there is no doubt that all of the African participants at the inauguration of the commission in late 1958 were concerned with how to bring about the rapid transformation of Africa, without which it would be very difficult, if not impossible, for the continent to move forward into the modern world. With its collection of minuscule states and the fragmentation of its political economy, the perspectives of the ECA were regional and subregional.

Some of the key elements of the various development frameworks, strategies, and charters which would emerge from the ECA debates in the 1970s and 1980s were already identified in December 1958 at the ECA's inaugural session and in its first biennial work program of 1960–1961. But the challenge of decolonization occupied pride of place. Although it did not feature explicitly in the program of work, it was a recurrent theme in all discussions and activities from 1958 until 1991. Three phases are discernible in this drawn-out process of political decolonization: the pre-1960s, the 1960s, and the 1970s to the early 1990s (table 5.1).

Clearly, the world of 1958 was very different from that of today. The ECA has had to adapt continuously to changing realities during the first four decades of its existence. One area in which change was most frequent and rapid was in its membership. Indeed, throughout most of its life, the commission has been serving a continent that has been in a lengthy transition from colonial rule to independence.

The insistence of the commission that Portugal's membership should be terminated by ECOSOC because of its failure to allow its dependencies—Mozambique, Angola, Guinea Bissau, and Cape Verde—to participate created much bitterness. There was also resistance from the council to the commission's decision to deprive South Africa of its membership because of its apartheid policy and officially sanctioned racism. The UN member states that voted against the ECA's resolutions at ECOSOC explained that the expulsion of Portugal and South Africa would be detrimental to the multilateral system which the UN was striving to attain. However, those states that supported the ECA felt that the continued flouting of UN decisions by recalcitrant member states threatened the very existence of the system.

Although both Portugal and South Africa were eventually deprived of their membership on the commission, the ECA paid dearly for it. When it was established, its members expected help from foreign powers. They were confident that given Africa's long history with Europe and America's support for decolonization, the West would provide a Marshall Plan–type program of aid to their countries under the aegis of the ECA, but this turned out to be a pipe dream, which was not surprising in view of the unfolding relations between the West and the independent African countries in the commission. The situation was further exacerbated in 1960 when the Congo crisis broke out.

During the second session of the commission, in Tangiers, it was announced that Belgium would grant independence to the Congo in June 1960. Unfortunately, at the independence celebration in Leopoldville (now Kinshasa), which

Table 5.1. Africa's Long Walk to Freedom

Phase	Period	Number of Countries Becoming Independent	List of Countries
I	Signatories of UN Charter	4	Egypt, Ethiopia, Liberia, and South Africa (which was later suspended from ECA membership because of apartheid; its membership was restored in 1994 after majority rule had been introduced)
	1950–1959	6	Ghana, Guinea, Libya, Morocco, Sudan, and Tunisia
II	1960	17	Benin, Burkina Faso, Cameroon, Central African Republic, Chad, Congo, Democratic Republic of the Congo, Cote d'Ivoire, Gabon, Madagascar, Mali, Mauritania, Niger, Nigeria, Senegal, Somalia, and Togo
	1961–1965	10	Algeria, Burundi, Gambia, Kenya, Malawi, Rwanda, Sierra Leone, Tanzania, Tanganyika, and Uganda
	1966–1969	5	Zambia, Lesotho, Mauritius, Swaziland, and Equatorial Guinea
III	1973	1	Guinea Bissau
	1975	5	Angola, Cape Verde, Comoros, Mozambique, Sao Tomé and Principe
	1976–1980	3	Djibouti, Seychelles, and Zimbabwe
	1990–1993	2	Namibia and Eritrea

Source: Based on UNESCO, *General History of Africa*, vol. VIII (Berkeley: University of California Press, 1999), Table 28.1, 831.

was attended by Ralph Bunche, pandemonium broke out as soon as independence was declared and the new prime minister, Patrice Lumumba, not only failed to express gratitude for colonial rule but, on the contrary, stressed the fact that the Congo had been a victim of colonialism.

Executive Secretary Mekki Abbas of the ECA was appointed to be the secretary-general's representative in the Congo, supported by some senior staff seconded from the ECA. However, when ECA affairs required that he should return to Addis Ababa, his deputy, Robert Gardiner, was appointed in his place. Within a few months, Mekki Abbas resigned and Gardiner was appointed his successor, but he remained in Leopoldville until June 1963. In spite of the positive role the staff of the new organization played in the Congo, the conflict had a very negative impact on the administration and leadership of the commission. The staff position was further weakened between 1960 and 1963 because the administration of the ECA was in the hands of a succession of officers-in-charge. The UN had assumed that the crisis would not last more than a few months, but it turned out to be highly complicated and very violent. But for the UN presence, Belgium might have attempted to reoccupy the Congo. Unfortunately, the direct involvement of the ECA executive secretary and some of his senior officials in the Congo operation did not make for a pro-ECA attitude in a number of chancelleries in Europe and elsewhere in spite of the sacrifice that the commission had made to the cause of peace and unity.

In the meantime, with the political independence of fourteen French territories, Zaire (now Democratic Republic of Congo), Nigeria, and Somalia, the number of independent African member states of the commission had more than doubled to thirty-six by the time of the commission's fourth session in February 1962. At the end of the 1960s, fifteen more countries had become independent, bringing to thirty-two the number of countries which had achieved independence in the decade. Thereafter, the struggle for independence by the few remaining colonies necessitated bloody wars of independence. By the time of the ECA's silver jubilee in 1983, the number of independent African states had risen to fifty-one; most of the newly independent states came from eastern and southern Africa. Indeed, by the end of the 1980s, the only remaining colony was Namibia, which became independent in March 1990. The Republic of South Africa still remained a bedrock of racism, and although it was a founding member of the commission, it remained deprived of membership until 1994 when majority rule was established.

In spite of the legacy of colonialism, the continent's long isolation from the rest of the world, and the protracted decolonization process, the commission quickly set to work in carrying out its mandate. But all these factors, and the Congo crisis in particular, inevitably affected the way and the ease with which it carried out its duties. Nevertheless, the general view is that it discharged its responsibilities creditably. For example, George Davidson, who was the president of ECOSOC at the session during which the resolution to establish the commission was given final approval and who later became the UN Under-Secretary-General for administration and management, testified that the ECA had succeeded in coping with the political evolution of the continent and had succeeded in maintaining an even balance between issues of economic development and social reform more successfully than some of the other regional commissions.[9]

During its first five years, the foundations of the relations between the Western countries and ECA were well and truly laid. First and foremost, the colonial status of most of Africa at the time of the establishment of the ECA and the anticolonial stance of the commission ipso facto marked ECA as anti-Western from the start. The aftermath of the antagonism between the commission and Portugal, Spain, and Belgium still hangs in the air. The dramatic change in the status of the former colonial powers from full members to associate members of the commission and the exclusion of the United States from the start would appear to have permanently prejudiced these relations, particularly in view of the fact that they do not suffer similar discrimination in ECLAC and ESCAP. In ECLAC and ESCAP, the OECD countries are full and active members, whereas in the ECA they are not only treated as outsiders but are also not allowed to forget it by the representatives of their former colonies. Not surprisingly, therefore, the ECA is not among the West's most popular regional commissions. However, international politics and diplomacy, particularly during the Cold War era, did not permit the open admission of this reality and consequently it could not be directly and forthrightly addressed.

For thirty-two years of ECA's existence (1958–1990), the Cold War between the great world powers loomed over Africa. In the fight against colonization, many African countries received arms and training from the Eastern bloc. Insofar as independent African countries wracked by civil war were concerned, Cold War considerations were decisive in obtaining support from either the Eastern or the Western bloc; it was always a case of "my enemy's friend is my enemy."

To escape from their dilemmas, most African nations joined the Non-Aligned Movement, but their economies remained firmly dependent on the West. Nevertheless, their involvement in the Cold War remained a potent factor in the development of African regionalism; many independent African countries remained indebted to the bloc that had supported them in their struggle against colonialism or in their civil wars. Indeed, many African conflicts were the by-products of the Cold War; the violent conflicts in Angola, Mozambique, and the Horn of Africa are prominent examples.

The exigencies of the Cold War era, which compelled the two competing major powers to support repressive regimes, were responsible for the pervasiveness of antidemocratic forces and political instability in Africa. U.S. support for Siad Barre, despite his repression of the Somalis, sowed the seeds of that country's tragic disintegration. Similarly, Soviet support for Mengistu Haile Mariam allowed him to decimate the Ethiopian people and sustain a senseless civil war for decades when the issues at stake called for diplomacy and statesmanship. The two superpowers fought many African conflicts by proxy through local factions.

Now that the Cold War era has ended and the political decolonization process has been completed, the time has come to revisit this sensitive issue of membership and put the ECA on the same level as ECLAC and ESCAP. This is not to suggest that the African peoples and governments should forget the past but rather that they should not allow it to haunt their present and their future. This requires a new approach to relations between the West and Africa based on trust and mutual respect for each other's ideas. One of the ideals expressed in the African Charter for Popular Participation in Development is the imperative for the African governments to yield space to their peoples so as to facilitate a true and dynamic democratic partnership.[10] The same principle could be extended mutatis mutandis to relations with the West.

Nevertheless, the ECA has been the creature of its context. First and foremost, unlike the OAU, which was established five years after the ECA, it was not an independent African institution. It was and still is an integral part of the UN. As an intergovernmental body, it is an organ of ECOSOC, through which it reports to the General Assembly and which provides it with budgetary resources. Its staff from the executive secretary downward are employees of the UN appointed by the Secretary-General. Thus, it is not simply a regional body but also part of the global system and, as such, African governments do not have the last word in its affairs. Nor do they have any responsibility in appointments to key positions in the secretariat—that is the job of the UN chief administrative officer. Unfortunately, decentralization, delegation, deconcentration, and devolution—the four Ds of good governance—are ideals which are more often honored than adhered to, and this is as true of the UN as elsewhere. Even when laws command their observance, bureaucracies rarely fail to frustrate them.

It is in this context that in spite of the emergence of a majority of independent African states in the ECA, its decisions are not final and sovereign.

Limiting the participation of non-African states to observer status at ECA meetings means very little because some of these "observers" are major influences at the higher levels of decision-making, such as ECOSOC and the various committees of the General Assembly, particularly the Fifth Committee, which is in charge of budgetary appropriations.

The rapidity with which African states became independent, paradoxically, had a negative impact on African solidarity. As was to be expected, their level of preparedness to assume the responsibility of sovereignty varied considerably. Those that were ill-prepared were very vulnerable to external pressure and became the weak links in the chain of solidarity. They were manipulated by donor agencies and countries. While this intensified the fear of external forces, it did not diminish their dominance and power over individual African countries.

Yet, potentially, the ECA remains an important instrument for advancing the cause of regionalism; for protecting small, dependent, and vulnerable states; and for promoting pan-Africanism and international cooperation.

Laying the Foundations of Postcolonial Economies in Africa

Political decolonization was only one side—albeit a crucial one—of the multidimensional challenge facing Africa since the independence decade of the 1960s. The rapidly growing number of independent African countries struggled tirelessly in the UN for the decolonization of Africa, and the establishment of the ECA was seen as an instrument for pursuing the decolonization strategy. Within a decade after ECA was established, not only had the number of independent African countries increased from nine (excluding South Africa) to forty-one, but the Organization of African Unity had also been born. With this historic development, the ECA ceased to play a frontline role in the struggle for political decolonization, which was now left almost exclusively to the new continental political organization. But the ECA still kept its doors open to the liberation movements in those countries remaining under colonial rule or racist domination. By Resolution 254 (XII), passed at its twelfth session in February 1975, the ECA's rules of procedure were amended to allow national liberation movements recognized by the OAU to participate in its activities and to provide assistance with the travel and other expenses of members of such movements. As a result, three liberation movements—the African National Congress, the Pan African Congress of South Africa, and the South West African Peoples' Organization—participated fully in all the activities of the ECA until South Africa became a majority-ruled state in 1994 and Namibia became independent in 1990.

Economic decolonization, however, was extremely difficult to deal with. The people of each newly independent country soon realized that their situation compared most unfavorably with the social and economic conditions prevailing in other regions of the world, particularly those in Latin America and Asia. Each independent state faced enormous problems in building a national infrastructure. These countries had emerged into statehood with economies characterized by a vicious interaction between excruciating poverty, abysmally low levels of productivity, serious deficiencies in physical and social infrastructures, weak research capabilities, and poor endowments of technological know-how and human-capital resources—all of which are indispensable for an integrated and dynamic national economy.

In specific terms, the structural characteristics of the typical African economy at the time of independence were:

- The predominance of subsistence agriculture and the pervasiveness of the informal sector and commercial activities;
- A narrow, disarticulated production base with ill-adapted technology;
- A neglected and extremely weak and underdeveloped formal sector;
- Lopsided development due to the urban bias of public policies in general and development policies in particular;
- Fragmentation of each national economy and of the regional economy;
- Openness and excessive dependence of each national economy on
  a) one, two, or three commodities for earning foreign exchange; and
  b) the import of key factor inputs, including technical expertise;
- Shortages of indigenous trained personnel in both the public and modern private sectors, including a scarcity of entrepreneurial capabilities to spearhead transformation and development;
- Weak institutional capabilities and infrastructure;
- A modern private sector that was limited in size;
- Environmental degradation resulting in and exacerbating drought, desertification, and soil erosion;
- Large-scale unemployment and underemployment and, particularly since the 1980s, high rates of unemployment among school-leavers and college graduates.

At the regional and subregional levels, these countries were new to international cooperation. During the colonial era, the only intergovernmental institutions in Africa were those established by the metropolitan powers to promote their own interests. The African members of the commission had no history of economic cooperation among themselves.

The commission's first program of work provides an indication of the intentions of the small group of independent African countries that had fought for a pan-African economic commission between 1947 and 1958. They were certainly earnest in launching a process of socioeconomic transformation at both the national and the regional levels in Africa, but the fundamental question is why Africa has remained economically backward and underdeveloped in spite of the efforts of the commission. Why has structural change and transformation continued to elude the continent? Is it because it has pursued inappropriate development paradigms? Is it due to a lack of the will to develop on the part of the people and their governments? Is it due to exogenous factors? Or, as the World Bank asked some years ago, is the lack of a breakthrough in development in Africa due to a failure to fully comprehend the nature of African problems, particularly as seen from the perspective of the well-meaning donor community and the international financial institutions?[11]

In other words, what role have ideas played in the African development problematic? No one can dispute the crucial role of ideas in human progress and more particularly in the development process. In developing societies, people have too often underestimated the power of ideas while they have been overly impressed by the idea of power, with disastrous consequences. Or, to paraphrase a Yoruba saying, the ideas of elders which are scoffed at and laughed at in the morning invariably become the popular folklore wisdom by sunset. Keynes put it even more sharply when he wrote that "the ideas of economists and political philosophers, both when they are right and when they are wrong, are more powerful than is commonly understood. Indeed, the world is ruled by little else."[12]

However, the origin, and originators, of ideas are crucial factors to their acceptance or rejection. Ideas that emanate from the center are more likely to be taken more seriously than those coming from the periphery. And the world, particularly the Western world, has yet to accept that ideas coming from Africa are worthy of serious consideration. Matters are made worse if the proponents or progenitors of such ideas are not in a position to back them up with the necessary resources to facilitate their acceptance. More often than not, ill-digested or irrelevant ideas become beacons for policy and action because they are backed by resources, usually foreign. Or the media, both print and electronic, may proselytize such ideas. Selling a refrigerator to an Eskimo may sound improbable, but it can be done if the source of the idea and the incentive to adopt it (the price) are right and there is strong political support or pressure to do so. Sometimes old ideas which have been found faulty and have been discarded can be recycled by the strong and powerful and imposed on the weak and ignorant. But in the battle between good ideas and ill-conceived ones, the former ultimately prevail—but usually at a price, after considerable losses have been imposed on the victims. Usually good ideas become internalized in the corpus of knowledge while ideologies sooner or later become spent forces.

The ECA came into existence almost a decade and a half after World War II, after the Bretton Woods Conference and the establishment of the World Bank and the International Monetary Fund (IMF). It was created at a time when the literature on the problems of underdevelopment was increasing rapidly. Most of these writings drew inspiration from the Keynesian theory of employment and growth. The ECA came into existence during the period when it was also becoming increasingly clear that the theory of underdevelopment propagated in the literature was no more than an adaptation and extrapolation of the Harrod/Domar version of Keynesianism. (Keynesian theory is primarily concerned with short-term equilibrium, while the Harrod/Domar model is one of long-term growth. Nevertheless, both underline the importance of investment and demand.)

There was, however, an overlap with the very small corpus of literature that was striving to shift the discourse from underdevelopment to development and from growth to structural transformation and which found the Keynesian analytical tools rather restrictive. For example, Raul Prebisch's *The Economic Development of Latin America and Its Principal Problems*[13] was published in 1948 and was followed three years later by a seminal UN report.[14]

What impact did these ideas and others have on the newly born ECA, which was grappling with the problem of forging a future for Africa? Did the commission accept the proposition of Dag Hammarskjöld that it should serve as a well-organized clearinghouse for the exchange of information and experience, supplemented by some measure of analysis and critical appraisal? Did the commission see itself as the forum where the socioeconomic needs of the African people would be discussed or as the generator of the development of an African-centered model of sustainable development that would meet the basic needs of its people?

The latter question touches upon traditional UN secretariat activities; namely, research, data collection, analysis and dissemination, and institution-building. Consequently, two vital subjects included in the first program of work of the commission were staff development and correcting the lack of adequate statistical data and research through capacity-building at the national level.

Because of the acute shortage of high- and medium-level staff in virtually all the newly independent African countries, the first session of the commission also asked the executive secretary to establish and develop a system of advisory services and training for member and associate member states.[15] This was followed at the commission's second session by two resolutions[16] requesting training programs in the field of economic development and planning and for assistance in overcoming the widespread shortages of both teaching and research staff. In response to these requests, the executive secretary convened a panel in December 1961 to consider the scope and functions of an African institute for economic development and planning and an economic projections and programming center, both to be established under the auspices of the commission.

The Institute for Economic Development and Planning (IDEP), which was located in Dakar,[17] inaugurated its nine-month course in November 1963. Meanwhile, the commission had decided to institutionalize the Conference of African Planners[18] in order to facilitate the coordination of national development plans. By 1965, most countries, with the encouragement of the donor community and the World Bank, had introduced development planning as a means of achieving an optimal allocation of resources for rapid economic and social advance. However, except in East Africa, no attempt was made to coordinate development among countries.

The major problems of the initiation of any development plan are the inadequacy of basic statistical and technical data and key planning personnel. Indeed, right from the very beginning, the commission saw statistics as one of the most important areas needing immediate attention and action. The first Conference of African Statisticians was held in 1959, within months of the establishment of the commission. Since then, the conference has met every two years and, under the aegis of the commission, a network of statistical training institutes has been established in different parts of Africa; as a result, greater uniformity in data-gathering and statistical classification and analysis has been achieved. So rapid was progress that by the time of the second Conference of African Statisticians, nineteen governments had programs for the expansion of statistical services. Due to these efforts by the ECA, as countries became independent, they began to appreciate the value of quantitative data for planning purposes and to allocate substantial funds for statistical development, especially in activities devoted to conceptualization, assessment of statistical needs, and statistical organization and training.

One of the most remarkable achievements of the commission is its success in institution-building. Following the establishment of IDEP, the commission embarked on setting up an African development bank at its fourth session in February/March 1962.[19] A committee of nine member states was set up to prepare the proposed bank's charter, make recommendations on its location, and make all necessary contacts to promote and obtain the support and cooperation of all African governments and the international community—all within six months. In June 1963, the Conference of African Ministers of Finance adopted the charter, which was signed almost immediately by thirty of the thirty-three countries eligible for membership.[20] By historic coincidence, the OAU was inaugurated in May 1963, a few days before the ministers of finance conference, and lent its support for the rapid establishment of the African Development Bank. On September 10, 1964, the agreement establishing the bank came into force and the bank's Board of Governors held their inaugural meeting in Lagos from November 3 to 7, 1964. All the members of the commission were fulsome in their praise of the executive secretary for assisting them to achieve their objective so quickly.

By the time the commission celebrated its silver jubilee in April 1983, it had successfully put in place an impressive institutional landscape consisting of almost forty institutions in the following sectors: financial and banking services (five); earth resources (seven); industrial development and services (seven); social and economic development planning and management (seven); trade and transport (seven); and ECA Multinational Programming and Operational Centers (MULPOCs)—recently renamed Subregional Development Centers (five) (table 5.2).

These institutions have provided valuable services to African governments, including advice on policies and strategies and help in the mobilization of human resources in their respective fields of competence. Although they are sponsored by the commission, they are owned and managed by member states—under the leadership of the ECA—which pool their resources to provide services that are beyond the financial means of individual countries.

Finally, mention must be made of the ECA Training and Fellowships Programme for Africa, which has been in operation since 1965. This program complements national capacity-building for development and good governance. It identifies and secures training opportunities for Africans in fields that are critical in advancing progress. It provides fellowships and finance and administers and monitors the training. The program mobilizes and awards fellowships for study in institutions within and outside Africa at undergraduate and graduate levels for short and medium-length courses. In all, almost 3,000 Africans have benefited from the program, which during the decolonization period was also used to provide cadres in non-independent African states with the skills required for managing a modern state. Thus, in 1979 a special component of the program was developed in collaboration with the United Nations Institute for Namibia (UNIN) to train Namibians in development administration and management skills. It is from

Table 5.2. ECA-Sponsored Multinational Institutional Landscape

I. Financial and banking services	**V. Trade and transport**

I. **Financial and banking services**

African Development Bank
Association of African Central Banks
African Centre for Monetary Studies
West African Clearing House
Association of African Tax
   Administrators

II. **Earth resources services**

Regional Centre for Training in Aerial
   Surveys
Regional Centre for Services in
   Surveying, Mapping and Remote
   Sensing
African Regional Remote Sensing
   Council
Eastern and Southern African Mineral
   Resources Development Centre
African Association of Cartography
African Regional Centre for Solar Energy
Regional Centre for Remote Sensing

III. **Industrial development and services**

African Regional Centre for Engineering
   Design and Manufacturing
African Regional Centre for Technology
African Regional Organization for
   Standardization
African Institute for Higher Technical
   Training and Research
Eastern and Southern African Mineral
   Resources Development Centre
African Regional Industrial Property
   Organization
The African Organization for Intellectual
   Property

V. **Trade and transport**

Association of African Trade Promotion
   Organizations
Port Management Association of West
   and Central Africa
Port Management Association of
   Eastern and Southern Africa
Port Management Association of North
   Africa
African Regional Organization for
   Standardization
Trans-African Highway Authority
Trans-East African Highway Authority

IV. **Social and economic development
planning and management**

African Institute for Economic
   Development and Planning
Regional Institute for Population Studies
Institut de formation et de recherche
   demographiques
African Centre for Applied Research and
   Training in Social Development
Eastern and Southern Africa
   Management Institute
African Regional Centre for Technology
United Nations Institute for the
   Prevention of Crime and the
   Treatment of Offenders

VI. **ECA Multinational Programming and
Operational Centers (recently
renamed Subregional Development
Centers)**

West African (Niamey-based) MULPOC
Eastern and Southern African (Lusaka-
   based) MULPOC
Central African (Yaounde-based)
   MULPOC
Economic Community of the Great
   Lakes Countries (Gisenyi-based)
   MULPOC
North African (Tangiers-based)
   MULPOC

Source: ECA, *Twenty-Five Years of Service to African Development and Integration* (Addis Ababa: United Nations, 1983), 58.

this cadre that the top echelons of independent Namibia's administration have been recruited.

Of course, the progress in institution-building inevitably had to face a multitude of problems, among which are:

- A lack of sustained political will on the part of some of the African governments that pressed for the establishment of a particular institution. The result is that not all countries eligible for membership have joined the institution or are meeting their budgetary obligations once it is created.
- The few African countries which have signed are left alone to carry and nurse the institutions. The financial burden on such countries becomes greater than it should have been and this has disincentive effects—particularly as non-participating countries benefit from the services of the institutions.
- The perception that there are "too many" institutions has led to a clamor for rationalization. But the governments that make this criticism are those that have always resisted any attempt at rationalization, particularly if the institutions likely to be affected are located in their own countries or if the chief executives are their nationals.
- The impression that the ECA secretariat is no longer as active in its support of the institutions as it used to be and that its advocacy and supervisory role has slackened considerably in recent years.

The expectation that the ECA would continue to promote these institutions in the interest of its overarching objectives of collective self-reliance and sustained development was a major factor in the decision of member states to establish and support them. However, critics of ECA have argued that its member states have created too many institutions without clear priorities that have minimal interconnectivity and are too thinly staffed and poorly financed. But in spite of these criticisms, the various evaluations commissioned by the ECA Conference of Ministers have consistently reaffirmed the need for the various institutions and, indeed, have strongly advocated that they be strengthened.

From Imported Models to an African Development Strategy

Since the ECA had been established only in 1958 and over four-fifths of its potential member states were still in political tutelage, Africa was not in a position to participate fully and effectively in determining the strategy, policy framework, and priorities of the UN First Development Decade of the 1960s.

However, the commission's first biennial program of work and priorities, 1960–1961, made it clear where the priorities in the development field should lie.

Africa and the First and Second Development Decades

Between January 1959 and February 1969, the commission passed 216 resolutions covering a wide range of subjects. Thus, from the onset, the commission mistook resolutions for resolve and adopted a "pork-barrel" approach to setting strategy and priorities. This may, of course, reflect their relative inexperience in international relations and the rapidity with which the number of independent countries increased, each with its own perception of priorities but all assuming that they only needed to pass resolutions in order to have the international community come to their assistance. Nevertheless, the failure to focus on a few well-selected priorities that would have strong multiplier effects dissipated the commission's effort and reduced its impact. No wonder some commentators have likened African governments to physically unfit soccer players who play without understanding the rules but who expect their opponents to let them win!

To really make themselves fit for the game, they should have clearly worked out a development paradigm appropriate for their countries and for the African region, even if the conclusion of their deliberations was that extant development theories were adequate and appropriate. At least the conclusion would have been reached in a rational rather than an assumptive manner. Unfortunately, close critical analysis of extant theories with a view to determining their appropriateness in the African situation was not begun by the ECA until the second half of the UN's Second Development Decade. That analysis was stimulated by the failure to launch a process of sustainable development despite adherence to orthodox development models. This failure became frustratingly manifest and indeed turned into a major economic crisis of unprecedented proportions in the 1980s—Africa's lost decade.

This failure also exposes one of the many paradoxes of which Africa was a victim—the inherent inability of African governments to match their rhetoric with reality. A few countries did associate economic decolonization with the idea of directing their societies toward socialist goals, even if socialism had different connotations in different countries—African socialism, democratic socialism, cooperative socialism, Arab socialism, and so forth. It was in Tanzania that socialism was pursued most seriously and relentlessly. *Ujamaa vijijini,* or village socialism, was Tanzania's radical new socialism articulated in the Arusha Declaration of 1967. In theory, *ujamaa* was based on the traditional values of the village and the policy of self-reliance. It emphasized group

and mutual support in contradistinction to the individualistic and exploit-
ative values of capitalism. But in terms of content, socialism in Africa, regardless of the national brand, meant the pursuit of four overarching objectives:

- Pervasive state intervention in the development process and state
  control of the economy;
- Limitation of the role of the private sector and of private investment;
- Nationalization of major economic institutions, particularly banks,
  insurance companies, foreign trade, manufacturing enterprises, and
  large agricultural estates;
- Imposition of a one-party system of government.

In spite of the rhetoric, the inherited colonial economic system remained
intact because colonial economic policies and strategies continued to be pursued. Besides, African socialist experiments rejected any massive expropria-
tion of foreign or private property. Monoculturalism also flourished and
dependence on foreign aid increased significantly. Indeed, over the years, the
socialist ideology, even as rhetoric, was replaced by the more pragmatic policy
of indigenization.

Socialism no doubt failed to take root in Africa because of the barrenness
of the sociological and material soil. Ethnicity has remained far stronger than
class consciousness in Africa. Needless to say, neither the ECA as an intergovernmental body nor its secretariat involved itself in this ideological contradiction. For member countries, the divide between the socialist and
non-socialist states in effect meant the divide between the African countries
within the sphere of influence of the Soviet Union and its communist allies
(the so-called progressive states) and those which were overly dependent on
the West, particularly the United States, and the former colonial powers of
Great Britain, France, Belgium, Germany, and Portugal (the conservative
states). On their part, the senior members of the secretariat were intellectually more at home with the historical approach to development than with the
ideological approach or the normative development scenario. It was not until
the mid-1970s that the secretariat took up the gauntlet of seeking alternatives
to ideological and neocolonial development paradigms for Africa.

The lack of an African development paradigm accounts for the fact that
a miscellany of projects from different sectors were put together and labeled
a "strategy for development" in the 1970s. The inherited colonial structure
of production remained intact and national self-reliance remained a delusion
as resources continued to be devoted to commodity production for export. It
took many years before African governments and leaders fully realized that
massive internal social and economic transformation must precede and

accompany accelerated development and economic growth.[21] It took the member states of the commission many years to realize that marching toward the future hand in hand with its colonial monocultural economic legacy held no dignified future for Africa at all. As long as African governments and people continued to just nibble at the inherited colonial economic system, they would fail to achieve any breakthrough in socioeconomic transformation. As Immanuel Wallerstein rightly pointed out, dependent development leads nowhere.[22] Of course, this failure to seek an original and innovative pro-African development paradigm also has to do, inter alia, with the origin, nature, and intellectual orientation of development economics as a new discipline.

Development economics emerged as a subdiscipline within the field of the economics of growth, which focuses on the sources of and obstacles to economic growth. It is linked to the neoclassical mainstream which since the beginning of the twentieth century was increasingly preoccupied with the analysis of short-term equilibrium analyses and the maximizing of efficiency in resource allocation. It was thus the neoclassical growth theories of the industrialized economies that were universalized and extended to developing countries. Yet it is clear that mainstream growth economists were not particularly interested in long-term growth or in the conditions of underdevelopment. Keynes's claim to any significance in the development debate is based on his placing the question of the relationship between markets, employment, and state on the agenda in his *General Theory of Employment, Interest and Money* (1936).[23]

Among the early development economists, it was only Joseph Schumpeter who made an explicit distinction between "growth" and "development."[24] Growth was the gradual extension of the capital apparatus and increasing production, while development occurred when technical innovators introduced new production techniques, new products, or new ways of organizing production. In this manner, more fundamental changes are brought about and new rules of play introduced into economic life.

Unfortunately, development theories were not immune to Cold War ideological propaganda. Africa inevitably suffered from the competition for hegemony, intellectual and ideological, from both sides of the Iron Curtain. A system of client states emerged in which leaders were maintained in power as a reward for their allegiance to one of the superpowers and opposition to the other. Cold War tactics led to a strong propensity to tailor so-called development theories to political ideologies. Such theories are derived a priori from long-held dogmas and ideologies and are then coated in "scientistic" terms in order to engender the belief that they have a sound analytical and empirical basis. Friedrich von Hayek[25] described as scientistic (in contradistinction to scientific) the tendency of social scientists in general and economists in particular to imitate the methodology of the physical sciences. This approach is decidedly unscientific in the true sense of the word, since it involves a mechanical and uncritical application of habits of thought to fields different from those in which they originated.

It is this scientistic approach that led development economists to confine their analyses to what is measurable and, by so doing, to anchor development economics in the primacy of "things" or a macroeconomic framework—gross domestic product, foreign-exchange gap, balance-of-payments equilibrium, debt and debt servicing, budget deficits, and so forth—rather than the primacy of people and human capital. From the very beginning, economic development was thus identified with the growth of national income, not with human development and improving the quality of life; with saving, investment, and incremental-capital output ratios, not with economic, political, and gender empowerment. The strong advocacy (of Arthur Lewis) for developing countries to move from a low savings ratio (5 percent) to a high savings ratio (of at least 10 percent) was the theoretical underpinning of large injections of financial assistance from developed countries to make up for the low level of domestic savings. This advocacy drew a lot of strength and considerable credibility from the outstandingly successful effort of the Marshall Plan in bringing about the economic reconstruction of Western Europe after World War II.

This two-gap model gave foreign capital and foreign aid a central place in the development process and, by so doing, exacerbated the dependency syndrome of African economies and laid the foundations for the current debt burden. The experience of oil-producing countries such as Nigeria, which, in spite of their access to huge financial resources are not only debt-ridden but also remain underdeveloped, proves the weakness and inadequacy of this theory. By focusing almost exclusively on those indices of development that are amenable to quantification, by chasing material things to the neglect of people, development economics inevitably proved inadequate to the task of providing an analytical and policy framework for propelling the economies of Africa into self-sustaining development.

Lastly, there is the influence of prejudice and bias, which although they are hardly ever articulated, are nevertheless implicit in the attitude of the early development economists, most of whom were from the West. As Albert Hirschman ruefully admitted:

[These Western economists] were convinced that developing countries were not all that complicated: their major problems would be solved, if only their national income per capita could be raised adequately. At an earlier time,

contempt for the countries designated as "rude and barbarous" in the eighteenth century, as "backward" in the nineteenth and as "underdeveloped" in
the twentieth had taken the form of relegating them to permanent lowly status,
in terms of economic and other prospects, on account of unchangeable factors
such as hostile climate, poor resources, or inferior race. With the new doctrine
of economic growth, contempt took a more sophisticated form: suddenly it
was taken for granted that progress of these countries would be smoothly linear. Given what was seen as their overwhelming problem of poverty, the underdeveloped countries were expected to perform like wind-up toys. In sum,
like the "innocent" and *doux* trader of the eighteenth century, these countries
were perceived to have only *interests* and no *passions*.[26]

It is therefore not surprising that orthodox development theories failed woefully in tackling the central problem of persistent underdevelopment by
bringing about a fundamental structural transformation of the African economies and people. Virtually all the first- and second-generation development
economists viewed the underdeveloped world from the perspective of their
own developed countries and thought that all that was required was for the
developing countries to imitate the development experience of the industrialized market economies. In this regard, they had many disciples among African economists.

While no one should doubt the potency of ideas which emanate from
knowledge, it must always be borne in mind that not all ideas matter and not
all intellectual work, particularly in the social sciences, which deal with peoples
and their societies, are amenable to universalization. Societies and peoples
are to a large extent culture-bound and are greatly influenced by their history
and political development, even in an era of globalization. The essence of the
teachings of the philosophy of science and the sociology of knowledge is that
because of the differences in history, politics, and culture, institutions differ
considerably in their responses to both internal and external impulses. Therefore, the attempt to globalize and universalize the experience of particular
societies and economies can do more harm than good.

In this connection, it is significant that even the World Bank, after insisting
for almost two decades that there was no alternative to its structural adjustment
paradigm, was obliged to express doubts about its relevance and intellectual
validity because of its persistent failure to generate sustainable development
in the countries where it has been applied. "Does Africa face special structural
problems that have not been properly understood?" the World Bank asked.
"Has the institutional dimension been neglected? Have recent reform programs been too narrow or too shallow? Have the external factors been correctly assessed? More fundamentally, is there a long-term vision that is both

credible and energizing?"[27] These are pertinent and fundamental questions, but they should have been asked and answered before designing development strategies, not after they had failed, causing severe hardship and rending the fabric of African societies.

In the circumstances, it was not surprising that the Preliminary Assessment of Long-term Development Trends and Prospects in Africa, which was undertaken in 1976 at the request of the General Assembly[28] and which covered the first post-independence decade and a half (1960–1975), showed falling rates of GDP growth in Africa. Its performance was substantially below all the targets except the target for imports, which grew on average by 10 percent per annum instead of the targeted 7 percent (table 5.3).

The most serious shortfalls were in agricultural output and commodity exports; both sectors had negative growth rates. Not only was the performance of Africa very poor in absolute terms in virtually all sectors, but it also fared worse than all the other regions of the world.

This overall picture, of course, concealed growing differences among the countries of Africa. While the average annual growth rates of the four oil-producing countries was 6.9 percent, five non–oil-producing countries—the Congo, Cote d'Ivoire, Sao Tomé and Principe, Tunisia, and Zambia—grew on average by an annual 5.8 percent. In the remaining thirty-six countries, growth rates were well below the target. From the picture presented in table 5.4, one can see that sub-Saharan Africa's growth has persistently lagged behind North Africa during the past five decades, in terms of both overall GDP rates and GDP per capita.

The inescapable conclusion of the assessment was that Africa not only performed worse than the other Third World regions but was faced with a development crisis of great portent. In spite of the region's ample natural resources,

Table 5.3. Targets of the Second United Nations Development Decade and Africa's Actual Performance

	Performance Strategy Target	Actual Performance (%)
Annual GDP growth rate (at constant price)	6	4.5
Imports	7	10.0
Exports	7	−2.8
Agriculture	4	1.6
Manufacturing	8	6.0

Source: ECA, "Preliminary Assessment of Long-Term Development Trends & Prospects in Africa," in *Long-Term Trends in the Economic Development of the Regions of the World, Report of the Secretary-General* (document E/5937/Add.3), March 29, 1977, Tables 10–15.

Table 5.4. Africa's Average Annual Growth Rates of GDP and Per-Capita Growth Rates of GDP by Decade (by Percent)

Africa's average annual growth rates of GDP

	1951–1960	1961–1970	1971–1980	1981–1990	1991–2000
Sub-Saharan Africa	4.0	4.5	2.4	1.4	2.8
North Africa	5.3	11.0	4.1	2.3	3.4

Average annual growth rate of GDP per capita (in 1980 US$)

		1961–1970	1971–1980	1981–1990	1991–2000
Sub-Saharan Africa	—	1.8	−0.4	−2.6	−0.4
North Africa	—	8.2	1.2	−0.3	0.6
Developing countries (excluding China)	—	3.3	2.4	0.1	1.1

Source: World Bank, *World Development Indicators 2000* (Washington, D.C.: IBRD/World Bank, 2000).

of a favorable ratio of population to natural resources; in spite of the generous and even undiscriminating incentives for foreign private enterprise; and in spite of adherence to orthodox theories and prescriptions, neither high rates of growth nor diversification nor an increasing measure of self-reliance seemed to be within reach.[29]

The Search for Alternative Development Models

The findings of the Preliminary Assessment of Long-term Development Trends made it imperative for the ECA to begin in earnest to search for an African development paradigm that would enable Africa to participate more fully in the preparation of the strategy for the Third United Nations Development Decade. This time around, the secretariat took the lead and successfully mobilized the OAU in this endeavor. The starting point was to ensure that Africa was a net beneficiary of any changes in the global economic system and in its management that might emerge from the ongoing negotiations for a new international economic order. There was a firm belief that unless Africa first put its own house in order it would remain marginalized and peripheral in any reconstructed international economy. Therefore, at the national level, each country has to put in place a new national economic strategy based on the principles of self-reliance and self-sustainment, on freeing each national economy from the shackles of excessive external dependence, and on the recovery and establishment of national self-confidence. Such a new national socioeconomic order must be designed to maximize not only the rate of economic growth but also human development, social justice, and equity.

Similarly and complementarily, a new African regional economic order must be put in place to achieve an increasing measure of collective self-reliance. Given the large number of minuscule states in Africa, intra-African economic cooperation and integration is a necessary condition for the achievement of national economic and social goals. Politically, this requires Africa to learn to protect economic-cooperation institutions and arrangements from political differences.[30]

Accordingly, the ECA secretariat came out, in 1976, with its first landmark document setting out a framework for a new economic order in Africa, entitled the "Revised Framework of Principles for the Implementation of the New International Economic Order in Africa."[31] Its importance lay in the intellectual and theoretical foundation it provided for the subsequent Monrovia Strategy and the Lagos Plan of Action (LPA), including the Final Act of Lagos (FAL). Its immediate impact was the challenge it posed to the conventional wisdom concerning African development and its systematic exposé of the inappropriateness of that strategy for transforming the economy of the continent. Its lasting contributions lay in its clear and precise definition of the meaning and scope of self-reliance for Africa and in its identification of the means for bringing about the fundamental change in strategy that it was advocating.

After noting the dominance of the interests of the former metropolitan countries as one of the major determinants of Africa's continued economic backwardness, the Revised Framework drew two conclusions from Africa's experience of socioeconomic development since independence. The first was that the available pool of knowledge and experience of how economies grow and how socioeconomic change can be managed was limited. The second was that even after independence, policymaking in Africa, in most cases, was a succession of responses to diagnoses of social and economic ills originating outside the region. Both the diagnoses and prescriptions were greatly influenced not only by a firm belief in the efficacy of international trade and its associated economic relations as an engine of desirable economic growth and social change but also by strong adherence to a particular interpretation of the genesis of international trade.

The ECA questioned the validity of the hypothesis of international trade as an engine of growth because it depends on the products that constitute the basis of trade. International trade based on the export of one or two commodities and the import of consumer goods, including the basic necessities of life, cannot be an engine of growth. Such a pattern only unleashes the forces of boom and bust and, consequently, economic and political instability while increasing dependence on the export of primary commodities. Also questioned was the conventional linear thinking by which economic growth is regarded as a semi-mystical process, the outcome of which is measured by increases or decreases in the GDP or GNP and which is the result of a semi-mystical input called investment which consists mainly of resources from abroad. In such a conventional approach, the role of indigenous factor inputs is hardly examined at all nor is it given a central place in the development process. Because of the lack of national or multinational programs for the production of such indigenous factor inputs, there is heavy reliance on foreign exchange as the means of obtaining these inputs. Hence single-product export, the net inflow of foreign private investment, and the search for foreign gifts and loans to supplement these two are vitally important in this model.

Of course, the greatest weakness is not simply the perpetuation of colonial economic policies and strategies or the lack of coherent policies and institutional arrangements for accelerating economic growth and structural change, nor is it the excessive external dependence of African economies. More fundamentally, the model's weakness is the lack of any vision and long-term perspective on the part of the political, social, and industrial leaders of what the African countries, individually and as a group, might become. It is this capacity to conceive a voluntarist image of its own future that is a condition of policymaking and strategy design in every developed and semi-developed country. Without it, no reliable path toward the future can be constructed and followed either by individuals, communities, countries, or groups of countries. And without it, it becomes easy to go astray or to be led astray.

Accordingly, the Revised Framework proposed three overarching objectives of any credible development strategy for Africa. These are:

- The deliberate promotion of an increasing measure of self-reliance;
- The acceleration of internally located and relatively autonomous processes of growth and diversification;
- The progressive eradication of unemployment and mass poverty and a fair and just distribution of income and the benefits of economic development among the people.

The ECA's basic proposition was that an increasing measure of self-reliant and self-sustaining development and economic growth was a most important accompaniment to political independence since it would lead to the economic decolonization of Africa. Self-reliance is defined as a triple process involving:

- The internalization of the forces of demand which determine the direction of development and economic growth and the patterns of output;

- Increasing substitution of factor inputs derived from within the system for those derived from outside;
- Increasing participation of the mass of the people in the production and consumption of the social product.

Increasing self-sustainment is taken to mean the deliberate installation of patterns and processes of development and economic growth in which the different components mutually support and reinforce each other so that when related to the internalization of the forces determining demand and supply, the whole system develops its own internal dynamic. A development strategy based on these four main pillars—self-reliance, self-sustainment, the democratization of the development process, and the fair and just distribution of the fruits of development—calls for a complete break with the past. It is inward-looking rather than externally oriented. It does not make a sacred cow of foreign-exchange earnings and therefore does not attach much importance to trade in primary commodities as a basis for development. It puts domestic markets, including subregional and regional markets, rather than foreign markets at the heart of the development effort. And when it emphasizes indigenous factor inputs, it means African scientists and technologists, African entrepreneurs, African market analysts and distributors, and African technology. In the new development strategy, external trade based largely on primary-commodity export and the importation of basic consumer goods, including food, is not seen as constituting the heart of the development effort.

Thus, even as far back as 1976, the ECA was deliberately trying to evolve a development strategy that would not suffer from the limitations of foreign ideologies, which Africa was obliged to imitate. In other words, a development strategy which was genuinely African and not imitative was considered imperative. A close examination of the variety of socialist and market-economy patterns of development and lifestyles shows clearly that, notwithstanding the problems of justice and equity and of providing the material as well as the non-material needs of a society and its people, there are no models of socio-economic development which are universally valid and applicable. Each society has to develop its own pattern of development and lifestyles which, while borrowing from other societies, does not alienate its people from their cultural heritage. None of the extant models which have been pressed so hard upon Africa by outsiders, as well as by many of Africa's foreign-trained intellectuals, will enable the African people to achieve the kind of development that Africa needs and deserves.

It will, of course, be obvious that to have any operational meaning, such a development strategy will require governments to play a large and central part.

They will act as planners; as providers of basic infrastructure; as developers; as promoters of social and technological innovations; as facilitators of an enabling environment for enterprise and development, including personal, community, and national security as well as the security of property; and, as allocators of national resources through fiscal and monetary policies and a structure of incentives and disincentives. But, as argued in the Revised Framework, this is not statism; instead, it requires African governments to move from being predatory to becoming developmental.

The Revised Framework was not only approved by the Executive Committee of ECA in 1976 but was also endorsed by the Assembly of Heads of State and Government of the OAU in June 1977. Although the ECA secretariat regarded this as marking the beginning of a breakthrough, it recognized that much still remained to be done. Accordingly, between 1976 and 1979, the ideas contained in the Revised Framework were expanded and improved upon through numerous internal ECA secretariat brainstorming exercises and a series of specialized meetings such as the Joint OAU/ECA Colloquium on Perspectives of Development and Economic Growth in Africa up to the Year 2000, held in Monrovia in February 1979, and the joint ECA/UNEP Seminar on Alternative Patterns of Development and Life Styles for the African Region, held in Addis Ababa in March 1979.

The continuing search of the ECA for a genuinely African approach to development was stimulated by the need to prepare the International Development Strategy (IDS) for the Third United Nations Development Decade. Not having participated effectively in the preparation of the two earlier development decades, the ECA was determined to ensure that its voice would not only be heard this time but would also play a crucial role in determining the contents and scope of the third IDS.

Accordingly, at the ECA Conference of Ministers of Development and Planning and the fourteenth session of the commission held in Rabat, Morocco, in March 1979, the "Development Strategy for Africa for the Third United Nations Development Decade" was prepared.[32] In addition, the ministers, having decided that the Strategy should be submitted to heads of state and government at their meeting in Monrovia four months later (July 1979) as well as to the UN, also decided to prepare for submission to them a draft "Declaration of Commitment of the Heads of State and Government of the Organization of African Unity on Guidelines and Measures for National and Collective Self-Reliance in Social and Economic Development for the establishment of a New International Economic Order."[33] Upon the adoption of both the Strategy and the Declaration of Commitment by the Heads of State and Government at their meeting in Monrovia, these documents were respectively christened the Monrovia Strategy and the Monrovia Declaration of Commitment. It was also at the Monrovia meeting that the heads of state decided to hold an economic summit in Lagos in April 1980, an economic summit that the ECA secretariat had been promoting since 1977.

The ECA Conference of Ministers at its Addis Ababa meeting early in April 1980 prepared for the endorsement of the Heads of State and Government the "Plan of Action for the Implementation of the Monrovia Strategy for African Development."[34] After its adoption by the Lagos Economic Summit it was entitled the Lagos Plan of Action for the Economic Development of Africa 1980–2000.[35]

Both the Monrovia Strategy and the Plan of Action carried the analysis and argument of the Revised Framework farther by emphasizing:

- The importance of the domestic, subregional, and regional markets for the supply and organization of factor inputs and the demand for final consumer goods and services.
- The imperative need of the natural resources base, not only for determining product lines but also for planning the internal development of the skills required for the identification, exploration, evaluation, and development of such resources and for organizing and managing production and distribution.
- Planning in terms of multiple objectives (both from the supply and demand sides) in real terms, as opposed to planning based on a single main objective (i.e., economic growth).
- The intrasectoral and intersectoral linkages and the intragroup and intergroup and spatial considerations that such an approach to planning demands. Thus, the industrial sector is designed to supply the bulk of the industrial inputs required for agricultural production, processing, storage, and transportation (agricultural chemicals, equipment, including implements and tools, etc.) as well as building materials, metal and engineering products, and chemicals for the transport and communications, mining, energy, and other sectors which make use of capital goods. The food and agriculture program (which includes forest products and fibers) should provide not only inputs to the processing industries but also markets for industrial products of the kind just listed. The importance of intrasectoral and intersectoral linkages is also stressed for other sectors, such as transport, communications, energy, science and technology, and human resources development.

• Finally, in both the Monrovia Strategy and the Lagos Plan of Action, the need to involve, at all stages of the formulation and implementation of development plans, all the principal decision-making agents in the economy, as well as subregional development organs such as ECOWAS (Economic Community of West African States), UDEAC (Customs and Economic Union of Central Africa), and the ECA's MULPOCs.

The adoption of the Monrovia Strategy in 1979 proved, even to the most cynical, that the welcome and support which the Revised Framework received in 1976 was not an aberration but the beginning of a process. It showed that the governments were increasingly aware of, if not alarmed about, the growing gap between promises and performance and, recognizing that continuing with the historical colonial trends was not only futile but also inimical to their national and regional interests, were willing to try a new approach to development.[36]

It is also fair to add that in adopting the Monrovia Strategy and the Plan of Action, the African leaders were aware of at least three crucial factors—time, sacrifice, and assistance from abroad. In all development efforts that require that problems be identified and analyzed and that decisions be taken to solve them, time is very important. African policymakers are not so naïve as to think that the goals and objectives, which they have set themselves, will be achieved overnight. Indeed, they are aware that the process will be a lengthy one. Similarly, they are also aware of the basic truth that there is no way of avoiding either the sacrifices required or the real costs of development and economic growth and reconstruction. Finally, they are also aware of the need for assistance from abroad, although such assistance needed to be supportive of the new approach to development.

The Heads of State and Government made all this abundantly clear in their Declaration of Commitment as follows:

1. That we commit ourselves individually and collectively on behalf of our Governments and peoples to promoting the social and economic development and integration of our societies with a view to achieving an increasing measure of self-reliance and self-sustainment;
2. That we commit ourselves individually and collectively on behalf of our Governments and peoples to promote the physical integration of the African region in order to facilitate social and economic intercourse;
3. That we commit ourselves individually and collectively on behalf of our Governments and peoples to establish national, subregional and regional institutions which will facilitate the attainment of the objectives of self-reliance and self-sustainment;

4. That, most specifically, we commit ourselves, individually and collectively, on behalf of our Governments and peoples to:

a) Self-sufficiency in food production and supply;

b) The successful implementation of the program for the United Nations Transport and Communications Decade in Africa;

c) Subregional and regional internally located industrial development;

d) Co-operation in the field of natural resources exploration, extraction and use for the development of our economies and for the benefit of our peoples and the setting up of appropriate institutions to achieve these purposes;

e) The development of indigenous entrepreneurial, technical manpower and technological capacities to enable our peoples to assume greater responsibility for the implementation of our individual and collective development goals; and,

f) Co-operation in the preservation, protection and improvement of the natural environment.

We hold firmly to the view that these commitments will lead to the creation at the national, subregional and regional levels of a dynamic interdependent African economy and will thereby pave the way for the eventual establishment of an African Common Market leading to an African Economic Community.[37]

It must be emphasized that the Plan of Action was an attempt to operationalize the Monrovia Strategy, which drew its inspiration from the ECA's Revised Framework. The Monrovia Strategy was in turn the springboard for the Declaration of Commitment, which clearly identified the priorities which all African governments committed themselves to pursue between 1980 and 2000. It is because of this five-year-long evolutionary process and the interconnection between the three documents that the Lagos Plan of Action focused exclusively on the sectoral actions to be undertaken in the implementation of both the Monrovia Strategy and the Declaration of Commitment. The sector-by-sector approach in the Plan of Action would of course be meaningless without the links to the guiding principles and macroanalytical framework, strategies, and priorities provided by its three precursors. The Final Act of Lagos completes the quartet.

Seven of the LPA's thirteen chapters focus on Africa's seven strategic sectors—food and agriculture, industry, natural resources, human resources, transport and communications, trade and finance, and energy. The remaining chapters are on such crosscutting issues as the environment, science and technology, gender, and least developed countries. Throughout all the chapters run the overarching themes of self-reliance, self-sustainment, the democratization of the development process, and what today is referred to as sustainable human development.

A universal criticism of the Plan of Action was its "lack of a pragmatic blueprint of how to achieve set objectives, the time table for their achievement, and a price tag. The necessary quantitative (physical or financial) linkages between sectors and sub-sectors is missing, as is any indication of the host of assumptions which must inevitably underlie such scenarios."[38] But it was also universally acknowledged that the Plan of Action was, in a very real sense, a genuinely historic document, representing the first continent-wide effort by Africans to forge a comprehensive and unified approach to the economic development of Africa.

Battles for the African Mind

The publication by the World Bank of its study of development in sub-Saharan Africa, *Accelerated Development in Sub-Saharan Africa: An Agenda for Action,*[39] within a year of the adoption of the Lagos Plan of Action, fomented strong criticism, as it was in many ways the antithesis of the plan. Where the plan emphasized self-reliance and self-sustaining development based on integrated and dynamic national, subregional, and regional markets, the Bank put the emphasis on the external market and the continuation of the colonial export-oriented economic structures inherited at independence. While the Bank identified agricultural export as the motor for African development, the Lagos Plan of Action recognized that the motor in each country will depend on the content and nature of its natural resource endowment. Because it fully endorses the perpetuation of an economically dependent development strategy based on export, it is quite logical for the Bank's *Agenda for Action* to argue that African trade and exchange-rate policies are the reason for the weak incentives to export in much of Africa. The Bank then draws the mistaken conclusion that it is poor export performance rather than the worsening external economic environment (manifested in the collapse of the commodity market) that is responsible for Africa's poor overall economic performance.

But even more significant, the Bank failed to appreciate the strength of the attachment of African governments and their leaders to the Lagos Plan of Action, which, as already stated, was the first effort by Africans themselves to recover their self-confidence and create confidence in their capabilities to initiate and organize their own concepts, policies, and strategies. The Bank's *Agenda for Action* was perceived, perhaps wrongly, as yet another attempt by foreigners to diminish Africa's own initiative and collective effort to forge its future. Such discouragement tended to undermine the recovery of Africans' nascent self-confidence.

The Battle for the African Mind: The First Round

The World Bank's *Agenda for Action* was viewed as its vision of how the global economy should be ordered. According to this—which is also the Western vision—the self-reliance and self-sustainment advocated in the Lagos Plan of Action was "inimical to Western interests and consequently should be ignored or ridiculed."[40] By emphasizing global rather than regional interdependence, the World Bank's *Agenda for Action* would ensure that Africa remains "the storehouse of natural resources necessary for the maintenance of the West's industrial manpower and leadership—hegemony if you wish. It was felt that the West and the World Bank saw in the self-reliant development strategy and the almost inevitable de-linking from the capitalist system too much orthodox Marxist thinking, which must be counteracted."[41]

But since the World Bank study was initiated at the request of the African governors of the bank, it would be improper to impute ulterior motives. The World Bank responded to this request with a genuine and honest analysis and prescriptions based on well-established orthodox theories of development. But there is also no doubt that while the Lagos Plan of Action was Africa-centered, the *Agenda for Action* saw Africa from the perspective of the Western world. Chester A. Crocker, then U.S. assistant secretary of state for African affairs, put this with admirable honesty and succinctness in a speech at the Georgetown University Center for Strategic and International Studies:

> There is a striking contrast between African and Western perspectives. . . .
> The African viewpoint . . . must assume a future that is economically viable
> and politically sustainable. It must assume industrialization and, at least, a
> promise of technological equality with the West (including Japan). It must
> encompass spiritual health and self-reliance as well as material well-being.
> The perspective is quite naturally African-centric.
>
> The Western perspective is . . . that of the policy-maker. . . . Africa does
> not dominate his perspective, it is only one of a panoply of global concerns.
> Unlike the African politician, the Western bureaucrat is not compelled to
> assume politically viable solutions within Africa, nor does he take for granted
> the feasibility of rapid economic progress. Quite the contrary, he is usually
> more impressed by the negative, short-term implications of Africa's economic crisis, particularly its effect on political stability. . . .
>
> These differing perspectives, African and Western, are reflected in two
> much-discussed documents, the "Lagos Plan of Action" and the report of
> the World Bank entitled "Accelerated Development in Sub-Saharan Africa:
> An Agenda for Action."[42]

As is well known, the African governments were unanimous in their rejection of the World Bank's *Agenda for Action*. The ECA Conference of Ministers, the institutional architects of the Lagos Plan of Action, declared that the World Bank strategy was in fundamental contradiction with the political, economic, and social aspirations of Africa. In contrast, the ministers reaffirmed that "the goals and objectives defined by the African countries for themselves in the Monrovia Strategy and the Lagos Plan of Action remain the authentic and authoritative goals and objectives for Africa."

The ECA's historic "Declaration on the Agenda" leaves no doubt as to the gulf existing between Africa and the World Bank over which development path is to be followed. It reads as follows:

> We, the African Ministers responsible for Economic Development and Planning, assembled in Tripoli for the eighth meeting of the Conference of Ministers of the Economic Commission for Africa and the seventeenth Session of the commission, having carefully examined the World Bank Report entitled *Accelerated Development in Sub-Saharan Africa: An Agenda for Action* in the light of the basic guidelines for the achievement of the objectives of self-reliant and self-sustaining development in our respective countries and in the African continent as a whole; conscious of the imperative need to reduce the present extreme dependence of our countries on the export of primary commodities and the import of almost all the strategic inputs required for promoting development and economic growth; and, convinced that externally-oriented and primary-commodity-based strategies of development have hitherto not helped and cannot be expected to help our countries in the restructuring of their economies in initiating the process of internally-generated self-sustaining and reliant development and economic growth and in reducing progressively and finally eliminating the present burden of external debts.
>
> Declare that the strategy recommended in the World Bank report, which emphasises export orientation in general and primary commodity export in particular, regards industrialization and economic co-operation and integration in Africa as longer-term issues, and completely disregards external factors as being major constraints on Africa's development and economic growth, and which adopts approaches, concepts and objectives which are divergent from those of the Lagos Plan of Action and the Final Act of Lagos is in fundamental contradiction with the political, economic and social aspirations of Africa.
>
> We further declare our firm commitment to the promotion of multinational, subregional and regional economic co-operation as a major instrument for restructuring the economies of our countries and for the economic integration of our continent.

> We accordingly affirm that the goals and objectives defined by African countries for themselves in the Monrovia Strategy, the Lagos Plan of Action and the Final Act of Lagos remain the authentic and authoritative goals and objectives for Africa.
>
> We therefore call upon all States members of the Economic Commission for Africa to continue with the full and effective implementation of the Lagos Plan of Action and the Final Act of Lagos at the national, subregional and regional levels.
>
> We hereby urge the international community to provide aid and technical assistance to African countries within the framework of the goals, objectives and philosophy of the Lagos Plan of Action and the Final Act of Lagos.[43]

The fact that this decision was in the form of a declaration (rather than the usual UN resolution) and the fact that it was unanimously adopted in spite of pressure and arm-twisting by senior World Bank officials at the meeting showed a great deal of courage and commitment. Some of the ministers confessed during the debate that they had received threats that their countries would be denied new loans if they went along with the declaration. Some were warned that their ministerial jobs would be at stake if they openly rejected the World Bank's orthodox development paradigm as contained in the *Agenda for Action*. Nevertheless, the declaration was adopted unanimously on April 30, 1982, at the seventeenth session of the commission. Although there is no overt ideological discussion in the text of the *Agenda* (nor is there in the Lagos Plan of Action), the market-oriented bias of the World Bank is unabashedly evident throughout.

The FAL—the last of the quartet—is both an integral part of the LPA and at the same time separate from it. It was adopted with the LPA and annexed to it because the desired national self-reliance and self-sustainment depends largely on the extent to which regional and subregional collective self-reliance is achieved. The balkanization of Africa during the colonial era made this imperative.

To its credit, the ECA had always appreciated this vital point. Even since 1958, it had linked the concept of regionalism with development (what is now referred to as "developmental regionalism"), and from 1975 it saw regionalism as a tool to combat and reduce external economic dependence ("developmental nationalism"). Not surprisingly, therefore, the African leaders resolved to adopt a far-reaching regional approach in the FAL. So central are the concepts of developmental nationalism to the achievement of the goals of the LPA that the ECA has never tired of pursuing the cause of integration regardless of all the difficulties and frustrations and in spite of the lack of any breakthrough for many years.

In the 1970s and 1980s, the effort at last began to yield some positive results. ECOWAS was established in 1975, thanks primarily to the initiative of
Nigeria and Togo but with significant ECA input. This was followed in 1980
by the establishment of the Preferential Trade Area for Eastern and Southern
African States (PTA) and in 1983 by the Economic Community of Central
African States (ECCAS). All of these, together with a large number of technical and specialized regional and subregional institutions to which reference
has already been made, were sponsored or inspired by the ECA. And, as envisaged in the FAL, in June 1991 at Abuja, Nigeria, the African Heads of State and
Government signed the treaty establishing the African Economic Community. (There are in addition a host of non-ECA-inspired groupings, notably
the Southern African Development Community [SADC].)

These persistent efforts of the ECA to foster regionalism and pan-Africanism
was given a new fillip after more than four decades when in July 2000 the Heads
of State and Government at the summit meeting of the Organization of African Unity/African Economic Community adopted the Constitutive Act of the
African Union,[44] a follow-up to the Sirte Declaration[45] of September 9, 1999.
This act establishing the African Union has since been ratified by more than
two-thirds of the potential membership. Its objectives include, inter alia:

- Achieving greater unity and solidarity between African countries and the
  people of Africa;
- Accelerating the political and socioeconomic integration of the continent;
- Promoting sustainable development at the economic, social, and cultural
  levels;
- Promoting cooperation in all fields of human activity to raise the living
  standards of African peoples;
- Coordinating and harmonizing the policies between the existing and future
  regional economic communities for the gradual attainment of the
  objectives of the African Union.

This is no doubt a decision of immense portent for Africa and the world.[46]

The Crisis of the 1980s: Africa's Lost Decade

The trend was clearly discernible in the data on the performance of Africa
during the first decade and a half of independence—Africa, more precisely
sub-Saharan Africa (SSA), was heading toward a socioeconomic cataclysm
early in the 1980s. Between 1971 and 1980, the average annual growth rate of
GDP was 2.4 percent while GDP per capita was falling by an annual 0.4 percent (table 5.4). Compared with the performance of other developing countries (excluding China), SSA had done very poorly. Its condition worsened in

the 1980s with GDP per capita falling by 2.6 percent a year while developing countries as a whole still managed to maintain a very modest increase of 0.1 percent. ECA's description of the 1980s as "Africa's lost decade" was therefore most apt.

True enough, the debt crisis and the great drought of 1983–1984 accelerated the decline, but all the signals during the waning years of the 1970s were ominous. The ECA agonized over a reappraisal of the economic situation and the search for a new economic model. While these could not reverse the downward trend easily, the hope was that it could be slowed down and subsequently reversed if a new development paradigm was vigorously pursued. But this did not happen.

Sub-Saharan Africa was virtually prostrate by the dawn of the 1980s. By the middle of the decade, African economic conditions had become quite desperate. The whole region was in economic regression. While its share of world population kept increasing, its shares of world GDP and world trade were falling. Thus, to all intents and purposes, SSA had become de facto de-linked from the rest of the world—accounting for only 1 percent of world output and trade. The African situation was, of course, seriously exacerbated by the long world depression of the 1980s, which followed the second oil shock of 1979.

The weak production base and the predominantly exchange-oriented, monocultural, and excessively open nature of Africa's economies makes them susceptible to the boom-and-bust cycle that is the plight of dependent primary producing economies. The "Dutch disease" is also a characteristic of these boom-and-bust cycles: It emerges whenever there is a sudden rise in the influx of foreign exchange arising from a sudden escalation of commodity prices, which in turn causes the real exchange rate to appreciate and consequently reduces the competitiveness of other exports. The Dutch disease also changes the relative profitability of traded goods (mostly agriculture) versus non-traded goods (mostly public services); the latter are encouraged at the expense of the former. This process naturally has adverse effects on the agricultural growth rate, which fell from 2.7 percent in the 1960s to only 1.4 percent in the 1980s. Not surprisingly, the continent's food self-sufficiency ratio fell from an annual average of 102 percent in 1967–1970 to 70 percent in the 1980s, thus necessitating both increased food import and food aid, given the rapid rise in population.

Africa's failure to escape from its inherited colonial economic structures meant that the foundations for the fundamental transformation of the productive structure were yet to be laid. In such circumstances, the economic crisis that engulfed the continent was inevitable. The great African drought of 1983 and 1984 drove home in a devastatingly tragic manner some of the consequences of inaction. By the middle of the decade, a consensus had been reached by African governments and the international community, particularly the Bretton Woods institutions and the donor community, that the structural transformation of the African economy must begin with food and agricultural development and the revitalization of the rural sector. This meant addressing Africa's excessive dependence on rainfed agricultural systems, its outmoded agricultural techniques, its inadequate application of science and technology, and its persistent land degradation and inefficient utilization of land. It also meant achieving significant improvements in the incentives given to farmers, particularly food-crop farmers, who are predominantly women. It meant putting in place efficient marketing and distribution systems and adequate institutional support. Finally, the neglect of women farmers, who are responsible for between 60 and 80 percent of food production and about 90 percent of food-processing activities, has to be rectified.

Unfortunately, this consensus was not followed by action—either by African governments or by the donors and the international community. Instead of implementing the structural transformation policies as envisaged in the Revised Framework, the Monrovia Strategy, the Lagos Plan of Action, and the Final Act of Lagos, structural adjustment programs (SAPs) were put in place with funding from the international community.

The conceptual problem that SAPs face in the context of Africa's monocultural economies is adjustment to what? From all the available evidence, the answer appears to be adjustment to a system that perpetuates the monocultural economic system, the narrow production base, and the persistence of excessive dependence on external aid, which renders these economies highly susceptible to external shocks, to cycles of boom and bust, and to the Dutch disease. In other words, SAPs take for granted, and indeed accept, the existing structure of the African economy and its production systems. SAPs ignore the vital need for fundamental change if SSA is to be rid of pervasive poverty and perpetual crises.

Diversification and structural transformation through a process of industrialization had failed to materialize. This was to have been the jewel in the economic crown. Although during the first two post-independence decades, industrial growth had averaged over 6 percent per annum—a rate much higher than that of the economy as a whole and those of all other sectors except mining—the sector consisted of a heterogeneous collection of industrial products, many of which are of marginal significance, particularly in terms of linkages—forward, backward, and lateral—to other sectors and are unlikely to be capable of launching a process of sustainable diversification and transformation. The high tariff wall around African industries and import-substitution policies which allowed a rise in the imports of raw materials and intermediate and capital goods resulted in the manufacturing sector becoming highly dependent on import. Transnational corporations and other foreign investors operating in Africa joined with their African partners to establish what is known as "last stage" factories, which are excessively dependent on imported inputs. Thus, the industrial-development process became a major consumer of scarce foreign exchange.

Industrialization in Africa was thus a disappointment in spite of its relatively high rates of growth during the first two decades after independence. With the onset of the crisis in 1980, industrial output fell, on average, by between 2 and 4 percent a year, the cumulative effect being tantamount to a process of deindustrialization. The direct involvement of governments in industrial investment exacerbated the situation; such investments are invariably wasted. Governments borrowed huge amounts abroad to finance white elephant projects; so instead of providing a dynamic thrust to the African economy, the industrial sector joined the growing list of crises afflicting the beleaguered continent.

Unlike agriculture and manufacturing, the mining industry has made considerable progress since independence. The spectacular increase in mining production began in the 1950s—the pre-independence decade—and from 1960 to 1975, these high growth rates were not only sustained but were substantially improved upon. It was during this period that a growing number of African countries, beginning with Algeria, Nigeria, Libya, and Gabon, entered the ranks of the world's major oil exporters. By 1975, Africa had increased its share of world output of crude petroleum from only 1 percent to 11 percent. Since then, other countries, notably Angola and Congo (Brazzaville), became oil-producing countries with crude petroleum, mining, and quarrying now constituting by far the largest sector of the economy, contributing between 30 and 50 percent of the GDP.

The cumulative effect of all these developments is that African governments have only succeeded in nibbling at the colonial economic inheritance, while the four millstones, "dispossession, colonization, dependence, and marginalization,"[47] have remained intact. In other words, SSA's past has continued to haunt its present and future. The oil-producing countries have come to realize that dependence on oil exports is no more than a substitution of one type of monoculture with another, apart from bringing other serious economic and social problems in its wake.

The debt overhang in the 1980s became Africa's Achilles' heel. The foundations of the debt crisis were laid in the 1970s by two major events: a) the first watershed in the history of the post–World War II international economic order occurred in 1971 when the United States unilaterally abrogated its obligations under the Bretton Woods system of fixed-exchange rates by de-linking the dollar from gold and introducing floating exchange rates with a consequent escalation in the rates of interest; and b) the oil-price increases in the autumn of 1973 enabled a few oil-producing nations (the OPEC countries in particular) to make vast profits (the so-called petrodollars) which were deposited in the banks of rich countries. This money was lent very liberally to the developing countries of Latin America, Asia, and Africa with little concern as to how it would be repaid. In the case of Africa, most of the loans came from the industrial countries, the international financial institutions (the World Bank and the IMF), and from the regional development bank (the ADB).

This wave of lending, reckless as it now appears in retrospect, no doubt saved the world economy from collapse in the 1970s. The slowing of economic growth during this period was accompanied by inflation, monetary instability, high interest rates, and growing unemployment. In the South, and particularly in Africa, there was also the collapse of the commodity markets. All of these factors compounded and aggravated the debt problem. Due to unfavorable developments in its terms of trade, SSA has been losing every year since 1980 (which was a relatively good year for commodity prices) an amount equivalent to an annual unconditional grant of US$13 billion (in 1980 prices). Compared with the conditions prevailing in 1980, the total loss between 1980 and 1992 amounted to some US$170 billion. Had Africa's export prices kept pace with the rise in its import prices during the period, the region could have paid for all its import from export earnings and its debt would have been 45 percent lower. Thus, the collapse of commodity prices, the sharp increases in interest rates—most debts had been contracted at variable rates and in the 1970s real interest rates were seductively low—and the constant fall in the exchange rate of the U.S. dollar all undermined the debt-servicing capacity of the sub-Saharan African countries.

Over the years, the multilateral debt burden, both in terms of stock and debt-servicing obligation, has grown faster than total debt. Whereas in 1980 multilateral debt was only 8.9 percent of the total, by 1994 its share had increased to 24 percent. The share of multilateral debt servicing has also increased correspondingly. It is now generally accepted that multilateral debt servicing constitutes a significant obstacle to development in the world's poorest countries, absorbing, according to Oxfam, two out of every three dollars disbursed from IDA returns to the World Bank in the form of debt repayments.[48]

The third factor that made the 1980s a lost decade for Africa is the widespread violence and pervasive lack of democracy. In the course of the past four decades, virtually every African country has been engulfed in one political crisis or another, usually involving violence.

Grave as the economic crisis has been, it is but the consequence of an equally grave political crisis which has engulfed SSA since independence. During the past four decades, SSA has acquired the reputation of a violent continent, of a continent at war with itself. In the 1980s and early 1990s the imperial notion of Africa as the Dark Continent returned with a vengeance.

In less than four decades there have been more than eighty violent changes of government. In the 1980s and 1990s these became a regular occurrence in thirty of the forty-eight SSA countries. Nigeria is at the top of the league table with six violent changes of government, followed by Sudan, Uganda, Ghana, Burundi, and Benin, each with five. Sierra Leone, Chad, and Burkina Faso have each had four such eruptions, while Ethiopia, Congo, Comoros, and Central Africa have had three each. But these do not provide the full picture of the scope and pervasiveness of violence, brutalization, and mass killings in the bloody struggles to obtain or retain power.[49]

In Liberia, a civil war raged for a decade and a half in the struggle for power. The power struggle between the FLNA and UNITA in Angola began in 1975, and, in spite of several attempts by the international community, remained unresolved until 2001 when UNITA leader Jonas Savimbi lost his life in the battlefield.

The Democratic Republic of the Congo (formerly Zaire) is currently engaged in yet another civil war barely two years after the bloody one that overthrew the Mobutu regime in 1996. The war in Sudan has lasted more than three decades and it is still raging. Currently some twenty SSA countries are wracked by armed conflict or civil strife, while another ten face severe political crises. In addition to civil wars, some countries are at each other's throats (Ethiopia and Eritrea). Others are helping to quash rebellion in their neighbors' territories (Senegal in Guinea Bissau, South Africa in Lesotho), and many of the states bordering or close to the Democratic Republic of the Congo have been drawn into the fighting there. Intervention, which is prohibited by the OAU Charter, has become commonplace. At the dawn of the new millennium, Africa has become increasingly devoured by warfare; almost two-thirds of SSA countries are embattled and paralyzed.

The Battle for the African Mind: The Second Round

Thus, SSA has been crippled by drought, conflict, external shocks, and debt, and of these, the most debilitating are external debt and the commodity crisis. The inability of many countries to service their debt turned debt rescheduling into a matter of survival; without it there would be default with serious political and economic consequences for the international economy. To be eligible for debt rescheduling and additional credits, the club of creditor nations—the Paris Club—has always insisted that the debtor nations must have in place an SAP with the Bretton Woods institutions. Despite the deficiencies of these programs, African countries, one after another, had to accept this condition, which gave the Bretton Woods institutions unprecedented power over their economic fortunes. "African governments now have virtually no sources for significant increases in foreign exchange other than international financial institutions," writes Carol Lancaster. The Bretton Woods institutions not only conditioned their lending on policy reforms but also influenced African officials through seminars and policy dialogues, and "where necessary and possible, international financial institution officials have circumvented official channels of communication (e.g., ministers of finance) and taken their views or recommendations directly to heads of state."[50]

In all, some thirty-five countries south of the Sahara had adopted IMF- and World Bank–supported stabilization and SAPs by 1988. By the end of the decade, the overall judgment was that the SAPs had failed woefully, even in terms of their own specific targets. In its relentless justification of the programs as the solution to Africa's economic crisis, the World Bank made one evaluation after another, but the general conclusion was that SAPs had not succeeded in easing the African crisis and laying the foundations for sustainable development. In a report in 1988,[51] the World Bank admitted that countries implementing SAPs had experienced:

- A decrease in rates of GDP growth from 2.7 percent to 1.8 percent;
- A decrease in investment/GDP ratios from 20.6 percent to 17.1 percent;
- An increase in budget deficits from 6.5 percent to 7.5 percent of GDP;
- An increase in the debt-service/export-earning ratio from 17.5 percent to 23.4 percent;
- A slight improvement in the current-account deficit/GDP ratio from 9.4 percent to 6.5 percent.

Yet in another World Bank Report,[52] prepared jointly with the United Nations Development Programme (UNDP) and published early in 1989, the assessment was reversed to such an extent that it provoked a sharp reaction from the ECA in particular and the international community in general. The reaction to this World Bank/UNDP publication was so sharp that the African ministers for economic planning and development asked the ECA to prepare a paper which "should be widely disseminated so as to put the record straight. The paper should highlight the technical and statistical variances contained in the World Bank/UNDP report, for an objective evaluation of the economic situation on the continent." The ministers were deeply concerned that "in many respects the World Bank/UNDP report is at variance with the mid-term review of the implementation of the United Nations Programme of Action for African Economic Recovery and Development (UNPAAERD) conducted by the forty-third session of the General Assembly of the United Nations and with the reality of the African economic situation."[53]

Among the points made in the ECA's subsequent report[54] the following are worth recalling. It was noted that:

> The World Bank's main hypothesis was that the growth rate of the 1970s (which had averaged about 5 percent per annum) was an aberration, while the decline of the 1980s (when per capita incomes were falling) constituted a return to normal. Secondly, World Bank had also argued that to obtain a more accurate picture of sub-Sahara Africa's economic situation, the relatively more important countries, especially the oil-exporters, should be excluded from the analysis. This was consistent with Chester A. Crocker's assertion that the Western perspective of Africa does not include the possibility of rapid economic progress.
>
> The report also suffered from one-dimensionality and selectivity in the compilation and presentation of data. It did not include a data set, a common practice in other publications, to show the numerical basis for its conclusions. Nor did it clearly define the criteria for classifying countries into those having strong, weak or no reform programs.
>
> The Bank gave the distinct but false impression that SAPs began to be implemented in Africa between 1985 and 1987. Yet many African countries had adopted them with the support of the Bretton Woods institutions since 1980. This is the case for 33 Sub-Sahara African countries.
>
> One assertion that has evoked a lot of concern is that which down-plays the chronic vulnerability of African economies, due to its dependence on commodity exports, rainfed agriculture and a lack of supporting infrastructure.
>
> Most serious of all is that in a matter of a few months, the World Bank had prepared three reports all relating to Africa's economic condition in the context of SAPs and yet reached very divergent conclusions which ranged from reporting them as success stories, as in the Report in question, to judging the results with much skepticism. The falsely optimistic conclusions were based on insufficient and faulty documentation. The most glaring example was the choice of 1970–73 as the base period to show that Africa's terms of trade were 15 percent higher in 1986–87. But this base period was marked by exceptionally low terms of trade, which obviously skewed the comparison. Had 1970 been taken as the base period, Africa's terms of trade in 1986 would have been about 14 percent lower, and if 1986 had been compared with 1980, the fall would have been more than 30 percent.

On the whole, neither the Africans nor other members of the international community were deceived by the manipulations in the World Bank/UNDP report. The warm reception that the ECA's *Statistics and Policies* received, particularly in the Western press, proved so embarrassing to the authorities of the World Bank that they launched their own counterattack, not publicly but by quietly approaching the media in Europe. After a visit by the World Bank's president, London's daily, *The Independent,* noted: "There is no doubt that these criticisms have greatly irritated Mr Conable, and they represent a challenge which the World Bank cannot afford to ignore. Half of the lending by its soft-loan arm, the International Development Association, goes to Africa. To suggest that structural adjustment in Africa is not working is to raise fundamental questions about the role of the World Bank."[55]

As predicted, the Bank's president convened a "peace" meeting in Washington, D.C., on May 10, 1989. Box 5.1 reproduces the full text of the joint statement issued by the UN and the World Bank at the end of that meeting.

On the basis of an exchange of views among senior officials, it was agreed that every effort must be made by all the organizations concerned to promote consensus-building on African development strategy and policy (box 5.1). It is significant that representatives from UN headquarters, particularly the Office of the Director-General and the Department of Economic and Social Affairs, were not invited to the parley. This no doubt is a reflection of their passive role throughout the entire debate.

When the ECA embarked on its search for an African alternative to SAPs, it constituted an international advisory board with a view toward reaching such a consensus—first, among African countries and second, between Africa and its bilateral and multilateral development partners. The Bretton Woods institutions, particularly the World Bank, served on this board. In the search for consensus, the findings and conclusions of the board were submitted to an international workshop of African and non-African economists held in Addis Ababa from January 3 to 5, 1989, from which a preliminary draft framework emerged.[56]

Globalizing Regional Problems, Perspectives, and Programs

Although the ECA has persisted in its search for a uniquely African development paradigm, it has never wavered in its conviction that international cooperation and support is a necessary condition for accelerating the process of socioeconomic transformation and development. As far back as 1977 it decided to bring its regional problems to the global level. As an organ of ECOSOC, and like the other regional commissions, it submits its annual reports to the

Box 5.1. A Joint UN/World Bank Statement on Africa's Long-Term Development

1. At the invitation of Mr. Barber B. Conable, President of the World Bank, the heads and senior officials of several major United Nations agencies committed to Africa's economic and social progress, as well as of the Organisation for African Unity and the African Development Bank, met to discuss issues related to the region's economic recovery and long-term development. The meeting was held at World Bank headquarters in Washington, D.C., on May 10, 1989.

2. Following upon recent reports by the World Bank/UNDP and the Economic Commission for Africa (ECA), participants exchanged views on the serious development challenges facing Africa, and particularly on the structural adjustment programmes currently being implemented by many African governments. While participants recognized that areas of disagreement remained, they emphasized their determination to work together and collaborate in the wide areas of consensus that exist. They agreed to strengthen mechanisms to achieve that result.

3. It was emphasized that policy reforms, whatever their form, must be relevant to specific country situations and must be designed, implemented and owned by the African countries themselves. It was further noted that the process of gaining public understanding and acceptance of the need for adjustment measures and economic transformation should be as broad-based as possible within the countries concerned.

4. Among the other major points of consensus agreed upon by the participants were the following:

   a) As the basic approach to adjustment issues has evolved, it has become clear that adjustment must be seen as part of a long-term development approach and that it must take full account of the human dimension. Stronger efforts are required to assure that this consensus is translated into action. The future challenge is to assist Africa to transform the condition of its economies still threatened with stagnation and decline to sustainable growth with equity.

   b) While sustainable economic growth is imperative, it is only the means to the overarching objective of improving human welfare—for example, reducing infant mortality, increasing educational opportunity, improving health and ensuring food security. Economic adjustment must lead to the long-term improvement in the quality of life of the African people. Particular attention should be given to protecting vulnerable groups during the adjustment process, including protection of core budget expenditures on social sector programmes. Special emphasis should be placed on employment opportunities.

   c) The shortage of technical skills and weak institutions are major impediments to Africa's growth and development. Priority should be given, therefore, to human resource development and national capacity building.

   d) The sustainable development and modernization of agriculture is central to Africa's future growth. New and appropriate agricultural technologies, and effective extension services, should be pursued.

e) Conserving Africa's natural resources base and protecting the environment are urgent priorities. No time should be lost in designing and implementing environmental action plans.

f) The process of increasing and improving regional economic cooperation and integration in Africa should be accelerated.

g) Promotion of the private sector is of vital importance.

5. Participants agreed that while Africa's major efforts to achieve economic growth and recovery should be recognized, the continent continues to be confronted by major problems, including weak commodity prices and terms of trade. The donor community has responded with substantial flows that are being monitored in the context of the UNPAAERD which was established following the 1986 special session of the U.N. General Assembly. Increased donor assistance is, however, required to support the efforts of the African governments to expand their reform programmes, and promote sustained economic growth. Substantial debt relief measures are needed, since the external debt burden remains a severe constraint on African development.

6. The distinctive and complementary roles of the various agencies working to support Africa's development were recognized. It was agreed that further steps should be taken to strengthen collaboration and the channels of communication among the Bretton Woods institutions, UN agencies and the African regional organizations. It was agreed that this process of consultation should be continued. Participants expressed appreciation to UNDP for its offer to host the next meeting. In addition, participants agreed that it would be useful to further explore issues of structural adjustment, based on studies and major reports prepared by various agencies represented at this meeting.

council, through which they are transmitted to the General Assembly. Traditionally, regional economic commissions had never engaged the General Assembly directly in their development problems.

The commission included transport development and industrialization in its first program of work and priorities for 1960–1961 because these two sectors were the most backward in the colonial economies inherited at independence.[57] Transport and communications systems in Africa have remained the least developed in the world because during the colonial era they were planned to facilitate the export of raw materials and agricultural products to the metropolitan countries, not to develop the domestic economies and promote intra-African trade.

The need to address these problems urgently was such that the first West African subregional conference on the transport sector in early 1961 decided inter alia that the ECA secretariat should "conduct a thorough study and as-

7. Mr. Barber B. Conable was commended by participants for his constructive initiative in convening the meeting. The exchange of views was welcomed and widely viewed as being beneficial to Africa's long-term development prospects.
8. Among those attending the meeting were Professor Adebayo Adedeji, Under-Secretary General and Executive Secretary of the Economic Commission for Africa; Dr. Bertram Collins, Coordinator of the Steering Committee on the UN Programme of Action for African Recovery and Development; Mr. William Draper III, Administrator, Mr. Arthur Brown, Associate Administrator, and Mr. Pierre-Claver Damiba, Assistant Administrator and Regional Bureau for Africa, UNDP; Mr. Richard Jolly, Deputy Director, UNICEF; Mr. Babacar N'Diaye, President, African Development Bank; Mr. Ide Oumarou, Secretary-General, Organisation of African Unity; Mr. G.E. Gondwe, Deputy Director, African Department, International Monetary Fund; and Mr. David Whaley, representing the Director General for Development and International Economic Cooperation. The World Bank was represented by Mr. Barber B. Conable, President; Mr. Moeen A. Quareshi, Senior Vice President, Operations; Mr. Edward V.K. Jaycox, Vice President, Africa Region; and Mr. Stanley Fischer, Vice President and Chief Economist. The African Executive Directors to the World Bank, Messrs. Benachenhou, Funna and Milongo, also attended.

Source: ECA and World Bank, "Joint Statement on Africa's Long-Term Development," meeting on Structural Adjustment in Sub-Saharan Africa, Washington, D.C., May 10, 1989.

sessment of the technical and economic problems and means of financing transport facilities across the Sahara."[58] The commission entered into an agreement with the International Telecommunication Unit (ITU) in 1964 to refurbish and expand the intra-African telecommunication network. This initiative subsequently evolved into the Pan-African Telecommunication Network Plan (PANAFTEL) in 1967, jointly sponsored by the ECA, the ITU, and the OAU.[59] Meanwhile the executive secretary was asked by the commission at its tenth session in February 1972 to enter into an agreement with the governments of Cameroon, Central African Republic, the Democratic Republic of the Congo, Kenya, Nigeria, and Uganda on the construction of the Lagos-Mombassa Trans-African Highway.[60]

In spite of all these initiatives, however, the development of the transport and communications sectors, both nationally and regionally, remained rather slow. Consequently, the commission decided at its thirteenth session, held in

February 1977, to call upon the General Assembly to proclaim a Transport and Communications Decade for Africa (UNTACDA) during 1978–1988 in order to:

- Mobilize active global support for the overall strategy for the development of transport and communications in Africa and for the application of that strategy for the purpose of solving the problems of the continent in this sector;
- Mobilize the technical and financial resources required to achieve the objectives of the Decade.[61]

The commission appealed to the international community for its full cooperation, and by Resolution 32/16061 of December 19, 1977, the General Assembly proclaimed the UNTACDA. The significance of this decision was twofold: first, for the first time ever, a regional problem had been fully recognized as deserving the attention and assistance of the entire international community; and, second, the recognition that Africa's transport and communications problems were to be viewed from an integrated regional perspective as opposed to the less effective modal approach.

Because of the general satisfaction with the accomplishments of the first decade, UNTACDA, an in-depth evaluation of which concluded that it "gave a major boost to the future development of transport and communications by equipping Africa with a strategy and policy as well as institutions and mechanisms" to implement the decade,[62] the General Assembly agreed to the ECA request that a second decade for transportation in Africa be declared from 1991 to 2000.[63]

Since 1977, the General Assembly has taken up other sectoral and macro-development problems of Africa. It declared a first (1981–1990) and then a second (1991–2000) Industrial Development Decade for Africa. At the height of the African economic crisis during the 1980s, an unprecedented Thirteenth Special Session of the General Assembly was held in May/June 1986. This special session was due to the initiative of the ECA and its secretariat, which did all the preparatory work, including basic documentation. Again, no support or substantive leadership came from the UN headquarters.

Through the ECA, Africa succeeded in making the international community in general and the UN General Assembly in particular aware that its development problems were grave and continued to deteriorate and that it was in the interest of the world to render all necessary assistance to arrest and reverse these problems. The fact that the international community accepted the need for a special session of the UN General Assembly devoted to the socioeconomic problems of Africa was in itself a measure of international solidarity. The output of the special session will remain one of the organization's seminal documents.[64]

The African Alternative Framework to Structural Adjustment Programmes for Socio-Economic Recovery and Transformation (AAF-SAP) was finally endorsed by the General Assembly in the autumn of 1989.[65] All members of the UN except the United States endorsed it. The document had earlier been approved and adopted by the ECA in April and by the OAU summit in July of the same year.

The Search for Consensus: The Third Round of the Battle for the African Mind

The impetus to search for an African alternative to SAPs came from the international community. During the debate on Africa's economic crisis during the Thirteenth Special Session of the General Assembly in 1986, the focus was on how to ensure that the recovery of the African economies was linked to long-term development and transformation on the basis of the Lagos Plan and not SAPs. Because many delegates, especially from Africa, complained bitterly about the negative effects of IBRD/IMF SAPs, the General Assembly, during its forty-third session in 1988, challenged African countries to "increase their efforts to the search for a viable conceptual and practical framework for economic structural adjustment programs in keeping with the long-term development objectives and strategies at the national, subregional and regional levels."[66]

In accepting this challenge, the ECA wanted to use it as an opportunity to build a consensus around an alternative paradigm that the Bretton Woods institutions would respect and accept. Consequently, the search by the ECA for an alternative was conceived as a process of extensive consultations both within and outside Africa. The ECA was anxious to have the bilateral and multilateral institutions sit side by side with African experts and policymakers in working out this alternative, so an international advisory board was set up to provide broad orientations for the study. Among the international institutions on this board were the World Bank and the IMF.

Economists throughout Africa, particularly in the adjusting countries, were recruited to undertake assessments of SAPs in their respective countries. This was followed by a conference of African and non-African economists in January 1989. At the intergovernmental level, a conference of senior government officials from ministries of planning and development and finance together with officials of Africa's central banks met in Blantyre in March 1989 to examine the proposals. Their recommendations were submitted to the twenty-fourth session of the ECA in April 1989. Thereafter, a joint session of the African ministers of development and planning and of finance took place on April 10 to adopt the AAF-SAP.[67] In the Addis Ababa joint statement by the ministers, they agreed that the AAF-SAP, because it was consistent with the Lagos Plan and the United Nations Programme of Action for African Economic Recovery and Development (UNPAAERD), should constitute the basis for constructive dialogue with Africa's development partners for designing country programs that would ensure self-sustained development and equity.

The AAF-SAP was the first alternative to the World Bank/IMF SAP. Until it came out in July 1989, there was no discourse about alternatives to the orthodoxy of the Bretton Woods institutions. A 1988 report by UNICEF protested against the falling standards of living among the poorest sections of the population due to such adjustment programs.[68] It argued against making the poor bear the brunt of the burden of adjustment and called for greater investment in social services and safety nets for the disadvantaged. Although accurate and compelling, the UNICEF critique went no farther than to suggest modifications of the orthodox adjustment programs. It did not offer an alternative holistic plan for development. As one eminent African economist remarked, calling for "adjustment with a human face" is like attempting to give a "monkey a human face"—the animal will still remain a monkey.[69]

The AAF-SAP was not merely an attempt at modification. Rather, it identified four major areas for policy action, namely:

- The strengthening and diversification of productive capacity;
- Improvements in the level of income and the pattern of its distribution;
- Radical change in the pattern of expenditure for the satisfaction of required needs;
- Establishment of an appropriate institutional framework in support of adjustment with transformation.

The AAF-SAP also abandoned the dichotomy between short-term crisis management through adjustment and long-term development objectives, and by so doing laid the foundation for Africa's socioeconomic transformation through radical changes and improvements in the structure of production and demand and of people's attitudes toward productive resources. The significance of the AAF-SAP and its path for adjustment is that it provides Africa with a coherent framework for a complete refocusing on domestic development and the mobilization and optimal utilization of indigenous factor inputs that will support the policy measures and priorities enunciated in the Lagos Plan and UNPAAERD. AAF-SAP was overwhelmingly endorsed by the General Assembly in the fall of 1989. The only negative vote was that of the United States.

Three months after the publication of the ECA's AAF-SAP, the World Bank came out with *Sub-Saharan Africa—From Crisis to Sustainable Growth: A Long-Term Perspective Study.*[70] Unlike the *Agenda for Action,* which was the antithesis of the Lagos Plan of Action, the long-term perspective study sought to achieve consistency with the AAF-SAP. This marked a significant change of position by the World Bank. Because of its broad convergence with African perceptions of Africa's problems, the Bank's report is a major contribution to the emergence of common ground in laying the basis for concerted action in forging a brighter future for Africa (box 5.2).

This does not mean that the World Bank agreed with the ECA on all issues. But at least, for the first time ever, it publicly acknowledged that it might not have all the answers to Africa's development problems and might not always have been asking the right questions. It is very significant that this long-term perspective study began by raising some searching questions, namely: Does Africa face special structural problems that have not been properly understood? Has the institutional dimension been neglected? Have the structural adjustment–related reform programs been too narrow or too shallow? Unfortunately, answers to these questions were not pursued to their logical conclusion. Perhaps they are easier to raise than to answer because thinking them through might lead the Bank to the conclusion that SAPs were merely a diversion with tragic human, social, and political consequences and should be abandoned. But like most big and powerful institutions, the

---

Box 5.2. Foreword to the World Bank Long-Term Perspective Study on *Sub-Saharan Africa: From Crisis to Sustainable Growth*

A central theme of this report is that although macroeconomic policies and an efficient infrastructure are essential to provide an *enabling environment* for the productive use of resources, they alone are not sufficient to transform the structure of African economies. At the same time, major efforts are needed to *build African capacities*—to produce a better-trained, more healthy population and to greatly strengthen the institutional framework within which development can take place. This is why the report strongly calls for a human-centered development strategy made by the ECA and UNICEF.

Source: Barber B. Conable, President of the World Bank, "Foreword," October 16, 1989, in World Bank, *Sub-Saharan Africa: From Crisis to Sustainable Growth* (Washington, D.C.: IBRD/World Bank, 1989), xii.

Bank is not prone to responding quickly to changed circumstances, particularly when such a change would prove politically embarrassing. In such circumstances, it took the easy course by remaining faithful to its past, to its record, and to its ideology.

Perhaps if the authors of the report had remembered the admonition of Professor Hayek that economists should be modest about their claims to have found solutions to complex human problems,[71] and if they are not to do more harm than good in their efforts to improve the social order, they will have to learn that in this, as in all other fields where essential complexity prevails, they can never acquire the full knowledge which would make mastery over events possible. Above all, they will have to acknowledge the cultural, social, and institutional differences that exist among societies if they are to do more good than harm. Unless development economists and other social scientists approach their discipline with humility and realism, they may turn out to be tyrants over their fellow human beings and the destroyers of civilizations which no single brain has designed.

The Bretton Woods institutions' operational and lending arms were apparently not impressed by the Bank's long-term perspective study, and consequently its message and promise diminished over time until it totally disappeared. SAPs still hold sway. This stubbornness no doubt forced James Wolfensohn, president of the Bank, to admonish his colleagues in a memorandum to the board, management, and staff dated January 21, 1999:

> We cannot adopt a system in which the macroeconomic and financial is considered apart from the structural, social and human aspects and vice versa. Integration of each of these subjects is imperative at the national level and among the global players. . . .
>
> The international financial architecture must reflect the interdependence of macroeconomic and financial, with structural and social and human concerns. . . .
>
> Unless we adopt this approach on a comprehensive, transparent and accountable basis, we will fail in the global challenge of equitable and sustainable development and poverty alleviation. We will fail to build a sustainable international architecture for the coming millennium.[72]

That Wolfensohn had to remind all concerned of these rather elementary points a decade after the joint UN/World Bank meeting and the publication of the ECA's AAF-SAP and of the Bank's own long-term perspective study illustrates the seriousness of the African situation because it looks as if, rhetoric apart, those operators in charge of Bank lending are determined to stick to SAPs in spite of their dire consequences for the people of Africa and their economies.

The ECA's Successful Attempt to Reach the Bretton Woods Institutions'
Main Constituencies through the Media

Because the World Bank is accountable to its owners, principally the donor community, it was essential that these countries, particularly their civil
societies, be convinced about the credibility of the African alternative. It was
therefore decided to launch the AAF-SAP not in Addis Ababa or elsewhere in
Africa but in the heart of Europe, London, on July 7, 1989, and to have it
published simultaneously in New York and Washington, D.C. As a result, the
AAF-SAP received substantial media attention in Europe and in the rest of
the world.[73] Virtually all the most influential newspapers and magazines in
the donor countries, Asia, Latin America, the Middle East, China, and Eastern
Europe welcomed the AAF-SAP, even though some of them picked specific
issues for criticism.

The coverage was on the whole very positive. Even a conservative newspa-
per such as the *London Daily Telegraph,* in an editorial of July 10, 1989, advocated careful study of the AAF-SAP on the grounds, inter alia, that while SAPs
might have brought about better balance-of-payments figures, they had failed
to achieve progress toward more fundamental goals such as self-sufficiency in
food and higher levels of education and health. In an editorial comment, the
Daily Telegraph remarked: "As a think tank, the commission lacks the resources
of the IMF and the World Bank to implement its alternative approach. But its
document is a valuable contribution, from Africa itself, to the aid debate. It is
encouraging that the Bank is showing signs of flexibility over lending policies. Certainly, the record of the 1980s gives no ground for complacency."[74]

When the prestigious *Financial Times* of London published an editorial
under the title "Flawed Plan for Africa" in which the ECA was criticized for
"yearning for statism" and failing "to set out convincing alternatives to the
main principles underlying the World Bank-led Africa recovery programme,"
it was severely criticized by Stanley Please, a former vice president of the World
Bank: "What is now required is to get the toughness of the ECA on the important policy issues which are impeding development in Africa, allied to the
toughness on year-to-year financial and economic programme formulation
and implementation. Your editorial simply aggravates the attempt to achieve
consensus among the regional and international institutions involved in Africa; a consensus which has been called for by both the head of ECA and of
the World Bank."[75] Sir Douglas Wass, former permanent under-secretary to
the treasury during Margaret Thatcher's premiership in Britain, wrote: "What
the ECA is concerned about—as anyone who studied the current state of Sub-
Saharan Africa must be—is the need progressively to transform the potential

of the continent to be self-reliant, and to offer its people some prospect of rising living standards."[76]

The Last Decade of the Twentieth Century and the Beginning of the New Millennium

At the end of its Thirteenth Special Session on June 1, 1986, the General Assembly adopted the United Nations Programme of Action for African Economic Recovery and Development 1986–1990 (UNPAAERD).[77] The pervasiveness and intensity of the development crisis had led to the adoption by the African heads of state and governments of the ECA's African Priority Programme for Economic Recovery (APPER) at the July 1985 OAU summit.[78] This was essentially a five-year program to deal with the crisis situation and lay the basis for an accelerated implementation of the Lagos Plan of Action. There is little doubt that the focus on SAPs had held back the long-term transformation process of the African economies. Instead of vigorously pursuing policies to diversify the economies and increase their capacities, attention was diverted to increasing commodity exports and reducing domestic demand (by closing down educational and health services) in order to generate surpluses to service the external debt. APPER was an attempt to return Africa to the fundamentals of development. Both the Abuja Statement (June 1987)[79] and the Khartoum Declaration (March 1988)[80] pointed clearly to the long-term perils of persisting with SAPs. Indeed, the Khartoum Declaration, which came out of the ECA's International Conference on the Human Dimension of Africa's Economic Recovery and Development, puts it plainly:

> This Declaration affirms that the human dimension is the sine qua non of economic recovery. We, the delegates here assembled, will not abide economic rationales, will not tolerate economic formulas, will not apply economic indices, will not legitimize economic policies which fail to assert the primacy of the human condition. That means, quite simply, that no structural adjustment programme or economic recovery programme should be formulated or can be implemented without having, at its heart, detailed social and human priorities. There can be no real structural adjustment or economic recovery in the absence of the human imperative . . . (which is) that the vulnerable and the impoverished, the uprooted and the ravaged, women, children, youth, disabled, aged, the rural poor and the urban poor, every group and individual in society who is in some way disadvantaged, must be given paramount consideration in the socioeconomic development process. This is a sacrosanct principle. And in the service of that principle health, education, welfare and all related social sectors become indispensable components of every national policy . . . every regional or sub-regional collaboration.[81]

Reginald Green, who was one of the ECA resource persons at the Khartoum conference, expressed his own ideas about the macroeconomic context that is the overriding concern of SAPs—export earnings, reduction of import bills, government revenues, inflation, and devaluation:

> The crisis of falling export earnings and import capacity, of eroding government revenues and inflationary deficits, of inefficient policies and under-utilized capacity are very real. But they are not more real nor more important than the crisis of rising numbers living in absolute poverty, rising infant mortality, the re-emergence of killer diseases like yaws and yellow fever, virtually eliminated by the end of the 1950s, school systems near collapse and peasants without tools or seeds. . . . Therefore, one basic test of all stabilization and structural adjustment programmes is whether they will improve the human condition. . . . If a programme cannot pass that test in prospect or in operation, it is fatally flawed and itself in need of structural adjustment or total design.[82]

As part of the attempt to mobilize the international community behind APPER, the ECA submitted the document to the Thirteenth Special Session of the General Assembly, which then unanimously adopted the UNPAAERD.[83] This program—the first ever adopted by the UN on any region—represented a unique agreement between African states and the international community, with both sides committing themselves to specific and far-reaching efforts to accelerate Africa's development.

The UNPAAERD consists of two central elements. First, the determination and commitment of African countries a) to launch both national and regional programs of economic development as reflected in APPER; b) to continue to vigorously pursue appropriate policy reforms; and c) to mobilize domestic resources for the successful implementation of the UNPAAERD. The five priority areas were development of the agricultural sector, development of sectors that support agriculture, anti-drought and anti-desertification programs, human development (particularly education and public health), and socioeconomic policy reforms. The second central element in the compact is the international community's commitment to support and complement Africa's development effort, provide financial and technical support, grant debt relief and debt forgiveness, and create an enabling environment for Africa's recovery and development.

New Challenges and Initiatives

Every year after the adoption of the UNPAAERD, progress reports on its implementation were submitted by the Secretary-General to the General Assembly. Unfortunately, by the end of 1990 it was evident that more vigorous efforts on the part of the international community were needed, even though African countries had put in place fundamental political and economic reforms between 1986 and 1990. Hence, at the final review and appraisal of the implementation of the UNPAAERD in 1991, the General Assembly, realizing that Africa's socioeconomic conditions had actually worsened between 1986 and 1990, decided to renew the commitment of the international community to support Africa's effort to achieve self-sustaining growth and development by refocusing world attention on the socioeconomic difficulties which continued to face Africa. The result was a commitment to an agenda of cooperation for sustainable social and economic development of Africa in the 1990s—the United Nations New Agenda for the Development of Africa in the 1990s (UN-NADAF).[84]

Like the UNPAAERD, UN-NADAF has two parts: Africa's responsibility and commitment and the responsibility and commitment of the international community. The structural transformation of the economies to achieve growth and development on a sustained and sustainable basis (AAF-SAP); the promotion of regional and subregional economic cooperation and integration (FAL); the intensification of the democratization process (The African Charter for Popular Participation); human development; investment promotion; combating desertification (the Bamako Convention); the systemic integration of population factors into the development process (the Kilimanjaro Programme of Action for African Population and Self-Reliant Development [1984]); and agriculture, rural development, and food security constitute the main components of Africa's responsibility and commitment.

The responsibility and commitment of the international community has seven components:

- The solution of Africa's external debt problem through cancellation or reduction of official development assistance (ODA) debt and debt service and the encouragement of the write-off of private commercial debt.
- Increased resource flows to achieve an average annual growth rate of 6 percent of real GNP in the course of the 1990s. The UN Secretary-General estimated that a minimum of US$30 billion in net development assistance would be required in 1992, increasing thereafter at an average growth rate of 4 percent per annum.
- Diversification of commodity exports and a substantial reduction in or removal of trade barriers to boost earnings.
- Support for the diversification of African economies. To this end, it was agreed that subject to a feasibility study, a proposal for the

establishment of a diversification fund for Africa's commodities
should be submitted by the Secretary-General to the General
Assembly in 1993.
- Support for regional economic integration, particularly in the fields of
environment, science, and technology.
- Non-African NGOs should assist in the formulation and
implementation of development assistance projects and in promoting
African NGOs at national, subregional, and regional levels.
- The expansion and intensification of the role of the UN system in the
implementation of the New Agenda and in particular the Second
United Nations Industrial Development Decade for Africa and the
Second United Nations Transport and Communications Decade for
Africa—both of which were initiated by the ECA in the late 1970s and
the 1980s.

The final evaluation of the UN-NADAF by the General Assembly is scheduled for the end of 2002. It will provide an opportunity for a comprehensive
intergovernmental review of development in Africa during the 1990s. But judging from the report of the panel on independent evaluation of the UN-NADAF,
it would appear that it has suffered the same fate as the UNPAAERD due to
the failure of the international community to fulfill their obligations, the pursuit of inappropriate reform measures, and the lack of any breakthrough in
debt-service relief and debt cancellation.[85]

On March 15, 1996, Secretary-General Boutros Boutros-Ghali launched the
United Nations System-wide Special Initiative on Africa (UNSIA).[86] This was
conceived as a global effort to mobilize support for African development and to
strengthen UN coordination and rationalization of that support. Because the
Secretary-General had described the initiative as reflecting "his personal determination, and that of the Heads of all United Nations agencies, to work collectively for the enhancement of African development,"[87] there was some suspicion
that it was related to the question of his reelection as Secretary-General. Hence,
widespread skepticism surrounded the initiative. Yet the UNSIA could trace its
origin to the UN-NADAF, which was based on shared responsibility and full
partnership with Africa, with the UN system expected to play a major role in its
implementation. Accordingly, organizing the system to discharge this responsibility seemed logical. It was therefore unfortunate that the Secretary-General
personalized the initiative. Inevitably, the donor community was not enthusiastic. They questioned the value of the initiative at a time of shrinking aid resources and were generally reluctant to accept the premise that they needed to
redirect their programs in order to meet African priorities as identified by the

UNSIA. Even within the UN system itself, there was abundant evidence that the initiative had not been internalized in any meaningful way.

The introduction of the United Nations Development Assistance Framework (UNDAF)[88] by Kofi Annan, Boutros-Ghali's successor, provided an alternative mechanism for improving coherence and coordination of UN programs at the country level. However, the General Assembly, on the recommendation of the Committee for Programme and Coordination (CPC), decided that the UNSIA should be regarded as the operational arm of the UN-NADAF.[89] Henceforth, the UNSIA was referred to as the United Nations System-wide Special Initiative for the Implementation of the United Nations New Agenda for the Development of Africa in the 1990s.

Serious tension persisted between the UN-NADAF and UNSIA because of widespread doubts and skepticism regarding the UNSIA. The latter's credibility was not improved after the CPC declared that it was an instrument for the implementation of the UN-NADAF. In any case, the different origins of the two initiatives had a negative impact on the UNSIA, which was a product of UN agencies, while UN-NADAF was intergovernmental in character. The failure to mobilize additional resources and the absence of effective links with UN field offices and country programs reduced the UNSIA to a modest regional coordination mechanism. An independent evaluation of the UNSIA recently asked whether it was proper to designate this modest mechanism as a "special initiative" of the UN.[90] Concerned by the burden the proliferation of initiatives intended to foster development in Africa placed on its countries, and their external partners, the independent evaluators concluded that the elimination of one of them might be a salutary step toward a genuine partnership in support of African-owned development.[91]

This was the same conclusion reached by the UN Joint Inspection Unit (JIU) about UN-NADAF itself as far back as 1995. The JIU found that UN-NADAF "had no impact on the ground four years after it was launched" and that "there was still general lack of awareness of the existence of the Agenda among United Nations system field personnel in Africa, who ought to be on the sharp edge of its implementation."[92]

However, the CPC at its mid-June 2001 meeting decided to disregard the conclusions and recommendations of the UNSIA independent evaluation and to have the UNSIA and all other similar initiatives on Africa reviewed at the time of the UN-NADAF evaluation in mid-2002. The JIU in its report of 1995 went beyond UN-NADAF in its concern that there were far too many UN initiatives for Africa. An ECA website identifies thirty current initiatives! Little wonder that the JIU stated that "because the existence of so many overlapping programming frameworks inevitably creates confusion, complicates development coordination at country level, and strains the absorptive capacities of host governments, the Inspectors recommend that consideration be given to establishing a moratorium on the adoption of new regional programs, and that efforts be concentrated instead on strengthening the central and sectoral capacities of African Governments to integrate and manage existing programmes."[93]

Indeed, this was exactly the view held by the ECA Conference of Ministers in May 1991 in a memorandum in which they argued that "given the global political and economic climate, it cannot be expected that a repetition of UN-PAAERD, no matter how modified, would yield results different from those of the previous programs. If anything, it might exacerbate the marginalization of Africa by removing its main concerns from current global concerns and treating them as special problems. It will thus be a political mistake to relegate Africa to a 'back burner' position by invoking yet another program with an appellatory character which, as everybody knows, would lead to nothing."[94]

This was the collective wisdom of African governments in May 1991. If they had been listened to, the 1990s would have been more profitably utilized in establishing and strengthening national, subregional, and regional capacities to successfully manage existing programs. Africa and the international community would have been saved from the UN-NADAF, the UNSIA, and all the other UN initiatives on Africa.

Although the ECA was inevitably involved in the articulation of the various initiatives, in the 1990s it ceased to be on the front line when the leadership role passed to the headquarters of the UN in New York, where two small African economic secretariats had been set up—the Office of the Special Coordinator for Africa and the Least Developed Countries (OSCAL) and the Office of the Coordinator of the UNSIA. The combined effect was to put UN headquarters in the place of the ECA on regional African matters. In the meantime, the ECA changed its focus to establishing mechanisms for dialogue and consultation on selected development and public-policy issues whose overarching objective is to mobilize all stakeholders in the African development process. Three such forums were established during the second half of the 1990s. They are the African Development Forum (ADF), the "Big Table" of OECD-African countries' consultation on the ECA's partnership program, and post-conflict reconstruction and development.

The ADF has been described as the flagship of the ECA. So far, three forums have been held—ADF I, whose theme was "The Challenge to Africa of Globalization and the Information Age," took place in October 1999,[95] while ADF II, which focused on "AIDS: The Greatest Leadership Challenge," took place in December 2000.[96] ADF III (March 2002) focused on regional integration.[97] These are important themes for Africa and its future development.

Among the forces that have launched the process of globalization, accelerated it, and turned it into an unstoppable phenomenon is the revolution in
information and telecommunications technologies (ICTs). The combination
of old and new ICTs has created an interactive information society everywhere except in sub-Saharan Africa, which has:

- The lowest teledensity in the world (1.89 percent) with only 2.0 percent
  of total telephone lines in the world; 1.2 percent of total world
  Internet users; and virtually 0 percent of global ICT production.
- Low computer penetration.
- Low Internet connectivity. There are three key indicators of Internet
  development: the number of host sites, the number of users, and the
  number of Internet service providers (ISPs). It must be emphasized
  that low computer penetration and low Internet connectivity
  account for the low diffusion of recent technological innovations in
  Africa.
- A technological and digital divide between the urban and rural areas
  and population, between the high-income elite and the rest of the
  population, and between males and females. All these factors continue
  to exacerbate internal marginalization.
- Inadequate provision of electricity—less than 40 percent of SSA's
  population have access to electricity, the overwhelming majority of
  which live in urban areas.
- A high percentage of illiterate population—more than 40 percent of the
  population of SSA is illiterate. Even among young people, one in four
  is illiterate.

Little wonder that the technology achievement index (TAI) of Africa—
that is, the composite index of technology creation, diffusion of recent innovations, diffusion of old innovations, and human skills—is very low. The
capacity to participate effectively in the technology age depends on the level
of the TAI. No society or country can leapfrog into the globalization highway
unless and until it is able to successfully address the many hindrances standing in the way. The information revolution is often said to be Africa's last
"chance to catch up." If this is to materialize, it is imperative that all corrective
measures are initiated to launch the catching-up process.

Consequently, the focus of ADF I on globalization and the information
age was a step in the right direction for these meetings. But to have an impact,
there must be perseverant follow-up. Nine hundred and fifty participants
exchanging views in five working days was a good start, but the challenge

requires a much longer investment in terms of time, skills and knowledge, and social and private investment. ADF I was intended to be the foundation of a structure for dialogue among the various stakeholders. But as the Independent Evaluation of the United Nations System-wide Special Initiative on Africa has proposed, if the ADF is to become the foundation of a structure for dialogue with African countries to ascertain and refine African development priorities as identified by Africans as well as address collaborative relationships between Africa and the donor community, it will need to be streamlined; "enriched and expanded by policy dialogues at the sub-regional level which will in turn be informed by inputs from the country level. The sub-regional and country-level focus would facilitate the dissemination of successful approaches and good practices and, if desired, monitoring through mechanisms such as peer review of performance in addressing common problems."[98]

ADF II focused on "AIDS: The Greatest Leadership Challenge." It took place in December 2000 and was co-sponsored by UNAIDS, the International Labor Organization, and the OAU; the ECA was the convener. Its primary purpose was to "serve as a major launching pad for a renewed commitment to more concerted action against HIV/AIDS in Africa by highlighting positive local, national and regional experiences and by generating the highest level of scientific, technological, traditional and intellectual leadership possible, at all levels of society and the development community towards addressing and mitigating the impact of the pandemic in Africa."[99]

Fifteen hundred participants from Africa and elsewhere took part. The lack of political will and leadership to make HIV/AIDS a top priority on the development agenda and to invest the necessary resources to fight the disease was the major concern of the Africa Consensus and Plan of Action which emerged from the forum. This calls on leadership at all levels—family, community, workplace, schools, civil society, government, and international—to overcome the threat of HIV/AIDS across the continent.

The theme of ADF III (March 2002) was "Defining Priorities for Regional Integration." In view of the commitment of the African heads of state to the establishment of the African Union,[100] ADF III provided the opportunity for a large-scale public discussion of how to implement this commitment in such a way as to build on the progress made so far and to accelerate the process of regional economic integration. The African Union having been led so far by governments, ADF III provided a well-timed opportunity for emergent development partnership initiatives. This is a most appropriate role for the ECA to play, as it has been in the forefront of promoting economic cooperation and integration since 1958 and has been advocating a new regional economic order for Africa since 1975.

In November 2000, the ECA hosted an African-OECD ministerial consultation which has been tagged by the secretariat the "Big Table." Eleven African ministers and ten bilateral donors from OECD countries, joined by five high-level representatives from international organizations, were involved. This process must be linked with the ADF. Its agenda should derive from African priorities, which emerge from the ADF and other types of dialogue. It would be more effective if it is institutionalized along thematic and/or sub-regional lines with specific "Big Tables" dealing with particular issues not merely with words but also by action, commitment, review, and evaluation.

What is emerging from the various dialogues is the reaffirmation of the earnest desire of African states to consult and seek advice on their development priorities. Indeed, they have never shown any reluctance to admit their faults and adjust their priorities in the light of such consultations. Unfortunately, concrete actions to translate these into commitments have been lacking or at best have come too little too late. In spite of the HIPC (Heavily Indebted Poor Countries) Initiative, Africa's debt burden is still unbearable, and poverty, instead of falling, is rising rapidly. SSA joins South Asia as two regions in the world where the incidence and depth of poverty have been escalating. It is, therefore, imperative in the review of the UN-NADAF that all the different consultative initiatives should be pulled together and focused on promoting and monitoring the implementation of any successor arrangement.

The Neglected Political and Social Dimension

In the battle to forge a future for Africa, the ECA has taken the lead in promoting a holistic development paradigm and steering away from the narrow focus on economic growth. Of course, it is realized and stated repeatedly that the pervasive lack of democracy in Africa creates a basic conflict between state power and people's power and that Africa's socioeconomic decline in the 1980s was due largely to political failures associated with the lack of popular participation. This was the reason for the ECA's international conference on popular participation in 1990 and the Charter on Popular Participation for Development, which emerged from it. But this was a charter that was adopted by governments from one-party states and by countries governed by military juntas. In other words, the effort fell short of dealing with the form and kind of government which is conducive to popular participation; good governance; pluralistic political party systems; free and fair elections; freedom of association, including complete freedom to form political parties; and the supremacy of the rule of law.

Nor have the various discourses on forging a credible, dynamic, and stable future for Africa done anything to reduce the many conflicts, civil strife, and wars in the various countries of the continent. The ECA was not involved in the prevention of civil wars or in post-conflict reconstruction and development. Although it was involved in the Congo conflict from 1960 to 1963, it has not been allowed to play any role in conflict resolution since then because the UN established a separate department in New York to look after conflicts throughout the world.

However, in July 1999, the UN Secretary-General asked the executive secretary of the ECA to lead the efforts of the UN system and other partners to develop a subregional program of post-conflict reconstruction and development for the Mano River Basin countries of Guinea, Liberia, and Sierra Leone. Accordingly, the ECA launched the Mano River Basin Initiative, whose aims include the revitalization of the Mano River Union; capacity-building for economic policy and management; and the reestablishment of a framework for good governance in the three countries.

More than ever before, there is a widespread recognition within Africa and the international community that peace and development are fundamentally intertwined and that good governance is imperative for both. Accordingly, and under the auspices of the United Nations System-wide Special Initiative on Africa, the UNDP and the ECA launched the Africa Governance Forum (AGF) in 1997 with the following four major objectives:

- Provide a platform for African governments, civil-society organizations, and the continent's external partners to sustain a dialogue on the state of governance in Africa;
- Promote partnership among participants and encourage the exchange of information, experience, and good governance practice;
- Assist African governments to develop nationally defined governance programs and strengthen coordination mechanisms to permit long-term resource mobilization in support of these programs;
- Discuss best practices in various areas of good governance through consultations among African governments, international partners, and civil-society organizations.

AGF sessions have been held annually since 1998. The first was in Addis Ababa, at which fourteen African countries were invited to present papers on their governance programs. AGF II (June 1998) focused on the issues of accountability and transparency, while AGF III (November 1999) dealt with post-conflict governance challenges, peace-building, and development. The basic document used at this 1999 AGF was a book by the African Center for Development and Strategic Studies,[101] based on a study funded by the UNDP.

The ECA is currently working on a project on "Setting Goals and Monitoring Progress towards Good Governance," which will develop indicators for monitoring good governance in the administrative, political, and economic management fields; promote the adoption by countries of good governance targets; and monitor the status of implementation once every two years. Based on this, the ECA will publish a report on "The State of Governance in Africa," which will synthesize and disseminate "best practices" in selected aspects of governance.[102]

As already pointed out, ADF II was focused on HIV/AIDS, which together with tuberculosis has become Africa's greatest killer disease and the most serious drain on human capital. As is argued by the UNDP in the *Human Development Report 1996,* governments that do not take the AIDS threat seriously now or shy away from action will pay the price later. The ADF II initiative came at a critical juncture in the development of the disease in Africa. At the end of 1999, 33.6 million men, women, and children worldwide were living with HIV/AIDS, 95 percent of them in developing countries. It is estimated that about 25 million of these are in Africa. Without effective national programs and massive international support, the pandemic will continue to spread in Africa, thus accentuating the poverty of its people. The response to the ECA and other UN initiatives throughout Africa has been tremendous. In April 2001, a summit meeting of African heads of state on HIV/AIDS, tuberculosis, and other related infectious diseases was held in Abuja, Nigeria— just before the Special Session of the UN General Assembly on HIV/AIDS in June 2001. Also before the special session, the wives of African heads of state organized a similar conference in Yaounde in January 2001 alongside the France/Africa summit. There can now be no doubt about the general awareness of the HIV/AIDS menace—the ECA's ADF II has had a salutary multiplier effect.

Global Dreams and Regional Visions: The Interactive Impact of UN Global Conferences

Since its establishment more than fifty years ago, the UN at the initiative of the General Assembly has convened a number of global conferences on political, economic and social, and cultural issues that require some clarity of ideas and ideology in terms of conceptualization to explore all the possibilities of maximally exploiting the way and manner in which the outcome of such conferences can contribute toward shaping the future of the world.

Global conferences on the environment, sustainable human development, education, water, population, women in development, and social development have turned out to be landmarks in the evolution of ideas, strategies, policies, and programs. In fact some of these issues have been more than one-shot affairs. An evolutionary process has thus been embarked upon to the benefit of the international community. For example, at least three UN global conferences have been held on each of these issues—population, women and the environment, and sustainable development—during the past three decades. Although policymakers and multilateral diplomats and technocrats talk about "global conferences fatigue," they are nevertheless still taking place even though it is becoming increasingly difficult to reach consensus on some of the most strategic and crucial issues, particularly those of direct interest to the less developed countries of the South. What is even more significant is that they are increasingly held at the summit level of heads of state and government. The 2002 Johannesburg Conference on Sustainable Development is reported to have attracted as many as 100 heads of government.

No doubt some of these UN global conferences have become repetitive both in their coverage and scope and in their agreements or the lack thereof. Often one finds, particularly with regard to some of the latter-day global conferences, that almost everything on the menu of one conference has been served up before at another conference. Development targets are often rehashed from one conference to another, and new aid packages from rich countries invariably turn out to be anything but new. They are usually warmed-up pledges that were first made several years before.

With such high propensity to not achieve global consensus on the issues that matter most and with such a persistent failure to honor pledges, implement decisions, and ratify protocols, one wonders why these conferences continue to be held. One can only hazard the guess that in continuing to make the decisions to organize these conferences, the General Assembly believes that dreams are perhaps the only reality while the member states are convinced that one of the principal ways that their visions can become actualized is never to give up making the attempts, on the ground that no problem is solved until it is solved aright.

But one indisputable fact about these global conferences is that they mobilize the entire UN system during their preparatory process. Invariably, regional preparations involving both experts and (nowadays) representatives of civil society and governments are held to determine respective regional positions before the global perspective is unleashed through a global preparatory mechanism put in place by the General Assembly. In this process, regional commissions, as the regional arms of the UN, play a particularly crucial role and carry a great deal of responsibility. It is more at the regional than at the global level that the opportunity abounds for truly participatory encounters, as the regional preparatory forum is often turned into a "marketplace of ideas" in which participants are provided with virtually limitless opportunities to use their talents and ingenuity.

But the origin and the originators of ideas are crucial factors in their acceptance or rejection. And ideas coming from the center are more likely to be readily acceptable and universalized than the ones coming from the trenches. Nevertheless, ideas do, and indeed have, come from the regions that have influenced the outcome of and subsequent follow-up to the global conferences.

In this connection, it will be instructive to trace the ECA's contribution to the evolutionary process of ideas, vision, strategies, policies, and programs in the area of women and development as a case of the strategic leadership of a regional commission. The ECA has been very much ahead in the UN family.

With all the debate that took place at both ECOSOC (1957) and the General Assembly (1958) on the terms of reference of the ECA in view of the insistence of the few African delegations who were member states of the UN that the social aspects of economic development and the interdependence of economic and social factors be incorporated therein, it is not surprising that it was accorded high priority in the commission's very first program of work and priorities for the biennium 1960–1961. Accordingly, in its Resolution 109 (VI) of March 2, 1964, the commission embarked on work on the methods and techniques of social development planning, the integration of social programs with economic programs, the criteria for the allocation of resources for social development, and the definition of social-development objectives and policies in relation to the need for accelerated economic development. Without doubt, the commission was well ahead of its time because there was no room in the orthodox development theories at the time for measurable social development indicators.

In the pursuit of this holistic approach, the ECA social development division, under the leadership of the late Riby Williams, began to lay emphasis on promoting women's activities with special reference to the integration of women in economic and social development. In this endeavor, the ECA, following its Regional Conference on Education, Vocational Training and Work Opportunities for Girls and Women in Rabat in May 1971, prepared a five-year program (1972–1976) on pre-vocational and vocational training of girls and women toward their full participation in development. Second, it inaugurated in 1975—the International Women's Year declared by the General Assembly—

the African Training and Research Centre for Women (ATRCW) as one of the commission's major activities to commemorate the year. This was renamed the African Centre for Women (ACW) in 1994. Third, it began to help member states to establish national, subregional, and regional machineries to foster the integration of women in development. Fourth, it established the Africa Regional Coordinating Committee composed exclusively of representatives of member states whose primary responsibility was to coordinate and harmonize programs at national, subregional, and regional levels. Fifth, following the first global conference on women in development held in Mexico in 1975, it held a regional conference on the integration of women in development in Lusaka, Zambia, and decided to institutionalize a triennial regional conference on the integration of women in development.

The ECA African Training and Research Centre for Women played a proactive role in all the UN activities for women in development, continuing to blaze a trail which can be traced back to the ECA's work on women in the early and mid-1960s. Among the ECA's pioneering publications was one on *The Status and Role of Women in East Africa*[103] in 1967, issued three years before Ester Boserup published her pioneering study on *Woman's Role in Economic Development.*[104] Also, on the basis of statistical country studies, the ECA was able to publish in 1974 *The Data Base for Discussion on the Interrelations between the Integration of Women in Development, Their Situation and Population Factors in Africa,*[105] in which some of the first estimates in the world were made of women's contribution to rural labor and to GNP. All these helped to emphasize the centrality of women in development.

Not withstanding these efforts, glaring gender disparities still exist in Africa. The UNDP's gender-related development index (GDI) and gender empowerment measure (GEM) indicate the magnitude of the disparities. The picture which emerges is that despite many efforts to equalize opportunities, women still constitute 70 percent of the region's poor, and gender-related discrimination is still widespread in education and employment, in nutrition and health care, and in economic and political empowerment. Not only is it imperative for more opportunities to be opened to women as a matter of rights, but society as a whole would gain if women's skills and capabilities were better used in society at large. The Lagos Plan of Action has encapsulated what concrete measures must be taken to actualize this vision.

Finally, the ECA was the first-ever UN organization to mobilize civil society—African and non-African—en masse for its historic February 1990 international conference on Popular Participation in the Recovery and Development Process in Africa: Putting the People First (Arusha, Tanzania). The output of the conference was the African Charter for Popular Participation in Development and Transformation—the "African Magna Carta."[106]

Of its 350 participants, over 60 percent were from African and non-African NGOs, voluntary development organizations, grassroots organizations, trade unions, women's organizations, youth organizations, and the media. Government representatives (African and non-African) accounted for only 20 percent of the participants. The charter therefore was the voice of the people. It well and truly led the drive for democracy in Africa.

This bold initiative brought considerable criticism to the ECA, particularly its executive secretariat, at the UN General Assembly but gave representatives of civil society an opportunity to make a significant contribution during the negotiations of the UN-NADAF. It is therefore not surprising that the 2002 independent evaluation of the implementation of the UN-NADAF testified to the increasing involvement of NGOs, both African and non-African. It was the African Charter—the African Magna Carta—that had spelled out in considerable detail the role of civil society—particularly African civil society—at the ECA conference in February 1990.

African Leaders Take Up the Gauntlet Again

For the preparation of the first-ever Special Session of the UN General Assembly on Africa's Economic and Social Crisis in May/June 1986, African governments submitted a special memorandum to guide the international community in their deliberations.[107] The document was exceptionally frank: The governments fully and openly admitted their failures and accepted responsibility for them. They admitted that in spite of all the effort made since independence, the basic economic structures of the African economy have not fundamentally changed.

After reviewing the past performance and present characteristics of the African economy, the memorandum proposed a way forward which is essentially based on a reiteration of the Revised Framework, the Monrovia Strategy, the Lagos Plan of Action, and the Final Act of Lagos. Africa's Priority Programme for Economic Recovery streamlined the quartet into a holistic five-year reconstruction program while AAF-SAP provided the long-term variant. Unfortunately, both the UNPAAERD, which came out of the special session in 1986, and the UN-NADAF of 1991 have received much lip service but have not been implemented by either the African countries or the international community at significant levels. The former have been obliged to pursue SAPs and have consequently been derailed from the path of restructuring and transformation, while the latter have continued with the "business as usual" approach that is often backed by help that is too little too late. The international community's response to these initiatives gives credence to Chester Crocker's remark that the Western perspective of Africa's political and economic development prospects is negative,[108] or, as Michael Crowder has put it, "the mood, the exhilaration and the optimism of the 1960s have been shattered and replaced by a profound disillusion whereby Africa has become the world's basket case, a permanent *mezzogiorno* for which there is little, if any, hope. In the Chanceries of the West, officials wish Africa would just go away."[109]

The cumulative consequence of the failure to act and implement the various programs has been the persistence of Africa's vulnerabilities—drought and desertification, dependence and dispossession, destabilization and excruciating debt burdens, and, last but by no means least, demographic explosion.[110]

The failure of Africa to lay the foundations for a holistic, human-centered, long-term socioeconomic transformation has prompted a resumed search for appropriate development paradigms—this time by the top echelons of the political leadership. The resumption of this effort gives the lie to the efforts that were made in the late 1990s to show that the African economies were moving forward. Indeed, valiant attempts were made to see some silver linings in Africa's dark clouds. But as *The Economist* of London correctly assessed the situation, it was an illusion. The cheerful statistics were the result of good rains and bad accounting. Sub-Saharan Africa, as a whole, had an annual GDP growth rate of less than 3 percent in the 1990s, which just about kept pace with the rate of population growth. So on average, no one got richer.

The optimists can, however, still argue that in spite of the relatively small achievements in the economic domain, fundamental changes are taking place in the political sphere, that the process of democratization has unleashed a number of forces which, in due course, will help to consolidate economic reforms and have a profound impact on the dynamics of Africa's political economy. However, such optimism will disappear if Africa's so-called democratic revolution turns out to be no more than "donor democracy"; that is, just enough of fair elections, good governance, and respect for human rights to satisfy the aid donors. In other words, once donor support is withdrawn, democratic gains may collapse like a pack of cards. In many African countries there are elections but there is little democracy. It is feared that there would be few elections were it not for outside pressure, to the extent that donors actually fund many such elections. Hence, the view is widespread that democracy in the continent is often a sham.[111]

Recent decisions of the heads of state to resume the struggle to forge a better future at least confirms that they are convinced that Africa is not yet out of the woods. The direct intervention of African heads of state has occurred in two different ways. The first was the decision to transform the Organization of African Unity into the African Union in order to accelerate the implementation of the Abuja Treaty of June 1991, which established the African Economic Community, and to fulfill the ideal of generations of pan-Africanists to achieve a full-fledged African unity. The idea that the African Union is the only real solution to Africa's manifold political and economic problems has been floated since the First Pan-African Congress in Manchester, England, in 1945. The LPA, although ignored by African governments and derided by the donor community and the international financial institutions, was no doubt inspired by the pan-African spirit when it proposed pan-African programs for food security, infrastructural facilities, the exploitation of natural resources, and so forth.

The idea of pan-Africanism has always been very popular in Africa, even though Westerners have tended to discount it and African leaders have always shied away from it. They have preferred the national flag, the national anthem, and the pomp and pageantry that the minuscule nation-state can provide. Thus, for four decades, those who have held the reins of government have distanced themselves from African unity, from pan-Africanism. Given their caliber—ignorant military officers, malevolent authoritarian presidents, and a rent-seeking bureaucratic bourgeoisie—they failed or refused to see the folly of perpetuating the partition and balkanization of Africa.

The signing and ratification of the Constitutive Act of the African Union is therefore of historic portent. Implementing it will be far from easy but should receive the full support of all Africans and the international community. If for no other reason, the provision that no government which comes to power through unconstitutional means shall be allowed to participate in the activities of Union makes the support of the international community mandatory as this has the potential of turning Africa's fledgling (donor) democracy into a people-centered sustainable democracy.[112]

In July 2001 at the Lusaka summit, the New Partnership for African Development (NEPAD)[113] was adopted. Like the LPA, it is an African-initiated and African-driven framework for eradicating poverty and promoting gender-sensitive human development and a framework for interaction between Africa and the rest of the world. NEPAD, which will now be the framework for sustainable development in Africa, is a merger of the Millennium Partnership for the African Recovery Programme (MAP), spearheaded by South Africa with the support of Algeria and Nigeria, and the Omega Plan launched in

June 2001 by Senegal with the support of Egypt at an international conference of economists. It was endorsed by the extraordinary OAU Summit in Setre, Libya, where the establishment of the African Union was also declared in March 2001. An Implementation Committee of heads of state and government, whose task is to monitor the implementation of NEPAD, has been set up under the chairmanship of Nigeria.

It was in this capacity that Nigeria presented the new African initiative to the summit of the industrialized market economies plus Russia (the G8) and to the British prime minister at Chequers in September 2001 in the presence of selected African leaders. Nigeria also presented NEPAD to the European Union (EU) in October 2001. NEPAD's Implementation Committee is determined that NEPAD should predominate over all other initiatives on Africa.[114] It is to be hoped that this decision will also be respected by the UN. The final outcome of the review of UN-NADAF and the UNSIA as well as of all the other UN initiatives in the second half of 2002 will be a test case. Now that the request for a moratorium on African initiatives has come from the very top of the African political leadership, it is to be hoped that the UN and the international financial institutions will at least not demur. To achieve this will call for much discussion and negotiations by the Implementation Committee with the Bretton Woods institutions over SAPs and with the General Assembly and other UN bodies over their strong propensity to come out with a new program at the end of any review. If Africa is burdened by SAPs and debt, the future of the continent will, without doubt, remain hopeless.

Within Africa itself, there is a no less formidable task waiting for attention. The NEPAD initiative, which is slated to supersede all other initiatives, apart from being little known in the continent, needs to be fine-tuned so that it is consistent with the LPA, the AAF-SAP, the FAL, and the Constitutive Act of the African Union. NEPAD was prepared without consultation with the stakeholders and key actors in Africa's development. No public debate has been held on it, particularly on the extent to which the paradigm on which it is based corresponds to the African reality and is consistent with the aims of a holistic, human-centered, and transformational development strategy which is fully democratized. There is also no evidence that national parliaments have been kept fully informed of both the Constitutive Act and NEPAD.

And finally, there has been no specific reference to the UN Millennium Development Goals although the UN Secretary-General in his report to the fifty-sixth session of the General Assembly on the follow-up to the outcome of the Millennium Summit has welcomed the new African initiative as evidence of a greater resolve on the part of Africa's leaders to take ownership and control of the continent's destiny.[115] Once there is a mutual recognition of the imperative of accepting African ownership and management of any new program without prejudice to honoring the UN Millennium Declaration and, in particular, the well-targeted millennium development goals, a moratorium on new initiatives and programs will be effective.

6

ESCWA: Striving for Regional Integration

Blandine Destremau
With Anne-Sophie Saywell and Julien Barroche

- **The Long and Painful Birth of the Economic Commission for Western Asia**
- **The 1970s: The Initial Years, the Age of Prosperity**
- **The 1980s: The Years of Recession**
- **The 1990s: New International Order, New Regional Perspectives, New Economy**
- **Concluding Remarks**

The Long and Painful Birth of the Economic Commission for Western Asia

The region covered by the Economic Commission for Western Asia (ECWA), which later became the Economic and Social Commission for Western Asia (ESCWA), is marked by a number of special features: broad economic inequalities between member states; great instability; and the problem raised by the question of Israel. These particularities not only influenced the role the regional commission could play in diffusing ideas but also explain its late creation (1973).

Wide Disparities between Countries

The ECWA region is quite heterogeneous. The area of its countries ranges from 598 sq km for Bahrain and 11,000 sq km for Qatar to 2,150,000 sq km for Saudi Arabia. The small emirates of Bahrain and Qatar have fewer than 1 million inhabitants, while in Egypt there are well over 60 million. The population density of Saudi Arabia is ten inhabitants per square kilometer, while

Lebanon has 412. In 1997, Yemen had a gross national product (GNP) per capita of US$270 and Egypt, Jordan, and Syria had between US$1,000 and $1,500, but the rich oil-producing countries enjoyed much higher incomes: US$7,150 per capita in Saudi Arabia and US$8,640 in Bahrain. In 1996, commercial energy use per capita ranged from 187 kilograms of oil equivalent in Yemen to more than 11,000 kilograms in Bahrain, Qatar, and the United Arab Emirates.[1] Other indicators reinforce the picture of disparities, be they related to mining or hydraulic resources, agricultural productive capacity, education, or health. Differences between countries are larger today than they were before the oil boom, although the economic crisis has tended to generate similar problems in the various countries.

Three major profiles emerge, which constitute three categories of ECWA member countries: sparsely populated, desert oil–exporting countries enjoying large revenues, grouped in the Gulf Co-operation Council countries (Bahrain, Kuwait, Oman, Qatar, Saudi Arabia, and the United Arab Emirates); densely populated countries with some natural resources and a rather diversified economy, labeled "diversified economies" (Egypt, Iraq until 1990, Lebanon, Jordan, and Syria); and finally the poorer and least developed countries (the two Yemens, then the Republic of Yemen after their reunification, and Palestine). Iraq joined the group of poorest countries in the 1990s.

These disparities allowed for some complementarity and exchanges between countries in the fields of oil and labor power. The 1990 Gulf War, however, showed the extent to which these exchanges were asymmetrical and unequal. Compensatory and redistributive mechanisms, through emigration or aid, have proved to be inadequate in reversing unequal relationships.

A Highly Unstable Region

The explosive birth of the state of Israel inaugurated long-lasting tensions between Israel and its Arab neighbors. The Arab-Israeli conflict gave a political dimension to the relationships between the region and the international community which tended to relegate the region's social and economic development to the background. Consequently, the possibility of creating a United Nations regional commission for the Middle East was crippled by the problem of respect for the principles of universality and non-discrimination, which was strongly supported by the Western countries. The UN could not envisage the establishment of a regional intergovernmental organization which would exclude one of its member states.[2]

The Arab-Israeli conflict, however, was not the only factor of instability in the Middle East. A number of conflicts within and between Arab countries plagued the region. Saudi Arabia and North Yemen on the one hand, and Oman and South Yemen on the other solved their border differences only recently; Iran and Iraq were at war for many years (1980–1988) and Iraq and Kuwait had several armed clashes even before the 1990s; and prior to their reunification in 1990, the two Yemens had several open conflicts. Furthermore, the Lebanese civil war plagued the area for sixteen years, there were several episodes of domestic tension in Syria and Iraq, and Oman remained in a state of internal warfare for many years.

In addition to postponing the creation of the regional commission until 1973, regional instability led to its headquarters being moved, and its staff evacuated and relocated, several times from one country to another. At its first session in Beirut in 1974, the location of the commission's headquarters was the object of strong competition among the member states. Lebanon, Iraq, and Syria each put forward a proposal. Lebanon, which played a decisive role in the creation of the commission, was in a strong position, and the disagreement between Iraq and Syria allowed it to temporarily host the headquarters on its territory. In 1976 at a special session on the question held in Qatar, it was decided that Iraq would host the commission's permanent headquarters because of the quality of services available there, despite Lebanese protests and the Syrian proposal.

The same year, due to the war in Lebanon, ECWA and its staff were evacuated to their home countries and then temporarily relocated to Amman before returning to Beirut for some months. In 1982, after another evacuation of the families of ECWA staff members from Beirut in June 1980, the commission moved from Beirut to Baghdad in a convoy protected by UN troops, as Beirut was under Israeli bombing. In 1988, the conditions created by the Iran-Iraq War led to the evacuation of the families of the commission staff from Baghdad to their respective homelands, but at the end of the war in June 1988 the commission reaffirmed its will to maintain its permanent headquarters there. The commission then had a two-year period of stability. After the beginning of the Gulf War, however, the Secretary-General decided to evacuate all staff members from Baghdad after the invasion of Kuwait on August 2, 1990. Most of them were placed on temporary evacuation leave and were dispersed to their home countries. In 1991, the commission was temporarily relocated in Amman, where it remained for six years. At the seventeenth session of the commission, in May 1994, it was decided, by vote, to return to Beirut. The decision was endorsed on July 29, 1994, by Resolution 1994/43 of the UN's Economic and Social Council (ECOSOC),[3] and Kofi Annan inaugurated the permanent headquarters in Beirut on March 20, 1998.

The Long and Painful Birth

In 1947, aware of the serious economic problems threatening the stability of the Middle East after World War II, the General Assembly invited the Economic and Social Council "to study the factors bearing upon the establishment of an economic commission for the Middle East."[4] The fundamental idea underlying this proposal, which was reactivated two years later, was that collaboration between the countries of the Middle East would help to strengthen their economies and raise living standards and that "such measures would be facilitated by close collaboration with the United Nations and its subsidiary organs as well as with regional organizations in the Middle East such as the Arab League."[5] But the opposition of Arab states to the participation of Israel and of the Western countries to any discrimination led to a stalemate.

In the absence of a UN commission for the Middle East, some countries joined existing regional commissions. Egypt and Ethiopia joined the ECA, Afghanistan and Iran joined ECAFE, and Greece, Israel,[6] and Turkey joined the ECE. But the other independent countries of the region (Iraq, Jordan, Libya, Saudi Arabia, Syria, and Yemen) and the Arabian Peninsula territories under British trusteeship were unable to join any regional commission.

The UN could not exclude the Middle East from its development efforts altogether, all the more since the 1955 Bandung Conference had inaugurated a new approach to Third World issues and the General Assembly had decided to decentralize UN economic and social activities in the framework of the First United Nations Development Decade and to enhance the role of the regional commissions. In 1963, the ECOSOC resolution for the establishment of a United Nations Economic and Social Office in Beirut (UNESOB) was endorsed by the General Assembly, thus creating a UN regional body for the Middle East.[7]

Thus, through an unusual procedure and thanks to the support of the Group of 77, the Middle East acquired a UN regional organization. It was a substitute economic commission that fulfilled some of the same functions as a regional commission and its director attended ECOSOC's meetings on an equal footing with the regional commissions' executive secretaries. Despite this assimilation, UNESOB did not have, in real terms, either the status, power, or resources the General Assembly accorded the regional economic commissions.

As Paul Berthoud, the first director of UNESOB, recalled: "The assimilation of UNESOB to the secretariats of the other regional commissions was pursued as far as possible, but the lack of an intergovernmental cooperation machinery denied the region the status enjoyed by the other regions of the third world."[8]

In addition, the establishment of the United Nations Economic and Social Office in Beirut, when Israel and some Western countries wanted it to be located in Cyprus, had reactivated the problem of including the state of Israel in its sphere of competence. Paul Berthoud was commissioned by the secretariat to carry out a reconnaissance mission in Israel in 1964 in order to explore the ways Israel could collaborate to the activities of UNESOB. He thus stated:

> The question of whether such an involvement would have been tolerated by the Governments of the Arab countries never arose, for the Israeli Government refused me any co-operation and declared me *persona non grata* in Israel; it refused to have any dealings with UNESOB as long as Israel did not have access to it on an equal footing with the representatives of the Arab Governments.[9]

Later, in 1972, when the representative of Lebanon proposed the creation of an economic commission for the Arab countries at the fifty-fifth session of ECOSOC,[10] consideration was deferred to a later session because of Western and Israeli pressure. But the geopolitical balance of power had changed since 1948, as reflected in the balance of forces within the UN. After the 1960s, voting in the General Assembly and ECOSOC was no longer controlled by Western countries. Also, the accession to independence of new oil-producing countries together with the changes in the distribution of oil income to the benefit of the countries of the Middle East had convinced the international community of the necessity to improve the integration of the region into the world economy. At the 1973 session, the Lebanese delegation reiterated its proposal, arguing that the UN failure to have the twelve Arab states of the Middle East represented in a regional commission constituted a gap in the system and even discrimination against the Arab world.

In a spirit of conciliation, Lebanon changed the name of its proposed body to "Economic Commission for Western Asia," and the proposal was put on the provisional agenda.[11] The Israeli observer, Reuven Hillel, supported by the United States and the Netherlands, spoke against this proposal, arguing that it was "contrary to the principles of universality and non-discrimination" and that such a commission "constituted an ethnic group of countries united by their hostility toward Israel, in flagrant violation of the principles of the Charter and the practices of the United Nations."[12] Italy supported Israel and proposed a suspension of the debate. In reply, the representative of Lebanon noted that the commission in question was in no way ethnic, stating inter alia that all the friendly countries of the region could participate in it with a view to fruitful collaboration. The principles of equality of rights and universality would not be impaired by ECOSOC's decision. The countries to suffer were in fact the twelve Arab countries interested in the creation of the commission, for they had been denied exercise of the rights stemming from those two principles for twenty-five years.

China, Pakistan, Spain, Yugoslavia, and Arab countries such as Egypt, Tunisia, and Yemen supported Lebanon's arguments and proposal. In contrast, the United States urged that the International Court of Justice should give an opinion on the legality of such a commission. Fearing that the debate would become bogged down in a long political wrangle, Lebanon called for a vote on the U.S. proposal, which was heavily defeated. Finally, the draft resolution was adopted by 33 votes to 8 with 9 abstentions.[13]

On August 9, 1973, thanks to the fighting spirit of the Lebanese delegation supported by the countries of the South and the socialist countries, the Economic and Social Council established the Economic Commission for Western Asia (ECWA) by its Resolution 1818 (LV).[14] The newborn regional commission was composed of the twelve Arab countries which enjoyed the services of UNESOB: Bahrain, Iraq, Jordan, Kuwait, Lebanon, Oman, Qatar, Saudi Arabia, Syria, the United Arab Emirates, and the two Yemens.[15] On December 26, 1973, Secretary-General Kurt Waldheim appointed Said Al-Attar, the permanent representative of Yemen to the UN, as the commission's first executive secretary.[16] On January 1, 1974, the commission was able to begin work at its temporary headquarters in Beirut, taking over UNESOB. The birth of this regional intergovernmental organization was enthusiastically welcomed by the governments of the region, which saw in it a means of putting the region on an equal footing with the other regions of the world. At last, twenty-seven years after Europe and Eastern Asia and the Far East, twenty-six years after Latin America, and sixteen years after Africa, the Arab countries of the Middle East had secured for themselves a regional economic commission of the UN.

The questions of the admission of Egypt and the representation of Palestine quickly arose. Egypt already belonged to the ECA, but its status as a regional power in the Middle East and the fact that part of its territory, the Sinai, was in Western Asia argued strongly in its favor. It became a member of ECWA in 1977. As far as Palestine was concerned, the General Assembly's recognition of the Palestine Liberation Organization (PLO) in 1974 authorized ECWA to grant the PLO the right to join the commission. In 1975, the PLO was accepted by ECWA as a permanent observer.[17] In 1977, the PLO became a full-fledged member of the commission. ECWA is the first international body in which the PLO took a seat with the same rights and prerogatives as other governments. In 1990, the unification of the People's Democratic Republic of Yemen and the Yemen Arab Republic into a single state reduced the membership of the commission to thirteen; the League of Arab States had twenty-two members.[18]

The Regional Commission as a Promoter of Ideas

The idea that regional cooperation between developing countries was a decisive factor for development was the basis for the creation of each regional commission. In the Middle East, the creation of ECWA was delayed by the political considerations mentioned above but also by the fact that it took time for the countries of the region to nurture a regional consciousness. Awareness of the region's economic interests had developed through the work of the League of Arab States, the Organization of Arab Petroleum Exporting Countries (OAPEC), and even UNESOB itself.

As a regional commission, ECWA was and is the regional arm of the UN and is responsible for providing input to assist ECOSOC and the General Assembly in their tasks and for supporting member countries in complying with the principles, norms, and policies adopted by these two bodies. On an operational level, ECWA was created to promote economic and social development by coordinating cooperation among the countries of the region[19] and UN organizations operating there while at the same time involving the many regional bodies. Its mandate responded to the needs of its member states for surveys and studies of the region's economic, social, and technical problems on which development programs could be focused. Additionally, the commission's mission was to enhance the capacities of state administrations, all of which were relatively new and lacked experience, by collecting, evaluating, and disseminating economic, social, technical, and statistical information and providing training and advisory services at the request of the governments of the region. The statutory functions of ECWA which lead to the generation of ideas are threefold: identifying development problems; raising awareness of the impact of these problems and the policies that may assist in their solution; and serving as the main general economic and social development forum for the exchange of ideas among ECWA countries.[20]

This chapter will try to analyze these ideas, relating their nature and content to the region's political, economic, and social conditions as well as to the global context and to the major orientations given by the UN system. It will also question the role of ECWA in producing, diffusing, and promoting ideas in its region. "Has the Commission played the role of a leader or advisor helping countries to identify or react to regional challenges and changes?"[21] will be one of the questions this chapter will attempt to answer. The importance and content of these ideas will be assessed through the regional commission's various publications, actions, and collaborations through which these ideas found expression. A number of interviews were conducted that provided valuable guidelines and inspiration in the interpretation and understanding of the commission's ideas. Part of the information concerning the history and structures of the commission was drawn from *ESCWA (1974–1999): Twenty-Five Years of Service to the Region's Development,*[22] with which the author of this chapter closely collaborated from its inception.

This chapter obviously suffers from several limitations: Only major areas of involvement will be dealt with, which means that each period will be characterized by some key ideas only, others necessarily remaining in the background. Furthermore, because of the nature of the documents used and the limitations in size, it was often not possible to track ideas from their origin to the end of the period, or to identify their genesis. Another weak point concerns the internal workings of the commission: It was difficult to access information concerning the debates that took place between member states, how they reacted to an idea coming from outside, and which changes led to an original proposition. As will be repeated in the conclusion, the commission carefully maintains a homogeneous and uniform official position toward the outside and internal differences tend to be considered essentially politically sensitive, as are several key issues. This situation typifies the region itself, where free and open public debate is often muffled and conflicts and tensions are widespread, but it is also linked to the nature of the role of the commission and its need to build its legitimacy and credibility.

This chapter follows a chronological outline. The first part deals with the first years of the commission; that is, the second half of the 1970s, when ECWA took over from UNESOB and became more involved in development issues. The 1980s are marked by a slowdown in economic prosperity and the beginning of the crisis of the post-oil boom; the second part will analyze how new ideas influenced the regional commission's positioning on major economic choices. As shown in the third part, the Gulf War and the end of the Cold War deeply altered the political context of the region, just as liberalization, globalization, and impoverishment posed new economic challenges in the 1990s. Considering the degree of instability in the region, the frequency and gravity of armed conflicts, and the heavy role of political factors, each section will start with ECWA's perspective on regional integration as a crucial element of its capacity to fulfill its role. The major economic challenges and the commission's main choices and ideas regarding development and growth will then follow. Finally, as a link between politics and economics, social issues and ECWA's approach to such questions as the position of women, demography, poverty, and so forth will be tackled.

The conclusion will express the author's ideas, analysis, and point of view, based first of all on present research work but also on many years of academic research in the region and several episodes of gratifying work with the regional commission.[23] It is in no way prescriptive and does not pretend to make recommendations.

The 1970s: The Initial Years, the Age of Prosperity

From a political and diplomatic point of view, the 1970s were dominated by three events: the October 1973 War; the international recognition of the PLO in 1974, ten years after its creation; and the Camp David Agreement, which was signed on September 17, 1978, between President Anwar al-Sadat of Egypt and Prime Minister Menachem Begin of Israel. The latter was followed by a peace accord signed by Egypt and Israel on March 26, 1979, in the presence of the United States. This bilateral agreement has symbolized the division of the Arab countries, which have stigmatized the Egyptian compromise. Meanwhile, another front opened with the start of the Lebanese war in 1975.

ECWA as a Promoter of Regional Institutionalization

Although political discourse insisted on the existence of an Arab nation, the effective process of regionalization was still in its infancy. ECWA felt that the priorities of regional cooperation were institutional, sectoral, and technical bases. Beginning in 1975, it developed relations and signed cooperation agreements with a number of regional intergovernmental organizations of Western Asia. The main ones were the League of Arab States and its various satellites such as the Arab League Educational, Cultural and Scientific Organization (ALECSO), the Arab Organization of Administrative Sciences (AOAS), the Arab Standards and Metrology Organization (ASMO), and the Council for Arab Economic Unity (CAEU).[24] The Industrial Development Center for the Arab States and the Arab Labor Organization were also among the first regional organizations to work in partnership with ECWA. In 1976, in order to increase the region's financial contribution to the various ECWA projects and programs of work, the commission initiated new forms of cooperation with Arab economic development funds such as the Arab Fund for Economic and Social Development and the Kuwaiti, Abu Dhabi, and Saudi economic and social development funds. ECWA made its scientific skills and its knowledge of the institutions of the UN system available to these organizations, which were often represented at the ministerial sessions and at many seminars, conferences, and training workshops.

In order to cope with the development problems of the region, ECWA deemed it necessary to build appropriate human and institutional structures. The identification of appropriate expertise and know-how constituted a major problem of development. Devices such as directories could be useful in that regard. The commission argued that "the pooling of regional expertise should also serve as a means to struggle against brain drain outside the region. Playing on countries' respective comparative advantages could encourage graduates to remain within the region."[25]

Another common issue was water. The development of water resources was given high priority by all ECWA countries, given their scarcity in the region, the fact that all the main sources of water are located outside the Arab world, and the importance of water in the Arab-Israeli conflict. The member states made an explicit demand of the regional commission, whose position was that the protection, management, and optimal and equitable sharing of water resources depended on achieving a high level of regional cooperation. Water is an area in which ECWA played an innovative role, insofar as it was the first regional organization to elevate water security to a priority issue and to take such a strong stand in favor of regional cooperation in this regard.

Regional cooperation rested on solidarity as well. Special attention was paid to the member states in the most precarious situation: the least developed countries of the ECWA area and Palestine. In its original work program, presented in 1974, ECWA stressed that "certainly, the twelve member-states will wish to benefit from the help of ECWA in the fields where their needs exist. . . . This type of assistance, focused on precise needs, can particularly apply to the circumstances of the region's least developed countries."[26] The member states were repeatedly asked to pay special attention to the specific needs of these countries, for which a program was designed. This position explicitly rests on a strong position in favor of cooperation among developing countries, as formulated in a 1977 ECWA resolution, which was considered to be an intrinsic part of regional cooperation. It was also inspired by the general framework of the new international economic order (NIEO), as set out in a UN General Assembly resolution of 1974.[27]

ECWA's strongest regional stand concerned Palestine. The Palestine Liberation Organization was founded in early 1964, and the Fatah Movement was born on January 1, 1965. One of the feasible and relevant ways for ECWA to support development in Palestine was to collect data in order to testify to the effects of war and occupation on the Palestinian people: A few years after the 1967 Israeli occupation of the West Bank and Gaza strip, which caused another wave of displaced persons and refugees, little was known about the social and economic living conditions of this scattered people.[28] In 1976, ECWA thus launched a major project: a general study of the situation and the economic and social possibilities of the Arab people of Palestine in Western Asia. This study would take seven years to be realized because of numerous difficulties such as defining terms of reference, gathering relevant information, recruiting suitable staff, and gaining access in the field. This work was entrusted to the Team International research agency and was largely funded by Qatar, the UN regular budget, and a contribution from the United Nations Fund for Population Activities (UNFPA). The same year, in coordination with the PLO and the UNFPA, ECWA set out to conduct a census of the Palestinian people, the first steps of which were to establish definitions and methods for gathering data: Because the population lived in diaspora and was marked by high rates of mobility and migration, the quantitative reality of the Palestinians was difficult to determine.

The Challenge of Setting the Foundations for Economic Development

The use of petroleum as a weapon, by limiting production in order to maintain high prices, generated the oil boom that started in 1973–1974 with a considerable increase in the oil revenues of the producing and exporting countries. This major event affected both the economic and social development of the whole ECWA region. The oil-producing countries benefited from the oil rents[29] and the incomes derived from them as well as various types of international aid and subsidies linked to geostrategic interests. These revenues stimulated strong economic growth, which led to an improvement of overall welfare, particularly of the poorest groups. The non–oil-producing countries of the region experienced a similar situation to that of the oil-producing countries, although to a much lesser extent. Their incomes and revenues rose mainly because of the large remittances of their emigrant workers in the Gulf, but also because of grants and concessional loans from the Gulf countries as well as international aid to support public budget and military expenditures.

However, it was soon apparent that prosperity, and even economic growth, were not the same as development. Deciding how to spend, allocate, and invest their increasing—often skyrocketing—revenues represented a real challenge for the countries of the region. One paradoxical consequence of the oil boom was to increase the dependence of the region upon world trade and the technology of Western countries. The import of sophisticated manufactured products, equipment, and services and the necessity to call upon skilled labor power to run the economy made the region perhaps more vulnerable than any other region of the world. The rentier model of development, which characterized the economies of the region, made the search for technical progress all the more difficult because labor productivity was low and the productive structures were very weak and concentrated in oil. Furthermore, "up to the mid-seventies, interest in developing scientific and technological capabilities was largely confined in most ECWA countries to the armed forces and se-lected branches of the extractive industries. Integrated and comprehensive policy statements dedicated to advancing national Science and Technology (S & T) capabilities were largely absent in most ECWA member countries. Isolated articles of legislation, a variety of laws, rules and regulations, gave rise to implicit de facto S & T policy regimes that were often fragmented, and sometimes incoherent."[30]

The development challenges the commission had to face consisted of help-ing the member states engage in patterns of economic growth that could sup-port development in the medium and long term, secure their food supplies, invest in modern industrialization, establish efficient public administration, and tackle some of the newly emerging social issues. In conformity with the recommendations of the UN's first and second decades for development, ECWA gave priority to agriculture and industry, focusing on capital forma-tion, raising productivity, and improving planning.

Representatives of the member states and various executive secretaries never ceased reiterating their calls for the strengthening of regional cooperation through the coordination of different development programs and the estab-lishment of a regional system for the exchange of development information.

However, not all countries needed the same model of development or faced the same problems, which made it difficult for ECWA to promote a unified and homogeneous vision of regional development and build overall acceptance, le-gitimacy, and credibility among its member states. More generally, questions were also raised among the member states about the relevance and appropri-ateness of the UN agenda for an area boosted by the oil boom, specifically for the powerful and wealthy oil-producing countries, which had their own means, priorities, and preoccupations. Often the ideas put forward by ECWA collided with those of the oil-producing countries. At the same time, countries with a socialist orientation tended to be suspicious of the whole UN system.

In the end, only two countries really benefited from ECWA and took ideas from it: Jordan and Yemen.[31] Nevertheless, ECWA never stopped promoting the idea that regional cooperation was necessary for the economic develop-ment of all countries of the region. In 1974, the question of an Arab common market was revived and ECWA began to recommend regional cooperation in sectors such as technology, industry, and trade and took a lead in the harmo-nization and improvement of statistical and accounting methods for interna-tional comparisons (purchasing-power parities, for example).[32]

Agricultural Development Focused on Food Security

ECWA adhered to the common vision of the 1970s that agricultural de-velopment should aim at improving food security, promoting moderniza-tion, and supplying inputs for industrial activities. Nevertheless, because food security was a major problem for most countries of the ECWA region, it became the priority in the work of the joint division established by ECWA and Food and Agriculture Organization (FAO). The work of the expert group meeting on Constraints in Agricultural Planning and Resource Mobiliza-tion for Food Security Programs in the ECWA Region (1983) demonstrated that

> the gap between food production and demand in the ECWA region [was] widening at an alarming rate and posing a serious threat to the food secu-rity of the region. This [called] *inter alia* for an action plan to exploit inter-country complementarities in resource use through interlocking of their diverse resource endowments. However, in view of the constraints placed by the long gestation period inherent to agricultural development, a cur-rent action plan to ensure food security based on the availability of food supplies in the international market [was] an imperative need of the ECWA region.[33]

The commission also insisted that food security could not be solved at the national level, and ECWA therefore introduced and promoted the concept of regional food security, which was not easy to achieve because of the weakness of intraregional trade and the lack of cooperation among countries.

ECWA's strategy followed three main directions: the improvement of plan-ning at national and regional levels; the development of techniques to adapt new technologies in order to increase productivity; and the adoption of an integrated approach to rural development, aiming to reverse the situation of growing rural unemployment and underemployment and to help rural com-munities escape economic stagnation and participate in national construc-tion.[34] Agricultural development planning and the intervention of the state in the management of the agricultural sector were given prominence in the 1970s.[35] They were considered the principal means for securing food security, sustainable development, and policy coordination and required the estab-lishment of an accurate database. Agricultural management also demanded staff who were qualified in the areas of the preparation of agricultural plans; the identification, preparation, and implementation of projects; and in man-agement, monitoring, and evaluation.

Food security and agricultural development were directly affected by the environmental fragility of the region and its limited water resources, which in

turn called for regional cooperation in resource conservation and management. The protection of natural resources and the fight against desertification were major imperatives for the region, which has the largest proportion
of land in the arid and semi-arid zones of all the UN regions. The commission developed a systemic policy-oriented approach to desertification that
has guided all its initiatives in this field:

> Agricultural problems have resulted, partly, from long-term, chronic and per-
> vasive physical processes associated with environmental changes and partly
> from the shortfalls in the established institutions and management practices.
> In most cases, the technology to combat the physical dimension of degrada-
> tion exists, but all too often the application of this technology is weakened by
> inadequate knowledge of the social and economic context and the non-avail-
> ability of management skills, and because the process has been insufficiently
> well identified.[36]

PLANNING AND COORDINATING INDUSTRIAL DEVELOPMENT

During the 1970s, the industrialization effort in the region, and more generally the promotion of economic development, was led by the public sector.
This was clearly indicated in the national economic plans and programs and
was confirmed by the levels of investment, output, and employment in publicly owned industry and by market regulation. At the same time, modernization was an important factor in establishing the legitimacy of most of the
member states, and this was associated with industrialization. For this reason
as well as for purely economic considerations, the governments of the region
had a major stake in industrialization.

Non–oil-exporting countries, for which the bill for imported manufactured goods was a concern, albeit covered by migrant remittances, tended to
engage in import-substitution strategies. These policies led to some diversification of output and were responsible for most of the growth in industrial
output in the 1970s. Having completed the first stage of an import-substitution strategy, however, these economies ran into the classical obstacles when
they tried to move on to the second stage of developing intermediate and
engineering industries; namely, a lack of investment capital and a scarcity of
skills and technology.

In oil-exporting countries, the dependency of export revenues on a single
primary commodity soon raised awareness of their intrinsic vulnerability,
which pushed these countries toward attempts at industrial and economic
diversification. They pursued an export-oriented capital-intensive strategy
after the 1973 oil boom, but the transformation of crude oil into a range of

manufactured products still lagged behind. Although oil in the Gulf Co-op-eration Council countries could have sustained a much more diversified development of the petrochemical, fertilizer, iron and steel, and cement industries, the oil economies of the region could still be characterized as rentier economies.[37] In the course of the 1970s, as was the case in most countries with controlled economic systems, the oil-exporting countries introduced more liberal industrialization policies and measures and encouraged the growth of the private sector.

ECWA established a joint division with the United Nations Industrial Development Organization (UNIDO), which collaborated with various regional partners, in particular the Arab Industrial Development and Mining Organization (AIDMO), which had long been established in Baghdad. From 1974 to 1985, the joint division drew up the framework of an import-substitution strategy for the countries with diversified economies (e.g., Iraq, Egypt, and Syria) and with the aim of enhancing the value and diversity of exports from the Gulf countries. Furthermore, the division conducted a major effort to boost awareness of new technologies, particularly microelectronics and software industries, information and communication technologies, biotechnologies, and new material technologies, with the aim of building scientific and technological capacities. The transition to a knowledge-based economy should enhance capacities in a wide range of areas.

At the same time, the first industrialization plans were being produced. Many governments were interested in studies on the subject, but few were carried to the stage of concrete action; industrial-development planning in the region was often no more than an institutional framework for giving priority to projects based on political prestige rather than economic rationality. The success of development plans and programs undertaken by ECWA countries depended on the continuity of their efforts to develop an administrative machinery that was responsible not only for the coordination of various policy measures but also for the effective mobilization of capital and human resources for industrial development. In a 1981 report,[38] ECWA pointed out that the lack of continuity in industrial strategies had led to short-term industrial policies and the neglect of more far-reaching issues and objectives, such as the possibility of combining import-substitution strategies with the promotion and diversification of manufactured exports; the choice between pursuing an integrated industrialization strategy and giving priority to the markets for final goods; and the absorption of more advanced technology.

As was the case for agricultural development, the main axis of ECWA's ideas in promoting industrialization at this time was that regional cooperation was of utmost importance for the region's industrial development and that planning was to be a major tool to secure policy continuity. Cooperation was to take the form of concerted planning and industrial joint ventures, which underwent real development in the region in the late 1970s. The results, however, were limited, as many projects did not move beyond the stage of feasibility studies. For the sake of continuity and cohesion, ECWA tried to assist in the development of long-term policy guidelines for regional cooperation. But these initiatives had little impact on the industrial development of the region, as they implied a degree of regional cooperation for which the states were not prepared. Nationalist policies based on the imperatives of national defense prevailed in the region and were a serious obstacle to economic cooperation. Moreover, the commission decided to end its involvement in industrial issues, which were covered by UN specialized agencies, and to expand in areas not addressed by specific agencies.

ECWA's Commitment to Population and Women's Issues

The role of the state was—and still is—outstanding in the Middle Eastern rentier-type economies. Through redistribution, it established social cohesiveness and reduced relative poverty. It employed a considerable share of the national labor forces, thereby distributing a large proportion of total wages. Bureaucracy, central administration, and public services expanded, reflecting the process of building the state apparatus and the means of intervention. Socially and politically, public employment contributed to create or consolidate a middle class that was largely urban and generally devoted to the state, which came to constitute the state's most stable source of legitimacy and support. The abundant revenues in the region not only stimulated strong economic growth but also led to a considerable improvement in the situation of the poorest social groups by generating employment and financing the development of public services.

Remarkable progress was achieved in education and health, thanks to considerable public investment in equipment and personnel (national or foreign). Child mortality, illiteracy, and fertility rates fell considerably in all countries, although not to the same extent. Nevertheless, large inequalities remained in the distribution of welfare benefits and opportunities. Poverty, as defined by the United Nations Development Programme (UNDP), is high in Western Asia compared with the other regions. It is also much higher than indicated by monetary indicators. The most alarming indicator is that of illiteracy and school dropouts, particularly of women. Moreover, the oil boom intensified the migration of population toward the Gulf countries, which resulted in an acceleration of urbanization in cities not equipped for welcoming migrants and in rural migrants who were not prepared for urban lifestyles. New social problems thus emerged from changes in the pattern of regional labor markets.

ECWA's involvement with social issues was circumscribed by several factors: first, most of what had to do with poverty at large was tackled under the heading of development. Second, the wealthiest countries were reluctant to raise issues that might question the pattern of their economic growth or their political balance. The precariousness of internal cohesiveness, state legitimacy, and external relationships generated conservative attitudes which made it difficult to start a debate on issues such as women, wealth distribution, or rentier patterns of development and their negative impact on production and productivity. "Moral" social questions such as drugs, prostitution, corruption, poverty, and so forth, were considered very sensitive as well, which had the effect of limiting ECWA's intervention to technical studies. Third, Islam and its various prescriptions were perceived, partly in a defensive manner, as the best way to combat most social evils, including poverty. Member states would deny that the UN system, and implicitly the West, had anything to teach them in matters of social management and would insist that their own culture, habits, and religion were better adapted to address local problems.[39]

Two issues, however, were directly tackled by ECWA, partly as a response to the concerns of some countries or specific groups and partly as a result of impulses coming from UN international conferences: the issues of women and population. All through its history, ECWA has remained strongly involved in these fields, which remain particularly salient in most Arab countries today.

In the 1970s, women did not represent an effective social force; in most countries of the region—except Lebanon, where the tradition of female education is among the oldest in the region—female schooling lagged considerably behind that of men. In the early 1970s, only in Lebanon were more than 10 percent of women active in the public sphere.[40] The commission cooperated with the United Nations Development Fund for Women (UNIFEM) in order to enable women of the region to play a larger role in economic and social development. It took a strong and progressive stand in this regard, considering the cultural environment, and declared that the social integration problems in ECWA-region national societies are particularly reflected in the status and role of women in the development process. Factors such as political and legislative reform (voting rights, new personal-status laws), the development of education opportunities for girls, industrialization, and urbanization processes (including employment) are the major problems to be taken into account.[41]

Following the International Women's Conference in Mexico in 1975, the idea of promoting the integration of women in development grew in ECWA. During the 1970s, most of the commission's activities regarding the promotion of women's roles in development had to do with collecting statistics and data and producing studies. It turned out to be pioneering work which is an indispensable reference for researchers and governments of the region.[42] By disseminating information on the condition and needs of women, ECWA contributed to the initiation of a number of operational projects that demonstrated that it is possible to secure concrete improvements in the situation of women. ECWA and UNIFEM have also raised funds to support NGOs for women in the region and reinforce their role in society.

When ECWA was established in 1974, the population of the region was estimated at 76 million people. Twenty-five years later, it had increased to about 160 million. With the exception of Egypt, population-growth rates were extremely high: Between 1980 and 1985 they reached around 4 percent a year. The problem, however, did not affect the various countries equally. The Gulf countries had a problem of relative population and labor-power scarcity, while most of the others suffered from a growing gap between economic and population growth.

The commission underlined that for the countries of the region, there was a clear link between population (growth and structure) and development: Development planning had to take population increase and structure into consideration, especially in relation to social services and the labor market. ECWA promoted the idea that demographic changes, including fertility, mortality, migration, and urbanization, were all deeply affected by economic policies and development planning. Conversely, all kinds of transformation in the population had important economic implications for infrastructures, social services, and the labor market. Understanding the relationship between, on one hand, the unusual population situations prevalent in the region—high birth rates, low death rates, considerable population movements, rapid urban population growth, and the national composition of population—and, on the other hand, the nature and structure of development is crucial for the formulation of rational development policies.[43] In particular, ECWA insisted that if a qualified and modern labor force, able to fulfill the requirements of development, was to be realized, the educational needs of the growing population needed to be addressed. The link between population and the use of limited natural resources was also crucial.

This perspective explains the focus of UNESOB and ECWA on documenting demographic facts, measuring population, evaluating social needs,

assessing the demographic transition, following urban growth and urbanization, and appreciating the importance of migrant and refugee groups.[44]

It can be argued that the sensitivity of the population question, the differences between the respective situations and interests of the member states,
and the fragile legitimacy of the regional commission discouraged ECWA from
taking an explicit stand in favor of such issues as the control of demographic
growth. But it cannot be denied that the establishment of a reliable statistical
database and efforts to raise consciousness about what was at stake in matters
concerning demographic growth and structure were in themselves a significant contribution to the improvement of demographic conditions in the region. Census experts that were provided to the member states also played a
role in highlighting the magnitude of the problems.

The 1980s: The Years of Recession

The Iran-Iraq War violently shook the Middle East in the 1980s, pitting the
two largest states in the region against each other with serious local, regional,
and international consequences. During the war, the Arab states were unable
to form a unified front, and lasting divisions split the Arab world. Thus, for
example, the Syrian Arab Republic, which allied with Iran, forbade Iraq to use
the pipelines crossing its territory toward the Mediterranean. Saudi Arabia,
Jordan, and Turkey, however, were reliable allies of Iraq. At the end of the war,
Iraq considering itself the victor, claimed a leading role in the Middle East,
and in order to reinforce its military strength and rebuild its economy, it invaded Kuwait in August 1990. The Lebanese war was also becoming more
intense. On June 6, 1982, Israel, with its "Peace of Galilee" operation, launched
a large-scale invasion of Lebanon, pushing all the way to Beirut. After August,
the invaders gradually withdrew, confining their occupation to the so-called
security zone.

Mobilizing the Region on the Issues of Palestine and the Environment

ECWA constantly demonstrated its determination to take into account the
Occupied Palestinian Territories in its activities. In 1982, when the PLO asked
for assistance, the executive secretary was asked by the member states to use
the scale for assistance to the least advanced countries of the region. A resolution passed in 1985 stressed the fact that data on the Palestinian Territories
had to be included in every ECWA regional study.[45] The ECWA program of
action vis-à-vis Palestine was mainly based on two projects formally adopted

at its 1976 session, which were to be widely debated at subsequent sessions, where they prompted many declarations and resolutions.

The report on the situation and the economic and social potential of the Arab people of Palestine was submitted to ECWA members and to the International Conference on the Question of Palestine held in Paris in 1983. Its ten volumes included many sectoral and specific studies, which were annexed to the main text. Beyond its documentary value, this report was meant to provide a guideline for aid and practical measures to improve the living conditions of the Palestinian people. The Voluntary Contributions Fund of the member states was expected to finance most of these activities. As a result, in 1984–1985, a working group was set up to study and boost ECWA's participation in the development of the Occupied Palestinian Territories. It was active until its collapse in 1990–1991, when the Gulf War increased tensions among the member states and weakened support for Palestine in some of them. The commission then initiated various types of support for the Palestinian population: feasibility studies for technical and vocational training in agriculture (1988), the industrial sector, and a livestock project (1989), as well as a study on household spending and income;[46] vocational training; technical cooperation services for the Palestinian Central Bureau of Statistics and the Open University in Jerusalem; and an emergency aid project to support small-scale farming initiatives.

The second project was the census of the Arabs of Palestine living in the Palestinian Territories and in the rest of Western Asia and even beyond.[47] It encountered many difficulties, notably the problem of defining who should be regarded as a Palestinian, since many of them living abroad had acquired the nationality of their host country. Moreover, some Arab countries were reluctant to communicate, or even obtain, information about their Palestinian populations, which was often a politically sensitive issue. Several proposals were made in order to complete the project, which was entrusted to the Palestinian Central Bureau of Statistics, located in Damascus.

The strong cohesion of member states in their solidarity with Palestine led them to react to the signing of the Egyptian-Israeli Peace Treaty. In 1980, the executive secretary received a note from the heads of delegation of all member states except Egypt, stating that "Inasmuch as the government of Egypt has abandoned the will of the Arab nation and has concluded treasonous agreements with the racist Zionist entity . . . the delegations of the following countries wish to record their reservations and their strong objection to the participation of the government of Egypt in the meetings of the Commission."[48] Heated debates continued at the next session, but Egypt's exclusion was not mentioned again in reports after 1982. Again taking a political stand, a joint declaration was issued in 1988. It supported the Palestinian *intifada* as a righteous struggle of a suffering people, requesting from the "international instances" the implementation of the various resolutions in its favor and the respect of inalienable human rights.[49]

Water and environmental problems, including desertification and marine waters, remained major issues for the regional commission and a fundamental challenge for regional cooperation. Because of the size and dimensions of the environmental challenges confronting the Arab countries, ECWA argued for more regional and subregional cooperation in order to pool resources and exchange experience for better environmental resource management and to achieve a better balance between growth and ecology. ECWA stressed that regional bodies were needed in order to coordinate and harmonize legislation, policies, and plans for the protection of the environment in various fields. Environmental concerns were increasingly connected to agricultural and rural development, making integrated approaches to agricultural development more relevant. The commission expressed renewed concern about "the persistent shortfall of domestic food supplies, which has necessitated an alarming growth in food imports."[50] For ECWA, low productivity and low cropping intensity certainly played a role in this increased dependency, but environmental factors and the lack of adapted technology, and thus of research and management planning, were also highly relevant.[51] These considerations led to the organization of the first regional seminar on alternative models of development and lifestyle in the Middle East. ECWA and the United Nations Environment Programme (UNEP) strove to increase awareness of environmental problems in the region, especially with regard to drinking water, seawater, and the fight against desertification. The commission also stressed that labor power that specialized in water-related fields needed to be trained at technical and university levels, within and outside the region. The region lacked not only specialists but also the education and training facilities needed to produce them.

The question of new, renewable, and alternative sources of energy, a major theme of the UN conference held in Nairobi in 1981, boosted consciousness about the exhaustibility of oil resources. It prompted ECWA to encourage the search for alternative and renewable sources of energy with a view toward reducing the dependency and vulnerability of the region. Because the economic crisis threatened the balances and prosperity attained in the 1970s, a review of the viability of current modes of life and prevailing economic models became unavoidable. It necessarily took fragile and endangered natural resources into consideration. In 1987, the UN General Assembly adopted the report by the World Commission on Environment and Development, *Our Common Future*.[52] The emphasis this report put on the concept of sustainable development helped make the environment a priority for the regional

commission, which, in turn, urged all its member countries to develop policies consistent with this concept.

Facing the Mounting Economic Crisis

In the 1980s, the main factor hindering economic development and trade
in the region was the persistence of weak oil prices. They began to fall after
1981, then to collapse in 1986, when the export price index fell to 50 percent
below its 1985 level and more than 40 percent below that of 1980. Thus, the
revenues of the oil-exporting countries, and to an extent of the region as a
whole, were gradually reduced: Between 1980 and 1986, Arab oil revenues fell
by three-quarters with devastating effects on the "indirect income" of governments and households, not to mention cutbacks in intraregional and international financial transfers. The recession in the Gulf states spread to all
countries of the region through the reduction of trade and aid, and the repatriation of foreign currency by emigrant workers in the high-income countries. Thus, all countries in the region saw their revenues fall and domestic
sectors of production were unable to cushion the drop in per-capita incomes.

Moreover, the external debt of the region increased considerably, reaching
a total of US$153 billion in 1990. An increasing proportion of the diminished
oil revenue had to be used to reduce budget deficits and foreign debt. For
some countries, such as Egypt, Jordan, Syria, and Yemen, the situation was
critical. By depriving them of precious foreign exchange, debt servicing absorbed development resources and undermined their capacity to invest and
to cope with their rapid demographic growth. The recession also had an impact on the monetary situation, and there were more frequent currency de-
valuations after 1987.

Economic growth was seriously reduced from the early 1980s, and the economic crisis only deepened with the Gulf War. The ECWA countries which
had averaged growth rates above 10 percent per annum in the 1970s now faced
a dramatic decline to stagnation. Several sectoral trends are worth noting:

• The striking decline in the relative contribution of mining and quarrying (primary oil extraction) to GDP. This sector represented more
  than 55 percent of the combined ECWA countries' GDP in 1980. In
  1990, its contribution was no more than 24 percent. Organization of
  Arab Petroleum Exporting Countries (OAPEC) oil revenues declined
  from about $214 billion in 1980 to $51 billion in 1986.
• The contribution of manufacturing to GDP remained relatively small;
  in the major oil-exporting countries, the increase in the share of the

manufacturing sector was greater than the regional average, while in
Syria it declined.
- The increased contribution of trade and services was linked to a high
dependency on imports, the anti-productive bias of the rentier
economy, and the expansion of the state apparatus.
- The increasing share of the public sector in GDP. In a number of
ECWA countries there was a striking increase in the share of governmental services (including community, social, and personal services),
while in Egypt, Jordan, and Syria it declined.

At the international level, the World Bank and the UN emphasized the need
for new development policies. Support for economic planning, public spending, and industrialization dwindled. In the emerging liberal context, the hyper-
trophy of the state apparatus in most ECWA countries made it a priority to let
other actors play a larger role in the economy. ECWA conveyed the view that
states should be less involved in the management of production and more in
the promotion of private-sector production, providing support services, and
changing the structure of incentives. In the second half of the 1980s, ECWA
stressed the need for structural changes in favor of the productive sectors (manufacturing and agriculture) in order to develop productive (versus distributive)
economies in the long term. It also reiterated its calls for special support for the
two Yemens, which were affected by high rates of child mortality and hunger.

Promoting a Private Sector–Led and Outward-Looking Development

The 1980s recession shook the fragile economic foundations of the countries
in the region. ECWA had pointed out the inherent weakness and vulnerability of the Middle East mode of accumulation. The deteriorating international
economic situation, manifested by falling terms of trade, variable exchange
rates, rising interest rates, a slowing of the exports of developing countries,
and growing protectionism in the industrialized countries, led to severe negative effects on the Arab economies and a high debt burden.

ECWA now paid more attention to the region's integration in the international economy. Market and regional trade development became one of its
central preoccupations. The dominant idea was that structural changes in the
industrial sector implied and required a reconsideration of foreign-trade policies as well as new industrial-export strategies.[53] The diversification of export
markets and the development of new export products could be sought through
joint projects with foreign partners. The participation of the private sector in
the formulation of regional and national trade policies was considered crucial

for sound economic development. One of the challenges was to identify specific market needs and tastes for manufactured imports.

Because of the proximity of ECWA member countries to the European Union market, the commission encouraged them to adhere to existing quality standards and related requirements and to develop more sophisticated marketing techniques. It also stressed the importance of improving the international competitiveness of products and reducing the high dependence of the ECWA region upon world trade. The developed countries absorbed more than half of the exports of the ECWA countries; Japan and the European Union led the way, and the United States quickly increased its share. Two-thirds of imports into Western Asia were coming from industrialized countries, European countries ranking first.

The industrial production of the region was characterized by a narrow range of outputs and low levels of specialization. As a consequence, it imported manufactured goods and exported mainly commodities (oil and agricultural products). ECWA recommended strategies and policies that would aim at developing an integrated and competitive industrial sector capable of exporting manufactured goods, developing the use of advanced technology and associated labor-power skills, and promoting an integrated regional development in this field.[54]

ECWA thought that industry could be best supported through major institutional changes; namely, by questioning the role of the state, which had been overwhelmingly predominant in the region's economies; by promoting the private sector; and by improving trade and marketing. These new directions reflected the efforts of the joint ECWA/UNIDO division to adapt to a changing regional situation as well as the emerging liberal orthodoxy incorporated in structural adjustment reforms.

The joint division thus directed its activities toward private-sector export-development strategies that emphasized the dynamic role of small and medium-sized enterprises (SMEs). Most large productive firms were owned by the state, which dominated the "modern" economic sector. Private economic activities continued to be of the traditional type; they had no banking support and little technical innovation. ECWA argued that SMEs represented the real economic and productive complements to large-scale industries. An entrepreneurial culture needed to be fostered to increase the participation of indigenous entrepreneurs in the national economy. A study of six countries (Jordan, Egypt, Yemen, Syria, Lebanon, and Iraq) stressed that for an enterprise culture to be promoted, potential entrepreneurs had to be helped to identify and establish viable operations.[55] Additionally, financial and other assistance (e.g., training) also needed to be provided to existing entrepreneurs.

Furthermore, the study recommended that the role of the bureaucracy be reduced and administrative procedures simplified. Small-business centers for the collection and dissemination of information should be created and should contribute to establishing a network of information and extension services to small industry. In 1990, this led to the idea of "business incubators" that would help identify the problems facing small businesses in the ECWA countries and make recommendations for improving the existing support systems (legal, training, information, communication, etc.). Four objectives were identified:[56] research about technological innovation in products and services for both domestic and export markets; decentralization of economic activity away from urban areas and mobilization of local resources; promotion of industrial subcontracting via links with large-scale industrial complexes; and integration into the global economy by providing foreign companies with potential entry into the domestic market. Although privatization of existing large publicly owned enterprises was not yet on the agenda, these were attempts to introduce more flexibility and entrepreneurship in the regional economies.

In agriculture, however, planning was still the main focus of the regional commission, although improving both agricultural and productive efficiency was judged to be necessary. Two main directions were taken during this decade: first, to build capacity in the institutions involved in planning and policymaking at the national, subregional, and regional levels and train staff and planners in management and analysis; and second, to "identify the distortions in the agricultural sector, and determine comparative advantages of major crops, as well as recommend alternative policy options for eliminating distortions from agriculture, with the aim of encouraging competitiveness and enhancing efficiency."[57]

Promoting Regional Economic Cooperation

The promotion of markets and the development of trade also had to take intraregional trade into consideration. ECWA was particularly concerned by this issue, not only because regional integration was and remains one of its main endeavors but also because it believed that intensifying trade and reinforcing complementarities were necessary steps to a restructuring of the economies of its member countries and the improvement of their efficiency.[58] In the 1980s, trade among the Arab countries was very limited. Restrictions on international payments, trade, current transfers, or capital movements were largely determined by political considerations, but they constituted obstacles to the growth of a regional market. In value and in volume, the oil countries accounted for the largest share of intraregional trade, especially of exports.

Trade flows within the region consisted mainly of hydrocarbons and of the re-export of manufactured goods to other destinations.

In 1985, ECWA published a study of economic integration that analyzed the relationships between integration, economic development, regional planning, subregional cooperation, the role of the private sector in integration, the identification of intraregional investment opportunities, and the development and integration of financial markets.[59] The publication also described the various regional cooperation bodies and joint ventures and presented regional trade data.

ECWA strongly supported the idea of an Arab common market capable of competing on the world markets, and it was supported—at least verbally— by most of its member states. The commission hoped that the dismantling of intraregional trade barriers would widen the regional market, raise the levels of national productivity and competitiveness, increase domestic and foreign investment, and promote a more efficient allocation of regional investment.

However, according to the study, a change of perception from trade liberalization "to the promotion of co-operation in the field of production" had occurred among member states. This was mainly due to "the limited progress achieved on [the front of trade liberalization and the establishment of a common market] and the new prospects arising from the substantial increase in the overall financial capabilities."[60]

Existing trade and production structures, and behind them political rigidities, hindered trade liberalization; a strong and shared political will would be needed to implement a long-term plan to dismantle barriers to a free flow of capital resources. In fact, it was not until 1998 that an Arab Free Trade Agreement with a ten-year implementation period was introduced.[61] Alone, however, the countries of the region were powerless to alter the level and patterns of production.

ECWA supported this new emphasis on cooperation in production, believing that complementary production structures were a prerequisite for the expansion of regional trade. Trade was the goal and cooperation in production the means, insofar as it could foster exchange and the diversification of exports. At the same time, intraregional trade contributed to export diversification and industrial development; that is, growth and diversification. The weakness of manufacturing and the rentier patterns of economic growth, as reflected in the structure of trade, were the main obstacles to a qualitative change in the regional economy, and cooperation thus constituted a means and an end. In fact, "heavily dependent as they are on exports of primary commodities, export diversification was seen as synonymous with raising the share of manufactures in total exports."[62]

Integration would enlarge the possibilities for economies of scale, a more efficient use of resources, and a higher level of resource utilization. In the field of agriculture and food security, ECWA saw cooperation as more and more necessary: "The lack of regional cooperation results in high import costs and undesirable shortages and waste in various member countries. Lack of appropriate food security arrangements has in several countries led not only to a precarious food situation but has also upset national development efforts through unexpected reallocation of capital resources towards food imports."[63]

ECWA felt that the factors inhibiting effective cooperation were regional economic structures, such as the disparities between national development levels, dependence on outside markets for exports, and the small size of national markets. Differences between national economic policies, competition, and the lack of coordination compounded these difficulties. Furthermore, the commission felt that "what mattered more than the fact that the industrial goods produced by ECWA countries tended to be competitive rather than complementary was that national markets were shielded by tariffs and other forms of protection."[64]

The study's recommendations to overcome these obstacles were congruent with the economic liberal view emerging in the 1980s while taking into account the political dimension of economic policies. It argued that regional integration should not disrupt economic relations with the outside world but should rather rest on the maximization of gains from interaction with world markets. The various external restrictions, notably on the circulation of capital and labor, should be limited as much as political circumstances would allow. However, as the freedom of capital movement is more readily acceptable than that of labor, labor policies should be coordinated and not left entirely to market forces to avoid unpredictable economic, social, and political imbalances. If ECWA countries were to move closer to one another economically, steps toward political harmonization were thus also necessary.

The sensitive issue of food security required regional food security arrangements. The commission studied their feasibility and the development of food and feed-grain policies such as collective imports and regional stocking policies. The prevailing political climate, though, was not conducive to the establishment of regional food security arrangements and so, in the mid-1980s, the commission shifted the emphasis of its food security program toward practical activities and the evaluation of the technical and economic factors and policies affecting food production.[65]

The commission had no choice but to be concerned by regional balances and stability, including their political dimensions. It had limited trust in the capacity of market mechanisms to play an integrative role and feared that the benefits of integration might translate into a "substantial degree of polarization in the development of the integrated area."[66] It insisted on the need to reconcile efficiency and equity. For the commission the answer lay in planning in order to direct resources toward the most promising economic activities and in the coordination of policy measures to ensure an acceptable distribution of costs and benefits among the integrating countries. ECWA went as far as proposing mechanisms for balance-of-payments adjustment, suggesting that the financial resources available in the region be used to deal with the balance-of-payment problems of non–oil-exporting countries. The awareness of the risks arising from inequalities, however, was limited to those between countries. The threat generated by inequalities within countries would not be taken into consideration until the 1990s.

In a rather innovative fashion, the study asserts that grassroots support is necessary for the promotion of regional cooperation and integration, thus ensuring a better chance of survival and permanence for those regional arrangements. It said that a "bottom-up approach, including all sectors of the society, and particularly the private sector and civil society, should be adopted, to minimize dependence on political good will"[67] and to promote efficiency and equity of the integration process. ECWA was thus taking what appears to be a rather balanced position, adapting the global theoretical and doctrinal economic trends of the 1980s to regional circumstances. On one hand, considering political obstacles to regional economic rapprochement, it advocated the diversification of agency and a wider participation in related decisions; but on the other hand, it did not go so far as to dispossess the state of its planning and decision-making functions.

Toward the end of the decade, however, regional cooperation and integration became less important in the commission's ideas. Regional cooperation was now seen from the perspective of globalization and the reinforcement of regional poles, as illustrated, for example, in two studies on trade in services[68] produced against the background of the GATT Uruguay Round.

Labor Markets and Population Movements: A Growing Concern

The 1980s saw the growing interest of ECWA member states in social issues and social development. The mounting economic crisis encouraged awareness of the issues of human capital and the relationship of institutions to social development, but the most prominent issue was that of the relationship of labor markets to population movements, which acted as a mirror for other social concerns. Other changes were taking place, shaking the economic and social basis of the region and bringing social issues more and more into the open: Westernized younger generations were becoming distant from their tribal and religious affiliations, university graduates facing unemployment were putting pressure on state governments, and female elites and groups wanted change. These emerging social forces were concerned about social issues and supported ECWA's proposals. In response, member states requested the adoption of the name Economic and Social Commission for Western Asia in order to bring out clearly the social dimension of development in the activities of the commission.[69] As a result, in 1985, ECWA became ESCWA.

The regional context brought forward the demographic issues. On the one hand, population growth in the region remained one of the world's highest, resulting in heavy pressure on health, education, and housing services and, more generally, on development strategies. One of the commission's challenges, however, arose from the fact that issues of birth control and family size were a problem only for countries where the burden of demography constituted an obstacle to development: The relative positions of countries vis-à-vis population issues could be very different.

Huge migration flows generated major challenges both for sending countries—for example, scarcity of skilled labor and sectoral polarization—and the receiving ones—for example, social cohesiveness and the demographic weight of immigrant groups. In the period 1986–1988, the rate of growth of the non-national population, mainly Arab and Asian, in the six Arab Gulf countries (Bahrain, Kuwait, Oman, Qatar, Saudi Arabia, and the United Arab Emirates) reached its peak. The proportion of expatriates reached 70 percent of the labor force in Kuwait, 81 percent in Qatar, 50 percent in Saudi Arabia, and more than 85 percent in the United Arab Emirates. Indigenous labor forces suffered from a generally low level of educational attainment.

The rentier pattern of labor-market development was also a source of concern, for example, the erosion of the incentive to work by blurring the relationships between efforts and rewards.[70] To respond to concerns of the Gulf States about the growing population of non-nationals, ESCWA endeavored to develop tools for labor-market management and to improve communication between labor-sending and labor-receiving countries (Jordan, Lebanon, and Syria being both).

During the boom period of oil revenues, unemployment diminished considerably in all ESCWA countries; the shortage of labor in the oil-producing countries virtually eliminated unemployment in the region as they absorbed large flows of immigrants. Remittances sent by the workers to their home countries (Jordan, Egypt, Yemen, and the Syrian Arab Republic) totaled $7.1

billion in 1984; in 1986 they were $5 billion. These remittances were equal to two-thirds of the value of exports from these countries and covered half of their trade deficits.[71] However, ESCWA noted that "exporting labor has caused severe shortages of certain types of labor, particularly among skilled workers and technicians, and hence has become detrimental to development efforts in capital-deficit countries."[72] There were debates among the member states about whether migration between countries should be regulated in order to limit their negative impact on the development of both the labor-sending and labor-receiving states and the brain drain within the region and about whether inter-Arab migration should be left free to maintain the cultural, social, and economic interaction between Arab peoples.

Expectations were that Asian labor would increasingly fill the gap between the demand for and supply of labor in the region. In this context, planning seemed of the utmost importance to the commission, although it was virtually non-existent in the ESCWA countries, in order to deal with labor-power bottlenecks, to design immigration policies, to prepare for the education of nationals and the participation of women, and to cope with the brain drain.[73] Programs that were better-documented and better-coordinated, more voluntary, and more finely tuned were required to complement general education policies. In particular, the commission felt that women should be encouraged to participate in the labor force, in spite of the traditional cultural environment, while also attempting to avoid moves that could be perceived as unnecessarily provocative.[74] Women should take their full place in social and economic development; documenting the facts should necessarily constitute the first steps toward that goal.

Finally, the commission turned its attention to the hundreds of thousands of refugees and displaced people, which were mainly the result of the Arab-Israeli conflicts and the Lebanese civil war. These forced migrations created economic uncertainties and fluctuations of employment in the sending countries. In the latter part of the 1980s, some ESCWA countries had to cope with returning migrants, displaced people, and refugees. The end of the Lebanese conflict and then of the Gulf War led many migrants to return to their home countries. This massive population movement was the largest in recent history and had a long-term and disruptive impact on all the countries of the ESCWA region.[75]

The economic crisis also drew attention to the problems of deprivation. One of ESCWA's priorities concerned social welfare programs. They aimed to improve the standard of living of the poorest classes and to integrate these groups in the general development process. The commission's position toward social protection developed considerably in the course of the 1990s.

The 1990s: New International Order, New Regional Perspectives, New Economy

Two major events affected the political context of this decade and prompted the commission to adapt and reinforce its position in favor of regional integration: the Gulf War in 1990–1991, which strengthened the domination of the United States and launched the post–Cold War era in the region, and the attempts to negotiate peace between Israel and its Arab neighbors.[76] Under the umbrella and influence of the United States, a peace process between Israel and its Arab neighbors was initiated immediately after the Gulf War with the ambitious aim of reaching a comprehensive political solution to the Arab-Israeli conflict. A peace treaty was signed in 1994 between Israel and Jordan. However, no feasible solution has been found for the termination of the Israeli occupation of the Palestinian territories, and after September 2001, the situation degenerated into an armed conflict, "the second *intifada.*"

The Strengthening of Regional Integration Efforts in the Context of Globalization

The context of ESCWA's commitment to the development of Palestine had thus changed. In the aftermath of the Gulf War, especially with the start of the peace negotiations between Israel and its Arab neighbors, the different ESCWA divisions were often asked to produce research on the question of Palestine. In 1991, a study was made of unemployment, and in 1992, several documents were published in connection with the International Day of Solidarity with the Palestinian People. Since 1993 and the start of the peace negotiations, ESCWA has been in a better position to undertake many studies on the question of Palestine and the impact of the peace process.

In 1994, following the first Oslo Accords, ESCWA created a new task force to assist the Palestinian people in building their national economy and institutions. It gave due emphasis "to the role of ESCWA in promoting and providing technical assistance and implementation of projects that are within the scope of Palestinian national development."[77] As always, the commitment of ESCWA to the Palestinian issue was both economic and political: As a response to a UN resolution condemning the continued construction of new settlements by Israel, the commission regularly issued and updated reports about the Israeli colonies in the Palestinian territories and the Golan Heights and their impact on the economic and social situation of the Palestinian people. The commission's determination to produce studies and reports is remarkable in a context in which, until the 1990s, little information filtered through on the economic and social conditions of the Palestinian people under occupation.

Regionalization and economic cooperation are tightly linked with a new mode of integration in the global context, and both are narrowly tied to the peace process. As expressed in 1996 by Hazem El-Beblawi, ESCWA executive secretary, the beginning of the peace negotiations between Israel and its Arab neighbors meant that a new vision of regional development could be born and that efforts and resources could be redirected toward sustainable development. In the foreword of a book dedicated to the issue, he writes:

> Peace is a pre-requisite for sustainable development.... In the field of economics, the expected dividends of peace have been publicized to such an extent that it has almost been taken for granted that with peace, everyone will be a winner. This is not true, however, at least not in the short run. Peace will bring major changes to the region, and with it there will emerge new risks and opportunities, losers and winners. However, in all major changes—peace being a case in point—the gains do outweigh the losses.[78]

In the optimistic context of the start of the peace negotiations, the enactment of the peace treaty between Jordan and Israel, the signing of the first agreements between Israel and the Palestinian Authority, the tightening of economic relationships between Israel and some Arab countries (especially Jordan and Egypt), and one year after the economic summit (which was attended by Israeli representatives) took place in Amman, ESCWA organized an expert meeting called The Impact of the Peace Process on Selected Sectors.[79] There, several papers on the Israeli economy were openly presented and discussed. The goals of the organizers were to "consider whether change in trade relations [would] be the major aspect of economic relations between Israel and its neighbors"[80] and to examine

> how mechanisms of industry relations and technology transfer may emerge as well, possibly leading to a new geographical distribution of production, through bilateral arrangements such as subcontracting, joint ventures or the possible relocation of industries from Israel to its neighbors. The newly emerging industrial pattern may result in Israel's concentrating on selected high-technology products (geared mostly to Western markets) and on the transfer of technology, while ESCWA member countries may continue to promote labor-intensive and/ or less technology-intensive industries, such as food processing and textiles and garments.[81]

The lines quoted above express explicit concerns about the economic consequences for ESCWA's members of opening industrial trade relations with

Israel, as did the various contributions to, debates within, and conclusions resulting from the meeting. But the move was extremely courageous on the part of the regional commission, considering that there was considerable opposition to the peace process among member states and within member countries. As the peace process weakened and as tensions were again exacerbated toward the end of the decade, ESCWA's political legitimacy to pursue such a path dwindled.

Parallel to the increased institutionalization of regional economic blocs and the growing importance of globalization, the liberalization of international trade, and the World Trade Organization for the region, the commission was more than ever committed to promoting regional integration:[82]

> As a result of the changing international political and economic context, the world is now characterized by both greater complexity and greater interdependence than ever before. Because individual countries are finding it increasingly difficult to face new demands, regional cooperation is becoming stronger. . . . Today's development issues and problems are of a global nature, [and] their application and solutions can only be sought within the context of the specific circumstances and conditions prevailing in the various regions.[83]

The regional commission was convinced of the necessity to conclude "a series of multilateral trade agreements within the framework of the World Trade Organization and the emergence of a large number of economic blocs [which] will transform the international trading system in the future."[84] The main idea was that the various countries needed to define their position toward international trade negotiations and the creation and development of economic and trade blocs and to coordinate these positions among themselves. ESCWA stressed that privatization, microenterprises, and entrepreneurship were among the core issues for the economies of the region, as were the bias toward a strong state and the concomitant weakness of the private sector in most member states.

The commission also continued to insist on the importance of managing shared resources—particularly water—and improving communications between countries, two issues of real geostrategic importance in the context of the peace negotiations. The preparations for the 1992 United Nations Conference on Environment and Development (the Rio Summit) brought environmental issues to the fore at the beginning of the 1990s after the Gulf War had led to a major ecological disaster in Kuwait. The summit itself provided a further incentive to emphasize the environment.[85] Within the framework of Agenda 21, a list of twenty-one priority measures for the promotion of sustainable development, ESCWA argued for a transitional period which should be used to initiate and stabilize a number of actions to achieve sustainable development and to gradually incorporate environmental considerations into development planning. The commission argued that national environmental action plans, national water strategies, and national land policies should be systematically related to each other and to the overall national development plans of the different sectors of the economy because a multidisciplinary, rather than a sectoral approach, was needed. Two of the most important actions to be taken were the incorporation of environmental objectives into tax, investment, and foreign-trade policies and the establishment of a system of incentives affecting the pricing of goods and services. The regional commission endeavored to convince its member countries of the fact that they could not promote economic development at the expense of the environment and that environmental management should be seen as a means to achieve the wider objectives of sustained economic growth and the alleviation of poverty. The commission proposed the creation of a database which governments could utilize when formulating and implementing investment plans that involved the use of natural resources. It also considered necessary the development of training programs in environment-related areas through the establishment of regional training centers.

After the launching of regional peace negotiations in 1993, the involvement of the commission in environmental issues provided a decisive geostrategic dimension that reinforced its position in favor of regional and subregional cooperation. The need to maintain a multilateral approach in the negotiations and a common front to defend the collective interests of the Arab countries of the Middle East against Israel seemed more crucial in this new context. Meetings of experts were devoted to the questions of institutions (1994), management (1995), and legislation (1996) related to water. The commission stressed that in any major mobilization against desertification, strategically crucial water resources needed to be managed carefully and national and regional plans needed to be formulated.[86]

A committee for transport was established in 1997 on the premise that integrating transport networks would contribute to the acceleration of regional cooperation, considering "the important role of the transport sector in facilitating the flow of goods and passengers among countries and regions, thus contributing to the liberalization of international trade, the promotion of tourism and the growth of exports, particularly within the context of the growing trend towards globalization."[87] The framework of the peace negotiations has also prompted an interest in relating the environment to transportation. A recent ESCWA study on the harmonization of environmental standards in the transport sector in member countries[88] recognized the need to establish national standards and harmonize them at the regional level:

The issue of land transport pollution has not received the attention it deserves in the region, mainly because there is not enough awareness about the future magnitude of the problem, and because of the absence of reliable data on air pollution. It would be more effective and appropriate in this context to take steps that address the major catastrophic problems related to city pollution from vehicle operation. The high rates of population increase in the region and the consequent increase in the number of vehicles, concentrated in already congested urban areas, will ultimately result in pollution crises in the major cities in the region.[89]

Liberalization and Structural Reforms at the Heart of ESCWA's Development Efforts

The 1990s were years of economic adjustment for the countries that were most affected by the economic crisis. A number of ESCWA countries undertook stabilization programs and structural reforms. The Gulf countries followed the recommendations of the International Monetary Fund, as did Lebanon and Syria, while others, particularly Egypt, Jordan, and Yemen, engaged in formal structural adjustment programs. The reform policies have had some positive macroeconomic impacts, such as stabilizing the exchange rates, rebuilding hard-currency reserves, and reducing inflation and budget deficits. But these results were achieved at considerable social cost: increased levels of unemployment and poverty and deterioration in the conditions of the middle class. International organizations and globalization have played an increasing role in the region's major economic decisions.

Overall, the commission has adopted the new dominant economic orthodoxy and defended the neoliberal ideas and theories conveyed by the International Monetary Fund and the World Bank. It views structural adjustment as having three components: the promotion of market-based economies, the opening of markets to foreign trade, and the rationalization of public investment. ESCWA has continued to recommend that its member countries create a stable macroeconomic environment with a strong private sector through the deregulation and commercialization of economic activities, on the one hand, and the privatization of public enterprises, on the other hand, in order to encourage evolution toward a free-market economic system and modern and competitive economic structures.[90] According to conventional wisdom, policies to establish macroeconomic stability must be accompanied by trade reforms and restructuring that will enable the ESCWA economies to fully benefit from their opening to world markets and to better manage their external dependency. In fact, the ESCWA countries remain highly dependent on the markets of the industrial countries and their technological know-how.

The commission's position is that the ESCWA economies must become more open and must maintain either liberal or relatively liberal systems in order to cope with the new era of globalization. The opening up of the domestic economies to world markets is supposed to stimulate national productivity and sustain economic growth. Greater access to foreign direct investment and the latest available technologies, production methods, and management techniques will contribute to improving the technological base. Spending on research and development, which has been very low in the ESCWA countries in comparison with the Western world, is also necessary. ESCWA has recommended close cooperation between the private sector and the universities in order to promote research and development; that is to say, to develop human capital and to invest in human resources. Information technology is one of the fields in which ESCWA is involved.

The reform process should thus enhance the development of domestic capital markets that can increase capital mobility and provide the private sector with the credit needed for effective economic development. In turn, the development of these markets is expected to stimulate domestic savings and investment and attract foreign capital; in other words, to mobilize resources and the supply of capital to companies and firms and thus for privatization. Moreover, stock markets facilitate the inflow of foreign investment in the regional economy, which in turn makes the ESCWA region stronger and more integrated in the world economy. Governments should facilitate access to financial markets for new businesses and encourage the wide distribution of stocks to broaden the ownership base.[91] ESCWA has been very involved in promoting the development of stock markets in the region, which would link it to the privatization process and the increased participation of the private sector. Unfortunately, except for Egypt and Lebanon, stock markets in the region are still in their infancy because of the lack of laws, regulations, and accounting systems.

The commission supports the idea that this process necessarily entails the disengagement of states from direct intervention in the marketplace as both producers and traders. It feels that states should refocus on their fundamental tasks and reduce their involvement in economic activity (particularly in the productive sector) and concentrate on upgrading and developing social services.[92]

Eliminating subsidies to the public-sector enterprises that do not turn a profit, either by privatizing those that can attract private-sector investors or by liquidating non-viable enterprises, would reduce budget deficits. In this theory of privatization, breaking up state-owned monopolies (which will increase competition) and allowing the private sector to buy the assets of selected public-sector enterprises will reduce the current and capital burdens on state budgets, create the necessity for enterprises to adhere to rigorous management constraints, mobilize savings and investments, and energize emerging financial and stock markets.

The commission believes that privatization in the region still lags behind other areas of the world and that it must be a priority of the member states. It feels that privatization should not be seen as the simple transfer of ownership from public to private management but as a comprehensive reform of all those institutions that directly and indirectly affect the behavior of the actors in the marketplace. In a crucial study,[93] ESCWA pointed out the significance of institutions (conventions, norms of behavior, common law, regulations, etc.) and their effects on economic performance. Believing that institutions are the necessary foundations for regional economic cooperation, ESCWA has emphasized the importance of establishing systems for good governance and a legal framework to support better economic and social development.

Because of its high social costs and its demanding reforms, which challenge the legitimacy of political regimes, structural adjustment depends essentially on political feasibility. Often the implementation of unpopular reforms, coupled with some political liberalization, tends to reinforce opposition movements and/or social instability. In the ESCWA region, a highly explosive and strategic area of the world, donors and international organizations fear political and social instability above all. The move toward privatization, market systems, and a reduced role for the state has therefore been slow compared with other regions of the world.

ESCWA shares the now widespread view that there is a relationship between economic and political liberalization and that democratization is a requirement of economic development. Democracy, governance, and civil society have emerged as fields of activity. Overall, political pluralism and liberalization has progressed in the Arab world.[94] However, in the context of wars, extensive militarization, and high levels of defense spending, the possibility for Arab countries to implement responsive governance has been weakened. Control over opposition in civil society and the press is still the rule, and the separation of judicial, legislative, and executive powers is a remarkable exception. The position of the regional commission is that the lack of democracy, demonstrated by the lack of alteration in the political leadership; the high degree of state centralization; the disrespect for human rights; and, to a large extent, the state's domination over civil society are among the main obstacles to development in the Arab world.[95]

A paper presented at an ESCWA conference called on NGOs "to fill the vacuum caused by globalization mechanisms and the new values accompanying them" and noted that such organizations "would permit the re-establishment of new concepts of development that are far from state ideas and hegemony," especially in the framework of "the legitimacy crisis which often plagues governments and states." NGOs have a role both "in transforming the benefiting segments into interest groups" and in "filling the vacuum created by the unorganized withdrawal of the state from social welfare."[96]

The regional commission argues that promoting democracy is strongly linked to the fight against poverty, as poverty reveals the challenges democracy must face and questions the effectiveness of governance. The only efficient way to empower marginalized groups and the poor is to extend democracy. Giving more political power to these groups in civil society will give them more influence on public policy, but this idea is opposed by the governing elites behind a façade of modernization and liberalism. ESCWA has played a significant role in promoting new attitudes without calling into question either the cultural and religious heritage of the region or the Islamic legal framework which prevails in many of its member states.

Unemployment, the Alleviation of Poverty, and the Empowerment of Women

The eradication of poverty was incorporated into the policy programs of most Arab governments in their first decades of existence, particularly in the states where socialists had come to power. It was integrated into development programs, mainly under the heading of land redistribution and the satisfaction of basic needs. During the 1980s, better management of labor markets and the improvement of human capital were expected to be the major factors of social development. The regional commission adopted this approach in its work programs. In the 1990s, global poverty became a major concern of international organizations (particularly the UN), researchers, and governments alike. The issue emerged in the ESCWA region as well, prompted by the objective facts of increasing poverty in several countries after the Gulf War, the spreading economic crisis, and the policy orientations of most international organizations.

ESCWA adopted the orthodox position that because of the political stakes in the overall reform process, the negative social effects of reforms should be compensated for by specific programs. It feels that the pursuit of liberal economic reforms should be accompanied by a strong commitment to increasing employment and alleviating poverty. The commission has produced several studies on the consequences of the economic crisis and structural adjustment, the impact of macroeconomic policies, and the possible effects of specific policies on social development and poverty in the region.[97]

One of the original strands in ESCWA's analysis is that poverty may be caused by a disjuncture between political, economic, social, and cultural policies in a country. The persistence of structural imbalances in an economy leads to an ultimate slowdown in economic growth which, in turn, adversely affects the standard of living. In a basic-needs perspective, the linkages between the availability of food and access to education and health ought to be explored. Thus, ESCWA analyzes agricultural and social-sector policies which have an impact on food security and the development of human resources among the poor. It also deplores the fact that in most countries, spending on education and health has been reduced as a percentage of total capital expenditures while defense spending has continued to increase.

The commission's analysis thus gradually took into account the impact of the region's many wars, the specific features of its integration into the world economy, the situation of women, the problems of corruption and bribery, and the lack of transparency and democracy on the evolution of and the prospects for eradicating poverty. It has developed a comprehensive approach to poverty that integrates political, economic, social, environmental, and cultural dimensions at national and international levels:

> Most countries in the region are still attempting to deal with the general decline in socio-economic conditions, which were greatly exacerbated by the series of crises and finally the Gulf war. . . . These conflicts have drained economic resources, which have been directed to security and armaments instead of development. They have also influenced population distribution, contributing towards urbanization and the primacy of major cities. . . . They have contributed to increasing unemployment and poverty.[98]

ESCWA specifically pointed to the great damage caused to the Iraqi economy by the Gulf War with a view to showing the extent to which the armed attack and the subsequent embargo has contributed to the drastic impoverishment of Iraq's population.

The commission also highlighted the demographic dimension of poverty. It stressed the links between environmental degradation, poverty, and rapid population growth. The International Conference on Population and Development (held in Cairo in 1994) emphasized the relevance of population planning and policy programs in alleviating poverty and providing equitable social services in a framework of sustainable development.[99] It also related poverty to population movements, be they caused by armed conflict or socioeconomic necessity: Millions of people are in a precarious and unstable situation in the ESCWA region.

Several countries have suffered greatly in the aftermath of the Gulf War, which caused considerable unemployment and impoverishment. Unemployment has become a problem most of the ESCWA countries share. Large numbers of returnees are a burden on countries that were relying on migration to solve their unemployment problem. Unemployment also generates political problems: New entrants to the labor force who do not find suitable jobs represent a greater threat to social stability than the long-term unemployed who may have joined the informal sector. After the Gulf crisis, return migration became a major focus of attention. The regional commission has published many studies on the issue of the impact of the Gulf War on migration in the Arab world; it has paid special attention to returning migrants.[100] The Expert Group Meeting on the Absorption of Returnees in the ESCWA Region (held in Amman in 1991) stressed that the long-term absorption of returnees into the national economy must be carried out within a framework of improving the national economy and reducing the rate of unemployment; that is, by pursuing the structural reform and growth policies adopted in the 1980s.[101] However, return migration caused by the Gulf War put a particularly severe strain on Jordan, which could not cope with the sudden and huge influx of migrant laborers and was unable to follow through with its economic adjustment program.[102] Some years after the Gulf War, the problem of absorbing the returnees has decreased because many of them have returned to the Gulf countries, where their relative weight in the local populations has again become a subject of concern. In 1996, the largest proportions of non-nationals in the population were to be found in Kuwait (66 percent), the United Arab Emirates (73 percent), and Qatar (77 percent).

The commission has noted that the rapid growth of education throughout the ESCWA region and the modernization of production and business practices has led to a considerable upgrading in the regional labor force and an increase in the proportion of employees in managerial, technical, and professional occupations. The commission notes that in spite of the fact that the "brain drain may currently account for over 10 percent of university-trained manpower . . . the Arab countries have come to attain levels of manpower development . . . which . . . enable them to build a firm economic/technological base for sustained future development. What is required here are the appropriate policies which would help attain these goals."[103] The relevance of education to labor-market demand still seems to be underestimated in some of the ESCWA countries: Graduates suffer from unemployment and do not have the technical skills their countries need, to the point where countries are forced to import workers in vocational and technical occupations.[104] Vocational training remains a weak point in labor-market management in most of the region's countries.[105] This lack of interest and capacity seems to originate in the pattern and ideological model of development which has predominated in the region: Higher value is attached to white-collar activities and recruitment of workers into public service is seen as a benefit to society, while there is often a weak tradition of manufacturing skills. Imports and exports of labor power have led to underestimates of the need for technical skills in most states.

Human development was adopted as the most suitable way to approach poverty in the regional context, from theoretical, methodological, and comparative standpoints. In 1995, the ESCWA Human Development Section established a "theoretical model combining the percentage of poor and the following variables: the per capita private consumption expenditure, the actual per capita calorie intake as a percentage of the required calorie intake, the total primary enrollment ratio and the infant mortality rate."[106] ESCWA thus formulated its own poverty indicator, based on the UNDP approach, making a contribution to the debate among experts at the international level. It estimated that the poverty rate in Western Asia fell after 1975 but increased again at the end of the 1980s, reaching 27 percent in 1992. The poverty statistics included non-nationals, which was an unusual practice for some Gulf states. The poverty rate as estimated in 1992 is indicated in table 6.1.

Various tracks have been explored in the quest to alleviate poverty, but nevertheless the commission realizes that "a sustained reduction in poverty is a function of the rate and the pattern of growth. The poor need to be beneficiaries of—and indeed partners in—the process of growth. . . . The focus of development planning then is on increasing the participation of the poor through greater availability and ownership of assets—physical, financial and human."[107] In 1999, the commission again affirmed that "economic growth is not social development's magic wand and it does not necessarily ensure it."[108]

The involvement of the commission in the 1995 Copenhagen World Summit for Social Development certainly played a role in propelling the theme of social development forward within the commission and among its member states. The Arab Declaration on Social Development, which was drafted after this first phase of involvement, was the outcome of a preparatory meeting of experts organized by the UN and of a resolution of the Council of Arab Foreign Ministers (Cairo, December 1994).[109] Among other things, it advocated cultural pluralism as a right for all citizens and social groups; it would open societies up to other cultures and give credence to the concept of democracy as part of the Arab heritage (that is, respecting human dignity and freedom of expression). It also took a stand in favor of the democratization of higher

Table 6.1. Poverty Rate in Western Asia, 1992[a]

	Poverty Rate (%)
Western Asia	27
United Arab Emirates*	3
Qatar*	11
Kuwait*	11
Bahrain	15
Oman*	17
Lebanon	19
Saudi Arabia*	21
Egypt	22
Syria	22
Jordan	23
Iraq	45
Yemen	47

Source: *Poverty in Western Asia: A Social Perspective*, Eradicating Poverty
Series no. 1, (document E/ESCWA/SD/1995/8/Rev.1), 16.
*Total population, including the non-nationals.
[a]Proportion of the total people living in poverty, defined according to a
multidimensional indicator based on private consumption, nutritional intake,
enrollment in primary education, and infant mortality rate (ibid., 15).

education and the promotion of equal opportunities for all. The draft said
that eradication of poverty required a just distribution of material and non-
material assets and a reconsideration of taxation policies with a view to
achieving equity. This declaration was to have been included in the documents submitted to the Copenhagen Summit, but its contents were no doubt
too ambitious in terms of the social and economic reforms envisaged, and
it remained at the draft stage without being adopted by the League of Arab
States.

ESCWA believes that high levels of poverty and unemployment lead to
low levels of social integration. Social development should therefore include
both equity and integration—that is, specific policies in favor of refugees,
minority groups, and displaced persons—and not simply a general welfare
system.[110] The 2000–2001 *Survey of Economic and Social Developments in the
ESCWA Region*[111] emphasized building social capital, "a crucial factor" that is
still being neglected by policymakers. Social capital would include "the Arab
family" and NGOs as well as institutional reforms and the emerging role of
local authorities. In this framework, social policies are now being explored
from a holistic integrated perspective with a view that encompasses not only
poverty levels but also gender equality, economic growth, social and cultural
integration, popular participation, and citizenship.

It is mainly in this context of poverty analysis and alleviation that women's issues have been dealt with in recent years. The United Nations Fourth Conference on Women, held in Beijing in September 1995, drew general attention to the fact that poverty was the major problem and obstacle facing the development of women and highlighted the issue of the feminization of poverty. Several studies by the commission have explored this issue and the link between poverty and women's development. They show that, among the poor, women tend to be more marginalized and impoverished than other sectors of society, especially when they are heads of households. One ESCWA study noted that "women in the ESCWA region are still disadvantaged in terms of access to resources, level of education, participation in economic activity and participation in the development process and institutional support activities. Another important issue facing women in the region is the growing conflict between women's public and familial roles."[112] The employment opportunities available to poor women constitute a case in point: Although unemployment rates among the poor are usually much higher than those among the non-poor, the situation is even worse if female unemployment rates are compared.[113] One study also pointed to the specific difficulties women experiences when they are also handicapped.[114]

The work done by ESCWA in connection with the preparation of and follow-up to the 1995 world conference on the status of women has prompted widespread regional debate and the adoption of a number of joint declarations on the question of women. ESCWA believes that "the Arab states should be encouraged to waive out their reservations with regards to the Convention on the Elimination of All Forms of Discrimination against Women."[115] Gender issues have become more central to all types of development discourse. The primary justification is most often moral, based on the ethical value of gender equity/equality. But its economic dimension is clearly mentioned as well:

> Empowering women through education and productive employment and institutionalizing family planning within the context of reproductive health care are key goals for sustainability. The role of women is considered crucial in determining the future demographic structures of society . . . and in harmonizing the relationship between population and sustainable development. Women are essential elements in the participatory development process because of their direct involvement in the development of human resources.[116]

More gender equality and empowerment for women should be central in increasing their productivity and participation in the labor force, raising household incomes, and generating social and demographic changes. NGOs play a vital role in the region, and women can make use of them as pressure groups, as agents of change in social development, as service providers, and as advocates for change with respect to human rights and national legislation.[117]

Employment offers the major opportunity for women to increase their mobility in society. To facilitate their integration in the workforce, educational attainments and other contextual factors such as fertility and health have to be improved. Data has to be gathered on working women, their occupational status, and their living and working conditions.[118] And tools are needed to support individual projects such as microcredit lending, which is expected to contribute significantly to the alleviation of women's poverty and contribute to their empowerment.[119] ESCWA's statistical output is an indispensable reference source for researchers and governments in the region and is contributing to the emergence of a new awareness of the status of women in the region. In its capacity to fuel new and sensitive debates, the commission has a unique position in the regional landscape, even though its scope remains constrained by cultural values and conflicting interests.

ESCWA takes the position that in order to promote the development of women, close attention must be paid to the demographic characteristics, household composition, family life, health conditions, educational attainment, and employment status of women as well as their participation in public life. Information and data are thus necessary for any policy design.[120]

The work done by ESCWA in collecting, processing, and disseminating accurate statistics on the situation of women in the region has helped to clarify phenomena about which little was previously known and to establish rational foundations for policies aimed at improving the status of women. A paper presented at an ESCWA conference in 1999 shows that "the majority of the Arab countries agreed to give highest priority to three domains: women and poverty, women and environment, and women in decision-making positions. . . . All Arab countries established social mechanisms to follow up the implementation of the Beijing resolution."[121]

Concluding Remarks

ESCWA has been operating in an unstable area, where political priorities and cultural sensitivities are translated into various degrees of resistance to the adoption of the ideas it has sought to promote. A gap has existed between the global ideas the regional commission has tried to promote and the prevailing regional ideas and orientations in areas such as the status of women, labor rights, poverty and inequality, and democracy. As economic recession settled in most countries of the region, requiring political and economic change, the circumstances affected not only the perceived relevance of new ideas but also the readiness of governments to alter their standpoints on given issues. As the regional arm of a global entity, the commission has constantly striven to disseminate global ideas by adapting them to the conditions of the region and making them acceptable to its member states while remaining at their service. It has also taken a strong stand in urging the region to become more cohesive and thus to strengthen its position in a context of globalization. The regional commission has acted as an agent of integration and modernization and has contributed to changes in the overall framework of development in the Western Asian region while at the same time attempting to voice and defend some of the main regional positions within the UN system, the Palestinian question certainly being the main one. This role as mediator, which is often difficult to perform, is not without its ambiguities.

The Ideas of the Regional Commission Face Political Constraints

The region in which ESCWA has been operating for over a quarter of a century has undergone deep and radical changes within a short time span: Modes of living, thinking, organizing, and ruling have been dramatically transformed. All the state structures that emerged in the 1950s and 1960s and all the economies of the commission's member states are profoundly different from what they were some decades ago. Continuities are strong, nevertheless, in the social and cultural spheres, and alternatives to dominant Western values often express themselves through conservative ideologies and reactionary movements. ESCWA countries are often defensive against what they perceive to be attempts by external interests to change their identity, values, social organization, and political structures.

ESCWA's ideas have often been considered provocative. Any initiative to reduce population growth is liable to be perceived as a defensive attempt by the West to weaken a potentially threatening Muslim Orient. Suggestions to increase the role of women in development are readily seen as attacks against the integrity of the region's cultural and moral values as well as its social cohesion and balance. Analyses of poverty and especially income distribution, or surveys of migration, which touched the delicate issue of the conditions of labor and life of migrant workers in the rich Gulf countries, are readily considered as threats to the political legitimacy of regimes, Arab solidarity, or the cohesion of oil-exporting countries.

Another factor which has hindered the acceptance of ESCWA's ideas by its member states is that some of them felt that such ideas did not meet their needs at the time the commission was proposing them. Ideas about planning, regionalization, privatization, administrative reforms, population, the labor force, and so forth, failed to raise general interest among the member states when they were first suggested. This was apparently a consequence of the focus of governments on resolving their problems in national contexts, but it was also a result of their heterogeneity and their political differences.

In promoting regional cooperation, ESCWA saw its ideas hindered by multiple conflicts and tensions among the countries of the area. During the twenty-seven years of ESCWA's existence, the Arab-Israeli conflict has brought a political dimension to most of the relationships between this region and the rest of the world, and issues of regional socioeconomic development have been somewhat relegated to the background. The presence of a UN economic commission in the Middle East has been haunted by the problem that the UN's principles of respect for the principles of non-discrimination and universality pose for member states. But this conflict was not the only one, as member states repeatedly found themselves at war or in states of tension with each other. Thus, development, however much it was stressed as a need and a government program, always had to be framed within a highly unfavorable context of insecurity, wars, refugee flows, extensive militarization, and high defense expenditures. ESCWA's efforts to elevate economic and social concerns above geostrategic and political interests, efforts which are still on the agenda today in the framework of the peace negotiations, have often collided with regional and national political priorities.

A large number of issues are considered politically sensitive and thus are only reluctantly admitted to public debate. Disagreement in itself may also be considered politically sensitive. It would seem that the quest for consensus prevents the polarization of ideas in a political arena. One of the main functions of debate is to arrive at a consensus and to separate differences in approach from political or ideological positions. But the stifling of debates that could filter out of the regional commission often reaches the point where ESCWA's official position ends up sharing almost everybody's point of view: that of its member states, of the UN, the World Bank, and so forth.

Constrained by the various differences between its member states, ESCWA often has had no other means of action than to multiply the arenas of participation; that is, by creating committees, discussion groups, expert meetings, and so forth, with the effect of slowing down the process of adopting policy guidelines. The multiplication of intermediary discussions, preparatory meetings, and the like and the apparent necessity for the commission to reach a consensus often leads to a considerable weakening of its original ideas whenever they are liable to provoke polemics. This necessity to present a unified position, at least in official statements, probably explains why recommendations and decisions about multilateral activities and programs frequently fall back on raising awareness, on training, on the production of studies, and on the gathering of information and statistics. That is not to say that these activities are not needed, useful, or relevant; quite the opposite.

When political conditions were unlikely to support regional cooperation and broader visions, another coping strategy the regional commission may have used was to shift the emphasis toward more practical activities and technical assistance at the bilateral level. The fields where ESCWA apparently found sufficient leeway to promote ideas and innovative programs were in those areas that were not considered politically sensitive, such as alternative energies, transport, rural development, or microcredit.

ESCWA has been, and still is, very determined to support institutions that can sustain regional cooperation and stabilize intraregional relationships. In addition to agreements, norms, and common research centers, the commission has made constant efforts to foster a unified position with respect to regional institutions. There again, however, the ideas of the commission have been dominated by political factors. The construction of nation-states, which are crucial for development and for political stability, have contributed to the strengthening of nationalist ideologies and structures, to the point where a regional institution that promotes regional cooperation was unlikely to raise great interest in the past.

Constructing Legitimacy: ESCWA as an Agent of Modernization and Regional Integration

Over time, more and more of ESCWA's innovative ideas have succeeded in achieving some degree of legitimacy among its member states. This has been the result of several interrelated factors. Changes in the discourse at the global level—that is, the rise of a new orthodoxy that the member states could not entirely ignore—have played an important role. This is certainly the case for gender and environmental issues, and even perhaps for the issue of poverty. In the ESCWA region, as in others, for example, few institutional programs can find international support or even acceptance without including gender issues and sensitivity to environmental issues. The policy issues that most states felt compelled to adopt—for example, those concerning international trade or monetary management, participation in the global economic system, or the pressure exerted by international conventions—have also contributed to reinforce governments' international responsibility and accountability. Changes within the countries themselves, in particular those linked to the coming of age of a new generation whose members have often been trained in the West as technocrats, have also played a role in the legitimization of challenging issues and the emergence of a more liberal spirit.

Changes of attitude also owe a great deal to the increasingly felt relevance of some of the issues brought forward by ESCWA, issues which may have seemed out of context some years before but which have finally reached the official agenda of member states. This was the case for population issues and the issues of food security, water, and industrial diversification. In a way, reality caught up with ESCWA's prescient ideas, generating a greater interest from the countries of the region. The regional commission also somewhat succeeded in becoming a forum for Arab intellectuals who were willing to discuss new ideas.

ESCWA felt that part of its mission was to encourage the redistribution of resources at the regional level and to direct them toward investment for development. In the first decade, the focus on infrastructure, agriculture, and industry answered the obvious needs of most of these countries, but these issues were also the dominant focus of development economics at the time. They also matched the modernizing needs of the member states, and progress in these three areas was one of their main routes to gaining legitimacy. This rested on a vision of development which took the nation as the basic unit but also viewed international exchanges as a way to foster national development. In its first years of existence, ESCWA served mainly the poorer countries of its region, as shown by the origin of its secretaries-general and personnel, the commission's attendance at various meetings, and the main recipients of its services.[122] This was a time when the dominant visions of the developing world emphasized the negative effects of dependency, the unequal relationships between center and periphery, and the need for the Third World to unite to defend its needs and rights.

Progressively, however, as "Third-Worldism" ceased to dominate the development discourse, mainly because of the realization of the profound diversity of the "underdeveloped" world and the toll of structural adjustment, and as the economic crisis started to spread to the oil-producing as well as the poorer Western Asian countries, the Gulf Co-operation Council member states became more ready to participate in ESCWA. As it gained experience, the commission accumulated solid technical expertise on a number of issues, which helped to convince the member states of its usefulness. These human resources play a crucial role in ESCWA's growing capacity to play an innovative and supportive role in selected fields, such as poverty and migration, the environment, technology, water, and population. In the 1980s, as problems arose in the region as well as globalization in its present form, a stronger normative element entered the commission's vision of regional development.

In the 1990s, the global scene imposed itself more and more in setting the goals of regional development, in reinforcing the necessity of strengthening intraregional ties for better integration into the global economy, and in deciding what tools can be used to that end. The more interventionist character of international organizations, rules, and conventions gives the commission more leeway to formulate analyses that infringe upon the political sphere and "politically sensitive" issues, such as democracy, civil society, the empowerment of women, corruption, and so forth. ESCWA's activities and ideas display a constant effort to transform a set of differentiated countries, with various and often contradictory interests, into a functional entity. The concepts and ideas it has used to promote development have always been linked to the struggle for peace and to the fight against the region's centrifugal tendencies in order to reinforce interdependency, cooperation, harmonization, and so forth among its member countries. During the numerous political crises in the region, ESCWA has provided a platform for discussion; after the Gulf War, for example, it served as a forum to diffuse tensions between the two camps.[123]

In its conferences, seminars, training programs, and technical services, ESCWA has always attempted to bring together divergent interests and to create forums for the exchange and debate of ideas, including forums with regional multilateral organizations and affiliates or branches of the UN system. Its most outstanding effort may be the dissemination of information and statistics, the promotion of harmonized national accounting and statistical systems, and the publication of reports and studies.

ESCWA's handling of the issue of Palestine has legitimized it among its member states and has united them behind the commission's position. It has steadfastly striven for Palestine to be given full status as a member state, it has testified to the effects of the Israeli colonization on Palestinian economic and social conditions, and it has carried the voice of the Middle Eastern states to the international powers. On this extremely sensitive issue, which is central to the region but raises many points of view, the commission took a clearly practical stand and drew attention to socioeconomic issues rather than limiting itself to the political question.

The Regional Commission between Ideas and Ideologies

Overall, ESCWA has tended to be a follower rather than an innovator of ideas at the world level: Its main inspirations have generally come from either theories and currents of thought developed in other regions of the world or from global conferences. In general, the ideas ESCWA propagates are not ambitious theories, new conceptualizations, or daring analyses. For a quarter of a century, ESCWA has been a mirror of the evolution of international ideas regarding development. In its first years, it was strongly influenced by the NIEO, but in the 1980s, and even more so in the 1990s, it became more pragmatic and very open to the approaches of the UNDP, which it mixed with elements of neoliberal orthodoxy. However, the commission has been very innovative within its region, striving to bring in new and progressive ideas, values, and concepts; to initiate debates; to move the frontiers of some issues considered to be sensitive; and to challenge existing convictions.

The underlying drive behind the commission's activities and ideas has been to influence the policies and attitudes of its member states toward rational decision-making—basically understood as Western rationality. In most of its ideas, ESCWA has implicitly taken the position that politics should be at the service of the economic interests of nations and of the region as a whole and that ideologies ought to be stifled if they interfere with dominant—although often contradictory—political interests and the course of globalization. Until the end of the 1990s, ESCWA did not take into account culture or identity, although they play an important role in the region. In spite of their apparent neutrality, their "self-evident" and technocratic nature, most of ESCWA's activities and discourses are not devoid of ideas. Indeed, this may well be the form that ideas tend to take when economic and social affairs are handled in the absence of open and verbally expressed political competition: They become apparently depoliticized and pragmatic, denying that the dominant orthodoxy represents only one of the possible paths to development and that other alternatives exist. More than ideas, then, the regional commission certainly conveys an ideology.

Like its equivalents in other regions, ESCWA has a double face: It is both the emissary of the UN system in the region and a regional body composed of and supported by its member states. It thus plays a double function of mediation: It acts as a vector of globalization, modernization, and integration for the region it represents in the UN system and it acts as a spokesman for its region's major interests, including its resistance to exogenous ideas, when they come into conflict with global doctrines.

In the context of a historical trend toward the domination of Western values over regionally embedded cultures, the ideas carried by the regional commission in the economic field have generally been vehicles for the dissemination of a global model of capitalist development, based on and legitimized by the ideologies of modernization and the homogenization of the modes of thinking, living, consuming, organizing, and ruling. Conflict remains, however, between contradictory ideologies, and this may be reinforced by the fact that the rapid integration of the world economy, in addition to economic growth, has also brought about environmental degradation and increasing inequalities in the Western Asian region.

In the social field, debates organized by the regional commission have tended to challenge the validity of global prescriptions for the specific context of the region and to attempt to genuinely adapt, reconceptualize, and reappropriate resources. In a context in which the clash of civilizations, the affirmation of cultural differences, and a questioning of a single path proposed by globalization are emerging everywhere in the world, it may that ESCWA's ideas will play a more innovative and integrative function in the future.

Appendix: Evolution of Membership in the Five UN Regional Commissions, 1947–2000

	ECE Members	ESCAP Members	ECLAC Members	ECA Members	ESCWA Members
1947 *March 28*	Belgium Byelorussian SSR[1] Czechoslovakia[2] Denmark France Greece Iceland Luxembourg The Netherlands Norway Poland Sweden Turkey Ukrainian SSR[4] United Kingdom United States USSR[3] Socialist Federal Republic of Yugoslavia[5]	Australia China France India The Netherlands The Philippines Thailand United Kingdom United States USSR[3]			
Later		Pakistan			

(continued)

Appendix (continued)

ECE Members	ESCAP Members	ECLAC Members	ECA Members	ESCWA Members
1948				
February 25				
		Argentina		
		Bolivia		
		Brazil		
		Chile		
		Colombia		
		Costa Rica		
		Cuba		
		Dominican Republic		
		Ecuador		
		El Salvador		
		France		
		Guatemala		
		Haiti		
		Honduras		
		Mexico		
		The Netherlands		
		Nicaragua		
		Panama		
		Paraguay		
		Peru		
		United Kingdom		
		United States		
		Uruguay		
		Venezuela		

	ECE Members	ESCAP Members	ECLAC Members	ECA Members	ESCWA Members
Later		Burma[6]			
		New Zealand			
1950		Indonesia[7]			
1953		Afghanistan			
1954		Cambodia			
		Ceylon[8]			
		Japan			
		Republic of Korea			
		Vietnam			
1955	Albania	Laos			
	Austria	Nepal			
	Bulgaria				
	Finland				
	Hungary				
	Ireland				
	Italy				
	Portugal				
	Romania				
	Spain				
1956	Federal Republic of Germany				
1957		Federation of Malaya[9]			
1958					
April 29				Belgium[10]	
				Ethiopia	
				France[11]	

(continued)

Appendix (continued)

	ECE Members	ESCAP Members	ECLAC Members	ECA Members	ESCWA Members
				Ghana	
				Italy[12]	
				Liberia	
				Libya	
				Morocco	
				Portugal[13]	
				Spain[14]	
				Sudan	
				Tunisia	
				Union of South Africa[15]	
				United Arab Republic[16]	
				United Kingdom[17]	
Later					
1960	Cyprus	Iran		Guinea	
				Cameroon	
				Central African Republic	
				Chad	
				Democratic Republic of the Congo	
				Republic of Congo	
				Côte d'Ivoire	
				Dahomey[18]	
				Gabon	
				Madagascar	
				Mali	
				Niger	

	ECE Members	ESCAP Members	ECLAC Members	ECA Members	ESCWA Members
1961		Mongolia	Canada	Nigeria Senegal Somalia Togo Upper Volta[19]	
1962				Mauritania Sierra Leone Tanganyika[21] Algeria Burundi Rwanda Uganda	
1963		Malaysia[9] Western Samoa	Jamaica Trinidad and Tobago	Kenya Zanzibar[21]	
1964	Malta			Malawi United Republic of Tanzania[21] Zambia	
1965		Singapore		Gambia	
1966			Guyana	Botswana Lesotho	
1967			Barbados	Equatorial Guinea Mauritius Swaziland	
1971		Nauru Tonga			

(continued)

Appendix (continued)

	ECE Members	ESCAP Members	ECLAC Members	ECA Members	ESCWA Members
1972	Switzerland[20]	Bhutan			
1973	Canada German Democratic Republic[22]	Bangladesh			
August 9					Bahrain Democratic Yemen[23] Iraq Jordan Kuwait Lebanon Oman Qatar Saudi Arabia Syrian Arab Republic[24] United Arab Emirates Yemen[23]
1975			Bahamas Grenada	Cape Verde Comoros Guinea-Bissau Mozambique Sao Tomé and Principe	
1976		Maldives Papua New Guinea	Suriname		
1977				Angola Djibouti Seychelles	Egypt[25] Palestine

	ECE Members	ESCAP Members	ECLAC Members	ECA Members	ESCWA Members
1978			Dominica		
1979		Fiji	Saint Lucia		
1980		Solomon Islands	Spain Saint Vincent and the Grenadines	Zimbabwe	
1981			Antigua and Barbuda Belize		
1983			Saint Kitts and Nevis		
1984		Vanuatu	Portugal		
1985		Brunei Darussalam Tuvalu			
1990	Germany[22] Liechtenstein		Italy	Namibia	
1991	Estonia Israel[26] Latvia Lithuania Russian Federation[3]	Kiribati			
1992	Belarus[1] Bosnia and Herzegovina[5, 28] Croatia[5, 30] Republic of Moldova Slovenia[5, 32] Ukraine[4]	Azerbaijan[27] Kazakhstan[29] Democratic People's Republic of Korea Kyrgyzstan[31] Marshall Islands Micronesia Tajikistan[33] Turkmenistan[34] Uzbekistan[35]			

(continued)

Appendix (continued)

	ECE Members	ESCAP Members	ECLAC Members	ECA Members	ESCWA Members
1993	Andorra			Eritrea	
	Armenia[36]				
	Azerbaijan				
	Czech Republic[2]				
	Georgia[37]				
	Kyrgyzstan				
	The former Yugoslav Republic of Macedonia[5, 38]				
	Monaco				
	San Marino				
	Slovakia[2]				
	Turkmenistan				
	Uzbekistan				
1994	Kazakhstan	Armenia			
	Tajikistan				
1996		Palau			
		Turkey			
2000	Yugoslavia[5, 39]	Georgia			

Source: United Nations, *Yearbook of the United Nations* (New York: United Nations, various issues).

Notes: The table includes all the members of the five regional commissions until 2000. More information about some countries can be found in the footnotes.

Three regional commissions have changed their name since their creation: ECAFE (Economic Commission for Asia and the Far East) became ESCAP (Economic Commission for Asia and the Pacific) by ECOSOC resolution 1895 (LVII) on August 1, 1974. ECLA (Economic Commission for Latin America) became ECLAC (Economic Commission for Latin America and the Caribbean) by ECOSOC resolution 1984/67 on July 27, 1984. ECWA (Economic Commission for Western Asia) became ESCWA (Economic and Social Commission for Western Asia) by ECOSOC resolution 1985/69 on July 26, 1985.

[1]The Byelorussian Soviet Socialist Republic, whose name changed to Belarus on September 19, 1991.

[2]The former Czechoslovakia. Czechoslovakia was an original member of the UN from October 24, 1945. The Czech and Slovak Federal Republic ceased to exist on December 31, 1992, and the Czech Republic and the Slovak Republic, as successor states, were admitted as individual member states on January 19, 1993.

[3]The Union of Soviet Socialist Republics, which was an original member of the UN from October 24, 1945. In a letter dated December 24, 1991, the president of the Russian Federation informed the Secretary-General that the membership of the Soviet Union in the Security Council and all other UN organs was being continued by the Russian Federation with the support of the eleven member countries of the Commonwealth of Independent States.

[4]The former Ukrainian Soviet Socialist Republic, which was an original member of the UN from October 24, 1945. Its name changed to Ukraine on August 24, 1991.

[5]The Socialist Federal Republic of Yugoslavia was an original member of the UN, the charter having been signed on its behalf on June 26, 1945 and ratified October 19, 1945, until its dissolution following the establishment and subsequent admission as new members of Bosnia and Herzegovina, the Republic of Croatia, the Republic of Slovenia, the former Yugoslav Republic of Macedonia, and the Federal Republic of Yugos avia. See footnotes 28, 30, 32, 38, and 39.

[6]Former Burma, whose name changed to Myanmar in 1989.

[7]By letter of January 20, 1965, Indonesia announced its decision to withdraw from the UN "at this stage and under the present circumstances." By telegram of September 19, 1966, it announced its decision "to resume full cooperation with the UN and to resume participation in its activities." On September 28, 1966, the General Assembly took note of this decision and the president invited representatives of Indonesia to take seats in the General Assembly.

[8]Data refers to former Ceylon, which became a member of the commission ir 1954 before it joined the UN on December 14, 1955. In 1972 Ceylon changed its name to Sri Lanka.

[9]The former Federation of Malaya, which joined the UN on September 17, 1957. On September 16, 1963, its name was changed to Malaysia, following its admission to the new federation of Singapore, Sabah (North Borneo), and Sarawak. Singapore became an independent state on August 9, 1965, and a member of the UN on September 21, 1965.

[10]Belgium has been an observer state of the ECA since 1963.

[11]France became an associate member of the ECA in 1963 and renounced this status in 1978.

[12]Italy ceased to be an ECA member on July 1, 1960, when the former trust territory of Somalila nd under Italian administration (together with Somaliland Protectorate) became the independent state of Somalia.

[13]Excluded from the ECA since 1963.

[14]Spain became an associate member of the ECA in 1963 and renounced this status in 1976.

[15]On July 30, 1963, the council decided that South Africa should not take part in the work of the commission until conditions for constructive cooperation were restored by a change in South Africa's racial policy. Readmitted to membership by the Economic and Social Council on July 29, 1994 (dec. 1994/303).

[16]The former United Arab Republic was established on February 21, 1958, by a union of Egypt and Syria and continued as a single member of the UN. The same year it also became an ECA member state. On October 13, 1961, Syria, having resumed its status as an independent state, resumed its separate membership in the UN and the United Arab Republic continued as a member of the UN. On September 2, 1971, the United Arab Republic changed its name to the Arab Republic of Egypt.

[17]The United Kingdom became an associate member of the ECA in 1963 and renounced this status in 1976.

[18]Dahomey, whose name changed to Benin in 1975.

[19]Upper Volta, whose name changed to Burkina Faso in 1984.

[20]Switzerland was admitted to the ECE on March 24, 1972, and to the UN on September 10, 2002.

[21]Tanganyika was admitted to the UN and to the ECA on December 14, 1961; Zanzibar was admitted on December 16, 1963. Following ratification of the Articles of Union between Tanganyika and Zanzibar on April 26, 1964, the two states became a single member: the United Republic of Tanganyika and Zanzibar. Its name changed to the United Republic of Tanzania on November 1, 1964.

(continued)

Appendix (continued)

[22]The Federal Republic of Germany and the German Democratic Republic were admitted to membership in the UN on September 18, 1973. Through the accession of the German Democratic Republic to the Federal Republic of Germany, effective from October 3, 1990, the two German states united to form one sovereign state. Before their union, the Federal Republic of Germany had been an ECE member since February 21, 1956, pursuant to ECOSOC resolution 594 (XX).

[23]Yemen was admitted to membership of the UN on September 30, 1947, and Democratic Yemen on December 14, 1967; both of them were original ECWA members. On May 22, 1990, the two countries merged and have since been represented as one member with the name Yemen.

[24]Egypt and Syria were original members of the UN from October 24, 1945. Following a plebiscite on February 21, 1958, the United Arab Republic was established by a union of Egypt and Syria and continued as a single member. On October 13, 1961, Syria, having resumed its status as an independent state, resumed its separate membership of the UN.

[25]On September 2, 1971, the United Arab Republic changed its name to the Arab Republic of Egypt.

[26]Admitted to the ECE on a temporary basis; Israel has been a member of the UN since May 11, 1949.

[27]Azerbaijan has been a member of the UN since March 9, 1992.

[28]The Republic of Bosnia and Herzegovina was admitted as a member of the UN by General Assembly resolution A/RES/46/237 of May 22, 1992.

[29]Kazakhstan has been a member of the UN since March 9, 1992.

[30]The Republic of Croatia was admitted as a member of the UN by General Assembly resolution A/RES/46/238 of May 22, 1992.

[31]Kyrgyzstan has been a member of the UN since March 2, 1992.

[32]The Republic of Slovenia was admitted as a member of the UN by General Assembly resolution A/RES/46/236 of May 22, 1992.

[33]Tajikistan has been a member of the UN since March 9, 1992.

[34]Turkmenistan has been a member of the UN since March 2, 1992.

[35]Uzbekistan has been a member of the UN since March 2, 1992.

[36]Armenia has been a member of the UN since March 2, 1992.

[37]Georgia has been a member of the UN since July 31, 1992.

[38]By resolution A/RES/47/225 of April 8, 1993, the General Assembly decided to admit as a member of the UN the state provisionally referred to for all purposes within the UN as "The former Yugoslav Republic of Macedonia" pending settlement of the difference that had arisen over its name.

[39]The Federal Republic of Yugoslavia was admitted as a member of the UN by General Assembly resolution A/RES/1955/12 of November 1, 2000.

Notes

Foreword

1. Midge Decter, *The Liberated Woman and Other Americans: On Being a Woman, on Being a Liberal, on Being an American* (New York: Coward, McGann & Geoghegan, 1971), 135.

1. Unity and Diversity of Development

1. Donald Winch, *Economics and Policy: An Historical Study* (London: Hodder and Stoughton, 1969), 19.

2. The exceptions tend to be bodies such as the IMF, which have large research divisions and publish academic-style journals with authored contributions by staff members and outside academics. UN staff members also contribute to academic journals, often on the basis of work initially presented in UN publications, but citations will of course refer to the individual authors and not to their organization.

3. See Seamus Heaney, *The Redress of Poetry: Oxford Lectures* (London: Faber and Faber, 1995): "If we know in what way society is unbalanced, we must do what we can to add weight to the lighter scale (3)." Perhaps there is a parallel here with the important role of a "loyal opposition" in a healthy parliamentary democracy.

4. *The Times,* London, 28 August 1978.

5. Palamadai Lokanathan, *ECAFE: The Economic Parliament of Asia,* Bound Pamphlets on the United Nations, no. 87 (Madras: Madras Diocesan Press, 1954).

6. Louis Emmerij, Richard Jolly, and Thomas G. Weiss, eds., *Ahead of the Curve? UN Ideas and Global Challenges* (Bloomington: Indiana University Press, 2001).

7. Translation of the definition given in Paul Robert, *Dictionnaire Alphabétique et Analogique de la Langue Francaise* (Paris: Société du Nouveau Littré, 1976).

8. The wording here is from UN, *Terms of Reference and Rules of Procedure of the Economic Commission for Europe* (Geneva: United Nations, 1993), 1.

9. Richard Jolly, Louis Emmerij, Dharam Ghai, and Frédéric Lapeyre, eds., *Contributions of the United Nations to Development Theory and Practice* (Bloomington: Indiana University Press, forthcoming).

10. "Restructuring of the Economic and Social Sectors of the United Nations System" (General Assembly Resolution 33/202), 29 January 1979, part V, 131.

11. "Restructuring of the Economic and Social Sectors of the United Nations System" (General Assembly Resolution 32/197), 20 December 1977, annex, part IV, para. 20, 124.

12. Not everyone will agree with this. There is the alternative thesis that research and operational activities mutually reinforce each other. See chapter 4, note 36.

13. One of the conclusions and recommendations of the 1994 OIOS report on ECE was that technical assistance be limited to help for countries to implement policies adopted and agreements reached in intergovernmental bodies.

14. In Asia the Allies had not established mechanisms to deal with transport, energy, and services as in Europe. The ECE inherited these "E-organizations," as they were called, which gave it an immediate legitimacy. ECAFE had to start sectoral cooperation from scratch.

15. UNDP, *Human Development Report 2001* (New York and Oxford: Oxford University Press, 2001); World Bank, *World Development Indicators 2002* (Washington, D.C.: World Bank, 2002).

16. WTO, *International Trade Statistics 2001* (Geneva: WTO, 2001), chapter 3.

17. UN, *Yearbook of the United Nations* (New York: United Nations, various issues); UN, *Statistical Yearbook* (New York: United Nations, various issues).

18. Freedom House, "Freedom in the World 2002: The Democratic Gap," available at <http://www.freedomhouse.org/research/freeworld/2002/essay2002.pdf>, accessed 14 April 2003.

19. UNESCO, *Statistical Yearbook 1999* (Paris: UNESCO and Bernan Press, 1999), available at <http://www.uis.unesco.org/en/stats/statistics/yearbook/YBIndexNew.htm>, accessed 14 April 2003.

20. This story is elaborated in another volume of the UNIHP series. See Michael Ward, *Quantifying the World* (Bloomington: Indiana University Press, forthcoming).

21. In their study *La régionalisation dans les organisations universelles: les commissions économiques régionales des Nations Unies* (Bordeaux: Société Française pour le Droit International, 20–22 May 1976), Jean Siotis and Melvyn Fagen noted that "its first executive secretary, the Indian economist P. Lokanathan, deliberately modeled its organization on the ECE, not only because he considered it a pioneer and personally appreciated the qualities of Gunnar Myrdal, but also because it was necessary to rebuild the region and, above all, to replace the UNRRA, whose functions were coming to an end" (13). Translated from the French by the author.

22. Gunnar Myrdal, "Preface," in ECE, *A Survey of the Economic Situation and Prospects of Europe* (Geneva: United Nations, 1948), iii.

23. ECAFE, *Economic Survey of Asia and the Far East, 1947* (Shanghai: United Nations, 1948), chapter 1, 1.

24. "Foreword," in ECA, *Economic Survey of Africa*, vol. II, *North African Sub-Region* (New York: United Nations, 1968).

25. Gunnar Myrdal, "Preface," in ECE, *Economic Survey of Europe in 1949* (Geneva: United Nations, 1950).

26. ECAFE, *Economic Survey of Asia and the Far East, 1947,* chapters 1 and 2.

27. John Toye and Richard Toye, *International Trade, Finance, and Development* (Bloomington: Indiana University Press, forthcoming).

28. ECLA, *Economic Survey of Latin America, 1949* (New York: United Nations Department of Economic Affairs, 1951), 14.

29. Ibid., 20.

30. Ha-Joon Chang, *Kicking Away the Ladder: Development Strategy in Historical Perspective* (London: Anthem Press, 2002).

31. Myrdal, "Preface."

32. See Toye and Toye, *International Trade, Finance, and Development.*

33. ECE, *Economic Survey of Europe in 1989–1990,* 16; and ECE, *Economic Bulletin for Europe,* no. 46 (1994): 7.

34. Oral history interview of Samir Amin (30 April 2002), 20–22, in the Oral History Collection of the United Nations Intellectual History Project, The Graduate Center, The City University of New York.

35. ECAFE, *Economic Survey of Asia and the Far East, 1950* (New York: United Nations, 1951), chapter 6.

36. Quoted by Paul Rayment, in "Washington Consensus or Development Economics?" *Third World Economics,* no. 274 (1–15 February 2002): 11–14.

37. Ibid.

38. William Lazonick, "Public and Corporate Governance: The Institutional Foundations of the Market Economy," *Economic Survey of Europe,* 2001, no. 2 (New York and Geneva: United Nations, 2001): 59–72.

39. Isebill Grunh, *Regionalism Reconsidered: The Economic Commission for Africa* (Boulder, Colo.: Westview Press, 1979), 113.

40. Robert W. Gregg, "The UN Regional Economic Commissions and Integration in the Underdeveloped Regions," *International Organization* 20, no. 2 (Spring 1966): 213.

41. Grunh, *Regionalism Reconsidered.*

42. The debate took place in Bangkok in February 2000 between Secretary-General Rubens Ricupero of UNCTAD and Executive Secretaries K. Y. Amoako, ECA; Yves Berthelot, ECE; José Antonio Ocampo, ECLAC; Adrianus Moy, ESCAP; and Hazem El Beblawi, ESCWA.

43. ECE, "Globalization: A European Perspective," a note prepared for the interactive debate with heads of the UN regional commissions at the UNCTAD X meeting, Bangkok, 12–19 February 2000, 10. This note was written by Paul Rayment, who was then the director of the Economic Analysis Division of ECE.

44. ESCAP, "Asia-Pacific Perspective on Globalization and Development: Trade, Investment and Finance," report prepared for the interactive debate with heads of the UN regional commissions at the UNCTAD X meeting, Bangkok, 12–19 February 2000, 19.

45. ECE, *Globalization: A European Perspective,* 12.

46. Ibid., 4.

47. Henry Kissinger, "Globalization and the World Order," a lecture delivered at Trinity College, Dublin, 12 October 1999, quoted in ECE, *Globalization: A European Perspective*, 4.

48. Toye and Toye, *International Trade, Finance, and Development*.

49. A more balanced view on the development decades is found in Jolly et al., *Contributions of the United Nations to Development Theory and Practice*.

50. Oral history interview of Margaret Snyder (28 March 2002), 31, in the Oral History Collection of the United Nations Intellectual History Project, The Graduate Center, The City University of New York.

51. Ibid., 42.

52. The ECE secretariat lagged behind for gender statistics and was authorized, thanks to the lobbying of NGOs, to mobilize some resources on the condition of women in the region only in preparation for the Beijing Conference.

53. ECOSOC, *Regional Co-operation Study on Regional Structures, Report of the Secretary-General*, 15 November 1972, *Economic and Social Council Official Records*, 54th Session (E/5127). Hereafter *Economic and Social Council Official Records* will be *ESCOR*.

54. The Commission on Global Governance, Our Global Neighbourhood (Oxford: Oxford University Press, 1995), 291.

55. Ibid., 286–291.

2. The ECE

1. Eric Hobsbawm, *Age of Extremes: The Short Twentieth Century* (London: Michael Joseph, 1999), 49.

2. Mark Mazower, *Dark Continent: Europe's Twentieth Century* (London: Penguin Books, 1999), 217.

3. Ibid., 26.

4. M. Djilas, *Conversations with Stalin*, translated from Serbo-Croatian by Michael B. Petrovich (New York: Harcourt, Brace & World, 1962), quoted by Mazower, *Dark Continent*, 217.

5. On the contrast between the Western European economies in the aftermath of WWII and those of Eastern Europe after the revolutions of 1989, see ECE, "Economic Reform in the East: A Framework for Western Support," in *Economic Survey of Europe in 1989–1990* (New York and Geneva: United Nations, 1990), 5–26.

6. ECE, *Economic Survey of Europe since the War* (Geneva: United Nations, 1953).

7. On the importance of gradualism as a key feature of democratic systems, see Richard Kozul-Wright and Paul Rayment, "The Institutional Hiatus in Economies in Transition and Its Policy Consequences," *Cambridge Journal of Economics* 21, no. 5 (September 1997): 641–661.

8. See, e.g., Barry Eichengreen, "Institutions and Economic Growth: Europe after World War II," in Nicholas Crafts and Gianni Toniolo, eds., *Economic Growth in Europe since 1945* (Cambridge: Cambridge University Press, 1996), 38–72.

9. André Newburg, "The Changing Roles of the Bretton Woods Institutions: The Evolving Concept of Constitutionality," in Mario Giovanoli, ed., *International Monetary Law: Issues for the New Millennium* (Oxford: Oxford University Press, 2000), 82.

10. Joseph Gold, "Transformation of the International Monetary Fund," *Columbia Journal of Transnational Law*, no. 20 (1981): 227, quoted by André Newburg, "The Changing Roles," 82.

11. John Maynard Keynes, *The Economic Consequences of the Peace* (London: Macmillan, 1919).

12. ECE, *Economic Survey of Europe in 1948* (Geneva: United Nations, 1949), 5.

13. David Thompson, *Europe since Napoleon* (London: Penguin Books, 1966), 17.

14. These came into effective operation, respectively, in May, June, and September 1945.

15. ECE, *A Survey of the Economic Situation and Prospects of Europe* (Geneva: United Nations, 1948), 3.

16. "Reconstruction of Countries Members of the United Nations Devastated by War," General Assembly draft resolution proposed by the delegation of Poland, Report of the General Committee, document A/22, in *General Assembly Official Records*, 1st Part of the 1st Session, 22nd Meeting, 2 February 1946, 331. Hereafter *General Assembly Official Records* will be referred to as *GAOR*.

17. A detailed account of the negotiations from February 1946 to their conclusion in March 1947 is given in Václav Kostelecký, *The United Nations Economic Commission for Europe: The Beginning of a History* (Göteborg: Graphic Systems AB, 1989). Kostelecký joined the ECE secretariat in 1948 and became one of Gunnar Myrdal's closest collaborators. This section draws on his account.

18. "Discussion of Draft Terms of Reference for the Economic Commission for Europe," in *ESCOR*, 1947, 4th session, 80th meeting, 27 March 1947, point 58, 199.

19. "Reconstruction of Countries Members of the United Nations Devastated by War," 335.

20. Ibid.

21. Ibid., 336.

22. ECOSOC, *Report of the Economic and Employment Commission*, in *ESCOR*, 1st year, 2nd session (E/40), annex 5, 249.

23. ECE, "Economic Reform in the East: A Framework for Western Support," in *Economic Survey of Europe in 1989–1990* (New York: United Nations, 1990), 5–26; ECE, "Postwar Reconstruction and Development in South East Europe," *Economic Survey of Europe*, 1999, no. 2 (New York and Geneva: United Nations, 1999), 1–21.

24. "Discussion of Draft Terms of Reference for the Economic Commission for Europe," point 58, 198.

25. ECOSOC, "Amendments Proposed by the Delegation of Soviet Socialist Republics to the Draft Terms of Reference Submitted by the Committee on the Economic Commission for Europe," (E/363/Rev.1/Add.1), 22 March 1947.

26. ECOSOC, "Committee on the Economic Commission for Europe: Draft Terms of Reference for the Economic Commission for Europe," (E/363/Rev.1), 20 March 1947.

27. Albania, Austria, Bulgaria, Finland, Hungary, Ireland, Italy, Portugal, Romania, and Switzerland. Switzerland continued to participate in accordance with Article 8 of the commission's terms of reference until it joined the UN in 2002.

28. "Resolution Concerning the Voting Rights of European Nations Not Members of the United Nations," ECE Resolution 1 (VII) (E/ECE/150), March 1952, 20.

29. "Admission of New Members to the United Nations," General Assembly Resolution 995 (X), 14 December 1955.

30. ECE, *ECE, The First Ten Years, 1947–1957* (Geneva: United Nations, 1957), II-3.

31. Kostelecký, *The United Nations Economic Commission for Europe*, 25. More precisely, the idea of an ECE appears to have come from Walt W. Rostow:

Early in 1946, while serving in the German-Austrian Economic Division of the Department of State, I concluded that if the United States restricted itself to housekeeping tasks within the American zone of Germany and of Berlin, it would ultimately preside over the split of Germany and Europe and harm the prospects for a sound European recovery. Consequently I wrote a memorandum advocating a concerted approach to the continent's economic and security problems, which envisaged an offer of assistance to all of Europe, including the U.S.S.R., and was committed to proceeding in the West if Moscow's response was negative. This plan gained the backing of top State Department officials including Dean Acheson and William Clayton, but James Byrnes, then Secretary of State, rejected it, preferring to present the Russians with a proposal for a 50-year disarmament of Germany. Byrnes did, however, endorse the proposed Economic Commission for Europe, in which I later served within the office of the executive secretary.

Walt W. Rostow, "Lessons of the Plan: Looking Forward to the Next Century," *Foreign Affairs* (May/June 1997): 206.

32. Gunnar Myrdal, "Twenty Years of the United Nations Economic Commission for Europe," *International Organization* 22, no. 3 (Summer 1968): 617–628; and Kostelecký, *The United Nations Economic Commission for Europe*, 37.

33. Peter Pulzer, *German Politics 1945–1995* (Oxford: Oxford University Press, 1995), 40.

34. Charles Bohlen, *Witness to History 1929–1969* (New York: W.W. Norton & Co., 1973), 262–263.

35. Kostelecký, *The United Nations Economic Commission for Europe*, 89.

36. Ibid., 89–90.

37. Note from H. J. B. Lintott of the Board of Trade to Roger Stevens at the Foreign Office, PRO-UE 4615/168/53, quoted by Kostelecký, *The United Nations Economic Commission for Europe*, 108.

38. ECE, *Report of the 1st Session (2–14 May 1947) and the 2nd Session (5–16 July 1947)* (E/451), 18 July 1947, 9.

39. Paul R. Porter, "From the Morgenthau Plan to the Marshall Plan and NATO," in Constantine C. Menges, *The Marshall Plan from Those Who Made It Succeed*

(Lanham, Md.: University Press of America, 1999). Porter played an important role in the early development of the ECE and was the U.S. resident representative to the ECE from 1947 to 1949.

40. See his interview "Jetzt größere Schritte," *Der Spiegel*, no. 43, 23 October 1989, 26.

41. W. W. Rostow, "A Commission Europe Should Revive," *International Herald Tribune*, 20 April 1990.

42. Gunnar Myrdal, "The Research Work of the Secretariat of the Economic Commission for Europe," in *25 Economic Essays in Honor of Erik Lindahl* (Stockholm: Economisk Tidsknift, 1956), 267–293.

43. In addition, the secretariat published the *Economic Bulletin for Europe*, which appeared variously on a quarterly, trimestrial, biannual, and annual basis. Due to cuts in the resources available for economic analysis, publication of the *Bulletin* ended with the 1997 issue. To simplify the text, general references to the *Survey* should be taken to refer to the *Bulletin* as well.

44. "Economic Commission for Europe. Statement Made by the Executive Secretary on Item 8 of the Agenda" (ECOSOC document E/ECE/49), 15 July 1947. It is interesting to note that at the fifty-sixth session of the ECE in 2001, the ambassador of the Czech Republic praised the most recent *Surveys* for their quality, adding that "the *Survey* provides us with a large quantity of internationally comparable data and comments of high quality. . . . With its *Survey* ECE continues to be in a unique position among international institutions providing economic analysis. We appreciate . . . the fact that the *Survey* generalizes from current experience, gives warnings as to possible risks in future economic developments, and recommends measures designed to avoid them." Remarks taken from a copy of the Czech ambassador's speech, which was circulated at the 56th session of the commission.

45. Myrdal, "The Research Work," 270.

46. One of the unfortunate economies resulting from the UN's recurrent financial crises of the 1980s and 1990s was the elimination of full reports of the proceedings of the commission and other intergovernmental bodies. One may thus read what conclusions were reached but not how they were reached or what the positions of individual governments were. The words quoted above were taken from a sound tape of the proceedings, but whether such tapes will survive as well as paper for future researchers is open to question.

47. Myrdal, "The Research Work," 270.

48. The pressure was resisted and the study was published in ECE, *Economic Bulletin for Europe* 42/90 (New York: United Nations, 1991), 109–129.

49. ECE, "Enlarging the EU to the Transition Economies," *Economic Bulletin for Europe* 48 (New York: United Nations, 1996), 7–18.

50. Donald J. Johnston, "Japanese Decision to Allow OECD Report's Release Commendable," *Financial Times*, London, 24 January 1997, 14.

51. Thus, issues of adjustment and the distribution of its costs are often brushed aside with questions such as "Are you in favour of the market economy or of central planning, of free trade or autarky?"

52. Arthur I. Bloomfield, "Review of ECE's *Economic Survey of Europe since the War* and OEEC's *Europe—The Way Ahead*," *The American Economic Review* XLIV, no. 1 (March 1954): 194–197.

53. An Ipsos-Reid World Poll of 20,000 adults in thirty-nine countries in the summer of 2000 asked respondents to rate their level of confidence in six global institutions—the IMF, the UN, the United States, the World Bank, the WTO, and multinational corporations—for addressing the economic problems of countries around the world. The UN "was the institution that overall seemed to engender the most confidence" and multinational corporations the least. "Ipsos–Reid Press Release," 28 September 2000, available at <http://www.ipsos-reid.com/media/ dsp_displaypr_cdn.cfm?id_to_view=1080>, accessed 14 April 2003.

54. In Central Europe, extensive extracts from the *Survey* were translated and published in the official press, and economists in countries such as Poland and Hungary could easily obtain copies of the complete text from their contacts in Geneva. Danuta Hübner, a former executive secretary, and now Poland's minister for European integration, recalls the publications of the ECE as "a breath of fresh air, the only reliable source of information on the economic situation in other Eastern European countries and USSR, making it possible to compare the situation in Poland with that in those other countries." She went on to say that "ECE publications and meetings played a role, indeed difficult to measure, in the evolution of ideas in the East and, at the end of the 1980s, in the acceptance that dramatic reforms were necessary." Conversation with Yves Berthelot, 2001.

55. Stanislaw Raczkowski, "A Few Thoughts on the Occasion of the United Nations' 50th Anniversary," in Marie Lavigne, ed., *Almanac(h)* (Pau: Lavigne, 1997), 134.

56. "Economic Commission for Europe," ECOSOC Resolution 36 (IV), 28 March 1947, in *ESCOR*, 4th session, 1967, 11.

57. ECOSOC, "Presentation by Executive Secretary Gunnar Myrdal," in *Report of the First and Second Sessions of the Economic Commission for Europe* (ECOSOC document E/451), 18 July 1947.

58. ECE, *ECE, The First Ten Years, 1947–1957*, I-6.

59. Ibid.

60. Ibid.

61. "Opening Statement by the Executive Secretary to the Eleventh Session of the Economic Commission for Europe" (ECE document E/ECE/242), 11th session, 5 April 1956, 5–6.

62. Robert Marjolin was a French economist, professor, and civil servant who served as Secretary-General of the Organization for European Economic Cooperation between 1948 and 1955. Hal B. Lary, an American economist, was deputy director to Nicholas Kaldor and then director of the UNECE's Research and Planning Division in the late 1940s and 1950s. His work on international economic issues, including the U.S. balance of payments and foreign investment, was well known. His book *Imports of Manufactures from Less Developed Countries* (New York: National Bureau of Economic

Research, 1968) had considerable influence on subsequent empirical work on changes in international trade patterns.

63. Willy Brandt, the future German chancellor, however, refused Myrdal's invitation to become the ECE's first press officer. Willy Brandt, "Jetzt größere Schritte," 26. Evgenyi Chossudovsky was a career UN official from the 1940s to his retirement, an exception for a Soviet national. He later served in UNCTAD and was involved with UNITAR.

64. Kostelecký, *The United Nations Economic Commission for Europe*, 85.

65. In addition to those in *The New Palgrave Dictionary of Economics and Law*, we may note Hal B. Lary, Tibor Barna, Ester Boserup, Mogens Boserup, Karl Brunner, Albert Kervyn, Robert Neild, Rudolf Nötel, and Alfred Maizels.

66. Myrdal had published a warning concerning postwar optimism at the end of 1944: *Varning för fredsoptimism* (Stockholm: Albert Bonniers, 1944), translated only into German, *Warnung vor Friedensoptimismus* (Zurich and New York: Europa Verlag, 1945). Kaldor had contributed an extensive appendix to the 1944 Beveridge Report; see Nicholas Kaldor, "The Quantitative Aspects of the Full Employment Problem in Britain," in William H. Beveridge, *Full Employment in a Free Society* (London: Allen & Unwin, 1944), 344–401.

67. Gunnar Myrdal, *An American Dilemma* (New York: Harper & Brothers, 1944).

68. *Ex ante* and *ex poste* are concepts that were developed by Gunnar Myrdal in his *Monetary Equilibrium* (London: W. Hodge & Company, 1939) in order to introduce expectations and uncertainty into macroeconomic analysis. *Ex ante* refers to the anticipated or desired level of an activity or variable and *ex post* to the actual outcome. If expectations are not fulfilled, *ex ante* and *ex post* will not be equal and a process of dynamic adjustment will occur.

69. J. Herbert Furth, "Review of Economic Survey of Europe in 1949," *The American Economic Review* XL, no. 5 (1950): 954–957.

70. A. K. Cairncross, "Review of the *Economic Survey of Europe in 1951*," *The Economic Journal* 62 (December 1952): 945–950.

71. See Furth, "Review of *Economic Survey of Europe in 1949*"; and Furth, "Review of the *Economic Surveys of Europe in 1950 and 1951*," *The American Economic Review* XLIII, no. 4 (1952): 652–657.

72. ECE, *A Survey of the Economic Situation and Prospects of Europe*, 83.

73. ECE, *Economic Survey of Europe since the War*, 134.

74. Myrdal can also be credited with raising the general issue of the deleterious effects of corruption when it was still a taboo subject for most Western governments and development economists. See "Introduction to the Papers from the ECE Spring Seminar, May 2001," in ECE, *Economic Survey of Europe*, 2001, no. 2 (New York and Geneva: United Nations, 2001), 58.

75. ECE, *Economic Survey of Europe since the War*, 135.

76. Ibid., 133.

77. Ibid., 137.

78. Ibid., 135.

79. Ibid., 138.

80. Ibid., 135.

81. Ibid., 139.

82. Ibid., 140.

83. ECE, *A Survey of the Economic Situation and Prospects of Europe*, 105.

84. Ibid., 107.

85. ECE, *Fifteen Years of Activity of the Economic Commission for Europe, 1947–1962* (Geneva: United Nations, 1964), 97.

86. ECE, *ECE, The First Ten Years, 1947–1957*, XI-1.

87. Ibid., XI-2.

88. Ibid.

89. Ibid., XI-3.

90. Ibid., XI-4.

91. Per Olaf Kjellström, "Coal: The Way Ahead," in ECE, *The Economic Commission for Europe: A General Appraisal* (Geneva: ECE, 2 May 1957), IV-2.

92. Ibid., IV-1.

93. ECE, *International Classification of Hard Coals by Type* (Geneva: United Nations, 1956).

94. Ibid., IV-3.

95. Paul Levert, "Les problèmes de transport en Europe," in ECE, *The Economic Commission for Europe*, IX-20.

96. Jean Monnet (1888–1979), "the father of Europe," was a visionary economist who conceived many of the ideas and initiatives for the unification of Europe, such as the French proposal for the creation of the European Coal and Steel Community. This new institution placed French and German coal and steel production under a common high authority and was also open to other European countries. This plan was presented as the "Schuman Plan," named after the foreign minister Robert Schuman (1886–1963), who officially proposed it in May 1950.

97. Myrdal, "The Research Work," xi–6.

98. Egon Glesinger, "The ECE Timber Committee: The First Ten Years," in ECE, *A General Appraisal*, VI-7.

99. See ECE, *The European Housing Problem: A Preliminary Survey* (Geneva: United Nations, October 1949).

100. ECE, *European Rent Policies* (Geneva: United Nations, August 1953).

101. Barrie Davis, "The Conference of European Statisticians," in Myrdal, "The Research Work," X-5.

102. Ibid., XI-11–12.

103. Conference for Security and Co-operation in Europe, *Final Act*, Helsinki, 1 August 1975, 1, available at <http://www.osce.org/docs/english/1990-1999/summits/helfa75e.htm>, accessed 10 April 2003.

104. Ronald Reagan, "Remarks at the Annual Convention of the National Association of Evangelicals," Orlando, Florida, 8 March 1983, available at <http://www.ronaldreagan.com/sp_6.html>, accessed 10 April 2003.

105. "The President's News Conference," 29 January 1981, available at <http://www.reagan.utexas.edu/resource/speeches/1981/12981b.htm>, accessed 14 April 2003.

106. Gorbachev's speech to the Supreme Soviet, 27 November 1985, quoted in Jean-Jacques Roche, *Chronologies des relations internationales de 1945 à nos jours* (Paris: Montchrestien, 1997), 62. Translated from the French by the authors.

107. Dusan Sidjanski, *The ECE in the Age of Change* (New York and Geneva: United Nations, 1998): "Through a conjunction of circumstances or a convergence of ideas, the Monnet method came to coincide with the mechanism of integration as formulated in the functionalist theory supplemented by the *spillover* concept of Ernst B. Haas, according to which integration initiated in one sector necessitates integration in related sectors, thereby producing a cumulative effect. . . . This mechanism provides an effective response to real needs" (5).

108. The Senior Economic Advisers held two first meetings in 1961 and 1962 before their group was established as a permanent subsidiary body of the Economic Commission for Europe. In 1997, this body was dismantled.

109. Ingvar Svennilson, *Growth and Stagnation in the European Economy* (Geneva: ECE, 1954), 3.

110. Ibid., 6.

111. Ibid., 7.

112. Ibid., 41.

113. Edward F. Denison, *The Sources of Economic Growth in the United States and the Alternatives Before Us*, Supplementary Paper no. 13 (New York: Committee for Economic Development, 1962).

114. ECE, *Economic Survey of Europe in 1961*, Part 2, *Some Factors in Economic Growth in Europe during the 1950s* (Geneva: United Nations, 1964), chapter 5, 23.

115. Ibid., chapter 7, 11.

116. Ibid., chapter 7, 12.

117. See ECE, *Structure and Change in European Industry* (New York: United Nations, 1977), especially chapter 3.

118. "Is European Monetary Policy Too Cautious?" in ECE, *Economic Survey of Europe*, 2001, no. 1 (New York and Geneva: United Nations, 2001), chapter 1, 7.

119. ECE, *Incomes in Postwar Europe: A Study of Policies, Growth, and Distribution* (Geneva: United Nations, 1967), chapter 1, 1.

120. Ibid., introduction, 1.

121. Ibid., chapter 1, 5.

122. Ibid.

123. Ibid., chapter 1, 6.

124. Ibid., 7.

125. Ibid., 15.

126. Ibid.

127. "Some Key Problems of Economic Development in Southern Europe," in ECE, *Economic Survey of Europe in 1953* (Geneva: United Nations, 1954), chapter 15, 184.

128. Ibid., chapter 12, 161.

129. Ibid., 177.

130. Ibid., 180.

131. Ibid., 181.

132. ECE, *Economic Bulletin for Europe* 23, no. 2 (1972): 75.

133. ECE, *Economic Survey of Europe in 1953*, 203.

134. Ibid., 183.

135. Ibid.

136. Ibid., 188.

137. Ibid., 191.

138. Marie Lavigne, *The Economics of Transition* (London: Macmillan, 1995), 32.

139. Ibid., 13.

140. ECE, *ECE, 1947–1987* (New York: United Nations, 1987), 34.

141. Christopher Freeman, *A Commentary on the Papers and Discussion in Policies and Means of Promoting Technical Progress* (New York: United Nations, 1968), 3.

142. Ibid., 5.

143. Ibid., 6.

144. Jacques Baudot, "Methods of Analysing the Qualitative Aspects of Long Term Economic and Social Development," in ECE, *Long-Term Planning: Papers Presented to the Seventh Meeting of Senior Economic Advisers to ECE Governments* (New York: United Nations, 1971), 33.

145. Ibid., 34.

146. Michael Bacharach, "The State of Mathematical Economic Planning in the Countries of the Economic Commission for Europe," in *Macro-Economic Models for Planning and Policy-Making* (Geneva: ECE, 1967), 10.

147. ECE, *Factors and Conditions of Long-Term Growth* (New York: United Nations, 1974), 1–9.

148. ECE, *Employment, Income Distribution and Consumption* (New York: United Nations, 1979), 4.

149. ECE, *Distribution Policies in Long-Term Development Planning*, papers presented to the Tenth Session of the Senior Economic Advisers to ECE governments (New York: United Nations, 1973).

150. ECE, *Employment, Income Distribution and Consumption*, 8.

151. "The Development of Foreign Trade," ECE Resolution 3 (XXIV), 23 April 1969 (E/ECE/747).

152. ECE, *Analytical Report on the State of Intra-European Trade* (New York: United Nations, 1970).

153. Ibid., 135.

154. Ibid.

155. ECE, *Economic Survey of Europe in 1956* (Geneva: United Nations, 1957), chapters 5 and 6.

156. Myrdal, "The Research Work," XI-1.

157. ECE, *The Price of Oil in Western Europe* (Geneva: United Nations, 1955), 23.

158. Ibid., 37.

159. Ibid., 39.

160. Ibid., quoted on cover page.

161. ECE, *Energy Problems in Europe,* progress report by the executive secretary (document E/ECE/768), 25th session, 10 February 1970, para. 6, 2.

162. ECE, *A Comparative Study of Some National Energy Models* (document ST/ECE/ENERGY/13), 22 March 1972, 17.

163. ECE, *The Commission's Activities and Implementation of Priorities, Report by the Executive Secretary* (document E/ECE/817), 31 January 1972, 28.

164. ECE, *Preliminary Report on Some Medium- and Long-Term Problems of the Energy Economy in the ECE Region, Prepared by the Executive Secretary* (document E/ECE/847), 14 March 1973, 22.

165. Ibid., chapter 3, "Conclusions—Present Needs, Opportunities for Further Co-operation amongst Governments of the ECE Region," 54–57.

166. *Annual Report, 28 April 1972–18 May 1973* (ECOSOC document E/ECE/855).

167. Conversation with Jacques Royer on 22 February 2001.

168. ECE, *Annual Report, 28 April 1972–18 May 1973,* 66.

169. ECE, *ECE Symposium on Problems Relating to the Environment* (New York: United Nations, 1971), 2.

170. Ibid., 12.

171. Ibid., 3.

172. Ibid.

173. Ibid., 4.

174. Karin Bäckstrand, "What Can Nature Withstand? Science, Politics and Discourses in Trans-boundary Air Pollution" (Ph.D. dissertation, Lund University, 2000); and ECE, *Economic Survey for Europe in 1989–1990* (New York: United Nations, 1990), 23.

175. Bäckstrand, "What Can Nature Withstand?"

176. ECE, *Economic Survey for Europe in 1989–1990,* 5.

177. ECE, "Productivity Trends in Eastern Europe and the Soviet Union, 1970–1983," in *Economic Survey of Europe in 1985–1986* (New York: United Nations, 1986), 209–223.

178. ECE, "Economic Reform in the East: A Framework for Western Support," in *Economic Survey of Europe in 1989–1990* (New York: United Nations, 1990), 5.

179. ECE, *Economic Survey for Europe in 1989–1990,* 13.

180. Ibid., 14–15.

181. Ibid., 23.

182. Ibid., 24.

183. Adam Smith, *The Wealth of Nations,* vol. 1 (Oxford: R. H. Campbell & A. S. Skinner, 1976), 469. Ricardo recommended a similarly gradualist approach to England's removal of restrictions on the import of corn after 1846.

184. ECE, *Economic Survey for Europe in 1989–1990,* 16.

185. Address by Jacques Delors to the European Parliament, "Presenting the Commission's Programme for 1990," EC Press Release, Strasbourg, 17 January 1990.

186. Louis Emmerij, Richard Jolly, and Thomas G. Weiss, eds., *Ahead of the Curve? UN Ideas and Global Challenges* (Bloomington: Indiana University Press, 2001), 162.

187. It cannot be argued that the *Survey* of 1989–1990 passed unnoticed, even though its print run is small compared with the publications of other international institutions. It was the first international report on Eastern Europe to appear after the 1989 revolutions and it received massive coverage in the press, radio, and TV. It was a lead item on the main evening news program in France on channel TF1, its star presenter, Patrick Poivre d'Arvor, holding up the *Survey* before the camera so everyone could see what this obscure publication looked like.

188. This assumption was also behind the metaphors which decorated the rhetoric of the early 1990s: "jump starts," "big bangs," and, of course, "shock therapy" were all prescribed as quick fixes for setting up a market economy. It seems to have escaped those who employed it that a "jump start," for example, applies to a mechanism when all the constituent parts are in place and in working order and just one spark of energy is required to get the whole system working. This was not an illuminating or helpful metaphor for a transition economy.

189. "The IMF's first big mistake [with Russia] was its failure to support the reformers of the early 1990s with something akin to a Marshall Plan. . . . Because a Marshall Plan was not forthcoming, Russia today looks more like Germany after the Treaty of Versailles. Of course, blaming the IMF for this historic failure misses the point: The US had no vision. Neither did its partners in Europe. It was too easy to believe that the move to a market economy would solve the problem itself." Rudiger Dornbusch, "Nothing Left to Steal," *Financial Times*, London, 23 September 1999.

190. Thus, German Foreign Affairs Minister Hans-Dietrich Genscher thought that a plan for Russia along the lines suggested by the ECE was desirable, and in the United Kingdom's House of Commons, Leader of the Opposition Mr. Kinnock asked the prime minister whether he accepted "the need for a co-ordinated international aid and support programme—a modern Marshall Plan—as proposed by the United Nations Economic Commission for Europe? Does he not agree that such a programme, amongst other things, would establish an effective linkage between western support for economic development and the response from the newly independent States in terms of schedules for comprehensive, verifiable and quicker disarmament?" *House of Commons, Hansard Debates for 3 February 1992* (London: HMSO, 1992), column 23.

191. Dame Margaret Anstee, Under-Secretary-General and director-general of the UN office in Geneva in the early 1990s, was deeply concerned by what she judged to be a very dangerous situation in the countries of the former Soviet Union. She tried to persuade Mr. Boutros Boutros-Ghali that the UN should take a lead in persuading the West to make a major effort to help them with a very difficult transition, but "he did not think that this was a very good idea at all." Ms. Anstee was unaware at the time that the ECE secretariat in Geneva shared her concerns and was publishing detailed arguments in support of the line she was proposing to the Secretary-General. See Oral History Interview of Dame Margaret Joan Anstee (14 December 2000), 133–134, in the

Oral History Collection of the United Nations Intellectual History Project, the Graduate Center, The City University of New York.

192. ECE staff members frequently wonder whether their senior colleagues in New York are aware of what they do or even where they are. In his recent book *Peacemonger* (London: John Murray, 2002), Marrack Goulding complains about the limited research capacity that was available to back him up when he was the UN's Under-Secretary-General for Special Political Affairs and describes his unease at his "poor understanding of the deeper currents of Yugoslavia's ethnic politics at this time" (299). But in the ECE there were people in the Economic Analysis Division with a deep knowledge of the Balkans and an extensive network of contacts, within and outside the region, who could be called on to fill the gaps in their knowledge of the region. It would have been a simple matter to organize briefings or set up some specialist seminars for Goulding and his colleagues, as in fact the ECE did on the subject of reconstruction after the Kosovo bombing—but no one in New York thought of asking.

The experience of both Mr. Goulding and of Ms. Anstee (see note 191) suggests that senior staff at UN headquarters are not very familiar with the substantive work being done in other parts of the UN system. Considerable resources are devoted to maintaining central control and "coordination" of budgetary and personnel issues, many of them of quite minor importance, and there are perennial calls to eliminate "duplication," but very little is given to understanding the underlying substance of the various programs and how they might relate to one another. The experience of Mr. Goulding shows that not only is direct analytical support for important activities such as peacekeeping woefully inadequate but that no one at headquarters appears to know how to compensate for such gaps by drawing on the expertise and the specialized country and regional knowledge available in the wider UN system.

193. Anyway, those who never go against the stream will never end up ahead of the curve.

194. ECE, *Economic Bulletin for Europe* 48 (1996): 13.

195. Ibid., 18.

196. ECE, *Economic Survey for Europe,* 1999, no. 2 (New York and Geneva: United Nations, 1999), 1–21.

197. ECE, *Economic Survey for Europe,* 2000, no. 1 (New York and Geneva: United Nations, 2000), chapter 5, 155–187.

198. Ibid., 171.

199. Ibid., 183.

200. To mention just a few points at random: The *Survey* was well ahead of other international institutions in warning (*Survey* of 1990–1991) that the recovery from the 1990 downturn would take much longer than the official forecasts were assessing because of the adjustment to high levels of personal and corporate debt in the United States and parts of Western Europe. The *Survey*'s prediction of a severe recession after 1989 and the rapid collapse of intra-CMEA trade and the slow return of the transition economies to economic growth were fairly accurate, although they were not popular. Its

forecast of the likely date of the EU enlargement appears to have the most accurate of all the assessments that were made in the mid-1990s.

201. ECE, *A Survey of the Economic Situation and Prospects of Europe,* 27–30.

202. ECE, "Aspects of Intra-industry Trade in Manufactures," in *Economic Survey of Europe in 1987–1988* (New York: United Nations, 1988), 87–92.

203. For example, the estimation of consistent exchange rates among the former CMEA members to obtain better estimates of the value of their international trade.

204. ECE, "Wage Rigidity in Western Europe and North America," in *Economic Survey of Europe in 1987–1988* (New York: United Nations, 1988), 99–113.

205. ECE, "Globalization: A European Perspective," Geneva, UN/ECE, January 2000. Paper prepared by the UN ECE secretariat for the Interactive Debate with Heads of UN Regional Commissions at the UNCTAD X Meeting in Bangkok, February 2000, available at <http://www.unece.org/ead/misc/UnctadX.pdf>, accessed 4 March 2003.

206. In 1986, M. Etienne Dreyfous (a director of Air France), chairman of an ECE working party on trade facilitation, estimated that the agreement on an international standard for the electronic exchange of trade documentation, reached in September 1986, would save some $600 from the production cost of a passenger car (U.S. Mission, *Daily Bulletin,* 26 September 1986). On the basis of passenger-car production in 1982, a recession year, that would imply a cost reduction of some $16 billion for the global car industry. The U.S. industry alone would have gained $3 billion, which compares with the UN's regular budget at the time (which the U.S. was seeking to cut) of $700 million and with the $13.4 million that the Plaza Group was trying to "save" from the UN budget by abolishing the ECE. More recent estimates of the potential reduction in the transaction costs of international trade go to more than $4 trillion (although the basis for the estimate is not clear). UNECE Press Release, ECE/Trade/01/04, Geneva, 3 April 2001.

207. ECE, "Europe: A Common Will," Conference Room Paper submitted to the fifty-fourth session of the commission, May 1999.

3. From ECAFE to ESCAP

I must thank Mr. Sivsankaran Thampi, special assistant to the executive secretary of the commission, for his invaluable assistance, based on his deep knowledge of ESCAP over a long period. He will not necessarily agree with many of my interpretations of ESCAP history. Mr. Janintr of the ESCAP library has been a source of valuable information. Mr. C. Suriyakumaran, who was a senior official in ECAFE in the late 1960s and early 1970s, working closely with U Nyun, provided me with many interesting insights into those early days. I am grateful for their assistance.

1. The acronym ECAFE is used when describing events prior to 1974, and ESCAP is used for subsequent years. Whenever the commission's entire history is considered, it is referred to as either ECAFE/ESCAP or as "the regional commission" or as "the commission."

2. David Wightman, *Towards Economic Cooperation in Asia: The United Nations Economic Commission for Asia and the Far East,* published for the Carnegie Endowment for International Peace (New Haven, Conn., and London: Yale University Press, 1963). This book provides a comprehensive history of ECAFE's early years.

3. ECAFE, *ECAFE: Twenty Years of Progress* (New York: United Nations, 1967).

4. ECAFE, *ECAFE: 25 Years* (New York: United Nations, 1972). Also see ECAFE, *ECAFE: 25 Years, Record of Observances* (Bangkok: Thai Watana Panish Press, 1973). This is a compendium of the observations made by eminent persons inside and outside the region on the occasion of ECAFE's twenty-fifth anniversary.

5. ESCAP, *ESCAP 1947–1987: Regional Cooperation for Development* (Bangkok: ESCAP, 1987). Also see ESCAP, *ESCAP Today: Over Four Decades of Cooperation in Developing and Modernising the Asia-Pacific Region* (Bangkok: ESCAP, 1997).

6. ESCAP, *ESCAP, 1947–1997: 50 Years of Achievement* (Bangkok: ESCAP, 1997).

7. These Central Asian states also joined the Economic Commission for Europe (ECE).

8. *The Quarterly Bulletin for Asia and the Far East* and the *Annual Survey,* published by ECAFE, are replete with policy prescriptions for economic development in which the state plays the dominant role. Also, discussions with the late C. Hart Schaff, who was executive secretary of the Mekong Committee in Bangkok in the early days and was later UNDP resident representative in Colombo, Sri Lanka, in the early 1970s and who was a personal friend of the author. His article "The United Nations Economic Commission for Asia and the Far East" (*International Organization* 7, no. 4 [1953]) is illuminating.

9. Japan was already a global economic power, being a member of G7.

10. See Wightman, *Towards Economic Cooperation in Asia,* 137–140.

11. Bernard Molitor and Göran Ohlin, "Independent Review of UNCTAD and the Regional Commissions," April 1996, an unpublished document for internal use by the directors of the UN administration. Bernard Molitor was president of the OECD Working 3.

12. "Restructuring of the Economic and Social Sectors of the United Nations System," General Assembly Resolution 32/197, 20 December 1977, document A/32/45.

13. This was also partly due to interpersonal relationships at the time; personal knowledge and discussions with UNDP and ESCAP personnel.

14. ESCAP, *ESCAP, 1947–1987,* 32.

15. The Asian Development Institute, established in Tokyo by the Asian Development Bank, further enhances these capacities.

16. Personal knowledge and discussions with many concerned officials.

17. For example, the South Pacific Centre.

18. This issue will be discussed in a later section.

19. The Lahore Declaration or Agreement was based on proposals made by Executive Secretary S. Lokanathan to the Seventh Session of ECAFE held in Lahore from 28 February to 7 March 1951; see ECAFE, *Future of the Commission: Note by the Executive Secretary* (document E/CN.11/278), 18 January 1951.

20. See Wightman, *Towards Economic Cooperation in Asia,* 20–52.

21. Ibid., 19 and 35. Also see Nicholas Mansergh, "The Asian Conference," *International Affairs* 23 (July 1947).

22. See "Temporary Sub-Commission on the Economic Reconstruction of Devastated Areas," ECOSOC Resolution 2/6, 21 June 1946, 393–395.

23. See Wightman, *Towards Economic Cooperation in Asia*, 55–70. Also see *Preliminary Report of the Temporary Sub-commission on Economic Reconstruction of Devastated Areas* (General Assembly document A/147), 26 October 1946.

24. See "Economic Reconstruction of Devastated Areas," General Assembly Resolution 46 (1), 11 December 1946.

25. See "Economic Commission for Europe," ECOSOC Resolution 36 (IV), 28 March 1947 (E/402), and "Economic Commission for Asia and the Far East," ECOSOC Resolution 37 (IV), 28 March 1947 (E/405).

26. See Wightman, *Towards Economic Cooperation in Asia*, 21–36.

27. The Netherlands was present at the next session of ECAFE.

28. See Wightman, *Towards Economic Cooperation in Asia*, 50.

29. See ECAFE, *Report of the Economic Commission for Asia and the Far East (Seventh Session) to the Economic and Social Council*, 13th Session, 1951, supplement no. 7 (E/1981), para. 341, 41.

30. See Wightman, *Towards Economic Cooperation in Asia*, 21–37. Also see "Economic Commission for Asia and the Far East, 1st Session," summary records of the 1st–4th meetings, held at Shanghai on 16–17 June 1947 (ECOSOC document E/CN.11/SR 1–4).

31. See ECAFE, *Regional Working Relations with the Specialized Agencies, Note by the Executive Secretary* (ECOSOC document E/CN.11/37), 23 October 1947.

32. See *Report of the Commission for Asia and the Far East on Its First and Second Sessions* (ECOSOC document E/606 & Corr.1), 8 January 1947.

33. Ibid.

34. See Wightman, *Towards Economic Cooperation in Asia*, 285.

35. See ECAFE, "The Establishment of a Committee on Industry and Trade," ECAFE Resolution, 5 April 1949 (ECOSOC document E/CN.11/AC.11.8).

36. See "Establishment of a Bureau of Flood Control," ECAFE Resolution, 10 June 1968 (ECOSOC document E/CN.11/110); ECOSOC, *Report of the Third Session of the Economic Commission for Asia and the Far East* (E/839), 4 July 1948, 52–53; and Wightman, *Towards Economic Cooperation in Asia*, 49.

37. Malaya and Singapore were one country at the time.

38. *Report of the Economic Commission for Asia and the Far East* (ECOSOC document E/CN.11/306), 28 February–7 March 1951.

39. See Wightman, *Towards Economic Cooperation in Asia*, 62–65.

40. Over the last fifty years, the commission has produced a large literature on various policy aspects of economic and social issues. A major component has addressed regional trade. The commission has been instrumental in analyzing emerging patterns of trade and investment in the region. What is attempted here is a brief summary of the commission's own approaches to these issues.

41. These sectoral issues are dealt with in the section entitled "Regional Action at the Sectoral Level."

42. The influence of the London School of Economics can be noted here.

43. See A. Gosh and J. Guha, "Macro-economic Planning Models: The Indian Experience," in D. B. Gupta, Y. C. Halan, and P. B. Desai, eds., *Development Planning and Policy: Essays in Honor of Professor V. K. R. V. Rao* (New Delhi: Wiley Eastern, 1982), 271–272. This model analyzes the impact of savings and trade gaps on development.

44. Two areas in which ESCAP has not been engaged, although the UN system has emphasized them in recent years, are human rights and governance.

45. See "Accelerated Measures for Regional Economic Co-operation for Development of Trade and Industry," ECAFE Resolution 45 (XIX), 13 March 1963 (ECOSOC document E/CN.11/627).

46. See ESCAP, *ESCAP, 1947–1987*, 13. Also discussions with former ECAFE officials. See "Establishment of the Asian Development Bank," ECAFE Resolution 65 (XXII), 31 March 1966 (ECOSOC document E/CN.11/739/Rev.1).

47. ECAFE, *ECAFE: 25 Years*, 50.

48. "Establishment of Regional Centre for Development Administration," ECAFE Resolution 112 (XXVI), 24 April 1970 (ECOSOC document E/CN.11/932).

49. Annual reports of the commission to ECOSOC during this period contain many references to the constraints, especially financial, which have confronted this institution. There is also evidence from discussions that it was adversely affected by the quality of its personnel, which were not of the level expected of a prospective center of excellence.

50. It is now called the Statistical Institute for Asia and the Pacific (SIAP).

51. See the successive histories of ECAFE and ESCAP and the annual reports to ECOSOC; also discussions with Dr. Ananda Meegama, former director of SIAP. I evaluated SIAP for UNDP and ESCAP in 1996. Its full potential has not been realized so far, and another strategy is called for if it is to be a dynamic regional organization.

52. See successive histories of the commission and its "Annual Reports" to ECOSOC, published in *ESCOR*.

53. Personal knowledge. I was a delegate for Ceylon to the meeting on the Asian Reserve Bank, held in Bangkok in 1972. It is curious that the commission never actively pursued this proposal. Some observers attribute this to a failure of leadership in subsequent years. Apparently there were strong pressures from several developed countries, and possibly the ADB and IMF, not to proceed with the proposal.

54. "The Asian Coconut Community," ECAFE Resolution 95 (XXV), 26 April 1969 (ECOSOC document E/CN.11/868).

55. "Asian Rice Trade Fund," ECAFE Resolution 136 (XXIX), 21 April 1973 (ECOSOC document E/CN.11/1101).

56. "Regional Co-operation in the Development of Coarse Grains, Pulses, Roots and Tubers," ESCAP Resolution 174 (XXXIII), 29 April 1977 (ECOSOC document E/ESCAP/58).

57. "Mekong Committee," ESCAP Resolution 189 (XXXIV), 17 March 1978 (ECOSOC document E/ESCAP/97).

58. See successive histories and the annual reports of the commission to ECOSOC for information on these institutions.

59. See ESCAP, *ESCAP, 1947–1987.*

60. Although it was a favorite phrase of U Nyun (he used this phrase when I met him in Burma as late as 1986), it was probably first used by the first executive secretary, S. Lokanathan. See P. S. Lokanathan, "ECAFE, the Economic Parliament of Asia," *Indian Yearbook of International Affairs* 2 (1953).

61. Personal knowledge. I was closely involved with the development of this proposal as an official of the government of Sri Lanka.

62. See the annual reports of the commission to ECOSOC.

63. See "Restructuring the Conference Structure of the Commission," ESCAP Resolution 48/2, 23 April 1992 (ECOSOC document E/ESCAP/889), 104–107. See also ESCAP, *Report of the Group of Eminent Persons on Intergovernmental Structure Subsidiary to the Commission* (ECOSOC document E/ESCAP/798), 28 January 1991.

64. The report of the task force was presented to a Regional Preparatory Meeting on the Review of the Conference Structure of the Commission held in Bangkok, 24–28 February 1997. See "Report of the Task Force on ESCAP Reform," in ESCAP, *Review of the Current Conference and Programme Structures of the Commission, Including Its Thematic Priorities: Findings and Recommendations of the ESCAP Secretariat Task Force* (ECOSOC document [E/ESCAP] PMD/CSC/1), 6 February 1997.

65. See "Rationalization of the Conference Structure of the Economic Commission for Asia and the Far East," ECAFE Resolution 143 (XXX), 5 April 1974 (ECOSOC document E/CN.11/1153), annex III.

66. Discussions with officials and government representatives. There are, however, many who are satisfied with the current arrangements.

67. Extensive information on these activities is to be found in ESCAP's annual reports to ECOSOC and other literature produced by the various divisions of ESCAP.

68. The UN University in Tokyo has done more extensive work in this field than ESCAP has ever done.

69. See the occasional paper by ESCAP (Statistics Division), *ESCAP Conferences for Regional Statisticians* (Bangkok: ESCAP, 1988). This is a historical record of ESCAP's work in statistics, prepared by the chief of the Statistics Division. It illustrates the very useful work done by ESCAP in this field.

70. See ECAFE, *Report of the Conference of Asian Economic Planners (Second Session)* (ECOSOC document E/CN.11/673), 12 November 1964.

71. Even a flagship project of this kind has its limitations, as noted in the ESCAP annual report for 2000, where it is stated that the Bangkok Agreement has made only a modest contribution to trade among member countries.

72. "Population Growth and Economic and Social Development," ECAFE Resolution 54 (XX), 17 March 1964 (ECOSOC document E/CN.11/662/Rev.1).

73. "Regional Co-Operation in the Field of Population," ECAFE Resolution 74 (XXIII), 17 April 1967 (ECOSOC document E/CN.11/791).

4. ECLAC

1. To adapt to changing realities in its own region, the name of ECLA was changed to the Economic Commission for Latin America *and the Caribbean* (ECLAC) in 1984. Thus, in this chapter, the acronym "ECLA" is used for all references to the institution prior to 1984, and "ECLAC" is used for succeeding years.

2. For a sample of the history of ECLA as well as its link to the history of development thinking, see ECLAC, *La Cepal en Sus 50 Años: Notas de un Seminario Conmemorativo* (Santiago: ECLAC, 2000); ECLAC, *Cincuenta años de pensamiento en la CEPAL: Textos Seleccionados* (México: Fondo de Cultura Económica, 1998), 2 vols.; ECLAC, *El pensamiento de la CEPAL*, Colección Tiempo Latinoamericano, ed. Fernando H. Cardoso, Aníbal Pinto, and Osvaldo Sunkel (Santiago: Editorial Universitaria, 1969), especially chapter 1, "La evolución del pensamiento de la CEPAL," 13–45. See also C. Furtado, "Desarrollo y estancamiento en América Latina: un enfoque estructuralista," in A. Bianchi, ed., *America Latina, ensayos de interpretación económica* (Santiago: Editorial Universitaria, 1969); A. Gurrieri, comp., *La obra de Prebisch en la CEPAL* (México: Fondo de Cultura Económica, 1982); C. Mallorquín, "Aventuras y desventuras de un economista brasileño," in R. Prebisch y C. Furtado, *El Estructuralismo Latinoamericano* (México: Benemérita Universidad Autónoma de Puebla, 1999), 33–135; F. Pazos, "Cincuenta años de pensamiento económico en América Latina," *El Trimestre Económico* 50 (4), no. 200 (October–December 1983); O. Rodríguez, *La teoría del subdesarrollo de la CEPAL* (México: Siglo Veintiuno Editores, 1981); and P. Streeten, "Development Ideas in Historical Perspective," in B. Minhas, ed., *Towards a New Strategy for Development: A Rothco Chapel Colloquium* (New York: Pergamon Press, 1979).

3. Raúl Prebisch, *El desarrollo económico de la América Latina y algunos de sus principales problemas* (Santiago: ECLA, 1949). Published subsequently in ECLA, *Boletín económico de América Latina* 7, no. 1 (1962).

4. ECLA, *Economic Survey of Latin America, 1949* (New York: United Nations Department of Economic Affairs, 1951).

5. E. Dosman and David H. Pollock, "Raúl Prebisch: The Continuing Quest," in Enrique V. Iglesias, ed., *The Legacy of Raúl Prebisch* (Washington, D.C.: Inter-American Development Bank, 1993), 11–42; Joseph L. Love, "Las fuentes del estructuralismo latinoamericano," in R. Prebisch and C. Furtado, *El Estructuralismo Latinoamericano* (México: Benemérita Universidad Autónoma de Puebla, 1999), 17–32.

6. ECLA, *The Latin American Common Market* (New York: United Nations, 1959).

7. This is not to say that all members of the secretariat agreed on all points. On the contrary, heated debates have always taken place within the secretariat; see C. Furtado, *La Fantasía organizada* (Buenos Aires: Editorial Universitaria de Buenos Aires, 1988), 159–162; translated from the original, published in Portuguese in Rio de Janeiro by Paz e

Terra, 1985. But the flagship documents usually veiled these conflicts and projected a single institutional opinion.

8. The points of reference are marked by Raúl Prebisch and Enrique Iglesias, who had the longest tenures as executive secretaries (thirteen years each): Prebisch from 1950 to 1963 and Iglesias (who is currently president of the Inter-American Development Bank) from 1972 to 1985.

9. Most ECLA documents are readily available at both the library at ECLAC headquarters in Santiago and the Dag Hammarskjöld Library in New York.

10. The most complete examination of ECLA's genesis, which is furthermore a firsthand account of one of the institution's progenitors, can be found in H. Santa Cruz, *Cooperar o Perecer,* vol. 1 (Buenos Aires: Grupo Editor Latinoamericano, 1984), 143–162 and 454–458.

11. Ibid., 144.

12. The other members were Belgium, Chile, China, Cuba, India, Norway, Lebanon, Peru, Turkey, and Venezuela.

13. It should be noted that in the same session of the General Assembly, Egypt and Lebanon launched the initiative to create an Economic Commission for the Middle East. In their draft resolution, both countries noted the decision of ECOSOC to study further the creation of an Economic Commission for Latin America; see Santa Cruz, *Cooperar o Perecer,* 152. See also chapter 6 of this volume.

14. As an interim measure, the secretary-general of the Pan American Union (and future first secretary-general of the OAS), Alberto Lleras Camargo, testified that, in his judgment, the creation of ECLA was not incompatible with the work of the Inter-American Economic and Social Council. When it finally met in May, the council agreed, thus overcoming one of the potential objections of the United States, which nevertheless insisted on the need for close cooperation between the future commission and the OAS.

15. *Report of the Ad Hoc Committee on the Proposal for an Economic Commission for Latin America,* ECOSOC Resolution 106 (VI), 25 February and 5 March 1948 (E/712/ Rev.1), Article 1. The functions of the secretariat are further described in its rules of procedure. These include:

(a) Provide substantive secretariat services and documentation for the Commission and its subsidiary bodies; (b) Undertake studies, research and other support activities within the terms of reference of the Commission; (c) Promote economic and social development through regional and subregional cooperation and integration; (d) Gather, organize, interpret and disseminate information and data relating to the economic and social development of the region; (e) Provide advisory services to Governments at their request and plan, organize and execute programmes of technical cooperation; (f) Formulate and promote development cooperation activities and projects of regional and subregional scope commensurate with the needs and priorities of the region and act as an executing agency for such projects; (g) Organize conferences and intergovernmental and expert group meetings and sponsor training workshops, symposia and seminars; (h) Assist in bringing a regional perspective to global problems and forums and introduce global concerns at the regional and subregional levels; (i) Co-ordinate its activities with those of the major departments and offices at United Nations Headquarters, specialized agencies and intergovernmental organizations with a view to avoiding duplication and ensuring complementarity in the exchange of information.

16. Ibid., 5.

17. Santa Cruz, *Cooperar o Perecer,* 454–458; and Celso Furtado's account in his book *La Fantasía organizada,* chapter 8, "Goliath and David," 97–101.

18. The formal decision of ECLA was ratified in one sentence of a lengthy decision (ECOSOC Resolution 414 [XIII], September 1951) on the organization and operation of the council and its commissions. The relevant paragraph (number 40 [2]) says "to continue the Economic Commission for Europe, the Economic Commission for Asia and the Far East and the Economic Commission for Latin America."

19. A. Bianchi, "La CEPAL en los años setenta y ochenta," in ECLAC, *La CEPAL en sus 50 años,* 44; F. H. Cardoso, "The Originality of a Copy: CEPAL and the Idea of Development," *The CEPAL Review,* no. 4 (1977, 2nd Semester), 30; J. Hodara, *Prebisch y la CEPAL: sustancia, trayectoria y contexto institucional* (México: El Colegio de México, 1987), 73–76; and O. Sunkel, "Introduction: In Search of Development Lost," in O. Sunkel, ed., *Development from Within: Toward a Neostructuralist Approach for Latin America* (Boulder and London: Lynne Rienner, 1993), 3.

20. See chart 1, page 23, in Ricardo Bielschowsky, "Evolución de las ideas de la CEPAL," *Revista de la CEPAL, CEPAL cincuenta años. Reflexiones sobre América Latiina y el Caribe,* Número Extraordinario (October 1998), document LC/G.2037-P.

21. See, e.g., Raúl Prebisch, "Five Stages in My Thinking on Development," in G. M. Meier and D. Seers, eds., *Pioneers in Development,* World Bank Publication (Oxford: Oxford University Press, 1984). See also the comments by Albert Fischlow and Jagdish N. Bhagwati that appear on pp. 173–204 of the same publication.

22. Among the names that come to mind are Jorge Ahumada, Celso Furtado, Regino Boti, Juan Noyola, and, a bit later, Anibal Pinto, Victor Urquidi, and Osvaldo Sunkel. For an engaging description of the early years, see Furtado, *La Fantasía organizada,* 47–49 and 63–70. Furtado made especially significant contributions, both within and outside of the secretariat; see, e.g., Furtado, "Desarrollo y estancamiento."

23. As suggested above, some would argue that the OAS fulfilled some of the functions that ECLA was called upon to perform, although it was not strong in conceptual and analytical work. Furthermore, in comparison to the proliferation of subregional and regional institutions of subsequent years, ECLA was virtually alone as a regional organization to promote development, especially as seen from the Latin American perspective.

24. See D. H. Pollock, "Some Changes in United States Attitudes towards CEPAL over the Past 30 Years," *CEPAL Review,* no. 6 (1978, 2nd half): 57–80.

25. See, e.g., J. Viner, *International Trade and Economic Development* (Glencoe, Ill.: Free Press, 1952), 61–64. Gerald M. Meier chastises ECLA in his textbook *Leading Issues in Development Economics* (New York: Oxford University Press, 1964, 78) for "its highly protectionist and interventionist policy recommendations."

26. See Pollock, "Some Changes in United States Attitudes towards CEPAL over the Past 30 Years"; and J. Levinson, and J. de Onis, *The Alliance That Lost Its Way* (Chicago: Quadrangle Books, 1970). In his book on the Kennedy years, *A Thousand Days* (Boston: Houghton Mifflin, 1965), Arthur Schlesinger Jr. notes: "The Alliance rested on the premise that modernization in Latin America required not just injections of capital or technical assistance but the breaking of the bottlenecks of economic development through reform of the political and social structure" (761). He also acknowledges that "a document of particular interest came in from the group of Latin American economists who had been foremost in the fight for development—Raúl Prebisch of ECLA . . ." (203).

27. F. H. Cardoso and E. Faletto, *Dependencia y desarrollo en América Latina* (México: Siglo Veintiuno Editores, 1969). It is noteworthy that Fernando Henrique Cardoso is only one—albeit the most prominent—of numerous ex-ECLA officials to subsequently assume leading roles in their respective countries. Arguably, ECLA's role as an incubator of what Jorge Domínguez called "technopols" must be included as part of the UN's intellectual heritage. See *Technopols* (University Park: University of Pennsylvania Press, 1997).

28. In Osvaldo Sunkel's words: "Economic thinking on development was vigorous and creative during the 1950s, particularly in our region. It was here that the concepts of center-periphery and structural heterogeneity and the structuralist and dependence approaches arose. But since the early 1970s, this school of thought has lost vitality and force, undergoing severe criticism from both the Marxist and neoliberal perspectives"; Sunkel, introduction, 3.

29. A fate that the Pinochet government seriously contemplated at one point, according to the Oral History Interview of Enrique Iglesias (3 and 6 November 2001), 102, in the Oral History Collection of the United Nations Intellectual History Project, the Graduate Center, The City University of New York. It should be noted that Iglesias's energies were channeled into important activities, including the defense of numerous persons (mostly, but not exclusively, secretariat staff), the decentralization of the ECLA secretariat, and the defense of the principles of the UN Charter in a frankly hostile environment.

30. See Bianchi, "La CEPAL en los años setenta y ochenta."

31. See ECLAC, *El problema de la deuda: gestación, desarrollo, crisis y perspectivas* (Santiago: United Nations, 1986); ECLAC, *La evolución del problema de la deuda externa en América Latina y el Caribe* (Santiago: United Nations, 1987); and R. Devlin, *Debt and Crisis in Latin America: The Supply Side of the Story* (Princeton, N.J.: Princeton University Press, 1989), 181–280.

32. Norberto Gonzalez of Argentina (1985–1987), Gert Rosenthal of Guatemala (1988–1997), and José Antonio Ocampo of Colombia (1998–2003).

33. J. Williamson, "Development Strategy for Latin America in the 1990s," in Enrique V. Iglesias, ed., *The Legacy of Raúl Prebisch* (Washington, D.C.: Inter-American Development Bank, 1993), 175–185; Enrique V. Iglesias, "Democracy and the 'Washington Consensus,'" *World Development* 21, no. 8 (1993): 1329–1336.

34. See ECLAC, *The Fiscal Covenant* (Santiago: United Nations, 1998); ECLAC, *Equity, Development and Citizenship* (Santiago: United Nations, 2000); and J. A. Ocampo, "Rethinking the Development Agenda," *CEPAL Review*, no. 74 (August 2001): 7–13.

35. Old ECLAC hands feel some kinship with the school of institutional economics espoused by economists such as Douglas North, Robert W. Fogel, Ronald H. Coase, and Oliver E. Williamson.

36. It should be noted that in addition to its conceptual or analytical output, ECLA was deeply involved in what the UN calls "operational activities," especially in the areas of training, technical assistance, and institution-building. It is difficult to separate these operational activities from the analytical work, since they mutually reinforce each other.

37. See Prebisch, *El desarrollo económico de la América Latina;* and ECLA, *Economic Survey of Latin America 1949*.

38. See ECLA, *Problemas teóricos y prácticos del crecimiento económico* (Santiago: United Nations, 1952), especially 14–25. In his book *La Fantasía organizada*, Celso Furtado remarked on this particular document of 1952: "The report represents, in my judgement, the most complete presentation of what has been called the *pensamiento* of ECLA. More precisely, the ideas spawned in that Commission, which came to have a decisive influence with the Latin American Governments . . . Much more than the theoretical chapters drafted by Prebisch for the 1949 Report, the new document had the mark of the ample debate that had involved the technical staff during the previous two years" (83).

39. The fact that Prebisch was strongly influenced by Keynes is supported by a treatise he wrote, which was published by the Fondo de Cultura Económica of Mexico in 1947 under the title *Introducción a Keynes*. He also acknowledged a debt to Paul Rosenstein-Rodan for the latter's classic work in Eastern and Southeastern Europe. Joseph Love and Joseph Hodara further speculate on intellectual debts to Mihail Manoilescu and Werner Sombart; see Love, "Las fuentes del estructuralismo latinoamericano," 22; and Hodara, *Prebisch y la CEPAL*, 60.

40. See H. W. Singer, "The Distribution of Gains between Investing and Borrowing Countries," *The American Economic Review* 40, no. 2 (May 1950): 473–485. Also see John Toye and Richard Toye, "The Origins of the Prebisch-Singer Thesis," chapter 3 of John Toye and Richard Toye, *Trade, Finance, and Development*, a forthcoming book in the UNIHP series.

41. This observation in itself gave rise to a great debate within academic circles; see, e.g., Viner, *International Trade and Economic Development*.

42. Raúl Prebisch, "Commercial Policy in the Underdeveloped Countries," *The American Economic Review* 49, no. 2 (May 1959): 261–264; also see J. A. Ocampo, "Raúl Prebisch y la agenda del desarrollo en los albores del siglo XXI," *La Revista de la CEPAL*, no. 75 (December 2001): 25–40, especially 25–27.

43. "Industrialization is an inescapable part of the process of change accompanying a gradual improvement in per capita income." Prebisch, "Commercial Policy in the Underdeveloped Countries," 251.

44. "A selective protection policy is a preferable instrument [to depreciation] . . . provided that protection has not been exaggerated to shelter inefficiency." Ibid., 257.

45. See, e.g., Hodara, *Prebisch y la CEPAL,* 79.

46. Indeed, Raúl Prebisch has never been fully accepted in the hallowed halls of academia. An anecdotal example can be found in Victor Urquidi, Sidney Dell, and Jan Tinbergen's repeated frustrations in not being able to progress with their nomination of Prebisch for the Nobel Prize in Economics.

47. E. L. Bacha, "La inflación y balanza de pagos: la influencia del pensamiento de la CEPAL en los años setenta y ochenta," in ECLAC, *La CEPAL en Sus 50 Años* (Santiago: ECLAC, 2000), 53.

48. Rodríguez, *La teoría del subdesarrollo de la CEPAL.*

49. O. Muñoz Goma, "The Process of Industrialization: Theories, Experiences and Policies," in Sunkel, ed., *Development from Within,* 258.

50. In his oral history interview in the Oral History Collection of the United Nations Intellectual History Project, The Graduate Center, The City University of New York (18–19 June 2000, 78), Victor Urquidi said: "I can swear that Central American integration was not in the mind of Prebisch, or anybody in CEPAL. It was an authentic Central American idea." A more accessible description of the times appears in V. Urquidi, "Incidentes de Integración en Centroamérica y Panamá, 1952–1958," in ECLAC, *CEPAL cincuenta años,* 259–267.

51. I. Cohen, *Regional Integration in Central America* (Lexington: Heath and Co., 1968), especially chapters 2 and 3, 13–35.

52. For a much more detailed analysis, see, among others, ECLAC, *Situation of the Central American Economic Integration Programme* (Santiago: ECLAC, 1965); and ECLA, *Evaluación de la integración económica en Centroamérica* (Santiago: ECLA, 1966).

53. Among these, Manuel Noriega Morales (Guatemala), Jorge Sol Castellanos (El Salvador), and Enrique Delgado (Nicaragua) were especially prominent.

54. According to Victor Urquidi's recollection in "Incidentes de Integración en Centroamérica": "The Americans, at the end of this thing, were very opposed when they got wind that we wanted industrial planning for Central America under a special agreement. This idea did not come from the secretariat—you cannot blame CEPAL for everything—it came from the countries themselves. It came, in fact, from Nicaragua."

55. See ECLA, *Evaluación de la integración económica en Centroamérica.*

56. That was the interpretation given to Article 20 of the General Treaty, which states: "The Central American Economic Council [CAEC] will be the organ in charge of facilitating the execution of the resolutions adopted by the Committee of Economic Cooperation [CEC] of the Central American Isthmus regarding economic integration." In other words, the CAEC (the main intergovernmental body of the General Treaty) implements; the CEC (a subsidiary organ of ECLA) only has the capacity to propose.

57. ECLA, *The Latin American Common Market.*

58. See ECLAC, *Bibliografía, 1948–1988* (Santiago: United Nations, 1989).

59. See, e.g., ECLA, "25 años en la agricultura de América Latina: rasgos principales," *Cuadernos de la CEPAL*, no. 21 (1983).

60. The term was coined by Albert Hirschman in "Ideologies of Economic Development," in *Essays on Development and Latin America: A Bias for Hope* (New Haven, Conn.: Yale University Press, 1971), 280.

61. See ECLA, *Economic Survey of Latin America 1949*, 89–490.

62. ECLA's vaunted Training Program on Problems of Economic Development was created in 1952 under the direction of Jorge Ahumada.

63. This document by ECLA is entitled "Economic Development of Brazil" (México: ECLA, 1955).

64. CEPAL, *Análisis y Proyecciones del Desarrollo Económico. V. El Desarrollo Económico de la Argentina* (México: UN Department of Economic and Social Affairs, 1959).

65. CEPAL, *Análisis y Proyecciones del Desarrollo Económico. IV. El Desarrollo Económico de Bolivia* (México: UN Department of Economic and Social Affairs, 1958).

66. ECLA, *Analyses and Projections of Economic Development. III. The Economic Development of Colombia* (Geneva: UN Department of Economic and Social Affairs, 1957).

67. CEPAL, *Análisis y Proyecciones del Desarrollo Económico. VI. El Desarrollo Económico del Perú* (México: UN Department of Economic and Social Affairs, 1959).

68. CEPAL, *Análisis y Proyecciones del Desarrollo Económico. VII. El Desarrollo Económico de Panamá* (México: UN Department of Economic and Social Affairs, 1960).

69. "The Cuban Economy in the Period 1959–1963," in ECLA, *Economic Survey of Latin America 1963* (New York: United Nations, 1965), 259–289. This was the last important study in Cuba for many years because of the reluctance of the government to open itself to external scrutiny. ECLA again started including Cuba in the yearly economic survey in the early 1980s, but based on limited and controlled information. It was not until 1995 that the secretariat was authorized to undertake a full-scale survey, which appeared, in book form, in 1997; see ECLAC, *La economía cubana: reformas estructurales y desempeño en los noventa* (México: Fondo de Cultura Económica, 1997).

70. The study was prepared by Mexican economists Juan Noyola and Oscar Soberón, in addition to Celso Furtado and Osvaldo Sunkel. In one of the less brilliant moments of the secretariat, Prebisch demurred to the complaints of the Mexican authorities and the study was not published, much to the dismay of the authors; see Furtado, *La Fantasía organizada*, 164–168.

71. Other studies include Costa Rica, Colombia, El Salvador, Honduras, and Nicaragua.

72. "Let us take one instance: the case of Argentina. This country has followed the very mistaken policy of trying to stimulate industrialization to the detriment of agriculture, instead of promoting a balanced growth of both. In the recent ECLA study prepared at the request of the Argentine government, we examined a series of measures

that might considerably increase exports. . . . Similarly high elasticities for imports have been found in ECLA's studies for Brazil, Mexico, Colombia and Peru." Prebisch, "Commercial Policy in the Underdeveloped Countries," 252–253.

73. See ECLA, *Problemas teóricos,* chapter 4, especially 26–36; and ECLA, *Estudio preliminar sobre la técnica de programación del desarrollo económico* (Santiago: United Nations, 1953).

74. "The elaboration of a development program does not necessarily mean a greater interference in the economy on the part of the State than that already existing in many Latin American countries, in the guise of exchange controls, price controls, etc. What it means, simply, is to increase and order investments aimed at providing greater strength and regularity to growth." Ibid., 4–5; see also ECLA, *Informe preliminar sobre el estudio "Las condiciones sociales del desarrollo económico"* (Santiago: United Nations, 1955), 7–18.

75. See A. Waterson, *Development Planning: Lessons of Experience* (Baltimore: John Hopkins University Press, 1965).

76. "Participating Latin American countries agree to introduce or strengthen systems for the preparation, execution, and periodic revision of national programs for economic and social development consistent with the principles, objectives, and requirements contained in this document. Participating Latin American countries should formulate, if possible within the next eighteen months, long-term development programs"; OAS, The Charter of Punta del Este, Establishing an Alliance for Progress within the Framework of Operation Pan America, 17 August 1961, Title II, Chapter II, point 1, available at <http://www.yale.edu/lawweb/avalon/intdip/interam/intam16.htm>, accessed 4 March 2003.

77. J. Noyola Vásquez, "Inflación y desarrollo económico en Chile y México," *Panorama Económico* 11, no. 170 (July 1957).

78. Osvaldo Sunkel, "La inflación chilena: un enfoque heterodoxo," *El Trimestre Económico* 25 (4), no. 100 (October–December 1958); see also O. Sunkel, "Un esquema general para el análisis de la inflación," *Economía* 18, no. 62 (1959).

79. Raúl Prebisch, "El falso dilema entre el desarrollo económico y estabilidad monetaria," *Boletín económico de América Latina* VI, no. 3 (October 1961), 1–10.

80. Ibid., 2.

81. Although Prebisch denies this in "El falso dilema entre el desarrollo económico y estabilidad monetaria." He begins by saying: "The economists of ECLA are frequently accused of having a certain tolerance for inflation. . . . Nothing is further from our thoughts." Ibid., 1.

82. D. Seers, "A Theory of Inflation and Growth in Under-developed Economies, Based on the Experience of Latin America," *Oxford Economic Papers,* no. 14 (1962): 173–195. Recognition of ECLA's work also appears in one of the classic surveys of inflation theory of the times: "In several Latin American countries, doctrines called *estructuralismo* and *Cepalismo* affirm that aggregate output responds to price increases with greater elasticity than to equal real-income increases achieved by noninflationary means. For this reason, as well as because inflation tends to lower real interest rates and

helps maintain industrial peace, many Latin American writers oppose monetary and fiscal controls over the price level." M. Bronfenbrenner and F. D. Holzman, "Survey of Inflation Theory," *The American Economic Review* LIII, no. 4 (September 1963): 610.

83. The proceedings and conference papers can be found in W. Baer and I. Kerstenetzky, eds., *Inflation and Growth in Latin America,* The Economic Growth Center, Yale University (Homewood, Ill.: Richard D. Irwin, 1964). See especially the introduction by Richard Ruggles (3–20) and Dudley Seer's paper "Inflation and Growth: The Heart of the Controversy" (89–103).

84. See, e.g., Bacha, "La inflación y balanza de pagos."

85. ECLA, *Introducción a la técnica de programación,* vol. 1 (Santiago: ECLA, 1955).

86. Ibid., 2.

87. Although Adolfo Gurrieri complains that Echavarría's first tasks in the secretariat were in the editorial services rather than in the social area. See A. Gurrieri, *La obra de José Medina Echavarría* (Madrid: Ediciones Cultura Hispánica del Instituto de Cooperación Iberoamericana, 1980), 18.

88. Prebisch, "Five Stages in My Thinking on Development," 181.

89. Cardoso, "The Originality of a Copy," 26.

90. In his last major document as executive secretary, Prebisch himself expressed some doubts regarding the benefits of foreign direct investment; see ECLA, *Towards a Dynamic Development Policy for Latin America* (Santiago: United Nations, 1963), 53–56.

91. Santa Cruz, *Cooperar o Perecer,* 460–469.

92. ECLA, *La cooperación internacional en la política de desarrollo latinoamericano* (New York: United Nations, 1954), vii.

93. Evaristo Araiza (Mexico), Rodrigo Facio (Costa Rica), Francisco Garcia Olano (Argentina), and Cleantho de Paiva Leite (Brazil).

94. See ECLA, *La cooperación internacional.*

95. Ibid., 131–133.

96. See Santa Cruz, *Cooperar o Perecer,* 460–469; as well as the resolutions arising from the Meeting of Ministers of Finance or Economy at the Fourth Extraordinary Meeting of the Inter-American Economic and Social Council, Quitandinha, Río de Janeiro, Brazil, November 1954. The meeting did, however, propose the creation of a working group to further study the matter. ECLA participated in the working group, which finally met in Santiago from 17 February to 15 April 1955, and which virtually endorsed the recommendation of the 1954 preparatory group. It took another four years and an intense effort on the part of President Juscelino Kubitschek of Brazil to persuade the Eisenhower administration to go along with these proposals.

97. See Levinson and de Onis, *The Alliance That Lost Its Way,* 63–70.

98. These were held, successively, in Santiago, Havana, Montevideo, and Mexico between 1948 and 1951. After that, the meetings were held biennially, in Quintandinha, Bogota, and La Paz between 1953 and 1957.

99. S. Dell, "Economics in the United Nations," in A. W. Coats, ed., *Economists in International Agencies* (New York: Praeger, 1986), 115.

100. Albert Fischlow, "The State of Latin American Economics," in *Economic and Social Progress in Latin America: 1985 Report* (Washington, D.C.: Inter-American Development, 1985), 123.

101. UN, *Toward a Global Strategy for Development: Report of the Secretary-General to the United Nations Conference on Trade and Development* (New York: United Nations, 1964), 9–15.

102. Ibid., 15–18.

103. As will be recalled, some of the "value added" by UNCTAD to ECLA includes: a) the need for international agreements on basic commodities; b) a system of non-reciprocal trade preferences for manufactured goods originating in developing countries; c) the need for compensatory financing in cases of abrupt declines in the prices of basic commodities; and d) a host of other mechanisms to "even the playing field" between the center and the periphery (ibid., 27–47). These matters are explored in a separate volume of the intellectual history of the UN.

104. Even Prebisch recalls, in "Five Stages in My Thinking on Development," that it was clear to him by 1960 "that the process of industrialization . . . had nearly exhausted the possibilities of further import substitution for the internal market of nondurable consumer goods" (181).

105. Fischlow, "The State of Latin American Economics," 129.

106. See ECLA, *Towards a Dynamic Development Policy for Latin America*. In the preface to the document, Prebisch writes: "This . . . report is the outcome of our great concern for the course of events in this part of the world [i.e., Latin America], a concern which, on the occasion of the ECLA secretariat's fifteenth anniversary, finds expression in the reflections set forth in the ensuing pages. They should also be viewed as representing a needful 'creative pause' on the part of one who has been in charge throughout almost the whole of that period" (vi).

107. "The days when foreign enterprise came in to do what Latin America could not are definitely over. We need the outside world to help us to cultivate our own ability, so that the population as a whole can be brought to share in the process of development. Thus, the foreign enterprise must be a nucleus for the dissemination of technology, as it already is in some cases"; ibid., 54.

108. ECLA, *The Latin American Common Market*, 1.

109. ECLA, *Economic Development, Planning and International Co-operation* (New York: United Nations, 1961), 84.

110. "Backward linkage" is a term coined by Albert Hirschman and is now widely used to denote links with inputs; inputs have forward linkages with integrated products. See Albert O. Hirschman, *The Strategy of Economic Development* (New Haven: Yale University Press, 1958).

111. "Latin America . . . will be unable to carry out its development plans, will be unable even to regain the rate of growth it achieved in the ten post-war years, unless it makes a sustained effort to establish within its own territory the capital goods industries of which it is in such urgent need today"; ECLA, *The Latin American Common Market*, 1.

112. ECLA, *Problemas y perspectivas del desarrollo industrial latinoamericano* (Santiago: United Nations, 1963).

113. See ECLA, *La fabricación de maquinarias y equipos industriales en América Latina* (Santiago: United Nations, 1962). For a complete list of the sectoral studies, see CEPAL, "Hacia un desarrollo sostenido en América Latina y el Caribe: Restricciones y Requisitos," *Cuadernos de la CEPAL,* no. 61 (1989): 147–162.

114. Typical of the mood of the meeting were the remarks of the then minister of economy of Chile, Domingo Santa Maria, in his inaugural address, when he said: "There is a basic need to make a determined fight against inefficiency, to raise productivity and quality, to work at economic costs, and to control profit margins"; see United Nations Industrial Development Organization, *Report of the Symposium on Industrial Development in Latin America* (Vienna: UNIDO, 1967), 49.

115. For an interesting analysis of this aspect, see Albert O. Hirschman, "The Political Economy of Import-Substituting Industrialization in Latin America," *The Quarterly Journal of Economics* LXXXII (February 1968): 1–32.

116. See ECLA, *The Latin American Common Market* (New York: United Nations, 1959).

117. Also, see Prebisch, "Commercial Policy in the Underdeveloped Countries": "The response to this [the splitting of the industrialization process into as many watertight compartments as there are countries] should be the enlargement of national markets through the gradual establishment of a common market" (268).

118. For an assessment of ALALC (which was converted into ALADI in 1980 through the second Montevideo Treaty), see ECLA, "Relaciones comerciales, crisis monetaria e integración económica en América Latina," *Cuadernos de la CEPAL,* no. 4 (1975): 56–85; and ECLA, "Integración y Cooperación Regionales en los Años Ochenta," *Estudios e Informes de la CEPAL,* no. 8 (1982), especially 11–56.

119. See ECLA, "Integración y Cooperación Regionales": "The assessment of the results of ALALC clearly showed its shortcomings" (62).

120. Ibid., 62–70.

121. See J. H. Boeke, *Economics and Economic Policy of Dual Societies* (New York: Oxford University Press, 1953); and W. A. Lewis, "Economic Development with Unlimited Supplies of Labor," *Manchester School of Economic and Social Studies,* no. 22 (May 1954).

122. See A. Pinto, "Concentración del progreso técnico y de sus frutos en el desarrollo latinoamericano," *El trimestre económico,* no. 125 (January–March 1965); A. Pinto, "Naturaleza e implicaciones de la 'heterogeneidad estructural' de la América Latina," *El trimestre económico* 37 (1), no. 145 (January–March 1970); and A. Pinto, "La 'Heterogeneidad Estructural': Aspectos fundamentales del desarrollo latinoamericano," *Modelos de Desarrollo en América Latina,* III-IT 11/72 (1972): 1–30.

123. See, e.g., ECLA, "Los cambios estructurales del empleo en el desarrollo económico de América Latina," *Boletín económico de América Latina* 10, no. 2 (1965); and ECLAC, *Bibliografía, 1948–1988* (Santiago: United Nations, 1989), 268–278.

124. See Raúl Prebisch, "El Porqué de la Planificación," *Panorama Económico,* no. 231 (1962): 147.

125. Ibid., 147–149.

126. A little-known fact is that Prebisch took some of ECLA's most prominent thinkers with him. Thus, ILPES turned out to be, in part, a new version of the old ECLA, leaving the parent organization debilitated by the loss of some of its key personnel as well as by some overlapping and duplication between the two organizations.

127. In fact, Prebisch did not relinquish this post even when he assumed the secretariat of UNCTAD in 1963. Rather, he took a leave of absence and left Cristobal Lara (Mexico) as acting director.

128. See ECLA, *Problemas y perspectivas del desarrollo industrial latinoamericano.* Technical assistance missions were also set up in Central America and the Andean region. These were funded jointly by ECLA, the OAS, and the IDB.

129. An intellectual contribution of ECLA that deserves specific mention is the landmark document prepared by Sergio Melnick in 1958 entitled *Manual on Economic Development Projects,* document E/CN.12/426.

130. Another classic was Gonzalo Martner's *Planificación y Presupuesto por Programas* (México: Siglo Veintiuno Editores, 1967).

131. Instituto Latinoamericano y del Caribe de Planificación Económica y Social, *Discusiones sobre planificación* (México: Siglo Veintiuno Editores, 1966).

132. See, e.g., ECLA, *Report of the Latin American Seminar on Planning,* prepared after the Tenth Session (E/CN.12/644), Mar del Plata, Argentina, May 1963; and Instituto Latinoamericano y del Caribe de Planificación Económica y Social, *Experiencias y problemas de la planificación en América Latina* (México: Siglo Veintiuno Editores, 1974).

133. An example is the text of Osvaldo Sunkel and Pedro Paz linking development theory with the Latin American experience, which has gone through various editions. O. Sunkel and Pedro Paz, *El subdesarrollo latinoamericano y la teoría del desarrollo* (México: Siglo Veintiuno Editores, 1970); as well as that of Antonio Barros de Castro and Carlos Lessa, *Introdução à economia: uma abordagem estructuralista* (Rio de Janeiro: Forense, 1967).

134. Cardoso, "The Originality of a Copy," 31.

135. José Medina Echavarría, *Consideraciones sociológicas sobre el desarrollo económico de América Latina* (Santiago: ECLA, 1963).

136. The following disclaimer appears on the cover of document E/CN.12/646 of 10 February 1963 (*Consideraciones sociológicas sobre el desarrollo económico de América Latina*): "Although the author is a staff member of ECLA, this work has been written under his own responsibility. Therefore, the ideas contained therein may not necessarily coincide with the organization he belongs to."

137. Also see Gurrieri, ed., *La obra de José Medina Echavarría.*

138. ECLA, *Social Trends and Programmes in Latin America,* prepared for the Tenth Session, Mar del Plata, Argentina, May 1963.

139. Enzo Faletto, "ECLAC and the Sociology of Development," *CEPAL Review* 58 (April 1996): 193.

140. What emerges less clearly from ECLA documents of the time is how the secretariat proposed to deal with conflict, although it is implicit that it believed that conflict could be held within tolerable bounds in situations of dynamic growth.

141. Some analysts reject the idea that there is such a thing as a dependency theory, dependency school, or dependency perspective, given the broad variety of points of view that fit under this umbrella. However, there is enough broad agreement on the essential features of what is commonly understood as *dependencia* to justify using the term here. See R. A. Packenham, *The Dependency Movement: Scholarship and Politics in Development Studies* (Cambridge, Mass.: Harvard University Press, 1992), 24–27; and G. Palma, "Dependency: A Formal Theory of Underdevelopment or a Methodology for the Analysis of Concrete Situations of Underdevelopment?" *World Development* 6, no. 7/8 (1978): 881–924.

142. In his text "Fernando Enrique Cardoso: Social and Institutional Rebuilding in Brazil," João Resende-Santos has called Cardoso and Faletto's *Dependencia y desarrollo en América Latina* "the classic statement on dependency análisis" (152); this text has been published in Jorge I. Domínguez, ed., *Technopols: Freeing Politics and Markets in Latin America in the 1990s* (University Park: Penn State Press, 1997).

143. The "probably" refers to the conflicting claims about whose contribution came earlier: Cardoso and Faletto's or that of Andre Gunther Frank, *Capitalism and Underdevelopment in Latin America· Historical Studies of Chile and Brazil* (New York: Monthly Review Press, 1967). See Packenham, "The Dependency Movement: Scholarship and Politics," 19–24; and Palma, "Dependency: A Formal Theory of Underdevelopment," 909.

144. See F. H. Cardoso, *Dependency and Development in Latin America* (Berkeley: University of California Press, 1979); and Joseph L. Love, "The Origins of Dependency Analysis," *Journal of Latin American Studies* 22, no. 1 (1990).

145. Resende-Santos, "Fernando Enrique Cardoso," 152.

146. Fischlow, "The State of Latin American Economics," 131; and Joseph L. Love, "Raúl Prebisch and the Origins of the Doctrine of Unequal Exchange," *Latin American Research Review* 15, no. 3 (Chapel Hill, N.C.: Asociación de Estudios Latinoamericanos, 1980).

147. Fischlow, "The State of Latin American Economics," 131.

148. Ibid., 132.

149. See, among others, "International Development Strategy for the Second United Nations Development Decade," General Assembly Resolution 2626 (XXV), 24 October 1970 (A/8028); "Declaration and the Programme of Action on the Establishment of a New International Economic Order," General Assembly Resolution 3201 (S-VI) and 3203 (S-VI), 1 May 1974 (A/9556); and "Charter of Economic Rights and Duties of States," General Assembly Resolution 3281 (XXIX), 12 December 1974 (A/9631).

150. It should be noted that ECLA was also under siege from the other extreme of the ideological spectrum. A group of countries, spearheaded by Cuba, Mexico, and Venezuela, proposed in 1974 the creation of a regional economic organization which would be more independent of the influence of Southern Cone governments and

developed countries. The Sistema Económico Latinoamericano (SELA) was created in October 1975, at least in part as a reflection of misgivings on the part of the more progressive governments of the region regarding ECLA's eventual orientation.

151. Bianchi, "La ECLAC en los años setenta y ochenta," 44.

152. Cardoso, "The Originality of a Copy," 30. However, farther on in the same article Cardoso allows that "for these ideas no epitaphs need be written. They have undergone changes and moulted their plumage, as *idées-force* often do, but they have continued to survive" (40).

153. "My generation of economists, formed in the 1960s, has been called neostructuralist. Today, I believe it would be more appropriate to call them *paracepalinos.* In other words, we evolved in parallel with ECLA, almost always in the same direction, although in a few rare instances with some crossed lines. One differentiating intellectual characteristic of that generation was that of having followed postgraduate studies in U.S. universities, although having received a strong influence of ECLAC thinking in our previous university studies, acquired in Latin America. That generation was responsible for the creation of postgraduate centers of economics in the region during the period in which military regimes predominated in the Southern Cone. It moved on to assume increasing responsibilities in policy-making in the region during the process of democratization from the 1980s onwards"; Bacha, "La inflación y balanza de pagos," 53.

154. See Bacha, "La inflación y balanza de pagos," 44–51. Also see the United Nations Intellectual History Project Oral History Interview of Enrique Iglesias.

155. Part of the executive secretary's attention during this period was devoted to other pursuits, especially to protecting the secretariat from the hostile environment of the Pinochet regime.

156. See, e.g., Centro de Estudios del Desarrollo (CENDES), "Estilos de desarrollo," *El Trimestre Económico* 36 (4), no. 144 (October–December 1969). But the work at CENDES was basically undertaken by Oscar Varsavsky, an ex-ECLA staff member.

157. Contributions of all three authors, based on drafts circulated within the secretariat in 1974, appear on this subject in the first *CEPAL Review.* See the three following articles: A. Pinto, "Notas sobre los estilos de desarrollo en América Latina"; J. Graciarena, "Poder y estilos de desarrollo: una perspectiva heterodoxa"; and M. Wolfe, "Enfoques del desarrollo: ¿de quién y hacia qué?" *Revista de la CEPAL,* no. 1 (1st Semester 1976): 97–194.

158. Pinto, "Notas sobre los estilos," 99.

159. See ECLA, *Income Distribution in Latin America* (New York: United Nations, 1971).

160. See ECLAC, *Bibliografía, 1948–1988* (Santiago: United Nations, 1989), 70–81.

161. See, e.g., O. Altimir, "La dimensión de la pobreza en América Latina," *Cuadernos de la CEPAL,* no. 27 (1979); and ECLA, *¿Se puede superar la pobreza?* (Santiago: United Nations, 1980), especially Sergio Molina and Sebastián Piñera, "La pobreza en América Latina: situación, evolución y orientaciones de políticas," 13–62. Also see, as one of the inputs to the study, Sebastián Piñera, *¿Se benefician los pobres del crecimiento económico?* (Santiago: United Nations, July 1979).

162. Osvaldo Sunkel and Nicolo Gligo, comps., *Estilos de desarrollo y medio ambiente en América Latina*, Lecturas, no. 36, 2 vols. (México: Fondo de Cultura Económica, 1980).

163. World Commission on Environment and Development, *Our Common Future* (Oxford: Oxford University Press, 1987). The impact of this report is covered elsewhere in the Intellectual History Project.

164. Also see ECLAC, *El desarrollo sustentable: transformación productiva, equidad y medio ambiente* (Santiago: United Nations, 1991).

165. ECLA, *Mujeres en América Latina: Aportes para una discusión* (México: Fondo de Cultura Económica, 1975).

166. ECLAC, *Desarrollo y Equidad de Genero: Una Tarea Pendiente* (Santiago: United Nations, 1993).

167. See the resolutions cited in note 149 above—2626 (XXV), 3201 (S-VI), 3202 (S-VI), and 3281 (XXIX)—for typical examples.

168. See, e.g., ECLA, *Latin America and the Second Development Decade* (Santiago: United Nations, 1971).

169. ECLA, "Las evaluaciones regionales de la estrategia internacional del desarrollo: Quito, 1973; Chaguaramas, 1975," *Cuadernos de la CEPAL*, no. 2 (1975); and ECLA, "Síntesis de la segunda evaluación regional de la Estrategia Internacional de Desarrollo," *Cuadernos de la CEPAL*, no. 5 (1975).

170. "Appraisal of the International Development Strategy," ECLAC Resolution 320 (XV), 29 March 1973 (ECOSOC document E.CN.12/958/Rev.1).

171. ECLAC, "Estabilización y liberación económica en el Cono Sur," *Estudios e Informes de la CEPAL*, no. 38 (Santiago: United Nations, 1984).

172. ECLAC, *Economic Survey of Latin America and the Caribbean 1997–1998* (Santiago: United Nations, 1998).

173. Devlin, *Debt and Crisis in Latin America*, 123–178.

174. By this time, the institution had added "and the Caribbean" to its title. Hence, from here on the term ECLAC is used in the present text.

175. Gert Rosenthal, "Development Thinking and Policies in Latin America and the Caribbean: Past and Future," in Louis Emmerij, ed., *Economic and Social Development into the XXI Century* (Washington, D.C.: Inter-American Development Bank, 1997), Part III, 192–193.

176. See Bianchi, "La CEPAL en los años setenta y ochenta."

177. ECLAC, *Economic Survey of Latin America, 1978* (Santiago: United Nations, 1978), 568.

178. See, e.g., Carlos Cáceres, "La vía chilena hacia una economía de mercado," *Estudios Públicos*, no. 6 (1982).

179. J. Ramos, *Neoconservative Economics in the Southern Cone of Latin America* (Baltimore: Johns Hopkins University Press, 1986), 13–23.

180. There is an ample body of work by the secretariat, beginning in the late 1970s and becoming increasingly sophisticated through the mid-1980s. For a sample, see ECLAC, "Monetary Policy and Balance of Payments Adjustment: Three Studies," *Cuadernos de*

la CEPAL, no. 29 (1979); ECLAC, "The Economy of Latin America and the Caribbean in 1983: Main Trends, the Impact of the Crisis and the Adjustment Processes," *Cuadernos de la CEPAL,* no. 49 (1985); ECLAC, "The Economic Crisis: Policies for Adjustment, Stabilisation and Growth," *Cuadernos de la CEPAL,* no. 54 (1986); ECLAC, "Latin America and the Caribbean Development: Obstacles, Requirements and Options," *Cuadernos de la CEPAL,* no. 55 (1987), document LC/G.1440-P, especially 41–50; and ECLAC, "Hacia un desarrollo sostenido," especially 77–83.

181. In this, ECLAC anticipated some of the arguments contained in UNICEF's "adjustment with a human face" approach. G. Cornia, R. Jolly, and F. Stewart, eds., *Adjustment with a Human Face* (Oxford: Oxford University Press, 1987).

182. See, e.g., ECLAC, "Estabilización y liberación económica"; ECLAC, "La política monetaria y el ajuste de la balanza de pagos: tres estudios," *Cuadernos de la CEPAL,* no. 29 (1984); ECLAC, "The Economic Crisis"; ECLAC, *El problema de la deuda;* and ECLAC, *La evolución del problema de la deuda externa,* especially 51–55. For an independent analysis, also see Bacha, "La inflación y balanza de pagos."

183. See, e.g., C. Massad and R. Zahler, "Dos estudios sobre endeudamiento externo," *Cuadernos de la CEPAL,* no. 19 (Santiago: United Nations, 1986), which contains a study first produced in 1977.

184. See, among others, ECLAC, "Políticas de ajuste y renegociación de la deuda externa en América Latina," *Cuadernos de la CEPAL,* no. 48 (1984); ECLAC, "The Economy of Latin America and the Caribbean in 1983"; ECLAC, "Latin America and the Caribbean Development," especially 116–128, and ECLAC, "La evolución del problema de la deuda externa"; as well as Devlin, *Debt and Crisis in Latin America.*

185. ECLAC, "Latin America and the Caribbean Development," 120–127.

186. From dealing with the problem case by case through debt restructuring ("muddling through") to the Baker Initiative of 1985 that advocated refinancing the debt of fifteen highly indebted countries to the debt-reduction strategy that emerged in 1989 through the initiative launched by Secretary of the Treasury Nicholas Brady.

187. ECLAC, *América Latina y el Caribe: opciones para reducir el peso de la deuda* (Santiago: United Nations, 1990); as well as Devlin, *Debt and Crisis in Latin America.*

188. See Bianchi, "La CEPAL en los años setenta y ochenta."

189. F. Fajnzylber, "Some Reflections on South-East Asian Export Industrialization," *CEPAL Review,* no. 15 (1981): 117–138; E. Tironi, "Relaciones comerciales entre los países de desarrollo intermedio de América Latina y Asia," *Comercio Exterior* 31, no. 12 (1981); and A. Bianchi and T. Nohara, eds., *A Comparative Study on Economic Development between Asia and Latin America,* JRP Series, no. 67 (Tokyo: Institute of Developing Economies, 1988), especially 11–66.

190. It was left to the World Bank to come out, in 1993, with their heralded—but also controversial—report on "The East Asian Miracle."

191. In point of fact, by the time the seminar was actually held, Iglesias had already assumed his new duties as foreign minister of Uruguay. He did, however, prepare the event, and he participated in it.

192. The documents that were produced left something to be desired in terms of overall coherence, but they did mark a departure in revisiting medium and long-term concerns; see ECLAC, *Crisis y desarrollo: presente y futuro de América Latina y el Caribe*, 3 vols. (Santiago: United Nations, 1985).

193. ECLAC, "Latin America and the Caribbean Development."

194. ECLAC, "Hacia un desarrollo sostenido."

195. Rosenthal, "Development Thinking and Policies in Latin America," 193–194.

196. Williamson, "Democracy and the 'Washington Consensus.'"

197. The so-called Treaty of Asunción was signed in March 1991, committing the four signatories (Argentina, Brazil, Paraguay, and Uruguay) to create a common market by 1994.

198. F. Fajnzylber, *La industrialización trunca de América Latina* (México: Editorial Nueva Imagen, 1983).

199. F. Fajnzylber, "Industrialización en América Latina: de la 'caja negra al casillero vacío,'" *Cuadernos de la CEPAL*, no. 60 (1990), document LC/G. 1534–P (Rev.1-P).

200. ECLAC, *Changing Production Patterns with Social Equity* (Santiago: United Nations, 1990).

201. In subsequent years, a further refinement introduced actions to be taken at the meso-economic level. The term was first used by ECLAC in 1994 and further refined in 1996; see ECLAC, *Latin America and the Caribbean: Policies to Improve Linkages with the Global Economy* (Santiago: United Nations, 1995), 151–193; and ECLAC, *Strengthening Development: The Interplay of Macro and Microeconomics* (Santiago: United Nations, 1996), 69–92.

202. See, e.g., Howard Ellis and Norman S. Buchanan, *Approaches to Economic Development* (New York: Twentieth Century Fund, 1955), 406–429.

203. See, e.g., ECLAC, *Equity, Development and Citizenship.*

204. ECLAC, *Social Equity and Changing Production Patterns: An Integrated Approach* (Santiago: United Nations, 1992).

205. The secretariat started publishing its now very popular *Social Panorama* in 1994.

206. ECLAC, *Education and Knowledge: Basic Pillars of Changing Production Patterns with Social Equity*, prepared jointly with the Regional Office for Education in Latin America and the Caribbean of UNESCO (Santiago: United Nations, 1992).

207. For example, Mexico's education plan, prepared under the aegis of then Minister of Education Ernesto Zedillo, was strongly influenced by the ECLAC proposal; see Poder Ejecutivo Federal, *Acuerdo nacional para la modernización de la educación básica* (México: Secretaría de la Educación Pública, 1992).

208. See ECLAC, *Changing Production Patterns with Social Equity*, 149–156; and Sunkel and Ramos, "Toward a Neostructuralist Synthesis," in O. Sunkel, ed., *Development from Within*, 7.

209. ECLAC, *La brecha de la equidad: América Latina, el Caribe y la Cumbre Social* (Santiago: United Nations, 1997).

210. See ECLAC, *El desarrollo sustentable*.

211. ECLAC, *Población, equidad y transformación productiva* (Santiago: United Nations, 1993).

212. See, e.g., ECLAC, *Changing Production Patterns with Social Equity*, 163–180.

213. ECLAC, *Open Regionalism in Latin America and the Caribbean: Economic Integration as a Contribution to Changing Production Patterns with Social Equity* (Santiago: United Nations, 1994).

214. Ibid., 7.

215. Final Declaration of the IV Iberoamerican Summit of Heads of State and Government, Cartagena de Indias, Colombia, 14 and 15 June 1994, points 9 and 25.

216. "We will direct the OAS Special Committee on Trade, with the support of the IDB, ECLAC, and other specialized regional and subregional organizations, to assist in the systematization of data in the region and to continue its work on studying economic integration arrangements in the Hemisphere, including brief comparative descriptions of the obligations in each of the Hemisphere's existing trade agreements." Plan of Action approved by the Heads of State and Chiefs of Government in Miami, 11 December 1964, at the Summit of the Americas, Chapter II, Section 9, point 7, available at <http://usinfo.state.gov/regional/ar/summit/plan.htm>, accessed 4 March 2003. And in the First Trade Ministerial Meeting, held in Denver on 30 June 1995, the trade ministers decided to "ask the tripartite committee—the OAS, the IDB and ECLAC— to provide analytical support, technical assistance, and relevant studies within their respective areas of competence, as may be requested by the working groups" (ibid., point 8).

217. ECLAC, *Strengthening Development*, 43.

218. ECLAC, *Latin America and the Caribbean*, 243–248.

219. Ibid., 235–240.

220. The first version of *Latin America and the Caribbean* was issued in March of 1994, in preparation for ECLAC's twenty-fifth session.

221. Ibid., 24.

222. C. Massad and N. Eyzaguirre, eds., *Ahorro y formación de capital: experiencias latinoamericanas* (Buenos Aires: Grupo Editor Latinoamericano, 1990); G. Held and A. Uthoff, *Indicators and Determinants of Savings for Latin America and the Caribbean*, ECLAC Documento de Trabajo Series, no. 25 (Santiago: United Nations, 1995).

223. ECLAC, *Strengthening Development*, 43–59.

224. ECLAC, *Latin America and the Caribbean*, 250–284.

225. See ECLAC, *Strengthening Development*, especially chapter 7, 93–110, entitled "Policies to Promote Saving, Investment and Financial Development."

226. These studies came out in a series called *Serie Financiamiento del Desarrollo: Pensiones*, which spans the period 1991 to the present. For a sample, see the following numbers: ECLAC, "Sistemas de pensiones de América Latina. Diagnóstico y alternativas de reforma," no. 9 (1991); ECLAC, "Fondos de pensiones y desarrollo del mercado de capitales en Chile: 1980–1993," no. 19 (1994), document LC-R.839; ECLAC, "On Economic

Benefits and Fiscal Requirements on Moving from Unfunded to Funded Pensions," no. 48 (1997), document LC/L/1012; ECLAC, "The Fiscal Covenant," no. 47 (1998), document LC/G.1997/Rev.1; and ECLAC, *Equity, Development and Citizenship.* In the same series, a number of studies were produced on the financing of health care through in-depth case studies of Argentina, Brazil, Colombia, Costa Rica, Chile, and Mexico.

227. See ECLAC, "On Economic Benefits."

228. ECLAC, *Serie Política Fiscal,* of which 114 numbers have been published so far.

229. For a compendium on the results of these seminars, see ECLAC, *La política fiscal en América Latina: una selección de temas y experiencias de fines y comienzos de Siglo* (Santiago: United Nations, 2000).

230. ECLAC, *The Fiscal Covenant.*

231. Ibid., 8–45.

232. Comisión Preparatoria del Pacto Fiscal, *Hacia un pacto fiscal en Guatemala* (Guatemala: 29 December 1999).

233. J. A. Ocampo, *La reforma del sistema financiero internacional: Un debate en marcha* (México: Fondo de Cultura Económica, 1999), 132; J. A. Ocampo, "A Broad Agenda for International Financial Reform," *Financial Globalization and the Emerging Economies,* Serie Libros de la CEPAL, no. 55 (2000): 41–62; and ECLAC, *Growth with Stability: Financing for Development in the New International Context* (Santiago: United Nations, 2000).

234. The report, under the banner of *Balance Preliminar (Preliminary Survey),* is presented with some fanfare by the executive secretary in the third week of December of each year, based on the most up-to-date information presented by member governments. It is thus an extremely timely publication.

235. See ECLAC, *Economic Survey of Latin America and the Caribbean 1997–1998;* ECLAC, *Economic Survey of Latin America and the Caribbean 1998–1999* (Santiago: United Nations, 2000); R. Ffrench-Davis, ed., *Reforming the Reforms in Latin America: Macroeconomics, Trade, Finance* (London: Macmillan/St. Anthony's College, 2000); and B. Stallings and Wilson Peres, *Growth, Employment and Equity* (Washington, D.C.: Brookings Institution Press, 2000).

236. ECLAC, *Strengthening Development;* J. M. Katz, *Structural Reforms, Productivity and Technological Change in Latin America,* Serie Libros de la CEPAL, no. 64 (2001), document LC/G.2129-P, especially 45–120; Stallings and Peres, *Growth, Employment and Equity,* especially 1–16.

237. A summary of the study is offered in chapter 7 of the book: "The reform results were neither as positive as supporters predicted nor as negative as opponents feared. Indeed, the reforms per se seem to have had a surprisingly small impact at the aggregate level, based on calculations using regional averages. It is only when we move to the country, sectoral and microeconomic levels that the magnitude of the changes begins to become apparent" (Stallings and Peres, *Growth, Employment and Equity,* 202–223).

238. ECLAC, *Equity, Development and Citizenship.*

239. Ibid., 11.

240. Ibid., 16.

241. Ibid., 50.

242. See "The Rise and Decline of Development Economics" in Albert O. Hirschman, *Essays in Trespassing: Economics to Politics and Beyond* (Cambridge: Cambridge University Press, 1981), 1–24, where Albert O. Hirschman virtually declared development economics defunct. However, W. Arthur Lewis disagreed when he said that "development economics is not at its most spectacular, but it is alive and well"; see W. A. Lewis, "The State of Development Theory," *The American Economic Review* 74, no. 1 (March 1984): 10. For his part, Amartya Sen also felt that "the obituary may be premature"; see A. Sen, "Development: Which Way Now?" *The Economic Journal*, no. 93 (December 1983).

243. Boutros Boutros-Ghali, *An Agenda for Peace* (New York: United Nations, 1992), 6–8.

5. The ECA

1. ECA, *Twenty-five Years of Service to African Development and Integration* (Addis Ababa: United Nations, 1983), xiv.

2. "Programme of Work and Priorities for 1960–1961," ECA Resolution 18 (II), 4 February 1960 (ECOSOC document E/CN.14/54).

3. "Proposed Economic Commission for Africa," General Assembly Resolution 1155 (XII), 26 November 1957 (A/3805).

4. It is worth noting that the British government left out all its territories south of Tanganyika (Tanzania), that is, south of the Limpopo River—Lesotho, Swaziland, Botswana, Malawi, Zambia, and Zimbabwe. The government had apparently decided to exclude them from the agenda for independence.

5. For the text of the draft resolution, see "Formulation of Social Policies Related to Economic Development," 3 October 1958 (General Assembly document A/C.3/L.666).

6. *North-South: A Program for Survival* (The Report of the Independent Commission on International Development Issues under the Chairmanship of Willy Brandt) (Cambridge, Mass.: MIT Press, 1980).

7. "Statement by the Secretary-General at the Inaugural Meeting," Addis Ababa, (ECOSOC document E/CN.14/18), annex VI, 29 December 1958, 21.

8. The title of Nelson Mandela's seminal autobiography (Boston: Little, Brown and Co., 1994), written and published after his release from prison following twenty-seven years in the infamous maximum-security Robben Island prison.

9. George Davidson, "Economic Commission for Africa in a Changing World: A Testimony ECA," in ECA, *Twenty-five Years of Service to African Development and Integration.*

10. ECA, *African Charter for Popular Participation in Development and Transformation*, adopted by the International Conference on Popular Participation in the Recovery and Development Process in Africa held in Arusha, Tanzania, 12–16 February 1990 (Addis Ababa: ECA, March 1990).

11. World Bank, *Sub-Saharan Africa: From Crisis to Sustainable Growth—A Long-Term Perspective Study* (Washington, D.C.: World Bank, 1989): "Does Africa face special

structural problems that have not been properly understood? . . . Have recent reform programmes been too narrow and too shallow?" (1)

12. J. M. Keynes, *The General Theory of Employment, Interest and Money* (London: Macmillan and Co., 1936), 383.

13. Raúl Prebisch, *The Economic Development of Latin America and Its Principal Problems* (New York: United Nations, 1950).

14. UN, *Measures for the Economic Development of Underdeveloped Countries* (New York: United Nations, 1951).

15. "United Nations and Multilateral Economic Aid to the Independent States and to the Territories Awaiting Independence in Africa," ECA Resolution 2 (I), 6 January 1959 (ECOSOC document E/CN.14/18, paragraph B).

16. "In-Service Training," ECA Resolution 16 (II), 4 February 1960; and "Training Facilities Available to African States," Resolution 17 (II), 17 February 1960 (ECOSOC document E/CN.14/54).

17. "Establishment of an African Institute for Economic Development and Planning," ECA Resolution 58 (IV), 1 March 1962 (ECOSOC document E/CN.14/168).

18. "Conference of African Planners," ECA Resolution 105 (VI), 29 February 1964 (ECOSOC document E/CN.14/290/Rev.1).

19. "Establishment of an African Development Bank," ECA Resolution 52 (IV), 1 March 1962 (ECOSOC document E/CN.14/168).

20. See the "African Development Bank" paragraph in the *ECA Annual Report, 1964* (ECOSOC document E/CN.14/290/Rev.1), 53–54.

21. Adebayo Adedeji, "Comparative Strategies of Economic Decolonization in Africa," in Ali A. Mazrui and C. Wondji, eds., *General History of Africa,* vol. 8, *Africa since 1935* (Paris: UNESCO, 1993), 393–429.

22. Immanuel Wallerstein, "The Three Stages of African Involvement in the World Economy," in Peter Gutkind and Immanuel Wallerstein, eds., *The Political Economy of Contemporary Africa,* Sage Series on African Modernization and Development, vol. 1 (Beverly Hills, Calif.: Sage, 1976), 30–57.

23. Keynes, *The General Theory of Employment.*

24. Joseph Schumpeter, *The Theory of Economic Development: An Inquiry into Profits, Capital Credit, Interest and the Business Cycle,* trans. Redvers Opie (Cambridge, Mass.: Harvard University Press, 1934).

25. See Friedrich August von Hayek, "The Pretence of Knowledge," Nobel Memorial Lecture delivered on 11 December 1974 and published in the *American Economic Review* 79, no. 6 (December 1989): 3–7.

26. Albert Hirschman, "The Rise and Decline of Development Economics," in Mark Gersovitz et al., eds., *The Theory and Experience of Economic Development: Essays in Honor of Sir W. Arthur Lewis* (London, Boston: G. Allen and Unwin, 1982), 388–399.

27. World Bank, *Sub-Saharan Africa,* 1.

28. "Examination of Long-Term Trends in the Economic Development of the Regions of the World," General Assembly Resolution 3508 (XXX), 15 December 1975, in *GAOR,* 1975, 30th Session, Supplement no. 34 (A/10034), 66–67.

29. Adebayo Adedeji, *Towards a Dynamic African Economy* (London: Frank Cass, 1989), 224–245.

30. Ibid., 234–235.

31. ECA, *Revised Framework of Principles for the Implementation of the New International Economic Order in Africa, 1976–1981–1986* (Addis Ababa: ECA, 1976).

32. See "Development Strategy for Africa for the Third Development Decade," ECA Resolution 332 (XIV), 27 March 1979 (ECOSOC document E/CN.14/725).

33. ECA, *Revised Framework.*

34. See "Plan of Action for the Implementation of the Monrovia Strategy for African Development," ECA Resolution 398 (XV), 12 April 1980 (ECOSOC document E/CN.14/781/Rev.1).

35. OAU, *Lagos Plan of Action for the Economic Development of Africa 1980–2000* (Geneva: International Institute for Labour Studies, 1981).

36. See "Development Strategy for Africa for the Third Development Decade."

37. Ibid., annex B, 133–134.

38. Robert S. Browne and Robert J. Cummings, *The Lagos Plan of Action vs. the Berg Report: Contemporary Issues in African Economic Development,* Monographs in African Studies (Washington, D.C.: Howard University, 1984), 23.

39. World Bank, *Accelerated Development in Sub-Saharan Africa: An Agenda for Action* (Washington, D.C.: World Bank, 1981).

40. Browne and Cummings, *The Lagos Plan of Action vs. the Berg Report,* 33.

41. Ibid.

42. Chester A Crocker, "Expanding the Development Dialogue," *Topic,* no. 147 (1981): 5–6.

43. ECA, "Declaration of Tripoli on the World Bank Report Entitled 'Accelerated Development in Sub-Saharan Africa: An Agenda for Action,'" 17th Session, Tripoli, 30 April 1982 (ECOSOC document E/ECA/CM.8/32/Rev.1), 53.

44. Organization of African Unity/African Economic Community, Constitutive Act of the African Union, adopted during the OAU Summit in Lomé, Togo, 11 July 2000, available at <http://www.Africa-union.org/en/home.asp>, accessed 4 March 2003.

45. Sirte Declaration adopted at the Fourth Extraordinary Session of the Assembly of Heads of State and Government at Sirte on 9 September 1999 (document EAHG/Draft/Decl.[IV] Rev.1).

46. OAU/AEC, "Constitutive Act."

47. Adebayo Adedeji, "From the Lagos Plan of Action to the New Partnership for African Development and from the Final Act of Lagos to the Constitutive Act: Whither Africa," keynote address prepared for presentation at the African Forum for Envisioning Africa, Nairobi, Kenya, 26–29 April 2002.

48. Adebayo Adedeji, "The Impact of Multilateral Debt on the Economics of Sub-Sahara African Countries" (mimeo), paper presented to the Seminar on the Debt Problems and the Nigerian Economy; Resolution Options, Abuja, May 1997; and Oxfam International Position Paper" (mimeo), London, September 1995.

49. For a summary discussion, see *The Economist*, 7 September 1996.

50. World Bank, *Report on Adjustment Lending* (Washington, D.C.: World Bank, 1988).

51. Carol Lancaster, *Africa Notes*, no. 97 (20 April 1989), 1–2.

52. World Bank and UNDP, *Africa's Adjustment and Growth in the 1980s* (Washington, D.C.: World Bank, 1989).

53. "The Current Economic Situation in Africa," ECA Resolution 671 (XXIV), 7 April 1989 (ECOSOC document E/ECA/CM.15/48).

54. ECA, *Statistics and Policies: ECA Preliminary Observations on the World Bank Report: "Africa's Adjustment and Growth in the 1980s"* (Addis Ababa: ECA, 1989).

55. *The Independent*, 4 May 1989.

56. "African Alternative Framework to Structural Adjustment Programmes for Socio-Economic Recovery and Transformation: Draft Resolution" (ECA document E/ECA/CM.15/6/Rev. 3), 17 November 1989.

57. "Programme of Work and Priorities for 1960–1961," ECA Resolution 18 (II), 4 February 1960 (ECOSOC document E/CN.14/54).

58. "Transportation across the Sahara," ECA Resolution 61 (IV), 2 March 1962 (ECOSOC document E/CN.14/168).

59. "Pan African Telecommunication Network," ECA Resolution 162 (VIII), 24 February 1967 (ECOSOC document E/CN.14/393).

60. "Trans-African Highway," ECA Resolution 226 (X), 13 February 1972 (ECOSOC document E/CN.14/554).

61. "Transportation and Communications Decade in Africa," ECA Resolution 291 (XIII), 26 February 1977 (ECOSOC document E/CN.14/683); "Transport and Communications Decade," General Assembly Resolution 32/160, 19 December 1977, in *GAOR*, 1977, 32nd Session, Supplement no. 45 (A/32/45), 97.

62. "United Nations Transport and Communications Decade in Africa," ECA Resolution 639 (XXIII), 15 April 1988 (ECOSOC document E/ECA/CM.14/42).

63. See "Second Transport and Communications Decade in Africa," General Assembly Resolution 43/179, 20 December 1988 (A/43/49), 135. This resolution followed ECA and ECOSOC resolutions proclaiming 1991–2000 as the second United Nations Transport and Communications Decade.

64. "United Nations Programme of Action for African Economic Recovery and Development, 1986–1990" (UNPAAERD), General Assembly Resolution A/S-13/2, 1 June 1986 (A/S-16/16).

65. "African Alternative Framework to Structural Adjustment Programmes for Socio-Economic Recovery and Transformation" General Assembly Resolution 44/49, 17 November 1989.

66. "Measures for Accelerating the Implementation of the United Nations Programme of Action for African Economic Recovery and Development 1986–1990," in *Report of the Ad Hoc Committee of the Whole of the General Assembly on the Review and Appraisal of the United Nations Programme of Action for African Economic Recovery and Development 1986–1990* (A/43/664), 3 October 1988, 45.

67. "African Alternative Framework for Structural Adjustment Programmes for Socio-Economic Recovery and Transformation (AAF-SAP)," ECA Resolution 676 (XXIV), 7 April 1989 (ECOSOC document E/ECA/CM.15/48).

68. G. A. Cornia, R. Jolly, and F. Stewart, eds., *Adjustment with a Human Face* (Oxford and New York: Clarendon Press, 1987–1988).

69. Bade Onimode in a remark made at a seminar held in Addis Ababa University in 1988 after the publication of *Adjustment with a Human Face* (by UNICEF).

70. World Bank, *Sub-Saharan Africa: From Crisis to Sustainable Growth.*

71. See von Hayek, "The Pretence of Knowledge."

72. James Wolfensohn, "A Proposal for a Comprehensive Development Framework," Memorandum, Office of the President, World Bank, Washington, D.C., 21 January 1999.

73. United Nations Department of Public Information, *African Alternative Framework to Structural Adjustment Programmes for Socio-Economic Recovery and Transformation: Selected Donor-Country Press Clippings Resulting from Press Kit and Media Outreach on the ECA Blueprint and Its Response to the World Bank's Assessment of Africa's Structural Adjustment Programmes* (New York: United Nations, 1989).

74. *The Daily Telegraph,* 10 July 1989.

75. "Letter Written by Stanley Please," *Financial Times,* 18 July 1989.

76. "Letter Written by Douglas Wass," *Financial Times,* 22 July 1989.

77. "United Nations Programme of Action for African Economic Recovery and Development 1986–1990," General Assembly Resolution S-13/2, 1 June 1986 (A/S-13/16).

78. OAU Summit Resolution A/40/666, adopted by the African Heads of State and Government at the July 1985 OAU Summit of an ECA-crafted African Priority Programme for Economic Recovery (APPER).

79. *Abuja Statement* (proceedings of the International Conference on Africa: The Challenge of Economic Recovery and Development) (Abuja, Nigeria: 1987), Para. 17, 18, and 25.

80. A. Adedeji, S. Rasheed, and M. Morrison, eds., *The Human Dimension of Africa's Persistent Economic Crisis* (London: Hans Zell, 1990).

81. ECA, "The Khartoum Declaration: Towards a Human-Focused Approach to Socio Economic Recovery and Development in Africa," ECA Resolution (ECOSOC document E/ECA/CM/14/RES/631), 15 April 1988.

82. Reginald H. Green, "The Human Dimension as the Test and a Means of Achieving Africa's Economic Recovery and Development: Reweaving the Social Fabric, Restoring the Broken Pot," in Adedeji, Rasheed, and Morrison, eds., *The Human Dimension,* 3.

83. "United Nations Programme of Action for African Economic Recovery and Development 1986–1990."

84. "Final Review of the Implementation of the UNPAAERD 1986–1990," General Assembly Resolution 46/151, 18 December 1991 (A/4649).

85. UN General Assembly, *Independent Evaluation of the Implementation of the United Nations New Agenda for the Development of Africa* (UN-NADAF) (New York: United Nations, 2002), passim.

86. "The United Nations System-wide Special Initiative on Africa," launched by the UN Secretary-General in March 1996, was adopted by the CPC at its 37th Session in 1997 as the implementing arm of UN NADAF which submitted in three successive years (1989, 1999, and 2000) progress reports to the CPC (E/AC 51/1998/7, 1999/6, and 2000/6).

87. Ibid., iii.

88. For the origin of UNDAF, see *Letter Dated 17 May 1997 from the UN Secretary-General to the President of the General Assembly* (A/51/829), 17 May 1997; and *Renewing the United Nations: A Programme for Reform, Report of the Secretary-General* (A/51/950), 14 July 1997.

89. "Mid-Term Review of the Implementation of the United Nations New Agenda for the Development of Africa," General Assembly Resolution 51/32, 6 December 1996 (A/51/49), 34.

90. CPC, *Report of the Independent Evaluation of the United Nations Systems-Wide Special Initiative on Africa, Note by the Secretary-General* (E/AC.51/2001/6), May 2001, 21.

91. Ibid., 31–32.

92. United Nations Joint Inspection Unit, *Evaluation of the United Nations New Agenda for the Development of Africa in the 1990s (UN-NADAF): Towards a More Operational Approach* (New York: United Nations, 1996), vi.

93. Ibid., paragraph 22.

94. "Memorandum by the ECA Conference of Ministers to the Ad Hoc Committee of the Whole of the General Assembly on the Final Review and Appraisal of the Implementation of UNPAAERD, 1986–1990" (document E/ECA/CM.17/L), Annex II, 15.

95. African Development Forum '99, "The Challenge to Africa of Globalization and the Information Age," report of the African Development Forum I, 24–28 October 1999, Addis Ababa, Ethiopia, available at <http://www.uneca.org/adf99/adf99reportintro.htm>, accessed 4 March 2003.

96. African Development Forum 2000, *Leadership at All Levels to Overcome HIV/AIDS,* report of the African Development Forum II, 3–7 December 2000, Addis Ababa, Ethiopia, available at <http://www.uneca.org/adf2000/docs.htm>, accessed 4 March 2003.

97. The theme of the African Development Forum III held in Addis Ababa in 3–8 March 2002 was "Defining Priorities for Regional Integration"; see <http://www.uneca.org/adfiii/adfiii.htm>, accessed 4 March 2003.

98. CPC, *Report of the Independent Evaluation of the United Nations Systems-Wide Special Initiative on Africa,* 28.

99. ECOSOC, *Report on the Work of the Economic Commission for Africa (ECA) 1998–2000* (document E/ECA/CM.25/4), 2 April 2001, 5.

100. OAU/AEC, "Constitutive Act."

101. African Center for Development and Strategic Studies and Adebayo Adedeji, *Comprehending and Mastering African Conflicts: The Search for Sustainable Peace and Good Governance* (London and New York: Zed Books in association with African Centre for Development and Strategic Studies, 1999).

102. This is a project sponsored by the Africa Union to assist in the peer review provided for in NEPAD.

103. ECA, Social Development Section, *The Status and Role of Women in East Africa* (New York: United Nations, 1967).

104. Ester Boserup, *Woman's Role in Economic Development* (New York: St. Martin's Press, 1970).

105. ECA, *The Data Base for Discussion on the Interrelations between the Integration of Women in Development, Their Situation and Population Factors in Africa* (Addis Ababa: United Nations Economic Commission for Africa, 1974).

106. ECA, *African Charter for Popular Participation in Development and Transformation* (Arusha 1990) (Addis Ababa: UNECA, 1990).

107. "OAU/ECA African Submission to the Special Session of the General Assembly on Africa's Economic and Social Crisis," *GAOR*, 1986, 13th Special Session (27 May– 1 June), Supplement no. 2 (A/S-13/16), 4.

108. Chester A. Crocker, "Expanding the Development Dialogue."

109. Michael Crowder, "Whose Dream Was It Anyway? Twenty-five Years of African Independence," *African Affairs* 86, no. 342 (January 1987): 9–10.

110. Adebayo Adedeji, *Towards a Dynamic African Economy*, 15–38.

111. *The Economist*, London, 13–19 May 2000.

112. OAU/AEC, "Constitutive Act of the African Union," Article 30.

113. Ibid.

114. "Communiqué Issued by the Implementation Committee of Heads of State and Government of NEPAD," 23 October 2001, paragraph 8 states that "all other initiatives promoted by individual African countries should be subsumed under the NEPAD process to represent a basis on which Africa can collectively and effectively cooperate with its development partners."

115. General Assembly, *Road Map towards the Implementation of the United Nations Millennium Declaration, Report of the Secretary-General* (A/56/326), 6 September 2001, 43.

6. ESCWA

We wish to thank all the persons who gave us valuable help and the staff of ESCWA's library, in particular Nabila al-Srougi and Pamela Nassar. We wish also to express our sincere thanks to François Burgat, director of the French Centre for Archaeology and Social Sciences (CEFAS) in Sana'a and Eric Huybrechts, the former director of the Centre for Study and Research on the Contemporary Middle East (CERMOC) in Beirut, for letting us use the facilities of their research centers and allowing two of their trainees to dedicate much of their time to this work. We would like to specifically thank Abdallah el Alem, a former ESCWA high-ranking executive, who carefully read this chapter, made numerous comments on it, and provided us with a lot of information, for all his time and careful attention. We are also grateful to Christophe Huss, who spent time assisting in the last exploration of documents. Furthermore, we extend our gratitude to all the persons who agreed to be interviewed in the framework of this project. Finally, Yves Berthelot and Sophie Theven have to be warmly thanked for spending many hours helping upgrade the original manuscript, as does Ms. Mervat Tallawy, the ESCWA executive secretary, who provided detailed observations and suggestions.

1. See UNDP, *Human Development Report 1999* (New York and Oxford: Oxford University Press), 201.

2. The UNDP has a Regional Bureau for Arab States, which evidently did not cause as much of a political problem to the UN. Remark by Mervat Tallawy, comments on an earlier draft of this chapter.

3. "Permanent Headquarters of the Economic and Social Commission for Western Asia," ECOSOC Resolution 1994/43, 29 July 1994.

4. "Study of Factors Bearing upon the Establishment of an Economic Commission for the Middle East," General Assembly Resolution 120 (II), 31 October 1947.

5. *Report to the Economic and Social Council of the Ad Hoc Committee on the Proposed Economic Commission for the Middle East* (ECOSOC document E/AC.26/16), 1 June 1949.

6. Israel joined the ECE in 1991.

7. "Decentralization of the Economic and Social Activities of the United Nations and Strengthening of the Regional Economic Commissions and the United Nations Office in Beirut," General Assembly Resolution 1941 (XVIII), 11 December 1963.

8. Interview quoted in Serge Nédélec and Blandine Destremau, *ESCWA (1974–1999): Twenty-five Years of Service to the Region's Development* (Beirut: United Nations, 1999), 30.

9. Ibid., 27.

10. Draft resolution proposed by Lebanon to ECOSOC at its 53rd Session, "Regional Co-operation: Establishment of an Economic Commission for Western Asia" (ECOSOC document E/L.1497), 19 July 1972.

11. In order to convince the members of the council, the representative of Lebanon first drew attention to the lack of a regional commission for the twelve Arab countries of the Middle East, although those countries were full-fledged members of the UN. He then emphasized that UNESOB was not an intergovernmental organization and did not have the power to make recommendations to member states or to negotiate bilateral relations. He dwelled for a moment on the discriminatory treatment of the region in the UN in terms of technical assistance and said that it would be pointless to wait for years to come for the solution of the political problems stemming from "Israeli aggression" before undertaking regional economic measures. Exercising his diplomatic skills, the representative of Lebanon tried to put across to the Western countries that the creation of such a commission was also in their interest: "Apart from many other advantages, the establishment of such a Commission will make it possible to increase the region's absorptive capacity and will serve not only the economic development objectives of the countries directly concerned but also those of the *International*

Development Strategy. The Arab countries need the co-operation of the developed world, just as the developed world needs the co-operation of the Arab countries, irrespective of political and economic system." See ECOSOC, *ESCOR,* 55th Session, 1868th meeting, 11 July 1973, 57.

12. See "Report of the Economic Committee," Agenda item 9, ECOSOC, *ESCOR,* 1973, 55th Session, 1878th meeting, 9 August 1973, 112.

13. The countries opposed to the proposal included Barbados, Bolivia, Denmark, the United States, Finland, New Zealand, the Netherlands, and Sweden, while Canada, France, and the United Kingdom, among others, abstained.

14. "Establishment of an Economic Commission for Western Asia," ECOSOC Resolution 1818 (LV), 9 August 1973 (ECOSOC document E/5400).

15. At the session of the General Assembly that discussed the ECWA budget, Israel reiterated its criticisms of the commission but found itself isolated. The first budget, for the biennium 1974–1975, amounted to $2,204,000 and was adopted by 76 votes to 1.

16. Mohammed Said Al-Attar, born in Yemen, was ECWA's executive secretary from 1974 to 1985; Mohammed Said Nabulsi, Jordanian of Palestinian origin, from 1985 to 1988; Tayseer Abdel-Jaber, Jordanian born in Jerusalem, from 1989 to 1993; Sabahidin Bakjaji, Syrian, from 1993 to 1995; Hazem El-Beblawi, Egyptian, from 1995 to 2000; and Ms. Mervat M.Tallawy, Egyptian, the first woman executive secretary, since 2000.

17. "Palestine Liberation Organization," ECWA Resolution 12/II, 9 May 1975 (ECOSOC document E/ECWA/28).

18. According to Mervat Tallawy, "The League of Arab States provides ESCWA with the political legitimacy to be able to cover all the 22 Arab countries, and not only its 13 member States." Personal communication with the author.

19. In its original work program, designed in 1974, the formulation of ECWA's general goal was "to encourage economic reconstruction and development in Western Asia," which shows the weight of conflicts on the national economies. See ESCWA, "Programme of Work and Priorities," *ESCOR,* 1974, 57th Session, Supplement no. 10 (E/5539), 8–34.

20. See UN Secretariat, "Functions and Organization of the Secretariat of the Economic and Social Commission for Western Asia," *Secretary-General's Bulletin: Organization Manual,* document ST/SGB/Organization, Section: ESCWA/Rev.1, 6 October 1994.

21. According to the formulation of Mervat Tallawy. Personal communication with the author.

22. See Nédélec and Destremau, *ESCWA (1974–1999).*

23. Blandine Destremau has a Ph.D. in Economics, and she is a permanent researcher for the French National Center for Scientific Research. In 1996, in Amman, she presented a paper in the seminar "The Impact of the Peace Process on Selected Sectors." She proposed that Dr. Hazem el Beblawi initiate a study on the institutional history of ESCWA and collaborated on the research paper that was published as a book under the title *ESCWA (1974–1999).*

24. Arab League Educational, Cultural and Scientific Organization (ALECSO, created in 1964); Arab Organization of Administrative Sciences (AOAS, 1961); Arab Standards and Metrology Organization (ASMO, 1967); Council for Arab Economic Unity (CAEU, 1957).

25. ECWA, *Report of ECWA on the 4th Session*, 24–29 April 1977, *ESCOR*, 1977, 63rd Session, Supplement no. 10 (E/5969), 39.

26. ESCWA, "Programme of Work and Priorities," 8–34.

27. "Declaration of the Establishment of a New International Economic Order," General Assembly Resolution 3201 (S-VI), 1 May 1974.

28. According to Mervat Tallawy, "ECWA/ESCWA was only able to address the situation of the Palestinian people by preparing a study in implementation of the ECOSOC and the Commission's resolutions." Personal communication with the author.

29. The word "rent" is used to designate the exogenous revenues.

30. Mervat Tallawy, personal communication with the author.

31. Interview of Fouad al Qa'id by the author, Sana'a, Yemen, 12 March 2001. Fouad al Qa'id worked for the UNDP for twenty-six years and was minister of planning of Yemen from 1981 to 1983.

32. These priorities and the ideas that UNESOB and then ECWA promoted were spelled out in a publication, *Studies on Development Problems in Selected Countries of the Middle East,* which at the creation of the commission was renamed *Studies on Development Problems in Countries of Western Asia.* At this time, it consisted of several sectoral and national studies. In 1978, ECWA started publishing a yearly overview, the *Survey of Economic and Social Developments in the ECWA Region.* Besides providing information and documentation, this publication expressed the views of the commission on regional development and major issues.

33. *Final Report of the Expert Group Meeting on Constraints in Agricultural Planning and Resource Mobilization for Food Security Programmes in the ECWA Region,* Baghdad, 18–21 December 1983 (Baghdad: ECWA, 1984).

34. ESCWA, "Programme of Work and Priorities."

35. Planning has been the subject of many training programs, described in a work published in 1980; S. S. Johl, ed., *Irrigation and Agricultural Development* (Oxford, New York, Toronto, and Sydney: Pergamon Press, 1980).

36. Mervat Tallawy, personal communication with the author.

37. ESCWA, "Programme of Work and Priorities."

38. ECWA, *Industrialization and Industrial Policy in the ECWA Region* (Beirut: ECWA, 1981).

39. Interview of Abdallah el Alem by the author, Sana'a, Yemen, 20 February 2001.

40. For more information, see ESCWA, *Statistical Abstract of the ESCWA Region* (New York: United Nations, 1997); and UNDP, in cooperation with the Council for Development and Reconstruction, *National Human Development Report: Lebanon* (Beirut: UNDP, November 1998).

41. ESCWA, "Programme of Work and Priorities," 27–28.

42. In 1975, ESCWA began a long series of statistical studies on the status of women with some financing from UNIFEM.

43. ECWA and UNFPA, *Population and Development in the Middle East,* foreword to the collection of papers presented at the two population conferences held in Amman in 1978 and Damascus in 1979 (Beirut: ESCWA, 1982).

44. Many statistical publications on the subject can be mentioned, such as *Estimates and Projection of Population, Vital Rates and Economic Activity for Members of the ECWA Region* (1978); and two series issued from 1976, entitled *Demographic and Related Socio-Economic Data Sheets for Countries of the ECWA* and *Fertility and Childhood Mortality by Mother's and Father's Education.* As a successor to the *Population Bulletin of the United Nations Economic and Social Office in Beirut,* issued in 1971, the *Population Bulletin of ECWA* periodically offered specific studies on the demography of the Arab countries and addressed questions of methodology and demographic theory. In 1981, ECWA produced a series of publications entitled *The Population Situation in the ECWA Region.* Each issue covered a member state and contained data on the main features of its population: size, distribution and structure, fertility, mortality, migration, growth, education, labor force, and policies. Furthermore, ECWA and the Lebanese government organized the first regional population conference in Beirut, from 18 February to 1 March 1974. A regional preparatory conference prior to the United Nations Conference on Human Settlements (Habitat I, Vancouver, May–June 1976) was organized by ECWA in collaboration with ESCAP in Teheran in June 1975.

45. "Economic and Social Conditions of the Palestinian People under Occupation," ESCWA Resolution 139 (XII), 24 April 1985 (ECOSOC document E/ECWA/XII/11).

46. ESCWA, *Household Income and Expenditure Survey* (Baghdad: ESCWA, 1987).

47. "Census of the Palestine Arab People," ESCWA Resolution 28 (III), 14 May 1976.

48. *ECWA Report on the 7th Session* (ECOSOC document E/ECWA/114), 19–23 April 1980; *Note by the Executive-Secretary* (ECOSOC document E/ECWA/110), 20 April 1980.

49. ESCWA, *Report of the Executive Secretary, April 1987–April 1988* (New York: United Nations, 1988).

50. ECWA, *Development Problems and Prospects of the Economic Commission for Western Asia Region in the 1980s* (E/AC.54/L.104), 3 February 1981.

51. Ibid.

52. World Commission on Environment and Development (Brundtland Commission), *Our Common Future* (Oxford and New York: Oxford University Press, 1987).

53. A joint UNCTAD/ECWA trade division carried out several important activities including the Multilateral Trade Negotiations and the Generalized System of Preferences projects.

54. ECWA, *Development Problems and Prospects,* 9–10.

55. ESCWA, *Promotion of Entrepreneurship in Small-Scale Industrial Enterprises* (Amman: United Nations, 1992).

56. ESCWA, *Establishment of Business Incubators in the ESCWA Region: The Cases of the Syrian Arab Republic and the Palestinian Territories* (New York: United Nations, 1995).

57. Mervat Tallawy, personal communication with the author.

58. It was not until 1993, however, that the *Survey* first included a section on regional economic cooperation and integration.

59. ESCWA, *Economic Integration in Western Asia* (London: Frances Pinter, 1985); this book followed a major expert group meeting held in 1980 on "Feasible Forms of Economic Co-operation and Integration in Western Asia."

60. Ibid., xii.

61. Some Arab League members have still not subscribed to this agreement, and the pattern of trade, including the weakness of intraregional exchanges, has generally remained unchanged.

62. ESCWA, *Economic Integration in Western Asia,* 89.

63. Mervat Tallawy, personal communication with the author.

64. ESCWA, *Survey of Economic and Social Developments in the ESCWA Region, 1998–1999,* Part 2, *Economic Developments in the ESCWA Region during the Last 25 Years* (New York: United Nations, 1999), 19.

65. Mervat Tallawy, personal communication with the author.

66. ESCWA, *Economic Integration in Western Asia,* 68.

67. Ibid., 216.

68. See ESCWA, *Trade in Services: Growth and Balance of Payments Implications for Countries in Western Asia* (New York: United Nations, 1987); and ESCWA, *Trade in Services and Development in the ESCWA Region* (New York: United Nations, 1988).

69. The session was held at a ministerial level and gathered representatives of the twelve ECWA member states. The Palestine Liberation Organization; governmental organizations, bodies, and agencies at the national, regional, and international levels; and a number of non-member states of ECWA participated as observers.

70. ECWA, *Development Problems and Prospects.*

71. ESCWA, *Return Migration, Profiles, Impact and Absorption in Home Countries* (Amman: ESCWA, 1993).

72. ECWA, *Development Problems and Prospects,* 36.

73. Ibid., 35.

74. Ibid., 37.

75. S. S. Russell, "International Migration and Political Turmoil in the Middle East," *Population and Development Review* 18, no. 4 (December 1992).

76. With the exception of Egypt, which had already signed a peace treaty with Israel.

77. ESCWA, *Revised Medium-Term Plan 1992–1997,* 2nd version (E/ESCWA/ID/ 1998/1), 25 June 1997.

78. Foreword to the *Proceedings of the Expert Group Meeting on the Impact of the Peace Process on Selected Sectors,* Amman, 23–25 June 1997 (Amman: ESCWA, 1998).

79. That which led to the publication of the *Proceedings of the Expert Group Meeting.*

80. Foreword to the *Proceedings of the Expert Group Meeting,* iii.

81. Ibid., introduction, 2.

82. The reform of the commission at the beginning of the 1990s affected and reflected its views on regional development. The sectoral structure was replaced by a

thematic structure, organized around three main priority areas: the management of natural resources and environment; the improvement of the quality of life of the people of the region; and the creation of an environment conducive to economic cooperation. Out of the five subprograms of work issued for the 1998–1999 biennium, two concern regional cooperation directly: the Coordination of Policies and Harmonization of Norms and Regulations for Sectoral Development and The Development, Coordination, and Harmonization of Statistics and Information.

83. "Cooperation among Developing Countries and Regional Organisations" (ESCWA document E/ESCWA/TCD/1997/4), 19 March 1997.

84. ECOSOC, *Regional Cooperation in the Economic, Social and Related Fields, Report of the Secretary-General* (ECOSOC document E/1995/40), 20 June 1997. This commitment was translated into the establishment of the Technical Committee on Liberalization of Foreign Trade and Economic Globalization in the Countries of the ESCWA Region in 1997.

85. In 1993, the Joint Committee on Environment and Development in the Arab Region was born, with the purpose to expand coordination between the regional organizations and the United Nations organizations in this field and to identify the regional priorities.

86. ECOSOC, *Regional Cooperation.* Starting in 1997, due to the prominence of the water issue, the frequency of the sessions of the Committee on Water Resources increased.

87. Ibid., 40–41.

88. *Harmonization of Environmental Standards in the Transport Sector in ESCWA Member Countries: Corrigendum* (E/ESCWA/TRANS/1999/5/Corr.1), 26 September 2000.

89. Ibid., 38.

90. ESCWA, *Industrial Strategies and Policies in the ESCWA Region within the Context of a Changing International and Regional Environment* (New York: United Nations, 1996).

91. ESCWA, *Reports of the Expert Meeting on Institutional Aspects of Privatization in the ESCWA Region* (Beirut: United Nations, 1997).

92. On this issue, ESCWA has organized several meetings such as that of experts on Institutional Aspects of Privatization in the ESCWA Region in Beirut, 1–3 December 1997, in collaboration with the Chamber of Commerce, Industry, and Agriculture of Beirut and Mount Lebanon and the Friedrich-Naumann Foundation of Germany.

93. ESCWA, *Industrial Strategies and Policies.*

94. Augustus Richard Norton, *Civil Society in the Middle East* (Leiden and New York: E. J. Brill, 1995–1996); Ghassan Salameh, *Democracy without Democrats: The Renewal of Politics in the Muslim World* (London: I. B. Tauris, 1994); and Rex Brynen, Bahjat Kourany, and Paul Noble, *Political Liberalization and Democratization in the Arab World* (Boulder: Lynne Rienner, 1995).

95. According to Freedom House, only Jordan is considered even partly free. Freedom House, *Annual Survey of Freedom, Country Scores 1998–1999,* available at <www.freedomhouse.org/ratings/index>, accessed 10 April 2003.

96. ESCWA, *Report of the Round-Table Discussion on Partnership between Governments and Civil Society in the Context of Follow-up to the Global Conferences*

(E/ESCWA/SD/1999/13), 13 December 1999. These lines express a rather political standpoint, away from the much milder formulation of activity reports.

97. ESCWA, *Impact of Selected Macroeconomic and Social Policies on Poverty: The Case of Egypt, Jordan and the Republic of Yemen* (New York: United Nations, 1995); and ESCWA, *Exploratory Study on Approaches to the Social Impact of Structural Adjustment Policies* (New York: United Nations, 1997).

98. ESCWA, *The Impact of Crises on the Social Situation in the ESCWA Region* (New York: United Nations, 1994), 2.

99. According to the UNDP, the notion of "sustainable development" may be defined as "the enlargement of people's choices and capabilities through the formation of social capital so as to meet as equitably as possible the needs of current generations without compromising the needs of the future ones." Tariq Banwi et al., *Sustainable Development: From Concept to Operation—A Guide for the Practitioner* (New York: UNDP, 1994), 7.

100. See, e.g., ESCWA, *Return Migration: Profile, Impact and Absorption in Home Countries* (New York: ESCWA, 1993); and ESCWA, *The Impact of Crisis on the Social Situation in the ESCWA Region.*

101. The meeting focused its attention on the following themes: the scope of the problem of returnees, the issue of returnees at the country level, an overall analysis of the problem of returnees, issues that stress the industrial sector, regional cooperation, and a dialogue between labor-sending and labor-receiving countries.

102. Jordan lost the bulk of its remittances, which were estimated at US$627 million in 1989—representing 10 percent of GNP—while the returnees added 8 percent to the country's population and 10 percent to its labor force; see ESCWA, *Survey of Economic and Social Developments in the ESCWA Region, 1990–1991* (New York: United Nations, 1992), 25 and 39.

103. ESCWA, *Survey of Economic and Social Developments in the ESCWA Region*, Part 2, *Economic Developments in the ESCWA Region during the Last 25 Years*, 10.

104. For example, the ratio of technical school enrollment to total secondary school enrollment was around 14 percent in 1996 in Lebanon, a ratio that seems to be inadequate given the strong demand for vocational and technical specialists because of the reconstruction process. See UNDP, *National Human Development Report: Lebanon.*

105. Between 1983 and 1991, studies were issued on vocational training and technical education (especially on Lebanon, Syrian Arab Republic, Egypt, and Palestine), but no specific and operational projects on vocational training were launched.

106. George Kossaifi, "Poverty in Western Asia: A Social-Political Approach," in UNDP, *Preventing and Eradicating Poverty: Report on the Expert Meeting on Poverty Alleviation and Sustainable Livelihood in the Arab States* (New York: UNDP, May 1997), 196.

107. *A Conceptual and Methodological Framework for Poverty Alleviation in the ESCWA Region* (E/ESCWA/SED/1993/19), 19 December 1993.

108. ESCWA, "The Role of Arab Non-Governmental Organizations in the Implementation and Integrated Follow-Up on the Recommendations of the Global

Conferences," paper presented at the Round-table Discussion on Partnership between Governments and Civil Society in the Context of the Follow-Up to the Global Conferences, Beirut, 4–5 October 1999. See document E/ESCWA/SD/1999/12 for the report of the discussion and a summary of the paper.

109. Resolution 220 (OS-14) adopted at the Fourteenth Session of the Council of Arab Ministers of Foreign Affairs, Cairo, 13–15 December 1994.

110. ESCWA, "An Agenda for Development," background document, ESCWA's contribution to the *Report of the Secretary-General* (Amman, 1 July 1993).

111. ESCWA, *Survey of Economic and Social Developments in the ESCWA Region, 2000–2001* (New York: United Nations, 31 May 2001), 106–126.

112. ESCWA, *Revised Medium-Term Plan 1992–1997*, 11.

113. ESCWA, *Women and Poverty in the ESCWA Region: Issues and Concerns,* expert group meeting on The Arab Family in a Changing Society: A New Concept for Partnership, Abu Dhabi (document E/ESCWA/SD/1994/4), 10–14 December 1994.

114. ESCWA, *The Situation of Disabled Women: Their Marginalization and Measures for Social Integration in the ESCWA Region* (New York: United Nations, 1995).

115. ESCWA, "The Role of Arab Non-Governmental Organizations in the Implementation and Integrated Follow-Up on the Recommendations of the Global Conferences."

116. ESCWA, *Survey of Economic and Social Developments in the ESCWA Region, 1999–2000* (New York: United Nations, 1 June 2000), 114.

117. Ibid., 139.

118. See, e.g., ESCWA, *Arab Women in the Manufacturing Industries,* Studies on Women and Development no. 19, issued in 1994; and see document E/ESCWA/ID/1994/5/Rev.1 for the revised version of 1995. This document consists of a series of studies of women's participation in traditional processing industries such as textiles and food processing and in modern industries such as pharmaceuticals and electronics.

119. ESCWA, *Feasibility and Operationalization of Micro-Credit Lending Facilities for Poor Women in Urban and Rural Areas in Selected Arab Countries: Theoretical Perspectives and Practical Considerations* (New York: United Nations, 1998), which contributes to establish a link between microcredit finance and poverty alleviation in three selected Arab countries.

120. See ESCWA, *Arab Women 1995: Trends, Statistics and Indicators* (New York: United Nations and ESCWA, 1997). This publication analyzes the status of Arab women in the twenty-two countries of the Arab region.

121. ESCWA, "The Role of Arab Non-Governmental Organizations in the Implementation and Integrated Follow-Up on the Recommendations of the Global Conferences." In January 2002, three of the most important UN agencies in the Middle East were headed by women: the UNDP, the UNFPA, and ESCWA.

122. Nédélec and Destremau, *ESCWA (1974–1999)*.

123. Mervat Tallawy, personal communication with the author.

Index

Note: Page numbers in **bold** refer to chapter topics. Page numbers in *italics* refer to graphs and tables.

About the Authors

Adebayo Adedeji is the founder and executive director of the African Centre for Development and Strategic Studies (ACDESS), which was established in 1991 after his retirement from UN service. From 1975 to 1991 he was an Under-Secretary-General of the organization and Executive Secretary of its regional commission for Africa. Between 1971 and 1975 he served as a cabinet minister in Nigeria in charge of economic development and reconstruction after the country's thirty-month-long civil war, 1967–1970. Educated at Ibadan, Harvard, and London Universities, he became a full professor at the age of thirty-six. He is a recipient of seven honorary doctorate degrees from African and non-African universities and of eight national honors from African governments. He has written and published extensively, and his works and intellectual contributions have been widely reviewed in learned journals and have become the focus of books such as S. K. B. Asante's *African Development: Adebayo Adedeji's Alternative Strategies* (1991) and Bade Onimode and Richard Synge, ed., *Issues in African Development: Essays in Honour of Adebayo Adedeji at 65* (1995).

Yves Berthelot is Senior Research Fellow at the CUNY Graduate Center and at the United Nations Institute for Training and Research (UNITAR). He is Director of the Geneva Office of the United Nations Intellectual History Project and President of the Comité Français de Solidarité Internationale. Until 2000 he was Executive Secretary of the Economic Commission for Europe. Before this, he was Deputy-Secretary-General of UNCTAD and Head of Research at the OECD Development Centre. As Director of the Centre d'Etudes Prospectives et d'Informations Internationales, a French think tank on global economics, he supervised the preparation of two books: *Economie Mondiale: La Montée des Tensions* (1983) and *Economie mondiale: 1980–1990. La Fracture?* (1985). He is author, with Jacques Debandt, of *Le Défi économique du Tiers-Monde* (1982) and, with Giulio Fossi, of *Pour une nouvelle coopération* (1976).

Blandine Destremau holds a Bachelor of Arabic and a Ph.D. in Economics from Georgetown University and is presently working as a permanent researcher for the French Center for Scientific Research. She has dedicated her work to Middle Eastern issues, mainly Israeli-Palestinian economic relationships, the Yemeni economy, rentier economic systems, and poverty alleviation. She has published many articles, directed collective works, and written two books. Among her main publications are *Mesures et démesure de la pauvreté* (2002), with Pierre Salama; *The United Nations Economic and Social Commission for Western Asia (1974–1999): Twenty-five Years of Service to the Region's Development* (1999), with Serge Nédélec; *Femmes du Yémen* (1990); and "Formes et mutations des économies rentières au Moyen-Orient: Egypte, Jordanie, Palestine, Yémen," *Tiers Monde* XLI, no. 163 (July–September 2000).

Paul Rayment is a graduate of Oxford University, where he was a Prize Scholar at Magdalen College. He spent several years doing research at the National Institute of Economic and Social Research, London, working with Alfred Maizels on international trade and development problems, before joining the United Nations as a staff member, first with UNCTAD and then the Economic Commission for Europe. From 1994 to 2001 he was Director of the ECE's Economic Analysis Division. He has published in a variety of academic journals, including the *Oxford Bulletin,* the *Economic Record,* and the *Cambridge Journal of Economics,* and has contributed to a number of collective works, particularly in the area of international trade. Most of his writing, however, has been for the ECE where, inter alia, he wrote all the opening chapters to the *Economic Surveys* and *Bulletins* between 1990 and 2001. He retired from the UN in 2001.

Gert Rosenthal is a Guatemalan economist. He received his undergraduate and graduate training in economics at the University of California at Berkeley. He served in various posts in the Guatemalan government between 1960 and 1974, as well as in the Secretariat of the Central American Common Market. He also taught development economics at the Rafael Landivar University in Guatemala. He joined the Economic Commission for Latin America in 1974 as Director of the Mexico City Office. He was promoted to Deputy Executive Secretary in 1986 and was Executive Secretary between 1988 and 1997. He is presently the Permanent Representative of Guatemala to the United Nations.

Leelananda de Silva was a member of the Sri Lanka Administrative Service, working at the district level and for the central government. From 1970 to 1977, with the Ministry of Planning and Economic Affairs, he was involved with international economic relations—with the UN (the World Food Conference of 1974, international commodity negotiations, and UN General Assembly special sessions), the Non-Aligned Summits, the Group of 77, and the Commonwealth Heads of Government Meetings. He was Secretary of the Economic Committee of the Non-Aligned Summit in Colombo in 1976. He was also the Secretary-General of the last annual sessions of ECAFE held in Colombo in 1974. Since 1978, he has worked as a consultant and senior advisor to more than ten UN agencies and with the International Foundation for Development Alternatives in Nyon, Switzerland; the Inter-Parliamentary Union in Geneva; and the International Council for Voluntary Agencies, Geneva. He has worked on UN assignments in more than thirty countries in Africa and Asia and has written extensively on development issues.

About the Project

The United Nations Intellectual History Project was launched in mid-1999 to fill a gap in the literature about the world organization. The project is analyzing the origins and evolution of the history of ideas cultivated within the UN family of organizations and their impact on wider thinking and international action. Certain aspects of the UN's economic and social activities have of course been the subject of books and articles, but there is no comprehensive intellectual history of the world organization's contributions to the shaping of past, present, or future international agendas.

This project is examining the evolution of key ideas and concepts about international economic and social development that were born or nurtured under UN auspices. Their origins are being traced, and the motivations behind them as well as their relevance and impact are being assessed against the backdrop of the socioeconomic situations of individual countries, the global economy, and major international developments. The project will publish fourteen books about human rights and key economic and social ideas that are central to UN activity. The first volume in the series, *Ahead of the Curve? UN Ideas and Global Challenges,* was published in 2001 by Indiana University Press.

The project also has completed seventy-five oral history interviews with leading contributors to crucial ideas and concepts within the UN system. A summary of the collection with excerpts will be published in 2004. The project is expected to be completed by the end of 2005.

For further information, the interested reader should contact:

UN Intellectual History Project
Ralph Bunche Institute for International Studies
The CUNY Graduate Center
365 Fifth Avenue, Suite 5203
New York, New York 10016-4309
212-817-1920 Tel
212-817-1565 Fax
UNHistory@gc.cuny.edu
www.unhistory.org